DATE DUE

4-13-04

BRITAIN, SOUTHEAST ASIA AND THE ONSET
OF THE PACIFIC WAR

BRITAIN, SOUTHEAST ASIA
AND THE ONSET
OF THE PACIFIC WAR

NICHOLAS TARLING

CAMBRIDGE
UNIVERSITY PRESS

Published by the Press Syndicate of the University of Cambridge
The Pitt Building, Trumpington Street, Cambridge CB2 1RP, UK
40 West 20th Street, New York, NY 10011–4211, USA
10 Stamford Road, Oakleigh, Melbourne 3166, Australia

Printed in Singapore by Kin Keong Printing Co.

National Library of Australia cataloguing-in-publication data

Tarling, Nicholas.
Britain, Southeast Asia and the onset of the Pacific war.
Bibliography.
Includes index.
1. World War, 1939–1945 – Diplomatic history. 2. Great
Britain – Foreign relations – Asia, Southeastern. 3. Asia,
Southeastern – Foreign relations – Great Britain. I. Title.
940.5322

Library of Congress cataloguing-in-publication data

Britain, Southeast Asia and the onset of the Pacific War/
Nicholas Tarling.
p.   cm.
Includes bibliographical references and index.
1. Asia, Southeastern – Foreign relations – Great Britain. 2. Great
Britain – Foreign relations – Asia, Southeastern. 3. World War,
1939–1945 – Asia, Southeastern. 4. Asia, Southeastern – History.
5. Great Britain – History – George VI, 1936–1952. I. Title.
DS525.9.G7T37 1996
327.41059–dc20   95–42787

A catalogue record for this book is available from the British Library.

ISBN 0 521 55346 6 Hardback

'At this moment of supreme danger
in the West diplomacy is really
our only weapon in the East.'

Smuts, quoted in telegram from UKHCSA,
18 August 1940, 533. CAB 80/19,
Public Record Office, London

For
Fiona, Rupert and Francis
with thanks and affection

Contents

Preface

Studies of the onset of World War II are, of course, numerous, covering both its origins in Europe in 1939 and the origins of the war in the Pacific at the end of 1941, and this book does not aim to duplicate them. Its aim is to relate the events they describe to those in Southeast Asia, which, interesting in themselves, also offer a clue to understanding the transition from European war to world war. The principal focus is on the role of the British and their relationships with the territories they did not formally control.

Britain's main aim in Southeast Asia in this phase was to continue to preserve the status quo, so far as it was possible, without getting involved in an additional war. That involved attempts not only to prevent the military expansion of the Japanese but also to restrict their penetration into the area, in particular by encouraging elements of resistance to the pressure they felt increasingly able to exert because of the course of the European war. If the invasion could be averted then it might be possible to prevent a Japanese takeover by other means. If the invasion could not be averted, it might at least be made more difficult.

What the British could do in either respect was limited. Unable to maintain effective land, sea or air forces in the East, they sought to use the other strengths, commercial and financial, on which their position in the world had long relied. They also drew on their diplomatic talents. But their diplomacy was unlikely to have much impact unless it could involve the Americans. Securing that involvement could indeed have drawbacks. Once engaged, the US might act with a boldness the British could not have envisaged and provoked Japanese reaction that would in fact destroy the status quo. In the event there was no alternative to that risk. The British perhaps underestimated it. But in any case such a development would have the advantage of involving the US and the UK ever more closely in a common cause, and that was the overriding consideration for the British at the end of two desperate years of European war. Southeast Asia abruptly ceased to be an area where the status quo was substantially preserved. It was suddenly and wholly overthrown.

Britain's policies towards the various territories in Southeast Asia, as might be expected, had an overall similarity of purpose and indeed of approach. Even in respect of territories under the formal control of the British their approach had to take account of the realities of power. Dealing with the government of Burma, or even the Raja of Sarawak, was in part a matter of diplomacy, as was dealing with Thailand. Dealing with the territories under other colonial powers had always been more complex and approaches more diverse. In these years the diversity increased. The Americans reinforced the Philippines; the French made a deal with the Japanese; the Dutch Government fled to London. Each of them had to be handled differently, although the common object was to uphold the status quo as far as possible. The British indeed sought to work with the Vichy regime in Indo-China rather than to overthrow it.

In the making of British policy Japan and the United States were, of course, of prime importance. The book thus takes their policies into account and indeed prompts some reflection about them. But for the Americans' interest in the outcome of the European war, the fate of Southeast Asia would have been of far less interest to them. At the same time the mobilisation of their power in order to cope with the European crisis of 1940 alarmed the Japanese and concentrated their attention on Southeast Asia, too.

In attempting to depict the interrelationship between the course of the war and the changes in Southeast Asia which British policy had to cope, I have divided the book into five chapters. Each covers a phase in the development of the war. The first is an introductory chapter, covering the period up to September 1939. The second covers the 'phoney war' phase and the period up to the fall of France. The third covers the three critical months between that crisis and the tripartite pact of September 1940. The fourth takes the reader up to the German invasion of Russia. The final chapter covers the six months that climax with the bombing of Pearl Harbor and the invasion of Malaya.

Each chapter is structured in a similar way. An opening section attempts to set out the policies of the British and of the other great powers and the relationships among them, also commenting on the policies of the Pacific dominions, especially Australia. Then the chapters examine each territory of Southeast Asia in terms of the policy the British attempted to develop towards it and to carry through. Netherlands India is dealt with first, then the Philippines, French Indo-China and Siam. Burma and the other territories under British control are given less detailed attention. Some reference is made to Portuguese Timor.

The making of British policy was a complex matter. In London it involved the Prime Minister, Cabinet and Cabinet committees, including the Chiefs of Staff and, later, the Defence Committee and the inter-departmental Far Eastern Committee. It involved the Foreign Office, with its own regional departments and its local representation, as well as the Colonial and Dominions Offices. It involved the dominions themselves, making a contribution either through the DO and the High Commissioners in London and the dominion capitals or more directly. The general thrust was determined by the Prime Minister and key Cabinet colleagues. But officials at the Foreign Office, in particular those of the Far Eastern Department, were persistent in their attempts to influence a policy that they were disposed to think should be bolder and more inventive in its attempts to make bricks with very little straw. Their analyses, dealt with in detail, throw light on the complex issues raised, for Britain and indeed for other powers, by the interconnectedness of events in Europe, the world, the region and the territories.

The book may be of interest to those concerned with international history, with British history and with Southeast Asian history. In general it should help to correct the tendency to see 1939 as the beginning of a world war. More particularly, it exemplifies the attempts of the British to play out their world role in the twentieth century in other terms than the mere application of force in which they were deficient. Thirdly, the book tells part of the story of the collapse of nineteenth-century imperialism in Southeast Asia. That region has always been open to the play of outside influences. Never was it more so than in these years. Outside influences brough catastrophe to the colonial regimes, although the war was followed by attempts to restore them. War brought revolution to the colonial peoples, mixing opportunity and catastrophe, but offering them a greater prospect of independence than they would have secured otherwise.

Studies of this phase have so far focused, on the one hand, on the activities of the main protagonists, Japan and the US, and on the other hand, on particular states and territories, above all Thailand. Writings on the British have concentrated on the inadequate defence of Malaya and the surrender of Singapore in February 1942. Writings on non-British territories other than Thailand have tended to be apologetic in nature. The present study attempts to fill some of the gaps without undue duplication, and perhaps to make the total more than the sum of the parts, by adopting a regional approach and by integrating an account of Britain's policy in Europe and the world at large with an account of its policies in Southeast Asia.

I have relied above all on unpublished records in the British archives, in particular those of the Foreign Office and the Cabinet in the Public Record Office at Kew. I have also drawn substantially on the documents published by other governments, in particular those of the US and Australia. Ranging so widely, I have certainly incurred many debts to other scholars but no doubt also fallen into many errors of my own. I am grateful to the *Journal of Southeast Asian Studies* and the *Southeast Asian Review* for publishing earlier versions of parts of this book, to Dr Brook Barrington for his comments on the typescript and to Mrs Elaine Hull, who typed it.

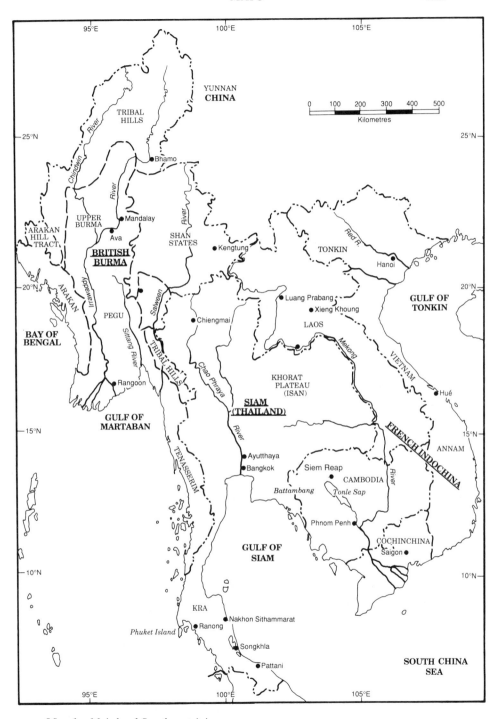

Map 1   Mainland Southeast Asia

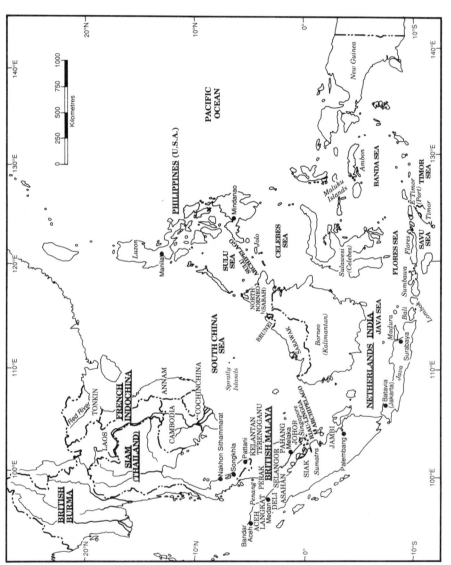

Map 2 Island Southeast Asia,

CHAPTER 1

Before September 1939

Britain and the world

The war of 1939 was a European war; it did not become a world war until 1941. Britain was a world power as well as a European power, which was a source of its strength as well of its weakness. It was also the reason for Germany's envy and for its frustration.

The European states had extended their influence in the world at large in substantial part because of their rivalry. By securing resources from outside Europe they could dominate other European rivals or secure independence from them. Rivalry with France, which had drawn Britain into India, culminated in the victories of Trafalgar and Waterloo. Britain enjoyed an unusually strong position among European powers by the mid nineteenth century. It was enhanced by its industrial pre-eminence. Indeed that prompted more moderate attitudes to territorial dominion than those of earlier European states with worldwide interests. Britain allowed the settler territories to govern themselves. It did not deprive other European powers of colonial opportunities. It tried to avoid creating further Indias.

Industrial pre-eminence did not last. The Industrial Revolution spread to other countries, in Europe and outside Europe. As a result Britain was faced with economic and political problems. Economically it faced the rivalry of other industrialising economies, sometimes more innovative, sometimes better resourced, often more protected. Britain met that rivalry in ways that were often thought inadequate. In some areas it met it head on with some success. Occasionally it resorted to a protected market, although it never indulged in full protectionism. It tended to turn to banking and investment and away from trade and manufacturing.

Politically Britain faced two major changes. First, it lost the security that the balance of power had offered on the continent of Europe since the defeat of France. With the unification and industrialisation of Germany, one state on the continent clearly became more powerful than any other. Furthermore, that dominance undermined the naval supremacy that Britain had established. Germany itself began to build a great navy, and it became all the more important that other navies of Europe should not threaten the British. Britain's own security was at stake.

Traditionally rivalry in Europe had prompted extension in the rest of the world. For Britain, however, to draw on resources in the rest of the world now in order to preserve the status quo in Europe was not easy, other than in economic and financial terms. First, its empire in the world rested in large part on economic links that were under challenge, rather than on political links. Second, other powers were emerging overseas, too. It would be necessary to seek their support. The emerging dominions would have to be won over; that was even more the case with independent powers like Japan and above all the US. Yet they, of course, had their own objectives, not necessarily consistent with those of the British.

What would be most damaging for Britain would be a challenge outside Europe and a challenge within Europe at the same time. In World War I that had been avoided, and indeed the resources of the world had been gathered into an alliance that finally secured an armistice with the Germans. While the Russians had been defeated, the French had not, and the Americans had been drawn in. While the Japanese were ambitious, they were yet allied to the British and thus restrained as well as encouraged by them. The position was very different by the opening of the war in Europe in 1939. But the role the rest of the world would play was important both to Britain and to Germany.

Hitler's ambition was, not unlike the Kaiser's, to replace Britain as the leading European power. A prolonged war was not to his advantage; it might overextend his resources and, as in World War I, draw in additional enemies. The British, by contrast, could only hope to outlast Hitler rather than defeat him. In the event he determined to attack Russia, while the mobilisation of American power prompted the Japanese to act. The British had differed among themselves about the way the resources of the world might best be made available. Was it better to preserve the status quo in the Far East? Was it better for the US not to become an active participant? In the event the US was directly involved. Britain was saved. But in the meantime it suffered great losses, and at the end of the war it emerged on the winning side rather than victorious.

The colonial structure of Southeast Asia had been created in the period of British primacy. It lasted until the Japanese incursion of

1941–42. This book examines Britain's attempts to preserve it during the struggle with Germany that began with the Nazi invasion of Poland at the end of August 1939. Essentially the strategies of the British were those they had adopted at the beginning of the century. Their main focus was on Europe. So far as it could be done they sought to maintain the status quo elsewhere. Their main means was diplomacy. Their military power was insufficient, which of course itself limited the effectiveness of their diplomacy. Through diplomacy they sought to contain the Japanese as well as to avoid provoking them.

Major changes since the beginning of the century had changed the context of diplomacy. They had also changed the relative power of the states concerned. They had not, however, dislodged the Southeast Asian status quo. The British were aware of their weakness, although cautious about displaying it. But it might be that success in preserving the status quo so far had produced an undue hope that it could still be sustained and contributed, along with the priority given to Europe, to the failure to provide adequately for its defence or to recognise fully the possibilities of disaster.

The impact of World War I

By the 1890s Southeast Asia included territories that Britain directly ruled, like Burma, conquered in three stages from British India; Singapore and the Straits Settlements, acquired as a protection for the Straits of Melaka; and Labuan, an island colony acquired in the 1840s as part of a Borneo policy never fully taken up. There were, however, three Borneo territories – Sarawak, Brunei and North Borneo – with which Britain had made protectorate agreements in 1888, and it had closer relations with several of the Malay states on the peninsula, which in 1895 had become the Federated Malay States.

Other colonial powers in island Southeast Asia existed partly on the sufferance of the British. The Netherlands were in the process of filling out their claims to a realm that extended from Sabong to Merauke. Internationally that had involved deals with the British, including the treaties of 1824 and 1871, as well as the policy of a commercial open door, marked, for example, by the tariff of 1872. Although without the same kind of specific treaty relationships, Spain in the Philippines recognised the primacy of the British in a somewhat similar way; it permitted them a major economic role, hoping thereby to diminish any political challenge. The French had established themselves in what they called Indo-China. To this the British had offered little opposition. Their concern had only been to limit French expansion. The main objective was to preserve Siam as a buffer between the empires. To that the diplomacy of the Thais, under the absolute monarchy of the Chakri kings, and their determination to maintain independence, substantially contributed. They succeeded, although having to make territorial concessions and 'unequal' treaties. Southeast Asia in the period of British primacy was a patchwork of jurisdictions, colonial, pseudo-colonial and independent European and Asian. On its remote verge stood a remnant of the earliest European empire, Portuguese Timor.

The form British primacy thus took naturally reflected Britain's interests. The main concern of the British, in Southeast Asia and in general, was to preserve and enhance the economic opportunity their security and their prosperity gave them. Their political interests seconded those objectives. Territorial control was not the prime objective; the aim was to ensure conditions under which commerce might flourish. India was an exception to prove the rule. There Britain had established a unique dominion, and it had its own political and strategic imperatives, which had a profound impact on the fate of Burma. But elsewhere Britain's interests lay in preserving the security of the sea lanes through Southeast Asia on which its connection with China depended and on preserving open-door access to the economic opportunities the area itself supplied.

The situation began to change in the 1890s above all as a result of changes in the world at large. The emergence of other industrial powers challenged Britain's primacy. Its attempt to meet the economic challenge was perhaps more limited than it might have been. Its attempt to meet the political challenge by a more assertive imperial policy was also limited; its dependencies had acquired considerable independence, and they had no intention of throwing it away. Its main thrusts were naval and diplomatic. There were limits to British naval power; other industrial powers also expanded navally. Even greater emphasis was placed on Britain's diplomatic resource. In a sense that had always been its approach. Britain had perceived the world as one of nations, tied above all by economic relations. That perception disposed it to adjustment, and the major changes after the turn of the century were perceived as continuing that policy. Perhaps that was mistaken: some have argued that the changes should have been greater. Perhaps it was misleading: the changes were after all substantial.

Indeed no options were likely to be very palatable. Some, however, were more palatable than others. What concerned the British most was the rise of Germany. The core of British policy had been and was to remain its security in Europe. That could be undermined by the rise of a power with aspirations to what its Kaiser called a Napoleonic hegemony.

The governments of the late 1890s and the early years of the twentieth century in vain sought an understanding with the second Reich but reached none. They adopted what came to be another prime feature in British policy: a relationship with the US that at the very least avoided conflict and that made the most of what the powers had in common. They also sought to diminish conflict with other European powers, in particular with France, and with Russia. With Russia the task was more difficult than with France. Russia had long been perceived as a threat to Britain's interests in Asia, and in particular to its dominion in India, and one that Britain, with its emphasis on naval power, had not felt entirely confident it could meet. Faced with changes in many parts of the world, but having to concentrate its strength more and more on Europe, Britain found it additionally difficult with the new thrust in Russia's Asian policy associated with Witte and the building of the trans-Siberian railway. It hoped to meet the Russian threat by its alliance with Japan of 1902.

Yet Japan itself wanted change. What form of change was not clear. It was concerned at the opportunities given the Western powers by the disintegration of China and in particular by the strategic threat of Russia. Would it aid the Chinese or would it emulate the West? Industrialising on a slender resource basis, Japan was also deeply interested in foreign economic opportunities. Could it acquire them or would frustration also drive it to imperialism? Britain's fundamental concern in the Far East had been China where it had led the way in making the unequal treaties but wished to maintain territorial integrity and the open door. There, as elsewhere, Britain wished to uphold the status quo as far as possible. Britain's relationship with Japan was likely to be ambivalent. Could it contain and channel the energies of the Japanese? Could they expect sufficient support against other European powers? None had been forthcoming in 1895 when Japan acquired Taiwan and secured the independence of Korea but was compelled by the Triple Intervention of Russia, France and Germany to disgorge its gains in Manchuria.

Britain's relations with its own dependencies themselves took on more of a diplomatic character. If they had become politically more independent that had been within the worldwide framework of Britain's economic and naval power. That framework was weakening, and the dependencies were increasingly faced with new foreign policy questions, indeed, it might be said, with the need for a foreign policy. 'Australia, in spite of herself, is being forced into a foreign policy of her own because foreign interests and risks surround us on every side,' declared Alfred Deakin, one of the founders of the recently established Commonwealth. 'A Pacific policy we must have.'[1] For Australia the rise of Japan, and Britain's increasing concentration in home waters, raised a major issue. Should it contribute to the British fleet, or should it defend its own home waters? 'A policy which disregards the Pacific, or leaves it to Japan', declared Frederic Eggleston, then in Australian municipal politics, in March 1914, 'cannot be regarded as a truly Imperial policy.'[2] A two-ocean dilemma now confronted the empire. New Zealand, more remote, smaller, concerned about markets worldwide, but above all in Britain, tended to favour the first option: one Empire, one Flag, one Fleet, in the phrase of its Prime Minister, Sir Joseph Ward.[3]

What happened in Southeast Asia was likely to be of increasing interest to these states. But before World War I the changes there were limited. The US acquired the Philippines in the course of its war of 1898 with Spain. Britain had been unable to prevent that acquisition. Its preference was for maintaining Spanish control, but American was better than German. Moreover, the US, by joining the imperialist powers in Southeast Asia, helped to preserve the nineteenth-century pattern. Change in the Philippines meant maintaining the status quo elsewhere. It was not so much that the Philippines revolution had been likely to spur on nationalism elsewhere, although US intervention certainly destroyed the first republic in Southeast Asia. More important, US intervention in the Philippines inhibited any intervention by the Japanese, already established in Taiwan. The ruling oligarchy of Japan was in any case cautious, chastened by the Triple Intervention. The aid given by Japanese extremists was limited.

The Britain–Japan alliance of 1902 tended the same way. In some sense it enlisted Japanese acceptance of the status quo at least for the time being. Indeed some Japanese then and since have seen it as a kind of alliance against nationalism: 'one of the main intentions of the Alliance was to contain the aspiration of Asian people for freedom'.[4] That view might exaggerate the strength and perceived threat of nationalism. But it has some validity. The alliance not only limited Japan's threat as a power; it also emasculated pan-Asianism, another form of international challenge to the British imperial framework, by supporting the real-politikers among the Japanese policymakers.

The Japanese came to terms with the other colonial powers, too. In 1907 they made an agreement with the French, accepting their claims over Vietnam, Cambodia and Laos, as did their allies the British who, pressed in Europe, had made the entente in 1904; the two governments

> having a special interest in seeing wider and peaceful conditions secured especially in the regions of the Chinese empire adjoining the territories where they have rights of sovereignty, protection or occupation, undertake to assist each other in assuring peace and security in the regions in order to maintain their respective situation and the territorial rights of the two contracting parties on the Asian continent.[5]

In 1912 the Dutch gave Japan most-favoured-nation treatment in the Indies.

In World War I itself, unlike World War II, there was no substantial conflict in Asia. But the war had dramatic effects both as to the framework within which empires were sustained and within the empires themselves. In the prewar period the British had already withdrawn some of their naval forces from East Asia, relying on their ally Japan to maintain the status quo. But the Japanese wished to change the status quo in their own interest; although restrained by their alliance partner, they were also encouraged. The absorption of Europe in the war gave them new opportunities in East Asia. They exerted pressure on China, particularly with the twenty-one demands of 1915. They were able to take over German colonies, including the Caroline and Marshall Islands, and German concessions in China, and although that was far from welcome to the Chinese or the Allies, it was accepted, even by the Americans when they entered the war in 1917. The Japanese also prospered economically, becoming for the first time a creditor rather than a debtor nation. It was not certain that these opportunities would satisfy them. The appetite might grow with feeding.

The war had its effect on India, too. The British, as ever, were concerned about subversion, and indeed the Germans were alive to the possibilities of Sikh extremism. At the same time the British found it necessary to involve India increasingly in the war. The spread of the war into Turkey involved Indian interests, and Indian labour was needed even in Europe. The involvement urged the British into new undertakings towards Indians. Towards the end they committed themselves to the goal of self-government along the lines of the settler dominions, the war precipitating a formulation so far only implicit. The policy for India, Edwin Montagu, the Secretary of State for India, declared, was 'the gradual development of self-governing institutions with a view to the progressive realization of responsible government in India as an integral part of the British Empire'.[6] That concession also had to be extended to Burma.

The collapse of the tsarist regime during the war left the way open for the Bolshevik seizure of power in 1917. That event had a message for the workers of the world, which indeed the Comintern was to take up. Its initial aspiration was for revolution in Europe amid the postwar chaos. Failing to achieve that, it looked to revolution elsewhere as a means of undermining capitalism. In particular it looked to the colonies and the underdeveloped countries, and its opposition was directed above all against the British, the predominant colonial power and the power that benefited most from the unequal treaties against which Chinese nationalists were now struggling. A traditional threat to the British-sponsored political system had come from imperial Russia; now it had a new ideological dimension. Moreover, that dimension crossed the frontiers in a way the old threat had not and reduced the isolation of opposition movements in the colonial and underdeveloped territories.

In a sense, however, the Bolsheviks had a rival. The US entered the war in 1917, making it a world war but also enhancing its ideological character. American power and ideals were now sure to play a larger part in the shaping of the world, and Wilsonian policies, with their emphasis on self-determination and nationality, were indeed to some extent competing with Bolshevik ideology. Both opposed the old colonial system and gave the redemption of China a special emphasis. The fact that the Americans in the Philippines lagged a little behind their own pretensions – despite the promises of the Jones Act and the 'Filipinization' policies of Governor F.B. Harrison – did not undermine the impact of their ideas in general. The fact that they did not join the League of Nations, which they had sponsored, did not destroy the impact of its agencies in colonial territories.

Yet the impact on Southeast Asia of all the wartime changes was limited. Britain's opponents had not effectively brought the war to Southeast Asia. Its Japanese ally restrained itself, concentrating on China, on economic opportunity and, at the war's end, on Siberia. The Indian troops in Singapore mutinied in 1915, which was disconcerting, and the lack of British forces in the area was shown up. Pan-Asians among the Japanese made rather more than the British liked of the assistance they afforded their ally. 'What is the significance to be attached to the fact that the flag of the Rising Sun was set up in the centre of Singapore?'[7] An alliance with the Japanese, although designed to maintain the status quo, always offered some threat to it. Now Japan seemed to be supporting the British almost too clearly, which showed that they needed support and not merely in respect of a threat from another power but within their own territory. Some Japanese would indeed have preferred a direct break with the British alliance. But no such break ensued, and the alliance continued till 1921–22.

Victory did not bring change either. The possessions of the defeated Germans in the Pacific were distributed, but they had acquired none in Southeast Asia. The Paris treaty offered no new opportunities, therefore, although it put Australia into New Guinea and Japan into the Pacific islands. The Washington international conference of 1921–22 provided an Asian counterpart to the Paris conference. Its decisions involved major changes, but the territorial framework even so appeared to be relatively secure. The Anglo-Japanese alliance itself was displaced, but the alliance had always had somewhat equivocal implications for Southeast Asia. While it had been displaced more because of American and

Canadian pressure than because of that of Britain's Asian or Australasian allies or dominions, its abandonment did not appear to be a source of concern. The pledges of the four-power, five- and nine-power treaties increased the sense of security. They supported the territorial status quo, diminished the prospect of naval rivalry and upheld the integrity of China and the open door. While the Netherlands was not directly involved in this security system, the powers, by identic notes, pledged to sustain the status quo in respect of Netherlands India too.

The changes were, however, perhaps more important, at least potentially, than the continuity. The treaties were made in the Washington spirit, but it was only that spirit that would preserve them; they contained pledges, but there were no sanctions behind them. The Japanese had accepted the treaties, despite the blow that the loss of the old British alliance seemed now to represent – 'A strong and healthy evergreen tree, which had symbolised peace in the orient for over twenty years, had been felled', as Ito Masanori, a journalist who covered the Washington conference, put it[8] – and despite the limits on their naval building under the five-power treaty. The system indeed provided security for Japan in East Asia. No other state could modernise its naval fortifications in the area, and the ratios in capital ships were such that, given the worldwide commitments of the UK and the US, they could not challenge Japan in East Asian waters. But Japanese interests in China were less secure. While the Washington powers envisaged a gradual accommodation between Chinese nationalism and outside interests, and thus the gradual dissolution of the unequal treaties, it was unlikely that such a process would satisfy an impatient Chinese nationalism, fuelled initially by a communist alliance and later sustained despite or because of a break in that alliance. In times of prosperity the Japanese might be content with the opportunities they still had in China. But if they determined to take more forceful steps to protect their interests, international treaties would provide few real obstacles in their way. The war had made the US the leading Western power. Whether it would use its power to uphold the settlement was quite uncertain. Indeed Charles E. Hughes, the Secretary of State, had made it clear that its interests would not require the US to intervene in China.

If the US were unwilling, the British would be unable. Their wealth had been greatly depleted by the war. Their navy, it was now quite clear, could only be a one-ocean navy. They could place it in the East only if there were no crisis in Europe. For the purpose they had to build a base in Singapore, which the Washington treaties permitted, but the cost would be substantial. The fact that it was built, coupled with the substantial development in Britain's economic involvement on the Malay Peninsula, which made it a dollar-earner when dollars were needed, both focused Britain's interest on the area and added to the conviction that it would be defended. But that could not happen if no naval forces were available or if those forces that were were not defended from the growing threat of air power. The concept that Singapore was a 'fortress', with intrinsic strength, was misleading. The two-ocean dilemma was recognised rather than resolved.

The 1920s saw change within China itself. The Kuomintang (KMT) and Chinese Communist Party allied in order to reunify China and undo the unequal treaties, and enjoyed success in the south and centre. Entrenched in the nineteenth-century system of unequal treaties in those regions, the British had borne the brunt of their attack. But they came to believe that they should try to accommodate Chinese nationalism and, working with the new élite as with the old, put their interests on a more collaborative basis. This was the purport of British Foreign Secretary Austen Chamberlain's policy of 1926, and it was in keeping with the general thrust of British policy in East Asia as elsewhere since the war, if not indeed since the beginning of the twentieth century. The essentials could be retained by adjustment within a more or less stable international system.

The Chinese with the Japanese were to find adjustment less easy. While the focus of the nationalists and their communist allies was on central China the Japanese did not feel threatened, and the policy of 'China Friendship' associated with the Foreign Minister, Shidehara, could be sustained. But when the Northern March reached the north the Japanese became more anxious over the protection of their rights and interests. Nor was the break between KMT and CCP that emerged with their very success likely to reduce Japanese anxiety. The KMT, anxious to show that the break would not mean that they would neglect China's status, sought the end of unequal treaties as demonstratively as ever, if not more so. The focus was Manchuria, and there the tension was apparent from 1928. Extremists in the Kwantung army of the Japanese had assassinated the Manchurian warlord, and his son hoisted the KMT flag. But it was the onset of the depression that made the next incident decisive. This time Japanese troops secured control of Manchuria, and the government at home lost control.

Japanese expansion in the 1930s

The realism of the Meiji phase had been modified by the internationalism of Shidehara. In turn it had given way to a more aggressive approach inconsistent with the Washington spirit and with the kind of adjustments the British envisaged. Moreover it increasingly invoked a Japanese nationalism that took up and reshaped early pan-Asian ideals and was conceived in terms of the reordering of the East Asian region. The states of the area would find their position within a Japanese sphere of influence. Japan would reconcile nationalism and imperialism by establishing puppet states.

Opposition from other major powers was ineffectual. There was no collaboration between the Soviet Union and the maritime powers, and the latter differed among themselves. None was disposed to intervene in Manchuria with force, and indeed none had force available. 'These acts do not imperil the freedom of the American people, the economic or moral future of our people', President Hoover declared. 'I do not propose ever to sacrifice American life for anything short of this.'[9] What the Japanese had done, however, defied the Washington treaty and the Washington spirit. The US took up a policy of non-recognition associated with Secretary of State Henry L. Stimson, although it had in fact already begun to develop the policy in 1917, if not in 1900. It insisted not that change could not be brought about but that it could not be brought about by force. If it were such change would not be recognised. The US was quite unwilling to do more, although later Britain was blamed for the inaction. Unable itself to act, Britain indeed had little enthusiasm for the non-recognition policy, and it was to remain a bone of contention between the two Western powers. What made non-recognition an easy course to adopt was not only a residual sympathy for Japan's position but also the assumption that Western disapproval might help to restrain the Japanese. In the past they had been unwilling to challenge the West openly and, although the old oligarchy was no longer in control, some caution yet remained. It diminished not only because of changes within Japan but also because of the impact on the other powers of the rise of Nazi Germany.

While complete success evaded them the objectives of the Japanese continued to expand throughout the 1930s. In 1934, with the so-called Amau doctrine, they spoke in terms of a Monroe doctrine for East Asia, paralleling the doctrine that the US had more than a century before adopted in respect of Latin America. At the end of the same year the Japanese determined to abandon the Washington naval treaty and aim for parity in naval building. Adopting Fundamental Principles of National Policy in 1936, Japan committed itself not only to establishing a lasting peace in East Asia by holding back both the Soviet and the maritime powers and, it was conceived, securing as a result its dominance over China; it also committed itself to taking 'footsteps' in Southeast Asia, of particular interest because Netherlands India was a source of oil. This now all-important fuel the Japanese mostly drew from sources in the US,[10] whose navy furthermore commanded the Pacific. The same year the Japanese enhanced their contact with Nazi Germany through the

Anti-Comintern Pact, designed, so far as they were concerned, to make the Soviet Union more cautious in East Asia and the colonial powers more ready to make concessions in Southeast Asia.

The Japanese were indeed aware of, although perhaps slow to recognise fully, the magnitude of the tasks they imposed on themselves. The general staff saw that a major mobilisation of the resources and labour available in Japan, Manchuria and northern China would be needed, and a long-term planned build-up would be needed also. Meanwhile it opposed additional external commitments. But it opposed them in vain. The Marco Polo Bridge incident of July 1937 escalated into an undeclared war with China. By the end of 1937 the Japanese were attacking Chiang Kai-shek's capital, Nanking.

The Premier, Prince Konoe, had never seen the peace as other than an attempt by the British and the Americans to maintain a status quo that suited them.[11] He allowed the episode to turn into a Great Patriotic Endeavour, outmanoeuvring the general staff, although, perhaps paradoxically, with the intention of driving through the legislation needed for the all-out mobilisation of resources and labour that they in fact wanted: 'in the China conflict, all interested groups found certain advantages'.[12]

Foreign powers also provide a context for the logic of Japan's decisionmaking. China was, of course, part of it. After the Manchurian episode the Japanese had a low estimate of the Chiang Kai-shek regime and tended to see its weakness rather than the strength of Chinese nationalism. That attitude had more than one result. It made them exacting and encouraged them to press ahead, even though success evaded them. It also led them to attribute China's continued resistance to intervention by other powers, who, they thought, must be keeping it alive. If they could exclude the influence of the Soviet Union and keep the Western powers at bay, they concluded, China must fall. Their estimate of other powers also derived from Manchuria. The Soviet Union, under Stalin's five-year plans, was rebuilding in the Far East, and it was conscious that Japanese troops were now back in strength on the mainland. In turn the Japanese army was anxious about the Soviet military threat, and the Japanese foreign ministry was concerned about Soviet political and propaganda activity. Although making them nervous, these factors tended to spur the Japanese to greater effort. So did the attitude of the Western powers. Protesting over Manchuria and resorting to the policy of non-recognition in 1932, they had nevertheless not interposed against the Japanese venture. The Japanese could well conclude that the Western powers might continue to resort to words rather than deeds. The traditional arguments for caution now had a diminished effect, and Stimson's doctrines were seen as provocative.

Japanese expansion in East Asia coincided from 1933 with the rise of the Nazi power in Europe. Britain's two-ocean dilemma was intensified. The European threat was, of course, the prime one since it affected the security of Britain itself. That led some British leaders, in particular Chancellor of the Exchequer Neville Chamberlain and the Treasury, to contemplate a compromise with the Japanese; indeed the concept of some accommodation with the Japanese remained a feature of Britain's policy. The main obstacle in East Asia itself was the position of China. Britain had long been committed to China's integrity and, although it had accepted infringements of it in the past, it was hard to contemplate the wholesale abandonment of long-held principles, and indeed of long-held privileges, that a deal with the Japanese was likely to imply unless perhaps it were part of an overall détente. Moreover such a deal would be a blow at Britain's prestige, a demonstration of its weakened position that might undermine its hold on its possessions and its standing with other states in Asia. But the main obstacle to the deal lay in the relationship with the US, and in the relationship of the Americans with China. The determination to avoid conflict with the US that had marked British policy since the beginning of the century had been followed by American intervention in the war. If the European balance were again upset, that help would again be needed. While US policy was uncertain, that possibility, it was generally thought, should not be foreclosed. The commitment of the US to China was itself uncertain, but it was likely to oppose an Anglo-Japanese agreement at China's expense. 'It may be that in no circumstances could we count on any assistance from the US. But by an alliance with Japan we should forfeit all chance of it ...', wrote Sir Alexander Cadogan. 'It must be the USA every time I think,' wrote R.G. Vansittart.[13]

American interests in China were indeed limited, as had been made clear at Washington. But that did not mean that the US was unconcerned about changes there. American missionary activities had helped to idealise China, and the US had identified with what had been British policies, the integrity of China and the Open Door. Wartime idealism had given these concerns a new context: China's redemption from the inequalities of the nineteenth century was associated with the end of imperialism and with a Wilsonian approach to world affairs. In what ways or to what extent the US would attempt to carry through this approach no one knew, and the onset of the depression added to the uncertainty prompted by isolationism. Its impact on China in particular was unclear. The Stimson answer – to disapprove of and not to recognise changes brought about other than by peaceful means – was repeated by the Roosevelt administration. 'We may have to, we may even wish to acquiesce. It does not follow that we must or we should give assent,' wrote

Stanley Hornbeck at the State Department.[14] The US seemed unlikely to do more than disapprove, even after the opening of the Sino-Japanese war.

Cordell Hull, the Secretary of State, indeed generalised the principles that Stimson had evoked. A press release of 16 July 1937 included the words:

> We advocate abstinence by all nations from use of force in pursuit of policy and from interference in the internal affairs of other nations. We advocate adjustment of problems in international relations by processes of peaceful negotiation and agreement. We advocate faithful observance of international agreements. Upholding the principle of the sanctity of treaties, we believe in modification of provisions of treaties, when need therefor arises, by orderly processes carried out in a spirit of mutual helpfulness and accommodation.[15]

Iteration of the principles, it was hoped, might promote adhesion to them. The approach, however, had two risks. One was that US pronouncements would appear to other powers to be impractical and irrelevant, and they might be tempted to ignore them. The other risk was that the US itself could not ignore them. The principles prescribed a framework within which it had to engage in diplomacy. At the same time as it emphasised such an approach to international relations, however, the US possessed great potential, and it did not doubt that it could deploy its potential if it so chose.

US policies were frustrating for the British. On the one hand, they inhibited any deal with the Japanese that might diminish the two-ocean dilemma. They did not, on the other hand, provide any effective restraint on Japan. The application of American power was not actual but possible. It might come too late to prevent a sudden move by Japan, another incident, another undeclared war. A sudden application of US power, by contrast, might produce a conflict with Japan in which the interests of Britain and the colonial powers would suffer. Attempting to secure a firmer or more definite commitment from the US, however, was not necessarily desirable. Some British leaders thought that it was not even worth trying. Others recognised that it would provoke isolationist and anti-imperialist tendencies and be self-defeating. In Sir Ronald Lindsay's time as ambassador in Washington, the British 'had to keep their heads down and their mouths shut, lest they be suspected of dragging America into unwanted foreign entanglements'.[16]

The policy has been described as 'waiting for FDR'.[17] Even that might, however, be a misinterpretation so far as East Asia was concerned. But for the war of 1939 Britain might have gone on waiting. The US endorsed principles for the conduct of international relations in East Asia, but it did not apply them even in the face of increasing Japanese violence.

It looked to an East Asian system built on respect for sovereignty and reciprocal trade. But for the violent methods of the Japanese it could have accepted their dominance. Even when their methods were violent it was doubtful about interposing. Indeed the US might have accepted a new order in East Asia provided it stopped short of the white dominions of Australasia. The idea of S.M. Bruce, the Australian High Commissioner in London, that the Americans were more likely to fight in the Far East than in Europe seems doubtful.[18] What was to make it possible was the importance they came to attach to Southeast Asia as a result of the impact of the European war.

In the meantime the policy of the Americans was easier to adopt, and easier for the British to accept, because of misjudgement of the Japanese, which was something they shared. The Western powers tended to depreciate Japan's chances of success in any case. They downplayed its determination and its capacity. Not only was it difficult for them to help China but also China did not really need it. Their gestures of disapproval, China's endurance and limited aid would suffice to bring the Japanese to a halt. That was a misinterpretation. The Japanese did not give up. In a sense the British, who had once relied on Japan to stem the Russian advance, now relied on the Chinese to stem the Japanese. They challenged the British program less. Indeed it seemed that they helped to blunt the challenge and to absorb the energies of the Japanese, whose determination the British were in any case inclined to underestimate. Meanwhile, it was thought, their involvement in China might at least keep them from Southeast Asia. But even that proved a mistaken appraisal. Frustration there contributed to the move south, although that was not its main source. Even then, the US and Britain tended to assume that joint opposition, strongly demonstrated, would halt the Japanese. 'The only thing that can really stop them would be the certainty that Great Britain and the United States would combine to stop them ...', wrote Frank Ashton-Gwatkin, a Counsellor at the Foreign Office.[19]

Australia and New Zealand recognised the threat that the rise of Japanese power involved. For them, as for Britain, the role of the US was all-important. What role it was prepared to play, however, was not apparent. The Australians tended to urge a deal with the Japanese. At the same time they were concerned about the implications for their defence policy. Would a fleet be available in Singapore in the event of a crisis, given the growing threat in Europe, marked by the remilitarisation of the Rhineland, the Anschluss and Munich? Should Australia contribute to that or concentrate more on its own defence? The British had offered assurances that hardly reassured. Sir Maurice Hankey had been unconvincing on his visit in 1934.[20] 'Great Britain is quite prepared to say in flowing language what the *objectives* of her policy are – such as cooperation, coordination and friendship etc etc with the great nations of the East,' wrote Sir John Latham. 'Such statements remind me of the noble candidate who states that he will not be deterred from pursuing at all costs the interests of the people.'[21]

Sir Robert Clive, the British ambassador in Tokyo, believed that American action was 'never likely to go beyond the writing of notes in order to defend the integrity of China. Japan's pan-Asian ideas are of vital interest to Great Britain. To the United States this interest is little more than academic.' Britain, Clive thought, could exert 'a moderating influence without provoking Japanese resentment'. At the Foreign Office Ashton-Gwatkin believed a policy of friendship with Japan unwise and immoral, but his colleagues tended to disagree. 'In general', wrote Richard Allen, 'we should aim at being as close friends with Japan as we can subject to not antagonising America, Russia or China ...'. 'We are ... driven, for the next eighteen months at least, to the conclusion', A.W.G. Randall added, 'that, while firmly maintaining our rights and allowing ourselves to be driven or cajoled into no dual arrangement which would compromise us with China, the USA or Russia, we must favour any reasonable détente between Japan and China and lose no opportunity of promoting a general Far Eastern détente as a necessary corollary ...'. 'We have to play for time, and to avoid clashes', Sir Robert Vansittart, the Under Secretary for Foreign Affairs, concluded. 'We have to feel our way carefully from day to day and year to year.'[22]

This qualified optimism diminished in the succeeding months. The Abyssinian crisis was followed by the remilitarisation of the Rhineland, and no new naval treaty replaced the Washington treaty the Japanese had abrogated. But there was some hope of a rapprochement with Japan in May 1937. The Foreign Office produced a memorandum on British policy in the Far East. Britain, it argued, had two main aims in the Far East, 'the absolutely essential aim, that of safeguarding Malaya, and the East Indian colonies, together with our communications to Australia and New Zealand', and 'the less vital aim, the maintenance and increase of British trade with, and commercial interest in China, Japan, Siam and the Netherlands East Indies'. Malaya and the East Indies were in many respects 'the nodal point of our overseas economy'. Their loss would be economically disastrous and, politically speaking, it 'must gravely affect and might well jeopardise our position throughout Asia'.

Yet Britain could not rule out a threat from Japan whose military action was now damaging British trade in China. The Japanese had seen that sanctions were a failure in Abyssinia but, if applied to them, might bring them to their knees. A policy of autarky had resulted, and that, and especially the need for oil, pointed to Southeast Asia, since even acquiescence in China could not give Japan all it wanted. Other motives

– fear of communism, consciousness of destiny, the desire to be a great power, to be accorded real racial equality – tended to strengthen Japanese attitudes. Much depended on European stability. A Russo-German war might permit Japan to descend on Borneo: British forces could not easily be spared from Europe at a time of such uncertainty, and Japan might expect German diplomatic support.

To discourage the Japanese Britain must show that it was not decadent or impotent. Netherlands India and the Philippines must be denied them. The possibility of cooperation with the Dutch, as well as the eventual destiny of the Philippines, 'cannot be without influence upon our defence requirements in the Far East', where the Chiefs of Staff wanted an effective defensive fleet to be available at the same time as a force was available in Europe to meet the requirements of war with Germany. Such measures would help to deter Japan's advance to the southward. But so, perhaps, would measures designed to encourage the abandonment of autarky: 'our policy should be to demonstrate clearly our determination to maintain the territorial integrity of South Eastern Asia; and at the same time to make every effort to aid Japan in fulfilling her legitimate aspirations'. The memorandum therefore discussed ways of improving relations with Japan and China and between Japan and the maritime powers.[23]

The Chiefs of Staff were far from certain that a fleet could be sent to Singapore in the event of a European war without prejudicing operations against Germany.[24] At the Imperial Conference of 1937, the Australian, New Zealand and Indian members of which secured a copy of their Appreciation, the British had kept their partners guessing, lest they cease to interest themselves in imperial defence and concentrate on the merely local, either out of confidence or lack of it.[25] The Foreign Secretary, Anthony Eden, spoke positively, however, of the prospects of American cooperation. The Australian Prime Minister, Joseph Lyons, went further. He spoke of a 'regional understanding and Pact of Non-Aggression by the countries of the Pacific', along the lines of the four-power treaty of 1922. He said he had mentioned the suggestion to Roosevelt, who said that he was ready to enter into an agreement to preserve peace, and 'that if serious trouble arose in the Pacific the United States would be prepared to make common cause with the members of the Commonwealth concerned'.[26] Yoshida's guarded welcome of the idea was followed by the Marco Polo Bridge incident.

The British had taken a somewhat more positive view of the prospect of US participation.[27] That had not been the case when Roosevelt's roving envoy, Norman Davis, proposed the 'neutralisation' of the Pacific. What did that mean? Apparently 'he had in mind an agreement between ourselves, the United States, and the Japanese, whereby the area covered

by the non-fortification clauses should be totally neutralised', no fortifications or naval bases being allowed. Hong Kong would be dismantled.
But would Japan do the same in Formosa?[28] The concept, said Vansittart,
was 'all wool', and, Eden added, 'the wool is certainly in no state to be
combed by the CID or the Imperial Conference'.[29] Sir Ronald Lindsay
said he believed that

> a neutralisation or rather disarmament policy in the Pacific could not possibly
> hurt the US strategically once they are rid of the Philippine commitment, even
> if the Japanese were to fail to keep their side of the bargain. Their influence
> for the protection of their commercial interests in China would of course
> diminish, but the average American voter would not worry about that ...[30]

It was best for Britain, James Dodds wrote from the Tokyo embassy, if the
US deferred playing its Philippines card.[31]

The war with China revived Eden's attempts to win more collaboration
from the US, particularly following the bombing of the *Panay* in
December 1937. The Brussels Conference – confused by Davis's
'thinking aloud'[32] – had got nowhere. The *Panay* incident, however,
prompted Roosevelt to suggest staff conversations with a view to a
prospective blockade of Japan, and he agreed to consider sending a
squadron on a courtesy visit to Singapore. The outcome was the visit of
Captain Royal E. Ingersoll to the UK early in 1938. The discussions, the
Americans stressed, were noncommittal and hypothetical, and their
caution was accentuated by what Reynolds calls the 'furore' in Congress
when news of the exchanges, supposed to be secret, leaked out.[33] Three
cruisers did visit Singapore for the opening of the graving dock on 14
February.[34] But the anxiety of the British over their naval weakness
conduced to the attempt to appease the Italians early in 1938 and the
Germans later in the year.

In the meantime there were some conversations with the new Japanese
Foreign Minister, Ugaki.[35] Sir Robert Craigie, the British ambassador in
Tokyo, believed in a positive outcome. The Foreign Office had, however,
shared the doubts the Dutch expressed. The Japanese would seek
recognition of Manchukuo and would pursue what they called their
interests in Netherlands India. The United States would view the
initiative with disapproval; 'likewise a keen reaction of the Chinese
Government and of the Chinese in the Netherlands Indies ... would be
inevitable ... from a selfish foreign standpoint anything is reprehensible
that might lead to the weakening of China's resistance ...'.[36] The talks
were terminated by Ugaki's resignation at the end of September.

More dramatic Japanese action followed. If Munich was influenced by
Asian as well as European concerns, the Japanese took the opportunity to
attack southern China. On 2 November Konoe called for 'a new order

which will insure the permanent stability of East Asia'.[37] In February 1939 the Japanese occupied Hainan and then the Spratly Islands in March. Hitler's coup against Czechoslovakia in March brought appeasement in Europe to an end. Hoping that the US could hold the situation in the Pacific,[38] the British sought to renew the naval conversations with the Americans. Unobtrusive talks followed in June,[39] the President insisting on secrecy.[40]

The Tientsin crisis, which began in April 1939,[41] brought near the threat of the war in Europe and Asia with which the approaches to the US had been designed to deal. The Americans declined mediation. Lord Chatfield, Minister for Coordination of Defence, believed that the British could send an effective fleet East only if it abandoned the Mediterranean, and Chamberlain urged a settlement. 'It is maddening to have to hold our hands in face of such humiliations but we cannot ignore the terrible risks of putting such temptations in Hitler's way.'[42] Late in July the President unexpectedly gave six months' notice of the termination of the US–Japan commercial treaty. The US no doubt wanted Britain to adopt a tough attitude in Europe, and the notice of termination can be seen as a gesture of moral support for those resisting Japanese encroachment. In fact, it seems, it was designed to forestall moves in Congress for or against sanctions; it was 'essentially a conservative step and a defensive one'.[43] The Soviet Union was probably more of a restraint on Japan in mid 1939 than the United States was.[44]

World War I had not disrupted colonial Southeast Asia, nor of course did the 1920s, as they were dominated by the Washington agreements and the Shidehara policy, and the chief concern of the colonial governments was over the penetration of communism into nascent political movements. In the 1930s the depression and the Manchurian incident affected Southeast Asia in general and in special ways. Southeast Asia was, of course, generally affected by the economic downturn that the crisis in America precipitated. Many of its markets collapsed; hardship, unrest and repression ensued. More broadly the depression can be seen as a major break in a phase of worldwide economic expansion that had lasted more than a century. That century had seen the shaping of many of the relationships of contemporary Southeast Asia, social, political and constitutional, and they were in that respect all challenged by economic collapse. Southeast Asia was also generally affected by the Manchurian incident. It added to international insecurity. Whatever the rights or wrongs of the matter, it showed the weakness of the League of Nations and of the postwar settlements. They could not be upheld. But the Southeast Asian status quo was not directly attacked. Instead it was subject to new tensions. The overall framework remained but came under new pressures, varying with the territory concerned.

The undeclared war had other effects. By absorbing Japanese energies it might protect Southeast Asia. 'We must leave the Chinese to fight their battle – or ours for us – and give them such assistance as we can', Cadogan wrote.[45] But if the Japanese were frustrated in China they might look to Southeast Asia in order to enhance their chances of success. In either case their activities would affect the Chinese in Southeast Asia and in turn the relationship of the Chinese communities with the Southeast Asian governments. In the latter case Japan might exert particular pressure on Southeast Asian territories that neighboured China, such as British Burma and French Indo-China. More remotely, others would be affected, too. Japanese advances in southern China, for example, affected Macau as well as Hong Kong. By making the Portuguese apprehensive about Macau they might be made more amenable in Timor.

Netherlands India

For the founder of the British settlement Singapore had been a fulcrum of British influence. In fact, for the rest of the nineteenth century, its importance had been rather economic than strategic; it had become an entrepôt for British trade with many parts of Southeast Asia. The changes of the early twentieth century, particularly of the period immediately after World War I, added to the strategic importance of Singapore. It became the second home of the one-ocean navy that now had to fulfil two-ocean commitments. It became, under the Washington agreements, a forward base for British naval power in the Far East. Whether a navy could be placed there in an Eastern crisis came, however, to be doubted as the crisis in Europe prompted by the reassertion of German power developed during the 1930s and as Italian ambitions grew. Moreover, while the navy was en route, the security of Singapore itself had to be ensured. That was one aim of the fortification. But it also depended on the position of neighbouring territories. Singapore could defend them if the navy were there, but in the meantime they could weaken its security.

To the north the British had strengthened their political control of the Malay Peninsula by establishing advisers in the northern states, claims over which had been transferred by Thailand in 1909. But they did not bring those states into the Federated Malay States, and the Straits Settlements remained separate. The attempts to create an all-Malayan union were not pressed in the 1930s. Nor was Malaya put in a position to defend itself; the British saw their role in traditional style as colonial arbiter and gave themselves the responsibility of defence. Their economic interests had become very substantial, above all with the rise of rubber, which, moreover, enjoyed a market in the US, and became a major dollar-earner, but defending them was to become more difficult. The rise of air power was also a threat. Elsewhere, it was used to back up Britain's deficiencies as an imperial power.[46] But in the hands of the Japanese it was a threat to Singapore. That meant that it was necessary to build aerodromes in Malaya and, of course, to provide fighters based on them. The threat increased as the Japanese advanced and as the range of aircraft increased.

To the south lay the Indies empire of the Dutch; indeed some of its islands were visible from Singapore. Before they decided to place the new Singapore base in the Old Strait,[47] the British gave some thought to acquiring islands south of Singapore from the Dutch – Bintang, Batam and Bulan – either by sale, by abandonment and occupation under the Anglo-Dutch treaty of 1824, by exchange, perhaps for territory in North Borneo, or by securing Portuguese Timor to Holland.[48] The GOC, Gen. D. Ridout, had recommended the acquisition. If neutral the Dutch might find it difficult to enforce neutrality in these islands. If Japan picked a quarrel with Holland it might cede certain possessions as the price of peace. Or Japan might take them in time of peace, and any action might involve Britain in war. The Japanese general staff, Ridout added, took a long view; many commanding positions were acquired for other than merely commercial reasons.[49]

The relationship with the Dutch was of long standing. Their possession of the Indies resulted from a British decision, marked by treaties of 1814, 1824 and 1871. They had sought to avoid total dependence, however, and they had opened up the Indies commercially to other powers as well,[50] even the Japanese. As de Waal, the Colonial Minister, told the States General in 1871, 'a liberal trade policy in our possessions will constitute an essential contribution to the defence of our territory against a foreign enemy'.[51] The early years of the twentieth century nevertheless caused them much anxiety. The rise of Japanese power concerned them not only because it excited their subjects but also because it appeared to be encouraged by an alliance with the British. Moreover, they were aware that the Japanese were short of oil, which was available in Sumatra and Borneo. In 1907 there was talk of a treaty with Japan, seeking maintenance of the status quo; there was talk also of some kind of participation in the Root–Takahira notes of 1908, in which the United States and Japan had pledged to respect each other's possessions in the Pacific Ocean.[52]

In World War I, by contrast to the second, the Netherlands were permitted by both sides to maintain their neutrality. The Indies became a base for German-backed subversion in British India.[53] But the British preferred not to break with the Dutch. The option their consul-general,

W.E. Beckett, offered them was certainly not attractive. He suggested making over part of Netherlands India to the Japanese; offering them a footing now might be better than trying to deal with their ambitions later. 'If the Netherlands Indies are not too friendly they are harmless. It would be quite another matter if the islands were in the hands of the Japanese and one would like to know whether the Admiralty would endorse Mr Beckett's views.'[54]

The Dutch, wrote Frank Ashton-Gwatkin, had been 'in terror of Japan; but when they realised that they had got through the war with their neutrality inviolate and therefore that the Indies were safe once more, a strong reaction set in in favour of encouraging the influx of Japanese capital.'[55] That would 'balance British and American interests in the islands and prevent any one country from getting a preponderant share'. But fear of the Japanese remained, and the Japanese, though having

> no definite political ambitions ... are obsessed by the idea that their country is one day destined to be the mistress of the Pacific and of its islands. They regard Holland as a very weak Power, and her colonial empire as doomed to disruption. Japan must have a say in the disposal of this rich empire. So she is steadily increasing her knowledge of the country, her vested interests therein, and the numbers of her merchants and colonists,

and keeping an eye on the native movement. The Dutch on the whole recognised that they could not defend the archipelago, and Ashton-Gwatkin felt that the long-standing envy and distrust of the British had diminished. That was 'gratifying; for the interests of the British and the Dutch are essentially similar, and we are clearly concerned in the maintenance of Dutch rule and the prestige of the white races in the archipelago ...'. The Dutch believed 'in the probability of an American–Japanese war, and in the likelihood of their own possessions being involved'. The result of such an upheaval 'might be most unwelcome both to us and to the Dutch'.[56]

The Dutch fears of the Japanese, evident prewar, persisted postwar, but in a different context. The British were even less likely to back them but also less able to restrain them. A war between Japan and the US was, however, likely to involve the Indies. The fears of the Dutch were reduced by the Washington agreements and the identic notes of 1922 but not eliminated. Their weakness, as 'a small country ... possessing such a vast Colonial Empire', was permanent.

> Holland realises the futility of endeavouring to defend unaided her Asiatic Possessions and ..., in the event of an armed conflict in the Pacific, she counts upon the protection of one of the Great Powers – in the first instance upon that of Britain. This crude admission has, of course, never been made officially by the Dutch, who content themselves with declaring that, in case of war, their chief purpose will be to maintain the neutrality of Netherlands India and that,

if an attempt is made to violate it, they will try to keep the enemy at bay until help arrives 'from another quarter'. But their reliance on Britain is implicit in such a statement, and they are willing to confess as much in private.

The menace could come only from Japan. Their chief desire was 'to remain neutral in any event, and ... they dislike intensely the thought of being compelled to take sides in a future conflict ...'.[57] The Dutch Colonial Minister spoke of strengthening the defences of the oil ports 'in order that the authorities may be enabled to maintain strict neutrality in the event of war between other Powers'.[58] In fact they were inadequate.[59] At most the Dutch would be able to render the oilfields useless to an enemy.[60] The sense of weakness was increased by the mutiny on *De Zeven Provincien* early in 1933 following pay-cuts.[61]

In the meantime the Manchuria crisis had undermined the Washington system, and it caused considerable apprehension in Netherlands India. In the Hague the Japanese ambassador denied that, in the event of a conflict in the Pacific, Japan would seize the oil supplies of Borneo.[62] Matsuoka introduced the idea of a nonaggression pact, the aim apparently being to ensure the supply of oil; the Dutch rejected it.[63] The British Consul-General in Batavia remarked that 'a certain feeling of uneasiness can well be understood'.[64]

> Present Japanese activities may be largely consistent with a policy of gradual economic expansion only, but seem more consistent with a longer view on the part of Japan – with a vision perhaps of the possibility that in a nearer or distant future she may wish to take more active measures to increase her influence, though a gradual expansion in the commercial sphere suffices for the moment ...[65]

In the Foreign Office W.R.C. Green agreed that there was some ground for suspicion. Pan-Asianism might promote a rising in which Japan could intervene on the plea of protecting its nationals. If Japan wished to attack Australia, or were involved in war with the US or Britain, it might feel compelled to occupy Netherlands India for strategic reasons. Certainly it would seek Borneo oil.[66]

Green alluded to the expansion of Japan's trade in the Netherlands Indies, promoted by the fact that the Dutch adhered to the gold standard and the Japanese abandoned it.[67] The Dutch proposed to close the Open Door gently rather than slam it. Quotas were introduced on imports and immigration, and the Dutch initiated discussions designed to lead to a new Dutch–Japanese commercial treaty.[68] The Japanese delegation claimed the right to share in the development of the Indies as an Asiatic land; that 'sounds so like Manchuria'.[69] The talks were stalemated.

The Japanese were suspicious that the British were securing favourable commercial treatment by promises of protection. General Lewin had visited Batavia in June 1934 and exchanged military information with General Koster. 'I cannot help feeling that such confidences are dangerous, *unless* we are willing to take on the obligations which must necessarily attach to a confidence', wrote Evelyn Shuckburgh at the Foreign Office. That was 'a question of high policy'. There was something to be said for understandings since Britain attached 'great importance' to the security of Netherlands India in time of war 'as against the Japanese. This must – or should – necessarily involve some previous consideration of the means of defence, and that in its turn would appear to necessitate some conversations with the Dutch authorities. But our eyes should be open. These initiatives cannot be left to generals.'[70] An admiral had already raised the issues. The Commander-in-Chief China, Sir Frederick Dreyer, pointed to the damage a Japanese coup in Netherlands India would do to the security of Singapore. The temptation would be increased if the US left Manila, but the Japanese might act as early as 1935, the 'critical year' for which they were preparing. Would the Americans come in or leave it to the British? A policy should be prepared, which might prompt the despatch of a fleet to the East. If the British planned to act they should tell the world.[71]

In the Far Eastern Department of the Foreign Office Allen thought that the main issue for Japan was oil. Ordinarily it was content to buy and store it 'against an evil day' and already had, it was said, two years' supply.

> There will, however, always be the risk of a moment when, from sheer nervousness, she may do something drastic, of incalculable consequences, in order to guard against what she conceives to be a menace to her supplies. Any hint of concerted action, 'sanctions', etc. (particularly if America is involved, since most of her oil supplies come from there at present) is apt to produce a crisis of this kind.

Allen did not 'see how, with the strategic distribution of our possessions in the Far East we could permit Japan to install herself in any part of the NEI'. The intervention might occur, as Green suggested, as a result of internal disturbance, as it had in Manchuria's case. In such a crisis 'neither the League of Nations nor America nor any foreign country (Siam would tend to be a catspaw for the Japanese) would be of any help to us'. America might withdraw its forces from the Philippines even before independence.

> To console us for the fear that America will 'leave us in the lurch', there are two factors to be remembered. On the one hand, Japan will certainly not move against the NEI as long as America retains any strategical hold, however nominal, over the Philippines. On the other, and paradoxical as this may sound, the more America keeps out of the Far East the less danger I think there is that Japan will ever do anything foolish in East-Indian waters. She will

neither need nor want to do so for the sake of oil so long as her supplies of it continue to be assured in a perfectly normal manner from across the Pacific.

Much depended on America's attitude – 'and who can say that the US will be prepared to disinterest themselves in the Far East for all time?' – and much also depended on the commercial opportunities afforded Japan, on its Manchurian 'adventure' and on its relations with Russia.[72]

Randall thought that 'the root of the question' was 'Japan's need for markets (which can best be expanded in peace) and oil (which can only become insistent and lead to war if there is fear of boycott and consequent panic)'.[73] C.W. Orde thought the matter ready for investigation, not decision. 'My own feeling is that Japan is too cautious to imitate pre-war Germany in pursuing all her objectives and antagonizing all her potential enemies at the same time; she will subordinate other strategical objectives till she has secured her position as against Russia.' Shuckburgh was concerned that Dutch restrictions on commerce 'would tend to have the same effect upon Japan as American interference in the Pacific or a threat to their oil supplies'.[74]

In the American Department Paul Gore-Booth agreed that no help would come from the US in dealing with a problem of this kind 'unless we found ourselves in a really critical position'. The US had a substantial trade in Japan, and the US public was in general averse 'to participation in a war which does not appear to concern it directly'.

> And although the US are retaining their Philippine naval bases until about 1947 at the earliest, and have spent considerable sums in modernizing their Hawaiian bases, there are few Americans who believe that a serious attempt could be made to defend the islands against Japan or that the use of them as a base in the event of a 'forward' Japanese policy would be a justifiable risk.

The only alternative for the US was 'a conciliatory Far Eastern Policy – tempered with the traditional "moral disapproval" of Japan'. That disapproval would be exercised in the event of Japanese action in Netherlands India, 'but there is apt to be a large gap between US moral disapproval and action'.[75]

The head of the American Department, Craigie, rather differed. It was impossible to count on the US at present: 'the normal degree of unreliability is today enhanced by a foreign policy impregnated with indecision and nurtured in ignorance'. But 'the present phase of defeatism in respect of Japanese aggression in the region of the Eastern Pacific is likely to be a passing one'. There was, Craigie thought, 'more than an even chance that the US would resist by force of arms an overt Japanese attack upon the Dutch East Indies – if only because of the future implications for the US in the success of such a stroke by Japan'.[76]

Ashton-Gwatkin thought a Japanese attack on Netherlands India 'a very remote contingency except in the case of a European war, or civil war in Great Britain and a collapse of British power'. To take all Netherlands India was a vast task; even if only parts of Borneo were seized, the transport of oil to Japan would be subject to attack. Japan had guaranteed the inviolability of Netherlands India in 1922. Manchuria was a very different case. Indeed, the Japanese adventure there lessened the likelihood of pressure south: 'Japan is so deeply involved on the Continent of Asia.' In the more likely case of war with Russia, Japan could get oil from the US as well as Netherlands India. 'To hold NEI Japan must have Singapore first.'[77]

Replying to the Admiralty, the Foreign Office suggested that, so far as British possessions were concerned

> (and there is a pretty close connection between them and the Dutch East Indies ...) the Japanese will ... only risk a general attack on British possessions in the Far East (whether as a part of, or distinct form, an attack on the NEI) if they regard themselves as absolutely safe in trying it, for instance, in the event of a European war and the complete collapse of British power in the Far East.

The seizure of the Indies would be 'an immense undertaking in any event'. But the question was not academic.

> The danger may be a real one in certain eventualities. Apart from a war which would keep us occupied the most dangerous situation would be one in which Japan felt able to count on Russian quiescence while America, after reducing herself to impotence in the Philippines, was on such bad terms with Japan as to make her nervous about her supplies of oil.

What should Britain do? 'The Dutch would probably be glad of some agreement with ourselves'; there was some suggestion on Lewin's visit to Java of an informal exchange of military information. Comment was being sought from the Hague, Batavia, Washington and Tokyo.[78]

The Japanese, the ambassador, Sir Hugh Montgomery, commented from the Hague, had aimed at something like 'an economic alliance' between Netherlands India and Japan. Their failure would not stop their attempts to increase their influence, and 'they may quite easily envisage the holding of the Archipelago in some kind of tutelage like Manchukuo'. The Dutch would destroy the Borneo oil wells if there was a danger they would fall to Japan. 'They are fully aware, they say, of the inadequacy of their defensive organisation but are determined not to yield an inch of territory without a stubborn resistance.' The solution to this paradox was that they rely upon having allies in any war with Japan, and particularly upon ourselves. This does not say however that they have the slightest wish to have such a contingency mentioned, indeed they would be insulted at the suggestion. As in Europe they take up the attitude that they are a neutral country and will not discuss their defence with anyone. In European affairs they are … preposterously touchy and as regards the Indies, where I think their danger is much more real, not less so.

Montgomery thus doubted that the Dutch would welcome an agreement with Great Britain. 'They are too afraid of getting off their fence, however agreeable they know our side to be, and they are fully aware of our interests in the matter.' Whatever conclusion the Committee of Imperial Defence reached, 'we should in no case, quite apart from our own disinclination to further commitments, make even a hint to the Dutch. The only possible position in the circumstances seems to be a sort of wordless understanding …'.[79] In Montgomery's view the Dutch believed that there was still some advantage in stressing their neutrality; it would, in a sense, sustain the spirit of the open-door policy and avoid provoking the Japanese. If need be, Britain's help could be relied on. The disadvantage of this attitude was that it meant that no real preparations could be made for joint defence.

The Washington Embassy's comment arrived after Japan had denounced the Washington naval treaty. The US had proclaimed its intention to build a navy second to none, and Quezon might be 'nervous of the liabilities of too great independence'. But on the whole it seemed that the Americans were 'disinteresting themselves increasingly in the Far East' and that they would stand aside if Japan suddenly occupied the Indies, using a local uprising as a pretext and presenting the world with a fait accompli. 'Also she would not run the risks inevitable in so serious a venture unless all the circumstances were extraordinarily favourable – first and foremost unless an Anglo-American combination against her as a result were out of the question'; Japan must act when relations were normal rather than strained. Disinclination to dollar diplomacy, the Hearst press, pacifism, commercial interest in Japan, all would argue against active intervention.

> To put it another way, if we ask ourselves whether the United States Congress, suddenly confronted by a Japanese occupation of the Netherlands East Indies – at a moment carefully selected by Japan – would decide on the delivery of an ultimatum to Japan threatening war unless that occupation were immediately terminated, we can only answer no. In the absence of some clear prior commitment – of far greater force than the Kellogg Pact – the United States would almost inevitably remain an anxious but ineffective spectator. The issue would be too remote …

Moreover, because of its sectionalism, 'in all matters of great importance, and especially in matters involving the issue of peace or war, America will always move very slowly indeed ...'. If Japan took Batavia, Swatow or even Hong Kong, the US would not act. 'But out of such seizure would emerge more or less slowly the truth that it must involve a disturbance of the whole balance of power in the Far East, and in the course of time America would discover that she could not under any conditions allow Japan to dominate the whole western coast of the Pacific ...'. But 'the change would not take place in time to be of direct comfort to the aggrieved Power'. Even Americans who favoured Anglo-American cooperation 'might not regard a Japanese attack on the Netherlands East Indies as an anti-British act'. The situation might be different if a Japanese attack, directed at Netherlands Indian oilfields, arose out of bad relations with the US. 'If in the course of any action which Japan took against the Netherlands East Indies, she happened – at a moment when American-Japanese relations were already dangerously inflamed – to commit some act which the United States regarded as a slight to their national honour ... an uncontrollable explosion of wrath here might result ...'.[80]

Occupation of even part of the Indies would be of great strategic disadvantage to Britain, Allen concluded, 'but their integrity could not be preserved against attack without the aid of British power at sea. Whether or not we should be prepared to go to war with Japan over such an issue would no doubt have to depend on the various circumstances and conditions of the particular case.' Help could be counted on neither from the US nor the League of Nations. The Dutch would help, and their submarine fleet was not without value, but they could not tie themselves down in advance. Japan, however, would be restrained both by US presence in the Philippines and by US moderation, and was preoccupied with China, Manchuria and the Soviet Union.[81] The memorandum implied that no commitment would be made. The Dutch emphasis on neutrality was, as Montgomery put it, 'far more convenient for HMG than any outright advances'.[82]

The Abyssinian crisis and the remilitarisation of the Rhineland seemed to provide the Japanese with a possible opportunity to strike south. Had there been a conflict in Europe, James Thyne Henderson suggested at the Foreign Office, there might well have been a 'Jameson' raid, as a Dutch columnist suggested. The Americans, his article said, were leaving the Philippines to its fate. Henderson thought an American move unlikely.

> In fact it might even suit the Americans to see the attention of Japan diverted towards the South-West. If and when the Powers owning colonies in the East Indies are financially able and willing to defend them some check might be set to the Japanese southward advance, but meanwhile the best defence is to absorb a large part of their energies in N. China by making difficulties for them there ....[83]

Henderson had also suggested that, 'the defence problem of the area bounded by Hong-Kong, New Guinea, North Australia, Java and Sumatra, and Rangoon' being 'essentially one problem', staff talks might have 'a salutary effect on Japanese nationalist aspirations'.[84] In fact the Dutch had become less hesitant about approaching the British. Colijn, the Prime Minister, had told the military attaché that he would value advice on armament. What option he would adopt for improving the defence of Java would 'depend on what he thinks or knows England would prefer him to do'.[85] Soon after, he discussed the matter with the ambassador himself.

> In his view it was such a vital British interest that the Dutch East Indies should not be taken by Japan, that there was little doubt that, if they were attacked by that country, Great Britain would come to the assistance of the Dutch. He said that he was precluded by the established policy of this country from suggesting any formal political arrangement for mutual assistance in that part of the world (and in any case he had doubts as to the expedience of a formal arrangement), but ... it seemed to him only commonsense to try to find out which form of defence would most usefully supplement British defence measures in those waters. He felt that he could quite well discuss the question informally with his friends in England.

'It seems to me all to the good', Montgomery commented, 'to take any opportunity that presents itself of encouraging the Dutch to be strong!'[86]

The officials at the Foreign Office agreed with Montgomery, but Eden, the Secretary of State, was dubious. Informal conversations 'might lead us rather far', he felt.

> My own feeling is that it is very much a British interest that the Netherlands Government should be in a position to defend their colonies in the East and that we should afford them as much technical assistance as we are in a position to do [Eden added the next phrase] in order to enable them to do this for themselves. We should encourage the Dutch to take all the necessary steps to defend their own colonies, but we must be careful to avoid committing ourselves to their defence ....[87]

Duff Cooper, the Secretary of State for War, thought that, before any discussions were agreed to, Britain must decide its policy in the event of Japanese aggression against the Dutch. 'We must be very careful to avoid in all this being committed in any way by Dr Colijn to defend the Dutch East Indies,' Eden wrote. The aim, the FO replied, was to give informal advice that did not imply any commitment.[88]

The Chiefs of Staff were able to define the strategic importance of Netherlands India but also stressed Britain's inability to provide adequately for it.

> We are of opinion that the integrity of the Dutch East Indies is vital to our security in the Far East, and the occupation of the Dutch Islands near Singapore by a hostile Power would be a most serious event.
>
> We do not, however, recommend that a guarantee of military support under all circumstances should be offered to the Dutch. Even if we intended to come to their assistance under all circumstances, it would be inadvisable to commit ourselves openly to this policy, which would no doubt cause the Dutch to rely on us and take little or no action to improve their defences. Moreover, with our present standard of naval strength, a one-Power standard, we are not in a position to undertake any additional commitment ...
>
> We suggest that our declared policy should at present be limited to a statement that the preservation of the status quo in the Pacific, including the integrity of the Dutch East Indies, is a major British interest ...

The Dutch should be encouraged to do all they could to prepare their defences. Informal advice would be formulated, together with proposals for British action.[89] Sir Horace Seymour thought a public statement would be seen as a guarantee and believed such would be 'premature'.[90]

At the subsequent meeting of the Committee of Imperial Defence, Vansittart stated the Foreign Office's viewpoint. Sir Ernle Chatfield, the First Sea Lord,

> suggested that Dr Colijn should be informed that the security of the Dutch East Indies is of great interest to us, and that his Government should be encouraged to do all they could to improve the defences. A declaration regarding the status quo, would, he suggested, be useful as a deterrent to the Japanese and thereby afford the Dutch additional security.

Vansittart thought Colijn could be told privately, if he pressed, that Britain was 'deeply interested' in the strategic position of Netherlands India. 'But he was opposed to any public or official declaration in the matter.' Neville Chamberlain, the Chancellor of the Exchequer, believed that the British should tell Colijn, if necessary, 'that we consider the Dutch East Indies a major British interest, but give them no guarantee of support. While agreeing that the integrity of the Islands is a major interest, it was not our only interest, and we should not in any way commit ourselves to a guarantee of assistance.' Chatfield pointed out that, if Britain could provide naval support in the event of a Japanese attack, the advice given to the Dutch might differ from that given if no such support could be provided. But the CID accepted the Foreign Office view: no guarantee, no declaration.[91] At Eden's suggestion the Cabinet refined the lack of commitment still further. He believed that it was unwise to tell Colijn that the integrity of the Indies was a major British interest. 'To use the language would be to encourage too great expectations. We would prefer to say that "It was a matter of concern to His Majesty's Government". This view was generally accepted.'[92] Eden told Colijn that Britain could accept no commitment, and Colijn replied that he had to insist on neutrality.[93]

> If the Netherlands East Indies were one of our Dominions whom we were advising on defence, we should point out that their security must rest ultimately on the power of the British fleet to control sea communications in the area ... and that their primary responsibility was to provide for their own local defence during the period before relief. We should, therefore, recommend that, after local defence requirements had been met, some form of naval contribution would be in the best interest of the Dominion.

But this line could not be adopted with the Dutch, the Chiefs of Staff pointed out; 'there is no agreement or alliance to guarantee our assistance in the event of war; and there is no Dutch fleet to send to the Far East'. The Dutch must concentrate on local defence, but 'the possibility of British assistance must to some extent be taken into account so that cooperation may be facilitated should the possibility materialise'.

The Chiefs of Staff also considered what the British might do to help the Dutch. It would involve war with Japan.

> In these circumstances our strategy of establishing the fleet at Singapore and controlling the sea communications in that area would be of direct assistance to the Dutch. The probable action of the Japanese, however, once our intervention was known, would be to establish themselves in a position from which to threaten Singapore, and the time factor would be all-important.
>
> Our naval forces on the China station would have to take such action as they could to prevent the Japanese from obtaining bases for this purpose. Apart from this action, they would be unable to afford direct assistance to the Dutch. Our immediately available forces in the Far East cannot face the Japanese fleet.

But with Dutch aerodromes, 'we might be able to reinforce by aircraft at the outset of hostilities. By this means we might increase the scale of aircraft attack that we could bring to bear against the Japanese'. This was a matter for the future, when modern aircraft, with increased ranges, were available.[94]

'Any addition to our present commitments must inevitably raise almost insuperable difficulties,' the FO declared in May 1937. But it raised the question of the Indies again; 'we seem already to be committed by our position' to their defence. A 'formal understanding' was undesirable; but 'should we not examine whether some recognition of that fact might not prove mutually advantageous?'[95] The China incident brought plans to improve relations with the Japanese to an end. It did, however, mean that they were 'pretty deeply implicated in a Continental venture', as H.H. Thomas put it. If adopted, the 'southward drive' policy of the navy would have meant armed conflict; 'whereas now we shall probably be able to restrict the fight (if fight we must) to financial and economic weapons'. A colleague at the Foreign Office pointed out, by contrast, that 'a prolonged campaign in China might cause difficulties in the oil and petrol situation' and turn Japan's attention to Netherlands India.[96]

The Brussels conference led Eden to give A.C.D. de Graeff, the Dutch Foreign Minister, assurances that the British would keep in touch with the Dutch over Far Eastern policy.[97] The Foreign Secretary had already asked the Far Eastern Department of the Foreign Office whether the CID should study the desirability of closer cooperation with the Dutch. John Chaplin wrote: 'Since it is admitted that the defence of the Netherlands East Indies is a vital British interest, it seems to be a matter of regret that we should not as yet have come to some practical understanding with the Dutch. Any formal arrangement is, of course, out of the question for both sides.' But the Chiefs of Staff obviously considered

> that some measure of common policy in regard to defence would be of great benefit. The Dutch cannot by themselves defend their own possessions against Japan; and they have no potential ally of any value but ourselves. They know, moreover, that if it lies within our power we will in our own interests defend the integrity of the Netherlands East Indies. Neither side could therefore become further committed by the institution of collaboration between the staffs at Singapore and Batavia.[98]

The Chiefs of Staff took a less positive stance than the Foreign Office: 'we view the prospect of closer collaboration with the Dutch on defence matters, even on the very limited scale suggested by the Foreign Office, with some misgivings'. Closer collaboration meant staff conversations, and they were 'apt to lead to commitments either actual or implied'. Moreover, although the integrity of the Indies was a major British interest, the islands were Britain's Achilles heel. 'If on the outbreak of war the Japanese were determined to seize those territories, there is very little we could do to prevent them unless the Dutch had been able to instal defences on a scale which ... is far beyond their resources to provide.' Closer collaboration would seem to the Dutch 'the prelude to some undertaking on our part to go to their assistance. While it might well be in our interest to do, we would hesitate to assume a commitment we might not be in a position to fulfil.' If, nevertheless, closer collaboration were decided on, the conversations should be in London, not in the East, so that they could be kept secret. If there were to be discussions with other powers in the near future those with the Dutch should follow them, not precede them. Antecedent to any discussions with the Dutch, moreover, the CID 'should lay down the precise limits to which we are prepared to go'.[99]

At the Foreign Office Orde thought the COS 'rather too nervous'. As planned in 1936, the British could make suggestions on Dutch defences, as Colijn had then requested.[100] 'The commitment exists already', Henderson insisted, whether the COS liked it or not. 'We are "committed" to defend Singapore, and so we are logically "committed" to prevent the seizure of such islands as would make that defence impossible or without further raison d'être. It is not a new commitment. It is as old as the decision to build Singapore.' The Dutch had concluded that Britain's attitude was based on fear.

> We are losing prestige – for nothing. If war came, we should have to prevent a Japanese seizure of the NEI. Why leave it to the last moment and then improvise inefficient and expensive measures, when we could do the same now at less cost, and by doing so probably ward off the danger. We must show some spirit if we wish to retain the respect (and valuable support) of the small nations, and show the gangster Powers that we are 'a strong man armed'.[101]

At the CID meeting Vansittart argued that technical advice was what the Foreign Office had in mind, and it seemed 'quite innocuous and non-committal'. The COS, Chatfield replied, feared that conversations with the Dutch would involve commitment to defend Netherlands India in the event of attack.

> Until our fleet arrived in the Far East, we could offer no undertaking that we should take concerted action with the Dutch in the defence of the Netherlands East Indies. Once the fleet arrived, although a period of two or three months might elapse before this happened, the Netherlands East Indies would be secure, provided it had not fallen in the interval.

The Secretary of State for Air, Lord Swinton, a personal friend of Colijn's, stressed that he wanted an exchange of information: 'we should meet Dr Colijn's desire for collaboration in the form of technical questions'. The CID resolved to do this through the attachés in London.[102] The Netherlands minister was told in February.[103]

The worsening of Britain's position in Europe and the Far East late in 1938 and early in 1939 was not accompanied by any change in the relations with the Dutch. The COS reaffirmed their view that conversations with the Dutch should follow conversations with 'more important powers', such as France.[104] Locally there were discussions between Vice-Admiral Sir Percy Noble and the Dutch naval authorities when HMS *Kent* and HMS *Falmouth* visited Batavia early in April 1939. 'Despite the strength of the Dutch goodwill towards us', Henry Fitzmaurice, the consul-general in Batavia, wrote, '... their devotion to the principle of neutrality is equally apparent ...'.[105] Noble indeed secured information about the measures the Dutch intended to take to preserve absolute neutrality in the event of a war between Britain and Japan, a 'fantastic' hope in the opinion J.P.E.C. Henniker-Major expressed at the Foreign Office.[106] At the same time as the Noble visit, Brig. G.N. Molesworth, Director of Military Operations and Intelligence of the Army in India, had visited Java, without uniform and without appearing on the passenger list.

> The readiness of the Dutch authorities concerned to discuss freely their own military and other precautionary measures once more emphasises their very friendly feeling towards us [Fitzmaurice wrote], though of course their earnest desire to maintain neutrality in any conflict which may break out between other nations is at least equally significant, and might, if these two inclinations clashed, prove to be the dominant factor.[107]

Beyond a visit to Netherlands India by the Air Adviser to the Government of Burma,[108] no more had been done when the European war broke out in September.

The Philippines

The US had recruited itself to the ranks of the colonial powers in East Asia by acquiring the Philippines through purchase and conquest. To that extent it had become a supporter of the status quo rather than a challenger. But how firm a supporter was it? The islands had been acquired amid criticism at home. During World War I, the Jones Act promised independence when a stable government was established. What that meant was uncertain.

> Must it be a government which under any circumstances can withstand aggression from without, and at all times be able to preserve its independence? If so, has there ever been a stable government in history ...? [the former Democratic Governor-General F.B. Harrison asked]. ... Must it conform exactly to American standards of government? If that is to be the test, must it conform to what we Americans would like to be, or to what we know of our institutions in actual practice? ...[109]

In practice politics determined the answer to these questions. Republican administrations tended to slow the pace to Filipinisation, Democrat to increase it. The Filipino élite was itself ambivalent. In some ways it was better to travel than to arrive. They increased their power within the islands while calling for independence. Some of them were more doubtful about securing independence. How would the political dynamics of the Philippines adapt? Would the US market for Philippines products remain? What would provide security for an independent republic?

The depression and its impact on the fortunes of other suppliers of sugar to the American market were to prompt some resolution of these issues. It was, however, in the form of a staged answer. Unlike the Jones Act, the Hare–Hawes–Cutting and Tydings–McDuffie Acts set a date for independence. In the meantime a Commonwealth of the Philippines was to be created with its own president but without control over foreign policy. Provisions both for American bases and for neutralisation added to the confusion. 'We should honestly and plainly declare our intentions', Hoover had urged in vain.[110]

The significance of these changes for the maintenance of the status quo was unclear. One possible concern was the example that the advance of the Philippines towards independence might give those who were ruled by other colonial powers. However, although Filipino nationalists occasionally talked of leading the Malay race, their nationalist struggle had little impact elsewhere. Much more significant were the indications the political changes in the Philippines offered of the extent and continuance of US commitment to the status quo in Southeast Asia. Coupled with the limitations of the Washington agreements, the moves towards independence caused concern in the 1920s. The establishment of the Philippines Commonwealth, with a deadline for independence ten years later, added to the concern. The Philippines were a barometer of American interest in East Asia. When the islands were taken that had been uncertain, and it remained uncertain. Indeed US policy in the Philippines seemed to typify its mixture of motives, its unfathomability; it tended not to indicate where the US stood but to show how difficult it was to tell where they stood. The British suspected that it wished to rid itself of the burden of the islands' security.

In some sense, of course, that was not wholly undesirable. Some Americans realised that possession of the Philippines gave them an impossible defence burden and a source of potential conflict with Japan. Even the British, apprehensive of the Japanese, were also apprehensive of the impact of an American–Japanese war on Southeast Asia, as Ashton-Gwatkin had pointed out in commenting on the security of Netherlands India. 'If the United States carry out their expressed intention of granting independence to the Philippines, the tendency will be for these islands eventually to drift into the orbit of Japan, which would bring that Power appreciably nearer to Australia,' he wrote. The current Republican administration was opposed to the 'surrender' of the Philippines. 'From the British point of view, this surrender ought not to be encouraged.' In assigning to Japan the ex-German Caroline and Marshall islands north of the Equator, he suggested, the Versailles peace conference 'had also given her the reversionary interest in the Philippines'. One outcome of an American withdrawal might be intervention by the Japanese Government in support of the immigrant community at Davao in Mindanao, over which the Australian authorities had expressed anxiety. On the larger scale, Ashton-Gwatkin pointed out, American withdrawal from the Philippines and Japanese domination of them would mean that 'the ring of Japanese islands round the coast of China would be closed' – 'a calamity for the British Empire'. But it was true 'that the evacuation of the Philippines might eliminate a possible danger to the peace of the Far East, inasmuch as they are strategically a source of weakness to the United States and a constant temptation to Japan'.[111]

The Manchuria episode added to the Hoover administration's concern over the moves for the independence of the Philippines. Opposing the recognition of Japan's regime, Stimson also insisted that the islands were 'a physical base for American influence – political, economic, and social in the Far East'. If American guidance were withdrawn, and the American market removed, chaos would ensue, 'followed ultimately by domination of the Philippines by some foreign power, probably either China or Japan'.[112] A Japanese source, however, reported the readiness to sign a treaty guaranteeing the independence of the Philippines if they were freed.[113] The Hare–Hawes–Cutting Act went ahead with its staged program. Quezon disliked it, perhaps not merely because he had not had the credit for negotiating it. His preferred alternative was an autonomous government, 'including the power to adopt measures to assume the responsibilities of an independent government'.[114] But the minor amendments provided by the Tydings–McDuffie Act did not convey this power. The US had the responsibility for foreign policy with all the uncertainty that meant. It was in this context that Quezon looked to the British and suggested joining the Commonwealth. But they did not want additional responsibility. 'The prospect of receiving a new Dominion into the fold', wrote Craigie, 'will no doubt warm the cockles of the D[ominions] O[ffice]'s heart – but such a liability would cause less enthusiasm amongst the Service Departments!'[115]

L.H. Foulds, British vice-consul in Manila, had pointed to the apprehension in the Philippines at the time of the Manchuria crisis. There was an American suggestion that the Pacific powers should execute a treaty guaranteeing the neutrality of the Philippines.

If this proposal is viewed in the light of American prejudice against foreign 'entanglements' and of the widespread popular determination to hold aloof from any difficulties which might affect an independent Philippine Republic in the future, it would seem to resolve itself essentially into a plan for making Great Britain responsible, with or without American assistance, for the defence of the Philippines Republic against a possible aggressor such as Japan, since Great Britain is the only other naval power in the Pacific ...

The US should be urged permanently to retain the island fortress of Corregidor and the naval station at Subic Bay. 'If she should prove obdurate in her determination to leave the Islands entirely, only one other alternative would appear possible, namely that these fortified points should be transferred by her to British sovereignty and occupation ...'. It would provoke 'an outburst of Filipino resentment' but, with the removal of American power, 'British goodwill would be of vital necessity to the Philippine Republic, and sooner or later the native government would be bound to recognise the fact, and to discover that British power was no more of a menace to them than to the Dutch in the East Indies ...'.[116]

By July 1933 Quezon was toying with the idea of entering the British Commonwealth. He was reported to have said at a private dinner that 'if the Philippine Islands were so unfortunate as to become independent within a year or two, he would go himself to London to ask the British Government to admit the Islands into the British Commonwealth of Nations, if possible with Dominion status. He said this would give them almost complete freedom, and also security as a unit of the Empire ...'.[117] After HHC was replaced by Tydings–McDuffie without significant change Quezon recurred to the idea: 'he has certainly hit on a very strange way of escaping the evils which the Act will bring in its train'.[118] One of his contacts, Frank Hodsoll of Warner Barnes & Co., raised it in conversation with George Sansom, counsellor at the British Embassy in Tokyo,[119] and again at the Foreign Office.[120] The Foreign Office decided to brief Hodsoll on British interests.[121]

'The general popular belief', Foulds wrote, 'seems to be that American withdrawal will inevitably be succeeded by Japanese domination, certainly economic, and perhaps political too.' The best way of avoiding a power vacuum was the permanent retention of the US bases, but American opinion tended to total withdrawal. The British rejoinder

> should be refusal to participate in a treaty of neutralisation for the Philippine Islands, because such a treaty would in effect transfer the burden of protecting the Philippine Islands from the United States to Great Britain without any quid pro quo and without any assurance of American support. The treaty could only be regarded as an attempt to ward off Japan, and that result would ... be more surely attained by a direct, and possibly informal, understanding between Great Britain and Japan

like that between Britain and France over Siam. Otherwise the weakness of the Philippine Republic 'may tempt Japan to seek to establish her hegemony in the country, repeating her exploits in Manchuria ...'. Then Japan would be athwart the line of communication between Singapore and Hong Kong and 'dangerously close' to British Borneo and British

Malaya, 'the eastern gateway of the Empire. It lies with the United States alone to decide whether the Philippine Islands shall be independent, but once independence is attained, its permanence will become a matter of importance to Great Britain.' The 'principal Filipino leaders' knew this fact and recognised its significance, 'and on it the future relations between Great Britain and the Philippine Republic may find a stable foundation ...'. Foulds suggested that offering an opening for Philippine sugar might increase British influence.[122]

Japanese domination of the Philippines, the British Admiralty believed,

> would be an unfortunate, even a dangerous, development, and would bring Japanese influence a long step nearer to Singapore and Australia. Should the situation develop so that the Japanese were ever able to use the Philippines as a base for their armed forces, our strategic position could be adversely affected and the potential threat to our interests in the Far East would be seriously increased.

British interests would be 'best served by the United States retaining at least the naval establishments'.[123] If Japan obtained the use of a Philippines base, declared the memorandum Paul Gore-Booth prepared for Washington, 'our strategical position would ... become so serious that the question even of armed resistance might arise'. There was a parallel with the Netherlands Indies. There the Japanese had advanced further towards economic domination, perhaps because, with the Americans in the Philippines, the Indies are 'the weaker of the two groups of islands vis-à-vis Japan'. The position would be reversed when the Philippines became independent, and then the Japanese, 'deeming perhaps the Philippines an easier prey', might 'transfer and concentrate their energies on them'.[124]

Quezon saw not only Hodsoll but also D.G. Osborne of the British Embassy. To the former he spoke of American bases, now that the naval treaty had lapsed, and of Douglas MacArthur's being employed to build up a military force.[125] Osborne, however, did not get the impression that the US had shifted its attitude. Quezon said that the Americans

> were still undecided and that their indecision was partly due to reluctance to spend the sums required for the requisite large navy and partly to uncertainty as to our policy in the Far East. He implied that if they were assured that we were determined to defend our interests against Japan (and I suppose this would assume that exclusion of Japan from the Philippines would be a British interest) and if there could be an understanding or engagement for cooperation by the two countries, then they would have no hesitation in assuming lasting responsibility for the Philippines ...

Osborne told Quezon 'that we thought a friendly and conciliatory attitude in Tokyo might be conducive to lessening the influence of the militaristic element there' and 'reminded him that we had a hitlerised Germany as a much nearer and more immediate menace'. Fortunately, Quezon did not suggest that Britain should assume responsibility for the Philippines. Osborne felt the US Government was more concerned about public opinion than about Britain. He pointed out 'that the knowledge of any understanding with us would almost certainly be greeted with execration by the Senate and reminded him of the mutability of United States foreign policy'. Quezon was 'fully alive to the eccentricities of policy and opinion in this country [i.e. the US]'.[126]

In view of the Americans' unreliability Orde thought the idea of an arrangement with them was 'risky' and 'rather premature'. He would 'deprecate giving them the slightest hint that we should welcome any alliance, as it were, directed against Japan. I cannot see the US being willing e.g. to guarantee the Dutch East Indies and British possessions against Japan, and I imagine the most we could hope for is that they will take measures to ward off Japanese domination of the Philippines ...'. Craigie welcomed the possibility that the US would establish naval bases in the Philippines: 'otherwise the full weight of any possible Japanese aggression in these parts will fall upon this country'. But the idea of promising the US support in defending bases in the Philippines was 'fantastic. A mutual Anglo-American guarantee of our respective positions in the Far East would be another matter, but at the moment this is not a matter of practical politics.'[127]

The newly inaugurated President Quezon toured the south with his friend the newspaper magnate, Roy Howard. In December Manila papers and the Scripps–Howard chain published an article that Quezon had read two or three times beforehand.[128] A Philippine Republic would not materialise, it declared. Congress would be requested to make Commonwealth status permanent; failing this, 'the business interests of the Islands will bring the full force of their influence to bear in an effort to persuade the insular government to make a direct approach to Great Britain to the end that the Islands be given a territorial status under the British flag ...'. Britain would welcome the Philippines, rich, English-speaking, strengthening its line of defence in the Far East. The Foreign Office was much less sure. 'The Filipinos are not the only people who would like to be independent and yet defended by and at the expense of, an altruistic Great Power who asked nothing in return ...'. 'One shudders to think that the day may come when the Philippines will be a member of the League, and their security become yet another obligation of the British navy ...'.[129]

Late the following year (1936) Hodsoll called at the Foreign Office. Quezon wanted to come to the coronation of George VI and then to sound out the British on protection in the event that the Americans hauled down their flag in nine years' time. His preference was 'incorporation' in or alliance with the British Empire. Alternatively the Philippines could join the League of Nations, although Quezon set little store by that; or an international treaty, with or without Japanese participation, could guarantee the integrity of the Philippines; or the republic could come to terms with Japan. At the Foreign Office J.M. Troutbeck pointed out that, while Japanese occupation of the Philippines would be 'a grave menace' to British possessions and communications, British occupation of the Philippines would be regarded as a menace by the Japanese. Moreover, news that 'we were even toying with the idea of the incorporation of the Philippines in the British Empire' would arouse resentment in the US as well. It was, however, undesirable to give Quezon 'a complete rebuff'; it might 'only lead him to make a deal with the Japanese and would almost certainly deflect him from his present very friendly attitude towards ourselves ...'. He should not be encouraged in his idea of joining the League. 'That would leave us with commitments, and the United States and the Japanese without them.' The neutralisation treaty seemed more advantageous; indeed it would be 'much more valuable' to Britain than to the US, and the latter 'might hesitate to take it on'. Perhaps, Troutbeck thought, Quezon should be told that, although no commitment could be made so far ahead, Britain would not exclude the idea of being party to such arrangement. Craigie was doubtful; Hodsoll should not lead Quezon to think that Britain could enter 'any fresh commitment'. 'Does not Sir R. Craigie mean "alone" (?),' asked Eden, the Foreign Secretary. 'The solution offered is a commitment, but a joint one.' 'Yes, I mean "alone",' Craigie replied. 'It seems rather fantastic that we should now have to deal with this nine year hence problem', Eden wrote, 'and what would the Americans say to our having talks with their protégé [?]' Could not Quezon be referred to the Americans?[130] In fact Craigie spoke to Atherton at the US Embassy, who said he was glad Craigie had raised the matter.[131] But the State Department in fact made it clear to Quezon that he could not hold conversations.[132]

When it had seemed likely that Quezon would visit the Foreign Office Vansittart had suggested a reference to the Committee of Imperial Defence.[133] The matter was raised again in March 1937. New Zealand, Troutbeck pointed out, wanted 'the strategic importance of the Pacific Islands' discussed at the Imperial Conference. Hodsoll had reported that, although the US Navy favoured retention of the Philippines, US military opinion was in favour of withdrawal, if possible earlier than 1946, and opposed MacArthur's defence scheme as 'impracticable and provocative'. At the State Department, where Hodsoll talked to Stanley Hornbeck and Joseph Jacobs, he had been asked if Britain would join in guaranteeing the Philippines as an independent state after 1946. He had answered affirmatively, and he also thought France and the Netherlands would, although it was suggested to him that they might be concerned at the 'impetus' Philippines independence would give to the unrest in Cochin-China and Netherlands India.[134]

A Foreign Office memorandum prepared for the Committee of Imperial Defence surveyed the provisions of the Tydings–McDuffie Act and portrayed the American attitude as undecided, torn between the importance of the Philippine market and the pressure of the sugar interests; a desire to be relieved of responsibility for defence and a 'feeling that the retention of naval bases might be of far reaching value in any conflict in which the United States might be involved in the Far East'. What made the question of Philippine independence an international one was the attitude of Japan. ' "South Seas expansion" is the object of a great amount of organisation and propaganda; though it is only economic at present on the face of it, the navy regards it as their special province and the Governor-Generalship of Formosa … is now more or less a perquisite of the navy …'. If the US severed all connection with the islands the Japanese would move on from economic to political domination. Quezon had been 'tentatively searching for some form of reinsurance against the possibility of the United States leaving the Islands entirely to their own resources …'. He had also explained his 'perplexities' to the US Government and a committee of experts had been set up. Britain's interest in the question 'arises from the danger of Japan unduly expanding her influence in the Islands should the US sever connection with them …'. If Japan were ever able to use bases in the Philippines, Britain's strategic position would become so serious that armed resistance might be called for.

Various alternatives had been suggested. One was incorporation of the Philippines in the British Empire or its alliance with the British Empire. This would mean that Britain 'would undertake a serious new commitment unaided', and it was therefore a policy of last resort.

> Moreover, it is a policy which could clearly not even be discussed with other Powers until the US Government had definitely decided to sever their connection with the Islands. Until that moment any suggestion that we were even considering the idea could not fail to rouse the keenest resentment in the US, nor would it be likely to be regarded as otherwise than a challenge by the Japanese …

A second alternative was Philippine membership of the League. Again this would imply commitments for Britain not shared by the US or Japan.

In itself it would not assist the preservation of Philippine independence. A third alternative, an Anglo-American guarantee against Japan, 'would give the impression of being an alliance directed against Japan and as such be open to objection, apart from the general risk of entering into an exclusive arrangement with so unreliable a Power as the USA'. A fourth alternative was, in the terms of the Tydings–McDuffie Act, a multilateral treaty for perpetual neutralisation. Such a treaty implied not only recognising but also guaranteeing the independence of the Philippines, and the guarantee, to be effective, must be 'several and not merely joint'. US intentions would no doubt be made plain in due course. The Japanese might agree; the Japanese delegation to the Institute of Pacific Relations Conference in 1936 had advocated such a guarantee. The French and the Dutch might want a guarantee of their possessions, too, if they were to join. This the US and Japan were unlikely to give, but French and Dutch participation was not essential. Clearly such a treaty was an additional commitment for Britain; indeed under it Britain might have to act alone. 'The unreliability of the US Government is here again a matter to be borne in mind. At the same time, failing the continuance of the status quo, this is the solution which would appear to give His Majesty's Government the greatest measure of security as compared with the degree of commitment involved ...'. But the preservation of the status quo, with the US solely responsible for the protection of the islands, was 'the best solution from the British point of view'.[135]

The Chiefs of Staff commented on the Foreign Office paper in June. While the US controlled the Philippines the Japanese would probably respect their neutrality in a war with the British. Any change in their status would, however, 'be liable to create conditions under which the maintenance of their neutrality in an Anglo-Japanese war would be doubtful ...'. This could affect the security of British communications, interests and possessions and the integrity of the Netherlands Indies. From bases in the Philippines the Japanese would be better placed to fight in the South China Sea and to attack convoys between Singapore and Hong Kong. Possibly they could launch an attack on Singapore or Borneo. Certainly aircraft based in the Philippines could reach areas further south than those now in range and, with increased ranges, would reach Singapore itself. The Philippines would also provide Japan with some of the raw materials it lacked and be 'a stepping stone to the oil and rubber of Borneo and the Netherland East Indies'. British naval, army and air forces in the region would have to be increased; permanent forces might be required in Borneo; Australia and New Zealand might need to boost their local defences.

On the other hand, the use of bases in the Philippines by British forces would strengthen the position of Hong Kong and simplify the problem of countering a Japanese threat to Australia and New Zealand through the mandated islands. The Japanese would resent any form of British control in the Philippines, checking their southward advance and threatening their security, and the expenditure would be high. But without forces in the Philippines in peace time, 'we could not rely on having the benefit in war of the advantages of being able to operate from the Philippines, while we should at the same time have the added responsibility of cooperating with the Philippines in the defence of their country if they were attacked'.

Any settlement making Britain solely responsible for the defence of the Philippines would be a heavy addition to its commitments and increase the risk of Japanese intervention against Britain in a European war. Either dominion status or League membership would involve major additional commitments for Britain. A guarantee of neutrality would be a satisfactory conclusion, if endorsed by the Americans, which would 'almost certainly' be prepared to assist in applying economic pressure, 'even if they were unwilling to support their signature to the extent of providing effective military cooperation'. But the best answer, the COS agreed, was the status quo.[136]

At the CID meeting on 17 June 1937, Chamberlain, the Prime Minister, alluded to the proposal for a regional pact in the Pacific, which had been put forward by Australia, and which the chief delegates of the Imperial Conference had supported in principle. It was decided that, as such a pact would cover the Philippines, 'it was unnecessary further to pursue enquiries into that particular question at the present time'.[137]

At the Foreign Office Cadogan indeed suspected that the Davis proposals were a means of spreading the responsibility for neutralising the Philippines.[138] Troutbeck thought the Americans might be playing 'rather a low game'; they would leave the Philippines, and the British have to dismantle Hong Kong 'to make their desertion easier'.[139] Fearful that the Americans would 'run out' of their commitment to neturalisation of the Philippines by 'some kind of woolly non-aggression' pact, Troutbeck thought Lyons' proposal 'unfortunate'.[140] 'I fear', wrote Holman at the Foreign Office on hearing of the CID decision, 'that the negotiation of a general Pacific Pact may give the US Government a pretext for getting out of their obligations under the Tydings–McDuffie Act. But they will probably do this anyhow?' 'Nevertheless', Troutbeck commented, 'it was surely a mistake to present them with this opportunity. Meanwhile the question of the defence of the Philippines is to be buried.' 'And meanwhile', Cadogan added, referring to the Marco Polo Bridge incident, 'the prospect of a Pacific Pact – vide the present situation in North China – recedes into the background.'[141] The Foreign

Office were anxious 'to keep President Quezon sweet without treading on the Americans' toes ...'. For 'serious consequences ... would follow for ourselves were the Japanese to establish a real footing in, or anything in the nature of control over, the Islands ...'. The Consul-General should keep 'a careful watch over any tendencies towards a *rapprochement* between the Philippines and Japan'.[142] But the British had 'little to offer'.[143]

Hodsoll found it difficult to maintain their influence with Quezon. The following year he had the impact of Munich to contend with. 'I sense ...', he wrote in February 1939, 'that European events during the second half of last year have shaken his faith in our desire and ability to protect the smaller nations of the world and I have naturally sought to correct any wrong impressions which have resulted from the very one-sided account of last September's international crisis which was presented by the American press ...'.[144]

In April 1937 Anthony Haigh, on the staff at the Washington embassy, had gathered that, in the event of a war with Japan, the US could not hold Guam or the Philippines for more than a month and would fall back on Pearl Harbor. He had been attempting to assess whether there was any chance that the Philippines would be retained and whether there was any chance that the US would go to war to prevent an independent Philippines from being annexed by Japan. The answer in both cases seemed to be 'some chance, but very little'. Haigh thus concluded

> that the United States could not prevent the Japanese from taking the Philippines (and Guam) off them if they wished to do so, though if the Japanese tried to annex the islands before US sovereignty over them is completely withdrawn the Americans would probably feel compelled, from motives of prestige rather than of economic interest, to go to war to get them back: but that if the Japanese annexed the Philippines after they had become independent, the United States would almost certainly not go to war on their account ...[145]

That might make the US more responsive to an earlier date for independence, an idea that Quezon had advanced because of his frustration over the ambivalent position of the Philippine Common-wealth regime. He did manage to negotiate a progressive decline of tariff preferences with the US, although what went through Congress was much less satisfactory.[146] But no change was made in the political arrangements of the Tydings–McDuffie Act. Nor did the US utilise its ability, following the lapse of the Washington naval treaty, to build up a base in East Asian waters, although MacArthur was employed by Quezon to build up a Philippines defence scheme.

French Indo-China

One colonial government in Southeast Asia, the Netherlands, was clearly a supporter of the status quo. It had, however, little strength to devote to it, and its frontline emphasis on neutrality, as well as the unwillingness of the British to assume any commitments, precluded any formal ties with the British. A second colonial power, the US, had the potential to support the status quo in Southeast Asia. But its program for the independence of the Philippines added to the uncertainty about its commitment, promoted by the attitudes of the Roosevelt administration, the isolationist pressures within the US, the doubts in the US Navy about the liability incurred by the defence of the islands and, more generally, by the disposition to accept change if brought about peacefully. The third colonial power, France, was in a different position again.

In some part the differences were, of course, geographical. Unlike the colonial possessions in island Southeast Asia, French Indo-China had a long and not impenetrable frontier with China. In discussing the Manchuria crisis the Asia–Oceania section at the Quai d'Orsay pointed to the danger in 'any solution' that produced 'a unified and disciplined China, which would constitute an immediate danger on the very frontier of Indochina'.[147] The French position over Manchuria was thus even more ambivalent than that of the other powers. European geography, however, also played a part. In Europe, of course, France had a frontier with Germany. The rise of the Nazis led the French to improve relations with the Soviet Union. Concluding the pact in 1935, the French tried to reassure a distrustful Japanese Foreign Minister that France aimed at being both an 'influential friend of Japan and a quasi-ally of Russia'.[148] But any relaxation of tension in the north they could promote might enable the Japanese to focus on China and perhaps Southeast Asia. In September 1936 there were indeed rumours of an attack on Hainan, which 'commands the Gulf of Tonkin, our ports of Haiphong and Tourane, and the Singapore–Hong Kong route'.[149]

The Anti-Comintern Pact, announced soon after, aroused new French apprehensions; it might even be expedient, the military attaché in China observed, 'not to neglect the aid that China could bring us'.[150] The outbreak of the Sino-Japanese war, which increased French apprehensions, added a complication to that concept. Hirota complained to the British ambassador about the supplying of China with war material via the Hanoi–Yunnanfu railway. Governor-General Brevié pointed to the weakness of Indo-China's defences if it were to face a Japanese-occupied Hainan and a Japanese-equipped and -officered Siamese army. 'The fact that Indochina is practically lacking all the means of maritime defence and has only an inadequate aviation can lead to an aggression or even a blockade of our coasts.'[151] The transit of war materials across Indo-China was banned. 'Since the transit can scarcely take place except through Indochina, we risk either, by refusing it, paralysing China or, by reopening it, provoking Japanese reprisals which in that case we do not wish to face alone.'[152] But no reassurance was secured at Brussels,[153] while the Japanese increased the pressure by suggesting 'the sending to Indochina of a Japanese officer to whom our authorities could provide proof of the reality of the closing of the frontier'.[154] A Chinese proposal for cooperation with France, now that its German advisers were departing, could not be accepted; 'the support that France can lend to China will be all the more efficacious as long as it remains discrete and we are careful not to compromise our moral authority and political position in the Far East by imprudent demonstrations'.[155] A somewhat bolder attitude in mid 1938 terminated with the capture of Canton in October; 'if arms or munitions continue to pass through Indochinese territory, the Japanese government will have to take efficacious measures to oppose the entry of this material into China'.[156]

The ban on munitions had been seen by the French as part of 'an informal understanding' with the Japanese, who for their part would not disturb the status quo in Hainan.[157] The occupation of Hainan thus led to a shift: the ban of the transit of war material would be 'less rigorous'. The change permitted 'transit shipments of anything susceptible to peace time use, such as motor trucks, civil airplanes, raw materials, and machinery, even that used in munition factories'. It did not lead to the cooperation with China that a former Governor-General suggested.[158] The subjection of the Spratly Islands to the Formosa government followed but did not change French policy any further. In May 1939, while reassuring Japan over the Russian conversations, the French Foreign Minister, Bonnet, became more anxious to keep China's resist-ance alive.[159] The Tientsin crisis, into which the French were drawn by the Japanese blockade, pointed to the risks of Japanese victory in China. The scholar René Cassin thought it would imply the loss of the European positions in the Far East, renew the Siamese danger and encourage Annamite rebellion. But not even Cassin would accept Chinese troops for the defence of Indo-China.[160] It would also show French weakness, and they would be hard to remove. France was a colonial power that recognised its incapacity but was not anxious to display it.

France shared Britain's anxieties over the Japanese and, increasingly, its hope that China's resistance might obstruct them. But, with its border with China, it was much more exposed to involvement in the developing Sino-Japanese conflict. The advance of Japan would undermine its security, but a countervailing reliance on China, whether or not it would be successful, would undermine its hold on Vietnam. That had meant an informal deal with the Japanese, setting off the transit ban with their abstention in Hainan. They had breached it, and the French had become somewhat firmer. But such a deal might presage the future.

The weakness of the French position internationally pointed in the same direction as their weakness in colonial terms. Facing the Nazi menace, they turned to Russia but doing so might only worsen their relations with Japan. From the Americans they, like the British, could expect little. The British, in turn, could offer little. They, on the other hand, could not receive much support from the French in maintaining the status quo in Southeast Asia. Yet the security of French Indo-China was essential to the security of Singapore.

Military conversations in Europe followed the invasion of Czechoslovakia in March 1939. The French opposed the Singapore strategy since the Italian coup in Albania made them apprehensive about the Mediterranean. It was decided that the matter would have to be determined when the need arose.[161] Conversations in Singapore followed those in Europe. They were held at Singapore in June 1939, chaired by Sir Percy Noble, and involved Gen. Maurice Martin, C-in-C of the French troops in Indo-China, and Admiral Decoux, the naval C-in-C. Two alternatives were considered: a European war, Japan not intervening, or a war in Asia as well, Japan having intervened. In the first case Japan must be deterred by reinforcement and diplomatic action. 'The importance of Indo-China was agreed upon as an advanced position in the defence of Singapore and Allied possessions in the Indian Ocean.' The security of Indo-China 'depended especially on the continuance and intensification of the effort now being made to complete the ammunition and material required for the use of the forces on mobilisation'. In the second case the British and French must act defensively until reinforced. The integrity of the coast of Indo-China, it was agreed, was a key position. 'The intention of the French Naval Commander-in-Chief is to base his forces generally in Singapore and to act from this base particularly to maintain sea communication with Indo-China …'.

The conference recognised the interconnection of French and British interests and the need for coordination. It also put on record

its grave concern at the present inadequacy of the Allied Naval and Air Forces in the Far East. This weakness places the Japanese in a position of such superiority that we can neither assure our essential communications nor prevent enemy occupation of advanced bases that directly threaten our vital interests. The Japanese can be expected to exploit this position in full during the period in which they are likely to hold such an advantage …

The conference did not believe naval forces would become available and concluded 'that Air Forces form the only mobile, effective and practical solution to the problem of preventing important Japanese successes at the beginning of the war ...'.[162]

More than once the French in Indo-China referred not only to their apprehensions of Japan and China and of Vietnamese insurrection but to their fears of the Thais. The establishment of their colonial realm in Indo-China had indeed often been at the expense of the Thais. They had claimed suzerainty over Laos and Cambodia, and the advance of French power had involved a major crisis between the two states in 1893. The weakening of the status quo in Southeast Asia as a whole might encourage the Thais to challenge this part of it in particular. Moreover, the overthrow of the constitutional monarchy in Siam in 1932 was to be succeeded by the regime of the Promoters, and increasingly the more irredentist of them gained prominence. The French, too, were apprehensive of Japanese influence among them.

For the British, Siam, although an independent state, was an essential part of the colonial status quo, even more important than Indo-China itself, for it lay along the borders of British Burma and British Malaya. There was likely to be somewhat more sympathy for them among the British than among the French. The chances of limiting Japanese influence also depended more on the British than the French. Once again Britain had the main burden in sustaining the status quo it had built up, although its power was less, its relative position was weaker and it had little help from others.

Siam

In the nineteenth century Siam retained its independence while all around were losing theirs. The major means the Thais used to attain this end was to come to terms with the major power in Southeast Asia, Great Britain. In the Bowring–Parkes negotiations of 1855–56 the Siam of King Mongkut accepted voluntarily what China had been forced to concede – extraterritoriality and tariff restrictions – as the price of maintaining political independence. Too exclusive a connection with the British was avoided, and connections were made with other states. The same principle was followed when, under King Chulalongkorn, the Siamese developed the practice of appointing foreign advisers; Britain had the lion's share, but citizens of other nations held some important posts. Through concessions to the Western powers, and through a degree of westernisation, Siam sought with success to preserve its independence. That independence also depended, of course, on the policies of the great powers and in particular on Britain's readiness to accept a substantially independent state as the outwork of its empire in India–Burma and Malaya. That readiness existed before the French established themselves in Indo-China, and it was reinforced by that event. The aim of the British was an independent Siam open to British commerce and amenable to British advice. It was on the whole attained, despite the problems caused by Thai claims in the Malay peninsula. Siam's position remained important in the twentieth century; indeed the development of air communications gave the country a new significance.

Siam responded to the changes brought about by World War I by attempts to improve its position. It sent troops to Europe and gained a seat at the peace conference.[163] Postwar it was able to renegotiate the unequal treaties. Britain still retained the predominant role as supplier of foreign advisers, and more Siamese students went to Britain than to other Western states. The continued influence of Britain indeed appeared to depend on such things. But what they, and thus continued British influence really depended on, was the continuance of Britain's power and prestige in East Asia as a whole. Britain's power had greatly diminished and, even before the revolution of 1932, a change of attitude had been noted in 'the governing oligarchy ... there is no longer the same uncritical and sentimental preference for everything British that so happily existed until quite recently ...'.[164] The revolution took the trend further. Britain's answer, somewhat prefiguring the approach it was to take to Quezon, was in keeping with its tradition with Siam. It would come to terms and work with the new government, as it had with the old, and so minimise the change in the status quo. The fear of foreign intervention felt by some Thais was groundless. Used with discretion, it could help the moderates. Otherwise it could be counterproductive.

In 1933 Siam abstained in the voting on Manchukuo at the League of Nations. *Phya* Abhibal told Cecil Dormer, the British minister, that its intention was to indicate neutrality between China and Japan, 'but Japan insisted on regarding it as showing support for her case'. Yatabe, the Japanese minister, was lecturing on Siam in his own country. The lectures, Dormer felt, pointed to Japan's interest in Siam and perhaps to a desire to be seen as a champion against foreign aggression.

> Among the Siamese of the older generation I have never found anything but fear and dislike of Japan, but they were evicted last June, and I should not be surprised if the youthful elements behind the Government today, obsessed as they are with the bogey of 'foreign (British or French) domination', are looking to Japan to hold us back in the event, as they think, of our interfering in their domestic disputes.[165]

Early in 1934 Prince Purachatra, in a conversation with W.A.R. Wood, the consul-general at Chiengmai, alluded to irredentism 'amongst the younger members of the new Government', who counted on Japanese support. Dormer thought that they had 'more urgent tasks to think about than extending their present frontiers. They must learn to work and to hold their own against the Chinese population; and they must learn how to live in harmony with each other.' Purachatra was trying to 'make our blood curdle', Orde wrote. Vansittart did not think it need be taken very seriously, 'though the idea of the decadency of the West – no new one – is interesting in its frequent manifestations'.[166] But after the Amau declaration Dormer wrote of 'a distinct tendency on the part of the younger Siamese to look to Japan. The idea that Great Britain might be involved in war with Japan has increased Siamese self-confidence almost to the point of arrogance.'[167]

The British sent an old hand back to Siam, Sir Josiah Crosby, who had also had experience in Netherlands India but had been a student interpreter in Bangkok in 1904.[168] The 'gang in power', he reported, were 'secretive' and reluctant

> to entertain direct relations with the foreign community ... I have ... made it abundantly clear to all those with whom I have spoken that I have not come out with a big stick behind my back, that there need be no fear of interference on our part, and that Britain wishes the new Siam all success in the process of working out her destinies under the conditions prevailing in the modern world today. The restoration of confidence in our own attitude and intentions should of itself help to correct any tendency on the part of the Siamese to orientate themselves towards Japan ...[169]

But, through its industrial and military activities, Japan had, as Crosby put it, attained a 'predominant position' in Asia, and Siam was bound to take it into account as 'one of the pivotal points around which her foreign policy must turn'.[170]

At the Foreign Office Randall suggested that the Japanese were 'steadily pursuing peaceful penetration' in Siam but that, unless it were done 'with great discretion, the suspicion of the Siamese is likely to be aroused and an anti-Japanese reaction would occur. Direct methods of counteracting the Japanese penetration are hardly possible, but it may be suggested that if our general prestige in the Far East is clearly maintained, the danger of our influence in Siam being destroyed would be obviated.' 'It illustrates the kind of thing that will happen to an even greater extent', Orde echoed, 'if we do not resist Japanese pretensions to behave as they like in the Far East.' Sir Victor Wellesley thought the Japanese held the 'trump cards ... They are determined to become, and will become, the dominant power in the Far East. I don't see how we can prevent it.' Lord Stanhope, the Parliamentary Under-Secretary, suggested that Japan could be kept lean. 'Japan's finances are far from being in a flourishing condition. She depends on China for a large part of her trade, and China is not prepared to eat out of Japan's hand unless she is urged by other Powers to do so ...'.[171]

Yatabe cautioned in 1935 that

> if a Japanese considers that present day Siam is attempting to rely solely on Japan, he would be seriously in error ... Siam wishes to be rid of the white man's oppression, but she has no desire to replace it with Japanese influence in Siam ... if there is anyone who believes that Siam can easily be gathered under the umbrella of the pan-Asian movement ..., that person is badly mistaken.[172]

'Suppose we do have "Asia for the Asiatics", what then?' the leading civilian Promoter, Pridi Phanomyong, asked in 1938. 'Do we have one nation trying to assume dominance? ... what has Siam to gain from such a policy? As it is now, open to all countries, we have the benefit of the culture, social and economic advantages, through intercourse with Western nations! And what is more, we have freedom!'[173]

The Western powers were, however, increasingly nervous that their own weakness, demonstrated in Europe or in Asia or both, would prompt the Siamese to look to Japan. The British feared that Siamese militarism would be encouraged by the German takeover of the Rhineland and the Italian conquest of Abyssinia.[174] Moreover Pibun and the military Promoters took up the irredentist cause that the Foreign Office had earlier rather discounted.[175] Luang Vichit Vadhakarn updated King Vajiravudh's nationalism and pushed it in a 'pan-Thai' direction.[176] Pridi concentrated on getting rid of the unequal treaties and securing complete autonomy, partly to counter the nationalist appeal of his military rivals.[177] His approach to the French, however, included a minor territorial claim that they found unacceptable.

He tackled the British first and proposed that they surrender at once the right of evoking cases in which British nationals were concerned from the Siamese tribunals.[178] Crosby favoured agreeing. In four years treaty revision would be due in any case, and 'we shall have no means at our disposal of forcing the Siamese to conclude a fresh Treaty of Commerce and Friendship with us upon terms which are repugnant to themselves'. Moreover, if the British did not respond, 'Japan (and, doubtless, other Powers as well) will be only too glad to step in and to rob us of that "kudos" for being the first to adopt an accommodating attitude towards the Siamese which the latter intend to afford us an opportunity of acquiring'.[179] Crosby felt that 'we have much to gain and nothing very material to lose, by consenting to negotiate with the Siamese for a new agreement upon those terms of complete equality which they have in mind ... let us make the best, rather than the worst, of it'.[180] Once the

British treaty had been made others followed, as had happened with the original 'unequal' treaties.

The treaty with the Japanese included, somewhat to their dismay, no special privileges,[181] though there were rumours that a secret clause provided for collusion in an attack on Indo-China.[182] It appears that the Siamese had broached with the French the issue of a slight territorial readjustment on the Mekong River, probably in order to make the boundary conform to the thalweg. In some places the French claimed the river up to the west bank. Aside from its inconvenience to river traffic, that was not in accordance with the accepted usages of international law.[183] The issue had in fact been raised during the renegotiation of the 1920s.[184] Then, and now again, the Indo-China authorities managed to avoid any change. The treaty of December 1937 merely reaffirmed the demilitarisation clauses of the original treaties and the unusual riverine frontier they had established.[185] But French fears of Thai irredentism were intensified by the growing clamour over Siam's 'lost territories' stimulated in army and navy circles by news of the Austrian Anschluss in March 1938 and by an article written by Luang Vichit.[186]

In mid 1938 the French relayed reports about Siam that seemed 'alarmist' to the British: a coup by Pibun was threatened; 'the Japanese ... were now endeavouring to make arrangements with the Siamese whereby they might be granted facilities in Siamese territory from which to threaten the Burma–Yunnan road'; they were also 'trying to persuade Siam to join the Anti-Comintern Pact'. Nigel Ronald of the Foreign Office told the French ambassador in London that, judging from Crosby's reports, the military party were not making any headway; 'still less had I gathered that the Japanese had succeeded in advancing much in Siamese favour ... There was always the danger that Siam, in her anxiety to be on the side of the strongest, might commit herself to some arrangement inimical to French and British interests.' But joining the Anti-Comintern Pact was unlikely.[187]

In fact, after Pibun became Premier in December 1938, he denied the rumours that Siam might associate itself with the Anti-Comintern Pact.[188] The Japanese were somewhat disappointed with Pibun. The newspapers they subsidised urged him to join the pact. Even one of the more neutral ones commented that, if war broke out in Europe, Japan would offer the Southeast Asian peoples support in their struggle for independence, and Siam would have to side with Japan and not the Europeans.[189]

Pridi was nervous. What were the British and the French doing to defend their interests in the Far East? What, he asked Lépissier, Crosby's French counterpart, could they do to help Siam to defend its neutrality if the Japanese delivered an ultimatum? The blow was likely to fall suddenly and the die to be cast before the British fleet reached Singapore.

If a squadron could not be based on Singapore, Crosby commented, 'the possibility must always exist of Japan being able to bring the Siamese into her camp through the threatened application of physical force. A crisis may, in fact, arise which the methods of diplomacy will be powerless to avert.'[190] The Siamese were 'pretty badly shaken' by 'happenings' in Czechoslovakia and Albania. Lépissier suggested that they should be offered a formal assurance of assistance in the case of an attack. Crosby favoured an assurance but given less formally and, he added, 'it will be necessary to convince them that we could come effectively to their aid at a moment's notice. There's the rub ...'.[191] No promise would indeed be made, it was concluded in London. But Crosby should be aware of what Chamberlain had told the Australians.[192]

The Anglo-French conference in Singapore in June 1939 was the cause of considerable speculation. One London newspaper reported that Britain and France had offered to guarantee the security of Siam. Alternatively, it was suggested that Thailand had sought such a guarantee, offering military facilities in return.[193] None of this was true, but the conference had expressed its concern that the attitude of Siam had 'deteriorated'. It recommended 'immediate diplomatic action ... to make Siam declare without ambiguity, her intentions; and ... to deter her from complicity with Japan'. Such diplomatic action, it recognised, would have 'a much greater chance of success if the Allied naval and air forces in the Far East were substantially increased. Unless the Siamese are able to see that the Allies are strong the diplomatic action may fail.' Its geographical position made Siam 'a vital factor in the security of Indo-China, Malaya and Burma'. The extension of Japanese influence and infiltration had to be countered.[194]

Crosby told the Foreign Office that the Thais would refuse such an assurance; their policy was one of strict neutrality. 'All classes of Thais, including the liberals who are now sympathetically disposed towards the democratic states, would be antagonised and a swing towards Japan would be only too probable.' Information from the French in Siam and Indo-China was often 'exaggerated, if not definitely false'.[195] The Joint Planners for the British Chiefs of Staff took note of this. The aim should be neutrality. Perhaps the arrival of reinforcements in the Far East would 'provide a suitable opportunity for diplomatic action'.[196]

For the British, indeed, the neutrality of Siam was important. As an outlier of the empire and then a buffer with another empire in the nineteenth century, it had to be kept free of a third empire. Britain's position in Siam had depended on economic and political connections, now much weakened. It also depended on a perception of Britain's power. The stronger that seemed the more likely it would be that Siam would resist Japanese pressure. Prestige was no substitute for power but the outcome of it which the matters raised at Singapore tended to show. The future was to show it ever more plainly. The Singapore conference pointed to another issue: the differing approaches of Britain and France.

The two colonial powers had recognised the significance of Indo-China in respect of the status quo in Southeast Asia. Their interests were not identical, however. The weakness of the French, and their relationship with China, inclined them to compromise with the Japanese. The attitude of the two powers to Siam also differed. With the Thais the French showed no disposition to compromise at all. Yet good relations with Siam had long been, and continued to be, an essential objective of the British. These differences were to become evident after mid 1940, but there was already some evidence of them. Differences between the British and the Americans were to become evident, too.

Burma

The 'alarmism' of the French had sought to arouse British concern over the Burma–Yunnan road. Britain's interest in Burma in the nineteenth century had been stimulated by hopes of trade with inland China, but they had been disappointed and, although upper Burma was acquired in 1885–86, subsequent railway-building did not extend beyond Lashio. The undeclared war of 1937 revived interest in the route as a means of keeping China's resistance alive through supply of war matériel over land. British Burma's frontier with China was, of course, far less penetrable than French Indo-China's. But the decision to build an all-weather road would attract Japanese attention to it. Indeed, in the Tientsin crisis, there was a report that the Japanese Government had demanded that the British close the road to shipments of arms and munitions. President Roosevelt 'stated that if the report were true and if the British Government intended to accede to this demand, the position of the United States would be that of a government which was attempting to give moral support to another government when the second government was deliberately undertaking to commit suicide'.[197]

The building of the road aroused controversy in Burma. Was it not an imperial interest rather than a Burmese one? Who should pay? Was Burma being exposed to an unnecessary risk? If these were issues that British officials in Burma might raise, they were also issues that would concern Burmese politicians. The political reforms, stimulated by the impact of World War I on India, had been extended to Burma. To that program the British adhered despite the depression and the Manchuria incident. In 1937 indeed Burma, formally separated from India, inaugurated a new constitution, which gave a Burman ministry, responsible to a legislature, substantial powers in the Burman-inhabited territories. While foreign policy remained in the hands of the Governor, he was bound to take account of the attitudes of the Burman ministry. Should taxes be used to construct the Burma Road? No explicit promise had been made that the goal for Burma was the status of a dominion enjoyed by Canada, Australia and New Zealand, but the British had increasingly to treat Burma like one. The relationship with Burma thus became more diplomatic and less directive. But the assumption that support would be forthcoming in case of crisis would be less soundly based in respect of Burma than in respect of Australia and New Zealand.

There was a paradox in the concept of the Empire–Commonwealth that had been both revealed and concealed in World War I. Dominions that had gained virtual independence might yet pursue foreign and defence policies that coincided with the interests of the British and their empire as a whole. To secure that, even in respect of the 'old' dominions, had required diplomacy, although there were ties of strategic and economic interest, financial ties, ties of kith and kin, to supplement it. Would the same be true of new dominions? That was the implicit assumption of the theorists of the Empire–Commonwealth. That assumption was optimistic, and indeed it could be undermined by the tensions of the intermediate phase in which Britain devolved some of the powers of an independent state but not all of them, and not indeed the main one, the power to deal with other independent states. In the meantime the burden of sustaining the security of the country had to be assumed by the British. Even Indian revenues could be utilised less readily.

Malaya and Borneo

These complications were not, however, the main reasons why the advance to self-government was much slower in the other territories for which Britain was directly responsible in Southeast Asia. Indeed between the two world wars the British were conscious of the need not merely for economic development there, but also for political advance. The problems, however, seemed intractable, and there was a risk that attempts to deal with them would fail. Failure might undermine the economic value of Malaya and, more generally, reveal the weakness of Britain's position and thus diminish the effectiveness of its diplomacy elsewhere in Southeast Asia. Since the problems were not after all urgent, it might be best not to stir up controversy by bold attempts to tackle them. The result, however, was that the territories lacked even the measure of coordination that was required to make the most of the capacity to defend them.

In postwar Malaya Governor Guillemard sought to economise and rationalise, but the obstacles, both institutional and personal, were too great. Conscious of the penetration of nationalism among the Chinese, his successor, Hugh Clifford, insisted that the peninsular states must remain Muslim monarchies; 'in these days, when democratic and socialist theories are spreading like an infection, bringing with them, too often, not peace but a sword, I feel it incumbent upon me to emphasize ... the utter inapplicability of any form of democratic or popular government to the circumstances of these States ...'.[198] The next Governor, Sir Cecil Clementi, took a different line. He sought to create a more unified Malaya, but the opposition overwhelmed him. The Straits Settlements feared subordination to Kuala Lumpur, the Unfederated Malay States to the Federation, the Malays to the Chinese. The Colonial Office afforded him no support; he had only stirred up trouble. The visiting Under Secretary of State, Sir Samuel Wilson, declared 'that the maintenance of the position, authority, and prestige of the Malay Rulers must always be a cardinal point in British policy: and the encouragement of indirect rule will probably prove the greatest safeguard against the political submersion of the Malays which would result from the development of popular government on western lines ...'.[199]

Clementi's successor, Sir Shenton Thomas, could make only cautious advances towards decentralisation, stopping well short of the recentralisation that was the ultimate objective. Bigger changes would provoke larger opposition. Internally they did not seem essential: Malays and Chinese and Indians lived apart. External threats did not dictate them. Attempts to make them might only show that the British were not strong enough to carry them through. It was not so much a policy of divide and rule as one of better leave alone.

Nor did Clementi succeed in rationalising British Borneo. He hoped to bring the four territories closer together and needed to assert a more effective British control in Sarawak and North Borneo. The British North Borneo Chartered Company's territory seemed the easier target. Its venture had never been very profitable, and the depression made the directors more ready to contemplate being bought out. But the very fact that made the bargain possible on their side made it impossible on the government's side. It was not prepared to spend money buying out the company. Nor was the Singapore government, which Clementi also tried. 'I can't understand Sir C. Clementi's mentality!' the Under-Secretary exclaimed. 'If there was ever a more inopportune time to make a suggestion of this kind I don't believe he could have found it ...'.[200] The Cabinet decided in June 1933, in the middle of the depression, that there was no call for such expenditure. The Colonial Secretary told it that the Company administered the state adequately. If the government took over the administration might be more efficient, but it would probably cost 'a good deal more'. 'Unless, therefore, some overriding Imperial interest arose (e.g. to prevent Japan from buying land) there appeared to be no strong reason for making the purchase at the present time.' From the point of Imperial defence the Cabinet were told that 'the value of North Borneo was negative. Our main object was to prevent any other country from obtaining possession. As long as the State was in the hands of the British North Borneo Chartered Company the War Office were satisfied ...'.[201]

Clementi made even less progress with his plans for Sarawak, still in the hands of the Brookes. His hope was to install some sort of regular system of British advice. But that, it was thought, might challenge the very foundation, as well as the raison d'être, of Brooke autocracy. The Raja, Sir Vyner Brooke, was characteristically evasive. His brother, Bertram, the Tuan Muda, was more explicit; it would be better for Brooke rule to cease than to be compromised. In subsequent years the Colonial Office remained anxious to improve the administration of Sarawak but cautious about taking the initiative. Defence became an additional argument. A tentative approach from Raja Vyner was welcomed in 1938 at the Colonial Office where Edward Gent told Vyner's emissary, L.F. Burgis, that the Eastern Department felt that the question of a takeover would come up in a matter of years. 'Not only defence requirements in the Far East, but also the increasing attention which was being concentrated nowadays on health, educational and other standards of administration would ... increasingly lead in that direction.' A colleague added that the defence departments had become more concerned about Japanese penetration in Borneo.[202]

This initiative got nowhere. But early in 1939 Vyner appointed his nephew Anthony (also known as Peter) as Raja Muda (heir apparent), which seemed an opportunity to press the arguments for a greater degree of British influence. Sir Shenton Thomas impressed on the Raja Muda 'that the Imperial Government while it may not desire unduly to interfere in the domestic affairs of Sarawak, must necessarily take into strict account the need for safeguarding native interests and the need for adequate defence'. The Raja Muda, he reported, would in fact like to have the services of a man like W.E. Pepys, General Adviser Johore, and he had been responsive to Thomas' further suggestion that the senior posts in future should be filled by seconding men from the colonial service. Sir Shenton sent a positive report home.[203]

> Sarawak is a territory of very great economic possibilities and of defence importance [Gent wrote] and it is essential to keep this iron hot and not lose the opportunity, which appears to present itself, to ensure an orderly introduction of modern ideas of progress (in its better sense) including progressive improvement of native society which the Raja himself has views on – but views which distrust any departure from the most conservative policy of protecting the natives against 'progress' in its worst sense.

The Colonial Office still hesitated to approach the Raja himself; it might, moreover, stir up opposition from the Ranee, as Lord Dufferin suggested.[204]

In the interwar period the British stuck to the policy of constitutional advance in Burma on which they had set out. In British Malaya and Borneo they had set out on no such course and, despite Clementi's initiative, stuck to that line. In both cases they wished, it might be argued, to give the impression of orderly development under their guidance. In a sense it was part of a policy designed to maintain the status quo. It purported to demonstrate that there was no need and no call for change.

Defence

The colonial powers were all concerned about Japanese penetration into Southeast Asia. Their attitudes differed. Partly that resulted from the difficulty in interpreting the objectives of the Japanese: were they long term or short term, political or economic? It also resulted from differences in motivation: their economic enterprise might be as welcome as their political enterprise was unwelcome. Was it right to term the Japanese venture in Mindanao 'Davaokuo'?[205] The location of the Japanese ventures might also affect the view the colonial powers took of them. Confusion and lack of coordination played their part, too. Even within the territories for which the British were responsible there was no coherent policy, it seems, on Japanese economic enterprise. In the Federated Malay States, for example, the expansion of Japanese rubber-planting was inhibited by the Rubber Lands (Restriction) Enactment of 1917, passed when Japan was an ally, and, although it was later withdrawn, Japanese rubber interests did not revive. On the other hand, iron-mining continued to be encouraged in the Unfederated Malay States in the 1930s.[206]

This was the negative side of the equation. If that was confused, the positive side was confined. That was the eliciting of support against the Japanese from the peoples of Southeast Asia. Of that, indeed, the colonial powers had little prospect. Two French experts, Albert de Pouvourville and François Deloncle, had said back in 1905 that Indo-China could be defended only if the French gave its inhabitants a reason to fight for the regime by treating them as partners.[207] That they had never done.

Even Britain, which, at least in Burma, took a rather positive view of nation-building, was not prepared to take the essential step of recruiting a Burman army. Its forces in Burma were drawn from external sources or from minorities, as was the Dutch colonial army in the Indies. The

Philippines could develop a defence force under the Commonwealth. Only the Siamese had an army they could deploy in pursuit of a foreign policy. The colonial powers had to retain a monopoly of force. But that also limited the prospect of support against a Japanese invader.

In Malaya the British had resisted the penetration among the Chinese of nationalism and communism, although increasingly recognising that in China those were the best defences against Japanese advance. After 1937 they became more tolerant. But the Chinese were not recruited to the defence force. Even the Malay regiment, formed in 1933, was to have only two operational battalions by 1941.[208] There was no Malayan army of the kind an inspector-general had seen before World War I as complementing the presence of the British navy.[209]

Yet, as the GOC Malaya, General Dobbie, pointed out, it was now essential to defend Malaya in order to defend Singapore.[210] On the one hand a landward advance from the north was now deemed both possible and threatening. On the other hand aeroplanes based in the north could help to keep the enemy at a distance. The fact that sending naval forces to Singapore was becoming increasingly problematic became, however, another argument for augmenting land-based forces in Malaya.[211]

The FMS had contributed more or less willingly to the financing of the navy. So, to some extent, had the dominions when persuaded. The task itself had become one of diplomacy. Yet sustaining a navy that could act worldwide was essential. The graving dock at the Singapore base was opened in 1938.[212] But without such a navy it had no purpose. 'It is becoming more and more important that all the component parts of the Empire should be prepared to assist us in shouldering the tremendous burden involved in building and maintaining a Navy that is adequate to carry out its task of protecting those vital arteries along which flows the life-blood of our Empire.' Getting the fleet to Singapore and defending the base were other issues again.[213] 'Is it really safe to rely on the capacity of Singapore to resist?'[214] The diplomacy the British Government followed with other powers, and indeed with the dominions themselves, was, in Cadogan's phrase, a matter of 'bluff'.[215]

The Australians came to suspect that. To the embarrassment of the committee's secretary they became aware of a discussion at the CID in January 1939, which questioned whether an adequate fleet could be sent to the Far East if Japan joined in a war in which the empire was fighting Germany and Italy.[216] The Prime Minister, Neville Chamberlain, telephoned Joseph Lyons, the Australian Prime Minister. 'In the event of war with Germany and Italy, should Japan join in against us it would still be His Majesty's Government's full intention to despatch a fleet to Singapore.' Its size would depend on the moment Japan entered the war and the losses the empire and its opponents had meanwhile sustained.

The object would be to prevent a major operation against Australia, New Zealand or India, to keep open sea communications and to prevent the fall of Singapore.[217] Lord Stanhope, the First Lord of the Admiralty, told A.T. Stirling, the Australian External Affairs officer in London, that it was 'extremely improbable that Japan will come in, owing to commitment in China, the immense distances involved and the grave risk of undertaking such an operation while there is a British fleet in being and there is a possibility of intervention by some other power'.[218] The US fleet, in the Atlantic for the World's Fair, was moved back to San Diego.[219] Norman Davis endeavoured to reassure Bruce,[220] but Roosevelt said that 'public opinion was not yet educated to the point of approving any commitments in this direction'.[221] At the end of June the new Prime Minister of Australia, Robert Menzies, again sought reassurance from Chamberlain[222] who reaffirmed what he had said to Lyons.[223] By this time the Tientsin crisis had hit the Far East. The Dominions Secretary, Lord Caldecote, told Bruce that no decision was being kept secret from the Australian Government. 'The fact of the matter was that no definite decision had been reached, and no definite plan formulated, in view of the fact that the position was still indeterminate.'[224]

'I cannot have a defence of Australia which depends on British seapower as its first element, I cannot envisage a vital foreign trade on sea routes kept free by British seapower, and at the same time refuse to Great Britain Australian cooperation at a time of common danger. The British countries of the world must stand or fall together.' So Menzies had broadcast late in April. But, as he added, what for Britain was the Far East was for Australia 'the near north', and he looked towards a 'concert of Pacific Powers'.[225] At the same time Australia gave particular attention to Timor.

Included in the remnants of the Portuguese colonial empire were Macao, in that part of southern China into which the Japanese were moving, and part of Timor not taken by either the Dutch or the British. In March 1939 a rumour circulated 'that Japanese are trying to do a deal with Portugal under which in return for Japan's guaranteeing Macao the Portuguese would adhere to the Anti-Comintern Pact, recognise Manchukuo and grant Japan air base in Timor'.[226] There was also concern over concessions to the Japanese. The Australians sought to 'counteract penetration ... by other foreign interests' by establishing an air service between Darwin and Dili.[227]

Whatever the Australians did, preserving the status quo in Southeast Asia essentially depended not so much even on the British, who were ready but not able to do it, but on the Japanese and the Americans, who were able but possibly not ready. Neither of them indeed had an interest in the preservation of Western colonialism in Southeast Asia. The US had acquired the Philippines but had signalled its determination to grant independence. It had put up with Japanese aggression in Manchuria, even in China. What was to make Southeast Asia different was the impact of the war in Europe. The Japanese shortened their timetable in the southern seas, and the Americans believed they had to interpose.

CHAPTER 2

September 1939 – June 1940

The great powers and Southeast Asia

In almost no sense is the origin of World War II to be found among the peoples of Southeast Asia. Although they had made and were making attempts to determine their fate, they yet remained, with the exception of Thailand, within a colonial framework. The framework had been established in the period of British primacy but had not collapsed with its passing. The Americans had in a sense recruited themselves to the ranks of colonial rulers; they did not offer their colleagues a direct challenge but instead a rather unconvincing example. The Japanese again avoided a direct challenge.

For most of their post-Meiji history the Japanese had been expansionist, but they had also been cautious. They were aware that they had more than one potential opponent, not only the Russians but also the maritime powers. In general they sought to work with the latter, which was indicated both by the Anglo-Japanese alliance and by the Washington treaties that replaced it. That approach had more than one effect. Its expediency tended to align them, so far as the Chinese and the Koreans were concerned, with other imperialist powers, and their pan-Asian idealism went for little. The approach also tended to encourage Western powers to depreciate their determination and their prowess. Their major struggle had been with the Russians. It did not seem likely that they would stand up to the maritime powers, particularly if Britain and the US demonstrably stood together.

The aims of the Japanese in Southeast Asia were a source of much uncertainty. The colonial peoples were at times inspired by their apparent success in dealing with the Russians, although the Chinese in Southeast Asia were among those bound to be more ambivalent. Their colonial rulers speculated about the Japanese, their settlements, their spies and their ambitions. In general the conclusion was that their aims were long-term; they were held to believe that the colonial regimes lived on borrowed time and that the area was in some way to be part of Japan's future. They were marking out significant strategic points and informing themselves of economic sources and political aspirations. Only insofar as those aspirations encouraged the Japanese to think that the future of Southeast Asia lay with them did the Southeast Asian peoples bear some responsibility for the involvement of the area in the war. Much more important were the resources of the area. What took place was a dramatic foreshortening of the timescale the Japanese had apparently set themselves.

This was the result of factors external to Southeast Asia. In that sense the war of 1939 led to the war of 1941. The European war was transformed or transformed itself into a world war. That was not in the event surprising since Europe had made the world one, and a struggle to be the leading European state, even when Europe had become only one of the world's centres of power, was bound to have an impact outside it.

What was at issue was the succession to Britain, the strength of which had been drawn from worldwide commerce and investment and worldwide formal and informal empire. Its primacy had ceased, but its worldwide influence had not been eliminated. The possibility of its passing affected the prospects, even the security, of the other powers, Russia and the US, Germany and Japan. If one power dealt it a severe blow the others would have to reckon with its potential effect. Should they support Britain? Should they join in against it? Should they ally with its opponents? Or should they follow a policy of expediency? The fact that more than one power was concerned meant a great deal of calculation and hesitation, particularly perhaps on the part of the traditionally cautious Japanese. But such phases of hesitation have often been broken, not only among the Japanese, by a burst of action, by casting caution to the winds, divine or otherwise.

It is the argument of this book that Southeast Asia was essentially drawn into the war because of the impact on the powers of the war of 1939 and its threat to the status quo that Britain had largely sustained. Southeast Asia's importance to the Japanese became more urgent because they needed its resources yet feared that they would be deprived of them and with that, they believed, the chance of pursuing that autonomous policy they had long sought cautiously to follow. The war might destroy the British, only to replace them with the Germans; would they lay claim to the Southeast Asian territories of the Dutch and the French? More worrying, the war in Europe caused the Americans to activate their potential, and they determined to build a two-ocean navy. Although the Americans retained their hold on the Philippines, their most advanced base was in Hawaii. But with a two-ocean navy they would be in a position to curtail the freedom the Japanese had won at Washington to dominate the East Asian region.

Moreover, the Americans gained a new interest in Southeast Asia. To some extent the Philippines had identified them with the cause of the colonial powers. The war of 1939 identified them much more closely with the British. The building of the two-ocean navy was a recognition that their own security, and that of Latin America, had in a measure depended on the British and their navy. A disaster for the British would be a disaster for the Americans. The British were to be kept going not only by aid and support, although not by direct participation. They were also to be kept going by making sure that the resources they needed continued to reach them, including the resources of the empire of the British that the Americans had so often criticised, in India, in Australasia and in Southeast Asia. The US, Hugh Wilson of the State Department argued, should not try to replace the British Empire in Southeast Asia; the far-flung empires of the nineteenth century could not be maintained in the twentieth. The West, indeed, could not be part of a new equilibrium in the Far East.[1] Wilson was perhaps a minority voice in the State Department, but he echoed an underlying conviction, which was only shifted by the impact of events in Europe. The Americans decided to maintain the status quo in Southeast Asia at a time when the Japanese became convinced they had to change it.

There was indeed considerable congruence in the longer-term views that Americans and Japanese had developed about the future of Southeast Asia. Neither supported the continuance of the colonial regimes. Both looked for their termination. They came to differ, as a result of the impact of the war of 1939, on the timescale. They also differed as to the mode.

The Americans had not set their face against change in Asia. Indeed they had no interests to justify opposing it. They had, however, stressed that change should be made peacefully, not by violence, and they had endorsed principles that accorded with that view. Here again there had been tension with the Japanese but no essential difference. Even their reaction to the Manchuria crisis had been in such terms. The Americans would not oppose change in itself but only change brought about in ways that defied the Washington spirit and the Kellogg-Briand Pact of 1928. They had believed that this approach might limit the Japanese and believed that it would have been more effective in doing so if the British had endorsed their line. But even if it did not do so in the short term it would do so in the longer term. Not currently accepting what was done in derogation of the principles held open the prospect that the principles could yet apply later. 'In our foreign policy', Stanley Hornbeck wrote, 'we lay more emphasis upon moral and legal interests than upon material interests. Our great problem in relation to current developments in the Far East is that of defending principles rather than that of salvaging investments. We are not immediately menaced as regards territory, either overseas or at home …'[2]

The Americans continued to adopt this approach after war broke out in Europe in 1939. They insisted on the principles they had long enunciated in an attempt to maintain the status quo as long as possible and put off the time limit their activation of potential was in fact pushing the Japanese to shorten. What had been an approach that prescribed peaceful modification of the status quo was not, however, entirely apt to a policy of maintaining it. How should Japan's defiance of that approach be handled? How did the approach cope with change achieved under duress, although not by actual force? Could the approach be modified by a policy dictated more by expediency than by principle? Could it cope with a status quo modified in part? What if the policy, relying on Japanese caution and on the effect of demonstrated Anglo-American unity, failed to restrain but rather provoked?

American policy was 'the outgrowth of belief in a number of fundamental and traditional principles'. Even the possibility that ad herence to them might lead Japan to turn to the Soviet Union or to attack the Indies did not justify abandoning them, Laurence E. Salisbury of the State Department's Division of Far Eastern Affairs wrote in November 1939. The policy was 'designed in the long run to demonstrate to Japan that that country cannot with impunity continue to violate those principles for her own advantage and to the disadvantage of other powers'. Compromise would destroy the long-range hope that the world would 'return to a sane and orderly procedure of international intercourse'. The US must adhere to its principles and so 'exert its influence to bring about a desired order out of the present international disorder'.[3] Warnings in respect of Southeast Asia would thus be based on the same principles as warnings in respect of China, and they had not been backed up. 'Stronger threats and plainer language would have required a clearer idea of the point in Southeast Asia where American interests became vital. Hull was unsure where that line was and was therefore vague.'[4]

The British were anxious to avoid a war in East Asia; above all they wanted to avoid adding to their enemies without adding to their allies. A war in the East as well as in the West would show up the weakness of their strategy and of their arms. A war in the Mediterranean as well would

completely undermine their strategy. An American policy that con
strained Japan while offering aid in Europe was helpful. As it developed
into a policy that might provoke Japan new calculations had to be made.
Would the US and Great Britain still be effective on constraining Japan
after all? If not, would the US assist the UK? Would that assistance be in
time? Would that divert American resources from Europe? Or was
American involvement the only means to victory in Europe, and a war in
the East the price for it that had to be paid?

Phase by phase the position of the world powers and their relationship
with one another changed in the years following the outbreak of war
among Britain, France and Germany in September 1939. In each phase
the position of Southeast Asia also changed. This book attempts to
outline the major changes that took place and to put the international
politics of Southeast Asia in that context. But for those politics it seems
likely that the war might have remained a European war even if the
Americans had entered it.

The phoney war

'For some time before September 1939 we had been nominally at peace
but practically at war. Now we were at war – but, except at sea, practically
at peace.'[5] On land, if not at sea, the initial phase was indeed one of
'phoney' war, the twilight war, the drôle de guerre, the Bore War, the
Sitzkrieg.[6] The Germans invaded Poland, and the British and, even more
reluctantly, the French declared war. Officially neutral, the Soviet Union
joined in against Poland. But nothing was done to help the Poles and,
after they had been crushed, the war was in a kind of suspended
animation. Neither side was yet ready for the next step. Indeed, although
what happened the following year is of course known to us, what was
going to happen was by no means clear at the time. There were 'periodic
scares'[7] about a German offensive against France, but the Western front
remained quiet. A Russo-Finnish war did not directly involve the
belligerents. Diversions were discussed, but the Allies did not wish to add
to their opponents. The French did not want the British to use their
bombers, fearing the retaliation would fall on them. Even action at sea
was intermittent.

The period seems in retrospect the calm before the storm. But as the
phoney war continued some had begun to conclude that the conflict
would not expand. There had been no immediate attack on London, nor
was there one in the following months. Chamberlain's policy was 'one of
passive firmness: "Hold on tight, keep up the economic pressure, push

on with munitions production and military preparations with the utmost energy, take no offensive until Hitler begins it. I reckon that if we are allowed to carry on this policy we shall have won the war by the spring."'[8]

In fact Hitler was not preparing for a long war; his strategy was blitzkrieg. In the event he ended the phoney war first by his attacks on Denmark and Norway in early April and then by his attacks on the Low Countries on 10 May. On 13 May the Dutch royal family left the Netherlands, and the Dutch Government followed, seeking to establish itself in London. Resistance ceased on the following day.[9]

With limited aid from the British, the weakness of the French, attacked through the Ardennes, became apparent. 'Well, if they must, let them crack and let us concentrate on our own defence and the defeat of Germany, instead of dribbling away to France all that we have that is good – and losing it,' Sir Alexander Cadogan, the Under-Secretary of State at the Foreign Office, wrote in his diary. 'But what a look-out! God give us courage.'[10] Courage came from Winston Churchill, made Prime Minister as a result of the Norway catastrophe. His position was by no means so unqualified as public statements suggested,[11] but he and his Cabinet determined to continue the war, even though France were defeated. On 14 June the Germans entered Paris. The French Government sought an armistice. 'Can a great nation give in on a threat?' General Ironside asked. 'Unheard of … Personally, if I didn't think we could still go on successfully I should still fight.'[12]

The course of the brief campaign had subjected the Anglo-French alliance to unbearable tension. On both sides statesmen were divided not only by personal ambition and political ideology but also by the challenge of the appalling problems that they had to face and to which there was no good answer. To what extent should Britain supplement its limited military aid by now using its air force? That might help France to resist for a longer period, but it might also mean that, if France were defeated, Britain would be unable to defend itself if or when Hitler turned his attention across the channel. Should France continue even so? There might be both long- and short-term views of the advantage of that. An early termination of the war might appeal to some, like Laval, for political reasons, but it could also be supported by rational argument. If France were defeated, might not Britain also be defeated too? France might do better to make terms with a victorious Germany while terms were available. Britain might only be fighting to the last Frenchman, prolonging the war in a vain hope of ultimate success. Alternatively, that success might ultimately be secured. Where would the French stand in a postwar world in which Germany was defeated and Britain victorious while France had ignominiously sought armistice?

These problems challenged judgement as well as attitude. They were given particular point by the question of the French navy. The French had been defeated on land, but they had not been defeated at sea. What was to be the fate of their navy? If Britain was to continue the war, it could be anxious to see such a force continue on its side or, if that were impossible, destroyed lest it augment the power of its opponents. For the French, on the other hand, it represented a bargaining counter with the Germans if they resolved on making terms. The navy could not be transferred to the British in the meantime; that would be a blow to French prestige, and a testimony that collapse was expected. But could it be made over to them, or even rendered useless to their opponents, during or after the conclusion of the armistice?[13] In fact the bitterness of the differences between the Allies was redoubled by the British determination to destroy the French fleet for fear it would be used against them. The major action was at the Algerian base, Mers-el-Kebir near Oran, early in July.[14]

Italy had joined in the war.[15] Cadogan had half rejoiced. 'Am rather glad. Now we can say what we like of these purulent dogs.'[16] 'All Winston said … was, "People who go to Italy to look at ruins won't have to go so far as Naples and Pompeii in future".'[17] Minor power that it was, however, Italy had a navy, which could only add to British concern about the balance of naval power in the Mediterranean and indeed beyond.

Dramatic appeals for United States intervention in the crisis had been in vain. Yet it was important for Churchill to believe, and to secure what assurance he could, that the US, although not in the war, would back continued resistance by the British. Rather as the French had failed to promise to make over the navy to the British in advance of defeat, by which time it was too late, Churchill was unable to offer any similar promise to President Roosevelt. The security of the US, however, depended in large measure on the existence of the British Navy, and that he did not fail to point out. One major result of the French catastrophe was indeed the US determination to build a two-ocean navy.

Sumner Welles asked R.G. Casey on 30 May 1940 'what I thought the British Fleet would do if Britain were overwhelmed'. Casey said that 'they would probably immolate themselves by an attack on German naval ports'. Welles thought that this would be 'unwise and illogical … because whilst the British Fleet remained in existence it was possible to retrieve the situation at some later date'. Unless Britain thought the US would enter the war it was doubtful, Casey replied, that such logic would prevail. As he reported, 'the eventual fate of the British Fleet is of great interest to this country. They have woken up to the fact lately that the British Fleet has been protecting the United States and the Monroe doctrine for a hundred years.'[18] Lest the US viewed too complacently a British collapse, 'out of which they would get the British Fleet and the guardianship of the British Empire', Churchill told Mackenzie King that he could not predict what policy a pro-German administration would follow if Britain were overpowered.[19]

> Although the present Government and I personally would never fail to send the Fleet across the Atlantic if resistance were beaten down here, a point may be reached in the struggle where the present Ministers no longer have control of affairs and when very easy terms could be obtained for the British Islands by their becoming a vassal state of the Hitler Empire ... The fate of the British Fleet ... would be decisive on the future of the United States, because if it were joined to the fleets of Japan, France, and Italy and the great resources of German industry, overwhelming sea power would be in Hitler's hands.[20]

Late in 1939 President Roosevelt had secured an amendment to the neutrality act that eliminated the arms embargo and placed trade with the belligerents on a cash-and-carry basis.[21] That helped the Allies, and he was convinced, unlike some of his advisers, that they could therefore keep going. The failure of the Allies to utilise the opportunity he had given them alarmed Roosevelt for, unlike Chamberlain, he believed the Germans would attack in the spring. He seems for a while to have hoped to promote a peace settlement, and he sent Sumner Welles to Europe in February and March 1940 partly with that in mind.[22] The idea died. But at least the mission might have helped Roosevelt to deal with the problem he had enunciated in December: 'how to get the American people to think of conceivable consequences without scaring the American people into thinking that they are going to be dragged into this war'.[23]

The Chamberlain Government wanted US help but on a limited scale. The Prime Minister wanted to end the Nazi threat to European security and to maintain Britain's position as a world power. A German collapse would achieve the former and, if it could be brought about without a full-scale war effort, the second objective would also be attained. He did not 'want the Americans to fight for us – we should have to pay too dearly for that if they had a right to be in on the peace terms'.[24] Chatfield criticised the Americans; 'They will indeed fight the battle for freedom to the last Briton, but save their own skins!'[25] But all-out American assistance was not wanted. 'God protect us from a German victory and an American peace' was a phrase the broadcaster Ed Munro often heard.[26] The Welles mission was viewed with distrust. It signalled Roosevelt's pessimism about the Allied cause; it gave comfort to the Germans.

The crisis in May changed the British attitude; large orders for armaments were placed in the US. It was recognised that the war effort in fact depended on the US. The US was also important in seeking cooperation from the Latin American states in the blockade. Increasingly it was felt that the US must enter the war. Not everyone agreed; David Scott at the American desk in the Foreign Office wanted maximum aid, not entanglement. Churchill believed US entry would have a 'tremendous moral effect' while it would ensure supplies in the long term.[27] He continued to look for American entry. The November presidential election became a focal point.

In the meantime the US had offered material support to keep the Allies' resistance alive. The French defeat, however, produced an emphasis on hemisphere defence and doubts as to whether Britain could survive. Only in August did Roosevelt feel more certain. Then he moved towards the Destroyers-for-Bases agreement. He had earlier been doubtful of that. 'I always have to think of the possibility that if the destroyers were sold to Great Britain and if, thereupon, Great Britain should be overwhelmed by Germany, they might fall into the hands of the Germans and be used against us.'[28]

The US was, of course, also of crucial importance for the Far East. American disapproval of Japan's expansion had, it appeared, been demonstrated by the nonrenewal of the commercial treaty, and Russian strength had been demonstrated at Nomonhan. Now the Russians had come to a deal with the Germans. The pact had produced a crisis in Japan, and the Hiranuma Government had resigned. The new Abe Government believed, however, that the European war that followed offered an opportunity to end the China 'incident' since it would facilitate the extrusion of Western influence on which the continuance of Chinese resistance was mistakenly thought to depend. The Japanese Government proclaimed its neutrality in the European war but on 5 September offered the powers involved the 'friendly advice' that they should withdraw their naval and military forces from occupied parts of China.[29] The British Government checked the views of the Americans. Hull told the British Ambassador in Washington, Lord Lothian, that the US would keep American forces in the Far East and that he hoped Britain would do the same. He had already told the Japanese ambassador that the US did not accept Japan's right to warn belligerents to remove their troops from China.[30]

Returning to Tokyo, US Ambassador Grew on 19 October condemned the New Order Konoe had proclaimed. The American people were opposed to the effort 'to establish control, in Japan's own interest, of large areas on the continent of Asia and to impose on those areas a system of closed economy'.[31] A compromise in East Asia, the British recognised, could only be at China's expense and so damage Britain's relations with the US. R.A. Butler hankered after a different solution.

> Russia and Japan are bound to remain enemies, and with our position in India and the East it would pay us to make a return to the Anglo-Japanese alliance possible. It does not appear that there are the makings of a war between

America and Japan; the American interests in the Far East are insufficient to justify a major war. I do not believe that it will in the end pay us to keep Japan at arms length, and distrust everything she does, for the sake of American opinion.[32]

In fact, although its interests were indeed limited, the attitude of the US meant that Britain could not seek a deal with Japan. Britain was really dependent on the US for security in the Pacific, 'and if we decided to come to terms with Japan at the expense of China, American opinion would certainly turn against us, and leave us to fend for ourselves'.[33] Indeed that applied not only to Asia but to Europe too.

We had constantly made it plain that we had no intention of deserting the general principles that had governed our policy *vis-à-vis* the Chinese Government, and we certainly had no intention of getting ourselves out of step with the United States Government ... On the other hand, it was very important for us, if we could manage it within these limits, to avoid any worsening of our relations with Japan and indeed, if this might prove possible, to try and improve them.[34]

The replacement of the Abe Government by the Yonai Government on 14 January did not appear to portend a change in policy. Indeed the Japanese remained cautious. The *Asama Maru* incident – in which a British warship had stopped a Japanese ship and removed the Germans on board – was settled by compromise, and settlement of the Tientsin dispute was advanced. The Germans' success in Scandinavia and the probability of their attacking the Netherlands gave Japanese policy a new turn. Only the fall of France, however, produced a decisive shift. New demands were put both to the British and to the French.

The French Ambassador Saint-Quentin asked Hornbeck if the State Department could request Japan to refrain from aggression.[35] Hull told Grew to suggest an agreement promising not to alter the status quo in territories belonging to belligerents.[36] The suggestion, Arita responded, 'might be difficult to accept'.[37] Given that neither Japan nor the US was a belligerent, 'the carrying out of the suggestion ... would in his opinion be a somewhat delicate matter';[38] 'it would give rise to very delicate relationships for Japan which has taken a position of non-involvement'.[39] No doubt the possible role of Germany was in Arita's mind, but his statement was not reassuring.

Furthermore, on 29 June, Arita made a statement on the sphere.

The countries of East Asia stand in close relationship to the regions of the South Seas in terms of geography, history, race, and economy. They are destined to enjoy prosperous coexistence by mutual help and accommodation and, by so doing, to promote the peace and prosperity of the world. It is a matter of course, therefore, to unite these regions into a single sphere on the basis of common existence so that the stability of that sphere be ensured ... In view of the mission and responsibility which the stabilising power of East Asia ought to accept, Japan hereby declares that she is gravely concerned about any consequence which the European war might have in these regions.[40]

The *New York Times* of 30 June was perturbed, although Arita insisted that the mission must be accomplished by peaceful means.[41]

The Americans, like the British, believed the resources of the empire essential for the continuance of the British war effort, and ensuring their accessibility was to play an important role in transforming the European war into the world war. What was at issue was the attitude of the Japanese. If they were involved the resources of the Pacific dominions and of Southeast Asia might no longer be available, either as a result of conquest or naval attack. Moreover, in order to defend them, Britain might have had so to weaken its forces in Europe that its opponents would make significant, perhaps conclusive, gains. At the outset, however, it appeared likely that the Japanese would remain neutral. In that case the resources of the Asian and Australasian parts of the Empire would be available. So, it was hoped, would be labour, ships and planes. The prospect that Japan would abandon neutrality made the Australians anxious and, as before the war, they looked for a satisfactory agreement with it.

Initially Britain looked to Australia for aircraft and for the despatch, when ready, of expeditionary forces that would operate in a main theatre or replace British forces in Asia.[42] Menzies had at once questioned whether Japan would remain neutral: 'She will probably play a purely selfish game and at any time during the war may engage actively without notice on either side and more probably with the enemy'. Peace with Japan might be too dearly bought, 'but without that peace I cannot escape the thought that communications between Australia and New Zealand and the United Kingdom, so vital to your supplies and our exports and internal economy, must rest upon a dangerous basis'.[43] In reply the British Government accepted 'that whether or not it will be possible for Australia to despatch oversea land and air forces to assist in the general war effort of the British Empire must be decided by the Commonwealth Government in the light of the conditions at the time when these forces are ready'.[44] Bruce looked not for concessions to Japan but for a general settlement, giving it commercial opportunities in China and the Empire.[45] Butler pointed out that the US was 'far from encouraging' this line.[46] By November the British were anxious that an expeditionary force should be sent.

Casey, however, raised 'a constant anxiety' of the Australians. 'Should we be in a position, if the need arose, to send any capital ships to Singapore?'[47] A memorandum prepared for the Australian and New Zealand high commissioners argued that, given Grew's outspoken speech and the termination of the US commercial treaty, Japan must be uncertain of US reactions and, together with concentration on China, this uncertainty gave others a measure of security. Moreover the British fleet, not committed in the Mediterranean, was less immobilised by threat from Germany than in World War I. Britain had sought to improve relations by settling the Tientsin incident and by allaying Japan's anxiety over raw materials. Japan would 'sit on the fence' so far as the war in Europe was concerned, concentrating its efforts on China.[48] Lothian himself believed that the US would enter a war if the Japanese expanded south. True, if Japan concentrated on British and Dutch possessions, American reaction would, he thought, be slower than if it attacked the Philippines.

> But partly because the Central Pacific is now regarded as a kind of American reserve, partly because the expansion of Japan overseas would eventually threaten the Monroe Doctrine and partly because a war with Japan would probably not involve sending abroad vast armies of conscripts, I think that long before Japanese action threatened Australia or New Zealand, America would be at war. This probability is probably enhanced by the fact that the army and navy and a great many publicists, though not yet public opinion, recognise clearly that the present form of American security and the Monroe Doctrine is, in the long run, just as dependent upon the British as on the American Navy. If the United States is to rely upon Great Britain to prevent totalitarian Europe from entering the Atlantic through the Straits of Gibraltar and the exits from the North Sea, the United States must themselves underwrite the security of the British Empire in the Pacific because they cannot afford the weakening of Great Britain itself which would follow the collapse of her dominions in the Pacific.[49]

A Japanese attack on Singapore was considered unlikely and the invasion of Australia 'even less likely'. The French fleet would have dealt with the Italians; even if that result had been long delayed, 'the Admiralty were prepared to close the Mediterranean at Gibraltar and Suez Canal and sacrificing important interests in that area proceeding to relief of Singapore or aid of Australia in the event of serious attack'. In fact Italy was neutral, and the British Navy could, if need be, provide a 'major deterrent' to the Japanese.

> The Admiralty regard the defence of Australia and of Singapore as a stepping-stone to Australia as ranking next to the mastering of the principal fleet to which we are opposed and the duty of defending Australia against serious attack would take precedence over British interests in the Mediterranean. It is very unlikely bleak choice will arise during next year or two ...[50]

The Australians hesitated even so: 'there is still some real uncertainty about the position of Japan which might become more acute if Germany invaded Holland and Netherlands East Indies were cut off from their mother country', and the situation in Europe did not appear urgent enough to justify the risk.[51]

At Casey's request, the naval appreciation was reconsidered. What would the position be if Japan encroached in the Indies, following probably a German invasion of the Netherlands? It was 'very unlikely' that the US would 'impassively watch' Japan's acquisition of bases west and southwest of the Philippines, which would compromise its whole position in the Pacific. Japan would weigh this with 'the utmost care', and the contingency was 'highly improbable, unless of course Great Britain and France are getting the worst of it, when many evils will descend upon us all'. If, however, Japanese encroachment began, or Britain got into war with Japan, 'the Admiralty would make such dispositions as would enable them to offer timely resistance either to a serious attack upon Singapore or to the invasion of Australia and New Zealand'. That would not necessarily mean stationing a fleet at Singapore but would involve making concentrations possible 'in ample time to prevent a disaster'.[52] Bruce thought the FO and Admiralty appreciations, designed to reassure Australia, 'drew a somewhat over-optimistic picture'.[53] But New Zealand had already decided to despatch a first echelon.[54] Casey advised Menzies to send the Australian division abroad too.[55] Menzies was 'incensed' at the New Zealand decision,[56] but the Cabinet agreed that the 6th Division could go overseas early in the New Year of 1940.[57]

In the French crisis the Australian Prime Minister, echoing the British, urged the US to intervene.

> I believe that even now, if the United States, by a magnificent and immortal gesture, could make available to the Allies the whole of her financial and material resources, Germany could be defeated. The effect upon the spirit of France would be transfiguring, while the whole of the English-speaking peoples of the world would, by one stroke, be welded into a brotherhood of world salvation.[58]

No such intervention ensued, and the fall of France redoubled the concern the Australians had felt on the fall of the Netherlands. Would the Japanese take the opportunity to overthrow the status quo in East Asia and the Pacific?

The British shared the concern. The defeat of Germany could be accomplished only by economic pressure, air attack and revolt in conquered territories. The British isles had to be the main base, and the risk was of an immediate attack. The task might be impossible without the full economic and financial cooperation of the American continent, but 'we should continue to fight as long as it was humanly possible to do so'. The struggle could not be continued by the fleet operating in America; it would have been used to prevent invasion.

The collapse of France would provide Japan with the temptation to take action against the French, British or Dutch interests in the Far East. We see no hope of being able to despatch a fleet to Singapore. It will therefore be vital that the United States of America should publicly declare her intention to regard any alteration of the status quo in the Far East and the Pacific as a casus belli.[39]

Like Bruce,[60] Craigie, the British Ambassador in Tokyo, wanted what he called a more positive policy. 'He feels that the United States policy, designed so to wear down Japanese resistance that the Army in Japan would be deposed from its paramount position, is now in view of the French collapse certain to be ineffective.' A declaration that the US would not tolerate an alteration in the status quo would be 'valuable if it means more than a repetition of non-aggression but ... if an eventual head-on collision between the United States and Japan is to be avoided, there should be a more positive side to the Anglo-American policy in the Far East'. Britain, Craigie believed, should on no account aim to involve the US in war in the Far East; 'it would divert the United States attention from Europe and seriously diminish the extent of the United States material assistance at a crucial point'. Rather Britain should aim to diminish the risk by giving Japan an option to 'stark aggression'. That had to include a settlement in China, based on its independence and integrity. The understanding would also cover Japan's neutrality, the status quo in respect of colonial possessions, financial and economic assistance to Japan, and guarantees against re-exports to foreign countries. The British Government sought American opinion on the approach to follow. 'If conciliation is the alternative to be adopted, then it is obvious that the weakness of our position in fighting Japan renders it undesirable that we should take the initiative on the matter.'[61]

Casey noted that, with the defeat of France, the US might move part of its fleet from the Pacific to the Atlantic. If that took place any approach to Japan would have less chance of success 'as Japanese would know they would have little opposition of any consequence to any move outside China they should care to make'. He thought, however, that, even if the US did not agree to alter its policy, Britain should negotiate, and preferably the American fleet would remain in the Pacific in the meantime.[62] The Australian Government was convinced Japan would not accept the proposal on China that Craigie outlined. A mediation proposal would only be worth pursuing if it produced a tripartite declaration on the status quo.

Generally, we agree with the view that it would be contrary to successful prosecution of war for the USA to become involved in war in the Pacific, and policy therefore must be based on realities of situation and common sense that we should not at moment take such action or by omission of reasonable action as will cause Japan to become involved in this war.[63]

Casey and Lothian put these views to Hull. The reply was that the US 'will not use force nor will they join the British Empire in negotiations with Japan and/or China'. It would not 'take responsibility of asking China to give up anything but if the British Empire evolves formula which they think worth proposing to China and Japan then the Secretary of State does not exclude the possibility that they would give consideration to it'. It was better, Hull thought, 'to acquiesce in Japanese demands under pressure of force majeure than to accept them as part of agreed settlement'. The fleet would remain in the Pacific for the present.[64] Britain had now to decide whether to make proposals and, in any case, how to meet the specific demands Japan had put forward. There was no change in the 'negative' policy of the US.

Hull had been told that the British could not resist Japanese demands to the point of war in the Pacific. The US should either impose an embargo or send ships to Singapore, recognising that war might result if these steps did not stop aggression. The alternative was to wean Japan from aggression.[65] He did not object to attempts to bring about Sino-Japanese peace, but indicated that 'the principles underlying the Japanese new order in eastern Asia would need negativing or at least serious modifying' and that peace should not be made with Japan at the expense of China or the principles enunciated in July 1937.[66] The Secretary of State saw no signs that Japan was willing to negotiate a satisfactory settlement or to be weaned away from a determination to impose its political will. He did not favour either of Britain's options. 'Acquiescence may be a matter of necessity. Giving of assent is, however, quite another matter.'[67] Hull did not oppose a British initiative but repeated US principles:

the principle of respect for procedures and conditions of law and order; the principle of respect for international commitments; the principle of modification of commitments and altering situations by peaceful processes; the principle of non-interference by nations in the internal affairs of other nations; the principle of equality of commercial and industrial rights and opportunities; and the principle of refraining from use of force in prosecution of positive national objectives ...[68]

The US adhered to its policy of opposing the Japanese by not recognising what they achieved through the application of force. The Americans' main aim at this juncture was still to demonstrate their disapproval of the policy Japan had adopted in China. The Japanese advance into Southeast Asia was not yet at hand. Indeed, Japan had indicated its support for the status quo in Netherlands India. The major change in Europe brought about by the French defeat might encourage them to alter that line. How could the British face such a challenge? They contemplated the wider deal they had contemplated before the European war. For that, a dubious prospect in any case, the US indicated little or no sympathy. If it began to attach more importance to Southeast Asia, that did not lead it into what the British called a 'positive' policy in regard to the Japanese. Indeed the Americans gave little indication of moving beyond 'non-recognition'. Talks in which Grew engaged with Arita, stressing the principles, suggested little prospect of success.

An embargo, the British pointed out, risked war. It was far from clear, however, that they wanted the US involved in a war in the Far East. That, they generally thought, would divert the resources they needed to sustain the war in Europe. The British had also recognised that in any Japan–US conflict their possessions, and those of the Dutch, would be likely to be initial victims.

That fear was to focus in 1941 on the economic sanctions to which the US was to turn. So far the US had not gone far, and what it had done had been designed further to demonstrate its disapproval of Japanese activities in China, the so-called 'moral embargo'. In fact the British had gone rather further. Their focus, however, was on the war in Europe. Both before and after the French collapse they attributed their hopes of victory to an effective blockade. Indeed supplies to Germany was one of the topics they envisaged in their proposed negotiations with Japan. Steps were taken to limit supplies of key commodities to Japan to normal proportions, 'partly to avoid the danger of important commodities being sent across the Siberian Railway, and partly to put pressure on Japan to induce her to sign a War Trade Agreement'.[69]

This course had caused some nervousness in Australia and New Zealand. The Australian Government thought it 'incumbent on us not to precipitate matters either with Italy, Russia or Japan', and the risk of any incidents must be avoided.[70] The New Zealand Government thought that the reprobation of Japanese aggression in China had been 'entirely inadequate' but 'that, at the moment, the main enemy is Germany, and there is little to be said for any course of action at this juncture which might conceivably add another enemy to the Allied cause or otherwise disturb the status quo in the Pacific unless such a step is clearly warranted as a necessary measure in the war against Germany'. New Zealand also deprecated a bargain with Japan; 'it must have the effect in some degree firstly of strengthening Japan's position in her attack on China and secondly of alienating neutral sympathy, particularly in the United States of America'.[71] The British began talks with the Japanese without imposing special restrictions.[72]

'America', Casey wrote, 'is mainly interested in diminishing Japan's effort in China. Britain, whilst interested most sympathetically with this aim, is more immediately concerned with stopping the re-export from Japan, through Russia and Germany, of commodities that Germany lacks.'[73] It was, however, a sign that Japan could hardly avoid implication in the European war. The French collapse made its opportunities seem wider. The US, moreover, did not appear to be stepping up its measures. But it did decide to build a two-ocean fleet and, as the Consul-General in Australia indicated, that 'seemed to be largely aimed at Japan'.[74] The building of a larger fleet, although designed for US defence, undermined the security in the Pacific that Japan had gained in the 1920s and maintained in the 1930s. That had implications for Southeast Asia, too.

The German invasion of the Netherlands

Two days before the war began in Europe, Germany and Great Britain pledged themselves to respect Dutch neutrality.[75] Three weeks after it began Craigie suggested that, if the Germans were 'seriously contemplating violating Netherlands neutrality', they would endeavour 'to secure Japanese assistance in some form through the offer of Netherlands East Indies'. The temptation for Japan would be great, even without such an offer, and Nomura, the Foreign Minister, thought that the US would not intervene. At the Foreign Office M.E. Dening of the Far Eastern Department thought this all 'rather far-fetched'. American public opinion was 'incalculable', as Nomura knew, and while Germany was no doubt 'offering much that isn't hers', Japan would not be tempted 'unless she looked like winning the war'. Craigie argued for the despatch of a British naval squadron to Singapore; 'normal temptation for Japan to obtain a footing in the Netherlands East Indies will be heightened, during the period of the present war'.[76]

Early in November 1939 there were rumours that Germany would invade Holland.[77] Craigie accepted that it was not possible for Britain to send a squadron to the Far East, but he suggested that the Japanese might be warned off the Netherlands Indies by the presence of American warships. The presence of the Royal Navy was precluded by Britain's belligerent status. 'It might ... be represented to the State Department that the integrity of the Netherlands East Indies is as direct an American as a British interest and that action proposed, if taken in time, might avert the danger of European war spreading to the Pacific ...' There was, as he had reported, no immediate danger to Australia and New Zealand, but action against Netherlands India was 'well within the bounds of possibility' if Germany conquered the Netherlands and Japan–Soviet tension was reduced.[78]

At the Far Eastern Department, Dening doubted the wisdom of making such a suggestion, although the British might give the Americans

> our thoughts on the Far Eastern situation ... If the US expected an attack on the NEI they will themselves be capable of gauging the effect on the world situation, and they will be moved to do something only if they feel that public opinion would support them. If Holland were invaded and overrun, sentiment in America might well support action to deter Japan.

The withdrawal of the British garrison from Tientsin had not been well received in the US, and asking for something now might well lead to the accusation that the British were 'asking the US to pull our chestnuts out of the fire. We must, I think, fortify ourselves with the hope that if the necessity arises, they will act on their own impulse. And I do not feel that the hope is necessarily a vain one.' Dening's colleague Ashley Clarke agreed. Lothian could speak at the State Department along the lines of the memorandum prepared for the Australian and New Zealand high commissioners, communicating British ideas on 'the likely developments' particularly after Wang Ching-wei set up his puppet government of Japanese-occupied China.

Ashton-Gwatkin recalled his visit to Netherlands India at the end of World War I: 'there was a saying among the Japanese that "when the old lady dies, we will have our share of the heritage". The old lady referred to Holland and the heritage to the Eastern part of the Dutch Indies.' These ideas were reviving. The US should be asked what its attitude would be following a German invasion of Holland and a Japanese threat to Netherlands India.

> It seems to me inconceivable that the Americans could stand aside and see the territorial control over a country of such immense economic and strategic importance pass into the hands of the Japanese. On the other hand, if there is any sign that Japanese aggression in this direction would be met by joint British and American action, Japanese designs on those countries would be put back into their pigeon hole.

R.G. Howe thought 'the main thing would be to stimulate the President's ideas and move them in the direction desired'. Cadogan did not mind giving the Americans 'our views on the possibilities of the situation, but I should be very careful not to make any suggestion to them for action on their part ... We shall not, by any suggestions we make, increase the readiness of the US to take any action: we shall only increase their suspicion of and resentment against ourselves.'[79] A draft was prepared.

Before the despatch was sent Lothian reported a discussion with Welles, which also turned partly on the question of Japanese reaction to

American pressure. 'I said that the root of the problem of Anglo-American relations in dealing with the Far East lay in the fact that if sufficiently strong economic or other pressure were exercised against Japan to produce retaliation that retaliation would not be against United States but southwards to us and the Dutch islands' and, unless it were known that the United States would help, Britain would have to yield or weaken itself in Europe and the Mediterranean. Welles appeared to expect some proposals from Japan before the commercial treaty finally expired, and Lothian suggested a compromise between Japan and China. The Foreign Office adjusted their reply. Generally it accepted Lothian's views. There was indeed a risk that Japan might move south, whether tempted by a German invasion of the Netherlands or pressed by American embargo. 'This does not mean that we would wish to discourage the US Government from taking a firm line with Japan, but we hope they will prepare in advance for the possible consequences not only for themselves but for us.' Lothian must be careful not to advocate peace moves in China that could be twisted into proposals to let China down.[80]

In another conversation Hornbeck criticised appeasement of Japan. He did not think that pressure would lead to retaliation. Japan had a year's oil reserves and would not need to attack Netherlands India, even if Germany entered Holland, and Japan would not attack British territories unless the war went against Britain in Europe. Foreign Office opinion was inclined to accept Hornbeck's conclusions.[81] The issues – implications, possibilities, responsibilities – had been raised with the US. That was as much as could be done, given the constraints on the policies of Britain and the US. More important, it was also felt that this was as much as needed to be done. The caution of the Japanese was taken into account, perhaps overestimated.

The impressions of US attitudes gained by Lothian's conversations were reinforced by a report from V.A.L. Mallet, on leave from the embassy in Washington. 'There is a definite determination among the people of the United States, reflected in Congress and the press, not to clear out of the Far East at anybody's behest.' Since the China incident began there was much less talk of abandoning the Philippines. China could not be dominated by the Japanese. Nor, Mallet reported, did the State Department think that economic pressure on Japan after the lapse of the commercial treaty would lead to a breakout southwards.

> Japan can get oil and other requisites from sources outside either the United States of America or the British Empire without a raid upon the Netherlands possessions which would entail the immediate blowing up of their own oil wells by the Dutch. But, of course, if contrary to expectation Japan made such an attack the reaction in America would be extremely violent, though not necessarily strong enough to drive America into war.

It would, however, ruin relations between the US and Japan, and the US fleet and the unconquered Chiang Kai-shek would be further deterrents. The US would not act as Britain's trustee, and Britain must not suggest it should. But 'we automatically become the beneficiaries of any strong action she may take'. The US realised that Britain could do little to steady the Far East but hoped that it would not give up positions by signing them away. The US would not act jointly but might act in parallel, 'and she will not refrain from pulling her own chestnuts out of the fire merely because a few British or French chestnuts happen to be there too ...'.[82]

Netherlands India itself had not shared British concern. 'The general feeling in this country since the Berlin–Moscow "alliance" is that the tension in Eastern Asia has to a large extent been relaxed. Japan, it is thought, will now reverse or, at any rate suspend, her southward expansion policy in order to be able to concentrate all her efforts upon a commercial campaign against Britain in China.' Nor did the Dutch think Germany would attack the Netherlands as it would 'stand to lose more than to gain by such a move'. Indonesian opinion, by contrast, was 'inclined to exploit the bugbear of a Japanese invasion as an opportunity for advocating the levy of a native militia, which might subsequently be used to promote nationalist ends'. The Dutch also thought the US had shown how it would act: a further warning would be 'superfluous'.[83]

At the end of 1939, following a report of a discussion in the Japanese House of Peers, Dening was more worried than the Dutch in the Indies, perhaps even more than he had himself been earlier. 'I am afraid we must count on trouble over the NEI, if Germany invades the Netherlands. It does not follow that Japan will stage a full dress annexation, but she will attempt to establish her right to "protect" the motherless NEI.' Ashley Clarke of the FO's Far Eastern Department thought Japan would be cautious, unsure of American reaction. 'But in the event of any overt act directed towards annexation our own position would admittedly be a difficult one as presumably the Netherlands would look to us for assistance. On balance I am still inclined to think that so long as things are not going too badly for us in the West Japan will be wary of embroiling herself with the US and ourselves.'[84] Howe echoed this view in the New Year.

> Not long after the outbreak of the war in Europe, fears were entertained that a German invasion of Holland might be accompanied by an attack on the Netherlands East Indies by Japan. It is, however, considered doubtful whether Japan would lightly embark upon such an adventure, since the United States could scarcely be expected to remain indifferent and since Japan's trade with America is of paramount importance to her.

Japan had denounced its arbitration treaty with the Netherlands but was ready to make a new one. The Foreign Minister had told the Diet that

Japan would be willing to conclude a non-aggression pact with the Netherlands. 'Emphasis has also been laid upon the fact that Japan's aims in the Netherlands East Indies are purely economic, and that she has no territorial ambitions ...'[85]

At the Foreign Office the general view remained that, as the commercial treaty expired, the US should not be dissuaded from exerting economic pressure on Japan in order to frustrate the New Order. Cadogan agreed with Chiang Kai-shek that 'we should be mistaken to try and restrain American policy when at last it is directed to the defence of our common interests and our common aims'. Although Craigie was doubtful, the view was, of course, supported by Clark Kerr, the British ambassador in China.[86] Dening agreed with him that a Japanese move, if it ensued, would be but a flash in the pan. 'We should, of course, suffer some damage in the course of it, but nothing is truer than that if Japan succeeds in establishing her new order in East Asia, we shall be more gravely menaced than ever before.'[87] Hornbeck asked Lothian late in February if the British Government were still afraid that American policy would drive Japan to attack British and Dutch possessions. 'I replied I did not think His Majesty's Government was alarmed about the present policy of the United States but would naturally be anxious about any developments which might lead to Japanese action on the high seas in the Far East so long as we had no fleet at Singapore.'[88] But the end of the phoney war, and the German successes that followed, revived British anxieties.

The invasion of Norway and Denmark in April 1940 ended the phoney war and presaged a widening of the conflict. The prospect of a German invasion of the Netherlands brought reports that Japan was 'considering vigorous diplomatic action to forestall military intervention by Powers in the Netherlands East Indies' and would be vitally concerned over any change in their status, including a protectorate.[89] There were also press reports that the US would interpose.[90] The Japanese Minister of Foreign Affairs, Arita, referred to economic ties of mutuality and expressed deep concern 'over any development accompanying aggravation of war in Europe that may affect status quo in Netherlands East Indies'.[91] Craigie urged an approach to the Americans: what were their intentions? Earlier a Japanese invasion had been thought impractical. But now the commercial treaty had lapsed and, despite the view Hornbeck had expressed, Japan, uncertain over the supply of American oil, might descend on Netherlands India. 'The danger is now more real than before the treaty lapsed. It will be still more real if Allies fail to repulse German invasion of Norway, for Japanese are imitative.' Craigie quoted the Anglo-Dutch treaty of 1824 as a 'pretext' for a British approach. Even if the American reply were unsatisfactory, 'we shall at least be in a better position to decide ahead of time what must be the limits of the British opposition to any Japanese movement against the Netherlands East Indies, and what line our diplomacy should follow in the meantime'.[92]

At the Foreign Office it was feared that the Japanese might 'act precipitately. They probably judge that we cannot put up any effective resistance if they should descend on the NEI, and that with the American Presidential nominations in the offing the USA. will do little more than protest. And they are probably right.' Britain wanted 'to prevent a situation from which there will be no escape', and a warning from the US might only bring about the crisis.

> We should rather aim at securing from Japan an undertaking that she will not act provided that we and the USA also take no action. That is to say we should aim at some kind of tripartite guarantee, or a gentleman's agreement between the three of us, which would declare that we are all interested in maintaining the political and economic status quo of the NEI in the event of the Netherlands becoming involved in the war.

The Japanese might agree and in any case the approach would make them aware of American views. 'Should on the other hand the US in reply to the Japanese gesture, make some ambiguous statement designed to be interpreted as a threat, then Japan may well be disposed to call the American bluff in the belief that it is nothing but bluff.' The first step was to ask the US if it would approach Japan as suggested. At the same time it should be asked what it proposed to do if Japan acted. 'We must try and convince the Americans that it will not be sufficient for them merely to strike an attitude and that if they threaten they must be prepared to implement their threats.'[93]

The Australian High Commissioner in London thought that 'the question should be taken up immediately with the United States Government'.[94] Menzies duly urged that the British secure the views of the Americans.[95] In fact the Foreign Office had decided not to make the approach it had contemplated: 'we are unlikely to get a useful answer out of the US Government – which will act when the time comes as the occasion prompts and as public opinion allows'.[96] As the Australian Government was told, an approach to the Americans might embarrass them, 'owing to their well-known dislike to committing themselves in advance to a course of action which on account of public opinion, or for other reasons, they might not be able to carry out when the time came'.[97] In the event Hull made a statement.

The Indies Government, Dickover, the Consul-General at Batavia, had told the State Department, would 'strive to exist ... as an independent nation', even if the Netherlands were conquered by Germany. The 1922 guarantee might not apply, however, if the Netherlands ceased to be independent. 'It is feared here that, should Germany invade the

Netherlands, Germans in the East Indies, numbering several thousands, might attempt a coup designed to take over the Government. This would give Japan an excuse "to protect" the Netherlands.'[98]

Concerned, as the Japanese were, over the possibility of a Nazi coup in the Indies,[99] Hull made a 'firm statement' on 17 April, which was based, according to Reuter, on the Root–Takahira note of 1908 and the note of 1922. It referred to the Japanese statement, and declared that any alteration in the status of Netherlands India would affect the interests of many countries, including the US, that depended substantially on it for certain essential commodities. Intervention in its domestic affairs or alteration of the status quo by other than peaceful means would be prejudicial to stability, peace and security not only in the Indies but also in the entire Pacific area. The statement concluded by expressing the hope that the policy of all governments in the Pacific and elsewhere would be based on the abandonment of force and on respecting pledges and the rights of others.[100] The Foreign Office still saw value in a diplomatic move designed to emphasise the Japanese interest in the status quo. Indeed it might support the Americans, who had taken the lead; that was better than appearing to lead them.

Dening had earlier commented on the newspaper reports. He suggested 'that we should first approach the Dutch and point out to them the danger as we see it that the Japanese might attempt to declare a protectorate over the Netherlands East Indies'. This, it should be added, Britain could not regard with equanimity 'in view of their proximity to British territories such as Malaya, Burma and India, and the strategic position which they occupy in relation to Empire communications between Great Britain and the Dominions of Australia and New Zealand'. The Dutch should be asked if they would agree that Britain should indicate to the Japanese its concern to see the status quo maintained during the European war and its desire to know whether they shared this view. This, Dening thought, 'would show the Japanese Government our interest in the matter without offending their susceptibilities. It would at the same time make it a little difficult for them to make the reply that they themselves intended to assume protection over the Netherlands East Indies' and forestall any attempt to 'take the world by surprise'. The Dutch might have approached the Americans; the Japanese would be opposed to their acting as protectors.

Howe had doubted the wisdom of approaching the Dutch. But he could see advantages in an agreement to respect the independence of Netherlands India – whether or not the Dutch were treated as allies in a German war or had technically to be treated as enemies because they submitted – if the Japanese would respect its independence also. Britain might thus avoid a collision with the Japanese, who might be tempted to act. Two or more British ships might be sent to Singapore, however.

Roger Makins, another Foreign Office colleague, added some other possibilities: that Netherlands India did or did not follow the home government's lead in resisting or in submitting, or that there was some sort of Nazi coup in the colony, which would be difficult to deal with. But the most likely course was resistance at home and abroad. In any case he did not favour an approach to the Dutch either; it 'would probably only alarm them'. Perhaps Britain should declare that the assurance it gave at the start of the war that it would respect Dutch neutrality applied to the Dutch colonies so long as others respected it. A further suggestion came from Gladwyn Jebb: the Dutch might be advised to appeal to the US. Some reciprocation to the Japanese statement, which had now arrived, was decided on. As Craigie was to point out, the Foreign Minister was really claiming the Western Pacific as Japan's 'special preserve' and indicating that it would not tolerate Western interference with the status quo. But it was, as Clarke put it, 'better tactics to take him literally at his word'.

On 16 April 1940 a meeting was held in the Assistant Under-Secretary William Strang's room, and a telegram to Lothian was drafted. It proposed to respond to another indication from the Japanese, although Cadogan did not quite like the admission of Japanese interest in the Indies. According to the Netherlands Minister in London, his counterpart in Tokyo had been told that the Japanese Government would not favour an alteration in the status quo in Netherlands India in the event of Netherlands involvement in the European war. 'We are now considering whether we should not say to the Japanese Government that we have heard of this communication, that we hold similar views and that, like them, we should be deeply concerned over any development in the European war which might affect the status quo in the Netherlands East Indies.' Should Britain tell the US and ask if it sees any objection?[101]

The US statement emerged at this point. 'The status quo was secured', Scott commented. 'Nevertheless I think it just as well that we should remind the Japanese that we also are interested in the NEI and cannot admit any exclusive rights on their part. By doing so, we shall be doing something to help the State Department maintain that they are not carrying our "baby" (though in fact they are).'[102] But Lothian was doubtful about the whole proposal. Britain's support of the status quo in Netherlands India had already been indicated by a statement in the House of Commons on 18 April. An approach to the US would raise difficulties over the Dutch West Indies, to which Britain planned to send forces on the invasion of the Netherlands in order to safeguard the oil refineries against German sabotage. The State Department might also wonder why the British Government was responding to a Japanese Government statement not addressed to it. Despite Lothian's discouragement, the Foreign Office decided to go ahead.[103]

The French had meanwhile suggested that the US, Great Britain and France should all assure the Netherlands of their fidelity to the 1922 note and tell Arita that they saw the Japanese statement on the status quo as confirming the assurance it contained.[104] Scott doubted the value of proposing a joint démarche with the Americans. The US was unlikely to join in; 'she always prefers to take action on her own in order to avoid the accusation of being tied to the chariot wheels of other nations'. If it did join in the démarche might precipitate Japanese action. Britain and France could follow Hull's lead, and that would help to retain US support, which would be vital if Japan seized the Indies in view of the 'shock' that it would administer to Britain's position in the East including India. Scott doubted whether, in view of their 'sensitiveness' to the Washington treaties, the 1922 note should be cited in the representation to the Japanese. Moreover, Britain would not wish to admit that the Japanese had any locus standi for objecting if Britain had to protect the Indies. Cadogan thought it might be cited only in the statement to the Dutch.[105] The French felt that a reference to the 1922 note would show that 'there was nothing for the Japanese to be alarmed about'. Welles had told the French that Hull had had the possibility of a Nazi coup in mind rather than an attack on the Indies. He also said similar action was more likely than concerted action.[106]

In the event, however, they decided not to make the reference, and, indeed, with the US standing out, no joint démarche was made. Instead the French ambassador in Tokyo was told to say that France noted the declarations made, interpreted them as confirming the 'intangibility' of Netherlands India and was delighted that other powers adhered to principles from which it had never departed.[107] Ambassador Shigemitsu made the British task easier by officially informing the Foreign Office of the Arita statement. Butler was able to say that Britain took a similar line.[108] The Netherlands Minister was duly told that the British Government had the 1922 communication in mind.[109]

The German invasion of the Netherlands began on 10 May. 'Would it be worthwhile', the press officer, William Ridsdale, wondered, 'to suggest to the Dutch Government that they should simulate – if simulation is required – a degree of anxiety as the security of the Netherlands East Indies, and request the United States Government to undertake the protection of their territory?' Roosevelt would be anxious to demonstrate his feelings on the latest aggression in a practical manner during the primaries, and such action could be presented as 'a logical projection' of Hull's statement. 'He could calculate on the general American sympathy with Holland, the "cash and kinship" connections of the two countries and the vital importance to the States of Netherlands East Indian rubber and other produce. Moreover, the American Navy, already steaming spaciously about the Pacific, would love to have something to take under its wing in a manner which might mildly irritate the Japanese.' A declaration of the kind might have a wider significance:

> it would mean that now America was in fact protecting a piece of Allied territory. A direct community of interest between the United States and the Allies would have been established and might perhaps be used as a precedent accepted for other forms of association. If the Japanese showed signs of perturbation, these would probably not go very far and might serve only to promote a healthy reaction from American public opinion. While the British Government would naturally have no overt part in this development, such help, extended by America to one of the Allies, could be effectively used to impress neutrals, dubious about the sufficiency of our powers, that America's sympathy might become increasingly practical.[110]

Made allies by the German invasion, the Dutch, Ridsdale was arguing, might become a means both of securing closer association with the Americans in the European war and preserving the Indies from the Japanese.

But his superiors generally thought the idea impractical. 'I should have thought', wrote Dening, 'that the US would be disinclined to go so far at present, because it might well lead to a head-on clash with Japan.' From the Far Eastern point of view he would prefer to leave things as they were. 'The Dutch have acted promptly against the Germans; the Japanese have said they expect the Dutch will be able to maintain the status quo and US Fleet is remaining at Hawaii.' If the Americans wanted to 'pick a quarrel' with Japan 'that is their affair, though we on our part are not anxious for a quarrel which can only affect our interests adversely'. '(a) The Dutch would not play (b) the Americans would not play.'[111] The Americans, it was indeed certain, would not wish to be drawn further into the European war, even by the violation of Dutch neutrality. A move on the East Indies might provoke the Japanese rather than preserve the status quo.

From Batavia Walsh, the British Consul-General, had reported that a Nazi coup was unlikely.[112] In Tokyo Pabst, the Dutch Ambassador, had told Arita that the Dutch did not intend to seek the assistance or good offices of any power in safeguarding its territory.[113] On the outbreak of war the government took effective steps to intern Germans and take over German ships. The Governor-General declared that government authority could be maintained: 'Assistance to this end from abroad from whatever side it may be offered will be refused as being unwelcome.'[114] The Dutch Naval Commander hoped the US would not 'take hasty action which might precipitate forestalling movement by Japan', and for the same reason opposed a conference with Allied forces.[115] As the Consul-General later put it, the government in Batavia was 'clinging to the shibboleth of neutrality' in its wish 'to maintain the status quo to please

Japan'. Would a stance that sought to minimise change – either by Nazi coup, or by talks with the British, or by seeking American intervention – be enough to restrain Japan?

On 11 May Craigie had talked to his Dutch colleague in Tokyo. 'We agree main danger probably lies in Navy's taking matters into its own hands.'[116] The same day he reported a conversation between Arita and the British Embassy's Counsellor. The Foreign Minister declared that if, as a result of Netherlands involvement in war, the supplies that Japan drew from the Netherlands Indies diminished, a situation would arise that it 'could hardly bear'. He agreed, however, that if the Dutch Government needed more, Japan might have to receive less. He said that he was making a similar communication to France and Germany. The Counsellor observed that the Germans could hardly make themselves felt in Netherlands India. Arita replied that he wished to prevent Germany's making a 'paper annexation'.[117] Hull asked Lothian[118] if Britain agreed that there should be no alteration in the status quo as a result of the invasion of Holland; if so, he proposed to invite the Japanese Government to make a similar statement. He was told, of course, that the British shared his view.[119] Hull made a statement recalling that in recent weeks several governments, including the UK, Japan and the US, had indicated their support for the status quo. This was in harmony with the 1922 pledges, to which he trusted governments would adhere.[120] The Australian Government also affirmed that it would take no step to alter the status quo.[121]

The British move on the Dutch West Indies raised complications, however.[122] President Roosevelt told Lothian that he was 'gravely alarmed' at the report from Tokyo that Japan was contemplating intervention in Netherlands India 'on the excuse of the British and French intervention in Dutch West Indies, in order to prevent it being possible for Dutch to invite assistance from British and French in East Indies as they had done in the West Indies'. He asked the British Government to state that it had no intention of intervening in the East Indies; if possible the Dutch Government should state that it had no need to invite assistance there. In addition the British Government should indicate that it would withdraw its forces from Aruba and Curaçao as soon as possible. A press statement was issued accordingly: the British Government retained its view that the status quo in Netherlands India should be maintained, had no intention of intervening, and had received no suggestion that it should.[123] A *Times* report promised that Allied forces would leave the Dutch West Indies when the Dutch were satisfied with security.[124] Reassuring telegrams were also sent to Craigie.[125]

Hull reassured Japan's ambassador Horinouchi Kensuke: he feared the Japanese would have made the British move in the West Indies a

pretext for a move in the East Indies.[126] The Germans were rather slower
to indicate their disinterest in NEI; they did it only on 22 May.[127]

Arita expressed appreciation of Britain's views and declared that Japan
had no intention of intervening in Netherlands India. His main
preoccupation was over the importation of raw materials from that
colony, but he appeared to think it natural that guarantees against re-
exportation would be required, as was the case with imports from Malaya
and the Straits Settlements. Craigie thought that 'we must do what we
can to cut ground from under feet of those pressing for positive Japanese
action'. A Dutch assurance that 'no drastic reduction in Japanese imports
of raw materials from Netherlands East Indies' was contemplated would,
he thought, be 'timely'.[128] At the same time a report from Paris that Japan
planned to descend on the colony led the French to suggest a
reassurance that oil supplies would continue. This the Dutch Government gave, and the Foreign Office authorised Craigie to replicate it
if they saw fit.[129] The ambassador did not agree that an attack on
Netherlands India was likely but thought the Dutch assurance would cut
the ground from under the feet of the extreme nationalists. He did not,
however, recommend that the British should endorse it: 'we must not
appear over apprehensive'. What would strengthen Arita's hands most,
Craigie added, would be 'a definite assurance from the Netherlands
Government that subject to their own prior requirements and to
guarantees against re-export to Germany every effort will be made to
meet legitimate requirements of Japan on normal supply of *raw* materials
from the Netherlands East Indies ...'[130] The Dutch Government told
Pabst to extend the assurance to all raw materials in the terms Craigie
had adumbrated.[131]

Craigie was still somewhat concerned over the Japanese extremists and
not without some justification; Yoshida restrained the more sanguine
strategists who tried out a manoeuvre based on transporting materials
from an occupied NEI.[132] The ambassador wanted the US to soft-pedal
any idea of embargoes against Japan.[133] But then he learned from Pabst
of 'far-reaching' Japanese economic demands on Netherlands India,
which threw an 'interesting light on Japan's present nervousness' as
regards its status.[134] The Japanese, he implied, were not merely
concerned that Netherlands India would become bound up with the
Allied war economy and its restrictions, as a *Times* report suggested had
been the view in Batavia.[135] Their 'wishes' were that Netherlands India
should refrain from prohibiting principal exports and modify import
restrictions on Japanese goods, alter regulations on the employment of
foreigners, control anti-Japanese press comment and extend facilities to
Japanese enterprises.[136] Arita listed certain commodities and quantities

Japan wanted to continue to receive;[137] 'an obvious effort to ensure invulnerability in case of American embargo', thought Craigie.[138] The immediate risk of an embargo seemed, however, small. Hornbeck had told Lothian that the fleet would stay in the Pacific, but provocation would be avoided. 'He thought that the Japanese were getting very exhausted and that they were unlikely to enter on any new adventure unless they were certain of fairly easy success.' Lothian thought Japan would not move unless the European situation led the US to move part of its fleet back to the Atlantic.[139]

In fact, at about the same time as the arbitration treaty had been denounced, the Japanese had indicated a wish to bring to an end the most-favoured-nation commercial treaty of 1912[140] and, as the Foreign Office now learned from the Dutch Government in London, they had, shortly after the termination of their commercial treaty with the US, handed in at the Hague a memorandum of general principles on promoting trade with Netherlands India.[141] The Dutch Colonial Minister saw the need to meet Japan's normal needs for raw materials, subject to satisfactory assurances from Japan against re-export to Germany. A collision with Japan must be avoided. Negotiations would be conducted in Batavia, and the Dutch would try to keep them on the economic plane. The minister agreed that it would be desirable to keep in touch with the United States Government on the matter.[142] The FO consulted the Ministry of Economic Warfare; how far would such demands affect negotiations with Japan on contraband control?[143]

Craigie had meanwhile again urged a more general British approach to the US. Economic pressure seemed to be Japan's plan, but 'we should be ready for any eventuality'. There was no need to ask the Americans for help; a frank statement of their views could be sought on what the counteraction might be. Cadogan admitted that the situation had changed since April. The West Indies operation was over, and discussions with the US would not lead to embarrassing questions about it.

> Our general misgivings as to the wisdom of inviting the United States Government to define their attitude in advance towards the situation which might arise in the Netherlands East Indies was that the Americans might be embarrassed to give us any answer at all; and if they did, their answer would hardly be likely to be helpful in view of the fact that their action in given circumstances would depend on the state of public opinion in America at the time ...

But these arguments might have lost some of their strength.

> Public opinion in America has been prepared by this week's events for the ultimate necessity of some action on their part on the side of the Allies ...

> Another consideration is that it has become patent to all how great a
> disadvantage we have suffered from being unable to conduct staff talks with
> Holland and Belgium before an attack was made ... Might not the same apply
> as regards the Netherlands East Indies? ...

Lothian was instructed to consult the President and, at the Admiralty's
suggestion, he was told that facilities for the American fleet would be
available at Singapore. The same night the ambassador talked to the
President. 'He said that in view of the situation in Europe he thought it
improbable that the United States today would declare war on Japan over
Dutch East Indies, though it would probably impose embargo and
cooperate in long distance blockade of supplies to Japan.' Roosevelt
made no direct answer on the question of staff talks, 'evidently thinking
that it was too full of political dynamite at the moment ...'.[144]

Hitherto the discussion of an American embargo had turned on its
relationship to Japanese policy towards the Indies. Would the fear of it
prompt the Japanese to act or not? But it was now asked, what, if,
prompted by that or by other factors, they acted in any case? The answer
seemed inadequate. Dening suggested that the President was speaking
'on impulse without a full consideration of the issues involved'. If it
imposed an embargo and blockade the US would have to be prepared to
implement them by war. Japan could not face complete blockade of
trade with the US and the empire; NEI resources would not make up for
it. The US could not 'evade the issue' in this way for Japan would have to
settle the issue by force of arms 'once she had made a move'. Probably
the President would realise this on fuller consideration.

> We ourselves are forced to allow affairs to look after themselves in the Far East.
> If the United States adopt a similar attitude, then the situation will indeed be
> grave, and since an embargo and a long-distance blockade are not in
> themselves sufficient to bring Japan to her knees in a short period, only the
> threat of force and the obvious intention to employ it if necessary will meet
> our mutual object.

Dening did not know 'whether it would be wise to press the matter
further at this juncture, but to leave it where it is, and to accept President
Roosevelt's views as final – if indeed they are final – would be dangerous.
If the US are prepared to risk an embargo, then surely staff talks,
however secretly conducted, are a pre-requisite.'

J.V. Perowne in the Foreign Office's American Department did not
favour pressing the Americans at this juncture, but Lothian could be
invited to speak 'as and how he thinks appropriate'. 'I don't believe that
what with (1) the state of military affairs in Europe (2) the unpreparedness of the US (3) the 5th column difficulties in South and
Central America (4) the forthcoming election the Administration will

dare to appear to commit themselves too far.' Howe was 'filled with misgiving'. If the US imposed an embargo and a blockade in the event of a Japanese attack on the Indies, 'they would certainly ask for our cooperation ... This would put us in a very awkward position with the Japanese in occupation of the Dutch East Indies a few miles from Singapore.' Staff talks were necessary.[145] A telegram was sent to Lothian:

> Imposition of an embargo and a long-distance blockade would not save the Netherlands East Indies and might well provoke Japan to open hostility in which case British interests and possessions would be the next to suffer. Prevention being the best cure, it is clear that only the threat of force by the USA. and the obvious intention to employ it would act as a deterrent in the circumstances, and if there is to be any concerted action between us, it seems essential that it should be preceded by staff conversations

for instance along the lines of the secret talks of 1939.[146]

Sir Ronald Lindsay, the minister, spoke to Hull in mid June. By then, as he put it, the centre of gravity had moved to the Atlantic, and he suggested staff talks in view of a possible German attack on England. Hull did not seem to think the time was ripe.[147] Dening believed that the Americans might be 'thinking of taking an entirely different line with Japan, i.e. to wean her from aggression. The US can do that, and we cannot; we should therefore do nothing to divert them for their purpose which, if it succeeds, would save us all a lot of trouble.' But if that did not succeed, the lack of staff talks would be regretted. 'We must, I suppose, leave it at that.'[148]

The French were concerned that the deterioration of the position in Europe might invite Japanese intervention in Southeast Asia, and no doubt Indo-China was in their minds as well as the Dutch Indies. Roché, the French chargé in London, spoke to Ashley Clarke early in June of encouraging the moderates in Tokyo rather than the extremists. The US aimed, it seemed, at reducing their deliveries of goods to Japan to pre-1937 level while the Allies wished to restrict supply to Germany via Japan. But it was important not to provoke the Japanese or give them 'a pretext for any adventure in the southern Pacific or for joining in the war against us'. France suggested an approach to the US that would adjust policy towards Japan by a renewal of commercial negotiations. Ashley Clarke discouraged the idea. Moderates and extremists were much the same but wanted different methods; adventures would be avoided unless the war went badly for Allies in Europe. The Americans did not intend to impose an embargo, or to reduce deliveries other than in specific commodities. 'The American policy was to hold the threat of an embargo like a Sword of Damocles over Japan, but to avoid provoking the Japanese into action by going any further for the present.' But it was inadvisable to suggest any sort of appeasement. 'While it was true that the Americans did not want

a conflict in the Pacific, they were equally resolutely opposed to con-
ciliating the Japanese, and we should probably arouse suspicion and
resentment in America if we were to propose a policy of this kind.' The
Dutch, Clarke added, felt that they could cope with their negotiations,
and Britain agreed that it was inadvisable to provoke Japan by interfering
in them.[149]

Generally his colleagues agreed with Clarke. In the longer term
Dening saw a risk.

> The Japanese technique is to take a certain line and to see if it works. This line
> about supplies from the NEI is working quite well, and Japan's vital necessities
> are therefore being impressed on everyone ad nauseam. We should be careful
> not to allow 'vital necessities' to develop into a 'life–line', for that will be the
> next step, after which the necessity for the physical possession of the NEI will
> be obvious.[150]

In the shorter term Dening saw no value in the French idea. It would
alienate the Americans, and it would not conciliate the Japanese, who
would take what they wanted if the Allies were defeated in Europe but
not otherwise; 'the policy we are at present pursuing is the correct one.
We are being conciliatory without giving anything away, and Anglo-
Japanese relations are, if not cordial, at any rate in a state of suspense
without any particular tension.' Any negotiations must avoid appeasement, Clarke agreed. The policy of the Ministry of Economic Warfare,
Seymour added, must avoid provocation.[151] Later it seemed, as Dening
noted, that the Americans might themselves try 'weaning' Japan from
aggression, but that would be their initiative.

Grew had in fact been authorised to talk to Arita, although Hornbeck
feared it might lead to appeasement.[152] The talks, however, emphasised
the 'principles'; 'stress the point that there can be no fundamentally
friendly relations between our two countries so long as the Japanese
continue to endeavor to achieve various positive national objectives by
use of force'.[153] Grew thought there was an opportunity, Hornbeck did
not; 'how would you like to try your hand upon diplomatic steps towards
effecting a rapprochment with Japan? Or, would you like simply to *trust
them* to respect a few interests, including ours, in the western Pacific,
eastern Asia, the Southern Pacific, and the Indian Ocean?'[154]

In Batavia the government had acted with vigour, dispelling earlier
fears of a Nazi coup or a Norway-type solution. But Walsh, the British
Consul-General, felt some doubt about it in the longer term. With the
Dutch Government in exile in London, he felt the Indies Government
might become independent of it and more conciliatory to Germany and
Japan. The government-in-exile prescribed contacts with the British
naval command in Singapore. This unofficial contact in the Far East

between those who were open allies in Europe was 'paradoxical' and could not long continue, the Consul-General believed.[155] 'A disposition on the part of the Netherlands East Indies to grow more conciliatory to Germany and Japan would create a very real danger', Dening thought. The Japanese must be aware that Britain would try to 'concert measures of defence ... now that we are allies. They will, of course, try to frighten us out of this as far as they can, and it would be advisable to conduct any conversations ... as unobtrusively as possible.' The Japanese attitude 'depends ultimately on the outcome of the battle in Europe, whether we like it or not. If we lose that battle, we shall have to be prepared to face an attack, not only on the NEI, but possibly on our own possessions in the Far East. To neglect staff talks with the Dutch now would in that event merely increase our danger.' The other task was 'try, through the Netherlands Government, to stiffen the resistance of the NEI towards Germany and Japan'.[156]

The GOC Malaya sought instructions on responding to a request from the Chief of Staff, NEI, for close liaison. The Joint Intelligence Committee concluded 'that if and when the Japanese intend to attack the NEI they will do so whether they have the excuse that we are holding staff conversations or not'. That the Dutch were now allies, moreover, made conversations only natural. The Dutch authorities, however, were not altogether to be trusted. Conversations should be held only on British territory, and secret matters should not be revealed. The naval authorities, who came from Holland, were more reliable than the army, largely recruited locally, and some of the civil servants. Any efforts to 'stiffen resistance' should be made through the government-in-exile. Unobtrusive staff talks were decided on.[157] Churchill favoured sending some of the Dutch troops evacuated in Europe and units of the Dutch fleet out to the East; but it must be done so as to avoid arousing Japanese suspicion.

> Since any interference by HM Government would be interpreted by the Japanese as an attempt to alter the status quo, it is essential that any reinforcement of the NEI by Dutch vessels or troops should appear as a spontaneous decision of the Netherlands Government. If any explanation were demanded of the Netherlands Government by the Japanese, they would then be in a position to say that the reinforcement of the NEI was designed to preserve the status quo and to render unnecessary the intervention of third Powers for the protection of the islands.[158]

'These various measures are useful', Seymour wrote: 'but the plain fact is that only the US could prevent Japan from occupying the NEI and present indications are that the US are not disposed to enter into any discussions as to what they would be prepared to do if an attack took place'.[159]

In fact, neither the War Office nor the Admiralty favoured Churchill's suggestion. The morale of the troops was not good; the morale of the naval forces was good, but they were more useful in Europe. In any case, as Dening pointed out, the situation had meanwhile 'developed to a point where any attempt to reinforce the NEI may be expected to have a very adverse effect on Japan'.[160] By this time France had collapsed and, as the FO had recognised, that encouraged the Japanese. The US, too, appeared to be concentrating on hemispheric defence while not encouraging concessions to Japan nor, indeed, succeeding itself in winning Japan from aggression.[161]

In the discussions on the Indies the British on the whole seemed confident that the Americans could stop the Japanese if they so decided, and the question was whether they would so decide. Prewar the Philippines had seemed a barometer of American determination. The discussions on the Indies did not refer to the Philippines. Yet, if the Japanese were to move on the Indies, the Philippines would in some sense be in their path. Moreover, while the barometer was not easy to read, the Americans had committed themselves to grant independence in 1946 but not earlier. The idea of an earlier independence, once sought by Quezon, had been abandoned. The Foreign Office wondered if it would come about at all. Even so, it might be that the Japanese could bypass the islands on their way south to attack Singapore and the Indies. Such was part of the plan developed late in May 1940 by Iwakuro of the War Ministry. It was based on 'separate dealings' with Britain and the US; 'we keep watch over the Philippines but refrain from any offensive action unless absolutely necessary'.[162] It is indeed conceivable that at that point this would not have provoked American action. The position was certainly going to be different the following year when the Americans were building their two-ocean fleet. The Japanese could not take the risk that they might have taken the previous year.

The implications for the Philippines

On the outbreak of the war in September 1939 the British Consul-General in Manila, Wyatt Smith, reported that the local press, American and Filipino, was sympathetic to the Allies. 'The Filipinos themselves, while their leaders are outwardly following the lead of the United States and expressing sympathy for democracy, are as a whole absolutely indifferent to the struggle in Europe save as it directly affects their pockets.' Prices of Philippine produce had risen, 'and the newspapers carry long articles detailing the rise in prices of local export products during the Great War and voicing the expectation that Filipino growers will reap great benefits by the present war'. Wyatt Smith felt that the

Filipinos were 'a most unfertile field for foreign ideological propaganda, for their interest is limited to local politics and to material benefits'.[163]

Local politics, however, might be affected by the war. What implications did the war have for Philippine independence, envisaged under the Independence Act for 1946? In October Smith reported several editorials as saying 'that the outbreak of war in Europe does not affect the forthcoming grant of independence and that, indeed, the Philippines are more likely to be drawn into war while under the US flag than if they were independent'.[164] 'In the present state of the world', Berkeley Gage remarked at the Foreign Office in London, 'sensible Filipinos should surely be reluctant to abandon the protection and commercial advantages to be derived from the American connection ...'.[165]

The question of earlier independence had, it seemed, been dropped. Following Roosevelt's assurance the US had modified some of the economic provisions of the Independence Act, and the Philippines Congress had accepted them in August.[166] The idea of a postponement of independence, or a modification of it, was, however, being advanced, in particular by F.B. Sayre and Paul McNutt. McNutt, Federal Security Administrator and presidential aspirant, addressed a *New York Herald Tribune* forum on 26 October on 'America's Pacific Frontiers'. America, he declared, should stay in the Far East, and therefore in the Philippines, 'where we have a perfect right to be by conquest, by purchase, and, I have every reason to believe, by invitation if and when we give any indication that such an invitation would be accepted ...'. In regard to defence McNutt predicted 'that so long as our flag flies over the islands no foreign power will trespass, irrespective of the military forces stationed in the Philippines'.[167] Sayre, the new US High Commissioner, had said the independence issue was closed unless the Filipinos wished to reopen it.[168] The same line he repeated on arrival in Manila:

> If ever the day should come when the Filipino people should decide to change their minds and alter the policy to which they have unyieldingly adhered for over 40 years and should bring such a request before Congress, it would be for Congress, and for Congress alone, to decide what course of action the United States should pursue ... in the light of such conditions as may then exist in the world and in the Philippines, and what these will be no one can foretell.[169]

Filipinos were unlikely to take up the invitation for they would lose face;'Filipino leaders generally, while for the most part afraid to ventilate their views publicly, are getting nervous as to the ability of a Philippines Republic to maintain its independence under present world conditions, especially after the Philippines has lost the great financial advantages of free trade with the United States'.[170] No one, Gage concluded, was really anxious for independence at present. 'Without US protection the

Philippines would soon fall into the Japanese maw', J.V. Perowne remarked.[171] For the British the continued presence of the Americans seemed still to be the best option. They would, it was believed, deter the Japanese. The movement of the American carrier *Langley* to the Philippines in October they had seen as a 'wise precaution'.[172]

Quezon went ahead with defence expenditure, arguing that it was part of the preparation for an independent existence. The European war, he said, showed that a small country could not long defend itself but, if the Filipinos were to become independent, 'they must assume the responsibility of defending themselves against external aggression'. He hoped for the neutralisation of the Philippines, as envisaged in the Independence Act, but did not place full reliance on any agreement that might be reached in respect of that,

> for international treaties had been violated time and again during the last few years. Moreover, even if the country were neutralized, it would be the obligation of the Filipinos to defend such neutrality, and the powers called upon to sign such treaty of neutralisation would be more willing to enter into such a pact when they knew that the Philippines did not depend solely on the strength, ability or willingness of the guaranteeing powers to defend it, but had its own force to maintain its neutrality.[173]

Gage did not think this had 'any serious significance'; Perowne thought independence in 1946 'quite uncertain whatever the "texts" may say'.[174]

In 1940, however, Quezon continued to insist that independence was the aim. The US would not give the full autonomy that was the only alternative. The present relationship could not be prolonged since under it the Philippines could not shape its own economy. 'An independent Philippines in 1946, even faced with danger of her security – and she could never hope to repel an invasion by a major power during her early years of independence – was … preferable.' Resistance to an invader would be possible only for a few months; only twenty-five years hence would the Philippines be able to defend itself. The problem was to avoid conquest meanwhile. That might happen, 'but unless we become independent we shall perpetuate this situation of dependence and powerlessness in which we now find ourselves'. And to be conquered would only be 'a temporary set back'.[175]

Arita told the Japanese House of Peers in February 1940 that Japan wanted 'coexistence and coprosperity' in the South Seas.[176] A message of reassurance followed; the Japanese wished to share prosperity with the Philippines and 'expand commercial and cultural ties, and they harboured no political or territorial ambitions'.[177] In the US, T. North Whitehead remarked, commercial circles generally assumed that the Filipinos preferred a continuing connection with the US for commercial reasons and from their fear of Japan. American commercial interests, especially in sugar, favoured a severance of the tie.

> Political considerations split the US into two unequal opinions – The majority opinion considers that the retention of the Philippines would enable the US to restrain the power of Japan in the Pacific – The minority, but influential, opinion believes that to retain possessions so far from the US and, relatively, so near to Japan is merely to risk entanglement in an area in which the US could not effectively use her sea power.[178]

The British drew comfort from the continued American presence. They were happy to believe, indeed, that independence would never come about. They assumed that the American presence would deter a Japanese attack. The alternative view was occasionally implied by Americans and Filipinos: that the Philippines was more vulnerable because of its connection with the Americans. In general, however, they followed the line the British followed. But it is not clear why the British did not squarely connect this conclusion with their concern to involve the US in the security of the rest of island Southeast Asia. It was, presumably, the US presence in the Philippines that led the President to suggest that he could pressure the Japanese if they attacked the Indies. That they might attack the Philippines as well did not seem likely.

The attitude of the Americans, whether or not it was demonstrated in the Philippines, was important to the other colonial powers. Those included, of course, not only the British and the Dutch but also the French. Their position was complicated, however, not only by their relationship with the Soviet Union but also by the proximity of their colony to China. The major feature of their position, however, was their weakness, evident at the outset of the war in Europe in 1939. Their catastrophic defeat in mid 1940 did not, however, destroy their hold on Indo-China. Like the Dutch, they continued to rule in Southeast Asia. But as a result of the surrender the French were in a position with regard to the British that differed from that of the Dutch. Maintaining the status quo in respect of Indo-China was even less straightforward than maintaining it in respect of Netherlands India.

Indo-China and the fall of France

The Nazi–Soviet agreement, alarming in Europe, offered the French some prospect that Japanese pressure would be alleviated in the Far East. They were disposed to use the opportunity to conciliate Japan, and the lifting of the ban on exporting iron ore from Indo-China pointed that way, as did the acceptance of a Japanese consulate at Noumea. The obstacle was, of course, China and, more particularly, US concern over

China. Under Secretary of State Sumner Welles told the French Ambassador, Saint-Quentin, that it would be 'as little opportune to pressure [the Japanese] as to appear to court them with too much solicitude'.[179] The French ambassador thought that the US 'counted on Russian military assistance to China holding Japan in check without the relations of this last power with the United States being compromised'.[180]

During the phoney war no major new initiatives were possible; if the UK and the US would not act, the French could not. The Governor-General of Indo-China, Catroux, told the US Consul at Hanoi, Charles S. Reed, that, while France was 'generally sympathetic to the Chinese cause', it could 'not afford to jeopardize Indo-China and will accordingly follow a policy of purely political expediency'. The French, Reed added, were apprehensive of Japanese action, and the Japanese were suspicious of the transit of goods to China.[181] The Japanese move into Kwangsi in November, and their capture of Nanning, was followed by a protest against the shipment of munitions together with a disclaimer of designs against Indo-China. The stationing of Japanese officials in Indo-China was also proposed. The French sent a firm response.[182] The issue remained,[183] and there was speculation that the Japanese would act more vigorously. The French took a special interest in their attitude towards the Dutch Indies. As the battle for France got under way Roché again suggested a conciliatory approach to Japan, but again that was not taken up.

The collapse of France enhanced the possibility that the Japanese would step up their activity in some form or other. At the same time the French in Indo-China were more exposed. Would the Germans aid, limit or ignore the aspirations of the Japanese? How would the British react to the continued retention by France of its colonial possessions, concerned as it had already shown itself to be about the fate of the navy that protected them? How would the Americans, concerned as they were by the overthrow of the status quo in Europe, react to the possible undermining of the status quo in Asia? In what ways, if any, would they support it? The omens were not good. Welles told Lothian that his government could not go beyond the declarations made in respect of Netherlands India.[184]

The policy of the British was, in Indo-China as in Netherlands India, to uphold the status quo as far as possible despite and because of dramatic changes in Europe. If the Japanese took their opportunity there the British would be greatly weakened and Singapore under direct threat. If the Japanese occupied Indo-China they would control Thailand; 'a new Japanese base at Saigon' would be a thousand kilometres from Singapore; it would provide air bases for operations against Malaya.[185] But upholding the status quo was rendered even more complex than in the case of Netherlands India as a result of the French defeat. The Dutch Government had fled and set up in exile in London. Its members were not to prove easy to deal with, and in the Indies the British Consul-General felt some apprehension over the attitudes of members of the bureaucracy and the armed forces. But in essence dealing with the Dutch was to prove a far more straightforward matter than dealing with the French. The armistice government, moving to Bordeaux and ultimately to Vichy, claimed the allegiance of French colonial authorities and overseas forces. In Africa and the Mediterranean the British were to step in so that French forces should not fall into the hands of the Germans and their collaborators. More controversially still, they were to attack the French naval units at Oran early in July. 'It was very necessary, but it was *not* pleasant! Like having a tooth out.'[186] In Indo-China a different line was followed, although the Oran episode made it no easier.

In Indo-China war had to be avoided, not prosecuted. Stepping in, even if the British had the power to do so, would provoke the Japanese by dislodging the status quo to which they had pledged themselves; abetting any Free French movement would also be dangerous. The British had to rely on the French colonial authorities to resist the Japanese, even giving them some help to do so, although not in a way that might provoke the Japanese, the Germans or indeed Vichy itself. Those authorities had a prime interest in avoiding a break in colonial authority, which it would be difficult to re-establish. That would tend to prevent their yielding to the Japanese. But there was also the risk that they would compromise with the Japanese in order to avoid the complete destruction of their authority. Such a compromise, moreover, might be pressed on them by the armistice government. In turn its action might depend on the attitude of the Germans. Would they be ready to second the Japanese cause rather than, as Arita had feared over Netherlands India, stepping in themselves? Warning them off was one purpose of his statement of 29 June 1940.

Armistice in Europe was based on the idea of survival. There was a counterpart in Asia. In their memoirs the French governors-general, Catroux and his successor Decoux, make it plain that their prime aim was to preserve the continuity of French authority in Indo-China.[187] Their tactics appear to have differed, but so also did the circumstances in which they found themselves. At the time of the armistice Catroux's plan was to offer concessions to the Japanese, even in advance of demand, in the expectation that they would not feel impelled to challenge or displace French authority. Such concessions must not, of course, undermine or discredit that authority. His policy, it seems, was a failure. His concessions and his acceptance of a Japanese inspection unit did not prevent the presentation of further demands by General Nishihara Issaku, commander of the unit, early in July 1940. These demands involved the admission of Japanese troops on a scale that Catroux recognised would undermine French authority. At the same time the Bordeaux/Vichy Government disapproved of Catroux's assumption of an independent negotiating position and his readiness to accept a Japanese inspection unit in French territory. 'Our weakness', Baudouin, the Vichy Foreign Minister, wrote, 'explains the attitude of General Catroux who was at bottom probably right in not meeting the Japanese demands with a blunt refusal, but who was wrong in the way he did it, for he acted as if he were a plenipotentiary of the French Government.'[188]

Vichy had decided to replace Catroux with Admiral Decoux. He did not take over at once and resolved to seek clarification from his superiors. Catroux argued that avoiding the change would avoid offering the Japanese an opportunity to assert that the French had changed the status quo so that they need no longer support it themselves.[189] He regretted that Vichy made known to the Japanese that Decoux was now Governor-General and he was not,[190] but his policy with the Japanese had already failed before that, and there was some truth in Decoux's view that he had only whetted Japanese appetites, particularly when Colonel Sato Kenryo of the South China Army joined Nishihara.[191] Taking over, Decoux was able to bring Catroux's policy to an end but only by indicating that negotiations were a matter for the metropolitan governments and not for the local authorities. This was in keeping with Vichy's views. But in Tokyo the Foreign Minister in the new Konoe cabinet, Matsuoka, was to adopt a more aggressive stance than his predecessor. Vichy was not prepared to take a firm line in response, and Decoux was in the end faced with an unpalatable agreement and an aggressive Japanese approach as well. The decision to move negotiations to Tokyo had cut him out of an effective role. It virtually invited the Japanese to build on Catroux's concessions, as Baudouin himself foresaw: 'when they have got as much as they can out of Hanoi, they will turn towards Vichy'.[192]

On the French capitulation the Foreign Office in London had telegraphed its consular officers in French territories in general:

> The British people, knowing that the French army has laid down its arms against its will and that of the French people, intend to continue the struggle. The greater part of France is now in enemy occupation but her overseas territories retain their freedom. The British Forces will therefore do all in their power to assist these territories to defend themselves against the enemy and the British people are confident that their cooperation will be forthcoming.

The Dutch and Belgian empires, it added, were 'resolutely prosecuting the war against Germany'.[193] Catroux replied to Consul-General

Henderson in Hanoi that, whatever happened in Europe, he considered the alliance and the Singapore agreement of 1939 'always valid' in respect of Indo-China. 'I rely solidly on British military cooperation in the event of attack by Japan which is now menacing us ...' He added 'that British decision to continue war until victory receives my entire approbation'.[194]

The British were thus faced not so much with a proffer of cooperation against Germany as with a request for support against Japan. The inter-departmental committee on coordinating action in respect of French colonial possessions discussed 'the extent to which it would be possible to render any direct military aid to French Indo-China and the repercussions vis-à-vis Japan which might ensue from such support, bearing in mind that the withdrawal of support was in effect disowning the alliance with France, and might in turn lead to a general landslide throughout French colonial possessions'. There were no British forces in Asia that could provide any effective assistance, and it was not clear what action, if any, the United States would take. Should Indo-China in these circumstances be 'encouraged not to resist in the hope that consequently Great Britain would not be involved in war with Japan, or should a show of resistance be made in order to give an example to other French territories?' An initial attempt should be made to preserve the status quo in Indo-China by diplomatic means, a memorandum argued. If this failed, would the fullest support to Indo-China be considered advisable, or 'a form of indirect assistance amounting to what was called "non-intervention" in the Spanish Civil War'? The latter would keep French resistance alive. The former would display Britain's fidelity to its alliance and might encourage other French possessions, but it would be 'courting another military defeat'.[195] Catroux was told that he could have British diplomatic support; but Britain's resources were needed in Europe, and the Governor-General would agree that it was desirable to avoid hostilities in the Far East. There was reason to believe, it was added, that Japan wished only to take measures to bring the China war to an end.[196]

Catroux said he was determined to carry on, but Sir Percy Noble, the British naval Commander-in-Chief, doubted whether he would be strong enough if and when Bordeaux made a direct communication with him; nor would Decoux be strong enough to withstand pressure from Bordeaux. 'This may lead to internal troubles.' Most people wanted to carry on. Setting up a French government in London would strengthen the Governor-General. Decoux was in 'a state of hopeless indecision', Noble added later, 'and will probably continue to let things drift and eventually obey orders from Bordeaux government when he receives them. His position is complicated by his being possible Governor-General designate and by position Indo-China vis-à-vis Japanese...'. A

virile French government should be set up lest the French lose heart.[197]
The same day Decoux as Commander-in-Chief indicated that he would
follow the armistice but also that Indo-China would be defended against
all aggression.[198] He took up the post of Governor-General in mid July
1940; Catroux retiring, according to the British Naval Liaison Officer,
only unwillingly and for fear of reprisals in France. Decoux had
reportedly told the French Government that he would retire if it could
not accept 'necessity for cooperation with British in special circumstances of Far East'.[199]

The British had wanted to avoid French Indo-China's joining the Vichy
regime, which would encourage the German cause in Europe and in
other overseas French possessions. If Germany seconded it Japan might
secure helpful instructions from Vichy to Hanoi. However, the price for
keeping Indo-China staunch, if it were possible, was at once evident; it
wanted guarantees against Japan. These Britain could not supply; it could
offer only limited diplomatic and economic support. Any attempt to do
more might mean defeat and bring the Japanese into the war against
Britain. There was, however, a prospect also of direct Japanese intervention. It might be promoted by too independent an attitude in French
Indo-China or by a shift in the allegiance of the regime, which could be
interpreted as a change in the status quo. The French Ambassador in
Tokyo, Arsène Henry, told Craigie that he feared that the change of
governors-general would give them a pretext,[200] a fear Catroux shared. If
it ensued the British could not hope to rescue Indo-China from a
Japanese invasion.

A French Indo-China still determined to resist Japan as effectively as
possible, but not provocatively, was the best the British could hope for.
That resistance might have to be tempered, like Britain's own, by compromise. Compromise would go too far if it amounted to de facto
Japanese occupation and not far enough if its inadequacy led the
Japanese to impose their own control. In this sense Britain's objectives
coincided with those of Catroux and Decoux. The British were in the
strange position of offering some support for a Vichy-instructed regime.
This paradox was the outcome of the impossible task they faced, that of
sustaining their interests in Europe and East Asia simultaneously. The
French were in the strange position of wanting British support in Asia
despite the armistice in Europe. Could this position be sustained? The
British could not offer much support. Not only had they little to offer;
offering too much might be provocative. Their hope, like that of the
French, was of US help; it was vain. The Germans might, however,
interfere. This would not necessarily help the Japanese cause; they might
have their own aims.

The Japanese were indeed nervous about German ambitions – as they
had been in respect of Netherlands India – and this might – as in that

case – help Britain to urge adherence to the status quo. *Nichi Nichi* and other papers stated, Craigie had noted on 19 June, that Japan would make friendly representations to Germany and Italy over Indo-China and 'seek reaffirmation of Japan's special relations with the colony owing to geographical propinquity and economic intimacy and serious hostility of colony as route by which assistance has been reaching Chungking...'.[201] On 29 June Arita told Craigie that Italy had given an assurance of disinterestedness: Germany had not replied. The whole situation might be complicated if Indo-China refused to accept orders from the legal government of France, although he did not say how. 'I said that the Bordeaux Government could not at present be regarded as more than a captive Government and that as long as Indo-China remained in French hands and adopted a friendly attitude towards Japan, this was surely all the Japanese Government could reasonably ask.'[202]

The Foreign Office had received other information from Craigie. Back on 17 June, he had reported that, according to Arsène Henry, Catroux had decided to stop the transit of oil and trucks to China.[203] Two days later he reported that the Japanese Government wanted railway material added to the list and sought the appointment of a Japanese military commission to see that the prohibitions were effectively enforced. Henry told Craigie that, in view of the army's pressure for an incursion into Indo-China, he had recommended to the Governor-General that these demands should be accepted.[204] In fact, as Craigie said, Catroux agreed on Arsène Henry's recommendation to close the frontier altogether as well as to accept Japanese inspection, which he hoped to limit to frontier districts: 'my French colleague believes this timely step will enable the Japanese authorities to control their extremists at least temporarily and prevent any direct action against Indo-China'.[205] He assured Arita that the change of Governor-General would not change the agreement thus reached between Japan and Indo-China.[206]

The attitude of the Thais was yet another complicating factor in respect of Indo-China. In pursuit of their irredentism, they might join in against the French. The British could not offer them support against the Japanese nor impose on them restraint in regard to the French.

Thailand's non-aggression pacts

The conclusion of the non-aggression pact between Nazi Germany and the Soviet Union, as Pibun realised, changed the international situation. The Anti-Comintern Pact collapsed and so did Japan's pressure on Thailand to join it. Pibun's adviser, Prince Wan, expressed the hope that the realignment would lead to a rapprochement between the Western democracies and Japan, 'thus further easing the pressure on Thailand'.[207] Certainly the Japanese Cabinet fell, and the military attaché left

Bangkok.[208] In Europe, of course, it led to war. On the outbreak Thailand proclaimed its neutrality, and the belligerent powers pledged to respect it. Sir Josiah Crosby was pleased to get in first.[209]

The French had suggested a non-aggression pact to Thailand. With the outbreak of war in Europe Pibun was to decide to take up the proposal. He told Crosby he was in favour of a non-aggression pact with Britain and France. Hitherto, Crosby believed, the Thais had been unwilling to provoke the Japanese suspicions by pursuing the idea. Pibun now said he was concerned about French preparations. But Crosby thought he had changed his mind because Anglo-Japanese relations were 'less strained'.[210] At the Foreign Office Henniker-Major favoured the idea. Not to pursue it would arouse Thai suspicions. 'Such a pact should also ... prevent the use of Thailand by the Japanese as a base for operations against us without encountering Thai resistance. It should also bolster up the Thai to resist Japanese influence.' For the French it was even more advantageous 'as it would remove the danger of an attack on Indo-China from both sides'. But Britain should not press as that would arouse the Japanese and 'might make the Thais think that we were afraid'.[211]

In the event the Thais revived the idea. Prince Wan, however, linked a French pact with revising the Mekong River frontier.[212] Crosby asked how a pact with the UK would fit in; the British would not want to be brought in 'afterwards casually, as it were, and by the way'.[213] Crosby and Lépissier supported the pact and wanted the British Government to support the 're-delimitation' of the frontier 'in order to meet possible objections from Government of Indo-China'.[214] So did Pibun.[215] French fears about Thai irredentism, Henniker-Major thought, were 'quite ridiculous'. He could not see that concessions over the Mekong frontier would encourage the irredentists to ask for more. 'It might have the opposite effect. The only circumstances under which Thai irredentism would probably be dangerous to ourselves and France would be the outbreak of war between ourselves and Japan. In that event, the previous cession or non-cession of islands in the Mekong would clearly have no effect on the Thai Government's policy.'[216] Prince Wan took advantage of Crosby's suggestion that he should not offer a pact to France alone; that made it more difficult for France not to agree to the delimitation, Henniker-Major observed.[217] He thought that Britain should attempt to allay French fears but, if that failed, conclude its own pact; 'it would at least do something to counteract Japan's being left with an open field'.[218]

Complete opposition from the Colonial Ministry was reported from Paris and surprise that the Thais had raised the issue with Crosby.[219] 'This', Henniker-Major commented, 'quite definitely eliminates the possibility of our using our good offices with the French to get them to agree to the redelimitation of the Mekong frontier ...'. He thought, however, that the two governments should both indicate that they were willing to make a pact and that the French minister should make a separate communication about the Mekong. That might seem to be forcing France's hand, but their objections to delimitation were based on 'groundless fears'. There was 'no real reason why we should risk prejudicing our position in Thailand because of them'.[220] It was decided to start discussion, keeping the delimitation question separate. The Thais might as a result have to clarify what they were offering to France and Britain, and it would not prejudice discussions about the Thai–Burma border.[221]

At the end of December Prince Wan told Crosby that Lépissier had asked that the British pact should not be signed before the French, and so the Thai Government was awaiting the result of his attempts to persuade his government to consent to the delimitation. The prince was, however, 'not in favour of waiting too long', and he asked Crosby what he thought was 'a suitable limit of time. I suggested the end of February, to which he seemed inclined to agree. He asked me not to relate the conversation to Lépissier.'[222] Henniker-Major did not think that there was 'very much harm in the French being pressed to be reasonable about the Mekong, but it should not ... be done in this way'. The linking of the issues now seemed to be a French wish, or was that part of Prince Wan's policy of playing off Britain and France?[223] Crosby thought Prince Wan was speaking the truth; Lépissier was trying to strengthen his hand with his own government.[224] The British minister rejected the French Foreign Office's belief that he was the instigator; he brought the subject up at the request of Pibun and of Lépissier himself. 'I am no favourite with the French die-hards in Indo-China or at Bangkok ... they look upon me as being Monsieur Lépissier's evil genius.'[225] Indeed, in a despatch that was rather more expansive than the telegram in which he related his conversation with the prince, Crosby stressed that he did not want to let it appear that there was jealousy or dissension between France and Britain. He recommended that, if the issue was 'forced upon us, ... we should inform the Thai Government ... that, whilst welcoming the conclusion of a non-aggression pact with them, we could not see our way to concluding one unless a similar opportunity were afforded to the French without reference to the question of the frontier ...'.[226]

The Foreign Office took a rather different line. The British Ambassador in Paris was told to ask what the French attitude was. 'Should the French not wish us to proceed with these negotiations, His Majesty's Government might wish to reconsider their present decision not to press them on the question of the Mekong frontier ...'[227] Perhaps another argument that could be used in Paris, Crosby suggested, was the risk that the Thais, failing to get a pact, might give the Japanese the rather larger agreement they seemed to want.[228] Crosby was certainly keen on the pacts. Their conclusion would 'stabilise conditions in South-Eastern Asia' and 'operate as a setback to the Japanese influence'.[229] A pact would be 'tantamount to a binding assurance from the Thais that they would not allow their country to be made a jumping-off ground for a Japanese attack upon British Malaya or our naval base at Singapore...'.[230] Crosby saw the prospect late in January that Thailand would recognise the New Order in China as an argument for prompt acceptance of the pact.[231]

In Paris at the French Foreign Office Chauvel suggested that, if no French pact were made, the British might include in their pact a clause providing for it to cease to operate in the event of Franco-Thai hostilities.[232] That the Foreign Office thought unacceptable. It would surely 'arouse needless suspicion as to French designs on Thailand'. The British could if needed give the French assurance of termination in the case of Thai aggression.[233] Chauvel suggested a general reference to the obligations between Britain and France. He also said the Ministry of Colonies were prepared to look at the Mekong issue on a 'purely administrative basis'.[234] If the latter was acceptable to the Thais, Henniker-Major concluded, the pacts could both go ahead. If not, the British should go ahead alone, perhaps making the general reference Chauvel wanted in an Anglo-Thai exchange of letters.[235]

In mid March 1940 Crosby reported that the French and Thais had found a formula. 'The idea now is that in order to facilitate the task of administration a deep water channel should be assured to the Thais which would be navigable all the year round, and that the islands between that channel and the Thai mainland should be held to belong to Thailand.' In order to implement the arrangement an expert would be sent out from France to preside over a committee to study the question.[236] The negotiations now got under way.

The Thais were, however, puzzled as to the need for an exchange of letters if the two pacts after all proceeded together.[237] Apparently the French had wanted this reassurance in any case.[238] If the pacts were signed together, however, 'the implication of the letter would be that one or other party ... had no intention of honouring their undertakings ...'.[239] The French argued for the letters. There would be a gap before ratification, even after signature, and negotiation over the Mekong administrative arrangements might take some months. The letters would remove the temptation to blackmail French negotiators.[240] Pibun opposed the exchange.[241] The deterioration of the position in Europe might lead him to cancel the pacts altogether.[242] The French agreed to drop the idea of an exchange of letters with Britain on 20 May.[243]

Their agreement with the Thais was signed on 12 June. At the same time they exchanged letters confirming the intention to fix the boundary on the thalweg of the Mekong and to appoint representatives to fix the borderline within a year. 'Moreover, it is understood that the French representatives will be led by an official of ambassadorial rank, who will also be empowered to negotiate other administrative problems which are still pending ...' Any benefits would operate only from the signing and ratification of the pact.[244] The French collapsed in Europe. On 19 June Crosby urged ratification of the British pact without waiting for them. The FO agreed on 24 June.[245]

Crosby had been anxious to pre-empt the Japanese. They had not even replied to Prince Wan's démarche in October. What they were looking for was not a Western-style non-aggression pact, but 'a special political understanding'. It would be the basis for political and military co-operation, which was seen as desirable as plans for a southward drive on Singapore were developed.[246] It was indeed unlikely that the Thais would accept a pact of cooperation while negotiations with Britain and France continued.

In April Direck, then the Thai Deputy Foreign Minister, pressed Japan for a reply to the October proposal. The Japanese equivocated. A pact was unnecessary because there was no common border; might not pacts with Britain and France offend Germany and Italy? No such objections were forthcoming.[247] The Japanese decided that it was too late to block the British pact. They would have to make certain that it was not turned against them by themselves securing a special pact with Thailand. It could not be the 'special political understanding' the military wanted; it was rather a stop-gap device designed to forestall any possible gains by the British from their pact. The basic points would include respect for territorial integrity and affirmation of friendship and peace, exchange of information on problems of common interest, and obligation not to assist enemy states in time of war.

Starting later, the Japanese wanted to conclude first. Their Minister Murai Kuramatsu told Direck on 22 April the agreement should be signed before the pact or on the same day.[248] Gage of the Far Eastern Department of the Foreign Office disliked the terms, but 'the most important thing seems to be to get our treaties signed as soon as possible'.[249] The Thais insisted that the agreement could not predate the pact. But the Japanese insisted that it should be signed in Tokyo so as to avoid the impression that it was related to the pacts with the western powers.[250] It was signed in Tokyo on 12 June, the day the French and British pacts were signed in Bangkok.

The fear that Thailand would not after all sign the non-aggression pacts proved invalid. Although in fact it did so, along with the treaty of Japan, apprehensions had not, however, been without some foundation. The irredentist Luang Vichit had indeed argued against making the pacts with the Western powers; they would serve no purpose, and Thailand could not defend neutrality. The US would not fight and Japan would move south; Thailand should align itself with the 'tiger'. But if the Japanese violated Thailand's sovereignty first there should be at least token resistance, and the presence of Japanese troops should be prevented or at least limited.[251]

The Thais, Crosby reported, had veered around to the conviction that the Allies were bound to lose the war. 'Like all Orientals, the Thais are vastly impressed by any overwhelming display of physical force and admiration for the German achievements in the field began to swallow up with many, if not most of them, the sympathy felt for the small neutral countries which had become so disastrously involved in the war.'[252]

The fall of France, however, made the Thais nervous. The Allies might be defeated, the status quo in Southeast Asia broken up, the Japanese left as 'the paramount power in the Far East'. The Thais, Crosby believed, had qualms about Japan's emergence as the regional power; 'what they have been hoping for ... was that the war would end in a draw, leaving both Britain and France, their two neighbours, still strong but not too strong, and with Japan remaining no more than a third and compensatory factor to offset, when desirable, the impact of the other two ...'. Now it was possible that Japan would occupy at least northern Indo-China and perhaps attack the Burma Road. Then 'the fat would be in the fire and Thailand would be faced with what she dreads most of all, namely, an Anglo-Japanese conflict immediately upon her own borders'.

There was another issue. If France lost control of Indo-China, Thailand's claims on Cambodia and Laos were likely to be put. What if Japan offered them to Thailand as a reward for adhering to the new order? 'Will the Thais be able to resist this bait if it is dangled before them? Much will depend ... upon the position in which Britain is going to be left in this part of the world if France should disappear as a ruling Power from the Asiatic Continent.' Crosby recurred to his usual theme. 'If we are able to maintain ourselves with unimpaired strength in Malaya and Burma, there is a good chance that the Thais will have sufficient courage to continue abstaining from too close an association with the policies of Japan.' But 'if they lose faith in our ability to protect ourselves, let alone them, they will walk over into the Japanese camp. There will be nothing left for them to do.'[253]

There were indeed two issues which the Thais had to balance. Were the Japanese to dominate Southeast Asia? In that case they must move to accommodate them if they were to preserve the substance of their independence as they had earlier accommodated the paramountcy of the British. In what ways, if any, were they to take advantage of the evident weakness of the French? One risk was that they would throw themselves further into the arms of the Japanese. The other was that they would alienate the British and the Americans. What, in turn, would the policies of those states be? The emphasis of the US would be on the status quo. What would or could it do to sustain it? What would British policy be?

Crosby told Pibun that in his personal view it would be to Britain's interest to raise no objection to the occupation of parts of Indo-China by the Thais. 'To oppose the aspirations of the Thais ... would not merely antagonise them, it would also force them to do a deal with the Japanese, which is the last thing that would suit us. Moreover, I take it that on the merits [of the case] we should prefer to see these regions occupied by the Thais rather than by the Japanese ...'[254] 'Our interest clearly lies in the maintenance of the *status quo*', Gage wrote, 'but if this proves impossible to maintain and the territory is partitioned with the tacit consent of the Indo-China authorities there would seem to be some advantage in our not opposing the Thai claims.' 'Our best course', Clarke commented, 'is to keep out of this business as far as we can.'[255] Indeed it was hard to believe that the French would make over territory to the Thais, hard therefore to avoid their receiving it in some way from the Japanese.

The Burma Road

In dealing with independent states Britain's approach had necessarily to be a diplomatic one. Increasingly that was true in respect of territories within its empire that were advancing towards statehood. It was the case already with the settler dominions; it was coming to be the case with those states that had been promised self-government within the empire. One of these was, of course, Burma, neighbour of Thailand and Indo-China, and of China itself.

Indeed the Burmans made use of the outbreak of war in Europe to secure a more definite promise of further political advance from the British. It 'caused an acceleration in the pace of Burmese politics'.[256] Ba Maw formed a Freedom Bloc with the Centre DAA and the All-Burma Students' Union, and this goaded Saw, the Forest and Agriculture Minister, to push for greater self-government leading to dominion status. He and other allies of the Pu Ministry attempted to form a Burmese United Front to counter its appeal. Anticipating the statement of November 1939 on the relationship of the war and India's constitutional future, the Pu Ministry sought a statement on Burma's future. The statement of 7 November indicated that the British Government would continue to use its best endeavours to promote the attainment of Burma's 'due place in the British Commonwealth of Nations'.[257] In the face of criticism Governor Cochrane sought an additional statement making it clear that Burma's due place was dominion status. 'Acrimonious' correspondence between him and Lord Zetland, the Secretary of State, led to the statement of 24 November that 'the natural issue of Burma's constitutional progress, through the gradual development of self-governing institutions with a view to the progressive realisation of responsible self-government in Burma, is the attainment of Dominion status'. A motion by U Ba Thi, opposing Burma's inclusion in the war effort against Germany, was carried in the House of Representatives in the first session of 1940, despite Pu's opposition to it. Saw, building his support, bided his time to secure the premiership for himself.[258]

The Burma Road, earlier a subject of some tension between the imperial and the Burman authorities, was open and working, helping to keep Chiang Kai-shek's resistance to the Japanese alive. The change in the position in Europe in mid 1940 led the Japanese to focus on it. At the same time as they demanded a further closing of the Indo-China frontiers they sought the closing of the Burma Road to war supplies. The Director of Military Intelligence of the Japanese General Staff, Wakamatsu, told the Military Attaché in Tokyo, Brig. B.R. Mullaly, that, given the collapse of France and 'Britain's impotence in the Far East', the Japanese people felt they must seize their opportunity and that the US was 'in no condition to prevent Japan from taking whatever action she likes in Western Pacific'. Positive action might be averted if Britain took its 'last chance', closing the Burma and Hong Kong frontiers and withdrawing its troops from Shanghai.[259] After signing the Tientsin agreement Craigie spoke to Arita, who said he would be discussing the three issues, but the 'form and substance of his communication would be entirely different'.[260] Arsène Henry told Craigie that he thought the campaign against Britain would 'greatly intensify with particular reference to British troops in the International Settlement and to transit trade via Burma. The opinion is that unless one can be sure of full American solidarity in regard to these matters we should be well advised to meet Japanese as far as possible on these questions...'.[261]

On 24 June the Vice-Minister, Ohashi, transmitted a 'friendly communication', designed to obtain Britain's cooperation, so that the transit of arms, ammunition, fuel and trucks along the Burma Road should cease.[262] Craigie favoured agreeing. A negative reply would not lead to a Japanese attack, he thought, but it would lead to other actions, such as a blockade of Hong Kong, and thus to incidents on which extremists would seize. The US would offer only goodwill, and a war with Japan could not be risked. The Chinese 'must realise that their fate will be decided in Europe rather than in east Asia and that our own security must be considered as well as theirs'. Giving way might lead to further demands, but if acquiescence were quickly followed up by some 'constructive effort' such as he had advocated, the situation would be 'stabilised'.[263]

Craigie's view was criticised in many quarters. Amery thought that the effect in India and Burma of any concession to the Japanese would be 'lamentable. Disasters elsewhere have not shaken public faith, because they have still left us presenting a bold and unbroken front.'[264] It would be a blow to the Chinese, Clark Kerr telegraphed, and affect 'American sympathy in general'.[265] Lothian thought it 'of the utmost importance from the point of view of American as well as Chinese sentiment that His Majesty's Government should not voluntarily agree to close it from the Burmese end though they may have to retreat before force majeure in Shanghai and Hong Kong'.[266] At the Foreign Office Dening thought there was point in the argument 'that we may have to succumb to force but should give nothing away under threats'.[267] 'Complete submission would invite further aggression', his colleague Sir John Brenan believed, 'while if the worst happens, a vigorous defence of Hong Kong, even if unsuccessful, will help to persuade the Japanese extremists to confine their immediate ambitions to the China seas.'[268]

Compliance might strengthen the US view that Britain was at its last gasp; a stand might increase US confidence and 'perhaps render the possibility of some help at a later and more critical stage in the Far East less unlikely'.[269] The FO drafted a reply that pointed out that the traffic in arms and ammunition along the road was limited and could make little contribution to the strength of the Chinese Government. Nor was Britain in a position to supply more. Other items, the draft continued, were part of the trade of India and Burma, while the road was also used for the passage of American products. The reply also pointed to Japan's unwillingness to restrict exports to Germany through Siberia. Finally the draft offered good offices to bring about 'a just and equitable peace' between Japan and China.[270] The FO raised with Craigie the idea of softening the blow by limiting the traffic to the 1939 level, which would prevent the diversion of material from the Indo-China route now closed.[271]

Craigie thought the British Government's course 'highly dangerous'. The suggested concession would 'immediately raise the question of inspection in an acute form'. In any case the Japanese were in no mood to bargain and would see the reply 'as tantamount to a refusal'. If they proceeded to enforce their demands, and Britain had to comply or failed to take strong counter measures, its prestige would suffer more than by closing the road now. The liquidation of the China incident was 'an obsession of every Japanese', and Craigie considered the Burma Road question 'the last big issue which Germany can effectively use to jockey this country into war with us'. Was Britain 'prepared to risk drifting into a state of war with Japan on this issue?' Even a ten per cent risk of war might not be justified. When Germany had been defeated the US and the UK, he hoped, would 'be able to teach Japan a lesson which she will never forget'. To precipitate a crisis now would jeopardise 'that ultimate re-establishment of a strong British position in the Far East on which I pin all my hopes'.[272] American 'sentiment', Craigie thought, was not a sufficient consideration; the US was in no position to oppose Japan by armed force and would be 'embarrassed' if the UK was involved in hostilities in the Far East.[273] 'We are told that we must consider our strategy and not our prestige. But what has maintained our strategy in the Far East for many years past if not prestige?'[274]

The British Government had explained the position to the Australians. Britain felt it should resist the demand to close the Burma Road to supply for China. 'At the same time, we have to recognise that the Japanese if they persist in their intention have means to enforce it.' A further complication that much of the traffic was American. 'Put bluntly, our problem is whether we are to incur both United States and Chinese odium by stopping traffic or face the consequences of refusal without the United States support.'[275] The Australians stressed the importance of 'a clear indication of United States policy'. In themselves, Menzies believed, the three Japanese demands did not

> vitally affect future or present security of Empire. The French acceptance of similar demands has further strengthened the Japanese position, and we can only arrive at the conclusion that if the United States is not prepared to give the most complete support, these demands should be conceded. The alternative is a grave risk of war against Japan, which cannot be contemplated in our present position.[276]

The Chiefs of Staff also favoured yielding; so did Churchill, Chamberlain and Lloyd, on the ground that Britain could not fight Japan as well as Germany and Italy, particularly now that the French fleet could not hold the Mediterranean.[277] Amery, who wanted 'a firm stand', decided that the Cabinet was 'still not what I should call a warlike body'.[278] Cadogan was against giving way. 'Quite apart from Chinese feelings, if we do, the Americans – or a large section of opinion – will say "the English are beat anyway". And we don't want that.'[279] Initially the Cabinet went down this track, taking account, too, of 'the very bad effect which the closing of the Burmese Road would have upon India, Burma and Malaya, which would be directly affected'.[280] Then the Cabinet 'took the wrong turning', as Cadogan put it.[281] The final form of the telegram was more satisfactory to him. 'Glad to say we *don't* surrender, but temporise.'[282] Churchill had declared 'that we could not afford the Japanese navy being added to the German and the Italian and possibly even coming round West …'. Amery would have preferred 'a brave front' and was glad Halifax sent 'a temporising reply'.[283]

The instructions to Craigie had been redrafted to leave open the way for future discussion. 'You may say, if you see fit, that our reluctance to comply with the Japanese request does not mean that we are not willing to meet the Japanese on questions which in our view are far more vital to their welfare.' The British Government, he might add, wished to understand Japan's economic needs and, as far as possible, to make provision for them. It was desirable 'to get the argument on to a wider basis'. The telegram recalled the earlier suggestions. If the Japanese showed any readiness to move in that direction, 'we would do our best to get a response from the Chinese side and also if useful to make constructive proposals ourselves'.[284] There was a hint here of the approach advanced by Bruce at a meeting of dominion high commissioners, that the present demands be dealt with as part of a general settlement.[285] The US had been far from encouraging about that but had not ruled it out.

Unlike the COS, the Foreign Office did not think Japan would resort to total war. Britain could not rely on armed resistance from America, but Japan could not be certain that America would not aid Britain. Its army was deeply involved in China. It would lose its trade in the empire, and a US embargo was at least possible. 'There is nothing in Japanese history to support the theory that the Japanese extremists, if they came to power, would throw all discretion to the winds. The Japanese are cautious by nature, and the method usually favoured is to choose a point at which to push, to withdraw if resistance is offered, but to push on if it is found that opposition is weak or yielding.' A refusal might lead to a limited Japanese reaction. Given the risk of a German invasion of Britain, rashness was to be avoided. Before a decision was taken to yield, however, its impact on other countries should be considered. The Soviet Union might aid China more or come to terms with Japan. The American leadership might understand the decision, although disliking it, but public opinion would regard it adversely, and the US would be less disposed to help Britain not only in the East, but also in the West. For China it would be 'a material and moral blow'.

> Anything likely to check the advance of Japan is likely to be welcomed in the surrounding countries, e.g. Thailand, Indo-China and the Netherlands East Indies. On the other hand, to yield would mean a loss in our prestige in all these countries, and especially in British territories, e.g. Malaya, Burma and India. It should not be forgotten that our position in the Far East has been defended in recent years by prestige rather than by military force, and we should not lightly allow it to be further diminished.

More demands would follow acceptance of these. Britain should not yield at least until an attempt had been made to bring about a comprehensive settlement.[286]

'Mr Arita's reception of our offer of assistance in terminating hostilities in China was not encouraging', Craigie reported. The Japanese 'are now in an exalted mood and feel confident of being able to snuff out Chiang Kai-shek with or without our help…'.[287] He rejected the overall solution.[288] The Japanese 'saw the trap into which we were trying to lead them', Dening commented.[289] Craigie favoured yielding for three months on the understanding that during that time special efforts would be made to bring about a 'just and equitable peace' in the Far East and that, if these should fail, the British would be free to permit resumption of the traffic.

The Cabinet in London resolved to take Craigie's line. At its meeting on 10 July the Dominions Secretary Caldecote, reported that Menzies favoured a 'realistic' approach while Bruce favoured a settlement on broad lines. In the discussion it was suggested that 'we were running a grave risk of being involved in war with Japan', that Britain was unlikely to get better terms, that the three months were in the rainy season and that, if the road were closed, 'it was not likely to be reopened unless and until we were in a strong military position'.[290] At the following day's Cabinet meeting, 'the view was expressed that no time ought to be lost in coming to terms with Japan. The present Japanese Government might at any moment be succeeded by an anti-British Government, who might declare war upon us.'[291]

Instructions were sent to Craigie. The preferred course was to limit the transit of materials for three months to the amount sent in the corresponding period in the previous year. If this were unacceptable the road would be closed to war materials.[292] The latter was decided on. A rather one-sided confidential memorandum was signed on 17 July.[293] Chamberlain was relieved that Churchill had been firmly against the bold line. 'Some think the Japs were bluffing but if they were mistaken – and we have to duel not with the Foreign Office but the truculent and ignorant Army officers who think we are going to be beaten by the Germans – we have not got the forces to fight Japs, Germans and Italians at once.'[294]

Lothian had told Hull that Japan was threatening war. 'I replied that I would not undertake to offer advice. I stated that one way of dealing with the threatened attack would be to devise parleys and protract the situation, adding that this was as a rule entirely feasible.'[295] 'He thought that our action in seizing French fleet [at Oran] would impress on the Japanese Government that we were not as weak as they might think.'[296] Lothian believed American opinion 'preoccupied with the possibilities looming up in the Atlantic'; it was 'not prepared to oppose force to the Japanese aggression so long as the European situation is in its present position'. More realistic than even a month earlier, American opinion would 'on the whole take our retreat as imposed upon us by the necessities of the European situation'. But Lothian did not think that meant that the British should formally agree to close the road.[297] Lothian relayed the British decision to Hull on 12 July. He 'expressed much regret and disappointment'.[298] He 'did not', Lothian reported, 'demur to its being inevitable in view of inability of United States to give us armed support'.[299]

Grew, however, had doubted that Japan meant war, and he thought Craigie was not 'correctly weighing certain considerations'.[300]

> Further evidence having been given of Great Britain's incapacity to maintain her position ..., Japanese morale becomes strengthened and Chinese morale becomes more susceptible of being undermined. The British decision may be regarded [Hornbeck wrote] as a new step in a diplomatic 'rear guard' action. It involves, however, a yielding of ground. It diminishes China's capacity to resist and it weakens the common front of the powers that are on the defensive, including the United States.[301]

Cadogan was disgusted. 'Craigie has given away 110%. I was always against it. We've been bluffed. But it was Winston who resolutely refused to call it.'[302] He found himself trying 'to dress up public statement, but ... it's like trying to walk an invisible tight rope in a dark room', 'making bricks not only without straw but also without clay'.[303] The outcome was the parliamentary statement of 18 July.[304]

The decision was unpopular. Arthur Rucker, Principal Private Secretary to Chamberlain, defended the concession on the ground that it avoided war. 'He claimed that our great fault in recent years had been to let our diplomacy outrun our strength, to threaten what we could not fulfil. It was essential to return to a system of *realpolitik*.'[305] By contrast the Assistant Private Secretary, John Colville, thought it 'a moral defeat to sacrifice in one part of the world the principles we are defending in another'.[306]

The Japanese had adopted more than one method. Col. Suzuki Keiji was sent to Burma in May 1940 as Minami Masuyo to contact Burmese dissidents, and he was to succeed in attracting Aung San, Ne Win and others to his cause.[307] He says he also met Saw, who asked if Japan would give military aid in Burma's struggle for freedom.[308] The Burma Defence Bureau had been aware for some time of Japanese contacts with Ba Maw, and it concluded that the crisis in Europe, 'when Britain appeared likely to meet with irretrievable disaster', had accelerated their negotiations.[309] Again, the war in the West affected the position in the East.

The Brookes

In respect of Borneo the Colonial Office continued in the early months of the war with its attempts to affirm British influence over Sarawak. Those attempts were not without reference to Britain's international position. They had related earlier to a concern that Britain was held responsible in League of Nations forums for activities for which it did not have effective authority. The stress on colonial welfare, although prompted by the crisis in the West Indies, had a wider and more urgent connotation. The new Colonial Welfare and Development Act was passed in 1940, and it was in some sense meant not only as an assertion of imperial responsibility but also as a demonstration of it to the United States.[310] The attitude of the Colonial Office to the Raj was influenced by this, as by the earlier concern over the League. If that was the main impact on its policy of the international position in 1940, it did not ignore the Japanese. But they seem to have been seen as a distant threat.

Early in 1940, the Raja, Sir Vyner Brooke demoted his nephew Peter (Anthony) six months after making him Raja Muda and Officer Administering the Government. It seems that he and the senior officers did not get on. A proclamation declared that he was 'not yet fitted to exercise the responsibilities of this high position'.[311] Correspondence Peter gave to the British minister in Athens included an extract from a letter of the Raja's of 21 December 1939. 'Pepys will be a kind of stepping stone towards intervention by the British Government. Sarawak would be absolutely safe under the B.G. and I see no alternative ... I shall have to make a definite statement at Council Negri next year and want to have everything arranged beforehand.'[312] British policy, Edward Gent thought, should aim 'at finding an opportunity if possible to strengthen the effective influence of British authority on the Sarawak regime' and securing a new treaty or agreement that made it 'answerable in the last resort to advice offered on any issue by HMG'. The Raja could be reassured over the protection of native interests, which was what he sought.[313] A telegram was sent to Sir Shenton Thomas.[314]

Thomas commented that neither the creation of the post of Raja Muda (heir apparent) nor its abolition affected the succession, which still lay with Anthony's father, the Tuan Muda. He did, however, think it possible 'that the Rajah would accept a new Agreement which would provide for the appointment of a General Adviser, and this would be a simple solution of the problem. Sarawak is tending more and more to look to Malaya for help and advice, and the Raja is more and more ready to leave matters to me whom he can trust.'[315] The issue was to be taken up in discussions when Thomas visited London.

A report from Pepys commented on the Raja's prestige. 'The crux of the matter seems to be the reconciliation of our position under the Agreement of 1888 and of the value which must be attached to the loyalty of the native population to their Raja with the fact that Sarawak has rather stood outside the main current of Colonial Development and Social Services in recent years ...' In a discussion with Thomas in London Gent and Cosmo Parkinson raised the question of 'regularising the Adviser system', which was now the Colonial Office's objective. Thomas thought the Raja might accept that, 'in view of the difficulties in which he found himself owing to the succession position', but was inclined to allow the Pepys experiment to 'run for a period'. Gent, however, wanted 'something settled before the question became further complicated by a restoration of Mr "Peter" Brooke to favour'.[316] As a result Thomas wrote to S.W. Jones, OAG, early in July. He was to consult Pepys in particular over the timing of an approach to the Raja over a new treaty.[317]

The question of reinforcing Malaya

The unhurried approach of the Colonial Office in respect of Borneo contrasted with the concern of the Foreign Office and the Chiefs of Staff in the summer of 1940. Nor did critics of the colonial administration consider that it was sufficiently active in Malaya and the Straits Settlements. It was, however, clear that the collapse of the French and the shifts in Japanese policy that followed it made Singapore more vulnerable. Not only might it be more easily attacked; it would also be hard to put forces there to defend it or to relieve it. Anxiety over the position had helped indeed to account for the decision on the Burma Road. It also boosted the anxieties of the Australians who had some influence on that decision.

On 25 June the COS had offered their preliminary views on the Far Eastern situation. 'The strategic importance of our position in the Far East remains as great as ever, particularly in view of our dependence upon the economic weapon to defeat Germany.' The chief counters to Japan's aggression were the US and Russia and its own heavy commitment in China. The US should be encouraged to declare its vital interest in the status quo in the Far East and Russia and to aid Chiang Kai-shek. No British fleet could be spared for the Far East at present. 'It is all the more important, therefore, that we should do what we can to improve our land and air defences in Malaya so that at the worst we retain a foothold in the area.' Troops could come only from India and Australia. Australia might be asked to send a division and two more squadrons to Malaya.[318] At the Cabinet in London it was pointed out that the US had declined a declaration of policy, but it was thought that Australia would send a division.[319]

Australia was asked to do so. 'The security of our imperial interests in the Far East lies ultimately in our ability to control sea communications in the South Western Pacific for which purpose adequate fleet must be based at Singapore.' But since 'our previous assurances in this respect' the whole situation has been radically altered by the French defeat.

> Formerly we were prepared to abandon the Eastern Mediterranean and despatch a fleet to the Far East relying on the French Fleet in the Western Mediterranean to contain the Italian Fleet. Now if we move the Mediterranean Fleet to the Far East there is nothing to contain the Italian Fleet which will be free to operate in the Atlantic or reinforce the German Fleet in home waters using bases in North West France. We must therefore retain in the European waters sufficient naval forces to watch both the German and Italian Fleets and we cannot do this and send a fleet to the Far East.

The importance of the Far East had meanwhile increased, both in terms of Empire security, and of the need to control essential commodities at source. The Japanese advance in China and Hainan had intensified the threat to Malaya, and any further advance in Indo-China, Thailand or the Indies would still further endanger Britain's position in Singapore,

> the key point in the Far East. Owing to the increased range of aircraft and the development of aerodromes, particularly in Thailand, we can no longer concentrate on the defence of Singapore Island entirely but must consider the defence of Malaya as a whole, particularly the security of up country landing grounds. For this reason and because we cannot spare a fleet for the Far East at present, it is all the more important that we should do what we can to improve our land and air defences in Malaya.

Placing one division and two squadrons of aircraft there would be 'an added immediate deterrent'.[320]

Bruce was indignant at the 'complete reversal' of Britain's naval policy in the Far East; the British Government was not, he thought, 'facing the great and fundamental issues that now confront us'.[321] Ismay accepted that before the war it had been the intention to despatch a fleet to the Far East in the event of serious trouble with Japan. It was also said 'that if it came to a choice of jeopardising either our Middle East and Mediterranean interests, or the security of our Empire in the Far East, we should not hesitate to sacrifice the former'. 'At present, however, it is not this choice which confronts us. The collapse of France meant that the Italian fleet might leave the Mediterranean and enter the struggle in the Atlantic and home waters.' Removing capital ships from the Mediterranean to the Far East would not only jeopardise the Middle East but also endanger the safety of Britain and its vital communications. 'This being so, it is clearly necessary for us to make certain of defeating the immediate danger in home waters, which is for the moment the decisive point, by concentrating our forces in this area.' The situation, it was hoped, would be of short duration and did not invalidate what was said in November when the British Government had stated that, if Japanese encroachment began, or an Anglo-Japanese war broke out, the Admiralty would make dispositions to offer timely resistance to an attack on Singapore or an invasion of Australia and New Zealand. Australia was not threatened by a serious Japanese invasion while the British fleet was still in existence and while Singapore was secure. 'The first condition still holds good, and it is to ensure the second condition that the Chiefs of Staff have asked Australia to send a Division and two Squadrons of aircraft to Malaya.'[322] Bruce had a discussion with the Joint Planning Committee.[323] The Australians determined to await the preparation of a new appreciation on the Far East.[324]

The image Australians were to conjure up of Singapore after its fall was like that of Louis Philippe at the première of *La Muette de Portici*: we are dancing on the edge of a volcano.[325] That suggested insouciance; it also suggested lack of preparation. In some sense the former derived from the latter. Sang-froid at least was seen as an indication that the British felt secure; an indication of concern would undermine the prestige on which, as Cadogan was to put it, they increasingly relied. In London 'dancing and gaiety ... were hailed by our newspapers as a sign of the indomitable spirit of the nation'.[326] Lack of preparation could also partly be explained by a perception, widely but not universally held, that the Japanese, challenged by the Soviet Union's army in the north, by involvement in China and by uncertainty about the US, would not undertake a major expedition in the south, especially given their generally cautious approach. Above all, however, it was explained by Britain's involvement in a European war for which it was unprepared and which had now expanded in an alarming way. While it was important to control the resources of the East, that objective had to take second priority to the defence of Britain and its sea routes.

'Certainly everything is as gloomy as can be. Probability is that Hitler will attempt invasion in next fortnight', Cadogan wrote on 29 June 1940.[327] 'As far as I can see, we are, after years of leisurely preparation, completely unprepared. We have simply got to die at our posts – a far better fate than capitulating to Hitler as these damned Frogs have done. But uncomfortable.' Hitler in fact did not invade. He commenced a tremendous air bombardment in the hope that would force the British to yield.

There were indeed arguments for yielding even before the Battle of Britain, and some historians have argued that Churchill misled the British by not doing so. The chances of victory, even perhaps of survival, were not good. Little could be done to attack the Germans; the only hope remained that of an effective blockade. Which power could hold out longer? It was by no means evident that it was to be Britain. If it was it would be as a result of support from the United States. Mobilising its resources would take time, and the British generally thought that it would be inadvisable for the US meanwhile to be diverted by any other call on its resources. That included a war in East Asia.

There, indeed, it therefore remained a matter of gaining time. Negotiations with the Japanese, although advocated by Bruce and Craigie, were always viewed with doubt, above all because of their likely effect on China and thus on the US. So, essentially the Americans would have to take the initiative if there were to be any negotiations. The Americans had limited interest in China but enough to prevent the British making a general settlement at China's expense. The British had to do what they could to hold the Japanese without provoking them. It might be impossible to prevent their advancing towards Singapore, but it might be possible to avoid their destruction of its strategic importance. Maintaining the status quo as far as possible coincided with the Americans' policy. Their implementation of it, however, was cautious. Conscious of the uncertainties of public opinion and of the approach of the 1940 election, Roosevelt and Hull were indeed inclined, although stepping up economic pressure a little, to adhere to the policy of non-recognition enunciated by Stimson at the time of the Manchuria crisis. Uncertain that Britain would survive, moreover, they tended to wait and see.

Only after the Battle of Britain and after the election did the Americans decide more squarely to back the British, and their policy towards the Japanese became firmer. Indeed they began to seek compliance from them by way of far more sweeping embargoes. It had always seemed possible, although not certain, that this would provoke rather than constrain the Japanese. The British had recognised that in that case their possessions, and those of the Dutch, would suffer. Would the Americans guarantee help in that case? they had wondered. And should the Americans become involved in a new war when their resources were needed to fight the existing one? Uncertainties remained.

Not that it was clear that the Japanese would so risk a conflict. The Americans and the British were inclined still to depreciate their determination. It was now indeed to acquire an element of desperation. One further outcome of the European crisis of 1940 was the decision of the US to build a two-ocean fleet. That meant that the Japanese had also to take account of time. For them it was a limiting factor. Increasingly they felt it might be necessary to use their local naval superiority while they still had the advantage of it and so guarantee access to raw materials and resources of which US policy and power might deprive them.

CHAPTER 3

July–September 1940

The US and the British Empire

In face of the surrender of the French the British determined to fight on. In retrospect that seemed a decision almost to go without saying. A compromise with the Germans had, however, not been ruled out. That there was no thought of peace was a myth that Churchill propagated. However, it is also a myth that the decision to fight on was Churchill's alone and that he is to be blamed for the monumental losses that Britain, albeit ultimately on the winning side, was to suffer. Faced with the disasters of May and June, the Cabinet had decided to continue. If there were to be compromise it believed that the terms then obtainable would be unacceptable and that fighting on might put Britain in a better position. There was also the thought, perhaps indeed stronger in Churchill's mind than in others', that the US would enter the war in Europe sooner rather than later. What was important, it seemed, was that Britain should survive the anticipated Battle of Britain and the period up to the US election. If it did the US might enter the war and ensure a victory that otherwise could be won, if won at all, through economic warfare and American supplies and support short of actual entry.

The fall of France alarmed the US. Even if they did not surrender, the British might be defeated. The connection of US security with the status quo in Europe that Lothian had pointed out became ever clearer. If the status quo was to be overthrown the security of the US was in question and so was the security of the Monroe doctrine countries. In face of this crisis the US not only expressed its wish for control of the British navy if Britain were defeated but also decided on a major naval-building program of its own. During these critical months considerable emphasis was given to hemispheric defence which reflected also a concern about Britain's survival in the summer onslaught. Should the focus be on helping the British so that they might survive or on building up hemispheric defences in case they did not? As the failure of the German campaign in the air became more evident, the Americans re-emphasised the strategy of supporting the British. But even Roosevelt's victory in the elections did not lead them to enter the war.

The strategy of keeping the British going was reflected in the policies the US adopted in Asia. Its main objective was to maintain the status quo in Southeast Asia, so that the resources of the area, and of India and Australia, should be available to the British Empire in its European struggle. That gave the Americans a new interest in the area. Their concern over the area had in the past been signalled chiefly by their policy towards the Philippines, marked as it indeed was by ambivalence. But the tactics they adopted did not greatly change from those they had adopted in regard to Manchuria and to China, where the Japanese had already challenged and in part overthrown the status quo. One tactic was Stimsonian, and Hull reaffirmed it. That was to enunciate principles in the conduct of international relations that stressed that change should not be brought about by force but rather by agreement. However, if challenged the principles were to be enforced only by protest. Yielding to force majeure without accepting its outcome would facilitate a readjustment when the world had returned to normality. These were views that could be adopted by a country which had limited interests in Asia and did not face immediate challenge. They were less appropriate to other countries with more significant or more threatened interests. They made compromise difficult; they were indeed in some respects opposed to it, which the US was to find for itself late in 1941. Meanwhile the British realised that it made it difficult for them to follow a policy of compromise lest they decisively alienate the US.

The approach was developed as a response to Japan's moves in China. It was to be applied in Southeast Asia as the focus shifted towards it during 1940 and 1941. But there it was less valid since US interests were more immediately involved, albeit indirectly. Increasingly the Americans needed to impede the Japanese, even to halt them, rather than take insurance for a future settlement when the world had returned to sanity.

Joseph C. Grew, the US ambassador in Tokyo, offered an analysis in mid September 1940. Some Japanese, he argued, saw the world situation as offering a golden opportunity. Others were beginning to see that Germany might not defeat Britain after all, and that the United States and Britain were drawing closer together while the United States was building a two-ocean navy. 'Nibbling' was likely to continue until the world situation became clearer. Drastic embargoes might, however, lead to some form of retaliation. Diplomacy was insufficient to deal with the 'predatory powers', among which Japan was now to be numbered.

He continued:

(b) American security has admittedly depended in a measure upon the existence of the British Fleet which in turn has been, and could only have been, supported by the British Empire.

(c) If we conceive it to be in our interest to support the British Empire in this hour of her travail and I most emphatically do so conceive it, we must strive by every means to preserve the *status quo* in the Pacific at least until the European war has been won or lost. In my opinion this cannot be done nor can our interests be further adequately and properly protected by merely registering disapproval and keeping a careful record thereof. It is clear that Japan has been deterred from taking greater liberties with American interests only out of respect for our potential power; it is equally [clear] that she has trampled upon our rights to a degree in precise ratio to the strength of her conviction that the American people would not permit that power to be used. Once conviction is shaken it is possible that the uses of diplomacy may again become accepted.

(d) If then we can by firmness preserve the status quo in the Pacific until and if Britain emerges successfully from the European struggle, Japan will be faced with a situation which will make it impossible for the present opportunist philosophy to maintain the upper hand. At [such] a moment it might then be possible to undertake a readjustment of the whole Pacific problem on a fair, frank, and equitable basis to the lasting benefit of both the United States and of Japan. Until such time as there is a complete regeneration of thought in this country, a show of force, together with a determination to employ it if need be, can alone contribute effectively to the achievement of such an outcome, and to our own future security.[1]

These views were like Lothian's. Grew stressed that the coincidence was 'purely fortuitous'.[2] But they were not the same as Hull's. Grew did not define the 'show of force' he proposed. Hull would not have used the words. He did not think it necessary to go so far, and he was not alone.

If more was needed to restrain the Japanese, it was not thought that much more was needed, and that view was perhaps the more readily accepted, given the tradition of US policy and the difficulty of galvanising public opinion in favour of a major change. The involvement of the Japanese in China, it was concluded, would absorb their endeavours, and the likelihood that, frustrated there and anxious over their future access to resources, they would turn south, tended to be discounted, especially in view of their insecurity on the Russian frontier. Economic restrictions were advocated as a further means of restraining the Japanese. If applied to any extent, or with any rigidity, they again might provoke the Japanese rather than restrain them. On balance it was thought that they would stop the Japanese. In the meantime, however, the Americans preferred to rely mainly on the deterrent effect that they believed mere uncertainty about their action had and would have. That had the further advantage of making it unnecessary to enter commitments to those powers, like the

UK and the Netherlands, on the territories of which any Japanese retaliation might fall.

The Japanese had always been cautious, it was often noted, and that gave the Americans more confidence that the policy they had devised for China, where their interests were limited, would more or less suffice for Southeast Asia, where they were becoming more committed as a result of the events of the war of 1939. The frustration of the Japanese in China would not, however, be the only factor in their policy. The commencement of a two-ocean US fleet made the Japanese more concerned for essential resources, especially oil, more determined to make the sphere a reality. At an army–navy liaison conference on 4 July 1940 Col. Usui of the Army General Staff explained its shift in policy away from the north:

> It seems to be an inevitable outcome of the European war that Germany and Italy will establish a bloc extending over Europe and Africa, separating Great Britain from the United States economically as well as strategically. As a counter-measure to this offence, Great Britain will try to secure a line of communication with the United States in the South Pacific, using India and Australia as their bases. In the meantime the enormous expansion plan of the US navy will have been completed in several years from now. The upshot will be the establishment of a strong Anglo-American bloc, economic as well as strategic, in the South Seas.
>
> Under such circumstances Japan's economy, which relied heavily on trade with the United States and Great Britain, would be greatly jeopardized. We have no choice but resolutely to forestall the United States and Great Britain by establishing ourselves in the South Seas. Otherwise, we will face great economic difficulty in the future ...[3]

Japanese experience of US policy was, however, as of a paper tiger, of protest rather than interposition. Nor was there a certainty that the Americans would defend the colonial territories. Even if the Philippines were involved their interest in Southeast Asia might be so limited as to suggest a negotiated settlement. Together with its growing concern about the US fleet such considerations might reduce Japan's traditional caution. What the Americans saw as a policy of constraint might be seen as a provocation.

It was in this way that the war of 1939 was to become the war of 1941. In some sense the US entered the war because of its determination to keep out of it, and in the process the war expanded. The aim of US policy in Southeast Asia was to enable Britain to go on fighting, with American aid short of entry, so as to maintain what could be maintained of the European and Atlantic status quo. That meant that the Americans had to contribute to maintaining the status quo in Asia, which they failed to do. Instead the Japanese went to war. The Americans joined in the war in a way that Churchill had not initially expected and many Britons had wanted to avoid.

Their concern had been to keep open the supply of American war matériel to Europe; a second commitment would reduce it, and it was taking some time to get American production geared up. Much less, it seems, was their concern about Southeast Asia itself. On the whole it was assumed once more that the Americans could, if they chose, bring the Japanese to a halt. At times the Chiefs of Staff recognised that, once lost, Southeast Asian possessions might take some time to regain. Too little attention was generally given to avoiding the loss in the first place. Given the demands of the European war, provision of adequate weapons and matériel was no doubt difficult, perhaps impossible. A tendency to depreciate Japanese determination and effectiveness made that a more easy position to accept. Still less attention was given to the longer-term implications of colonial defeat. The French were clear that colonies, once lost, would be difficult to regain; maintaining colonial authority, even in an attenuated form, was their preferred option. That was not to be an option the British were given nor, if they had been, would have accepted. But it seems unlikely that they realised the extent of the damage they would face short or long term in the event of an attack.

The Battle of Britain

'Funny pause', wrote Cadogan on 26 July. 'I should judge Hitler doesn't like the look of invasion and is trying to tempt us to parley ... But if that fails, I think he will attack. And I think that will fail too. And if it does, the whole face of Europe will be changed.'[4] By August the air battle was raging. 'This was the day Hitler was to be in London', Cadogan noted on 15 August. 'Can't find him ....'[5] 'Lots of air battles, in which we seem to be doing well', he wrote on 6 September.[6] 'We had a marvellous air battle late yesterday afternoon.'[7] 'Hershel Johnson [from the American embassy] at 1 [on 22 September] about a telegram from Washington that Pres. had news that invasion will take place at 3 p.m. this afternoon. It doesn't say whether its dep. Calais at 3 or arr. Dover!'[8] 'Invasion expected tonight', Cadogan wrote on 23 September.[9] It did not take place. By 12 October Cadogan thought it '*very* doubtful'.[10] Although the air battle continued, the British had won it. Meanwhile on 27 September the Germans had announced the Tripartite Pact with Italy and Japan.

Doubts about Britain's capacity to survive had affected President Roosevelt. On 27 June Lothian reported 'that there is a wave of pessimism passing over this country to the effect that Great Britain must now inevitably be defeated, and that there is no use in the United States doing anything more to help it and thereby getting entangled in Europe'.[11] The current state of US armaments and concern in Congress about hemisphere defence pointed the same way. So, too, did Roosevelt's own position. He was in the last months of the second term of his presidency. If he was, despite precedent, to seek a third term, his nomination had to appear like a draft. He also needed to pursue a cautious diplomacy, lest he be accused of war-mongering. Only in August did he give much further assistance to Britain.

In September 1939 Churchill had told the Cabinet of his desire to obtain US destroyers to fill the gap until mid 1941 when new British vessels became available. On becoming Prime Minister Churchill asked the President for a loan of forty or fifty old destroyers.[12] There was little chance of that during the following critical weeks when France collapsed, the US became concerned about hemisphere defence, and Britain refused to promise that its fleet would or could cross the Atlantic in the event that it too was defeated. When Roosevelt offered staff talks on 17 June he was, Reynolds suggests, 'more interested in strengthening hemisphere defence against the possibility of a British collapse' than in moving towards a military alliance.[13] Churchill himself probably recognised this. He was unenthusiastic.[14] Nor did he favour responding to the US interest in bases on British possessions in the Western Atlantic. Again that related to hemispheric defence. Churchill believed that there should be a quid pro quo. It took time to emerge.

The deal concluded in early September provided for Britain to receive fifty old destroyers and for the US to lease land for bases in eight British possessions; it also involved a statement by the British Government that if Britain fell the navy would not be sunk or surrendered.[15] Lothian had revived the issue of destroyers when the Democratic convention was over. The Foreign Office had urged the offer of bases as a means of winning collaboration with the US. Roosevelt and his cabinet agreed early in August that the destroyers were crucial for British survival, but a quid pro quo was needed. That must include not only the bases but also the assurance about the Royal Navy. Even that was unlikely to get the deal past Congress. But by 16 August the President had become persuaded that legislation for the transfer of destroyers was unnecessary.[16] Britain's survival also made the decision easier to take. In that American confidence had grown. Despite its doubts the British Government agreed. 'Winston agreed to give way to Americans on procedure.'[17]

David Reynolds points out that the destroyers–bases deal had more than one aspect, 'as with most of Roosevelt's diplomacy'. While in one sense it was strengthening Britain's capacity to continue the struggle in another it was an instalment of hemisphere defence. While Churchill described it in his memoirs as bringing the US 'nearer to us and to the war', that was not Roosevelt's intention; he was 'probably still hoping to avoid American belligerency if he could achieve his ends by less extreme means'.[18] 'This exchange is a big thing', wrote Lothian. 'It really links USA and the British Empire together for defence; but not for action in

Europe.'[19] In the House of Commons on 20 August Churchill had indeed spoken of 'the English-speaking democracies' getting 'somewhat mixed up together' and compared the process to the flow of the Mississippi. 'Let it roll. Let it roll on full flood, inexorable, irresistible, benignant, to broader lands and better days.'[20] If that affected the Commons it might also have affected the Axis powers. The deal spurred on the Tripartite Pact.

The US fleet had been kept in Hawaii from early May rather than returned to its West Coast bases, and that had been publicly announced.[21] It was believed to have helped to prevent the Japanese taking advantage of the crisis in Europe. The depth of that crisis, and the concern about hemisphere defence it induced, led some of Roosevelt's advisers to advocate bringing part of the fleet back to the East Coast lest Britain fell. That, of course, was not the wish of the British; they wanted it to stabilise the position in Asia. Their action at Oran not only persuaded the President of their determination. It also relieved the risks for the British and in turn the pressure on the President.[22]

The US also applied some economic pressure on Japan. Most of Japan's oil came from the US, and the hawks, Henry Morgenthau, Secretary of Treasury, Harold Ickes, Secretary of the Interior, Henry L. Stimson, Secretary of War, and Frank Knox, Secretary of Navy, all tended to urge firm action. Others, including Hull, Welles, Grew and Harold Stark, the Chief of Naval Operations, wanted a more cautious approach. Hull's policy in summer 1940, says Medlicott, was 'still one of all quiescence short of acquiescence'.[23] Strong action might drive the Japanese to attack the Indies in order to ensure an alternative source of supply, and a Far Eastern war would threaten the survival of Britain. Roosevelt sided with the moderates. On 2 July 1940 he proclaimed a list of products that, in the interest of national defence, could not be exported without a licence.[24] A further proclamation of 27 July added petroleum products, tetraethyl lead, and iron and steel scrap.[25] The petroleum products were, however, defined to include only aviation motor fuel and lubricating oil and the scrap to include only heavy melting scrap.[26] That was a stand, but a limited one. Japan could make do with lower-grade petroleum. Enough tetraethyl lead was available for Japan to make higher-quality aviation fuel. The scrap that was restricted accounted for less than a fifth of the export to Japan.[27] Furthermore, in pursuit of oil, Japan could exert additional pressure on the Dutch. Indeed even the modest American move was seen as a provocation.[28]

The Japanese on the whole, however, still hoped to secure their objectives in Southeast Asia without resort to force. Increasingly they were looking south. General Staff officers and officials from the Army Ministry drafted 'Main Principles for Coping with the Changing World Situation' in early July. The prerequisites for a southern move were security from attack by the Soviet Union, settlement of the China Incident and political alliance with Germany and Italy. The navy wanted southern expansion by peaceful means. Prime Minister Yonai refused to accept this as government policy. The army brought his Cabinet down.[29] The tasks of the new Konoe Government were hammered out in advance at a conference at his residence in the suburb of Ogikubo. The Cabinet agreed on an outline of Fundamental National Policy, and on 27 July the Liaison Conference ruled that the empire should strive to end the incident, control Indo-China, close the Burma Road and obtain resources from the Indies, 'for the present by diplomatic means'. Relations with the US might deteriorate, but if the situation turned favourable and the incident were settled force might be used in the south. That might make a clash with the US inevitable, and preparations should be made.[30]

In the following weeks pressure on French Indo-China was redoubled, and indeed it was further intensified, if also confused, by local army initiatives. A guarantee of oil from Netherlands India was sought. The tripartite pact was in some degree a response to the closer association of the UK and the US, apparently evidenced in the destroyers–bases deal. But it had been part of the Ogikubo package. Konoe saw it as a means of warning the US to keep out of the Far Eastern crisis and thus enabling Japan to achieve its aims by the more determined diplomacy on which his government had decided. Force might yet be avoided.

The pact had another objective. It would put an end to the ambivalence of Germany over the French and Dutch colonial possessions.[31] On 20 September Welles asked Henry-Haye, the French ambassador in Washington, if the Germans were backing the Japanese in Indo-China. The ambassador's opinion was that earlier Germany had hoped to take over French colonial possessions. But now he believed 'that Germany desired to immobilise the United States Navy in the Pacific and that in return for an agreement on the part of Japan to pursue a policy which would bring this about, had found herself obliged to give Japan in return the go-ahead signal for the occupation of French, Dutch, and British possessions in the Pacific'.[32]

The Cabinet in Tokyo had authorised Matsuoka to negotiate with Germany late in July, but he had found Ott, the Reich's envoy in Tokyo, unresponsive.[33] Hitler shifted during August and early September as Britain continued to resist and the US drew closer.[34] He was attracted by the 'peripheral' strategy advocated by Raeder and the 'continental bloc' diplomacy advocated by Ribbentrop. His object was to cut off Britain's imperial lifelines, just as the US sought to keep them open. He 'wooed' Franco and Pétain 'in an effort to close the Mediterranean and secure bases in the Eastern Atlantic'.[35] He also encouraged Mussolini's offensive in Libya, which would threaten Britain's hold on Egypt, Suez and the

Middle East. For him the pact also represented a warning to the US to stand off while the status quo in Europe was decisively altered in Germany's favour.

Ribbentrop's representative, Heinrich Stahmer, arrived in Tokyo on 9 September.[36] In the agreement negotiated between 9 and 27 September Germany, Italy and Japan undertook 'to assist one another with all political, economic and military means when one of the three Contracting Parties is attacked by a power at present not involved in the European war or in the Sino-Japanese conflict'. From this the Soviet Union was specifically excluded, and clearly the US was meant. The Japanese army had always had reservations about extending the Anti-Comintern Pact, and they were now met. The navy had been concerned about a commitment against the maritime powers, in particular, of course, the US. In fact it sought to ensure its freedom of action in an exchange of letters made at the same time as the agreement. Matsuoka, the Foreign Minister, endeavoured to insist that the question whether an attack had taken place must be the subject of consultation.[37] What mattered, however, was the public part of the pact. For it was designed as a statement that in itself would affect the international situation rather than as a commitment to action if it were affected. 'Germany and Italy intended to establish a New Order in Europe and Japan will do likewise in Greater East Asia', Konoe announced. '... it is inevitable that Japan, Germany and Italy should assist one another, and the pact may acquire the force of military alliance according to the circumstances.'[38]

What effect would it have on the US? Early in September Lothian had discussed with Hull the likely reaction to an immediate Japanese threat to the Indies. At the Foreign Office T. North Whitehead concluded that the United States

> would go as far as possible to cripple the Japanese short of a danger of war. The judgment as to what would provoke such a danger would be largely a matter for public opinion to decide. I do not think it wise to count on the United States Government taking a firm line in the event of Japanese aggression; public opinion might fear the danger of involvement.

But some measure of financial and/or economic support was likely.[39]

In response to Japanese moves in Indo-China, and then to rumours about the pact, the US announced a new loan to China,[40] and intensified its economic constraints. On 12 September the President placed under licence equipment that might manufacture aviation fuel from petroleum or tetraethyl lead.[41] On the 26th the press announced that all grades of iron and steel scrap would be placed under licence and licences issued only for countries in the Western hemisphere.[42] The hawks wanted to go further and spoke of an embargo on oil and of despatching the fleet to Singapore. No such actions took place. 'Tougher measures might prove provocative and the US had no reason to risk war in the Pacific when her primary interest lay in the survival of Britain.'[43] Stimson wanted a display of US power in the Indies to prevent a Japanese invasion. History showed that 'when the United States indicates by clear language and bold actions that she intends to carry out a clear and affirmative policy in the Far East, Japan will yield to that policy even though it conflicts with her own Asiatic policy and conceived interest'.[44] But Roosevelt and Hull agreed with Stark and Richardson and not with Stimson.[45] Welles opposed a visit to Singapore[46], a suggestion revived by Craigie.[47]

Following the announcement of the pact Lothian had raised the question of the Burma Road. If it reopened and that led to a Japanese attack would the US help? According to Lothian, Hull suggested that 'private staff discussions ... on technical problems' might be held among the Americans, Australians, Dutch and British.[48] Hull's own memorandum does not suggest that he went so far. He had spoken of a conference between the British and the Dutch. 'I had not suggested that my own country be in on this conference ....' Lothian suggested a naval representative attend a conference in London. 'The matter was finally left open ....'[49] On 7 October Hull suggested that Admiral Ghormley might have taken up the matter of a common defence without commitments 'some time ago'. 'A conference should be held in London or Washington at as early a date as possible ....'[50]

There had been contacts during the summer. A special American military mission had gone to London in August 'tasked to evaluate the likelihood of British survival'.[51] Rear-Admiral Robert L. Ghormley had stressed that none of the 'special observers' was 'authorized to make any commitments on behalf of their government'.[52] He stayed on, however, to discuss Admiralty ideas about the role of the US fleet if the US should enter the war. He had substantial conversations with the Bailey Committee, which had been set up in June to consider the forms of assistance desired from the USN.[53]

Hull, however, reverted to pre-election restraint. He felt it was 'necessary to proceed with great caution in view of shock to United States public opinion of realisation of possible consequences of deterioration of relations with Japan'.[54] Roosevelt felt it 'unwise ... that there should be anything that could be interpreted as commitment beyond international date line for the present'.[55] Hull's language remained strong. The Japanese called the embargoes unfriendly.

> I reiterated the view that it was unheard of for one country engaged in aggression and seizure of another country, contrary to all law and treaty

provisions, to turn to a third peacefully disposed nation and seriously insist that it would be guilty of an unfriendly act if it should not cheerfully provide some of the necessary implements of war to aid the aggressor nation in carrying out its policy of invasion ...[56]

Surviving the Battle of Britain, and stimulated by growing US confidence, the British had also taken a firmer line, which might indeed redouble US confidence. They decided to reopen the Burma Road. Its closure had been most unwelcome to the US and its reopening would at once assist China and indicate a congruence with US policy at a time when the pact seemed to be emphasising it. Closure had been for three months and accompanied by a commitment to serious discussions with the Japanese. These the FO had prepared for, but they had never got off the ground.

R.A. Butler had seemed to think a settlement possible. Japan, he argued, could be defeated only by a first-class power. 'We should be unwise to undertake the task and I doubt whether the Russians or Americans will.' So Britain should work for a settlement and not fall between two stools as in Europe before the war. 'Either we carry our settlement policy to its logical conclusion and produce a joint USA, Japan, British Treaty securing order in the Far East and Chinese independence; or we let Japan run into the USA and ourselves by continuing her policy of *taking* what she wants and more.'[57] J.C. Sterndale Bennett thought Britain too weak to take such an initiative.[58] So did Cadogan. The FO had considered possible terms before the war.

> But let us not, so long as the military situation remains as it is, imagine that we are going to have much influence in imposing it. And we shan't get the Americans to help. We lived on bluff from 1920–1939, but it was eventually called. Until we have made ourselves strong enough to maintain the position that we then aspired to hold, we shall have to play for time, which is neither dignified nor comfortable.

By 5 August Butler himself was writing:

> What we really want to prepare our minds for now is not so much a Peace Settlement but a Rearguard Action. I mean by that so to adapt British Policy as not to get into direct war with Japan but yet to impose obstacles to her indefinite ambitions. This may include "non-intervention". Though it may take years I am not hopeless about an ultimate satisfactory understanding with Japan. Meanwhile preparatory work for a settlement is legitimate.

A rather unconvinced letter was sent to other departments.[59] They doubted that a settlement could be made and doubted if it were in Britain's interests to make one.[60]

The Tripartite Pact had another effect; it intensified the conviction of those Americans who saw Germany and Japan as a joint threat to the democracies. In turn the British view of possible American belligerency shifted. Some had argued that US participation in the European war would lessen the availability of supplies to Britain and to the Allies. But that argument had now lost some of what strength it had. The Cabinet minutes of 27 September recorded that the pact might 'accelerate the entry of the US into the war. There was no support ... for the view, sometimes advanced, that the United States could lend us more help by staying out of the war.'[61] That was the war in Europe. What of a war with Japan? Cadogan thought that it was 'not in our interests that the United States should be involved in war in the Pacific'. Vansittart agreed: 'what reason is there for having a new enemy if it is to absorb the resources of our only friend?'[62] Lothian differed: the US would still see its priority in helping Britain and only a war would arouse the American public.[63] Churchill went further. Craigie should be told

> that entry of the United States into the war, either with Germany and Italy or with Japan, is fully conformable with British interests. That nothing in the munitions sphere can compare with the importance of the British Empire and the United States being co-belligerent. That if Japan attacked the United States without declaring war on us, we should at once range ourselves at the side of the United States and declare war upon Japan ...'[64]

These shifts of attitude were, of course, not merely connected with the Tripartite Pact. They indicated a clearer understanding, now shared more widely, that US entry into the war was essential if Germany were to be defeated. Britain had survived the Battle of Britain, but that did not mean victory. More was needed, more indeed than the gestures sought in May and June. If participation could be ensured by a war in the Far East, that should not be avoided. The potential scope of the war thus widened well beyond that of May and June, although its scope had widened then. That did not mean that Churchill wanted a war in the Far East.[65] He believed indeed that Japan could be deterred by a firm Anglo-American front and that, if a war did break out, it would not attack UK and US interests.

In June the Australian Government had been doubtful about Craigie's idea for a negotiation with Japan. With the closing of the Burma Road the UK was committed to try discussions. S.M. Bruce, the High Commissioner in London, had always been an advocate of a compromise and thought that the British Government had neglected the prospect. A settlement, Bruce now urged, must be comprehensive. 'If this attempt were to result in nothing more than the termination of Sino-Japanese hostilities, thus extracting [Japan] from bog she has landed herself in and freeing her for adventures elsewhere, our position would be seriously worsened.' The settlement must be of 'such a character as to ensure Japan observing it from self interest if for no other reason'.[66]

Menzies referred to his government's earlier views. There was an obligation to discuss the terms of a settlement, but 'there is little hope of promoting any general or lasting settlement with Japan while the European position is as at present'. Any weakness in bargaining would invite further demands; unless part of 'a really satisfactory general settlement', the termination of the Sino-Japanese war 'would simply leave Japan free to take full advantage of new opportunities occasioned by any set back in the European war'. Perhaps the better option was to play for time. 'It is a policy which at least keeps Japan at war with China and enables us to play for that necessary three months to demonstrate we are able to withstand the attack of Germany.' It might enlist the Americans' encouragement and 'more positive support after the elections'.[67] The New Zealand Government thought the Burma Road policy a mistake and did not favour appeasement.[68] Bruce told Halifax that, while his government had leant to appeasement, it was probable that it would now prefer 'a policy of standing up to Japan while she was still heavily engaged in China'.[69]

Bruce did, however, meet Shigemitsu, the Japanese ambassador in London, and offered his view 'that Japan's need of markets was the basis of the trouble that had arisen, and there was no reason why that trouble should not disappear if Japan were afforded an opportunity for obtaining her necessary supplies of raw materials and a reasonable market for her manufactured products'.[70] Bruce also sent Halifax a memorandum. In this he suggested that the US and the UK were both 'striving for the establishment of a durable peace in the Far East, based on a free and independent China, and which safeguards legitimate rights and interests of other nations'. The alternatives were pursuing 'a wide settlement', not merely extracting Japan from China, or 'keeping alive and increasing Chinese resistance, and at the same time intensifying financial and economic pressure on Japan so as to deter her from outside adventures and to bring her into a more reasonable frame of mind'. A frank exchange with the US was essential but had not taken place. 'Has not the position rather been somewhat nebulous suggestions on both sides with on our side an apprehension lest we might say something that would give United States the impression that we were relaxing towards Japan?'[71]

Menzies thought Bruce's alternatives were an 'oversimplification'. The only policy was the intermediate one the Commonwealth Government had suggested. To have a common policy in the Far East with the USA would be to 'the Empire's great advantage'. But given experience of the indefinite and variable USA policy in the Far East we can only conclude that even with agreement on common objectives we shall in fact be left to deal according to our own methods with each specific problem as it arises because it is obvious that present Japanese intentions are to ensure that such problems will be those primarily affecting British and not American interests.

Bruce's second option would precipitate war with no firm assurance of US support.[72] Casey agreed with Menzies. The Japanese would not negotiate pending the outcome of the Battle of Britain. No further concessions should be offered. Even the offer of future 'economic blessings' was inadvisable. The US would make no major policy commitments pending the elections. Casey did, however, favour keeping the US informed and in particular pointing out the risk in any further economic measures. 'Aviation petrol embargo was an unhappy example of unconsidered and undiscussed brainwave consequence of which will fall on us ....'[73]

At the same time the question of reinforcing Malaya, deferred by the Australian Government until it had been fully informed of the Far Eastern situation, was revived by the completion of the new Chiefs of Staff appreciation. Much of it was transmitted to Australia. It began by comparing the position with that in 1937. Then it had been assumed that the threat would be seaborne and that within ninety days Britain could send out a fleet sufficient to protect the dominions and India and give cover to communications in the Indian Ocean. Neither of these assumptions was now tenable. The Japanese advance in southern China and Hainan, the development of communications and aerodromes in Thailand, the situation in Indo-China, and the increased range of aircraft, all now enabled Japan to develop 'an overland threat to Malaya, against which even the arrival of the fleet would only partially guard'. Moreover, because of the fall of France, the threat to the UK, and the need to keep a fleet in Europe sufficient to match those of the Germans and Italians it had become 'temporarily impossible' to send a fleet to the Far East.

The paper outlined some general considerations. Japan's 'ultimate aims' were the exclusion of western influence from the Far East and control of raw materials from that area. They could not be attained without capturing Singapore, a potential threat to Japan's expansion while the British fleet remained in being. The war in China could not be relied on to deter Japan's activity elsewhere, although China's resistance would be increased if the Burma Road were reopened. Fear of Russian action would compel Japan to keep forces at home and in Manchuria. It might gamble that the US would not resort to armed opposition if its citizens and possessions were not attacked, but it could not be certain that the US would not intervene.

On the long-term view, Japan cannot stand the strain of a break with the British Empire and the Americans upon whom she is dependent for markets and for essential raw materials. Only if she could rapidly gain complete control of raw materials especially oil, rubber and tin, of Malaya and the Dutch East Indies would she have a chance of withstanding British and American economic pressure.

Japan might postpone any major advance until the situation in Europe were clearer, confining itself meanwhile to local military action.

The paper went on to insist that Britain must avoid a clash, seek to make a settlement or, failing that, play for time. The foundations of Britain's strategy were still to base a fleet at Singapore adequate to cover communications in the Indian Ocean and the southwest Pacific and to frustrate 'any large expeditions' against Australia, New Zealand or Britain's Far Eastern possessions. At present the fleet was not adequate, and the object would have to be to limit the damage to Britain's interests 'and in the last resort to retain a footing from which we could eventually retrieve the position when stronger forces became available'.

The COS considered possible actions by the Japanese. A direct attack on Singapore might be one, although no attack on Australia or New Zealand would be likely to follow until it had consolidated its position. Seizing bases and aerodromes there would not be difficult for the Japanese, and it 'might be effected without the United States breaking off economic relations'. Britain could not assist either Indo-China or Thailand. It was unlikely that the latter would oppose the Japanese by force, while the French forces could not prevent their occupying ports and taking over railways. 'If Indo-China adopted a hostile attitude to us, it is conceivable that Japan might be granted the use of bases in that country.' Such moves would be a threat to Singapore and make the defence of Burma and Malaya more difficult but under present conditions did not justify going to war. A third course would be to attack the Netherlands Indies. That would be a far graver threat to Singapore and to Britain's defence system and communications, but at present it could not be prevented. Fourth, Japan might attack the Philippines but, as that would mean war with the US, and the islands would be of no great economic importance, it was unlikely. An attack on the Indies might antagonise the US 'even if the consequences were confined to the economic sphere', and the Japanese would assume that it would bring war with Britain. Most probably Japan's first move would be into Indo-China or Thailand.

The paper then considered the defence options available in the absence of a fleet. 'If in addition to defending Malaya we could deny to the Japanese establishment of bases in the Netherlands East Indies, and if the movement of their naval forces through the line of these islands could be impeded, security of our interests would be considerably improved.' Hence the argument for strengthening the garrisons in Malaya, particularly needed in the absence of an adequate air force.[74]

The paper thus concluded by emphasising the request that the Australians had under consideration. It went to Australia with a message from Churchill. He thought Japan would not declare war unless Germany could successfully invade Britain. 'Once Japan sees that Germany has either failed or dares not try I look for easier times in the Pacific.' If it attacked the first objective would probably be the Netherlands Indies. 'Evidently the United States would not like this. What they would do we cannot tell. They give no undertaking of support but their main Fleet in the Pacific must be a grave pre-occupation to the Japanese Admiralty.' If Singapore were attacked it 'ought to stand a long siege', and a battle cruiser and an aircraft carrier could be based at Ceylon. The Eastern Mediterranean Fleet could be sent through Suez into the Indian Ocean or to relieve Singapore. 'We do not want to do this even if Japan declares war until it is found to be vital to your safety.' It would mean loss of the Middle East, and the prospect of beating the Italians in the Mediterranean would be gone. It was 'very unlikely' that Japan would invade Australia or New Zealand 'with a considerable army'. If it did, 'I have explicit authority of Cabinet to assure you that we should then cut our losses in the Mediterranean and proceed to your aid sacrificing every interest except only defence position of this island on which all depends'. Churchill's letter concluded with an account of Britain's growing strength on land and in the air. 'We ... feel a sober and growing conviction of our power to persevere through the year or two that may be necessary to gain victory.'[75] The Menzies Government welcomed the appreciation and the assurances and offered to despatch a division.[76] The British asked for it to go to the Middle East.[77]

The post-pact suggestion, which Hull allegedly made, that there might be staff talks involving the Americans, the British and the Dutch was relayed to the Australians by the British[78] as well as reported directly by Casey.[79] Churchill sent another message to Menzies. 'We gather ... that there is an impression in certain quarters that if the United States were to find themselves at war with Japan, we might stand aside.' The War Cabinet in London had no doubt that 'should the question arise we should certainly declare war on Japan. May we assume that ... the attitude of your Government would be similar?'[80] The answer was positive. 'It is assumed, of course, in regard to your earlier cablegrams ... on strategical position in Far East and assurances therein relative to naval dispositions designed to secure Commonwealth against major aggression that dispositions of combined Anglo-American naval strength would be such as to achieve the same end.'[81]

The impact of the Tripartite Pact was, however, muted by the approach of the American elections. For a brief phase it appeared that the pact would produce a more positive response from the US, and that the investigatory talks of the summer would be followed by conversations of a more definite nature. The British and the Australians had responded to that prospect with alacrity. But American caution had supervened. The elections had to be awaited. The reopening of the Burma Road was, however, announced, which helped to prepare the way for developing the relationship with the Americans after the election.

The talks envisaged were expected to involve the Dutch. Indeed the Netherlands Indies was an important consideration. As the COS pointed out, it was of the greatest strategic significance for the security of Singapore, and thus for the success of Britain's whole Far Eastern strategy. Furthermore, the continued existence of the Dutch Government added a possible means of influencing the US. Difficult as its members might be to deal with, they could provide an additional approach to Washington.

The question of assisting the Dutch in the Indies

Before the Australians sought a new appreciation, and indeed made it a condition of their considering providing reinforcements, the British Chiefs of Staff had begun to consider the situation in the Far East in more detail, and the Netherlands Indies was clearly in focus. The Joint Planning Staff emphasised how great an opportunity the Japanese had in the Far East and offered the view that, if no settlement could be secured, Britain must 'play for time' and 'cede nothing till we must'. It must build up defences, limit damage to British interests as far as possible in the absence of a fleet and at all costs retain a footing for retrieving the situation. If the Japanese moved into Thailand they would threaten Singapore, but it would not be desirable in present circumstances to go to war.

> The establishment of Japanese bases in the southern islands of the Netherlands East Indies would be a direct threat to our vital interests. We must ensure the retention of the line of islands Sumatra – Java – the Sumbawa and Flores groups – Timor to Darwin in friendly hands at all costs and we must seek the active cooperation of the Dutch forces to that end ...

A Japanese move into Netherlands India, menacing sea communications and Singapore, would normally lead the staff to recommend war. 'Under present conditions it is clearly impossible to mortgage the future in this way. Nevertheless we consider that in the event of a Japanese attack on

Dutch possessions we may have to liquidate some of our commitments elsewhere in order to provide the forces which would be required in the Far East ...'. British and Dutch interests 'coincide. Defence arrangements should be concerted', and the British should do all they could to assist the Dutch 'from the outset'.[82]

In their subsequent appreciation, however, the COS drew back for the time being from conversations with the Dutch. The Japanese could not be prevented by force from getting a foothold in Netherlands India. 'A combination of British and Dutch opposition, however, would constitute a considerable problem for Japan.' Britain should offer the Dutch 'all the support we can, including both military and economic action ... We should do this without a formal declaration of war, since the presentation of a bold Anglo-Dutch front to Japanese demands might cause them to abandon their demands without undue loss of "face".' The islands were of great importance both in respect of the defence of Singapore and in view of the trans-archipelagic channels to the Indian Ocean. Little could be done at present to dispute the passage of the channels, and invasion would be difficult to prevent. But Dutch assistance would help. 'The whole problem of defence in the Far East would be much simplified if we could be sure of Dutch co-operation and if we could concert plans with the Dutch beforehand.' They would probably be ready to prepare secret plans for the defence of their islands, although not to agree to assist against a Japanese attack on British territory alone. Since, however, Britain could not offer any effective military support at present staff conversations were undesirable. The problem of an Anglo-Dutch plan should be borne in mind, but it must await the boosting of British defences in Malaya by air and in the meantime by land forces. 'Our ultimate aim ... must be to secure the full Military co-operation of the Dutch.'[83]

This report had been much discussed by the COS. The First Sea Lord had differed from the Chief of Air Staff, the Chief of the Imperial General Staff and General Ismay over Britain's attitude to Netherlands India. A new draft version by the Joint Planning Staff had squarely proposed staff conversations.[84] The naval staff opposed them; it would be apparent that Britain could give Netherlands India virtually no military assistance. Britain would involve itself in war to no effect if resistance failed and had no justification for urging the Dutch to resist. 'That this is a highly unsatisfactory position must be admitted; but the facts are that, committed as we are in Europe, it would be the greatest folly to take any action that would involve us in war with Japan.'[85]

If we could be certain that the United States of America would go to war with Japan in the event of a Japanese attack on the Netherlands East Indies, we are agreed [the COS reported] that we should fight, irrespective of the attitude of the Dutch. In the absence of American cooperation, we are agreed that if the Dutch do not resist we should not fight, since we alone could not prevent a Japanese occupation of the Netherlands East Indies. We are, however, not agreed on the policy we should adopt if, in the absence of American cooperation, the Dutch decide to fight.

The majority maintained 'that the integrity of these islands is a vital British interest for the preservation of which we should give the Dutch all the support and encouragement we can, provided they fight'. But Sir Dudley Pound, the First Sea Lord, felt that in present circumstances Britain should on no account be involved in war. Britain, he believed, could not support the Dutch and should not undertake commitments it could not fulfil. A Japanese attack on Netherlands India need not lead to war, and the British should try to avoid adding to their enemies. Others pointed out that the Dutch were now allies in Europe, their forces helping to defend British interests in home waters; inaction would have a deplorable effect on the dominions, including South Africa; Australia might withdraw the forces being sent to Singapore; all chances of obtaining US support might disappear. The Japanese would ultimately move on Malaya in any case, and they would penetrate into the Indian Ocean; they might, however, be deterred by the prospect of Anglo-Dutch opposition, together with uncertainty over US reactions and the interest of the US in the status quo.[86]

Churchill had been asked for a ruling.[87]

I personally feel [he wrote] that an attack on the Dutch East Indies by Japan is an even greater menace to our safety and interests than Hong Kong, when it is admitted we shall have to fight. We should in fact be allowing ourselves to be cut off from Australia and New Zealand, and they would regard our acquiescence as desertion. I should hope the United States would not remain indifferent, as their position in the Philippines would also be affected. I was not aware that any such attack was imminent, and I do not quite understand the urgency for a decision. The American aspect might well be one to be discussed between the Staffs in the forthcoming conversations ...
Should a Japanese attack on the Dutch East Indies become imminent, we ought to tell Japan plainly that that will be war, with us, and not wait until Singapore is directly menaced. We should have to rely mainly on submarines and a few fast cruisers at the outset. I doubt myself whether the Japanese would wish to run the risks of such an adventure while they are entangled in China ...[88]

The Prime Minister's hint that the matter should be deferred and the US sounded had not, however, led to agreement among the COS.[89] The COS could get no further than to point to their continued disagreement on the course to be taken should the US not intervene but the Dutch resist. The First Sea Lord suggested that the alliance with the Dutch did not bring an obligation to defend their colonies. The Dutch would understand that the main object was to defeat Germany. If Japan were bent on capturing Netherlands India, 'there was little we could do to prevent her', and better a non-belligerent Japan in Netherlands India than a hostile one. 'Sir Dudley Pound maintained his opinion that in the present circumstances we should on no account take any action likely to result in war with Japan as a consequence of Japanese aggression in the Dutch East Indies unless we were sure of active American support ....'[90]

These arguments Pound had put again at the War Cabinet on 29 July when it tried to tackle the division of opinion. The discussion there on the whole testified to a wish to defend Netherlands India but also to the desirability of US support. Halifax, the Foreign Secretary, felt that a Japanese occupation of Netherlands India would mark a grave deterioration in the situation. But the Japanese would need new resources if they were to fight Britain, and possibly the US as well, and he thought that they might prefer peace. Churchill, too, suggested that Japanese occupation of Netherlands India would menace Singapore. But, he thought, 'if we made it clear that we should fight to preserve the integrity of the Netherlands East Indies, Japan might very well decide against attack. The danger of having to take on both this country and the United States of America was a powerful deterrent ...'.[91] Attlee, the Lord Privy Seal, believed British prestige would suffer 'a terrible blow' if Britain did not help to defend Netherlands India, and Lord Caldecote, the Dominions Secretary, expressed the concern of Australia and New Zealand, and pointed out that important convoys were due to leave Australia. Churchill told the Cabinet that Chamberlain, the Lord President, who was ill, 'had reached the conclusion that if the Dutch resisted Japanese aggression ... we ought to go in with them and try to shame the United States into joining in ...'. Lord Lloyd, the Colonial Secretary, thought that the Dutch might make an approach to the US; and it was suggested that Halifax could invite the Netherlands Govern ment to do so, saying that 'our capacity to help would depend considerably on what the United States would do'.

> The Prime Minister said that he thought there was no disagreement that we should take all steps in our power to keep the Japanese out of the Dutch East Indies. The real question was the adequacy of the means at our disposal to effect this, and the consequences which would be involved to the general strategical position. If the need arose, we might have to withdraw our Fleet from the Mediterranean in order to station an adequate Fleet at Singapore.

The COS appreciation of the position should show what would be involved in resisting Japanese aggression, and then the Cabinet would decide the policy question, taking account of the means available, which might be more adequate in a few months' time. The Cabinet thus invited the COS to draw up their paper on the supposition that Britain assisted the Dutch in resisting Japanese aggression, indicating plans of campaign with and without US support. The dominions would be asked their views. The Cabinet also agreed 'that, while no decision by the War Cabinet as to our action in the contingency contemplated was called for at the present time, it was important not to give the Japanese any grounds for thinking that we should stand aside ...'.[92]

Despite the apparent vigour of the Cabinet's concern over Netherlands India, the conclusions were much influenced by the First Sea Lord's view. Although the COS paper was to be prepared in a particular way, an actual decision on policy was still deferred. The potential importance in that decision of an American commitment was recognised by almost all who spoke. Churchill seems indeed to have steered the discussion in this direction; as in his earlier comments to the COS, he assented to the importance of Netherlands India but wanted British action on it left in suspense. Moreover, it was the Dutch who were to ask the Americans, not the British.

When the COS returned to their draft appreciation of the Far Eastern position Sir Dudley thus had the best of it, and hence it recommended that staff conversations with the Dutch be taken up only when Malayan defences had been improved.[93] The Far Eastern Department of the Foreign Office, not surprisingly, wanted a different approach. 'We feel', Dening wrote, 'that we should be much more likely to secure Dutch cooperation, and Dutch resistance to Japanese attack, if the Dutch were certain we should back them up. The most powerful deterrent we could furnish to Japanese aggression would be to convince Japan that we would fight if the Netherlands East Indies were attacked.'[94] The Foreign Office was unable to secure many changes in the final version of the appreciation. But, as a result of its efforts, that version did suggest that a Sino-Japanese settlement was remote, and it hinted at the reopening of the Burma Road.[95]

The Cabinet had meanwhile also considered a further paper in which the COS responded to its request for a plan of campaign with and without US support. What could Britain do in present circumstances? the COS asked themselves. With only financial and economic support from the US 'any attempt to produce an adequate naval concentration at Singapore in the present world situation would be unsound', they reiterated; it would mean abandoning Gibraltar and the eastern Mediterranean and reducing convoy work. The most that could be done would be to send one battle cruiser and one aircraft carrier to the Indian Ocean to be based at Ceylon to defend vital communications. That would not help the Dutch. Land defences in Malaya were inadequate and no assistance could be given to the Dutch on land. Air forces were again inadequate but, if Malaya were not attacked at the same time as Netherlands India, they could be directed against a Japanese attack on Sumatra or Java. Economic pressure would, however, have a great effect on Japan after a period of about twelve months, even given its occupation of Netherlands India. By contrast to this largely gloomy appraisal the COS were optimistic over the position if the US should intervene. If Japan were certain of this, indeed, they believed that it would not act. The assumption of the second half of their report was, therefore, 'that the Japanese would have no warning of American intervention'. The US could send a fleet to the Far East superior to Japan's 'whilst retaining a substantial force in their own home waters'. It would need to use Singapore and, to defend Singapore, the US could provide the necessary reinforcements. Whether the US used Manila or Singapore, the Japanese position would be 'hopeless unless they could succeed in making both Singapore and Manila untenable before the fleet arrived, which would scarcely be practicable in the time ...'.[96]

At its meeting the Cabinet again accepted Churchill's view 'that it would be premature to take a decision on the question of assistance to the Dutch in the event of Japanese aggression in the Netherlands East Indies'. It was concerned lest the dominions find the appreciation 'rather discouraging'. It concentrated on the nature of the communication to the dominions and approved the telegram to the prime ministers of Australia and New Zealand, which Caldecote thought would make a 'tremendous difference'.[97]

At the same time the appreciation was telegraphed to the dominions in a version that marked for further consideration all the statements that covered possible assistance to the Dutch. The views of the dominions were sought on the question of avoiding or entering war if the Japanese invaded Netherlands India, whether or not the Dutch resisted. Staff conversations, it was pointed out, would be deferred but, if they were held, Australia and New Zealand would be welcome.[98]

Halifax had talked to Michiels, the Netherlands minister, after the first Cabinet meeting. The first question was whether the Dutch would resist if Japan attacked; Michiels was 'sure that this was so' but would check with his government. No doubt, the Foreign Secretary continued, it would want to know Britain's attitude.

> That to some extent must inevitably depend upon the attitude of the United States Government. I therefore wondered whether the Netherlands Government would feel able to approach the United States Government and ask them what they would be prepared to do in this eventuality. It would be as well to know whether we could look for positive action to the United States; and ... we felt that the Netherlands Government would be likely to get more

out of them, if they felt able to make the approach. Moreover it was quite likely that if the Japanese had reason to believe that aggressive action on their part would land them in trouble, they might think twice ...

Halifax also wondered if it would have a deterrent effect to let it be known that the oil wells would be destroyed 'in the event of imminent danger of invasion'.[99]

The Dutch had already indeed approached the US. Dr Loudon, their ambassador in Washington, had talked to Joseph W. Ballantine of the State Department on 31 July. 'Although he was vague and indirect in language ... I gathered that he was trying to convey his apprehension lest the imposition by us of restrictions on certain exports to Japan might precipitate Japanese action against the Netherlands East Indies ...'.[100] A week later Michiels conveyed the 'not encouraging' impression gained by a Washington conversation with the Under-Secretary of State: the only answer was that 'as shown by public utterance' the US attitude 'has undergone no change'. As for the other points, the Dutch were likely to be non-belligerent if only Hong Kong were attacked but would 'almost inevitably' come in if Singapore were attacked. The Foreign Minister, van Kleffens, also indicated that the oil wells would be destroyed in the event of Japanese attack.[101]

In Australia the Dutch pointed out that they had told the British they would defend the Indies if attacked, but the British did not indicate whether their assistance would be forthcoming. They suggested that the UK Government's 'aloofness' was a threat to the Commonwealth's interests.[102] In commenting on the appreciation, however, the Australian Government concluded that no binding unilateral obligation should be made to Netherlands India; the policy should be to 'take a realistic view of such an act of aggression in the light of our military position at the time'. But the views of the empire should be put to the US with 'a suggestion for the adoption of a similar realistic attitude in event of the contingency arising'.[103] South Africa urged concentration on the Middle East.[104] New Zealand suggested a different line. Netherlands India could not be seen 'solely or even primarily as a military problem'. Honour and prestige were involved. If no action were taken the neutral world, and especially the US, would be 'gravely disturbed by what they would regard as another instance in which we have considered ourselves unable to assist our friends against piecemeal attack and destruction'. And that might militate 'against possibility of our receiving assistance from America'. New Zealand thought that the empire should act and let it be known that it would act; the Dutch should be urged to resist commercial advance and oppose aggression and asked to enter staff conversations; the US should be told, and its sympathy, and even its collaboration, sought.[105] Those views were welcome at the Foreign Office.

Over Netherlands–Japan economic relations, the Foreign Office had sought information in July. Sir Nevile Bland, the British ambassador, dined van Kleffens but got nothing out of him 'in spite of sherry, hock, claret and port'; an 'oyster-like attitude … not very satisfactory considering that the N.E.I. will be entirely dependent on us for any protection they may wish against Japanese aggression', wrote Gage of the Far Eastern Department.[106] Some information was secured from Pabst in Tokyo. On 6 June he had replied to the Japanese notes of February and May. The Netherlands Government would not obstruct Japanese acquisition of raw materials, but they must not fall into German hands. The Labour Ordinance could not be revoked nor separate treatment of particular countries agreed to. The Japanese had replied to this, interpreting the statement that they might buy raw materials as a guarantee, and the Dutch had sent an evasive response in return. Tokyo now planned to send a new economic mission to Netherlands India to conduct discussions, despite Dutch reluctance.[107] From Batavia, however, Consul-General Walsh reported that the Japanese were delaying the mission, 'awaiting the outcome of the present attack on England'. The Dutch, he added, would draw up a program for the discussions, dealing only with economic matters. To this the envoy would be asked to agree, and the preliminaries might take some time.[108]

In London Michiels had told Butler that the Dutch would have 'to concede many of the Japanese economic demands, while attempting to maintain their political independence'.[109] Gage feared that the Dutch would give in too readily. 'They might be told', the new head of the Far Eastern Department, Sterndale Bennett, suggested, 'that we recognise that it may be necessary to play for time (as we ourselves have had to do over the Burma Road) but I suggest that they should be encouraged to avoid any yielding on essentials and to keep us fully informed so that there may be opportunity for consultation before any crisis arrives'.[110] Although, as ever, unwilling to interfere much in these discussions, the Foreign Office wanted the Dutch to follow a policy of discreet firmness: neither give in to the Japanese nor provoke them. That was the best line to take, they believed; it was also the line most likely to be welcome in the US. It was neither appeasement nor war-mongering; it showed a desire to pull one's own chestnuts out of the fire.

The Dutch might concede too much, Dening agreed. 'If Japan intends to swallow them, it won't save them, and experience shows that it is a great mistake to accede to demands too readily … If they are not careful they will find that the Japanese have acquired a stranglehold before they know where they are …'. His colleague, Sir Horace Seymour, pointed out that Japan was pressing for more oil supplies following the introduction of American restrictions in July.[111] Bland talked to Van Kleffens again.

The Netherlands Indies Government contained people who knew how to deal with the Japanese, the Foreign Minister said. But 'the Japanese had so far not had a fair deal in respect of Netherlands East Indies raw materials', and if they could not obtain them by negotiation, they would be increasingly tempted to take them by force. Bland suggested that concessions might only encourage further demands. It was, Seymour concluded, still not clear what the Dutch meant to do.[112]

Late in August Kobayashi was appointed as envoy to the Netherlands Indies, and it was suggested that, as a cabinet minister, he would be able to have discussions with the Governor-General himself.[113] His instructions were vague, apparently because the Japanese were still awaiting the outcome of the German attack on Great Britain.[114] 'It is ... to be hoped that the Netherlands Government, without being too rigidly anti Japanese, (which is hardly likely) will adopt the "stone walling" tactics which we have adopted of late.'[115] According to a telegram from Batavia, a member of the Japanese mission revealed Kobayashi's real object:

> he had expected to be hailed as saviour of the Netherlands East Indies and to have long confidential talks with the Governor General, ending in a secret oral or gentleman's agreement. When asked on what subject agreement was to be, he said that aim of mission was to arrange that Japan will guarantee territorial integrity of the Netherlands East Indies and in return have a free hand economically there. They want an assurance that Japan would always be allowed to buy as much as she wants when she wants it ...[116]

These reports helped to account for the Foreign Office reaction to the Australian and New Zealand despatches. Dening had already observed 'that we are unlikely to get far with the Dutch unless we are in a position to let them know that we are prepared to fight. This knowledge would stiffen them (and if the Japanese get an inkling of it, would be salutary in that quarter also)'.[117] 'Our mutual hesitation is wasting valuable time, and we do not want to be caught totally unprepared – it has happened too often in the past.'[118] When the Australians' comment arrived, Dening observed that they would apparently prefer to let Netherlands India down if they could. In the present circumstances Britain, he agreed, should not enter a binding unilateral undertaking to go to its assistance.

> But without going as far as that, the time may very shortly come when we shall be ill advised to defer any longer our decision in the matter. For if the Dutch remain in doubt as to whether we will come to their support, their will to resist may well weaken, and they will progressively give more and more away to Japan until a point is reached where they may no longer be in a position to resist even if they want to do so.

Consulting the Americans might indeed be worth doing. No concrete support could be counted on, especially in the months leading up to the election, but the US might be more ready to help when the time came if informed of 'our intention to resist'. Anxious to push forward, Bennett wondered whether, once the decision on reinforcing Malaya had been taken, 'we could not have conversations with the Dutch without committing ourselves at the outset to any definite obligation. We might at least advance some way along the road in this manner though the discussions would probably show that a definite obligation was imperative in the long run.' R.L. Speaight agreed that it was important to let the Dutch 'see that being our Allies is not all give and take as the Nazis are constantly trying to impress on the Dutch people'. And it would help to keep alive the 'enthusiastic spirit' now evident in Netherlands India. 'The N.E.I. are vital', Butler wrote. 'It is important to show Germany that in the event of their overrunning a small European country, her large overseas children persist and flourish.'[119] The arrival of the New Zealand telegram prompted Dening to suggest preparing a paper for the War Cabinet.[120] The 'enthusiastic spirit' in the Indies was demonstrated by the organisation of a Spitfire Fund.[121] At a performance of *The Sleeping Beauty,* organised in September by the Indo-Europeesch Verbond, a fairy called out 'Long live the RAF' to loud applause.[122]

Lothian had stressed that the Dutch must avoid making long-term commitments on oil, undermining current American pressure and diminishing the chances of a stronger policy in the future.[123] He raised the issue with Hull.[124] American refusal of aviation fuel licences to the Japanese, he said in early September, had intensified their pressure on the Indies for long contracts. Resistance could be maintained only if the US indicated its support.[125] Hull's response was that the Americans were 'making almost a daily record of opposition to Japanese expansion and Japanese aggression' and that there was 'no more for me to say at this stage'.[126] But the Secretary of State reminded Consul-General Foote in Batavia of the importance the US attached to the status quo and asked to be kept informed of developments. 'Especially in the economic field, this Government would be prepared to give consideration to possible helpful action in regard to economic problems which might arise as a consequence of the cutting off of the Netherlands East Indies from normal markets and sources of supply and in connection with which this Government might practicably be helpful.'[127] If the US wanted the Dutch to conform to the embargo they must make it possible, the Foreign Office told Lothian.[128]

The Joint Planning Staff also considered the question of a commitment over Netherlands India in the light of the dominions' replies. They agreed with New Zealand that 'we could not afford to allow the

Japanese to enter into undisputed possession of the Netherlands East Indies' and even doubted whether, if Singapore were rendered unusable, it could be regained after Germany had been defeated. But they agreed with Australia that no binding commitment could be made. The aim must be to deter the Japanese, which involved obtaining the collaboration of the US. If deterrence failed resistance would be necessary. For that staff talks were required, and undertaking them might indeed encourage the US to take up a deterrent stance. Staff talks might, however, also reveal Britain's inability to help while obligating it to assist. The Joint Planners suggested that, once Malayan defences were on the point of being strengthened, staff talks, already planned with Australia and New Zealand, could involve the Dutch. But they need not involve 'binding obligations' since the Netherlands Government realised that Britain's attitude was 'largely influenced' by the US.[129]

News of the Tripartite Pact supervened. Grew thought that one of the most dangerous potential consequences of the pact was 'a possible ruthless application of power by Germany in Holland to bring about changes in the situation in the Dutch East Indies'. An officer in the Japanese Foreign Office sympathetic to the US and UK suggested that if the British offered US the use of Singapore, or a US squadron visited Singapore, that would give pause to the extremists.[130]

The COS had just completed a document, based on that of the Joint Planners, recommending staff talks with Netherlands India in the near future. It did not appear at first sight, they suggested, that the announcement of the pact affected that recommendation.[131] In response to the information from Washington that Hull had suggested technical talks, however, the COS argued in favour of them. They could be a deterrent since, although they were held secretly, the Japanese would become aware that closer collaboration was taking place. They would stiffen the Dutch attitude. They would improve defence planning and increase the chances of US military support in the event of Japanese aggression. The decision to open the Burma Road perhaps lent urgency to the talks. If the US wanted them immediately there was no need to await the strengthening of the Malaya garrison 'since with American support there is little fear that any weakness in our combined strength should deter the Dutch from resisting ...'.[132]

Some days later the COS even modified their conclusions on aid to the Dutch. The pact, they considered, strengthened the view that the British would be compelled to support them if they resisted a Japanese attack since it gave greater reason to suppose that the attack would ultimately turn against Great Britain. The prospect of American collaboration outweighed any discouraging effect British weakness might have, and conversations should proceed, more especially as some reinforcements were due in Malaya at the end of October. A bold front would deter the Japanese and encourage the Dutch. Britain could not alone bind itself in advance to support them, but it should come to an agreement with the US that they should together go to the aid of Netherlands India if it were attacked. If the US indicated that they would join in opposing Japanese aggression against Netherlands India British policy should be to aid Netherlands India, although that should not be an obligation in advance.[133] This, of course, still stopped short of what men like Dening now wanted,[134] but it was a step forward. The more positive stance of the Americans made possible a more positive British attitude to the Dutch.

Churchill wrote to Roosevelt on 4 October announcing the decision to reopen the Burma Road. Action spoke louder than words. Could an American squadron visit Singapore? Technical discussions might take place, and it would have 'a deterrent effect' on a possible Japanese declaration of war over the opening of the road.[135] Lothian reported that Welles, the Under-Secretary of State, did not care for a naval visit to Singapore. But he favoured staff talks, preferably in Washington, while Lothian suggested preliminaries in London.[136] And the Navy Department asked whether Singapore facilities would be available to the US fleet in the event of a Japanese reaction to the opening of the Burma Road, and whether US ships could use the base if Japan menaced Dutch or British possessions before war was declared.[137] The answer to this was, of course, affirmative. Churchill saw it as 'a message of the highest importance. It showed how great a mistake Japan had made in affronting the Americans …'.[138] Soon, however, Hull drew back.

The relationship with the Dutch in Southeast Asia remained during the summer of 1940 much as it had been before the war in Europe began, although the relationship with the Dutch in Europe had drastically changed. The pressure exerted by the Japanese after the fall of France – on the British and the Dutch, not merely on the French – did not produce new commitment between them. Although some of the British, particularly in the Foreign Office, urged the value of a commitment to the Indies – in order to stiffen the Dutch, deter the Japanese, prepare for defence – the view of the First Lord of the Admiralty and of the Prime Minister prevailed in London, and overseas the view of Australia prevailed over that of New Zealand. Backing from the United States would have made a difference. Various attempts were made to secure it, for instance, by pointing to the likely effects of uncoordinated economic restraints on the Japanese and their need to ensure a supply of fuel. Hull initially responded by no more than statements in support of the status quo, a policy that might at least make the Japanese uncertain of American reaction to an expansive venture. It might, however, do no more than that, and it might not suffice to stop them. Indeed British opinion remained quite uncertain that the US would interpose by other than fiscal or economic measures. The fact that Britain survived the Battle of Britain and was disposed to open the Burma Road made the Americans more forthcoming. The announcement of the Tripartite Pact led Hull to suggest technical military conversations. But, affected by the approaching election, he drew back. The prospect of a commitment by the Americans, and thus by the British, again receded.

The fact that the Americans remained in the Philippines was only occasionally invoked in these discussions. Presumably it was thought that, if they acted, the Japanese could by-pass the territory, while the USN could base only a limited number of ships there. It was clear, however, that the Americans were not leaving immediately, although it seemed likely that they would adhere to the date prescribed for independence under the Tydings–McDuffie Act.

The trade of the Philippines

Certainly Quezon had rejected any idea of postponing independence. He had concluded, indeed, that the semi-independence offered by commonwealth status prevented, rather than promoted, proper preparation for full independence since it gave the Philippines no power to pursue a foreign policy nor even an international trade policy.

This attitude was not seen as inconsistent with a desire to renegotiate the commercial provisions of the relationship with the US. In a broadcast on 17 September Manuel Roxas, the Secretary of Finance, appealed for their postponement. He stated

> that the Philippines had 150,000 trained men and did not expect American blood to be shed for her protection. She needed, however, arms, aeroplanes and other military equipment which the United States could supply, while at the same time safeguarding commerce between the Philippines and American with her fleet. The Filipinos would never believe that it could be the plan of the United States to 'leave the Philippines to her fate and permit her to be ruthlessly overrun by an invader'.

Then Roxas turned from defence to economics. The Philippines was now more than ever dependent on the United States. 'As a result of the war she had lost her trade with Europe while trade with China and Japan had been drastically curtailed.' The economic adjustment period should be extended, and the duties and quotas postponed until four years after peace had been re-established. The trade conference, planned for two years before independence, should be called at once.

Quezon endorsed Roxas' suggestions. Independence should not be put off. Otherwise the Philippines would be far worse off 'because her condition of entire dependence on the United States would continue and, at the end of the period which might be fixed for trade relations, the country would find itself in the same state of unpreparedness as before'.[139]

The Philippines offered no clear indication of US policy in Southeast Asia in general. In French Indo-China there had been a drastic change. The French had been pressed into a deal – privileges for Japan in return for a guarantee of territorial integrity – which seemed to influence Kobayashi's approach in Batavia. The deal prompted verbal support from Hull for the status quo and limited economic restrictions. Perhaps this was a stronger signal. Certainly a privileged role for the Japanese in Indo-China intensified the insecurity of Malaya and the Indies.

The Japanese move into northern Indo-China

The new Konoe Government had stepped up pressure on Indo-China. In Matsuoka's view that was still to take a diplomatic form, although an exacting one. The army was divided, some wanting to use force, some not, some increasingly interested more in the south than in China.

Admiral Decoux, Governor-General of Indo-China, refused new demands from Colonel Sato Kenryo presented early in August after General Nishihara Issaku had temporarily returned to Tokyo. He referred them to the governments themselves. Baudouin, the Vichy Foreign Minister, received an ultimatum from Tokyo. Matsuoka had given Arsène Henry, the French Ambassador in Tokyo, an aide-mémoire, asking that Japanese troops might cross Tonkin and occupy French aerodromes; failing agreement, they would proceed by force.[140] 'So, alas, all my fears are justified', wrote Baudouin. 'Such are the consequences of our defeat and of the concessions given by General Catroux. If we give way to this ultimatum, Indo-China will be rapidly and completely lost.' Baudouin got his Vichy colleagues to reject the demands as 'inadmissible in matter and form' but to offer a negotiation. 'We gave an order to Indo-China, to oppose by force any attempt on the part of the Japanese army to enter the country.' The telegram to Tokyo expressed readiness 'to accord exceptional facilities temporarily to Japan in return for a formal assurance that she has no territorial designs in Indo-China'. Baudouin told Sawada Renzo, the Japanese ambassador in Vichy, that France would expect recognition of its sovereignty in Indo-China and an assurance that the exceptional facilities would end with the conclusion of the Sino-Japanese war. He told the Vichy ambassador in Washington, Saint-Quentin, to point out that 'our resistance would largely depend upon American support'. He asked the American government to let the British government 'know what has happened, for my chief preoccupation is to rely so far as possible upon the two Anglo-Saxon Powers in withstanding Japan'.[141] Saint-Quentin reported, Baudouin subsequently noted, that the US Government, while supporting the status quo, 'does not contemplate any practical measures in support of this attitude'.[142]

The British embassy in Washington had reported that the US Government had received a communication from the Vichy authorities, 'stating that they had received what amounted to an ultimatum from Japanese government demanding right for the passage of troops through Tonkin and use of naval and air bases there in order that they might use them to bring the China war to an end'. The French Government asked the US to help and to inform the UK. The Under-Secretary of State told Lord Lothian that he thought that the American Government would reply 'in the same terms as it had used some months ago about the Netherlands East Indies, that it was opposed to any alteration in the status quo. In the present situation it was impossible for United States Government to go further...'.[143]

Saint-Quentin had been instructed to ask what support the US would give if France endeavoured to resist with its military forces in Indo-China.[144] Saint-Quentin's communication outlined the basis of the French response, 'emphasizing that, in the case the affair could be handled by means of negotiation, the resistance of the French Government to the Japanese would necessarily depend to a large extent on the nature and effectiveness of the support which the American Government would be disposed to give it'.[145] James Clement Dunn, political adviser at the State Department, told Saint-Quentin that his government was doing what it could 'within the framework of our established policies' to stabilise the situation in the Far East. Could the French 'delay discussions ... for a period'? Saint-Quentin thought this was impossible. He assumed Dunn's reply meant that the US 'would not use military or naval force in support of any position which might be taken to resist Japanese attempted aggression in Indochina'.[146] Grew was told to express US concern about the 'reported developments'. Welles recalled the statements about the Indies of 17 April and 11 May, opposing intervention, or alteration in the status quo by other than peaceful means, and indicating that these views were based on a doctrine of universal application. 'The same belief and the same observation naturally apply to French Indochina likewise.'[147] Grew told Matsuoka that the US attitude on the preservation of the status quo in the Indies 'applied in equal measure to the entire Pacific area including French Indo-China'.[148] 'That year of 1940', the American diplomat, Robert Murphy, later wrote, 'was a presidential election year and Roosevelt, as an astute politician, could never forget that any move which the voters might consider too war-like would jeopardize his chances for re-election, already uncertain because he was breaking precedent by seeking a third term.'[149]

Not all at Vichy quite agreed with Baudouin's approach. In the French Foreign Office, Jean Chauvel, head of the Far Eastern section, argued for resistance. It might hasten the evolution of American position: 'because of the ties established between Berlin and Tokyo, the Asian war and the European war were essentially the same war, which would be recognised one day'. The US would eventually enter the war through the Pacific, and France must avoid playing the Japanese game there. If it became absolutely necessary to accommodate Japan 'we must on each occasion drive the United States into a corner, to lead them to recognise their impotence to help us, to make them admit that the maintenance of a French presence ... was preferable to an eviction which had left all freedom to their adversary'.[150] Lémery, the Colonial Minister, favoured resistance and so did General Weygand, the Vichy Government's Defence Minister, and Gen. Buhrer, chief of the general staff. The Chinese ambassador at Vichy, Wellington Koo, inferred 'that Baudouin's idea in placing the question on the American door step is to enable France after a mild show of resistance in Tongking to submit to Japan as gracefully as possible ...'.[151] That was prescient. Later, in rebutting accusations from Hull over his policy, Baudouin pointed out that the US had several times declined practical help, that Murphy had said on 17 August that only 'a verbal condemnation' could be expected, and that Welles told Saint-Quentin on the 21st that, as the US could not come to its aid, it did not think it had the right to reproach the French Government for according military facilities to Japan.[152] In fact Chauvel's policy was not very different. The main aim of all was to preserve Indo-China to the French. What Baudouin's colleagues sought to do was to take more account than he of the role the US might play in the future.

Baudouin said he secured no reply from the British.[153] But they were not inactive. The Consul-General in Saigon had reported the new Japanese demands and had also reported that Decoux had been instructed to resist if need be by force. The French, he added, had few means of resistance. He also noted other acts of aggression: the occupation of two blockhouses near Langson, for which the Japanese later apologised, and aircraft flying low over Tonkin without permission.[154] 'What is interesting', wrote Gage at the Foreign Office,

is that the French Govt. should have asked the U.S.G. to inform H.M.G. of this [ultimatum]. One would like to know what attitude the Germans are adopting in the matter. It seems probable that in return for more active Japanese support for the Axis, they would be prepared to bring pressure to bear upon the French to give way. The U.S. refusal to do more than make a statement about the status quo seems categorical. It would presumably be useless to pursue the matter with them on the basis of the danger to China and to Singapore involved in this new Japanese move. But if they will not move, we certainly cannot ....

Dening agreed that the US would 'do nothing, as usual'. He also thought it useless to urge the administration 'to do something which the internal political situation will not permit', although he hoped that the press reports would help to make the public realise 'what is likely to happen in the Far East before long. Japan may try to hold us off with fair words or on the other hand she may not even bother to do that. But we should be under no illusions. From Indo-China it is but a step to Siam, and bases in Siam will at once put Malaya in grave danger.' Britain must stiffen its defences in Malaya as best it could 'and prepare for the worst. Because the worst is likely to happen, and we should not always be found completely unprepared.'

Dening's colleague, Ashley Clarke, agreed that the Japanese moves might be steps towards control over Indo-China, and then it was only a short step to bases in Thailand, 'with all the strategic implications which that would have for Malaya and the Netherlands East Indies'. The US would not react strongly, but the Japanese move should not pass without a British reaction. 'We are not in a position to come to the assistance of the French with force to resist Japanese pressure. But we are not entirely without weapons.' One course was to indicate that Britain would reopen the Burma Road. But threat was not the best way of dealing with the Japanese, and in any case Britain needed to avoid a crisis while withdrawing its Shanghai troops. The other option was to exert economic pressure, unobtrusively but so that it could be felt. Immediately, however, Craigie should make inquiry in Tokyo, as the American ambassador had done. 'We might add that we could not remain indifferent to Japanese action against Indo-China.' Sterndale Bennett agreed. 'We cannot threaten Japan at this stage but we can show close interest – and meanwhile prepare quietly for further action.' A Chiefs of Staff paper on Netherlands India suggested that Britain could hamper Japan considerably,

and that the Japanese are likely to be deterred if they know our attitude beforehand. The accepted view is that we cannot go to war with Japan over Indo-China. On the other hand, we cannot afford to let Japan take one strategic position after another, unhampered, so that at the end we are left to fight with every disadvantage, with our backs to the wall, at Singapore.

The proposal for an approach to Tokyo was put to the Foreign Secretary.[155] He raised it at Cabinet.

A Foreign Office memorandum suggested that the Japanese were carrying out a drive against Thailand and French Indo-China and pointed to its implications for Britain. The Thai Government, 'frightened of Japan', had been 'intimidated into sending a military and naval mission' there. New demands on French Indo-China amounted to an occupation. With that Japan

> would not only strengthen her position in her war against China, but she would also be able to bring pressure to bear on Thailand to grant her any concessions she might require. These are likely to be in the first place air bases from which Malaya and Burma could be attacked. A land attack on Malaya from Thailand is also conceivable. In the event of a Japanese occupation of Indo-China, Thailand would be unlikely to resist any Japanese demands.[156]

At the Cabinet Lord Halifax reported that in response to the American ambassador Matsuoka had disclaimed any intention of invading French Indo-China. He planned to get Craigie to put a similar question. 'The more disclaimers we had on record against the Japanese, the better.'[157] It was more a refusal to answer than a disclaimer, however, Clarke thought.[158]

Following the Cabinet meeting, a telegram to Craigie was drafted. It instructed him to inquire of Matsuoka as to the truth of the reports about the demands Japan had made of French Indo-China. Halifax deleted the phrase: 'adding that H.M.G. could not remain indifferent to any action on the part of the Japanese Government towards Indo-China which would affect the status quo in the Far East'. But the telegram did take up the American precedent by recalling the British Government's earlier statement that it agreed with the Japanese on the maintenance of the status quo in Netherlands India and declaring that it attached similar importance to the maintenance of the status quo in Indo-China and other territories in the Far East.[159] The Consul-General in Saigon was told to let the Hanoi government know of this telegram 'informally'.[160]

The Chinese were also told. Their ambassador in London, Dr Quo, approached Halifax on 13 August. He did not recount the conversation his counterpart, Dr Koo, had had with Baudouin in Vichy: the Chinese had warned against admitting Japanese troops, but the French minister had evaded revealing anything of the negotiations.[161] Quo told Halifax that he understood Decoux was opposed to the Japanese demands and, according to his colleague in France, the French Government was 'anxious to defend French interests in Indo-China, but were doubtful of their strength to do so unaided and were accordingly taking soundings in this country, the USA and the USSR as to what measure of support they could expect'. If Indo-China decided to resist and military operations followed, would the British refrain from interfering with French naval and military movements? Would they even help the French? Halifax replied that the problem was being considered. Much depended on the form in which it was presented and on the attitude of the French and US governments. He could not give a precise indication of Britain's attitude.

> I could say, however, that we certainly did not want to see the French empire break up. H.M. Government were in touch with the United States over Indo-China, but the attitude of the latter was not very definite though, like H.M. Government, they had made plain to the Japanese their attitude in regard to the maintenance of the status quo in the Far East.

Dr Quo could inform his government that the British Government 'were closely concerned with the events in Indo-China and were watching the situation and that they would certainly put no obstacle in the way should the Indo-China authorities decide to defend themselves against Japan ...'.[162]

Help of a kind might also be coming from the Germans, it seemed. True, a report from Vichy gathered from the Chinese embassy in Washington stated that they had been pressing the French not to 'provoke' the Japanese in the Far East. 'The French were disposed to resist this pressure, feeling that Indo-China, if lost would be lost for good, and that they might do better to decide to put up such a fight as they could against the Japanese, rather than give way as the Germans wished them to do.' The Germans would be the arbiters, C.E. Whitamore observed at the Foreign Office. Gage thought they would not press the French unless they secured a quid pro quo from the Japanese 'in the form of closer alignment with the Axis'. 'The Germans may not want the Japanese to get too strong a hold over Indo-China', Bennett added.[163]

A report from Kunming supported these rather optimistic views. It indicated on 14 August that the Chinese embassy in Berlin had learned that Germany had warned Japan against encroachment on French territories.[164] This Craigie could not confirm, but discreet inquiries at the Gaimusho suggested that 'latent antagonism between Japan and Germany is in fact developing over Indo-China'. Catroux, it seemed, got on well with the Japanese. 'He was comparatively independent of Vichy and took the line that if Japan would guarantee the integrity of Indo-China he would do what he could to oblige her ...'. Decoux had been 'more subservient to Vichy and proportionately more obstructive to the Japanese'. But the Japanese, it seemed, had not yet decided 'how far they dare go in Indo-China'.

If true, said Gage, this showed that Germany was behind Vichy's resistance. 'Thus indirectly and probably momentarily, German and British interests coincide in this matter. But the German motives are not clear. If by encouraging Indo-China to resist we could be induced to offer open support to that country and thereby become involved with Japan, the Germans would no doubt be delighted.' 'Britain's best policy will certainly be to make no move until this curious phase in German–Japanese relations has developed more clearly ...'. Perhaps, Clarke thought, the Germans wished to reserve Indo-China for themselves. Bennett did not think Britain should refrain from 'measures designed to show sympathy with Indo-China and to the French resistance there because this happens to suit the German book also for the moment. We do not want to encourage the idea in French minds in Indo-China that they are beholden to Germany.' 'The Germans would naturally be opposed to a premature division of parts of the French Empire, and there may be difficulties between them and the Japanese on this score', Sir Horace Seymour observed. 'But other evidence suggests that the Germans are very well in with the present Japanese Government and I would not found too great hopes on any difference of opinion.'[165] This was perhaps the most accurate assessment. Ribbentrop, the German Foreign Minister, had been rather unhelpful to the Yonai Government in July and, approached by Matsuoka, Ott had declared that Germany had little influence on French policy.[166] Germany was doing well, and pressure over Indo-China might only discourage French Africa from following Vichy.[167]

These assessments had helped to determine Foreign Office views on other proposals. Commenting on the Cabinet decision of 8 August, Bennett wrote: 'The question arises how to keep this matter of Indo-China alive. Would it be of any use to ask Sir R. Craigie to advise, after consulting the US Ambassador, whether there is any further step the two Ambassadors can take in Tokyo – on parallel lines?' Alternatively the Foreign Office could 'stir up Press interest in this country'. A *Times* report of 17 August suggested that Decoux had rejected Japanese demands for bases and for the use of the railway for troop movements to Yunnan. 'In view of the many indications that Indo-China authorities are successfully resisting Japanese demands, the less the matter is played up in the press here the better. I think we can safely wait on developments for the moment,' Clarke wrote.[168]

Direct contact with Hanoi had been broken following the British attack on French warships at Oran in Algeria.[169] Henderson, the British Consul-General in Saigon, conveyed the post-Cabinet British message to the Governor for transmission to Decoux. The Governor himself did not know the nature of Japan's demands. The British naval liaison officer, Henderson added, would be up in Hanoi from 12 August.[170] But wanting fuller information of what was going on, the Foreign Office suggested that Henderson should go up himself.[171] Henderson was prepared but said the Japanese were negotiating direct with Vichy.[172] Clark Kerr, the British ambassador to China, thought he might travel to Chungking via Indo-China and secure information from the Governor-General. The French ambassador had told him it would not embarrass the French authorities. 'On the contrary he was convinced that Admiral Decoux would welcome an opportunity to discuss current questions with me...'. Gage's first reaction was that, if Decoux were 'really willing', this was 'a good idea. It might have a healthy effect on the Japanese who, from information available, are receiving strong opposition from the Vichy Government (presumably backed by the German Government) and are treading warily. The only query is whether such a visit might raise issues with the Vichy Government beyond the question of Indo-China ...'. The visit, Clarke agreed, would demonstrate to the Japanese 'our interest in the situation in Indo-China'. The French Department agreed, and Seymour thought it 'a good plan .... The visit could puzzle the Japanese, which might be useful'. Sir Alexander Cadogan, the Under-Secretary, thought it 'a very good idea'.[173] Clark Kerr was told to go via Hanoi, checking with his French colleague that there was no objection.[174] Craigie, however, was critical of the idea.

> While I have no doubt that it is important for us to have unobtrusive contact with authorities at Hanoi, I suggest that visit of a high British official to the Governor General at this time, would attract considerable attention here and would tend to divert Japan's [resentment?] from Germany to ourselves, a development which should be in my opinion avoided at all costs ...

Halifax accepted this view. 'He felt that it was unwise to add to our difficulties with Japan if our object was already being achieved by the Germans: he would rather that all the odium fell on the latter...'. Bennett thought Craigie's argument 'over-subtle'.[175] But Kerr was told that, unless he had already consulted his French colleague about it and could not draw back, he should not visit Hanoi.[176] He did not go.

The Foreign Office were indisposed to release the aircraft carriers *Béarn* and *Ile de France* held in Martinique and Singapore. 'The French in Indo-China will have to make their attitude much clearer before we can release these ships', wrote Gage on 12 August.[177] But a different view was taken of the despatch of two training aircraft from Hong Kong. 'Our information shows that the Air Force is the most friendly of all the armed forces in Indo-China', Gage had written on 23 July. 'As it may be useful to us in the event of war with Japan, I think it will be useful to send these trainers.' The aircraft could 'make little difference one way or the other from a military point of view ...', Clarke observed, 'whereas their refusal would be taken ill in Indo-China where the authorities – perhaps even with the knowledge of Vichy – are taking care not to fall out with us ...'. In August the Foreign Office contemplated procrastinating over some de Havilland Tiger Moth training aeroplanes but in the event told the Air Ministry they should go. 'There are signs that the French wish to resist Japanese pressure, and that they are to some extent succeeding. We should naturally like to encourage them in this course, and would therefore favour the release of the seven aeroplanes ...'.[178]

The Foreign Office's decision on these planes was supported by the argument that the Hanoi authorities had asked for the return of the military and naval liaison officers sent away after Oran.[179] Captain Duncan, the military liaison officer, met General Martin in Hanoi on 17 August. Martin wanted to maintain relations in accordance with the decisions of the 1939 Singapore conference. Owing to weather conditions, he did not expect Japanese operations till mid November, but he thought them likely then.[180] Decoux had been unfriendly after Oran;[181] 'not very trustworthy', Gage thought, '... and Oran possibly rankles'.[182] Now he seemed 'better disposed',[183] 'more pro-British'.[184] The Foreign Office concluded in late August that

> it is safe to say that inasmuch as Indo-China has to face the same potential enemy as the British possessions in the Far East there is a tendency towards co-operation with Great Britain. The establishment of bases in Indo-China at which Japan is aiming represents a first step towards a position from which Japan could threaten British interests. Indo-China is therefore in a sense our first line of defence and it is in our essential interests that the French should be encouraged to defend it against the Japanese ...[185]

The Foreign Office tended to dismiss contrary information. The *Daily Express* of 12 August suggested that Pétain had told Decoux to give in. Clarke noted that such reports seemed to come from Chungking sources 'who have an obvious interest in making the situation more serious than it may be...'.[186] The Chinese Foreign Ministry reported late in August that the French Government had agreed to grant Japan a naval base in Tonkin Bay and the right to transport troops on the railway. Koo had been told that the Chinese Government would consider itself free to do what the Japanese did. The Japanese, however, had not gone ahead because 'they were awaiting the result of the air battles in England...'.[187] In London Quo gave Cadogan the same information. Cadogan told him in reply that British reports suggested that the French in Indo-China had 'rather stiffened in their resistance to the Japanese'. The British attitude remained as Halifax had put it.

> As regards what we should do in the event of Japanese encroachment, I said that Dr Quo would evidently not expect me to answer that question; the

answer must depend on the circumstances of the case, which we could not foresee. I repeated that we had no news to show that the French had yielded to the Japanese demands and there had recently been indications that the Japanese were going slower in various directions.[188]

The hope of preserving a fragile status quo influenced the reaction to press reports, later denied, of a rebellion in Indo-China in the name of the French National Committee in London. Craigie thought that such a rising would be 'most inopportune' and that it ought to be prevented. 'Our interests as regards Indo-China seem to me to be (1) to prevent any Japanese action there which would be a threat to our imperial security and (2) to exploit to the utmost the policy [? possibility] of clash of interests between Japan and Germany.' These objects Decoux was securing, and Craigie thought that the Japanese were 'seriously disconcerted by unseen presence of Germany behind other Powers opposing their designs on Indo-China'. A rising would give the Japanese an argument for intervening, would remove German interest in the status quo and divide the French among themselves. If the rising were successful and the Japanese did not march in, 'change of régime would ... simply divert Japanese resentment from Germany to ourselves without any proportionate advantage to us'. If, more likely, the rebellion failed and the Japanese intervened, the Chinese and Thais might intervene also; Britain would have to step in too or see an eventual extension of Japanese occupation to Cambodia and Cochin-China. Dening agreed with much of this analysis. Indo-China's adherence to de Gaulle would be welcome, but it would 'invite Japanese intervention at a time when we are not in a position to provide any effective counter-action. In these circumstances we feel that nominal subservience to Vichy may suit the General's purposes as well as our own for the time being, and that no attempt should be made on our part to force the situation.'[189] The Australians shared a similar view on New Caledonia. A local revolution might lead to a request for Australia to take over. That could be

misinterpreted in some quarters which would have far-reaching repercussions especially regards French Indo-China ... The solution seems to us to be to have an administration owing nominal allegiance to Vichy only but sympathetically inclined to the wishes of the local populace in regard to continuing the war effort – in other words to co-operate with the Allies as far as possible.[190]

Vichy and Tokyo in fact had been negotiating an agreement. If it resisted, the former believed, the Tonkin cities would be destroyed 'in short order'. If it complied, 'it will have at least a basis as flimsy as it may be, on which to assert a case for the future...'.[191] The agreement was signed in Tokyo on 30 August. The negotiations there had been between Matsuoka and Arsène Henry. On the 10th the former had made over a draft agreement in which the Japanese, in exchange for a vague formula of goodwill, would receive the right to send troops across Tonkin in the course of their military operations against China. This was not an ultimatum, but it was an insistent demand.

> It is impossible to answer in the affirmative [Baudouin wrote] for this would be to admit our complete weakness, as well as to call up trouble in Indo-China and perhaps in the other colonies. However, there can be no doubt but that our presence in the Far East forms part of the existing Anglo-Saxon plan for that part of the world. This plan is upset, but in the event of an invasion of Indo-China the United States will confine itself to a moral condemnation; such being the case we must come to terms with Japan, and maintain our position in Indo-China in agreement with her. We must, then, not reply by a direct negative, but must try to find a basis of agreement.

There was some opposition at Vichy to Baudouin's view, but he carried the day.

> The position is unhappily very simple; if we refuse Japan, she will attack Indo-China which is incapable of being defended. Indo-China will be a hundred per cent lost. If we negotiate with Japan; if we avoid the worst, that is to say the total loss of the colony, we preserve the chances that the future may perhaps bring us.[192]

The Japanese would bring in troops anyway. If the French refused to let them through, they would attack and Indo-China would be lost. If France tried to reach an agreement with Japan, 'this will begin by recognising our complete sovereignty over Indo-China, and we shall only partly lose the colony. It is true that the Japanese troops might remain in the country and annex it bit by bit but they might also respect French sovereignty, and withdraw once the fight against Chiang Kai-shek is at an end …'. With the support of Pétain and the Council of Ministers, Baudouin told Arsène Henry that the French Government was ready, on condition that Japan renewed the 1907 undertaking, to order the local military authorities to conclude a convention giving certain facilities to the Japanese army. He told Robert Murphy that the French attitude would have been 'a great deal firmer had we felt sure of real support from the United States'. Koo told him that Quo had seen Halifax but that the British could not act in the Far East. Baudouin suggested that the Chinese ambassador in Berlin might suggest that the Germans urge moderation on the Japanese.[193] On 27 August Matsuoka finally accepted the basis of the agreement Baudouin wanted.[194]

In the agreement finally made, registered in an exchange of letters between Arsène Henry and Matsuoka, the French Government recognised 'the supreme interests of Japan in the economic and political spheres in the Far East'. It expected assurances from Japan that it would 'respect the rights and interests of France in the Far East, particularly the territorial integrity of Indochina and the sovereignty of France over the entire area of the Indochinese Union'. Special military facilities would be available solely for the purpose of resolving the conflict with Chiang Kai-shek and along the Chinese border. The Japanese Government indicated that it had 'every intention' of respecting the rights and interests of France and the integrity of Indo-China, and accepted the proposal.[195] It was envisaged that the facilities would cover three air bases, the stationing of 5000–6000 troops and the right to transport troops for the China operations. So as to spare French dignity, these items were not included in the agreement, however. A military convention was to be negotiated in Hanoi.[196]

In Hanoi Nishihara, urged by Operations Division Chief Tominaga, pressed negotiations on Decoux even before he had received authority from Vichy.[197] He rejected the approach as an ultimatum,[198] and the Japanese agreed to negotiate. The outcome was the Nishihara–Martin agreement of 4 September, which barred Japanese movements into Indo-China until a definitive pact was signed. Then it envisaged the use of three air bases and it also limited the number of troops in Tonkin to a maximum of 25 000. Tominaga was restless and thought the French 'insincere'.[199] Indeed, Decoux was in no hurry to finalise the agreement, hoping still for American intervention.[200]

Up in Hanoi Henderson was able to report some of the events of this phase. He had been told by Decoux's 'righthand' man that Japanese officers had arrived, 'having taken for granted alleged statement by the French ambassador, Tokyo, that Indo-Chinese authorities were prepared to discuss passage of Japanese troops and munitions. This is denied here...'. They wanted the use of three aerodromes, introduction of 5000 troops to protect them, and the use of all railways. The Governor-General had refused and had asked Vichy for authority 'to resist by force as a moral obligation of the Colony'. Decoux had requested Henderson to inform the Foreign Office that he would adhere to the Singapore conclusions of 1939. The heads of the services had indicated their determination to fight. A conference of French leaders would be held the following day. 'I feel that the cross-roads have been reached ... Also that if the French face up to the Japanese the latter will not resort to force but they request at once British and American moral support ....'[201] The Japanese, Henderson reported later, had presented an ultimatum:

an attack would follow on the 5th if it were not accepted. General mobilisation had been ordered, and Decoux wanted diplomatic pressure on the Thais to refrain from military action.[202]

Bennett discussed the reports with Halifax. As a result telegrams were sent to Tokyo and Washington. Craigie was to ask if the reports were true: the British Government would find that difficult to believe in view of the declared attitude of the Japanese Government towards the status quo.[203] Lothian was to ask if the US Government would take 'corresponding' action,[204] and instructions were also sent to Sir Josiah Crosby in Bangkok.[205] A report that a long telegram had arrived from Vichy suggested that the Indo-China authorities might change their attitude.[206] Henderson was told that, if it would 'serve any useful purpose in stiffening resistance to Japanese', he could tell Decoux that Britain had taken the matter up with the Japanese, US and Thai governments.[207]

Late in August Hull had told the chargé at Vichy to inquire about the concessions reported to have been made and to say that they would create an 'unfavourable impression'.[208] Chauvel thought that the US already knew of the proposals. He read Matthews part of a telegram from Saint-Quentin reporting a conversation with Welles. Baudouin had suggested that the US should urge that, if Indo-China were occupied, the occupation should only be temporary. Welles had rejected this as 'quite inconsistent with our general policy of nonrecognition of the conquests of aggression …'.[209]

Now, as the Americans told the British, they were calling Japan's attention to its earlier statement of June on the status quo. Grew was to add 'that if the Japanese Government did take such action it would have a very bad effect on American public opinion'.[210] Matthews was told he might relay this to Vichy.[211] Ohashi, the Vice-Minister for Foreign Affairs, 'denied that he knew anything about an ultimatum', Grew reported from Tokyo. The passage of troops was a military necessity and implied no permanent occupation of French territory.[212]

Craigie also saw Ohashi. He said that discussions were proceeding in Indo-China and that he was 'unaware that anything in the nature of an ultimatum had been delivered. Certain proposals in regard to these matters had been made to the French Government but arrangements proposed were of purely provisional character.' Craigie said that even such provisional arrangements 'must definitely compromise neutrality of Indo-China and any attempt to force this acceptance upon the Government of Indo-China must necessarily have a bad effect on Anglo-Japanese relations – result which would be particularly unfortunate at a moment when prevailing ill feeling appeared to be abating …'.[213] The French ambassador in Tokyo, Grew told Craigie, had been discussing the question with the Japanese Government during the past few days.

Hearing of the alleged ultimatum, the French ambassador called on the Japanese Foreign Office. They were unaware of any such action and said the mission had been given no such instructions. The Vichy Government, Grew had been told, had agreed to give Japanese demands consideration, 'which was tantamount to an acceptance of the principle. French Ambassador was stated to hold the view that while as a matter of form diplomatic opposition would be offered to Japanese proposals, situation did not admit of any military resistance should demands be pressed.' Another source told one of Craigie's staff that no previous agreement had been made with the Germans. The source also stated that, as part of the agreement, the Japanese would guarantee the integrity of Indo-China for twelve months. Craigie concluded

> that Vichy Government and French Ambassador here would be prepared to enter into an agreement on this subject with the Japanese Government but that local authorities in Indo-China are of stouter heart and desire to make at least a show of resistance. It is greatly to be hoped that the procedure apparently favoured by the Government of Indo-China will prevail as our hand will therefore be strengthened in dealings with the Japanese Government, both now and when it comes later to securing the withdrawal of Japanese troops should they once enter Indo-China.[214]

The proposal for a guarantee was confirmed to Craigie by another source. 'I have the impression that Japanese are not alarmed by the possibility of Chinese counter-invasion since this would largely depend on the highly vulnerable Yunnan railway ....'[215]

Quo had alluded to this in a conversation with Halifax. The response was affected by a Cabinet meeting, which had discussed the question of reopening the Burma Road. The successful termination of the Battle of Britain might lead to a decision to do so, and the possibility should be left open, Halifax argued. But it was suggested that the Indo-China situation had overtaken the Burma Road situation. If Japan occupied Indo-China, this would bring Burma under threat from the air. Would aggression in Indo-China make Japan weaker or stronger? If Indo-China put up a good resistance the Japanese might 'become considerably involved, and *pro tanto* discouraged from further adventure'. Economic inducements might keep Japan on the path of virtue, Halifax thought. Could the United States be persuaded to take any action? it was asked. 'A great moral effect' would be produced if Roosevelt sent a cruiser squadron to Singapore 'on a ceremonial visit'. Churchill concluded that a successful end to the Battle of Britain would enhance Britain's prestige but would not materially affect the military position vis-à-vis Japan. 'A war with Japan would fundamentally affect our strategy in the Middle East. The right course was to go some way in offering inducements to Japan, and possibly also to go some way in using threats, but not to commit ourselves irrevocably to forcible action …'. The Foreign Secretary was to sound out the US Government and the Chiefs of Staff to assess the impact on Japan of hostilities in Indo-China.[216]

Quo called on Halifax the same day. He congratulated the British Government on its destroyer deal with the US, 'the significance of which he felt sure would not be lost on Japan amongst other countries'. He then reported that Indo-China was determined to resist Japanese demands and had asked China to consult on joint defence. Apparently it was acting contrary to instructions from Vichy. He asked what policy Britain would adopt towards such joint resistance and what aid it would afford. Halifax said there would be great difficulty in finding supplies for Indo-China, as for China. But the British were ascertaining the attitude of the American Government, 'which might be of great importance. There might well be an element of bluff in the Japanese attitude and if Indo-China resisted and the Chinese sent assistance the affair might become a larger proposition than the Japanese would be prepared to tackle.' Quo agreed. The Japanese had recently withdrawn from Kwangsi, which suggested that they could not reinforce themselves in the interior of China. If the US, backed by Britain, adopted a 'stiff attitude' and warned that economic action against Japan might follow any Japanese action affecting the status quo of Indo-China, the Japanese 'would hesitate not once or twice but thrice'. The Gaimusho denial of Nishihara's ultimatum suggested a 'hesitant mood', enhanced by Britain's success in the Battle of Britain, while the US had its fleet in Pacific. Quo thought conditions might soon be favourable for opening the Burma Road.[217]

Dening noted Quo's report that Decoux was acting against Vichy's instructions to give way. 'If this is true, it is interesting but not necessarily fatal, for if Admiral Decoux does not openly repudiate Vichy, it seems possible that Vichy might equally well not repudiate him.' If Vichy did repudiate him, or he Vichy, 'then there is nothing we can do, and we shall have to face up to any situation which develops in consequence as best we can …'.[218]

From Hanoi Henderson reported on the making of the Nishihara–Martin agreement and the subsequent attempts to implement it, interrupted by a border violation prompted by restless elements in the South China Army.[219] Decoux had shown him the ultimatum. 'Following morning the Japanese were prepared to discuss the position and the French are now presenting their terms. Agreement reached in Vichy and Tokyo is being followed in principle by the Governor-General although there is much opposition ….' Martin said the proposition was to allow 28 000 troops use of the railway, two-thirds of the number of French troops in

Tonkin. 'General intends to prolong the negotiations and make terms difficult as possible but he fears that the Japanese will accept ... Public opinion and services are in favour of resisting the Japanese and there is talk that the Governor-General may resign.'[220] On the 7th Henderson reported that the negotiations had been broken off, following a violation of French territory.[221] This involved, he said, Japanese planes flying over Langson and two companies of infantry crossing the frontier in war formation. Decoux seized the opportunity to break off relations. 'The French services and public will be pleased ...'. Nishihara expressed regret and made excuses. 'He is being pressed by aggressive military officers ...'. Decoux had referred the whole question to Vichy.

> Stated that his action together with American and British diplomatic pressure deterred any Japanese military action in the Far East outside China. He particularly asked that British propaganda should not attempt to disunite French in Indo-China by suggesting allegiance with General de Gaulle ... He evidently fears a split but I am of opinion that he will gain the support of all the French and native communities by this resistance to the Japanese who have made two mistakes which have given him an unexpected opportunity to retain his post: Firstly, ultimatum, second, military action yesterday.[222]

Reports came from Chungking, too, deriving from the Chinese ConsulGeneral at Hanoi. Negotiations were resumed after rejection of the ultimatum, which gave the Japanese 'something of a jolt', but they were 'still bent upon attaining their demands, if possible without a clash of arms'.[223] Kerr also reported a discussion with the Chinese Foreign Minister, which gave another view of Franco-Japanese relations. Laval had told Koo that the French Government had at the end of August agreed in principle to the establishment of naval, military and air bases, free use of the railway and passage of Japanese troops through Tonkin. It had rejected the right to exercise the prerogatives of an army of occupation. 'M. Laval had said that it was their intention then to spin out discussions on matters of detail as long as possible ....' Decoux refused to carry out the instructions and said he would rather resign. Then he received the Japanese ultimatum. He asked the Chinese Consul-General what help he might receive.[224] Washington learned of the agreement from Vichy. Japan was to recognise the French title to Indo-China, while France recognised Japan's special economic interests. Economic and military agreements were appended. The Japanese wanted to pass large forces through Indo-China, and the French wanted to limit them.[225]

> It seems [wrote Bennett] that the local Japanese military in Indo-China have overreached themselves and it is submitted that now is the moment for further representations from us and from the US. I do not think we ought to allow

ourselves to be fobbed off by the reply of the Vice-Minister ... a definite ultimatum was presented. Furthermore, the Indo-China frontier has been violated by the Japanese and if we pass by these latest developments without further representations the Japanese will be apt to take silence for consent.

Seymour did not think representations would have much effect, but they might be worth trying, 'rather from the point of view of the US than from any real results that we are likely to obtain'. 'I agree', wrote Cadogan. 'The US Government seem to have faith in words, and will like to see us doing this. It won't have much other effect.'[226] Bennett drafted a telegram to Craigie that indicated that the British were 'gravely disquieted' by news of an ultimatum, presented presumably without the approval of the Japanese Government. A sentence cut from the final version alluded to the negotiations discussed by Ohashi: apparently they affected the status and integrity of Indo-China.

It was 'difficult to escape the impression', the telegram continued, that advantage was being taken of the difficulties in which France and Indo-China found themselves 'to put pressure on them to agree to measures of profound political and strategic importance, affecting not only Indo-China and China proper, but all countries which have interests in the Far East'. Insofar as they were designed to facilitate a new attack on China they seemed inconsistent with the spirit of the Burma Road agreement 'since it would be cynical to assert that a new offensive can be regarded as a sincere effort to conclude a just and equitable peace'. Craigie should consult Grew before taking action since the US Government was being asked if it would make further representations.[227]

Craigie doubted if any action would be useful otherwise than in support of an American step. 'Important thing is that effort of Japanese extremists to rush Japanese Government into violent measures has failed ...'. In particular he deprecated a reference to the Burma Road agreement, which the Japanese could say did not preclude their prosecuting the war.[228] Bennett could not understand Craigie's attitude. 'It seems to me important that the Japanese should be left in no doubt about our views whatever their attitude may be ...'.[229] An instruction went to Craigie accordingly, although a phrase indicating that it was part of the policy of retaining maximum freedom of action over the Burma Road was cut.[230]

In his conversation Craigie nevertheless omitted all reference to the Burma Road. Matsuoka 'rejected with some indignation the suggestion that advantage was being taken of difficulties in which France and Indo-China found themselves ...'. The Japanese Government had reached an agreement with Vichy 'by process of friendly negotiations', and it was the settlement of details, left to authorities on the spot, which had given rise to the difficulty, the Governor-General 'being apparently unwilling to carry out not only instructions but also terms of a definite agreement entered into by his home Government'. He still hoped the matter would be 'satisfactorily settled', but the Japanese Government might have to take 'some effective steps' if Indo-Chinese authorities continued to flout the instructions of their own government. Although he had not intended to take the initiative, the Foreign Minister now wished to state that the Governor-General was in contact with British, American and Chinese consular representatives, 'all of whom were encouraging him in his policy of procrastination'. This Matsuoka thought 'very regrettable' as it amounted to encouraging local authorities to refuse to honour an agreement to which the Japanese Government was a party.

Craigie said he was sure the British Consul-General was not advising the Indo-China authorities to flout instructions from their own government. He was not aware of the terms of the agreement, but it appeared that they were likely to bring about a modification of the status quo to which the minister's predecessor had recently pledged himself and might profoundly affect British interests. 'It therefore seemed to me only natural that British consular officers should express their disapproval of any such demands if their opinion were invited.'

The minister said no change of the status quo was contemplated; the Japanese Government had guaranteed the integrity of Indo-China. He could not see that Britain could complain if the French Government afforded facilities for the struggle against Chiang Kai-shek for the duration of hostilities. He 'emphatically denied any British interest was affected or that there was any question of modifying the status quo ...'. 'Disingenuous', Gage observed.[231]

Hull had told the chargé in Vichy to express his 'surprise' on 'learning of the measure of assent on the part of the French Government that had been permitted to develop'. There was 'little if any warrant for entering into agreements which give affirmative assent to a derogation of principles'. The US Government deprecated 'the giving of a recognition by the French Government to a claim of a Japanese preponderance of interest and a privileged economic position in Indochina'. US interest in the maintenance of the status quo there 'arises out of and is a part of the general policy which this Government endeavours constantly and consistently to pursue of respect for the *status quo* except as changes may be and are brought about through orderly processes with due consideration for the rights and legitimate interests of all concerned ...'.[232] Hull said the same thing to Henry-Haye, the Vichy ambassador. The US Government 'had contested in every way short of military activities every inch of the Japanese movement of aggression', while the French had 'freely conceded to Japan superior influence and control in the Pacific area', without giving notice to the US.[233] Baudouin rebuffed this assertion. Statements of principle had not prevented the Japanese occupation of Manchuria or the development of the war in China. The French Government, unable to secure any naval support or war matériel, adopted 'the only line of conduct which took into consideration the factual situation with which it was faced'.[234]

The US put its faith, as Cadogan said, in words. Hornbeck had endorsed Henderson's view that the Japanese would not resort to force if the French authorities took a firm line; it was a pity, he had said, that they had not made this plainer sooner.[235] Replying to press inquiries Hull recalled the desire of the US Government that the status quo should be preserved, especially in Netherlands India and French Indo-China. The US was reluctant to credit reports of an ultimatum. 'It stands to reason that should events prove these reports to have been well founded, effect on public opinion in United States would be unfortunate.' 'Satisfactory as far as it goes,' Gage commented.[236] The effect of words was doubtful. Grew gave Craigie what Gage called Ohashi's 'rather stiff' reply to the American representations of early August. Japan, he said, was negotiating with Indo-China because of the need to construct a new order; it had no territorial ambition and would endeavour to avoid changes in the status quo as long as that did not interfere with the main objective. Old standards did not apply in a rapidly changing world. Japan had so far refrained from commenting on changes in the status quo in Europe. 'The effect of intrusion of the United States in an area so remote from that country as the Far East on Japanese public opinion is the same as that of the United States if some meddlesome third country intruded opinions on Western hemisphere affairs.'[237] The Japanese were certainly returning strong words for words; it was 'symptomatic of a new attitude to the USA', Clarke thought.[238]

Grew made an oral statement in reply, affected also by information of Craigie's approach.[239] The status quo was affected by the insistence on a right to send troops through and use aerodromes. There appeared to be an inconsistency between the stipulations being made on the authorities in Indo-China by the Japanese Government and its announced desire to maintain the status quo. The American Government urged on all governments 'employment of none but peaceful means in their relations with all other Governments and regions'. The attitude of the United States Government towards 'the unwarranted use of pressure in international relations is global'.[240] Reports of a threat to invade on 22 September, unless Hanoi, Haiphong and five airports could be occupied, prompted Hull to tell Grew to express 'great surprise', especially in view of the pledge to preserve the status quo in the Pacific area.[241] Grew found Matsuoka's replies 'illogical'.[242]

In London some further consideration was given to more than verbal support. Quo had called on Butler on 5 September with a telegram from Koo, who had been asked by Vichy if the British Government could assist French resistance in Indo-China in two ways. One related to the safe passage of two merchant ships to Djibouti; they would take rice and might bring back troops. Second, Vichy wanted help to transfer aircraft from the *Béarn* in Martinique to Indo-China. Quo said Decoux was consulting the Chinese, and he thought that French resistance was strengthening. Britain wanted 'to stiffen resistance in Indo-China' if it could, Halifax noted, but he did not know what difficulties these requests would cause.[243]

Bennett tried to disentangle the position from the reports so far received: an agreement between Vichy and Tokyo; an ultimatum; rejection on the basis of ignorance of the agreement; Decoux's learning of the agreement but still playing for time; the Japanese withdrawal of the ultimatum, because of resistance from the local authorities or interest shown by the US and Britain; negotiations continuing. 'We do not know whether the continuance of negotiations is mere face-saving on the part of the Japanese or whether ... they are waiting for a more favourable opportunity to make a fresh spring.' There was no guarantee that the requests Butler had received came from a French source. 'If we had them direct from Admiral Decoux we might consider them without a *quid pro quo*. But if we oblige the Vichy Government the question arises whether we should do so on conditions and to what extent we should inform General de Gaulle of what is happening...'. William Strang thought Vichy should make the request through Madrid or Washington. If it did, the Foreign Office would have to 'square the M[inistry of] E[conomic] W[arfare] about turning a blind eye to the Djibouti operation'. The aircraft on the *Béarn* were en route from the USA to France when France collapsed; the carrier was to be decommissioned; the aircraft were said to be rotting on the hillside. 'We badly want to get them ourselves, but the suggestion that they should be taken back to the United States and reconsigned to us has not borne fruit.' Any proposal to send them to Indo-China would have to be discussed with Washington. The matter was referred to the Committee on Foreign (Allied) Resistance, just as a direct request for the Djibouti troops came from Decoux.[244]

Various points were made in the committee's discussion. It was 'particularly desirable' that Indo-China should resist the Japanese if possible, and it was not desirable to refuse the requests from the 'relatively friendly' Decoux and the Chinese ambassador. 'There also seemed advantage from the point of view of our relations with the Vichy Government of at any rate giving the appearance of readiness to accede to these requests.' Four thousand Senegalese troops from Djibouti were, however, unlikely to make much difference, and the aircraft were unsuitable for the defence of Indo-China; 'all bombers and many of them ... never ... assembled. It was moreover most unlikely that these additions to French strength in Indo-China could arrive for a considerable time and it was moreover possible that the Japanese would prevent their arrival altogether.' The committee recommended no action over the aircraft since no direct request had been received. But it suggested that Decoux should be told that there was no objection to his sending two ships to Djibouti.[245] Henderson was telegraphed on 14 September that the passage of two ships would not be impeded, subject to contraband control at Aden.[246]

A telegram from him, dated the 6th, relaying a request for support for a French mission buying aircraft in the US,[247] and the decision over the *Béarn* planes, led also to a telegram to Lothian; the British Government was 'not in a position themselves to become directly involved or to assist with aircraft or munitions in present circumstances ...'. Was the US Government in such a position?[248] The telegram, urged by C.E. Whitamore on the ground that the Hanoi authorities wanted to resist Japanese aggression,[249] alluded to another suggestion made by Henderson on 7 September, that American army planes in the Philippines might be passed to the French, the Philippines then being supplied with types ordered by France in the US.[250]

Captain Duncan reported on 13 September that Vichy had ordered acceptance of the Japanese demands, and negotiations were continuing. General Martin thought the key was the arrival of fighter planes, 'even if only a few as a gesture'. Perhaps from Manila? 'Any action must be quick to save situation. General's attitude today is one of desperation but unwilling to cede anything to the Japanese ...'.[251] This was also referred to Lothian.[252] Henderson had noted that Decoux was 'hurt' that the Moths had not been released and asked 'how we can reconcile this action with our hope that he will resist Japanese demands'. Bennett favoured their release, and Seymour agreed, 'on the general principle of encouraging the French bluff, for I can't believe it is much more or that they could put up any resistance which would matter much to the Japanese'.[253]

There was thus rather more support from London than Decoux admits in his memoirs. Even in the Foreign Office there was doubt that it would be of any significance. At most it would encourage French bluff, French playing for time. But that was of no value if the US did not intervene. That, Decoux later indicated, was what he was waiting for.[254] He was not likely to get it. The US indeed doubted whether it should respond to the requests the British had passed on. Hull said the administration was trying to collect aeroplanes to send to Indo-China to justify its resistance. The difficulty however was to know what the real policy of France was. If aeroplanes were sent who[m] would they help? Was there a secret agreement between Vichy, the Germans and Japan? He had spoken most strongly to the new French Ambassador in this sense last week saying that if France valued American goodwill it must not become anti-British or [group undeciphered] as to Hitler or connive at Japanese aggression.[255]

Roosevelt's adviser, Alfred Berle, told the Counsellor at the British Embassy in Washington, however, that Washington believed that Decoux, while 'keeping in' with Vichy, was 'disposed to resist Japanese encroachment, partly in view of the strong local desire in that sense', and it wanted to support him. Aircraft could not be spared from the Philippines, but perhaps the Australians could supply fifteen to twenty oldish British machines to be replaced as soon as possible from American stocks. 'These would supply what Mr Berle believed that French Indo-China most needed, that was some moral support given promptly.' The Counsellor doubted that Australia would take action that Japan would see as unfriendly.[256] Berle asked Casey if Australia could supply fifteen or twenty. He thought this might 'tip the balance' and lead Indo-China to resist the Japanese. Casey thought it was 'too late'.[257] A report from Duncan that Nishihara had broken off negotiations led to a further request. 'It is considered this is not bluff this time. Is there any hope of planes immediately to oppose air attack if in our mutual interest?'[258] This was sent on to Lothian.[259]

The crisis was indeed at hand. The Foreign Office had gained the impression that Decoux was resisting Japanese pressure. It was, as earlier, inclined to discount contrary reports coming from Chinese sources. Quo had had another interview with Butler on the 13th, the object being no doubt to gain some commitment from the British; a vain one, of course. His information was that Decoux had agreed to allow 30 000 troops to land at Haiphong, but he was told that the British had no official confirmation of such a report.[260] In Hanoi the Chinese Consul-General again warned Decoux that the Chinese army would take action if France allowed the passage of Japanese troops.[261] The Chinese were apparently referring to the agreement of 4 September. Its implementation had in fact been suspended after the incident of 6–7 September and while the Tokyo and Vichy governments differed over the terms of their communiqué.[262] But now the Japanese Government, as Decoux puts it, lost patience. Indeed Craigie reported from 'a reliable official source' that Japan would act very soon not only because of the approaching expiry of the Burma Road agreement 'but also because of the danger that Germany may definitely make up her mind to warn Japanese off'.[263]

Although in the context of the Tripartite Pact soon to be announced the latter argument was faulty, the report itself was correct. The Tokyo government had agreed on 14 September to introduce troops into Indo-China on the 22nd, whether or not agreement had been reached, and, as Grew told Craigie, Matsuoka admitted that it had approved an ultimatum.[264] Tominaga reopened negotiations in Hanoi by demanding the stationing of 25 000 troops, the use of five aerodromes and the inclusion of Hanoi and Haiphong in the stationing area. This went beyond his instructions and, despite the operations staff and other extremists, Japan made some concessions. The agreement, finally signed by Nishihara on the 22nd, covered the stationing of 6000 troops, the transit of 25 000 and the use of four airbases. But major incidents were still to occur, both on the border and at Haiphong. They could have been avoided despite the fact that the agreement was signed only shortly before the deadline. The reason for them lies in the attitude of Tominaga, the Operations Division and the armies in South China.[265]

Henderson had tried to report the course of these events. On 17 September, he telegraphed, an agreement had been signed for the transit of 25 000 troops. The next morning, however, the demands were increased, and they had been refused. The French, said Henderson, now believed that the Japanese aim was to occupy Tonkin and to set up puppet states in Annam and Cambodia. The army would resist, but Hanoi and Haiphong could be bombed.[266] On the 21st he reported a new draft agreement, again aborted by the Japanese.[267] The following day he reported an agreement covering the use of Hanoi and two other aerodromes with 6000 troops to guard them. 'There must be conditions other than the use of these aerodromes', Whitamore commented.[268]

On the 23rd Henderson reported a Japanese attack on Langson. The agreement was suspended, but it was thought that hostilities would soon cease and that the undertaking over aerodromes eventually be carried out.[269] The following day Henderson reported further hostilities at Langson.[270] The French agreed to allow some troops to land at Haiphong, he telegraphed on 25 September, but doubted whether this would stop the Langson advance.[271] No heavy fighting had taken place for twenty-four hours, he later added. 'Tokyo ordered troops to cease attacking last night but they are filtering through on a frontier of 50 miles, concentrating on Langson which is practically surrounded.' The French had been ordered not to fire on them. Troopships were off Haiphong. 'Opinion is growing that Japanese will be allowed to enter peacefully.'[272] Some Japanese planes dropped bombs on Haiphong on the 26th, the Vice-Consul reported. But later tanks moved in peacefully, 'therefore I conclude that as far as Haiphong is concerned this morning's incident is to be overlooked'.[273]

The main issue in Hanoi, as Decoux makes clear, was the fear of an effective Japanese occupation. A central issue in the negotiations, therefore, was the number and disposition of the troops that the Japanese wished to introduce. Decoux tried to ensure that the army sent to attack the Chinese, or any sections of the South China Army being evacuated, were to be in Indo-China only transitorily. On this basis he made the agreement of 22 September and agreed with Martin that it must be upheld. The Japanese nevertheless infiltrated, and clashes ensued.[274] Some of them indeed wanted to occupy Indo-China, and there was a risk that this would be the outcome. These were, as Decoux puts it, days of drama and farce.[275] The events were certainly hard for the Foreign Office to follow, despite Henderson's reports.

'It is all still very obscure', Gage exclaimed on 21 September.[276] On the 24th Henderson was asked for the fullest possible authentic information on the Franco-Japanese agreement. 'Can you ascertain exactly what rights and privileges, economic as well as military, Japanese have obtained and subject to what conditions; what obligations French have undertaken; and in particular whether agreement includes any Japanese guarantee of integrity of Indo-China?'[277] Decoux's chief of staff told Henderson that the conditions of the agreement related only to landing 6000 troops at Haiphong to protect aerodromes and to the passage of troops towards Langson. The Japanese undertook to respect the sovereignty and integrity of Indo-China. Henderson had asked for a definition of this. Economic negotiations had been suspended but would no doubt be renewed with increased pressure now that Japanese troops had arrived. Henderson suspected a far-reaching Vichy–Tokyo agreement but thought he was not likely to be told of it. He could not yet describe the Governor-General as anti-British, but some leading civil servants were not pro-British, and Dakar was mentioned at each interview. French troops at Langson, forbidden to resist, had been captured. At Haiphong some 10 000 Japanese troops had been disembarked.[278]

A rather more accurate statement came from Bangkok whence Crosby reported a telegram the French minister had received from Decoux. The Vichy–Tokyo agreement dealt only in principle with the right to send troops. Details were to be settled at Hanoi, and agreement was reached on the 22nd on three aerodromes and 6000 troops. The army at Kwangsi then made additional demands over the passage of troops, the establishing of the general staff at Hanoi and the setting up of a military hospital. Decoux agreed, but no more than 25 000 Japanese were to be in Indo-China at one time. The Kwangsi army refused to accept the compromise and began an offensive. The Tokyo government then intervened.[279] The Foreign Office concluded that the Japanese were on the way to control of Indo-China. Dakar – the unsuccessful attempt by

British and Gaullist forces to seize that French West African city[280] – 'has not helped our relations with Admiral Decoux', Clarke thought. 'I don't know that the precise terms of the agreement make much odds', Seymour commented. 'The Japanese have entered Indo-China and the question whether they will ever leave will not be decided by paper promises.'[281]

An official announcement from Vichy did 'not elucidate the situation very much', as Whitamore put it. The communiqué repeated Japan's assurance that it would respect French rights in the Far East, the territorial integrity of Indo-China and the sovereign rights of France over it while seeking special facilities for the implementation of military and naval operations. The French Government did, however, state that its negotiations with Japan had been with a view to the creation of a new order and the solution of the affairs of China. Gage found this open endorsement of Japanese aims 'deplorable'. Dening agreed. 'But the French were pusillanimous to a degree even before Germany attacked, and it is therefore not surprising that a Government of so few principles should descend to such depths.'[282] In Tokyo the French ambassador told the government he had been let down: the Japanese announcement omitted the guarantee of integrity, declaring that the frontier clash had altered the situation. Craigie noted that France was prepared to contribute to the establishment of the new order. 'While the French acceptance of the agreement may be presumed to have been primarily due to defeatist sentiment prevailing at Vichy and in the French Embassy here, I cannot help feeling that there is also some understanding with Germany and that the French desire to embarrass us has played its part in this discreditable transaction.'[283] In fact Baudouin had sought German help in moderating Japan's demands in vain.[284]

The French military attaché in Tokyo gave his British counterpart a fuller account on returning from Indo-China, one hardly in accordance with the bland account given by the Japanese.[285] The agreement, he said, included respect for territorial integrity, and the agreed concessions covered only very small numbers of troops. The French authorities were determined to resist with force any attempt to widen the scope of the agreement, and the fighting was due to the Japanese army authorities in South China who broke its terms by entering Indo-China across the northern frontier. They had been told that they could cross the border if the agreement were not signed by 22 October. They were told it had been, but they still advanced. The Governor-General refused to ratify the agreement. The Japanese pleaded inability to control the troops. But Prince Kanin, Chief of the General Staff, secured an imperial mandate telling them to withdraw. The attaché was confident that they would withdraw and that the agreement would be carried out. He insisted that the Indo-China authorities would fight any extension of it. Martin kept Decoux, 'very anti-British', up to the mark. The attaché was 'too optimistic about Japanese good faith', Gage thought. 'It is interesting, if true', Bennett commented, 'that the French authorities in Indo-China still intend to fight against the extension of the Agreement. I fear they have not much chance, but we must watch for signs of further resistance and not take any unnecessary action to discourage them.'[286]

Despite Vichy's attitude, and the Japanese agreement, the Foreign Office thus favoured doing what it could to preserve the remnant of the status quo. There had indeed been second thoughts about the troops at Djibouti. The War Office preferred them to stay there and thought they would be of little use in Indo-China.[287] The whole thing, Catroux thought, was 'a device on the part of the Vichy authorities to get the troops out of French Somaliland on any excuse'.[288] Morton pointed out that the only assurance had been that French ships could go to Djibouti.[289] Bennett thought this a 'Machiavellian line'. But he agreed that further action should be held up when he heard of the breaking off of the negotiations. By 23 September, as Seymour put it, the whole proposal was 'washed out'.[290] The decision on the Tiger Moths remained, however.[291] The French still had 'some fight' left in them, Bennett wrote.[292]

Asked the reason for the delay between the agreement of 30 August and its implementation, the Japanese had blamed it on hostile third powers.[293] Besides the British and the Americans, these powers presumably included the Chinese. As well as warning Hanoi about possible intervention, and trying to elicit British and American help, they had also approached Vichy direct and had asked for the right to introduce their troops when Japanese troops landed and for the same facilities as afforded the Japanese. They had secured vague responses.[294] After the ultimatum Kerr reported that the Chinese Government was angry at the paucity of information it had received. Decoux now stated that he could not grant the Chinese right of entry without instruction from Vichy, which was 'making difficulties'. China had made military arrangements. What was Britain's attitude? Would it take concerted action with China and the US? Kerr told the Foreign Minister 'that it is idle to expect His Majesty's Government, with their present preoccupations at home, to take any effective action. But I gather that in spite of all that has been said, the Chinese still cling to the hope that circumstances will soon drive us into military co-operation with them ...'. 'There is ... the danger of driving China to make some kind of terms with Japan if we do not give her some fairly substantial comfort,' Whitamore noted. 'The US attitude towards Japan is getting stiffer.' Telling the Chinese the Burma Road would be reopened would be 'a concrete measure of support and encouragement equivalent and complementary to the American embargo on scrap iron to Japan and loan for China ...'. Bennett favoured a prompt opening of the road: 'any appearance of weakness and hesitation is more than ever to be avoided'.[295]

Craigie delivered a verbal protest in relation to the content of his earlier interview with the Foreign Minister: the agreement had not been freely negotiated, and the status quo had been changed. Burma, he added, was contiguous. That gave Britain an interest in the matter, and the government was giving the matter 'careful consideration'.[296] The US was becoming 'stiffer'. On 20 September Welles had rejected the Japanese Ambassador's suggestion that there was a parallel between Japan's action in Indo-China and the destroyers-for-bases deal, and indicated that the US might assist victims of aggression in the East as in Europe.[297] On 23 September Hull had repeated disapproval of changes of the status quo by duress and the following day stressed that Washington had not approved French concessions to Japan.[298] In a speech at Cleveland Welles reasserted the principles behind US policy: 'there is no problem presented which could not be peacefully solved through negotiation, provided there existed a sincere desire on the part of all concerned to find an equitable and a fair solution ...'.[299] The economic moves, more than mere words, did not prevent the announcement of the Tripartite Pact, designed in part to resolve any differences between Germany and Japan over the colonies but also to confront the US. Matsuoka had indeed hoped to defer the ultimatum to Indo-China because he thought the pact, forestalling American intervention, would lead the French to give in anyway. The military had determined otherwise.[300] The British decided to open the Burma Road. The Chinese decided to wait and see.[301] In fact the Japanese did leave Langson.[302]

The Cabinet on 4 September had asked the Chiefs of Staff to assess the impact on Japan of hostilities in Indo-China. The conclusion was the sombre one that the Japanese could subjugate all Indo-China and Yunnan and still be in a position to threaten Singapore. There would be little effective resistance; the Chinese might limit themselves to guerrilla action; and the population was 'largely disaffected towards the French'.[303] Halifax concluded: 'Not much encouragement for a robust policy here!' Bennett differed: 'the danger which Japanese penetration of Indo-China represents to us calls for as robust a policy as possible in encouraging resistance in Indo-China. If the Japanese enter Indo-China it is, I suggest, to our interest that they should be tied up there as much as possible since the difficulties of maintenance may increase with time ...'. Japan would gain economic benefits and would be working its way 'still further round our flank at Singapore'. Threats could not be employed, but 'our subsequent reaction ought to be as strong as possible and ... the danger justified some degree of risk ...'. The US, said Seymour, had the key to the position.[304]

A memorandum prepared in the Foreign Office on the action taken by the US and British governments to preserve the status quo in Indo-China was described in October as 'now only of historical interest'.[305] The endeavours had certainly been in vain. The Japanese had taken a decisive step, even though the extremists had not provoked the actual occupation that, as the British Chiefs of Staff saw, was fully within their capacity. In the next phase they preferred the pact diplomacy of Konoe. The US still believed that they would not resort to open attack. The British continued their attempts to uphold the status quo in East Asia, trying to encourage the Chinese without provoking the Japanese, trying to prompt the Americans to interpose, trying to sustain opposition in Indo-China. There they relied on the determination of the French to avoid a break in their colonial rule. That, it was clear, could lead to compromise, and it was to do so again in 1941. But it is hard to say that the determination of the French to retain their empire cost other colonial powers theirs. The Japanese, as the Chiefs of Staff saw, could have taken it easily. And it is far from certain that the US would have intervened.

The events in French Indo-China certainly marked a severe deterioration in the security of Malaya and the Indies, however. The reaction of the US was insufficiently complete or persistent to make up for it. The Thais, it seemed certain, would not resist Japanese pressure.

The Thai reaction

Sir Josiah Crosby, the British ambassador to Thailand, had suggested that the Thais had qualms about Japan's emergence as a regional power; they would prefer a balance between Japan and the colonial powers. They also had aspirations, however. Those might be achieved by accommodating to the regional power, which it would in any case be difficult to resist. If the primacy of Japan replaced that of Britain some of the territorial concessions made in the nineteenth century might also be undone. 'Thai Government is evidently scared to death of Japan and is at the same time anxious to have its share of the pickings if Indo China is to be dismembered. As I see it we must wait until we have won the war before we can strengthen our position in this part of the world...'.[306] 'The closing of the Burma Road has set a bad example', Ashley Clarke commented.[307]

In July the options for Pibun and his colleagues were yet obscure. Would Japan take over in Indo-China? Would it displace the French? How should Thailand pursue its interests? How indeed should it define them? Other Thais saw the collapse of the French as a golden opportunity for Thailand to regain the lost territories, and that impulse could not be ignored. Pibun's diplomacy was to be 'devious and thoroughly pragmatic'.[308]

Not surprisingly, Vichy was anxious to ratify the non-aggression treaty. But work on adjusting the Mekong frontier could not start until November when the rainy season ended.[309] Nor, the French indicated, could they send a high official out from Vichy; the minister in Bangkok would chair the negotiating party, including officials from Indo-China.[310] Direck told Crosby that future conditions in Indo-China were uncertain, 'and he thought the Thai Government would be well advised to postpone ratification until the proposals as to a new frontier had been carried into effect'.[311]

Early in August Pibun told Crosby that he wanted negotiations on the cession of all the right-bank territory to be associated with those over the promised surrender to Thailand of the islets on the river in connection with the non-aggression treaty. He thought that France would not agree, and in that case the treaty was unlikely to be ratified. He said 'that there was no point in the Treaty in view of the downfall of France unless Thailand was to have an adequate *quid pro quo*. He said also that if Japan was going to seize greater part of Indo-China, it would be safer to have her on the other side of Mekong.'[312] Prince Wan said the demands were less substantial: part of Laos ceded in 1904, and a triangle of territory ceded in 1907 based on a line drawn from Pakse westwards to the current frontier. Missions sent to Japan and Europe had these objectives in mind.[313] The Foreign Office did not oppose the claims as such. It told Crosby to emphasise that any change in the status quo at the present juncture was 'most untimely as it would give Japan excuse to demand more far-reaching concessions for herself'. The mission to Japan to secure its agreement would be 'prejudicial to Thai interests since the obligation under which Thailand would be placed would eventually be used as a lever to reduce that country to a state of complete subservience to Japan'.[314]

It turned out that the claims were more extensive than Prince Wan had said. Direck, the Deputy Foreign Minister, told Crosby that the mission to Japan would raise the question of Thai claims in case France had to relinquish Indo-China altogether. He was seeking the reactions of the UK and the US. 'Thailand would wish to recover all of the territory that she had at any time ceded to France, and she would wish to get the whole of Cambodia.' Crosby indicated that the UK was against disturbing the status quo, and it would consider the discussion 'premature'. Direck feared that Japan was about to seize Indo-China 'and it was imperative that they should enter their claim before it was too late'. The price,

Crosby responded, might involve becoming 'in practice a vassal of Japan'.[315] Gage thought Crosby 'a little too considerate to the Thais': put the pressure on, in view of British success in the air and Indo-China's resistance to the Japanese. Clarke preferred to stress the damage to Thai interests.[316] Crosby spoke to Pibun accordingly.

> As I see things the Thai Government can do no more than wait upon events. If the Japanese do not occupy Indo-China and if the French remain in full possession there the larger issue of the Thai territorial claims should lapse, though the Prime Minister ... is trying to get what he can out of the French as a condition of ratifying the treaty of non-aggression with them ....[317]

Crosby meanwhile put through the British ratification, just received.[318]

Pibun had been endeavouring to sound out the Japanese. Vanich Pananond, director of the Thai Rice Company, had gone to Tokyo at the end of July, ostensibly to discuss the export of Thai rice.[319] His brother-in-law, Admiral Sindhu, secretly visiting the legation in Bangkok, suggested that the goodwill mission also arranged could discuss military cooperation if Thailand's territorial interests were taken into account. This was the origin of the mission of Prom Yothi, the Deputy Minister of Defence. Officers of the War Ministry and army General Staff in Tokyo, meeting on 7 August, responded positively to the opportunity Thai irredentism appeared to provide. Eight additional officers were to join the Japanese military attaché in Bangkok.[320] Recalled for consultation, Tamura Hiroshi, the attaché, urged support for irredentism. But, he warned, even the pro-Japanese faction was wary about a Japanese advance.[321]

Prom visited Indo-China en route for Japan. His mission reached Hanoi on 4 September. Decoux was trying to prevent the Japanese moving troops into Tonkin in force. He had little time for Prom. In any case he mistrusted the Thais and thought they were colluding with the Japanese, 'an impression which Prom Yothi's visit', as Stowe puts it, 'did nothing to dispel'.[322] The Governor-General did not take Prom seriously when he suggested that Thailand would cooperate with France if the two Lao provinces on the west bank were transferred.[323]

Lothian had been told to seek the support of the US in bringing pressure to bear on Thailand if necessary.[324] Welles said that the US had already taken action.[325] He had in fact told Howard Grant, the American minister to Bangkok, that problems should be adjusted by peaceful negotiations and agreement and recalled the statement of 1937.[326] Direck told Crosby the US had referred to that statement.[327]

Grant thought that the Thai leaders were determined to regain the 'lost provinces' if the status quo in Indo-China were changed 'unless a very heavy restraining hand' were applied by Britain and the US. Crosby had urged restraint and hoped the US would too.[328] He was told 'discreetly' to exercise 'his influence' in the direction of discouraging action by the Thai Government that, if taken, might tend to complicate the already disturbed situation in Southeast Asia.[329] On 11 September the ambassador in Washington, Seni Pramoj, was counselled against the sending of Thai troops into Indo-China.[330]

Vichy had seen the agreement of 30 August as a restraint on the Thais as well as the Japanese[331] and hoped that the Japanese would uphold Indo-China's integrity against Thailand. Lépissier handed over a list of members of the French negotiating party on 10 September,[332] and he asked that the non-aggression pact should come into operation promptly.[333]

Now, however, that it was clear that the Japanese would not take over Indo-China, the Thais redefined their policy. Before it ratified the non-aggression treaty, Pibun told Lépissier, his government would require the cession of the islets in the Mekong and two pieces of territory on the right bank. In addition it wanted an 'assurance ... that in the event of France abandoning Indo-China, she would make over to Thailand as her legitimate successor, all the territories which the Thais have ceded to the French since the year 1893 ...'.[334] Direck sought Crosby's support for the more limited claim as giving Thailand a natural frontier along the Mekong. Crosby replied that Britain could give no help at Vichy. In the improbable event that Vichy agreed Britain would not, he thought, object.[335] More reasonable than expected though the claims were, Whitamore thought they should not be pressed; if they were satisfied the Japanese might seek concessions, and it might well be 'the prelude to the break-up of Indo-China'.[336] The Thai Government approached Vichy direct, suggesting that it would put the treaty into force immediately if the territorial transfers were made, and asking for a letter of assurance on the return of Laos and Cambodia if there were a change from French sovereignty.[337]

Vichy was unresponsive. Pibun told Crosby that it would negotiate only on the islands in the Mekong, and it wanted ratification first. If he agreed he would be forced from office. The Thai claims, Vichy had told Lépissier, were holding up the promulgation of Japan's undertaking to uphold the territorial integrity of Indo-China. Crosby feared that Prom might strike a bargain with the Japanese. He wanted the British Government to authorise him to tell Pibun that, while it was opposed to changing the status quo, it would, if a change did occur, consider Thai claims not unsympathetically. 'Without some such assurance, which should help us to retain Thai goodwill, I see real danger of Thailand going over to the side of Japan as a result of a bargain of the kind indicated ...'.[338] Bennett suggested that Britain's attitude to Indo-China thus far made it difficult to give the Thais any encouragement, especially as anything said might be twisted so as to give the French grounds to suspect 'that we are playing a double game and intriguing against their authority'. That was an important consideration if the French, as reported, were holding out against the Japanese.[339] A draft discouraging the Thais unless a change in the status quo should regrettably occur was displaced when news arrived that the French had given way.[340] The telegram sent suggested that Thailand might do better with a French than a Japanese frontier. The reported Japanese guarantee of Indo-China's integrity seemed to preclude the wider Thai claims. The British Government would not oppose settlement of narrower ones by free negotiation.[341]

Vichy's reply led the Thais to concede that the last point they had raised, the assurance, might be discussed 'if and when the need arises' but to insist that the territorial claims be satisfied.[342] 'This seems a moderate and not unreasonable reply', wrote Clarke, 'but it will not appeal to the French.'[343] Vichy was 'rather misguided to remain obdurate about ceding these two small pieces of territory'.[344]

Pibun expressed gratitude for the 'sympathy' of the language the Foreign Office told Crosby to use. The minister asked if he would resort to force and occupy the two right-bank pieces of territory if the French continued to reject the Thai conditions. The answer, it seemed, was yes, and he did not think Japan would object. Crosby asked about the larger question. Pibun thought that the Japanese would take over Indo-China but would let the Thais have Laos and Cambodia.[345] Crosby pointed out that gaining territory through the favour of the Japanese meant dependence on them. Pibun responded 'that what he desired most of all was the creation of a strong bloc consisting of Britain, the United States and the Netherlands which could keep Japan in check'. At present Britain could not resist Japan and the US would not use force and so, Crosby thought, Japan might seize Indo-China and Thailand thus secure the lost provinces. Britain, he believed, should even then still seek to maintain good relations with Thailand.[346] Clarke thought that Japan and Thailand were 'fixing things up between them' and that 'Japan's pound of flesh no doubt comprises bases in Thailand'. There was not much Britain could do. 'We cannot adopt one attitude towards the status quo with the Japanese and another with the Thais; and it may not be good policy to utter warnings (which we cannot back with force) as to the ill effects of granting bases to Japan...'. 'I would not quarrel with Thailand over this', Seymour wrote, 'and if Indo China is divided I think the more the Thais get the better.'[347]

The US had taken a different line. Grant had been apprehensive that Crosby would not insist on the status quo. 'It looks as though the British policy of appeasement is about to be applied to the Thai–Indochina affair.'[348] He was 'in a dilemma'.[349] Grant himself had argued that Thailand would have a better case for the territories at the end of the war if it did not act now.[350] Pibun told him that he was acting moderately. He did not, however, promise not to use force.[351] Hull thought that the US should do no more than reiterate the views it had already expressed.[352] Vichy insisted that it was determined to protect the political status and integrity of Indo-China. It could thus not agree to return territory on the right bank, and it considered the request for assurances over Cambodia and Laos 'groundless'.[353] Although the Thais sent their conciliatory reply, Grant reiterated that it was 'unwise' to make 'any move'.[354] Talking to Crosby on 1 October, Direck was 'disposed to accuse of Washington of being unsympathetic to the just aspirations of Thailand'.[355]

By this time Japan's 5th Division had begun to occupy Tonkin, and the signing of the Tripartite Pact had been announced.[356] Pibun seems to have gone the way Crosby feared and Clarke suspected. On 28 September he sent Vanich to tell the Japanese naval attaché, Torigoe, that he had resolved to rely on Japan, and he affirmed the pledge on 1 October. He would permit Japanese troops to cross Thai territory to attack Singapore in return for Japanese support for Thai irredentism, and he would agree to supply Japan with all the raw materials it needed. He declined, however, to put the promise in writing.[357]

Matsuoka now had the task of reconciling his pledge to French Indo-China with the new arguments the staff officers pressed on him for taking up Pibun's pledge.[358] The pledge to Indo-China might be burdensome in a way that differed from the pledge Kobayashi wanted to offer the Indies. But Matsuoka's difficulties were as nothing compared to those of the remaining colonial powers. The Japanese advance in Indo-China was a threat itself. They could not themselves prevent, nor help the Thais to prevent, advance into Thailand in one form or another even if they wished to do so.

The reopening of the Burma Road

Although Craigie had not wished to emphasise the point, the advances Japan made in Indo-China were inconsistent with the negotiations that were supposed to take place while the Burma Road was closed. They had never begun. Before mid October Britain would have to decide whether to reopen the road, Lothian had written on 21 August. By then Hitler might well have failed to invade Britain, and the anxiety that had paralysed US policy in the Pacific would have diminished. If Britain could get sufficient American support it should reopen the road and thus help to keep China going. What help would the US give?[359] In subsequent conversations Roosevelt 'somewhat cautiously' and Hull 'more definitely' expressed an interest in discussions with the British Government before the decision was taken in October 'with a view to seeing if, in the meantime, some common policy could be worked out by the two Governments'.[360]

No other assumption was possible, Bennett wrote, other than that Hitler would fail in the Battle of Britain. But a setback in Egypt or Sudan 'would have so disastrous an effect on our general position that we should not be able to afford to take the risk of reopening the Burma Road'. It was, however, desirable to prepare to reopen it if that should prove possible.[361] Preparation was particularly important lest the British should be manoeuvred into a position in which Japan might make it appear that they were breaching their undertakings. 'Japanese public opinion will be particularly accessible to a misapprehension of this kind, since it has never been made officially aware of the condition attached to the Burma Road agreement.'[362] A telegram to Craigie crossed one in which he had raised the question. He wanted to be able to show that the Japanese had failed to explore the opportunities for a general settlement.[363] The onus, the Foreign Office replied, should be on the Japanese. What had they done? If they sought concrete suggestions Craigie was to indicate that 'we should of course have to know on what precise basis Japan was prepared to deal with China'.[364]

Halifax took the matter to the Cabinet, arguing that the road should be reopened if it could be done without undue risk.[365] But the Cabinet thought the Indo-China situation had overtaken the matter; occupation by the Japanese would bring the road under threat from the air. The US was sounded out, as the Cabinet wished. Opening the road, like Dutch resistance, depended on US backing, Lothian said. Could this be demonstrated, for example, by parallel declarations in support of the status quo south of the equator, by threats of new embargoes and, if Hong Kong were threatened, by moving the fleet from Pearl Harbor to the Philippines? Hull called attention to his protest against threatened Japanese aggression in Indo-China and said he would leak a report that Britain and the US were consulting.[366]

Some days later Lothian and Casey called on Hull and referred again to the Burma Road and to the need for aid to Indo-China. Hull outlined American 'acts and utterances', 'including oral protests, protests in writing, protests in public statements and various moral embargoes, as well as the discontinuance of our commercial treaty and the stationing of our Navy at Hawaii'. Aid was difficult when the mother countries could not help, and the US Government had 'gone almost to the limit of resisting step by step Japanese aggression without the very serious danger of a military clash'. It had encouraged Indo-China, as it had Britain, to 'delay and parley', and in all probability Japan would not dare to make a military attack. The US would continue its protests. Involvement in war would not be wise for it would cut military supplies to Britain.[367]

Hull, Lothian reported, said that American action depended on the outcome of the Battle of Britain; if it became clear that Britain could hold out the US could take a stronger line in the Pacific. He would give notice before taking action that would intensify Japanese pressure on Britain or Holland. He implied that he would contemplate action that would bring war near but recognised that war would be against the interests of Britain, cutting off supplies from the European struggle. He hoped Britain would open the road. Cadogan found this 'a useful advance'. But he had reservations. New embargoes might bring pressure on Britain and Holland. Furthermore declarations about the status quo needed to cover territories north of the equator and in any case had little value 'unless the United States (and the rest of us) are prepared to make it clear that we mean to back up our announcement by force if necessary. The guiding principle in all this should be to create doubt and hesitation in the Japanese mind so that force will not be required in the event.'[368]

Craigie thought that, by contrast to July, in October, 'with the growing British prestige, Japanese extremists are less likely to get out of hand and any measures which the Japanese may take are therefore less likely to be of so provocative a character as to render outbreaks of hostilities reaching the inevitable'.[369] He thought a Franco–Japanese agreement for the passage of troops through Indo-China would afford ground for non-renewal of the Burma Road agreement,[370] although he also argued a few days later that the Japanese had determined to secure military facilities in Indo-China 'in order to neutralise effect of British refusal to renew the Burma Road agreement'.[371] He was indeed reluctant to void the Burma Road agreement without attempting the general settlement that it had envisaged. For this the Foreign Office had no enthusiasm.

> As regards the 'just and equitable peace' proposal, it is precisely this provision in the Burma Road agreement which has been subjected to the fiercest criticism, since it is obvious that the only peace the Japanese are likely to agree to in present circumstances is one on their own terms which it suits them to conclude in order to free themselves for more profitable adventures elsewhere.[372]

In fact Matsuoka spoke of the renegade Wang Ching-Wei as well as Chiang Kai-shek and told Craigie there were no other steps to be taken at that juncture.[373]

The Australians had also wanted to attempt a general settlement. After the agreement Bruce had taken up the argument he had made before it for a 'wide and lasting settlement' Japan would be ready to accept. Butler, who had his own ideas on the matter, termed his memorandum 'Assez jejune!'[374] Early in September Bruce discussed the position with Halifax. Craigie was planning to raise the question of a general settlement with Matsuoka, but the British had established no definite policy. Bruce insisted that it would be 'most dangerous' for Craigie to raise the question in the absence of clear proposals in respect of which Britain should be 'on side' with the US.[375] Caldecote telegraphed Menzies two days later. 'Nothing has happened to suggest that the Japanese Government are seriously prepared to fulfil their part of the bargain.' Britain was contemplating what should happen at the end of the three months. He explained the policy the Foreign Office was pursuing.[376]

External Affairs in Canberra recalled Australia's views in July with which, it said, the agreement had been generally in accord. 'Its essential feature was that it avoided immediate complications with Japan while being at the same time only a qualified acceptance of the Japanese demand.' But a settlement with Konoe's government was even less likely than one with Yonai's. Nor did it seem so likely as in July 'that the European situation will have clarified sufficiently by October to enable a clear-cut decision whether or not to resist Japanese pressure'. The problem, the department thought, was much as before; the policy must still be to play for time. It suggested some extension of the time period coupled with further investigation of possible negotiations.[377] The advice to the British was to temporise. Time might strengthen Britain's position if the Germans attempted an invasion and failed, if the US Government felt better able to collaborate after the election and if defences in the Far East had been strengthened.[378]

A telegram relayed some of the Foreign Office reservations over the Hull–Lothian discussions but added that the situation had to be reviewed in the light of the Tripartite Pact.[379] Reservations over the US repeated some old refrains. The US seemed ready only to help those who helped themselves. It would thus encourage the opening of the Burma Road and regret Dutch economic concessions. But even its help might be misplaced if, as seemed likely, it was to continue to take the form of economic restraints without political guarantees. The restraints of July had already provoked pressure on Britain and Netherlands India more than they restrained Japan. The Foreign Office did not, it seems, dissent from the State Department view that Japan could be stopped by measures short of war. Their belief was that, if embargoes were imposed, they should be accompanied by threats to use force, which would be enough. Indeed Cadogan and Vansittart were opposed to a Japanese–American war, which, as Hull had said, and Berle reiterated to Casey,[380] might prevent the US from helping to keep Britain's resistance to Germany alive. At a Cabinet meeting Churchill drew attention to this point as well as expressing interest in parallel declarations in favour of the status quo in the South Pacific. He questioned the view that it was not in Britain's interest that the US should be involved in war in the Pacific. The Foreign Secretary explained that the reservation derived from concern over the supply of arms for use against Germany.[381]

Halifax was already disposed to open the Burma Road. Failure to do so would have a bad effect in the US.[382] In Ashley Clarke's view the new American embargoes and the Tripartite Pact were arguments for a prompt repudiation of the Burma Road agreement. It would 'encourage the Americans on the right path' and give 'moral encouragement' to the Chinese. The intermediate course, suggested by Butler, was to announce that the agreement would lapse when it expired. That would seem like 'a half measure'. Inaction now would probably surprise the Japanese, 'and the extremists who have been urging a forward policy against ourselves will be justified and encouraged'.[383] Repudiation would give the Chinese more time to gather supplies before the Japanese could position themselves to bomb the road, while delay would allow the Japanese 'to work up an atmosphere of menace designed to force us into renewal of the agreement'. Repudiation might, however, 'over-dramatise the situation', and Britain had to 'weigh carefully' the risks involved.[384]

Lothian discussed the pact with Hull. The Secretary of State asked if the British and the Dutch had conferred on 'pooling their defense forces'. Lothian asked for his view as to the effect of an announcement that the road would be reopened on 17 October. The Secretary of State offered no opinion on that. But he set out again the 'definite and somewhat progressive line of acts and utterances' the US had pursued 'in resisting Japanese aggression and treaty relations'. He could not predict, 'much less make commitments, as to how fast and how far this Government may go in following up the various acts and utterances'; adding

> that, of course, the special desire of this Government is to see Great Britain succeed in the war and that its acts and utterances with respect to the Pacific area would be more or less affected as to time and extent by the question of what course would, on the part of this Government, most effectively and legitimately aid Great Britain in winning the war.

That general statement, coupled with the repeated statement that the US opposed the closing of the road, was 'self-explanatory'.[385]

The pact increased the importance of resolute action but also the importance of 'circumspection as regards method', Bennett argued.[386] The paper finally put to the Cabinet suggested a parliamentary question. This would indicate that the agreement contained no provision for renewal but, if it had, Britain would have been unable to agree to it.[387] The Cabinet decided to open the road accordingly.[388]

Within Burma the British had to win support as the position deteriorated. On 18 June the ministers had told the Governor they intended to issue a statement on the war and Burma's defence. This gave 'unconditional' support to the 'common task of making the forces of freedom and democracy triumphant' over the 'brute force' of Britain's enemies and urged HMG to state promptly that Burma would 'take at once her due place as a fully self-governing and equal member of any Commonwealth or Federation of free nations that [might] be established as a result of the war'. In response Governor Cochrane proposed that he be allowed to appoint a Burmese as Counsellor to the Governor who 'would be mainly concerned with explaining and popularising Defence measures and encouraging recruitment'. The War Cabinet agreed and indicated that, in the light of the world situation at the end of the war, Britain would be willing to discuss with Burma the attainment of dominion status.[389] Saw, the ambitious Forest Minister, considered this insufficiently categorical.[390]

Governor Cochrane discussed the possible opening of the Burma Road with the new Saw ministry on 21 September. Admiration for Japan in Burma had 'largely evaporated as result of clearer knowledge of Japanese methods in China'. The following of Ba Maw, now arrested, was unimportant. The ministers were thus 'friendly towards China', but they and the public wanted 'to avoid involving Burma in hostilities'. Some argued that renewal would remove the risk of aggression, but the Governor dissented; if Japan wanted a quarrel, it would do so regardless of renewal or non-renewal. He concluded from his discussion with them that the ministers would be 'loyal to any decision which does not unreasonably increase risk of attack on Burma'. But if an attack followed the non-renewal of the agreement 'wide expression would be given to view which would connect the two as cause and effect and blame Government for embroiling Burma unnecessarily with Japan ... This attitude might be reinforced by reference to state of Burma's defences ...'. The Governor's own view was that non-renewal would not inevitably lead to hostile acts unless the Japanese had already decided on other considerations that a war with the British Empire was worthwhile and, if they had so decided, renewal of the agreement would not prevent their finding another casus belli. Indeed, 'as renewal itself might be taken as a sign of weakness it might even encourage them to create an incident'.[391]

At the end of the month Cochrane discussed the idea of immediate termination with the Defence Council. Ministers were 'statesman-like', but 'unable to accept view that immediate removal of restrictions would not increase the danger of attack on Burma. The attitude which they would prefer and which of course is based on the teachings of Buddhism would be to be on friendly and peaceful terms with all countries.' The

Governor said that Japan had adopted Hitler's policy of aggression, and the only way to deal with it was by making it plain that it would not pay.

> Had I been in a position to add that determination of the Empire and U.S.A. to prevent further Japanese aggression is so strong as to preclude for practical purposes the threat of an attack on Burma, it is probable that Ministers would have accepted proposition as representing a sound policy. But as it was impossible for me to give the necessary assurances I was compelled to regard this as a long-term policy for which we could not forecast date of successful inception.

The discussion thus focused on the question of immediate reopening. That, the ministers thought, might give Japan an excuse for hostilities, such as an air raid attack on Burma. Whether or not reopening influenced such a decision, 'public opinion in Burma would link the two events, and Government would be subjected to serious attack for having provoked Japan unnecessarily'. Cochrane agreed with this estimate of public opinion, 'and these reactions might well be so strong as to interfere seriously with the successful prosecution of war. Ministerial attitude was summarised by Premier when he said "If Japan attacks us we will fight, but do not let us give them any provocation."' The Governor adhered to his earlier view, and so did the counsellors, but he could not hold that the view of the ministers was 'unreasonable'. He advised 'that if a Japanese attack followed the immediate removal of the restrictions it would have a most disturbing effect on the public mind and, if coupled with our inability to resist aerial attack, might lead to such a state of internal disorder as to divert important part of our Defence Force to maintain order'.[392] In fact the Foreign Office had already decided to avoid the more provocative approach.

'The Burma public should be reassured by the more recent information from Japan', Sir John Brenan wrote on 11 October, 'which shows that the Japanese are thoroughly alarmed at the result of their Axis pact on the United States and show no disposition to make trouble about the Burma Road.'[393] They handed Craigie a note verbale insisting that their moves into Indo-China and the pact were designed to bring about peace, but denying that the Burma Road agreement had been concluded on the understanding that attempts would be made to do so.[394] Scott saw this as 'a piece of impertinence'.[395]

The protection of Borneo and Malaya

If Burmans sought to exact a political price for collaboration in the crisis, the British used the crisis to exert some pressure on Sarawak. Burma might move more firmly towards dominion status; the Raj would become more like a protected Malay state.

The plan had been to use Pepys in approaching Raja Vyner over a new treaty. In fact Pepys had decided not to stay in Sarawak. Edward Gent thought that Sir Shenton Thomas should be instructed to open conversations with the Raja, indicating that the government wished to appoint a British Resident Adviser and would, if Sir Vyner agreed, be prepared to amend the 1888 agreement with the Raj accordingly.[396] A draft dispatch to Thomas was designed to convey the Secretary of State's conclusion that the agreement of 1888 was 'unduly restrictive' and prevented 'the Secretary of State's providing himself either with the requisite information about affairs in Sarawak or with the necessary authority and influence to help and direct the State administration towards the higher standards which are being achieved in Colonies and Protectorates elsewhere ...'. He wished to appoint a British Resident Adviser, who would concern himself not only with foreign affairs and defence, with which HMG must be particularly concerned as the protecting power, 'but also would have authority to be consulted at least, if not vested with the reserve power of "advice" on the model of the Malay States Treaties, on all matters affecting the administrative system and standards in Sarawak ...'.[397]

Sir Shenton approved the draft. Lord Lloyd, the Colonial Secretary, however, did not. Gent discussed it with him, but he preferred 'to find other means of pursuing this subject instead of communicating direct with the Governor on the lines of this despatch ...'.[398] Lloyd thought that, if any approach were to be made, he would be able to do it better himself; 'also he had some sentimental interest in Sarawak through acquaintance with the Tuan Muda ...'.[399]

The COS Appreciation recognised that a Japanese move into Thailand would threaten Burma with air attack. An invasion was 'a more distant threat' except in the extreme south where the aerodromes should be demolished. Elsewhere air forces and additional troops would be needed at Lashio, Rangoon and Tavoy. 'The defence of Malaya must, however, have precedence over Burma and the provision of such forces can only be a very long term project.'[400]

The priority was Singapore. Now all Malaya had to be defended as well. The forces available were insufficient to do so. Nor could other commitments be made, even towards Burma or the Indies, let alone Borneo, where Britain was busy playing the role of protecting power without the power to effect protection.

CHAPTER 4

October 1940 – June 1941

The prospects of American participation

'Everything – on paper – is against us', Cadogan wrote at the end of 1940, 'but we shall live. I don't frankly, see how we are going to win, but I am convinced that we shall not lose. And if you hang on – like a bull-dog – it's funny what things do happen. The enemy is a very good facade. But if it cracks, it will crack suddenly and cataclysmically...'[1]. Although the British indeed hung on, that, however, was not what happened.

Britain had survived the Battle of Britain. In itself that was a success for the British and a frustration for the Germans, but it by no means foreshadowed an end to the war in Europe. Indeed the war was more likely to expand further. Hitler would pursue alternative policies. Churchill would look with increasing urgency for the support of the United States, even for its participation. The United States, recognising that the British had survived, backed them more effectively after the election had returned Roosevelt for a third term. Participation was another matter.

The Japanese had taken advantage of the defeat of France by making advances in northern Vietnam through a deal with the Vichy authorities. Otherwise they had sustained their customary caution. That was promoted in part by their concern about the Soviet Union, which had demonstrated its military prowess in the Far East and then made a non-aggression pact with the Germans. Its presence and potential affected the calculations of the Japanese army leaders. In addition the China Incident had proved an absorbing challenge, difficult to bring to an end, even when the Western powers ceased to be able to offer the Kuomintang much support. But during the summer of 1940 there were increasing signs that neither the north nor China were going to remain

193

the main foci of Japanese concern. The Konoe Government looked more and more to the south. Moreover, more radical approaches were advocated at lower levels within the army.

These trends were related not only to the difficulties in the north or the frustrations in China. They were stimulated by the developments in the European war and in particular by the changes in American policy it provoked. The catastrophe of mid 1940 had encouraged an emphasis on hemisphere defence. The decision to build a two-ocean navy was, however, felt well outside the hemisphere. Above all, it concerned the Japanese and added to their anxiety to ensure a supply of oil from sources that were independent of the sources and the trans-Pacific supply routes dominated by the US. Initially they sought guaranteed long contracts from the Netherlands Indies. That might not suffice.

The US, moreover, had begun to give Southeast Asia an attention it had hitherto given no part of Asia. Its interest in China had been limited; its interest in Southeast Asia, even the Philippines, indeterminate. But the European war gave it a new importance. Hemisphere defence was a fall-back position. The continued resistance of the British to the Germans was seen to be of prime importance to the security of the Americans. If Britain's resistance was to continue, it would need resources not only from the US itself but also from its dependencies in India, Southeast Asia and Australasia. It became important to keep them open to the British. The Japanese could not be allowed to prevent that. They, however, began to see this as carving up the world and to find in it a further argument for the Greater East Asia Co-Prosperity Sphere.

Japan, Grew believed, had become a 'predatory' nation. 'A progressively firm policy on our part will entail inevitable risks ... but ... those risks are less in degree than the far greater future dangers which we would face if we were to follow a policy of laissez-faire ...'. The US must call a halt to the Japanese program, and the Japanese must be sure that the Americans would fight if need be.[2] One issue was American preparedness, which affected timing. Another prime factor in relations with Japan was the question whether getting into the war would so handicap American help to Britain as to make the difference between victory and defeat. 'In this connection it seems to me', Roosevelt wrote, 'that we must consider whether, if Japan should gain possession of the region of the Netherlands East Indies and the Malay Peninsula, the chances of England's winning in her struggle with Germany would not be decreased thereby.' The British survived because they were

able to draw upon vast resources for their sustenance and to bring into operation against their enemies economic, military and naval pressures on a world-wide scale ... The British need assistance along the lines of our generally established policies at many points, assistance which in the case of the Far East is certainly well within the realm of 'possibility' so far as the capacity of the United States is concerned. Our strategy of giving them assistance towards ensuring our own security must envisage both sending of supplies to England and helping to prevent a closing of channels of communication to and from various parts of the world, so that important sources of supply will not be denied to the British and be added to the assets of the other side ...'.[3]

In February Eugene Dooman, Counselor in the American Embassy, was to tell Ohashi:

So long as helping England in her war with Germany and Italy remains the dominant objective of the United States it would be idle to assume that the United States would remain indifferent to any threat, actual or potential, by Japan or any other power, to the lines of communication between units of the British Empire, which, by depriving England of foodstuffs and raw materials, would imperil her continued existence ...[4]

In Manchuria and China, scenes of earlier Japanese expansion, the Americans had reacted not by interposing force but by asserting principles. They believed that the Japanese would find China impossible to dominate and that their frustration and the fragility of their economy would lead them back to the more moderate policies associated with Shidehara and the Washington spirit. The principles might not restrain Japan meanwhile, but not giving in at this juncture would make it possible to restore the status quo later with such adjustments as might be fairly negotiated. This mainly verbal approach was coupled with a number of economic restraints, the chief of which was the abandonment of the US–Japan commercial treaty in 1940. They were designed to remind the Japanese of US interests, and they derived from the same sense of Japan's fragility that informed the non-recognition doctrine.

That approach suited the growing American interest in Southeast Asia less than its interest in China. China was seen as of importance in the longer term. Southeast Asia had become of immediate importance because of the European war. There was the possibility that words of disapproval, whatever importance they might have for the future, would have little impact on the present. The Japanese, themselves increasingly concerned about the resources of Southeast Asia, might increasingly discount words that they had heard too often before to take too seriously.

Economic sanctions came, therefore, more to the fore. Yet there was an increased risk that they would appear provocative. Would the Japanese react to curbs on oil supply by attacking the Indies? Again the image of their caution and their fragility persisted. While such a risk existed it was widely thought that they would not adventure a war with the US and the UK if they were convinced that one would occur. In the meantime the policy would be to keep them guessing, doing not enough to provoke them, but enough to worry them. That, of course, kept Britain and the Netherlands guessing, too. The Americans made no commitment to them in Southeast Asia, and that limited the commitments they made to each other.

The Division of Far Eastern Affairs of the State Department appraised the situation in April 1941. Full embargoes would not be in the best interests of the US: they would 'demonstrate to all elements in Japan that the only way of assuring Japan's future as a power with independence of action is to establish control through seizure or other means over an area which will be self-sustaining'. The US should not impose such restrictions unless it was prepared to accept the risk of hostilities in the Far East and partial diversion of energies and supplies from Britain. If 1941 could be passed with Britain still resisting in Europe, and Japan deterred, the balance of Japanese opinion might change. 'This Government's policy has had as one of its effective purposes the attrition of Japan's energies and resources by steps undertaken gradually on a basis designed to obviate creating the impression that they were in the nature of overt acts directed primarily at Japan.' At the end of 1941, with no quick German victory achieved and with the practical certainty that an attack in the Far East would involve Japan in a long war, Japan was likely to realise the difficulties facing its program. In the meantime it would react to events in Europe by continued opportunism. 'If Japan can be led to believe without question that the United States is able to resist and will resist by active intervention with its armed forces any aggression against British or Netherlands possessions in the Far East, Japan would hesitate to attack those areas.' At the same time the US should be willing 'to give honest and sympathetic consideration now to Japan's legitimate desire for changes in the economic *status quo* if Japan will abandon entirely its resort to and threat of armed force and aggression'.[5]

In September the Japanese and the Germans had joined with the Italians in the Tripartite Pact. For Hitler that was in some sense an alternative to the battle for Britain that had not brought him the results he expected; it would help to limit the support the US could give the UK. For Konoe it was designed to prise the two apart so that Japan might enhance its control over Southeast Asia not by force but by a more forceful diplomacy. The pact brought Japan and Germany closer together, although less close than they wished it to appear. It did not mean that war had come to Asia or even that it would. But, despite the hopes of its progenitors, it pushed the US and the UK closer together.

Churchill had come to the conclusion not only that US participation was essential to victory but also that the road to participation lay through Asia. Others, although doubtful at first, came to agree with him, though it is clear that neither he nor they recognised the damage a war in Asia would bring to the British Empire. It is far from certain in any case that the Americans took this view. No doubt their opinions also varied. But on balance it seems that they took the view that their policy would help to keep them out of the war, not, as it did, to get them into it.

The German attack on Russia

The war in the Mediterranean intensified in autumn 1940. On 28 October the 'dirty ice-creamers' attacked Greece.[6] The British sent planes to the kingdom, and they bombed Italy. On 11 November Cunningham delivered a great blow at the Italian battle fleet at Taranto.[7] 'Greeks are really whacking the ice-creamers, but of course it can't last and I suppose the Germans will snuff them out', Cadogan wrote. 'Our fighters seem to have cleared the sky of the Wops.'[8] On 12 December he recorded a 'sweeping victory over the Wops' at Sidi Barrani.[9] Early in February the Italians were driven from Cyrenaica. Then it was decided to help Greece militarily. 'On all moral and sentimental (and consequently American) grounds, one is driven to the grim conclusion. But it must, in the end, be a failure.'[10] At the end of March Rommel attacked the weakened British force in North Africa. A week later Germany declared war on Yugoslavia and Greece.[11] Things went badly. By the end of April Greece was in German hands. 'Awful news from Crete ... Certainly the Germans are past-masters in the art of war – and great warriors ....'[12] Rommel had driven the British back to Egypt but for a garrison in Tobruk.[13] A British offensive in Libya 'ended in a bloody nose – for us. Most depressing ...'.[14]

In March the Joint Intelligence Committee had suggested that an assault on Russia would be Hitler's next objective.[15] At the end of May the Chiefs of Staff concluded that Germany was prepared to attack Russia. 'I agree, but I believe that Russia will give way and sign on the dotted line. I wish she wouldn't, as I should love to see Germany expending her strength there. But', Cadogan concluded, 'they're not such fools (as our General Staff) ...'.[16] 'Germans are evidently ready to attack Russia. And they will do so if they don't get what they want. I think they will get what they want. I hope they won't, because that would give us time, and it must be *some* effort for them.'[17] The attack began on 22 June. Churchill announced that Britain would give what help it could. A British Military Mission arrived in Moscow on 27 June.[18] 'We seem to have no plan for harrying Germans in West', Cadogan lamented.[19] 'We are not prepared to take advantage of this Heaven-sent (and short) opportunity of the Germans being heavily engaged in Russia. We shall look awful fools!'[20]

'How are we going to pay for it all?' Hankey had asked back in July 1940.[21] Britain survived the air battle. Hitler's new peripheral strategy, however, redoubled the threat to its supplies. The US had become its major source. One question was production. Another was payment. The third was security.

Production in the US was not yet on a war footing. Its own requirements for hemisphere defence competed with the requirements of the United Kingdom. Payment was not yet a question of Britain's bankruptcy but of its ability to finance purchases in terms of dollars. During 1940 Britain's purchases were financed mainly by using its gold reserves. At the end of the year it would need help in realising its assets, and by mid 1941 massive credits would be needed. The closure of the Mediterranean and merchant shipping losses put pressure on the security of supplies.[22]

In this field, as in others, the British had to await the outcome of the presidential election in November. Hopes had been built on this; indeed some thought Roosevelt's victory would be followed by American entry into the war. 'Clearly', as Reynolds puts it, 'extravagant hopes had got the better of traditional doubts.'[23] Lothian was more realistic. He had told the FO in September: 'Public opinion here has not yet grasped that it will have to make far reaching decisions to finance and supply us and possibly still greater ones next Spring or Summer unless it is to take the responsibility of forcing us to make a compromise peace …'.[24] After the election a long statement of Britain's needs was prepared at Lothian's instance and finally sent on 7–8 December. Already, however, the President had been considering some kind of leasing arrangements mainly in respect of merchant shipping. The British letter helped to develop the idea into Lease-Lend, which the President aired at a press conference on 17 December. His fireside chat of 29 December spoke of the US as 'the great arsenal of democracy'.

> I make the direct statement to the American people that there is far less chance of the United States getting into [the war] if we do all we can now to support the nations defending themselves against attack by the Axis than if we acquiesce in their defeat, submit tamely to an Axis victory, and wait our turn to be the object of attack in another war later …[25]

The Lease-Lend bill was published on 7 January 1941. In Congress the Administration again argued that Britain was the USA's frontline and that it was designed to keep America out of the war.[26] The British Government said little for fear of provoking isolationists. It was signed into law on 11 March. Britain was 'not only to be skinned but flayed to the bone'. But Lease-Lend would, Churchill believed, help to pull the US into the war.[27]

After the election the British had renewed their suggestion of staff talks. Admiral Stark had produced Plan Dog on 11 November, postulating that the chief US interest was the defeat of Germany, for which an invasion of Europe would ultimately be required, and that a 'strict defensive' should be maintained in the Pacific, if possible avoiding war.[28] Army and President endorsed the plan in principle, and it guided the American planners in preparing for the talks. 'Atlantic First' was the strategy; there was no intention of moving part of the fleet from Hawaii to Singapore. Moving it a further 6000 miles, or even to Manila, would leave the Atlantic and the hemisphere too exposed; Hawaii was a compromise.[29] The American–British conversations (ABC) were presented as non-committal. The two sides agreed that the defeat of Germany and Italy was the priority, and that a defensive and deterrent policy should be maintained against Japan (ABC-1). Agreement was also reached that Britain would have first charge on US aircraft production until such time as the US might enter the war (ABC-2). The main controversy at this time was over Singapore. The US would not despatch ships there, as the Admiralty wished.[30] In the event it was agreed that it would transfer some ships from Pearl Harbor to the Atlantic so that Britain could send ships to Singapore.[31] The British could not press the US too hard and believed Japan could be deterred.'The first thing is to get the United States into the war. We can then settle how to fight it afterwards', Churchill wrote.[32] 'Britain was to pay dearly for this complacency ...'.[33]

Both the US and the UK were anxious to maintain Anglo-American control of the Atlantic. They agreed on the need as a result to keep Spain and Portugal out of the German camp, although they differed as to the means. They also differed over Vichy. Britain indeed backed away from its support of de Gaulle after the abortive expedition against Dakar on 23 September – 'Operation Menace had been an unqualified shambles'[34] – and made overtures to Vichy and to Weygand in Africa, but the bitterness engendered by the events of summer 1940 proved 'very difficult to eradicate'. The US maintained diplomatic relations with Vichy and indeed pressed Britain to modify its blockade.[35]

The German triumphs in Africa and the Balkans led US policymakers to question Britain's strategy and indeed renewed doubts about Britain's ability to survive. The regular night bombing of British cities intensified, and shipping losses worsened. The British were puzzled as to the propaganda line to follow in the US: 'the loss of *Hood* or the sinking of the *Bismarck*?' as Beaverbrook put it.[36] A few battleships were transferred to the Atlantic in mid April, more in mid May. Morgenthau concluded that the US would have to enter the war, and Berle thought it had to choose: entry, or a British compromise peace.[37] Roosevelt's reaction was the speech of 27 May, which announced a state of 'unlimited national emergency'. 'It goes further than I thought it was possible to go even two weeks ago', he told Churchill, 'and I would like to hope that it will receive general approval from the fairly large element which has been confused by details and allow them to see the simple facts.'[38] 'We are uplifted and fortified by your memorable declaration', the Prime Minister replied.[39] Roosevelt also told Halifax he planned to send US troops to relieve the British troops in Iceland. Hitler's invasion of Russia gave Roosevelt's policy of containing Germany by proxy 'new validity'.[40]

Hitler's moves in the Balkans had been seen as part of his 'peripheral strategy' against Britain. In fact they had been designed to assure his flank when he invaded Russia, a project to which he had finally committed himself after his meeting with Soviet Foreign Minister Molotov in November. The Führer allegedly told Prince Paul of Yugoslavia in March that he would attack Russia in June or July.[41] The invasion of Russia was initially seen as subordinate to the plan to conquer Britain. It would, it was thought, be but a brief diversion. Cadogan was not alone in thinking that Hitler would issue an ultimatum and that Stalin would give in. When it was clear that invasion would take place it was thought that the campaign would be soon be over. That proved a mistake, and a protracted struggle followed. Japan had not joined in but looked south. The failure of the Germans to secure a quick victory was to make the Japanese hesitate. It also left the US somewhat freer to exert pressure in the Pacific.

Naval dispositions there had been the subject of controversy in the ABC talks. The US wanted to retain its fleet at Pearl Harbor, a deterrent to Japan but not 'beyond range if a crisis developed in the Atlantic'.[42] The Admiralty sought to get the Americans to change their policy, partly because of their increasing fear that the Japanese were about to push into southern Indo-China. Churchill did not take this threat very seriously. Moreover, he did not wish to upset the US administration as it worked to secure the passage of the Lease-Lend bill through Congress. 'There is no use putting before them a naval policy which they will not accept, and which will only offend them and make it more difficult to bring them into the war', Churchill had written in December 1940.[43] Moreover, he did not believe the Japanese would besiege Singapore while a hostile American fleet was in the Pacific. 'Our object is to get the Americans into the war, and the proper strategic disposition will soon emerge when they are up against reality, and not trying to enter into hypothetical paper accords beforehand.'[44] The Prime Minister thought the Americans should simply be invited to use Singapore, not pressed to accept a strategy that seemed to them self-serving. His argument, Reynolds suggests, assumed that there would be time before a serious Japanese offensive developed to make the proper dispositions.[45] In fact the UK delegation in Washington recognised that time was needed to move land and air reinforcements or, a last resort, ships to Malaya. Hence the need 'to dispute the Japanese control of the sea communications in the South

China Seas ...'. Constituting a real threat to Japanese advanced sea communications, permitting at least their interruption, required one carrier and a division of heavy cruisers.[46]

A compromise was reached at the ABC talks.The Americans were, after all, anxious that the 'Malay barrier' should be held. This would be easier if the US Pacific fleet were, in the event of war, to attack the Marshalls and Carolines, and so divert Japan from the barrier. The US, moreover, would gradually shift its naval strength to the Atlantic, allowing the Royal Navy to send a British fleet to Singapore. That, of course, might be delayed by other contingencies and by Churchill's complacency.

Some ships were duly transferred to the Atlantic. The Mediterranean situation was alarming, but Hull and the President were also concerned about Japan. Matsuoka was in Europe and on 13 April made a neutrality pact with Russia, leaving Japan freer to move south through lessening its concern about the north. Not all agreed with Hull. Stimson argued that more ships should go to the Atlantic. That, and the fact that it would be interpreted as meaning the Americans were about to enter the war, would deter the Japanese.[47] Churchill supported Stimson. That was, in Cadogan's view, one of his 'midnight follies'. Menzies was right to make a stink about it.

> Anything more insane! ... But Winston very obstinate ... He who was convinced Japan was coming into the war last year [and] insisted on closing the Burma Road (a capital mistake), is now determined that nothing will make them come in. And he suffers from the delusion that any cold water thrown on any hare-brained US suggestion will stop the US coming into the war! Even the American naval authorities themselves were against this insane proposal.[48]

The advantages to be gained by the removal of a powerful American fleet would have to be 'very great and very definite' if they were to 'outweigh the very serious risk which that removal would entail'.[49] A telegram was sent on 8 May urging that the US had to maintain a deterrent in the Pacific and create one in the Atlantic.[50]

In the meantime ABC had also been followed up by talks at Singapore on 21–27 April, designed to further 'arrangements for mutual support'. The talks included representatives of the Dutch and the Australians as well. But the resulting ADB report was to be rejected by the US Chiefs of Staff in June, partly because it contained implicit political commitments, including the assumption that an attack on one would be seen as an attack on all. The American Chiefs of Staff also criticised the report because it made so little provision for a British naval presence at Singapore or elsewhere.[51]

The retention of ships in the Pacific had been important to Hull in April and May because of his talks with the Japanese ambassador,

Nomura. The talks had begun unofficially in March through the activities of the so-called John Doe Associates[52] and were designed to explore whether the governments shared any common ground. A draft understanding was produced on 9 April, largely the work of Col. Iwakuro, attached to Nomura's staff. Hull asked the ambassador if the Japanese Government wished it to be regarded as a basis for discussion. He also asked if it would accept a statement of the principles Hull considered fundamental. Nomura did not report this.[53] The subsequent American proposal of 21 June seemed as a result to be a hardening of the American position.[54]

The British were told little of these talks. Halifax and Casey had seen Hull on 15 February and discussed the talk Roosevelt and Hull had with Nomura the previous day. Hull told them 'that there had thus far been no discussion ... of any of the questions and other matters pending between Japan and the US'. The US had stated its position on two or three of the most vital questions and been 'absolutely firm'. It was important 'to have discussion of the policies and programs of our two countries during the past few years and ascertain the time and manner of divergence of the course of the two nations ...'.[55] When the proposals came in April, Hornbeck suggested that the British should be given 'an indication of what is going on and of our general thought in regard to the matter'.[56] Only on 16 May did Hull do so.[57] The FO, alarmed, feared that the Japanese were trying to split the British and the Americans. Hull, however, bitterly resented Halifax's criticism – the Secretary of State alluded to the Stimson–Simon controversy – and a soothing telegram replaced the aide-mémoire.[58] Britain could not itself take the initiative and had to leave it to the US. Indeed the US was the only power that could contain Japan and, if talks failed, it would be more convinced that it had to act. The British and the Dutch would, however, suffer most 'if things went wrong'.[59] They wanted more information about the talks, therefore. They could not get it. Nor could the British secure a firmer front among the three powers, the US, the UK, and the Netherlands (ABD). That might comprise joint or parallel warnings and a pledge of mutual support if deterrence failed. None of these were to be forthcoming.

In 1940 the Konoe Cabinet had resolved on a southern strategy, designed to make use of the opportunity Hitler's success in Europe had created. That success was less than complete, and the two powers came together in the Tripartite Pact with a view to increasing the pressure on the US, which they held responsible both for sustaining Britain's resistance in Europe and for the obstinacy of the British and the Dutch in Southeast Asia. The prospects were viewed initially with great optimism, but it was not borne out. In Europe Hitler began to pursue an alternative policy of which the Soviet Union was the focus. In Asia Japan enjoyed the limited success provided by its one-sided mediation in an escalating conflict between French Indo-China and Thailand. Its larger hopes eluded it, and it failed to prise Britain and the US apart.

The Japanese General Staff had not accepted the priority of the south over the north.[60] The deficiency was made up by the Army Ministry under General Tojo Hideki. One focus was on planning. The General Staff gave it little attention before July 1941. In July the War Ministry set up the Taiwan Army Research Division under General Itagaki and gave it the responsibility of preparing for the type of operation that Southeast Asia would require. It was the Army Ministry, too, that sent Colonel Iwakuro to 'assist' Nomura in the Washington talks. It hoped that, if it made some kind of offer on neutrality in the event of US entry into the European war, the US would support Japan's decision to obtain access to the resources of the Indies. Without some assurances that the US would accept a modus vivendi along these lines, the Liaison Conference ruled against making the proposal of 9 April formal. Iwakuro advised Tojo that Matsuoka's policy and personality stood in the way. A conference between Konoe and Roosevelt would be the best way to secure a settlement.[61]

On 17 April, four days after Matsuoka had made a neutrality pact with the Soviet Union, Imperial Headquarters adopted a new policy for the southern area. As Crowley points out, it no longer used the optimistic vocabulary of the previous year. The emphasis was now on self-preservation and self-defence. To that end it sought 'close' economic relations with Netherlands India and 'intimate and inseparable' relations with Thailand and Indo-China. Force would be justified in the event of an embargo by the US, Britain or the Netherlands, or 'when the encirclement of Japan by the United States, alone or in alliance with Great Britain, the Netherlands, and China becomes so restrictive that the situation becomes intolerable from the standpoint of national defense'.[62]

Early in June Oshima, the Japanese Ambassador in Berlin, warned that Germany might invade the Soviet Union. The options discussed by an emergency Liaison Conference were: (a) a move into Southeast Asia, (b) a compromise over Southeast Asia with the US and preparation for operations in Russia, or (c) military control over Indo-China and strengthening the Kwantung army, putting off the choice between north and south. The Army General Staff favoured the third option, but at the Liaison Conferences of 11 and 12 June Admiral Nagano secured priority for preparations against Britain and the US.[63] Despite Matsuoka, who argued for the Axis alliance, the Japanese adhered to this priority when Hitler invaded the Soviet Union on 22 June.

The Australian viewpoint

A Defence Conference at Singapore in October 1940, which included representatives from Britain, Australia and New Zealand, India and Burma,[64] had revealed what the Australian Government called an 'alarming position'.[65] It declared that it was 'gravely concerned'. The war had indeed to be won in 'the main theatres of operation', but 'the extent of Australian co-operation in overseas theatres is dependent on the Australian public's impression of the degree of local security that exists'. The land and sea threats to Malaya had been 'greatly increased' by the defection of France and the advance of Japan. The advice received from London, particularly in 1937, suggested that the defence situation would have been 'much better'. The Commonwealth Government outlined what it was prepared to do to help, including the despatch of a brigade group. But it urged 'immediate action to remedy deficiencies in Army and Air Forces both in numbers and equipment, which is all important, in view of inadequacy of Naval Forces'.[66] Perhaps, it added, some capital ships could be sent, in view of British naval successes in the Mediterranean, or at least the battle cruiser and carrier, based in Ceylon, contemplated in August.[67]

Churchill's reply was sent just before Christmas 1940. 'The danger of Japan going to war with the British Empire is in my opinion definitely less than it was in June after the collapse of France.' The German air force had been beaten off, and Britain had secured a decisive victory in Libya. 'It is quite impossible for our fleet to leave the Mediterranean at the present juncture without throwing away irretrievably all that has been gained there and all prospects for the future.' But with every weakening of the Italian naval power the mobility of Britain's fleet became 'potentially greater', and if the Italian fleet were knocked out, and Italy broken as a combatant, 'we could send strong naval forces to Singapore without suffering any serious disadvantage. We must try to bear our Eastern anxieties patiently and doggedly until this result is achieved, it always being understood that if Australia is seriously threatened by invasion we should not hesitate to compromise or sacrifice the Mediterranean for the sake of our kith and kin.' Churchill added that he was 'persuaded that if Japan should enter the war, the United States will come in on our side, which will put the naval boot very much on the other leg, and be a deliverance from many perils'. He could not be 'precise' about the number of aircraft that could be made available, and certainly flying boats could not 'lie about idle there on the remote chance of a Japanese attack'. The general aim was to build up forces in the Middle East, keeping them 'in a fluid position' to prosecute the war or 'reinforce Singapore, should the Japanese attitude change for the worse ...'.[68]

Concern over possible Japanese moves early in 1941 renewed Australia's worries. En route for London Menzies was advised by his Cabinet on 12 February to 'press for a frank appreciation ... as to the probable actions of Japan in the immediate future that would be looked upon as a casus belli and the possible moves that she might make which would be countered by other means ...'.[69] In Washington Australian diplomat Alan Watt discussed the evidence that Japan might 'spring' on a fixed date – such as 18 February – or at some date yet undetermined, perhaps after its intervention as mediator between Thailand and Indo-China had secured further bases to the south. He thought Japan would not take any step, such as an attack on the Philippines, which would inevitably mean war with the US, but it might attack Singapore by land or sea or both. What would the US do? It would fight if Japan attacked the Philippines; what it would do over an attack on Singapore was less clear. It could not base a battle fleet in Manila because of the state of its naval defences, and Singapore was the only place, besides Hawaii and possibly Sydney, where one could be based. The loss of Singapore would mean that Japan would control the Indies and cut off US supplies and augment its own; 'and it will be extremely difficult to throw Japan out of Singapore even after the conclusion of a successful war against Germany and Italy'. The current talks seemed to suggest that the Americans did not accept the importance of Singapore. Perhaps, however, their attitude was 'a gigantic bluff', designed to compel Great Britain to reinforce the fleet at Singapore, even though it must seriously weaken her situation in the Mediterranean by so doing.[70]

Casey discussed the threat with Hornbeck. He said there was 'no evidence that Japan intends early southward action. He believes it more than probable that they will consolidate Indo-China and prepare springboards for future use against possibly Netherlands East Indies and/or Singapore probably after Germany has demonstrated that she has reasonable prospects of success against Britain in the spring'. Asked by Casey what it was best now to say or do, Hornbeck suggested emphasising 'the vital importance of Singapore and the global aspect of the war effort against the Axis, stressing the fact that the integrity of Singapore is second only to the integrity of Britain itself, and that if Singapore were to fall to Japan, cohesion of the British Commonwealth war effort and of the Chinese resistance would be most seriously affected'. This view Halifax, now ambassador, and Casey put to the Secretary of State in the conversation of 15 February. Describing the President's interview with the newly-arrived Nomura, Hull indicated that the despatch of an ambassador 'professing love of peace' was 'a smoke-screen behind which the extremists will work just as actively as before'. Casey began to develop the theme Hornbeck had suggested, but Hull said he was already convinced of 'the supreme importance of Singapore'. Halifax left behind a memorandum, which more than hinted that, if Singapore were jeopardised, the Mediterranean might have to be abandoned, 'with the obvious setback to the British war effort against Germany and Italy in the main theatres of war'. Loudon saw Hull immediately after.[71]

In a speech at the Savoy on 3 March Menzies suggested that, although Japan had made the Tripartite Pact, it should not be assumed that conflict was inevitable. 'There was no difficulty that could not be resolved by the cultivation between nations of the utmost frankness.'[72] Dening was severely critical of the speech. The tension in the Far East was caused by Japan. Exposing its ambitions helped to restrain them and, if they could be deferred until Britain's defences were stronger, 'we may bluff Japan into putting off the date until the moment arrives when she decides that it would no longer be wise to embark on her great adventure at all …'.[73] Cadogan did not take 'too tragic' a view of the speech. Menzies insisted that it did not mean appeasement.[74]

He sought a plan for the contingency Churchill had outlined. How, if it proved essential, would the withdrawal from the Middle East be carried out? At the Admiralty the Vice-Chief of Naval Staff, Admiral T.S.V. Phillips, 'stated that we should not go to war with Japan over their occupation of any part of the Netherlands East Indies – this would only add to the number of our enemies, and if Germany could first be defeated we could turn to Japan later and deal with her'. If the Japanese were established in the Indies, Menzies countered, public opinion in Australia would insist on military action to eject them, as they would be able to threaten Singapore and attack Australia by air. It was desirable to develop a plan to reinforce Singapore by air and, gradually, by sea.[75]

The Australian Prime Minister also submitted a memorandum that was referred to the Chiefs of Staff. One issue was the defence of Malaya in the light of the 1940 report. The COS reported 'steady progress' on aircraft and did not consider the present situation critical. 'The majority of the 450 shore-based aircraft which the Japanese can marshal against us are of obsolete types, and … we have no reason to believe that Japanese standards are even comparable with those of the Italians.' The other was the plan for coming to Australia's aid in the event of a direct threat, including the possibility of sacrificing the Mediterranean. The intention, the COS commented, was 'to send a battle cruiser and carrier to the Indian Ocean at the start of war with Japan. Certain other heavy ships might be available, but their despatch to the Far East can only be considered in the light of the situation at the time.' Menzies had also suggested securing US support for a declaration that might deter Japan and drawing a line 'to indicate the point of aggression by Japan'. But in the absence of US support no definite policy could be adopted in advance.[76]

The withdrawal from Greece and reverses in North Africa led the Australian Government to fear that the position in the Mediterranean might prompt a Japanese breakout. It recalled the assurances of 11 August and 23 December 1940. They had been given in different circumstances, and they were subject to the condition that the defence and security of the Motherland must be assured, a condition with which the American emphasis on the Western hemisphere was consistent. A new appreciation was needed, 'candid and outspoken', 'shorn of any optimism', the Australian Cabinet declared.[77] The same day Viscount Cranborne, the Dominions Secretary, reported rumours that an expeditionary force in Formosa and Hainan would attack Singapore while Germany blocked Suez.[78] A full appreciation, Menzies was told, was being prepared. 'Churchill's attitude', he wrote, 'might be summarised by stating that he is so determined that the defence of Egypt must be made secure that the prospect of any alternative cannot be contemplated ...'. Menzies, however, wanted preparation for all eventualities.[79] He saw 'the Russian campaign while it lasts' as 'a breathing space of which the greatest possible advantage should be taken to improve our position in the Middle East'.[80]

The Australians had continued their search for reassurance over the Singapore strategy. That still evaded them. The naval defeat of the Italians in November 1940 improved the situation only temporarily. The spring of 1941 witnessed defeat in Greece and setbacks in Libya and as a result renewed concern over Egypt and the Mediterranean. At the same time the position in the Atlantic had deteriorated. The Lease-Lend Bill passed early in March. Not much pressure could be exerted on the US before that lest it evoked opposition to the bill. However, the passage of the bill, costly as it was, brought little immediate practical benefit, although it boosted morale. Some Americans felt once more that Britain might not after all survive. In this context Churchill's government found it impossible to offer greater assurances to Australia. Britain's defence forces were spread thinly. They must be used flexibly if they were to be used effectively. That, of course, meant that, in a crisis, time had to be won to move forces to the region concerned. It was thought that placing a limited force at Singapore, as contemplated in 1941, would sufficiently disrupt and delay a Japanese attack and win the time needed.

In February Grew again took stock of the Far Eastern situation as he had on 12 September. He thought that the Japanese were in a position where, 'with some added preparation', they could besiege Singapore. Its importance was, however, 'judgmental', and 'our expressed policy of supporting the British Empire dictates measures on our part to prevent the control of that strategically essential base from passing into hostile hands'.[81] Yet the American Chiefs of Staff, Casey reported, held that the retention of Singapore was 'very desirable' but argued that its loss would not have a decisive effect on the issue of the war. Japan could not invade Australia and New Zealand, the US could ensure their contact with the UK, and raw materials could be supplied from alternative sources.[82] Sending American forces to Singapore would impede hemisphere defence, and detaching a force from Pearl Harbor would make the fleet there less of a deterrent to Japanese action. Putting a fleet at Manila would invite attack, and it was 'politically impossible' to locate forces at British or Dutch bases in advance of war.[83]

These views contributed to the ABC compromise. The statements of the US COS were indeed perhaps something of a bargaining position, as Watt suspected. Certainly members of the State Department attached the utmost significance to the retention of Singapore. Sending ships there might indeed seem to the American public too much like defending imperialism and to the Japanese to be provocative. US diplomacy was, however, designed to keep the resources of Southeast Asia available to the British. That would help to keep British resistance to Germany alive and thus limit the threat to the US in the Atlantic. It was an argument that Lothian and Casey put, but one also put by Grew and increasingly accepted by the State Department and by the President himself. Again, however, they stopped short of commitment, which might not be acceptable at home. It might provoke the Japanese rather than restrain them. Keeping them guessing seemed to be preferable, and that was what the Americans saw themselves as doing.

It was not simply a matter of winning time. Time was indeed won, although at a cost of putting up with Japanese aggressions and advances. But that does not mean that such was the sole purpose in the sense of delaying an inevitable war. If the war in Europe could be won in time, a war in the East was thought to be unlikely. Then indeed the status quo could be restored with adjustments agreed on by peaceful means. Indeed, there remained some hope that agreement could be reached in the meantime. Those who had thought this way were even less hopeful than in 1940, it was true, but it was not ruled out. The agreement would, however, have to take account of the principles that Hull and the State Department had often enunciated. Developed in regard to China, they had been repeated when the Netherlands Indies and French Indo-China had been threatened in 1940. That made negotiations difficult. It made a different kind of approach, such as a modus vivendi, more or less impossible.

It was often thought that the Japanese could be halted by a firm demonstration of Anglo-American opposition and by measures, decisive but short of war, on the part of the US. That view perhaps made it more feasible to attempt the diplomatic approach; if it did not work, there was an alternative on which to fall back. The combination was problematic, however. The Japanese might be convinced that the US would not match words with deeds and find it impossible to accept a switch in US policy.

The policy was not indeed easy for the Americans to adopt. Joint statements with the British would, like other commitments, face opposition at home. Moreover, they might be provocative; it was not certain, although thought likely, that Japan would back down. US policy tended to be demonstrative and unilateral, which alarmed the British and the Dutch for, if the policy failed to work, it was their possessions that the Japanese were most likely to attack. They had, however, little influence over American policy in Asia in 1941.

In the first year of the war the British had in general been anxious to avoid a war in Asia. If the US did not join in the European war its supplies were essential and should not be diverted. If the US were to join in it should be in a European war. Increasingly the British recognised that the war could not be won without American participation and, furthermore, that might involve globalising it. Churchill saw that a war with Japan might be the only way America would enter the war in Europe in enough force and soon enough to be effective. Britain would suffer great losses in the interim. But the British tended to depreciate the fighting qualities of the Japanese, to exaggerate the chances that the US could bring them to a halt, and to neglect the extent to which their interests in the East might be permanently damaged.

The fate of Southeast Asia was even more in the balance than the fate of Australia. Its resources, particularly those of Netherlands India, had become ever more the focus of international rivalry as the impact of the European war was ever more widely felt. Hitler's invasion of the Soviet Union afforded some relief to the British in Europe and the Mediterranean. But it relieved the General Staff in Tokyo of some of its fears of the Soviet Union and intensified Japan's focus on Southeast Asia, which was to provoke a strong American reaction, above all new economic sanctions. They did not deter the Japanese.

Economic warfare

Economic restraints were not, of course, new nor applied merely by the US. Earlier in the war the British had been anxious to prevent supplies from reaching Germany through the Japanese conduit. After the fall of France the scope of economic warfare had broadened. Japan joined the pact 'while the security of British possessions in the Far East became directly threatened by Japan's declared intention of setting up a new order in Eastern Asia'. Japan had to be seen, as Hugh Dalton, the Minister for Economic Warfare, was to put it, 'not merely as a potential source of supply to the enemy, but as herself a potential enemy'. It was necessary 'to take steps to weaken her economy and prevent her from accumulating stocks which might make her invulnerable to blockade in the future' while avoiding 'any measures which might drive her to violent reactions'. In October 1940 the British Government suggested a co-ordinated approach to the empire governments, the US and the Netherlands. Although some emphasised 'the danger of marching ahead of the United States', the empire governments adopted a licensing system and a policy of limiting exports to normal figures in commodities regarded as German, Italian or Japanese deficiencies. 'The United States maintained and extended its specific embargoes, imposed haphazard, but showed much hesitancy in adopting a general system of rationing, being impressed by the danger of "encircling" Japan. The Japanese were thus able to increase their reserves' and by mid 1941 held about a year's stocks. 'Our objective can, therefore, no longer be merely to prevent the accumulation of stocks', the Ministry of Economic Warfare wrote early in July 1941, 'but to force Japan to draw on her reserves, which obviously creates a greater risk of violent reactions.'

Since the presidential election the Americans had subjected most important commodities to export licence 'and in practice when they place a commodity on the licensing list they normally refuse all licences to Japan'. The practice was more drastic than Britain's, but some commodities, like cotton and mineral oils (except aviation spirit and lubricants), were subject to no restriction at all. The United States had also extended its licensing system to the Philippines and to goods transhipped in the US, and begun a comprehensive policy of purchases in Latin America 'with the partial object of denying goods to Japan and to the enemy'. The Dutch were in principle anxious to cooperate but, in the absence of any assurance of assistance, had been unable entirely to resist. The Free French had introduced quotas for exports from the Pacific, and the British empire had 'gradually tightened' its restrictions on supply grounds or to conform with United States policy or for economic warfare reasons. 'The policy of the Dominions has not been easy to co-ordinate; Canada, for example, has imposed some embargoes against our advice, while Australia and South Africa have, on occasion, been reluctant to restrict their exports even to normal quantities.'

'[C]are is being exercised not to impose such restrictions to the extent of provoking Japan to war', the Ministry added. Little had been done to interfere with food supplies. But there had been protests, outbursts and appeals, which suggested that

our policy over the past eight months has begun to bear fruit. The Japanese
are, it may be hoped, finding it more and more difficult to avoid drawing on
their reserves ... By their control on Indo-China and by their pressure on
Thailand they have countered our efforts to restrict supplies of rubber and tin;
but they have had to share their loot with Germany and are not satisfied with
the position. While it would be foolish to claim that they are as yet seriously
weakened, it would be equally foolish to deny that they are becoming
increasingly alarmed.[84]

The purpose, Eden explained to Cabinet members, was to conserve
vital raw materials for the war effort, to prevent their reaching Britain's
enemies, and 'to prevent Japan from accumulating stocks of these
materials and thus to strengthen her power to make war on ourselves, the
Netherlands East Indies and the United States of America'. Insofar as the
reactions of the Japanese showed that they realised the disadvantages of
allying with the Axis, they were 'not necessarily undesirable'. Meanwhile
the Cabinet's Far Eastern Committee was being careful 'not to push
restrictions to the point of provoking Japan to war either by reducing too
drastically and suddenly supplies, e.g., of oil, considered vital by the
Japanese Government or by striking too brusquely at Japanese
enterprises within British territory'. But 'if and when Japan judges – for
whatever reasons – that the moment has come to strike at Malaya and the
Netherlands East Indies she will in all probability seize on our restrictions
as a justification of her action'.

The closing of the Siberian route as a result of the outbreak of the
Russo-German war gave Japan a pretext to demand relaxing the
restrictions. But possibly the Germans would be able to open it, and so
Japan should not accumulate stocks in the meantime. 'Apart from this, so
long as Japan remains tied to the Axis, she remains our potential enemy.'
Any change of policy would be premature 'until there are signs of a
radical reorientation of Japanese policy away from the Axis'.[85]

That was, of course, not to take place. Although the Japanese decided
not to join in against the Soviet Union, they resolved on a southern
policy that prompted more drastic sanctions. The expectation that they
would be effective is perhaps the more surprising in view of the
ineffectiveness of the earlier measures. Perhaps it was thought that their
unparalleled scope would make the difference. Earlier there had been a
wish to avoid 'pin pricks'. They would have little effect other than to
irritate. They would also mean that further measures would have to be
more drastic still. Within three weeks the British Government and its
partners had to decide on a new policy in the light of a new American
initiative.

The Australian Government had indicated that it was prepared to collaborate with the UK, US and Allied powers in the development of future economic policy towards Japan and was also 'in agreement with interim measures proposed to be put into force throughout the Empire to prevent Japan accumulating stocks of war materials'. But in taking unilateral steps Australia might fall between two stools. Piecemeal measures by the US seemed to have driven Japan into southward expansion. Pinpricks could only cause irritation in Japan without reducing its strength 'and produce a mental reaction that Japan can no longer be placed in a position where she can be dominated economically at the whim of a powerful neighbour'. Did Washington fully appreciate the 'consequences of tactics of irritation'?[86] Casey commented: 'I believe that pinpricks and provocation should be avoided by everyone particularly by countries that are vulnerable to Japan and we do not want to provide the maximum irritation with the minimum security'.[87] In April the British discussed suggestions for steps that might be taken in the event of further Japanese moves, including blacklisting one or two major firms and denouncing the commercial treaty.[88] Sir Frederick Stewart thought the measures quite inadequate: more pinpricks were useless, it was felt in Australia, and so was unilateral action.[89] What would be the result of the steps taken in July?

Dutch discussions with the British and Japanese

Netherlands India and its resources were increasingly the focus of rivalry in East Asia. The involvement of the British had two main aspects, economic and political, but they were connected. Netherlands India was important for the defence of British interests, in particular for the survival of Singapore. The British were unwilling, however, to commit themselves formally to come to the aid of the Indies if they were attacked. Their position seemed so much at risk worldwide that they believed their policy must be contingent, and they could make no unconditional promises even to the Dutch. Only if the US itself offered a commitment could the British themselves make one. No such commitment had been secured, even by encouraging the Dutch to seek it.

The resources of the Indies, in particular its oil, were what particularly interested the Japanese. Constraining their access to them might contain their imperial ambitions and render American and indeed British economic pressure more effective. But the Dutch might yield to Japanese demands unless more assured of British and American support. Indeed that was one of the hopes of the Japanese in making the Tripartite Pact.

The pact had encouraged Hull to suggest conversations, but then he had drawn back. Public opinion was anxious. He also thought the Dutch might be averse to anything that looked like formal defensive arrangements because of the effect on Japan and Germany, although he still appeared to contemplate private exchanges in London among service representatives and suggested that the Dutch might be brought into the Ghormley conversations. This shift was 'unfortunate', wrote Dening, but 'not surprising'. But was Hull right about Dutch apprehensions? Japanese pressure on them could be expected; if both Britain and the US hesitated, 'we may find at the crucial moment that they have lost heart'. It would in fact be a good thing if Japan and Germany knew that there were defence plans for Netherlands India. It would be a 'bulwark'; 'it is precisely for that reason that we have been urging joint consultation and a declaration – at the appropriate moment – that both we and the US will resist any attempt to infringe the *status quo* in the NEI'. Hopes must be deferred but not, Dening trusted, for long, 'because it is on our stand over the NEI that the future of the Far East depends ... And if ever evidence were needed that it pays to be firm, the Japanese reactions over the Burma Road have furnished ample proof.'[90]

> The firmness of the US and our reopening of the Burma road have undoubtedly caused Japan to pause and consider [Dening wrote]. But she will keep on pressing the weak points, and ... probably ... the capacity of the NEI to resist Japanese pressure will shortly be subjected to a test. I think that when that moment arrives we should all react vigorously, in order to make it clear to Japan that she has reached the danger point in her southward advance ...

But, as Bennett noted, the Americans were cooling off.[91]

The US had indicated that it could give no undertaking to support the Dutch.

> In a crisis [Lothian reported after a conversation with Welles] the American President can do almost anything because public opinion becomes interested and aroused, but before a crisis he can never give any kind of undertaking as to what he can do. Recent action in United States in indicating that it is not going to yield to Japanese threats and is preparing itself to meet hostile action should have been a great encouragement to Netherlands authorities. Though Administration has got to walk warily in this matter, I think the tendency will be for public opinion to consolidate in favour of common defensive action provided that it does not become entangled on the mainland of Asia.

Dening suggested that this should not hold Britain back. 'We should not be too timid just because we cannot get a cast-iron guarantee beforehand, and I think ... that we should be moderately safe in assuming that we shall get active support when the time comes.'[92] Bennett discussed the matter with Leslie Hollis, the senior Assistant Secretary in the War Cabinet office, and the COS made a suggestion to the Prime Minister.[93]

It was approved,[94] and a telegram went to Washington. It accepted that a staff conference must be deferred but stressed that the Dutch Government would see the US attitude as a key to theirs. The British would ask the Dutch to exchange information in London and to agree to exchange information at later stages of the Australia–New Zealand–British conference at Singapore. Would the US let the Dutch know that it supported this proposal?[95]

Nevile Butler discussed the proposal with Welles in Washington. Welles told Butler that staff conversations had to be limited strictly to an exchange of information; the US Government was 'not in a position to make any implied or direct commitment with regard to the course which it would pursue in the Far East in the realm of military operations'.[96] Then, on 18 October, Butler saw Roosevelt. The President repeated that conversations should for the time being be confined to exchange of information, although this might change in two or three weeks, that is, after the election. The US Government wished to be able to say 'that they had undertaken no new commitments'. Nor was any visit to Singapore possible in the meantime.[97] Halifax spoke to Michiels, the Netherlands minister, making the best of what little had come from the exchanges. Michiels said that the United States had asked for charts and information, which he regarded as encouraging. He thought the Dutch would be shy of attending at Singapore, which would be noticed by the Japanese.[98] In fact the Dutch preferred that a British officer in plain clothes go to Batavia.[99] This followed the final agreement of the Americans, pressed by Ghormley to send a representative to Singapore.[100] Although there was also some further discussion over a naval visit, it was recognised that this must await the election. But, said Dening, it was important that stagnation should not follow that event.[101]

Roosevelt's victory was as important as a naval victory, according to the Netherlands minister in London.[102] But at a meeting with the COS in London Lothian suggested that the presence of the American fleet at Singapore was unlikely: 'American opinion would take some time to educate up to this level'.[103] Roosevelt's re-election was a restraint but insufficient in itself [104] and, in the view of the Foreign Office, the position remained unsatisfactory. Unsupported, the Dutch might be too reserved over defence discussions with Britain, and they might yield too much in their negotiations with the Japanese. No promise from the US being forthcoming, despite the earlier hopes, the permanent officials were fighting an uphill battle.

In Batavia Kobayashi aimed at 'a gentleman's agreement' by which Japan would guarantee the territorial integrity of the Indies and in return have a free hand in economic matters. The Dutch resisted the attempt to shift the discussion to the political sphere and reacted to the Tripartite Pact by stressing that Netherlands India did not fall 'within living space of any Power, that Dutch will not admit leadership of any foreign Power, and will resist all attempts by others to alter status quo in the Netherlands East Indies …'.[105] The Japanese were thwarted but, affected by the US proclamation of July, put forward a demand for oil so greatly increased that meeting it would require the cancellation of other contracts. Pabst, the Dutch ambassador in Tokyo, believed that the aim was to apply maximum pressure before the US election.[106] Van Mook, Director of Economic Affairs and 'Minister Plenipotentiary', kept Consul-General Walsh informed. A renewed but vain attempt at political discussions, he said, led to the departure of Kobayashi, although another reason was given. But Mukai, the Mitsui representative, accepted the oil offer, which the Dutch had maintained was for the companies themselves to settle with reference to the supply situation and to existing contracts; the Japanese were given about half of what they asked for. Van Mook refused to discuss supplies of other products until the Japanese produced an agenda, which they failed to do.

> Mr Van Mook would prefer that the Dutch should break off discussions now for a good reason such as this rather than allow the Japanese to find a good pretext for doing the same thing later. He sees a serious threat to our economic war in the recent capitulation of Indo-China to Japan's economic demands. Backed by sources of supply in Indo-China …, Japan will be free to exert increased pressure in a politico-economic sense on the Netherlands East Indies …

That applied particularly to rubber. If Japan asked for more it would be for Germany and Italy, and the Dutch would have to refuse.[107]

Hull's view had been that a Japanese attack would be

> invited and accelerated by indications that the Dutch were willing to accede to whatever the Japanese demanded, whether reasonable or unreasonable, and, conversely, would be discouraged or retarded by efforts on the part of the Dutch to keep the current negotiations on an essentially commercial basis with indication of a willingness to meet reasonable desiderata but no intention of complying with excessive and discriminatory demands.[108]

The Dutch tried, it seemed, to move along these lines. They pointed out in London that they had sought to avoid undue tension in the Far East without yielding too much to the Japanese. The extra amount of oil was what usually went to the Mediterranean, and the contract was short-term.[109] The Dutch, as Clarke put it, were 'clearly pleased with themselves, as I think they have reason to be … But we have not heard the end of this yet …'.[110]

Handing over a memorandum on the discussions to R.A. Butler on 19 November, the Netherlands minister had said that the Dutch 'did not want to put the screw in on the Japanese to too great an extent'. He also said 'that speaking personally he himself had been mystified and disquieted by the fact that His Majesty's Government had never given to the Netherlands Government any undertaking that we should come to the aid of the Netherlands East Indies if attacked by Japan'. Butler assured him that Netherlands India was 'of vital concern to Great Britain and America. There had been circumstances which had rendered it inadvisable to press the American Government. Nor did I think it wise to exert undue pressure at this moment. Nevertheless the evident desire of HMG to engage in staff talks with the Dutch must have illustrated to the Minister the importance of this matter.' Michiels said that at an informal meeting of the Dutch Government 'he had himself put the point of view that it was of no value to indulge in staff talks unless the basis – a British undertaking to help defend the Netherlands East Indies – were forthcoming'. He hoped Butler would discuss it with the Foreign Secretary and reach some understanding that would satisfy the Dutch Government.[111]

In a memorandum, prepared following this conversation and a meeting of the new interdepartmental Far Eastern Committee, which had recently been set up, Butler connected the reservations of the Dutch with the development of the exchange of information at Batavia, which had proved unsatisfactory. He recalled the COS memoranda and the views of the dominions; the conclusion was against a binding obligation, but it was recognised that a guarantee would mean consulting the dominions again. In any case it would need to be carefully considered so that it did not encourage 'false hopes and subsequent accusations when the emergency arose that we had let the Netherlands East Indies down. It is doubtful in fact whether anything in the nature of a public guarantee would be advisable.' But the position could be explained to the Dutch. Given Britain's preoccupation in Europe, they might be told, 'the degree of help which we could give in Far East is necessarily limited and ... a great deal must depend on the attitude of the US. Nevertheless we should be so vitally concerned ... that our participation would be well-nigh inevitable if, as we assume ..., the Japanese aggression was resisted by the Dutch ...'. Bennett thought that the COS attitude – no obligation without a clear American indication – was unrealistic. 'I feel sure that if the Japanese did attack the Netherlands East Indies we should have to assist the Dutch and simply hope for the best as regards the USA. However it is unnecessary to pursue the point now as there is no question of giving the Dutch any binding guarantee at this stage ...'. In fact the conversations were going well after all, and maybe the preoccupation over a guarantee was particular to the minister. But the Foreign Secretary could well speak to the Dutch along the lines the Butler memorandum suggested.[112]

In a subsequent conversation with van Kleffens Halifax was able to express satisfaction that Dutch officers had now gone to Singapore.

> It was obvious much depended on the US, who were of the first importance to both of us. It was also obvious that anything affecting the position of Netherlands East Indies must be of direct importance to us. We would all like to send reinforcements to Far Eastern waters, but I could not say whether, in spite of Taranto, this would be feasible.

Van Kleffens said that the Americans were pressing for an exchange of information with the Dutch, but the Dutch did not want to commit themselves with the United States before the United States was prepared to commit itself further than it had at present with the Dutch.[113]

With the mauling of the Italian fleet at Taranto, the Foreign Office revived the proposal to send two British ships to Ceylon. It would be less provocative than sending them to Singapore but would show Britain's preparedness. The Admiralty declined. 'Surely the real deterrent to Japanese aggression ... can only be found in the willing and open cooperation of the United States.'[114] Passivity encouraged Japan and the Axis, Dening had written. 'A slap in the face to Japan at this stage, far from provoking war, might defer it indefinitely.'[115] The US and the Dutch had 'gone soft vis-à-vis the Japs recently', R.A. Butler told Halifax. 'The position in Saigon, Laos and Cambodia is steadily deteriorating. Our new air squadrons cannot reach the FE till March or April and the Navy cannot at present send ships.'[116] On Lothian's return concern was expressed over China, over Saigon, over Thailand;[117] some action was needed to restrain but not provoke Japan. If no naval visit to Singapore were possible, perhaps, as Hornbeck had advocated, some reinforcement of the US Navy in Asian waters would be?[118] Van Kleffens was pleased to learn some days later that the forces at Manila were to be increased. He added that negotiations were to continue at Batavia.[119]

Meanwhile the question of the Dutch Cabinet's attitude had been brought up again but with a shift of emphasis. According to Lord Phillimore, some of its members felt that the Dutch could do more but also felt that the British were unduly afraid of entering into commitments that might have to be fulfilled at the end of the war. They did not necessarily want an undertaking to preserve the integrity of their colonial empire; they would accept something along the lines of the assurance recently given to Bulgaria, that, if it did not assist Britain's enemies, Britain would do its best to ensure Bulgaria's independence and integrity at the peace. Bennett recalled the proverbial fault of the Dutch; all Britain was seeking was an exchange of information, and that would benefit the Dutch, too. But the Far Eastern Department was actually 'anxious to go as far as we possibly can to meet the Dutch, since our feeling is that if the NEI were attacked, we should have to join in and hope for the best from the USA'.[120] An informal meeting was held at the Foreign Office. It did not take up the Bulgarian parallel but, while rejecting a guarantee of territorial integrity, recommended 'that an informal assurance should be given orally on the lines that while the Netherlands Govt know that our resources in the Far East are at present very limited, they can rest assured that if the NEI are attacked, we shall do our best to help them ...'.[121] The concurrence of the COS was sought.[122]

The COS had meanwhile been considering a report on the conversations with the Dutch in Singapore in November.[123] The Americans had been persuaded to send an officer to the defence conference in Singapore the previous month, the attaché in Bangkok, A.C. Thomas.[124] That, Bennett thought, encouraged Dutch participation in November.[125] The COS adopted recommendations from the Joint Planners. The Dutch, the latter noted, would cooperate but, like the British, 'they will not commit themselves politically'. Liaison officers should be appointed, and mutual facilities secured at certain aerodromes.[126] The Netherlands Indies Government agreed promptly over liaison officers.[127] But the Dutch indicated that they would prefer not to take up immediately the invitation to the technical talks now getting under way in Washington.

The COS considered the new FO proposal in the light of these developments. They repeated their earlier conclusions.

> At the same time it is of considerable importance to the defence of our Far Eastern position that the Dutch should resist a Japanese move against the Netherlands East Indies and should agree to implement the recommendations of the Staff Conversations held at Singapore ...
>
> If the United States of America were to give us a clear indication that they would join us in supporting the Dutch against Japanese aggression, the position would be radically altered. While at present no such indication exists, the forthcoming conversations in Washington may lead to a movement of USA opinion in the desired direction.
>
> On balance, we consider that, unless the Foreign Office feel strongly that even a strictly limited oral statement would have the effect of stiffening the Dutch attitude, it would be better to leave the matter open until the conclusion of the Conversations at Washington.[128]

Bennett reacted in a way that could have been anticipated. He was influenced by further evidence of Dutch caution on the question of aerodrome facilities. The Dutch suggested that affording them might be seen by the Japanese as altering the status quo. They therefore wished to hold in abeyance a British request to use Sumatran aerodromes for patrolling in the Indian Ocean.[129] Bennett argued for the 'limited oral assurance' already suggested.

It is quite clear that we cannot stand by and see the Netherlands East Indies invaded and it seems high time that we stopped beating about the bush. We cannot of course guarantee that the assurance recommended will produce any specific result. But I suggest that we should take the line that those who have recently been in contact with the Netherlands representatives here have gained the impression that in the absence of some such assurance the Dutch and we are to some extent fencing with each other on defence questions and that an assurance would help to clear the air and facilitate collaboration.

Perhaps the assurances should be reciprocal.[130]

The Far Eastern Committee considered the idea on 16 January. The US seemed unlikely to be more forthcoming, but the lack of a British assurance was impeding Dutch cooperation.

On the other hand it was pointed out that the Dutch took a practical view of the situation; they knew that our power to assist them was limited; and it was doubtful whether the limited assurance we proposed would be likely to stiffen their attitude towards Japan ... There was a danger lest we should encourage the Dutch to be too stiff with the Japanese which might lead to their being embroiled in the Far East at a time when all resources were urgently needed at home.

The Foreign Office countered this view: 'there was little danger of their taking an unduly stiff attitude if, as was likely, they adhered to their long established practice of making concessions to the Japanese without yielding the whole demand ...'. The Foreign Office carried the day, and the committee recommended that the Foreign Secretary seek Cabinet authority 'to exchange orally with the Netherlands Government reciprocal assurances of actual help in the event of an unprovoked attack by the Japanese upon British or Netherlands possessions in the Far East'.[131] The C in C Far East wanted Dutch officers to take part in drawing up a combined Anglo–Dutch–Australian plan without political commitment. Bennett felt that 'we shall not get the Dutch to agree to this far reaching step without a definite undertaking that we will support them if they are attacked and resist ... more boldness on our part is required if the Japanese are to be stopped from penetrating the NEI as they are already penetrating Indo-China and Thailand'.

Clarke prepared a paper for Eden, the new Foreign Secretary, to present to Cabinet.[132] Eden cut out even a deprecatory reference to a declaration of the Bulgarian type. The paper recommended instead an assurance that the British would 'do their best' to help Netherlands India on the understanding that the Netherlands Indies would do its best if the attack fell on Malaya or British Borneo. Eden added that the dominions should be asked for their concurrence.[133] The War Cabinet on 6 February invited the Foreign Secretary and the First Sea Lord to discuss the matter

as a preliminary to a discussion by the Defence Committee
(Operations).[134]

Eden in fact met the Chiefs of Staff with Butler, Cadogan, Seymour
and Sterndale Bennett. The various arguments were rehearsed. The
failure to make formal arrangements with Netherlands India, it could be
said on the one hand, would lose the British cooperation and possibly
assistance if they were attacked; the Dutch were currently helping the
British; cooperation with the Indies had been developing. On the other
hand, British naval strength could not deal with the Japanese fleet; trade
east of the Cape and reinforcements to the Middle East from Australia
would be jeopardised if Britain had to go to war with Japan. If
Netherlands India were attacked British forces would be dissipated trying
to defend them and might not later be able to defend Singapore. 'The
Dutch must realise that the fate of the Netherlands East Indies is
dependent upon our winning the war. The longer we can remain at
peace with Japan, the more certain we shall be of a successful result.'
Eden decided that the COS arguments were strong enough to justify
further consideration of the question of a guarantee.[135]

Leopold Amery, the Secretary of State for India, thought, however,
that the Admiralty was 'rotten at the top' with 'timid old men' in charge[136]
and, in a letter to Churchill, had criticised its views as

> pusillanimous and shortsighted ... However weak we are in the Far East we
> shall gain nothing by telling the Japanese first mop up such Dutch forces as
> there are out there as well as occupy every strategic position in the Dutch East
> Indies up to the doors of Singapore, and then cut our throats at leisure. The
> logical conclusion of the Admiralty argument is that we shouldn't attempt to
> help either Malaya or Burma. After all, there are worse things than going
> under out there, for the time being, with credit, and our chances of not going
> under are, at the least, not worsened by our standing together.
>
> This is the material side. But how can we morally take the line of not helping
> Allies who have sacrificed their own home country – also they trust only for the
> time being – in order to stand with us? What of the Dutch sailors and airmen
> who are fighting with us if they hear that we propose to leave their comrades
> out East in the lurch? What of American opinion? Are we likely to enthuse
> America by the idea that we propose to let the Dutch East Indies be
> overwhelmed while we sit shivering in Singapore? Last, but not least, what of
> our own opinion at home?

Churchill referred this minute to Ismay.[137]

'The attitude of the Chiefs of Staff', Ismay explained, 'is that, on purely
military grounds, it would be most unwise to launch ourselves into war
with Japan on account of an attack upon the Netherlands East Indies,
unless we were certain of complete support by the USA.' It was for this
reason that they pressed for the joint declaration referred to in a

telegram just sent to Halifax in Washington.[138] That telegram, prepared on the basis of a COS aide-mémoire,[139] represented a reaction to Japanese moves in regard to Indo-China and Thailand. Japan might acquire new resources and advanced bases and, to meet a threat to Singapore, Britain might have to decrease its effort against Germany. 'Hence, it is clear that Japanese aggression against British interests in the Far East represents a serious threat to the United States of America, on account of its effect on our war effort as a whole.' It was essential

> in both our interests ... to prevent the Japanese from taking the plunge. We believe that this can only be done by a joint declaration to the Japanese by the United States of America and the British Empire that any attack on the Netherlands East Indies, or on British possessions in the Far East, will involve Japan in immediate war with both countries ...[140]

This Halifax sent to Hull on the same day.[141]

Harry Hopkins, Roosevelt's personal representative, had told Queen Wilhelmina that the President would regard any further southward movement as a warlike act. 'Unfortunately', van Kleffens added, 'Mr Hopkins had not gone on to say whether or not this meant that the United States would respond to it by war-like action.'[142] Halifax saw the President on 12 February.

> President said he had been anxiously considering what action the United States could take if Japan attacked the Netherlands East Indies, Thailand or Singapore. While the United States Government would declare war on Japan if latter were to attack American possessions he did not think that country would approve this action if Japan only attacked the Netherlands East Indies or British possessions.

Even if the US were involved in a war with Japan, Roosevelt felt that it would be 'a dangerous diversion of forces and material from the main theatre of operations which in his view was the Atlantic and Great Britain'. The US would have to fight a 'holding war' in the Pacific. The President showed Halifax a telegram from Grew, stressing 'the vital necessity of Singapore because of its importance to the general British war effort and disastrous effect of the fall of Singapore upon Chinese resistance'. Halifax pointed out that, if Britain had to fall back from the Middle East, Germany would be able to get Russian and Romanian oil by sea.[143]

Meanwhile the Foreign Secretary's reconsideration had not led him to amend his proposal, and Butler conveyed it to Churchill.[144] The Prime Minister told the First Sea Lord that 'this is all we can say in the circumstances. I doubt very much whether the issue will arise in this way.

It is more likely that we or British interests will be attacked directly ...'.[145] 'The American attitude', he added a few days later, was 'all-important, and it would not be wise to raise the matter again with them until after the Lease and Lend Bill is through, when the President will have a much freer hand ...'.[146]

The Admiralty restated its views, adding that staff conversations were about to take place, so that the absence of a guarantee was no obstacle. Without it there might be 'minor difficulties in the preparation of plans'. But neither these, nor the 'awkward political situation' in which Great Britain would be placed if it failed to go to the help of Netherlands India, could weigh against 'the dangerous strategical position in which we should be placed if, with no guarantee of American support, we became involved in war with Japan. Failing a guarantee of American support, it is vital that the decision whether or not to go to war with Japan should remain in our hands ...'. Yet the assurance that the British would do their best was a commitment: if a Japanese expedition against Netherlands India was within range of aircraft at Singapore they would be bound to attack it. The issue involved in war with Japan without US support was not simply the security of British possessions in the Far East but also the vulnerability of communications in the Indian Ocean and the threat to the war in the Middle East. 'With a guarantee from America obviously the whole position changes, and we should at once accept a joint Anglo-American assurance to the Dutch; but present indications show that America may well refrain from war with Japan should the latter attack the Netherlands East Indies. How, then, can we expect any guarantee?'[147] Churchill leaned towards the idea of a guarantee to maintain or return Dutch possessions at the end of the war. But he reaffirmed that further discussion should be deferred pending the passing of the Lease-Lend Bill.[148] The War Cabinet had agreed to this on 20 February.[149]

Meanwhile, as the Admiralty indicated, staff conversations had made progress. The C in C Far East, Sir Robert Brooke-Popham, wanted to carry the November discussions further now that liaison officers had been exchanged.[150] The Australian Prime Minister, visiting Batavia, found the Governor-General anxious to have a plan of operations drawn up and to receive a military mission from Australia for secret conversations.[151] Again Brooke-Popham, stopping at Batavia en route for Australia, found the Governor-General by no means lukewarm as some had reported. He wanted to maintain the status quo as long as possible and to give Japan no grounds for lodging complaints but was fully determined to resist aggression.[152] Brooke-Popham called again on his way back from Australia, and secret Dutch participation at Singapore was assured.[153]

In London the Foreign Office had approached the Netherlands minister, suggesting that, following the November conversations, 'mutual cooperation' should proceed a step further with planning discussions at Singapore 'of a purely technical nature'. The minister had stressed the need to avoid 'undue prominence' but saw no other difficulty and indeed thought the Governor-General could arrange the matter without additional instructions. He 'at one stage showed a disposition to raise once more the question of an assurance from us of support in the event of the NEI being attacked. But a telegram call interrupted the interview at this point and M. Michiels did not afterwards pursue the question of an assurance.'[154] In a conversation with R.A. Butler the next day – in fact the day before the Cabinet meeting on the 6th – Michiels indeed asked 'how things were getting along on the political side'. Butler 'thought that we both considered we ought to tie ourselves up a little closer to each other and the Minister said he would look forward to hearing further proposals ...'.[155]

On 18 February the Dutch Government was more forthcoming over the use of aerodromes.[156] But the following day the minister raised the question of guarantees. Butler did his best to offer comfort. 'We were after all Allies of the Dutch people and it would be in our interests to save their possessions from destruction ...'. The minister said that he understood the British Government's reluctance to offer the Netherlands Government in London a definite guarantee; 'but could we not take the matter a little further? Was our hesitation due to consultation with the Americans?' This gave Butler his opportunity to point out that it was necessary to choose the proper moment for that.[157] The Dutch Foreign Minister did not express any anxiety over the British attitude, but 'thought that the Americans still needed a great deal of educating ...'. He expressed some anxiety about Timor, 'one of the weakest and most vulnerable spots'. About to visit the Indies with Welter, the Colonial Minister, he 'showed every sign of a good spirit and a stout resolve'.[158]

A further factor in making the Netherlands more responsive was, no doubt, the attitude of the Japanese. That was manifested not only by their intervention between the Thais and the French in Indo-China but also in Matsuoka's speech to the Diet on 20 January. Hull had told the House Foreign Affairs Committee that Japan was 'actuated by ... broad and ambitious plans for establishing herself in a dominant position in the entire region of the Western Pacific'.[159] Matsuoka implied that Netherlands India was part of the Co-Prosperity Sphere.[160] The economic negotiations at Batavia were also at issue. As the British were informed both at Batavia and in London, the new head of the Japanese delegation, Yoshizawa, had finally produced an agenda.

It began, as van Mook told the Consul-General, 'with the usual tendentious and incorrect generalities alleging the close economic interdependence of Japan and the Netherlands East Indies and the urgent necessity for the former to help the latter to develop her resources for the welfare of the world'.[161] Although the New Order was not invoked, as the memorandum communicated in London commented, it was implied. The Japanese desiderata were not 'a workable basis for negotiations ... under less turbulent international conditions their very presentation might have constituted a sufficient reason for discontinuing the discussions. Under the present circumstances a somewhat more circumspect, though in practice not less firm line of action may recommend itself.' The desiderata included many old proposals – easier immigration, although in fact the existing quota had not been filled; removal of restrictions on prospecting; freer medical practice; 'favourable' and 'friendly' treatment of Japanese enterprises; fishing in territorial waters; direct air service to Japan by Japanese planes; removal of restraints on coasting trade – and one new proposal, a Japanese-managed submarine cable and the use of Japanese in telegrams. There were also unspecific proposals over import quotas and exports.[162]

The demands, as Dening put it, were 'preposterous'. At first sight they seemed 'the beginning of the end. But the Oriental sets his price high, expecting to be beaten down', and he doubted that the Japanese expected their case to be accepted. Nor was he certain that the Japanese had framed it so that its rejection might provide an excuse for aggressive action. 'I am more inclined to think that, while they may be shaping the shadows which events cast before them, they are simply adopting a spirit of aggressive diplomacy, backed by potential force, which must meet with the approval of their German mentors ...'. The demands involved 'a virtual relinquishment of sovereignty and complete penetration by the Japanese which, in effect, would paralyze resistance to any subsequent advance'. The Dutch, Dening thought, were aware of the dangers, and he imagined that 'they can be relied upon to play for time as long as possible'. He recommended that the US should be made aware of the demands. Bennett, Seymour and Eden agreed.[163]

After rebuffing Matsuoka[164] the Dutch replied to Yoshizawa in stonewalling style. Netherlands policy was based on welfare, progress and emancipation of the population, which required wide-ranging and non-discriminatory trade, although restrictions were unavoidable in wartime. The Japanese in fact enjoyed a far greater share of the import trade than of the export trade. But that was only possible by the increase of Netherlands Indian purchasing power through trade with other countries. Van Mook told the British Consul-General that he looked for some explanation of Japan's policy of 'soft words abroad and strong words at home'.[165] By mid February discussions had started. They were, van Mook said, 'pervaded by a bland, friendly feeling'. But he told Walsh that 'should Japan get bases in Indo-China and Thailand ... he intends to propose that Yoshizawa should return to Japan and economic discussions be closed'. Japanese conciliatoriness Gage ascribed to *rijstafel*.[166] Possibly, however, the Japanese were soft-pedalling while concentrating on the mainland to the north.[167]

The vexed question of a 'guarantee' was raised again with the arrival of the report of the Anglo–Dutch–Australian (ADA) conference at Singapore at the end of February and the passage of the Lease-Lend Bill on 11 March. The Singapore conference, attended by US observers, reached agreement on an ADA plan of defence, subject to ratification by the governments concerned. It argued that Japan's most likely move was to increase its hold on Indo-China and Thailand, 'leading to an attack on Malaya with object of capturing Singapore'. Unless it was certain that the US would not intervene it would have to retain considerable forces in Japan and keep a major portion of its fleet ready to deal with intervention. But the Allies could not rely on US intervention. The conference stressed the need to agree on cooperation against Japanese aggression, although not necessarily to announce it publicly, for failure to act together in face of a threat to one would weaken the military situation of all. 'Collective military strength can only be developed fully if governments agree to act together should any of them judge that Japanese action necessitated military counter measures.'

Governments should be advised to authorise such action, first, if Japan attacked British, Dutch, Australian, New Zealand or mandated territory; second, if Japanese forces moved into Thailand west of 100°E or south of 10°N; third, if large numbers of Japanese warships were clearly directed at the east coast of the Kra isthmus or Malaya or had crossed 6°N between Malaya and the Philippines, a line from the Gulf of Davao to Waigeou Island, or the equator east of Waigeou; fourth, if Japanese forces invaded Timor, New Caledonia, Loyalty Islands or the Philippines. In the third case, the decision could not await reference to London.

Commenting, Dening favoured this recommendation, but he recognised that it required the approval of the British Cabinet and the approval of the Dutch and dominion governments.[168] Indeed it went far beyond what the Admiralty had envisaged when suggesting that the lack of a guarantee was a quite minor obstacle to the preparation of plans. By contrast the conference argued that the Japanese threat really required a reduction of the contingency element, a high level of commitment and an unusual deference to local authority.

The issue had in fact already been raised at the previous discussions with Netherlands Indies officers at Singapore late in November. News of a Japanese expedition at sea might not be accompanied by certainty about its destination.

This is a very distinct possibility and emphasises the need for early cooperation. It is understood that the Dutch commanders intend to press for a Government decision that if a Japanese seaborne expedition should pass a certain parallel or certain islands, Dutch forces should be free to attack them without any declaration of war. This is considered to be important and it is thought that the British and Dutch Governments should agree on the stage at which they would authorize an attack on any Japanese seaborne expedition. It is suggested that the crossing of the parallel of 6°N between Malaya and Borneo by a formation of Japanese warships or a convoy of merchant ships should be regarded as a hostile act ...[169]

Vice-Admiral C.E.L. Helfrich had raised the matter again in a conversation with the British naval liaison officer at Batavia late in January. So far the decision on assistance remained with London. That meant, Helfrich said, that there would be no time for him to arrange effective Dutch assistance against a Japanese attack on Malaya.[170]

The Joint Planners and the COS noted that the ADA conference proposals raised the 'thorny question of an assurance to the Dutch', which awaited the Lend-Lease Bill. As for the 'chalk line' concept, 'what constituted an act of war could only be decided by His Majesty's Government in light of circumstances at the time ...'.[171] Bennett thought the COS reply 'too categorical'. But Seymour stressed another point of view. 'An important point here is the effect on the US of starting a war in some of the circumstances contemplated. It would be fatal to the chances of America coming in if we flew off the handle prematurely.'[172]

'What Napoleon or some other Old Guy said about the unwieldiness and low collective efficiency of Allies does come to mind', Admiral Thomas C. Hart, Commander in Chief of the US Asiatic Fleet, wrote to Stark from Manila.[173] But the comment was not entirely fair. The US was not an ally, and that made all the difference.

The Dutch again raised the question of an assurance.[174] Towards the end of March Michiels pretended some concern over the Singapore conclusions, suggested that they meant that the matter should be taken further and pointed out that the Lend-Lease Bill had now been passed. 'The Netherlands Minister is preaching to the converted, but he is in fact trying to jump us,' said Bennett. 'He has been the foremost protagonist of an assurance by us to the Netherlands. He knows perfectly well that the [Singapore] discussions ... were on a hypothetical basis without political commitment ...'.[175] The Far Eastern Department had in fact taken up an idea of Menzies, the Australian Prime Minister, who had visited the Foreign Office late in February.

Menzies believed 'that if Japan were told exactly where the chalk line was, she would hesitate to engage in a venture in which her navy might be defeated and her whole status consequently destroyed'.[176] At the FO in London on 26 February he said that the question was where the line was to be drawn which we could not allow the Japanese to cross and which we should let them know that we could not allow them to cross. The difficulty ... was that we might not be in a position to nail our colours to the mast without knowing the United States attitude. He felt, however, that drift was dangerous. Wherever we had taken a firm line it had paid.

Menzies raised the idea of a settlement. But the Japanese wanted 'physical control', not economic facilities, the Foreign Office pointed out, and 'it was difficult to see how any settlement could be come to which did not involve our throwing over China'. Menzies was afraid of 'a sense of inevitability on both sides. But he thought we ought to declare categorically to Japan that the Netherlands East Indies were vital to us and that we should have to watch Japanese activities elsewhere closely because they had a bearing on the security of the Netherlands East Indies ...'. 'What irresponsible rubbish these Antipodeans talk!' Cadogan wrote, although he did not take as 'tragic' a view of Menzies' public pronouncements a few days later.

A hard-and-fast chalk line as recommended in Singapore might be 'impracticable and perhaps undesirable', Bennett observed. But it seemed to be generally agreed that, if Netherlands India were attacked, 'we should regardless of any guarantee and with whatever forces were available, have to take action to support the Dutch in our own self-defence. If this is the fact, it is submitted that we ought to recognise it and utilise it to obtain the maximum cooperation both of the Dutch and of the United States'. The US should be told that the British would support the Dutch if they resisted an attack, and Halifax should be instructed to elicit from the US the best declaration possible along the lines of the Menzies suggestion.[177]

The US was not being pressed over the declaration proposed by the COS in February. On Craigie's recommendation the Foreign Office had itself suggested awaiting the outcome of Matsuoka's visit to Berlin, 'after which it might be necessary to take some counter-action'.[178] The new Menzies–Bennett idea – to turn to the US after making a statement to the Dutch – was supported by Lord Moyne at the Colonial Office, although he insisted that a decision about an act of war must remain with London.[179] Lord Cranborne thought that the situation was rather different from that in the previous August when the dominions' views had differed: 'we are not so weak in the Far East in terms of men and material as we were then'. Even more important, Hull had seemed more forthcoming in conversation with Halifax on 5 March.[180] The Dutch had suggested an approach to the US through diplomatic channels and the possibility of declarations not made public for the present.[181] Halifax mentioned the idea to Hull while on another subject. 'Mr Hull rather unexpectedly indicated in reply the readiness of the United States Government to do something on these lines not involving an unqualified threat ...'[182] A meeting of Butler, Menzies, Cranborne and Moyne on 8 April finally accepted the Menzies–Bennett idea: a mutual guarantee should be offered to the Dutch, and then the US should be approached. 'The Americans could not give a straight guarantee to protect the territory of a foreign Power but some form of words could no doubt be found to indicate that it was a vital American interest that the affected territories should not pass under the control of another Power ...'.[183]

The COS were, however, as Bennett put it, 'holding up' a political agreement, even though it had been agreed that the talks in Washington were to be followed up with a new Singapore conference with American, British and Dutch participation.[184] The Prime Minister and the COS in fact opposed a guarantee. Churchill supported what Amery called the Admiralty's 'illogical and immoral' view, 'which is in fact nothing less than the view that whatever action the little powers take it would lead to their being swallowed up anyway'. Nor would Churchill see that 'a shirking attitude' would have a bad effect in the US. 'If we are to be immoral it would be much better to promise the Dutch help now and go back on our promise when the time comes.'[185] The Defence Committee reserved the issue for further discussion by the Cabinet.

Bennett again marshalled his arguments and added some new ones. The lull in Japanese southward pressure was probably deceptive.

> German successes in the Middle East may quickly bring about their renewal ... The serious reverses in the Balkans and Libya surely provide an argument for and not against the re-insurance in the Far East which an understanding with the Dutch, and so far as possible with the United States, would constitute. Whatever happens in the Middle East, our commitments in the Far East and the Pacific, and more particularly to Australia and New Zealand, remain unaltered ...

The Prime Minister indicated that in his message to Australia and New Zealand in August and, in the interest of those commitments, a defensive barrier should be set up in Malaya and Netherlands India. The consensus was that Britain would have to fight if the Indies were attacked. It made sense to reassure the Dutch and, by a public declaration, to deter the Japanese. A commitment to the Dutch should be decided on, then the position should be explained to Roosevelt and he should be asked how far he could go by joint or parallel declaration to deter Japan. And that could help to counter any results from Matsuoka's new Soviet–Japanese non-aggression pact. Seymour thought that the joint declaration might be taken up as a response to the remarks Hull had made to Halifax, that is, not preceded by the assurance to the Dutch, which Churchill and the

Chiefs of Staff opposed. Bennett thought a commitment essential, at least after the declaration; 'a mere form of words' would be 'dangerous'. If the US agreed to a declaration, then it would be necessary at once to take up the question of assurance to the Dutch and to agree on the Japanese actions that would bring them into play.[186]

A telegram went to Washington on 19 April.[187] Eden spoke to John Winant, the American ambassador in London, on the same day,[188] and Menzies supported the approach at a Cabinet meeting.[189] The Dutch preferred using diplomatic channels, as they had suggested in February,[190] rather than making a public declaration; Halifax was authorised to discuss either, although the British preferred the latter.[191] Dutch support at Washington was sought at Bennett's suggestion and granted.[192] Casey also joined in.[193] But all was in vain. Hull's reaction was unfavourable. He saw Matsuoka's return to Tokyo as a bad moment; a declaration might be made at a later stage, not necessarily privately, but at this point it would be 'provocative'.[194] '... any more public declarations would do more harm than good'.[195]

On the other hand, the question of assurances had been revived by the arrival of the report of the American–British–Dutch (ABD) conference held on 21–26 April in Singapore. The report insisted that no political agreement was implied by its conclusions, which needed ratification. But, like the Anglo–Dutch–Australian report, it stressed that action against one power was 'of vital importance' to the others, that Japan might be deterred by their unity and that their strength would be fully developed only if cooperation were agreed on. Its chalk-line formula somewhat differed, however, from that in ADA. It urged the need for satisfactory procedures for a quick decision in the event of various Japanese moves, especially the move of a fleet south.[196] 'It is difficult to evolve any such procedure', wrote Bennett, 'in the absence of a definite commitment between the Powers concerned ...'.[197]

He tried again. German success in a drive to Suez would lead the Japanese to act.

> The object of pressing for joint or parallel declarations was (a) to deter Japan, (b) to encourage countries like China and Thailand to resist Japan, and (c) to pave the way for an exchange of assurances between the British Empire and the Netherlands East Indies which would facilitate the implementation of the plans which have been drawn up in recent staff talks at Singapore.

He thought the idea of declarations should not be dropped but that Britain should suggest that the declaration should be 'held in readiness for really speedy use should events take a turn for the worse in the Middle East or should Japan make some further move. Otherwise we shall certainly miss the psychological moment once more as we have done in the present case of the Soviet–Japanese pact.' The question of an exchange of assurances with the Dutch remained. Here the COS and the Foreign Office differed, while the Dutch, reluctant to join a public declaration without US participation, would adopt a different view of a confidential statement.

> Experience in Europe may not encourage us to enter into further commitments elsewhere, but the Netherlands East Indies are in a special case. We are already allied with the Netherlands Government against Germany. Thus, if the Netherlands East Indies were attacked by Germany's ally, both our moral obligation and the vital need to secure our communications with Australia and New Zealand would make it impossible for us to stand by and see the Netherlands East Indies overrun.

Plans had been worked out, 'and it now needs some political commitment to give confidence that they will be applied when the emergency arises'. Bennett suggested that the COS again be asked to approve an exchange of assurances with the Dutch. 'Armed with this we shall be in a stronger position to approach the United States Government again with a view to obtaining from her the maximum degree of solidarity which the United States Government feel capable of showing in advance of an actual emergency.' Cadogan thought that, in view of Hull's 'rather backward' attitude, the COS would be 'as reluctant as ever' to agree. 'Their objection is that, whatever we say, we can in fact do practically nothing. To which the purely cynical answer is that in that case we are committed to practically nothing. But, if by such a commitment, we increase the likelihood of the US Government making even a "parallel declaration", there might be positive advantage.' And the US should be continually reminded of the issue. Eden agreed.[198]

In the Far East Brooke-Popham had indicated in a press interview that Malaya–Netherlands India–Australia must be considered strategically as one.[199] An attack on any part must be regarded as an attack on the whole. That, van Kleffens declared in a broadcast on the Indies radio, 'seems to be a sensible opinion and one which should be taken to heart'. It was not Dutch to speak in challenging language, nor was it Dutch to let doubt arise 'regarding our will to fight if necessary and regarding our readiness should circumstances etc. lead thereto, to fight in alliance ... That America will give help to those who show themselves willing to assist in a struggle against unprovoked aggression, we all know.'[200] Although van Kleffens was more guarded in Sydney,[201] these remarks displaced Dutch reservations over a public statement; they also suggested the need for a British initiative. Bennett proposed endorsing the remarks, perhaps by a reply in the House of Commons. Seymour thought this would be too 'round about' and, more seriously, Cadogan pointed out that 'our internal controversy' had to be resolved first. Butler made a suggestion that Eden approved. The governments concerned, he thought, were

> guilty of the same hesitation as affected the Governments of Yugoslavia and European Holland. That is, we are not ready to concert before an attack even tho we all know that we are 'all in'.
>
> Now it appears that the American fleet is to move in part into the Atlantic, the Defence Committee should be asked to meet the Foreign Office view that – at least – parallel statements should be made by the Governments concerned about joint interest in the South Seas.
>
> Van Kleffens has done his duty. Could not the Defence Committee agree that the Foreign Secretary should take an opportunity to make a similar statement next week? Then the Americans can come along later.

A joint declaration was unlikely; this was the next best thing. Even this line, Cadogan pointed out, could not be followed before the domestic difference had been 'bridged'.[202] A memorandum was prepared for the Defence Committee, stressing the importance of the Dutch broadcast and the need to counteract the removal of part of the US fleet to the Atlantic. It suggested a statement endorsing van Kleffens' view, to be circulated in advance in the hope of securing support at least from Australia and New Zealand.[203]

At the Defence Committee Eden argued the Foreign Office case, adding that the Dutch were anxious to know whether Britain would 'ratify' the conversations. Sir Dudley Pound repeated his views. Without a tripartite declaration the British should not commit themselves to go to war if Netherlands India were attacked. 'Our Naval forces in the Far East were very weak and it would not be right to undertake to declare war automatically when such action might lead to a damaging attack on our trade. It would be better to keep an open mind and to decide at the time whether it was to our advantage to declare war or not.' Attlee said 'that we had often in recent months denounced those who had failed to make a united stand in face of danger. How could we justify ourselves if we adopted the attitude which we had denounced? A resolute stand by the Dutch and ourselves might prevent the danger ever arising.' Lord Beaverbrook, the Minister of Supply, David Margesson, the Secretary of State for War, Sir Archibald Sinclair, the Secretary of State for Air, even A.V. Alexander, the First Lord of the Admiralty, supported Eden. Churchill

> did not believe the Japanese would attack the Netherlands East Indies unless they were sure that the United States would remain neutral and unless they were prepared to go much further and attack us. He did not believe that such

a situation would arise. Why should the Japanese risk going to war with the Americans and ourselves when by waiting they could see whether the Germans were going to win the war. He agreed with the First Sea Lord that there was little we can do to help the Dutch and it was unpleasant in such circumstances to be committed to an automatic declaration of war.

But it was difficult to say nothing following the Dutch broadcast, and a public declaration would be a deterrent to the Japanese. They would behave 'like the Italians. They would enter the war when they thought that we were on the point of defeat, so that they could gather the spoils without danger to themselves.' Sir Dudley Pound suggested that the Dutch were adopting

> a short-sighted attitude. Holland was of more importance than the Netherlands East Indies. Yet if we became involved in war with the Japanese it might lead to our defeat. Thus in an endeavour to secure the Netherlands East Indies the Dutch would risk our failing to restore the independence of Holland. He felt that Van Kleffens was trying to trap us into a declaration by making his broadcast.

Cranborne 'suggested that as the United States were already involved in our victory they would be all the more likely to come into the war if we became embroiled with Japan in the Far East'.

Despite the First Sea Lord – and perhaps with some reluctance on Churchill's part – the committee decided on a public statement, subject to the concurrence of the dominions. The US should not be 'consulted' but 'informed beforehand'. The communications to the dominions and to the US should indicate 'that we felt we had no choice but to make common cause with the Dutch if the Netherlands East Indies were attacked by an Ally of the Axis, and that we had reached the conclusion that it was desirable to make this clear'.[204] Telegrams were sent to Halifax in Washington[205] and to the dominions.[206] The proposal was for a public declaration confirming that any attack on any part of the line must be dealt with as an attack on the whole. Churchill had shifted a little, despite his sympathy with Pound. But the proposal was not carried out; the communication to Washington brought down the idea.

Halifax had doubts about it. Hull, already perturbed by British comments on the Nomura talks, would be still further 'upset' . He would see a public statement as provocative. Casey pointed out that the Japanese knew of the three-way discussions. 'If we now announced defensive agreement with Dutch, Japan may well make capital out of non-participation of strongest party.' The Foreign Office reiterated its preference for a public statement; it might deter the Japanese, and they could not misinterpret it. In addition, 'it would be necessary to make private assurances much more categorical and precise than we are yet prepared for'. The US was 'more likely to take helpful action if impressed by our own resolution, and by the absence of anything which suggests that we are attempting to place the onus on them'. The aim was not to ask advice but to ascertain if it had any objection.[207] Among the dominions South Africa preferred to go no further without a US declaration.[208] Butler and Noel Hall from the embassy raised the matter with Hull on 3 June.[209] Neither Welles or Hull seemed to be opposed, provided a public statement were not provocative.[210] Casey also preferred a private undertaking with an indication in Tokyo that it had been given.[211] Canada did not reply. Only New Zealand fully approved.[212]

The Australians were, Bennett noted on 12 June, working on an idea said to have been started by the Dutch, but their objection that a public declaration without American support would indicate a lack of agreement appeared to apply equally to their own proposal. What made the whole idea additionally difficult to pursue was the report that the Japanese had broken off their economic negotiations with Netherlands India so that any declaration, public or private, would seem provocative. But if the Japanese now proceeded to more positive action 'then a declaration may be not only salutary but necessary'. Halifax should ask the US 'whether we could expect corresponding action by them'. But this, 'while preparing for *eventual* action designed to deter Japan (and, if the action was published, to encourage others, e.g. the Chinese, the Thais, the Dutch and our own people in Malaya and elsewhere), leaves the main problem unsolved'. That, in Bennett's view, was the question of a commitment to the Dutch to support the Singapore conclusions and 'to facilitate a rapid decision on military counter-measures to Japanese action which constitutes either an attack or an imminent threat of attack'. Consultation with the COS and the Dominions Office following the ADB conference suggested that there was no rapid procedure short of adopting the Singapore conclusion that certain acts must be met by force.[213] That need not, Bennett argued, mean a declaration of war, 'and there would be time for the Governments to consult each other as to whether full war measures would be necessary'. He urged 'ratification' of the conference conclusions and adoption of the 'chalk-line'. 'This in itself would be as definite a private assurance as the Dutch could wish for and it would be mutual.'[214] Bennett had urged that commitment must precede 'procedure'. Now he was urging commitment in the form the Dutch had suggested of 'ratification'. Perhaps he did not enhance his chances by adding an endorsement of the 'chalk-line', although he tried to draw a distinction between a reaction and 'full war'.

However, in the new context of the breakdown of the Batavia negotiations, the notion of a private warning made some progress. During March the Japanese had continued to appear 'indifferent to the success of their own proposals', van Mook had told Walsh. The Foreign Office presumed that the Japanese knew that they could not wring concessions from the Dutch, but their delegation could not leave empty-handed. They must be waiting on events, Dening suggested. They were 'not ready to exert pressure at this particular point yet', Clarke thought.[215] In fact the issues had become more intractable in any case. With its advance on the mainland Japan could supply its tin and rubber needs. To respond to its earlier demands on the Netherlands Indies for these products would enable it not only to build up its own resources but also to supply Germany and undermine the economic warfare that Britain had been developing since late 1940 and of which it reminded the Dutch.[216] In what turned out to be a final phase of the discussions, therefore, the original issues – on which the Dutch remained unyielding – were no longer the focus. The focus was on what had earlier been unspecific, the export quotas to Japan.[217]

Walsh felt that the Dutch were tempted to buy off Japan and acquiesce to demands for exports required by its Axis partners.[218] In fact, in May, the Netherlands delegation told the Japanese they reserved the right to raise or lower quotas of rubber and tin.[219] Their reply to the Japanese in early June in the event indicated that commitments could not be for longer than six months; allowed for the existing quotas of tin and a reduced quota of rubber for the rest of 1941, but suggested they might need to be cut; allowed one concession for oil exploration; and asked for increased Japanese imports of sugar, ebony and coffee.[220] The rubber quota, as the Dutch Government put it, might be high 'from the economic warfare point of view'. But it could not be 'detached from the reply as a whole which is very negative'.[221]

In Tokyo Matsuoka had asked for Craigie's good offices. Craigie had been tempted to seek a guarantee against re-export.[222] In London the Dutch Government had received a telegram, apparently indicating that the Governor-General intended to raise 'the whole issue of our military support for the Dutch in connection with the attitude now being maintained towards the Japanese requests for rubber'. The Dutch Government had not encouraged him but suggested that Craigie should participate in a joint discussion of rubber and tin exports. Clarke opposed this: no agreement could satisfy Japan and Britain; assurances over re-export would be valueless, and negotiations would worry the Chinese and the Americans, even though the Americans were themselves holding conversations with the Japanese. Craigie was told, too, that 'it would be highly inadvisable to admit that we are in a position to influence the Dutch',[223] a view supported by intelligence suggesting that the aim might be to present Britain as the source of difficulty.[224]

The idea had not been pressed by the Dutch, but the Netherlands minister in London did raise again the question of a declaration on the integrity of Netherlands India and suggested that 'we should not ask the Netherlands East Indies to be too restrictive in their policy of supplying the Japanese with rubber ...'.[225] Clearly the Dutch Government felt that the behaviour expected of it in the negotiations in their new context deserved a quid pro quo: they were expected to risk the security of Netherlands India and deserved support. Sir Frederick Leith-Ross of the Ministry of Economic Warfare thought the quotas finally offered 'as generous – and in some cases even more so – as the Japanese could possibly have expected ...'.[226] G.H.C. Hart was 'a little disappointed' with the comment, more especially as there was no British–Dutch–Australian (and preferably American) alignment to restrain Japan and make it easier to maintain an 'uncompromising' position.[227] In any case Yoshizawa told the Governor-General the reply was unsatisfactory and left.[228]

The Army Chief of Staff, Sugiyama, had opposed immediate military operations.[229] Craigie had, however, been concerned that a break-off would be followed by a Japanese attack, and Latham wanted to avoid provoking extremists.[230] There were suggestions both that the German Embassy was urging a Japanese attack and that ultra-nationalists wanted Japan to secure Netherlands India before Germany prevented its doing so.[231] The Tokyo Government's normal caution might be overcome by German pressure or a fait accompli. A declaration made at this juncture by Britain alone, Craigie thought, might 'touch off an explosion'. He suggested, however, that he might tell Matsuoka that he hoped the Foreign Minister would check any pressure for armed action, which 'must automatically involve my own country as ally of Holland'. The Japanese realised that American involvement was more likely if Britain came to the aid of Netherlands India rather than merely protested.[232] A public declaration, Craigie added, would be acceptable if the US made one, but that was unlikely, particularly in view of the Hull–Nomura discussions. Bennett, of course, favoured Craigie's suggestion. The exact phraseology – with its suggestion of automatic commitment – could not be used without consulting the COS and the dominions, but a different wording would avoid that necessity. Moreover, as Cadogan pointed out, it would avoid making it obvious that Britain had not got American cooperation: the ambassador would be expressing his view. Craigie was authorised to say that he hoped Matsuoka would check 'schemes which ... would produce a dangerous situation between Japan and my own country, as Ally of Holland'.[233] Craigie had in fact, already made such a statement that day to Ohashi, the Vice-Minister, when he referred to pressure for southward expansion.[234] In the event the Japanese merely discontinued the negotiations. No doubt, Craigie said, they were preoccupied with developments elsewhere. Would Germany secure close agreement with Russia or go to war?[235]

Clarke told Teixeira at the Dutch embassy that Craigie's statement had Foreign Office approval.

M. Teixeira said with a smile: 'That looks like the beginning of a commitment!' I said that it was hardly that, but in my personal opinion the commitment was one which we and the Netherlands had undertaken towards each other more than a year ago and that as far as the NEI were concerned there were certain geographical realities which could not be overlooked. M. Teixeira rejoined that this was no doubt so, but quoted the French phrase: 'It goes without saying, but it is better to say it.'

'Good', exclaimed R.A. Butler.[236]

Craigie had also discussed his proposed warning with the US ambassador in Tokyo. Grew asked his own government whether he too could speak to Matsuoka if Craigie were authorised by the British Government to speak. 'Line he suggested to his Government was that, as United States were doing everything in their power generally to keep Britain supplied across the Atlantic, it was obvious that they could not stand by and watch Britain's lifeline being cut in the Pacific through an attack on Singapore or Netherlands East Indies.' He received authority to speak if Craigie did. They decided to act if the situation again deteriorated or if Matsuoka gave a good opening.[237] The American decision affected the treatment of the suggestions Bennett had made on 'ratification'.

Not surprisingly, consultations between the Foreign and Dominions Offices and Joint Planners on procedures had concluded with some devices for making telegraphic communication more rapid in the event of a Far Eastern crisis but had stressed the importance of 'a wide measure of prior agreement'. A group of 'scattered democracies' was at a disadvantage in face of 'a totalitarian state having a wide choice of objectives and the advantage of initiative and surprise ...'. Indecision would not only increase 'our initial military disadvantage' but also 'encourage the Japanese to turn what might be restricted hostilities into total war'. The adoption of the list of cases as in the ADB report might be impracticable. 'Might it not at least be agreed that armed action by Japanese forces ... against the territory or mandated territory of any of the Powers concerned would at once be met by collective military measures on the part of those Powers?'[238] Bennett, it seems, had come to see that, by pressing for the chalk-line – which was too automatic, too 'devolved' – he might lose his whole case rather than gain it. The new proposal sounded more reasonable and would still be a commitment.

Meanwhile the Netherlands minister had formally raised the question of 'ratifying' the conclusions of the February and April conferences.[239] Over this notion, of course, the COS had reservations, which had been expressed by Pound the previous day; all that was necessary was to approve the plans.[240] The February report, then being considered, had indicated that it was subject to ratification and involved no political commitment. 'The Dutch', as Hollis put it, 'are presumably using this ...

as a lever for pressing us to enter into what is nothing more or less than a political commitment. I am sure that it was never the intention of the Chiefs of Staff that this Conference should be used for the purpose of engineering a political agreement with the Dutch ...'.[241] Bennett suggested that the term *ratification* was 'somewhat misleading, and what is really meant is the endorsement of the recommendations of these conferences'. At the same time he pointed to the conclusions reached by the discussions over procedure and submitted a draft telegram to Washington and a tentative memorandum for the Cabinet on assurances to the Dutch. Seymour thought that the question of assurances to the Dutch should be left alone for the moment for they would be unimpressive without US participation; the point was ratification, which, 'in whatever form gets round the political difficulty here', he favoured and which would, 'for practical purposes, be a sufficient assurance for the Dutch ...'. The draft to Washington was displaced when the news arrived that Grew had received authority to speak to the Japanese. Instead the British Government telegraphed its appreciation. The problem of 'getting round the political difficulty here' remained.[242]

The memorandum for the Cabinet pointed out that the proposed declaration of May was now inopportune, with the breakdown of Batavia negotiations, and so were representations to the Japanese. But the Dutch wanted to 'ratify' the conference reports, including the 'political' clauses in the April one, and it was 'hardly possible to continue to work on the basis of the report until we have decided that its political implications have been accepted'. Subject to dominion agreement, a statement might therefore be made, expressing the British Government's readiness 'to join with the other Governments concerned in a reciprocal agreement to co-operate to the full extent of their available resources in the event of any one of them being forced to take military action to counter armed action by Japanese forces against its territory or mandated territory...'. The other eventualities should be the subject of 'most immediate consultation'.[243] As Seymour pointed out to Cadogan, this statement contained 'a binding commitment. If this is thought so impossible as not even to be worth mentioning' the passage should be 'omitted. This, if approved, would result in the approval of the Singapore reports and a vague commitment defined only by the terms of the reports themselves.' Cadogan thought it could not be left out,

> because that is the whole question (which we have hitherto shied away from – but which we really must face) – are we, or are we not, to have a mutual commitment with the Dutch to help each other if attacked?
> Personally I think we *should*. I know that the Admty. say we can't do *much*, but I cannot conceive that, if our ally, who is helping to defend these shores, is attacked in her colonial possessions, we should do *nothing*. We should *not* do nothing: so let us say that we shall help to the best of our ability. It will be quite

understood that we can't transfer all our forces, naval, military and air, to the Far East.

Eden agreed.

C.J. Norton of the Foreign Office felt that the COS would not agree that Britain would be at war with Japan if Japan attacked Netherlands India. Bennett argued that the Defence Committee had in May already 'recognised the necessity of making common cause with the Dutch if the Netherlands East Indies are attacked and ... approved in principle an assurance to that effect'.[244] But Norton was proved right. The COS considered the full reports of the February and April conferences. They approved them as a basis for planning, adding in relation to the February one 'that no political commitment is implied' and that the British Government 'must retain complete freedom to decide what should constitute an "act of war" by Japan'.[245] They drew back even from this in respect of the April conference. The US had expressed some reservations about the proposed employment of the ships of the various navies and arrangements for naval command.[246] The COS did, however, reaffirm their conclusions on the ADA report.[247]

This, Bennett argued, produced 'a curious situation'. The Defence Committee had 'already approved the principle of mutual assurances between ourselves and the Dutch'; New Zealand had agreed and so had Australia on the understanding that the assurances were private. Yet the COS attitude would amount to 'a flat refusal to give any assurance' and 'produce the worst impression on the Netherlands Government'. Bennett advocated taking up the course already proposed but not yet put to Cabinet. 'Developments in Indo-China', he added, 'make it additionally urgent to get this long outstanding question settled.' 'We are now in the position that the Japanese southward drive is to begin almost at once and we have no political arrangement with the Dutch', Seymour added. 'It seems really impossible to allow this to continue, unless we do in fact contemplate letting the NEI be swallowed up without any help from us.' Eden again agreed.[248]

The new Japanese advance was not to elicit the assurances the Foreign Office had long sought. The relationship with the Dutch remained unchanged. Despite the pressure exerted by the Foreign Office, the British Government adhered to the views of Churchill and the First Lord. No promises could be made unless the US made a commitment. Otherwise forces were, they insisted, too widely dispersed to justify an automatic commitment. Immediate action might not be possible or desirable. But in reaction to the new Japanese advance the US was to undertake new moves that opened up an increased threat to the Dutch and the British without affording them a guarantee.

The Philippines flank

A sick Quezon had his speech read by another at the opening of the Philippine Assembly on 31 January.

> With regard to national defense the President admitted that with its own resources alone the Philippines was not in a position to defend itself. So long as the Philippines remained under American flag, its defense remained primarily the responsibility of the United States who had the exclusive right of determining whether they should be at peace or at war. He hoped that the program of national defense upon which the United States embarked included the Philippines, which was ready to cooperate with the United States and bear its full share of that responsibility ...[249]

The US had stopped short of major reinforcements in the Philippines, although it was clear that they would defend it if it were attacked. Attacking the Philippines would eliminate a threat to the flank of further Japanese expeditions to the southward, the ADB report pointed out. It would be the nearest objective to Japan and so 'easiest to cover as regards air support and lines of communication', and it could provide bases for further attacks. 'The disadvantages to the Japanese of an attack on the Philippines is that the economic resources of the islands are of comparatively little value for war purposes, so that it would be primarily a strategical move towards Japan's main object.'[250] The American Chiefs of Staff intended, Halifax reported, to adhere to their decision not to reinforce the Philippines in a major way.

> The principal value of the position and present strength of the United States forces in the Philippines lies in the fact that to defeat them will require a considerable effort by Japan and might well entail delay in development of an attack against Singapore and the Netherlands East Indies. A Japanese attack on the Philippines might thus offer opportunity to associated powers to inflict important losses on Japanese Naval forces and to improve their own dispositions.[251]

The US aimed to deter Japan by keeping sufficient forces in Honolulu. Keeping some in the Philippines might help. If the Japanese nevertheless moved south and attacked the Americans on their flanks, that would win the associated powers time and perhaps opportunity.

The contacts with the Decoux regime

The aim of the British was to preserve the status quo in French Indo-China. That had been their wish in 1940. The risk was that the French would compromise too much in order to sustain the continuity of their rule. Their aim was, as Chauvel of the French Foreign Office put it, 'at all costs to stay in Indochina. They feel that once they are forced out of the colony their chances of ever regaining possession ... would be slim indeed'.[252] Their concessions might, however, produce the same effect as a change in the status quo. But, despite the events of September, the British persisted with the policy for lack of an alternative.

One alternative the British did not pursue in the Far East was the support of Gaullism: any such venture might not only alienate Decoux, the Governor-General, but also encourage the Japanese to overturn the status quo. Another problem, with which the British proved unable to deal, was the Thais' desire to take advantage of Indo-China's weakness by regaining some of the territories lost in the colonial period. Trade was a third issue in relations between Britain and Indo-China. If Indo-China moved into Japan's orbit the British should step up their embargoes. But a more lenient policy might avoid its doing so.

In November the Foreign Office concluded that the situation in Indo-China was 'deteriorating'. Exports to the British Empire were prohibited, and no British ships were allowed into Indo-China ports. The Japanese, by contrast, were increasing their penetration, demanding rice, rubber, phosphates and other materials. 'It seems improbable that any effective resistance will be offered should the Japanese decide to extend their control to Southern Indo-China. Nor is it possible for His Majesty's Government to offer support in the way of aircraft or other war material or by military action.' Given Hanoi's subservience to Vichy, and Vichy's to Germany, 'there can be little hope of persuading French authorities at present of the unwisdom of their policy'. Britain should, however, react to the embargo as well as ensure that Indo-China did not become 'an entrepôt for British goods the supply of which to Japan we are endeavouring to restrict'. The plan was to stop all goods subject to licence in the UK and colonies from going to Indo-China, and for India to stop jute bags and cotton. The 'main purpose of our measures is to make Japanese encroachments as little profitable to Japan as possible', but 'the ostensible ground for taking these measures is the embargo on trade with British Empire'.[253]

Indo-China, however, denied stopping essential exports to British colonies, and a war trade agreement seemed possible.[254] 'It was desirable that the French should be encouraged to hold out against Japanese demands; but in any agreement we should not want to let Indo-China have any Japanese deficiencies ...'[255] Henderson, the Consul-General, was told that the government was inclined to 'let pressure continue' until Hanoi suggested conversations. If it did, Britain would contemplate 'a modus vivendi enabling some limited trade to continue'.[256]

In the event Decoux's aide-de-camp, Jouan, was despatched to Singapore and held discussions with the Governor and the C in C China:

'French authorities in Indo-China now find it imperative to reopen trade in their own interests and are definitely feeling the result of trade restrictions imposed by us'.[257] The Armistice Commission at Wiesbaden had authorised two French ships to go to Hong Kong per month and one to Singapore. At Decoux's request Vichy had, without the commission's concurrence, agreed to reciprocity. The Germans knew, however, about the movements of British ships in Indo-Chinese ports, presumably through the Japanese, and, to avoid reprisals, negotiations had to be secret and, if possible, ships had to avoid Haiphong. Gunny bags, supplied from India and used to export rice, were needed. But apart from them Indo-China could guarantee that no unlicensed imports would end up in Japan or enemy countries. 'Captain Jouan said that Indo-China could not carry on without her overseas trade, and if the British brought pressure on them by prohibiting this they must inevitably be forced into the arms of Japan, which would constitute an alternative source of supply for commodities now imported from British sources ...'. It was agreed that the supply of gunny bags should be limited to those needed for the rice exported to British possessions. An agreement between Decoux and Admiral Noble was reaffirmed to the effect that large and fast French vessels should not proceed off the China station and that there would be no hostile action between French and British warships on the China station.

Another topic was Free French propaganda. Jouan gave an account of the events of 1940 and their outcome, presenting the best case for Decoux. He

emphasised that the present situation in Indo-China was one of extreme difficulty for the French authorities. As things stood they could only wait for some more favourable turn of events before adopting any more active policy. For this reason they need all the support and co-operation that the British authorities can give. They point out that so long as the French remain in Indo-China there is a barrier between the Japanese and Malaya, but should Japanese occupation of Indo-China become general Malaya would be gravely menaced. Germany has clearly asked Japan to oppose and suppress any sign of a de Gaullist or Free French movement in Indo-China, and it is certain that, should such a movement become noticeable, the Japanese would immediately intervene and seize this pretext for occupying the whole of Indo-China.

The French in Indo-China all believed, he said, that 'a British victory is essential for the rehabilitation of France ... but in the present circumstances they are compelled to negotiate with Vichy and Japan if they are to continue to exist at all ... they were only asking assistance in order to maintain a position which must be of great importance to Great Britain'. A de Gaulle movement 'would give the Japanese a heaven-sent opportunity for further penetration'. Yet Decoux had information that

propaganda leaflets had been passed to the British Consul-General at
Haiphong for distribution. Sir Shenton Thomas said that any such
propaganda 'was entirely without the knowledge of the Straits Settlements Government and that it was the considered policy of that
Government not to do anything to cause divisions in Indo-China ...'.[258]

In London the Far Eastern Committee thought the Commander-in-
Chief–Jouan agreement on trade acceptable as a basis for discussion,
provided Indo-Chinese trade was not monopolised by Japan, and France
as far as possible restricted rubber exports to Japan that might be sent on
to Germany. The items agreed on 26 December became the basis of a
modus vivendi finally approved by Decoux and the British Government
in February 1941.[259]

The Straits Government told the Colonial Office that quantities of
Gaullist propaganda were indeed passing through Singapore from
Shanghai en route for Cochin China. Understanding that this was
'contrary to British policy', it had instructed the censor to detain the
material. This, Gage minuted, was 'quite correct'.[260] The Consul-General
in Haiphong reported that Decoux still suspected that the Consulate-
General in Saigon and British residents there were receiving and dis-
tributing Gaullist propaganda. 'There is no foundation whatever in these
suspicions and no proof is ever produced ....'[261] The British Government
sought de Gaulle's agreement to the undertaking 'not to do any de
Gaullist propaganda',[262] and his agent, de Schompre, stopped all Free
French propaganda.[263] 'We have lately entered into a gentleman's agreement with Admiral Decoux in which, with General de Gaulle's assent, we
have undertaken to refrain from Free French propaganda in Indo-China
in return for a similar undertaking by him in regard to Free French
territories in the Pacific.'[264]

Decoux's policy was 'one of delay'. Its features were: 'Maximum
negotiations before conceding any points, while always emphasising
territorial integrity and French sovereignty of Indo-China', making the
French population aware of this policy, strongly controlling the native
population, 'Discreet co-operation with British', increasing Indo-China's
military strength, and purchasing arms.[265] According to Meiklereid, the
British Acting Consul-General, Decoux entered the Singapore agreement, although he had accused the British of anti-Vichy propaganda,
partly because he feared that his unpopularity would increase as soon as
the terms of the economic agreement made with Japan were known, and
partly because essential imports were becoming scarcer. He told
Meiklereid that he intended to abide by it 'while at the same time
stressing the necessity of a common front by the white races against the
Japanese menace'. Meiklereid thought Decoux 'as small physically as in
mental outlook, and irascible to a degree which deprives him of all

charm ...'. Jouan, 'far-sighted', possessing accurate judgment, the chief instigator of the Singapore agreement, could be expected 'to do his utmost to maintain it in force, realising ... that the future both of this country and of France depends upon continued close co-operation with us'. He was influential, but on occasions had 'an uphill task' in persuading Decoux to adopt his policy.[266]

De Gaulle himself agreed that a Free French movement in Indo-China was not opportune. He had no objection to granting the Indo-China Government certain facilities for maintaining order and defending French interests, including the planes on the *Béarn*.[267] A telegram from Sir Samuel Hoare, the British ambassador in Madrid, indicated that the Vichy French wanted planes sent to Indo-China. Gage feared that, with the change in the position in Indo-China, Japan might get them.[268] The Air Ministry was prepared to see seventy go from metropolitan France.[269] Gage was referring to the crisis with Thailand. The border conflict had come to a head, and the Japanese intervened as mediators. The prospect was that they would, as a result, vastly increase their influence on the mainland and their threat to Malaya and Singapore.

Craigie had pointed out the implications of a possible partition of Indo-China. Japan might acquire bases within striking distance of Malaya and increase its strategic and political hold over Thailand. The British could make no 'effective movement' without 'full American support'. The Americans appeared to consider Japanese absorption of Indo-China 'inevitable, i.e. they are presumably not prepared to take any real effective action (as distinct from further economic pressure) when it happens'. The British should concentrate on the second threat 'by inducing American opinion, which has now recognised Singapore's value to America, to draw logical conclusions from this in regard to Thailand as key to Singapore'. Malaya's dependence on Thailand, for example in rice, might be shown. 'We might also emphasise how vulnerable Malaya would be to an amphibian Japanese attack via Isthmus of Kra and how easily Japanese forces established in South Indo-China could land on Thai territory e.g. at [Songkla?] for a [? march] on Singapore ....' Educating American opinion was the only option 'as we cannot apply military pressure alone'. The interest Americans now took in Singapore

shows such education as possible. The United States Government seem in fact to have drawn imaginary line north of Singapore and of parts of Netherlands East Indies, but south of Indo-China, and to be ready to react decisively only when Japan crosses this line ... Our first objective should be to convince them if possible to extend this line to cover Thailand, and ... once this has been done, we should see whether southern Indo-China cannot be included as well ...[270]

Clarke agreed that Britain should try to bring home to the United States 'that Japanese mediation in the Thai dispute means a big jump forward in the Japanese southward advance towards the showdown which will probably involve the United States in war with Japan'.[271]

The subsequent acceptance of Japanese mediation, 'with its enhancement of the Japanese prestige in overpowering eastern Asia and its open recognition of Japan's claim to leadership in this area', was, Craigie argued,

> a serious development from our point of view. An excess of defeatism has betrayed the French into a step which may well end in uniting the two Asiatic nations in an anti-European drive of which the French will be the first victims but Burma and Malaya the real objectives. The redeeming feature is that it connotes a success for Matsuoka's policy of political and economic penetration as against more direct and immediate action favoured by the Army and so gives the United States and ourselves a little longer to make up our minds on what line we propose to make our stand.

Had the United States offered 'clear or even sound advice' at Vichy, Craigie concluded, the French Government would have been encouraged to maintain its stand against Japanese mediation. That made it 'daily more necessary to know at what point, if any, the United States Government are prepared to join us in checking Japan's advance – by diplomatic means if possible, by force if necessary'. Craigie pointed to 'a general feeling amongst the Japanese' that the crisis in the Far East would come in the next few weeks because a German invasion of Britain was expected, or 'sudden tension' in Japan–US relations might lead to a break. He thought German–Japanese relations were becoming 'progressively more intimate' and that the 'German stranglehold on Japanese policy' was 'being tightened'. The best method of checking Japanese expansion and dispelling American hesitation was to strengthen British naval and air strength to form a deterrent, not merely to meet an emergency, although there were heavy calls in the Mediterranean and elsewhere.[272]

The Commander-in-Chief suggested that, since the Japanese had declared a visit to Singapore of a US squadron provocative, their move might be countered by a service mission.[273] Craigie suggested sending a US squadron to Manila. Could he say a landing at Songkla would be provocative? Dening thought that even one ship at Singapore would be something. Should Halifax ask the President or wait until the Lease-Lend Bill was through? Any British reinforcements would probably arrive too late. Over Songkla the Japanese might call the bluff, and that was all it would be. It might, Clarke added, be not a matter of reaction to events in Indo-China but of urgent defensive operations.[274]

In Washington Butler spoke to Hornbeck on 30 January of the need for a reaction. Hornbeck was thinking that the sword was mightier than the pen and referred to reinforcements at Manila.[275] Dening found it 'comforting' that Hornbeck felt that the point had been reached at which the sword was mightier than the pen. 'That is, I am afraid, true, provided of course the sword is not left in its sheath far from the scene of conflict.' Most of the contemplated reinforcements, American or British, would arrive too late, 'certainly for what has always been the main purpose of this Department namely to frighten Japan out of the war'.[276]

Early in February Latham reported from Tokyo that the southern move, which had seemed probable late in January, did not seem to be developing. But government and press were 'playing up' the idea that the acceptance of mediation meant the acceptance of Japan's leadership. He had told Matsuoka that Australia was not part of Asia and would not accept the New Order, and the Dutch ambassador, Pabst, had said the same of the Indies. It was important to stimulate 'self-respect rather than self-abasement' in Thailand and Indo-China, too. Any agreement should avoid reference to Japan's leadership. More generally, Britain should decide its policy in view of the threat to Singapore. Japan's hold on Indo-China was 'very strong'. Its domination of Thailand would be 'far more serious', and 'we should do what we can to strengthen our forces near Thai border, warn Thai Government against giving footholds to Japan and offer them all aid in our power to resist any attempt by Japan to take them by force. We should try to disabuse Thai of any idea that they will escape by yielding to Japan.' This policy should be adopted then explained to the Americans in the hope that 'they will stand by us if we are attacked'. It might bring about a Japanese attack, but more likely it would make Japan pause for 'I do not believe they want war especially as it means American intervention, but seek rather to advance peaceably by slow stages establishing each position before they make the next move ...'.[277]

Craigie declared that Britain must now be prepared to cope with Japanese control over Indo-China. He thought it possible that the Japanese might also secure bases in Thailand even if, as Crosby said, the Thais would wish to refuse and, if they secured bases on the west as well as the east coasts, 'they will be able in the case of war with us to by-pass Singapore completely and prey on our shipping in the Indian Ocean as if the fortress did not exist'. The Japanese would be able to attack Singapore 'in the most favourable possible conditions', or neutralise it, and meanwhile starve Malaya of rice. Again it was a matter of educating American opinion:

it is little use removing Axis threat to the Suez Canal if at the same time we allow the other main key to our Imperial position, value of which is already

recognised by United States opinion, to be compromised through inaction.
The great danger appears to be British and American opinion falling into a
kind of Maginot Line psychology as regards Singapore. Meanwhile Japanese
preparations elsewhere may be rendering its value nugatory.

The defeat of Italy in the Mediterranean might enable Britain 'so to
strengthen Singapore as to secure its outer glacis', but the only chance
of preventing Japan from establishing itself in Thailand in the meantime
was 'by securing full American co-operation'.

> First and most immediate necessity is to put some heart into the friends which
> we presumably still possess in Thailand and Indo-China. For this purpose it will
> be necessary to intimate clearly that neither British nor American Govern-
> ments can remain indifferent to any further modification of the status quo in
> this area and that they will be prepared to support in every way possible any
> resistance which those countries may be prepared to offer to further Japanese
> southward expansion.

Unless Thailand, Indo-China and the Indies could be 'made to feel *now*
that full strength of British Empire and United States will be behind
them in resisting further aggression, the pass will be sold'. Gains in the
Mediterranean 'will be to some extent offset by steady undermining of
our whole strategic situation in the Far East and Indian Ocean'.[278]
Bennett thought Craigie had 'done a public service in concentrating
attention in this telegram on a danger on which the Far Eastern
Department has been harping and hammering away for several months
past'. The Japanese were outflanking the British at Singapore, and
'unless we meet this threat boldly we shall find that the value of
Singapore has been sapped away when the moment comes'. The remedy,
in Craigie's view, was to convince the United States of the danger. Before
that, however, 'we must ourselves get the problem into proper per-
spective'. The British were in fact 'fumbling in the Far East. There may be
good explanations, i.e. our preoccupations elsewhere and the paucity of
our available forces', but the danger was not yet 'fully realised', nor were
the British 'going to the limit in meeting it'. The Chiefs of Staff have
refused to see Japanese penetration into Indo-China or Thailand as a
justifiable casus belli. 'They are even hesitating about the Netherlands
East Indies, though they must know perfectly well that we cannot afford
to see the Netherlands East Indies overrun by the Japanese.' But 'we are
in a much better position than would appear at first sight if only we act
with energy and determination'. True, Indo-China was virtually lost to
the Japanese. They were also 'in a fair way to establishing their influence
in Thailand', which was 'a serious potential threat' to Malaya and Burma,
'at all events from the air'. But the Japanese 'would clearly be operating

at considerable danger if they had on their left flank a solid block consisting of Malaya, the Netherlands East Indies and the Philippines, and if on the other side they were having difficulties in China'. They would try to ensure their flank by neutralising the United States, by knocking out the Dutch or 'by occupying British North Borneo and constituting so serious threat to the Dutch as to keep them quiet'. British policy should be not only to educate the Americans but also to tighten the bonds with the Indies and to hurry on preparation for military cooperation among Britain, the US and the Dutch. 'Simultaneously we should make sure that we are doing everything possible to maintain China's resistance and it is for consideration whether we can yet do anything to prevent Thailand from falling more completely under Japanese influence.' The Chiefs of Staff should 'think again with a view to deciding where our strategic interests really lie and what measures are open to us to strengthen our military position and to check the Japanese advance'.[279]

At the Cabinet Churchill thought, so far as Indo-China was concerned, that rapid developments were unlikely. So far as the US was concerned the point of immediate importance was the Lend-Lease Bill. The COS were invited to consider the strategic implications.[280] Japan, the Joint Planners concluded, would gain bases as a result of mediation. Its control of Indo-China would not directly affect Britain's vital interests. But the Indies would be its next objective, and penetration into Thailand would threaten Singapore. The US, they believed, should strengthen its forces in Manila. They also argued for a joint statement with Britain to the effect that the US would support the Indies in the event of attack.[281]

The mediation was to be a one-sided affair, but the view the FO took of Indo-China did not greatly change. The Far Eastern Department supported the continuance of the trade agreement. 'The overriding political consideration', Clarke wrote, 'is ... that we want the French to cooperate with us, and to resist the Japanese to the extent that they are able to do so. The Governor-General of Indo-China has gone a long way to meet our original desiderata ... '.[282]

> It is clear [Gage thought] that the Germans are taking a keen interest in all that is going on in this part of the world and, since they have granted permission for French ships to trade with British ports, they must clearly have an interest in it. One can only speculate that they wish to keep Indo-China going as a lever on Japan to follow their bidding in other respects ...[283]

On behalf of the Free French, Pleven and Escarra discussed Indo-China with Ashley Clarke on 4 March. There were, said Pleven, elements in Indo-China willing to resist, but 'Vichy was obliging them to be silent and to give way. General de Gaulle was considering whether the moment had not come to make a direct appeal to Indo-China to resist'. An appeal would be all the more effective if he could say that Indo-China would enjoy certain advantages, like Chad, which had joined de Gaulle. It could be either an appeal to resistance by force of arms or 'a moral appeal'. Escarra 'interjected that the former would require some prospect of military collaboration with Great Britain, the United States, China and perhaps the Netherlands East Indies'. Clarke thought that

> there was danger in making any form of appeal. It would be unwise to count on United States military support, the Chinese armies, though numerous, lacked the necessary organisation, and as for help from us, even if it were forthcoming it could hardly forestall the Japanese who were in a position militarily to step in very rapidly at key points owing to the foothold which they already had in the country.

Even a moral appeal 'might be used by the Japanese as a pretext for a military descent upon the rest of Indo-China'. The advice, Pleven concluded, was to do nothing. 'Would we prefer to see Indo-China fight with however little hope of success or struggle along as they were doing at present?' Clarke said the British preferred the latter. 'I added that the Dutch had been very successful in staving off Japanese pressure by means of temporising in one way or another.' Escarra said they faced no 'immediate military menace'. Clarke replied 'that this might be so, but it remained probably the best way of trying to hold the situation'. The recent agreement, made with de Gaulle's concurrence, might encourage Indo-China to keep going, and Pleven and Escarra agreed that the understanding with Decoux had been 'useful'.[284] Bennett thought 'the advice given was quite right'.[285]

The mediation did not proceed smoothly. Craigie thought that 'some form of Japanese armed intervention' would take place. A corollary of that would be the seizure of air and naval bases in southern Indo-China. 'Even if mediation is successful, it must be assumed that the army and navy will (using British re-inforcements of Malaya as pretext) continue to press the Government to sanction occupation of these bases.' Only two considerations would, Craigie thought, deter them: the possibility of armed American intervention, 'which however they frankly discount', and apprehension that indignation on Vichy's part might 'accentuate growing divergences between Vichy and Berlin and so impair Japan's relations with Germany'. Army and Navy thought they could seize southern Indo-China without risk of war, at least with the United States. What should Britain do if Japan occupied Saigon and Cam Ranh Bay? A 'strong protest ... would have the advantage of avoiding immediate precipitation of a conflict from which Germany and USSR would be the principal gainers'. A second option was to take counter-action, such as the occupation of Kra, further reinforcement of British forces in Malaya and Burma, or 'imposition of economic sanctions such as additions to restrictions on Japanese trade, at least far more severe rationing of Japan in contraband goods than is the case at present'.

The British Government's decision must depend largely on the action the United States Government was prepared to take. Halifax's telegrams suggested that it would be 'incapable' of any action like that in respect of Kra, 'which, unless supported by a full promise of American armed support, would land us in war with Japan'. But 'to content ourselves with a mere protest after recent indications of more determined attitude would greatly encourage war party and justify the general assumption by the Japanese public that the firmness of our attitude was more apparent than real'. The British must 'continue to do everything possible to deter the Japanese Government from embarking on this adventure. If we fail, however, things may move very quickly and there is every advantage in endeavouring to arrange with United States Government in advance what next step should be'.[286]

Intervention at Kra unsupported by the US, wrote Ashley Clarke, 'would probably land us in war with Japan, and there is little doubt that we should not get US support'. The Japanese might expect Britain to tackle Kra if they took action. But it would involve 'aggression' with Thailand, and it would be difficult to undertake from the political point of view unless Thailand gave bases to Japan. 'If she did so, it might then be a military necessity for us to undertake this operation.' The views of the Chiefs of Staff were needed on this, as also on the possibility of 'any signal reinforcement' as a 'counter-gesture' to an occupation of Cam Ranh Bay and Saigon. 'As for economic restrictions, something should surely be possible such as the complete suspension of rubber or tin exports.' This would need Netherlands Indies cooperation to be effective, and the effect would be 'greatly heightened' if the Americans simultaneously announced new restrictions on exports to Japan. Indeed action on the economic field seemed 'the most practicable reply to any occupation of bases in Indo-China'.[287] Dening suggested denouncing the commercial treaty. Japan would probably announce a trade treaty with Russia shortly. 'If she walks into Indo-China and we then denounce our Commercial Treaty the Japanese businessman will feel that Japan has exchanged the substance for the shadow, and the unpopularity of the present Government and its Russian policy will increase'.[288]

Crosby presumed that the British would not occupy Kra unless Japan had violated Thai neutrality; the non-aggression pact forbade it.[289] Clarke thought the answer – in fact the view of the newly created interdepartmental Far Eastern Committee – was: 'We agree'. Bennett doubted this was 'quite correct'. Certainly Britain could not 'occupy any portion of Thai territory merely in retaliation for some act of aggression by Japan against Indo-China'. Nor would Japanese acquisition of bases in Thailand necessarily allow Britain to take Kra. Only if Japan had declared war on Britain, or committed an act of aggression, would the Thais be precluded from granting facilities to the Japanese.

> I suppose that if we wished to occupy the Kra Isthmus, or any other portion of Thai territory we should have to show either that the Thais had broken the non-aggression treaty by assisting an act of aggression against ourselves or that the Thais were so much under the influence of the Japanese that they were no longer capable as an independent State of fulfilling their obligations under the treaty of non-aggression or in fact any other treaty ...

The Legal Adviser, Sir William Malkin, agreed 'that if Japan were to acquire bases in Thailand we should in all probability be able to demonstrate that these could only be required for the purpose of aggression against ourselves or a third Power ...'. Sir Horace Seymour preferred 'not to commit ourselves' as 'we might want to interpret our obligations in a rather different way at some later date'. Butler, however, favoured a telegram to Crosby in Bangkok that offered points for his consideration.[290]

The Joint Planners thought that an advance north of Songkla would help to hold up any Japanese attempt to advance through southern Thailand. The success of the move would depend on 'rapidity of execution', but the non-aggression treaty made it 'particularly necessary to avoid too precipitate a move'.[291] Contradictions continued to be connected with the concept.

While Kra was a question for the future, it was true that their mediation had greatly increased the influence of the Japanese on the mainland. They yet stopped short of moving into southern Indo-China. But their economic ties with the French regime intensified,[292] and the concern that Indo-China's rubber, sent to Japan, was reaching Germany, prompted renewed questioning of the agreement with Britain. The Governor in Singapore and the Commander-in-Chief favoured continuing it.

> There can be little doubt that denunciation of agreement would drive the Government further into the arms of Japan, who would then assume complete control of all exports from Indo-China. So long as we maintain some form of agreement with Admiral Decoux from which he himself derives some advantage, we shall continue to be able to exert some influence on extent to which Indo-China comes under Japanese domination.

Once relations were broken Britain would have no power to affect Japanese penetration. 'It is desirable to encourage even last shreds of resistance to Japan, even if we may appear genuinely weak by acquiescing in concessions which are to our disadvantage ...'.[293] Decoux drew attention to 'the very grave results a rupture of the agreement might have for both parties, particularly in regards to its symbolic value as evidence of solidarity of white races in the Far East'.[294] This did not impress the Far Eastern Department. Decoux's government had betrayed Britain to its enemies in Europe and the Far East.[295] At the end of June, however, when the Commander-in-Chief suggested an ultimatum that would demand assurances over rubber exports and over the release of Egal, a Free Frenchman deported from Shanghai, Clarke rejected such a change of approach. 'If the Japanese choose this moment to press on with their move southwards and intend to force Indo-China to grant them facilities of one kind or another, we should be ill-advised to do anything which would discourage Admiral Decoux from resisting to the best of his ability.'[296] The Far Eastern Committee agreed.[297]

The Thais and Japanese mediation

The position of the various parties over the mediation may be summarised in this way. The Thais were trying to maximise their diplomatic resources in order to win territory; Matsuoka was trying to reconcile his policies towards Indo-China and towards Thailand; the British were trying to maintain relations with Thailand without being able to offer alliance or more than a limited support for territorial change, since they wanted Decoux to survive; and the US supported the status quo.

Pibun's secret verbal pledge to Japan had stirred its hot-headed staff officers and challenged Matsuoka. But ambiguity still shrouded the Thai leader's policy. He told Grant, the American ambassador, that if Vichy did not cede the west bank enclaves soon he might resort to force.[298] Thai planes penetrated Laos airspace, and Vichit whipped up anti-French feeling.[299] Decoux decided that the Thais were the main threat and was angry that the British blocked his attempts to obtain the transfer of the troops at Djibouti, and the Americans hesitated to agree to the departure of aircraft at Martinique.[300] But the US was also concerned over the Thais: ten military planes, paid for by the Thais, were offloaded at Manila.[301] And the British had not surrendered in Europe. They gave Pridi's emissary, Thamrong, an honoured welcome in their dominions in Asia and Australia.[302] Pibun sent a confidant, Lt Kunjara, to Singapore, to sound out the situation. He seemed to take for granted that British and Thai forces would cooperate if the Japanese attacked Kra;[303] 'as gratifying as it is surprising', Crosby commented.[304] Then Kunjara asked, allegedly on behalf of Pibun, if the two countries would join in resisting the Japanese if they wished to pass through Thailand to attack Malaya.[305]

The Foreign Office had, however, concluded that Pibun had struck a bargain with the Japanese: 'we must reckon with the probability that after the Japanese penetration of Indo-China Thailand will also tend to come more and more under Japanese influence'. Britain must do all it could to maintain its 'friendly influence'. 'Frankness' was best: indicate understanding of Thai aspirations but stress that Britain could not be a party to attempts to upset the status quo. If Indo-China were dismembered or transferred the British looked for consultation with the Thais. The Foreign Office asked Crosby if it would be useful to warn them that granting bases would be an unfriendly act.[306]

Talking to Direck, the Deputy Foreign Minister, Crosby stressed that Britain was bound to discourage attempts to change the status quo by force but emphasised the importance of Anglo-Thai friendship. Direck said the Thais had just received a further refusal from Vichy to negotiate on territory other than the islets. Crosby deprecated forcible occupation. Then he asked Direck about the Thais' diplomatic mission to Japan; the British, he said, believed a bargain had been struck. Direck denied this. At least it looked as though one were contemplated, Crosby countered. Japan would exact a price for help in realising Thailand's territorial aspirations. Crosby expressed the hope that it would not include anything likely to injure Britain, in particular the use of bases in Thai territory. Direck rejected the idea altogether. Crosby did not favour making more any specific warning than the one he had delivered. The Thais had too much national pride to allow a foreign power to use bases, and he was reluctant to disturb the friendly atmosphere created by the ratification of the non-aggression treaty and the goodwill missions.[307]

The Far Eastern Committee tried to balance the interest in good relations with Thailand and the need to avoid giving the impression that Britain backed irredentism. The balance, Butler concluded, was 'in favour of maintaining friendly relations with the Thais, supported by such assistance as we could offer, the possibility of American intervention in the Far East being held in the background as a possible deterrent against co-operation with the Japanese'.[308] The Foreign Office accepted Crosby's advice.[309] Bennett, however, thought that before long 'words alone, however friendly, will not be sufficient to hold the situation against pressure from the Axis Powers. The Thais will ... be influenced by the extent to which we can either (a) assist them, or (b) harm them'. The military authorities should consider the situation in the light of the probability that Japan would penetrate further into Indo-China and the possibility that they would get bases in Thailand. What assistance could Britain give Thailand? What pressure could it exert to prevent its 'falling too much under the sway of Japan'?[310]

At the Far Eastern Committee it was felt 'that every effort should be made to help the Thais and to maintain friendly relations with them so long as they did not resort to force, and provided that they did not feel themselves beholden to Japan for any territorial gains'. The COS were asked to consider the military consequences of further Japanese penetration into Indo-China and possible acquisition of bases in Thailand. Was military cooperation with Thailand 'desirable and practicable'? What pressure could be put on Thailand to resist Japanese encroachments?[311] Crosby was told that the question was being studied. He was also told that the British were reviewing their attitude to Thai claims.

> In the event of Japanese over-running Indo-China, it might suit us best that Thailand should take over Laos and Cambodia provided that she does not thereby place herself under an obligation to Japan. What we have to guard against is hastening the break-up of Indo-China and alienating French authorities there by encouraging Thai claims now.[312]

The Far Eastern Committee questioned the wisdom of maintaining 'an unsympathetic attitude' to Thai claims.[313] But, despite the alarms of September, Indo-China still existed, and the Foreign Office still wished to avoid promoting its break-up by encouraging the Thais. If it did break up, however, it might be well if Thailand secured Laos and Cambodia and, if that were to occur, it would be better done without placing Thailand totally under an obligation to Japan. How all this could be achieved was less plain.

Crosby was concerned that the Thai Government and public resented misunderstanding on the part of the US and lack of sympathy for their territorial claims. Aircraft had been withheld at Manila; Hull had reproved the ambassador in Washington; Grant had told them not to seek territory even by negotiation. The American attitude was contrasted with Britain's

> more practical and realistic one, which is not unsympathetic provided status quo is maintained in principle and that resort is not had to force. The result is that warnings issued by Washington are tending to defeat their own object by making Thai irredentists turn towards Japan and Germany as the only quarters from which they are likely to get help ...

Crosby hesitated to raise the matter with Grant, 'who is inclined to be rigid and didactic but who doubtless reflects the views of his Government'. Could anything be done in Washington?[314]

Lothian had already been asked to draw attention to the Bangkok despatches.[315] Grant had told Crosby that he thought Britain's approach was appeasement, leaving the US alone to support the status quo. In the end Pibun's promise was worthless. But Crosby said he had to be 'realistic': Britain had vital interests, unlike the US.[316] Though Grant's view of the Thais was extreme – Crosby described him as 'doctrinaire, vain and extremely jealous'[317] – the State Department's stance was on the status quo. Later in October it acknowledged a memorandum from the British Embassy outlining the exchanges with Bangkok. It was gratified that the UK had expressed to the Thais its opposition to changing the status quo by force. The US had consistently tried to impress on the Thais 'the advantage of refraining from any action involving alteration of the status quo other than through peaceful means'.[318]

At the Far Eastern Committee R.A. Butler suggested that 'it was now perhaps time to move forward to support the Thai claims, a direction in which we had been moving for some time'.[319] A telegram from Crosby moved the Foreign Office a little further down that track but not so far. In conversation with Lépissier, Pibun had forecast rebellion in Indo-China and an offensive by Japan. He concluded that the Thais would then occupy the right bank territory. Crosby thought that, if they did, the British should not 'make a serious incident out of it, whatever Washington may say, for by so doing we shall assuredly drive Thais into the arms of Japan ... We cannot approve of break up of status quo in Indo-China, but if it comes about against our will we must make the best of the situation.'[320] If the Thais acted, Gage thought, there were three alternatives. Britain could oppose them in consultation with the Americans. 'This means words not deeds', and it would throw the Thais into the Japanese camp. Britain could instead 'adopt a positive attitude towards the Thai claims, on the grounds that the French have in effect already sold themselves and us to the Japanese and we should at least try to preserve the friendship of Thailand', which the Americans would see as appeasement. The third alternative, which was advocated by Crosby, was to 'let events take their course and decide on our policy afterwards'. That seemed the best course. There was no reason to be 'grateful' to Indo-China, while the US could not expect Britain to take action against Thailand and protests would have little effect except to annoy.

> If we could convince the Thais that we were strong enough to protect them against Japanese aggression, they would probably prefer to stay in our camp, for they know that what the Japanese give, they will also take away when it suits them. If we could be assured that the Thais would not sell themselves to the Japanese it may pay us to agree to them having the trusteeship of certain territories into Indo-China in the event of a collapse there ...[321]

The Far Eastern Committee accepted this line, although there was still talk of 'unobtrusive encouragement'.[322] But given the attitude of the US and the Free French, Clarke concluded, the line Crosby suggested, 'that if Indo-China is broken up we must make the best of the situation was about as far as we can go at the moment'.[323] '... it is becoming increasingly clear that our own policy should be to do nothing but endeavour to retain Thai goodwill, and at the same time avoid offending the US by appearing to be indulging in appeasement.'[324] The COS had affirmed that Britain itself was in no position either to support the Thais or to restrain them.[325]

Too stiff an attitude might drive the Thais into the Japanese camp, Nevile Butler was told.[326] He called on Maxwell Hamilton, Chief of the Division of Far Eastern Affairs, on 18 November. The UK was convinced that Japan would move on southern Indo-China. Should Britain or the US oppose in the event a Thai move to recover parts of Indo-China? Might not the Thais be more likely to give Japan bases if stopped by the UK or the US? Hamilton reiterated that the US adhered to the principles of 16 July 1937.[327] The reply, as Gage put it, was 'not full of constructive suggestions'.[328]

Pibun also, of course, looked to the Japanese. He evaded written promises to them.[329] He hoped, however, that they would come to his rescue by occupying Indo-China and allowing Thailand to reclaim its territory without recourse to force. He told Crosby 'with perfect frankness that he preferred to bide his time in the expectation of getting all that he wanted and not merely a small part of it'.[330] The Japanese took a different view. For the time being they had what they wanted from Indo-China.[331] What they now sought was an understanding with Thailand. The Four Ministers conference of 5 November decided that 'favourable consideration' would be given to Thai claims, 'especially concerning the recovery of lost territories in the area of Luang Prabang and Pakse', and attention would be given to mediation in Franco-Thai relations. Thailand would have to 'cooperate actively in the New Order in East Asia' and to recognise Manchukuo. Conferences would be held on cooperation in various fields, and far-reaching economic cooperation would be established. 'A gradual reform in the internal composition of the Thai government will be effected so that a Japan–Thai Alliance may be harmoniously realised.'[332] Chargé Asada, however, reported that the Thai Cabinet, influenced by a report by Prom, was leaning to the British and the Americans,'[333] and on 18 November *Asahi* published details of an Anglo–American–Thai alliance proposal. It was bogus[334] but invented by the Thais, not the Japanese.[335] That was in keeping with Pibun's diplomacy. Sounding out the Germans had, however, given him little help; Hitler wanted peace in the French empire.[336]

The Japanese were nevertheless stirred into action. After hurried conferences with army and navy leaders Matsuoka told the legation in Bangkok on 20 November that Japan would offer its good offices in the border dispute. In the mediation Japan would take Thailand's side and favour its recovery of Luang Prabang and Pakse. In return Thailand would agree to the conditions of 5 November.[337] Japan would also promise to consider the return of other lost territories in the future, especially those in British hands, and to furnish Thailand with economic and military aid. If Thailand was uncooperative Japan would support the French. If the French were uncooperative Japan would threaten to scrap the Matsuoka–Henry agreement and seek German pressure on Vichy.[338] In Berlin on 9 December, Ernest von Weizsäcker, State Secretary of the Foreign Ministry, told the Thai minister that he favoured the irredenta claim.[339] So did the Italian Foreign Minister, Ciano.[340] Hull suggested that France seek German help in restraining Japan.[341] Baudouin was against even asking: the Japanese would resent it.[342]

Pibun had speedily accepted the Japanese proposals, and negotiations culminated in a meeting between him and Asada on 28 November.[343] Tension was increasing, and there were border incidents. But the French took their time in replying to Matsuoka's offer of mediation, made on 2 December, and then gave a negative answer.[344] Matsuoka had indicated that the return of Luang Prabang and Pakse would be involved. France found itself unable to accept the kind offer from the point of view of its territorial integrity.[345] Junior army staff officers condemned Matsuoka's policy as soft and pressed for an immediate takeover of all Indo-China and Thailand. Tojo, the War Minister, argued that this action would provoke war with Britain and the US, for which Japan was not yet prepared, and the officers had to content themselves with supplying war equipment to Bangkok.[346] The Liaison conference of 26 December called for swift establishment of political, military and economic ties with Thailand and stressed the need to coerce Indo-China into accepting mediation.[347]

The escalating conflict on the frontier had prompted Gage to suggest that Japanese mediation could be expected. It was too late to exercise an influence, but Crosby might urge moderation.[348] Bennett wondered whether there was, 'in these days of "jungle" politics', any more effective alternative. 'I do not think that we want to get actively mixed up in this quarrel to the extent, say, of bringing economic pressure on the Thais to abate their claims.' Urging moderation might do little and 'only lead to our being ignored with damage to our prestige'. By contrast simply letting matters take their course might lead to difficulties between Germany, which virtually controlled Vichy, and Japan. Bennett was, however, inclined to revert to the orthodox course.

Although Germany may not relish Japan's further expansion, it is unlikely that she cares so much about the fate of south-eastern Asia at the present time as to quarrel with Japan for it, and the chances are that Japan would have a free run and would establish a dominating position for herself, both in Indo-China and in Thailand, as the price of imposing a solution of the present dispute.

Moreover, doing nothing to restrain the Thais might prompt criticism from the Free French. Perhaps Britain should urge moderation on both parties, pointing out that the dispute could only play into Japan's hands. Seymour preferred to follow Crosby's line: the concern should be to avoid a quarrel with the Thais. However, he could point out that a war with the French would help the Japanese to obtain such areas of Indo-China as they wished 'with awkward results to Thailand'. Butler agreed: 'I agree … stand back and see the dogfight but speak soothingly to yr. favourite dog'.[349] 'The best thing we could hope for', it was suggested at the Far Eastern Committee, 'would be to keep the Thais out of the Japanese orbit by presenting some token of Anglo-American goodwill to Thailand, possibly with the object of settling the dispute'. But it would be difficult to approach the US, given Grant's 'unhelpful attitude' and Hull's 'rigid views'.[350] A telegram was sent to Crosby along the lines the FO favoured.[351]

The prospect that Pibun would accept Japanese mediation in return for a military agreement, of which Crosby learned in Singapore, he found 'unexpected and disquieting'. There was, the Far Eastern Committee agreed, 'little hope' of joint Anglo-American intervention in the dispute.[352] Clarke thought Crosby should encourage the Thais to talk to France.[353] 'I think we should keep out of this for the moment', Bennett commented.[354] There seemed, Clarke remarked, little prospect of bringing the parties together. 'If we compose our trade differences with Indo-China shortly, we may get an opening, but failing this, or some unexpected accretion of our strength in the Far East, we are not in a position to exercise any influence on Indo-China in the sense desired.'[355] It had been suggested that bargaining with the French might produce a concession for Thailand. But Clarke preferred 'to rely on better relations with the French to give us an opportunity of suggesting a composition with the Thais', although he very much doubted that the advice would be taken.[356]

Back in Bangkok Crosby urged Pibun to remember that, in negotiating with Japan, 'he should see to it that the independence of Thailand was not sacrificed and that Anglo-Thai friendship was not impaired'. The Japanese, Crosby argued, were inciting France and Thailand to fight so that they might intervene to arbitrate.[357] But the FO now sought to go beyond lectures. Vichy had rejected Japanese mediation. Decoux had sought to involve the British and the Americans, one reason why Jouan also visited Singapore in December.[358] Knowing of the Torigoe talks and fearing Thailand might fall under Japan's military domination,[359] Britain made a new effort to involve the US. Possibly the French might be induced to cede the right bank territories as well as accept the thalweg in the course of an American or an Anglo-American mediation. An open mediation would be obstructed by Germany and Japan, 'but what we might aim at is a settlement brought about ostensibly by direct negotiations between Indo-China and Thailand with the United States and ourselves helping in the background'.[360] While repeating Crosby's warnings to the ambassador in London,[361] Britain approached the US on mediation. Neither Welles nor Hamilton wanted a 'concession to black-mail'. But the French were ready for mediation, and 'to allow the dispute to continue or to be settled by the Japanese' was 'to strengthen the Japanese in South-East Asia to the detriment of Indo-China, Thailand, Netherlands East Indies and British possessions, not to mention Great Britain and ultimately the United States themselves'.[362] Butler put the idea to Welles, suggesting that it 'would clearly not infringe United States principle that forcible annexation of territory should not be recognised'.[363]

Crosby thought that a settlement might be achieved by a prompt indication that the right bank territories could be transferred.[364] But the Americans opposed mediation in the current circumstances. Any settlement achieved was in any case unlikely to be permanent.[365] Butler said that even a delay in the Japanese advance was worthwhile, that the French would be better able to attempt this if their rear was not attacked by the Thais, that Thailand had everything to gain by keeping Indo-China as a buffer, and that concessions should enable the government to hold its own against the extremists.[366] This was all in vain. But Hull did warn the Thai ambassador of the risks of Japanese domination.[367] 'The American aide-mémoire is a typical production, reeking of Hornbeck', Cadogan observed.[368] The FO tried again. The US seemed to be relaxing its attitude to Japan. But remaining passive would accelerate its advance. 'If on the other hand the process of infiltration and absorption can be retarded and if Japan's doubts as to the wisdom and success of her policy can be increased, we may yet hope to reach a stage where the forces opposing her will have become so formidable that she will elect to abandon it.'[369] 'Settlement of the dispute will ... interfere with Japan's plans and gain time in which it may be possible to encourage and strengthen French resistance to Japan.' In that case it might hesitate to move on southern Indo-China 'whereas a policy ... of allowing matters to drift seems likely to render it more certain that Japan's advance will only be stopped by war'. Could the US not at least make some public statement on the desirability of negotiating a settlement?[370] Hull promised to consider the idea. He mentioned that the Thai minister had said that Thailand had revisionist claims against Britain, too. Butler replied 'that the risk of seeing these claims raised was a contribution that we were ready to make to a settlement of Thai–Indo-China quarrel'.[371]

Gage thought it was 'in the highest degree unlikely' that Britain would admit such claims if they were raised.[372]

Decoux complained to Henderson that back in October S.W. Jones, the OAG Straits Settlements, had told a Thai mission of British support for Thailand's just territorial claims against Indo-China. He also read passages of a report from Garreau, the French chargé, about a conversation with Crosby in which the latter allegedly said: 'I will do nothing against you but I must not hide the fact I can do nothing to calm Thai aspirations'; also that if he had to choose he would prefer Thai occupation of 'la chaine Annamite' to the Japanese menacing Malaya and India. Decoux also expressed surprise that Pibun's statement of 1 December, to the effect that Britain recognised the good foundation of Thai claims, had not been denied.[373] Crosby said his conversation with Garreau had been private and his views personal. They were that the frontier dispute could be settled only by Indo-China's acceptance of the thalweg as frontier and by cession of two pieces of territory on the right bank; that 'it will be best for everyone if France remains mistress of Indo-China'; and that, 'in the unfortunate event of France ever having to abandon Indo-China', he would prefer to see the Thais rather than the Japanese on the left bank of the Mekong.[374] Ashley Clarke thought Crosby's statement 'plain fact'. But he and Gage thought it necessary to make it clear, through telegraphing the C in C for Jouan, that the British were not, as Decoux suspected, egging the Thais on.[375]

From Tokyo about the same time Craigie reported that the French mission had been 'subjected to strong pressure by Japanese on the subject of alleged rapprochement between Indo-China Government and British authorities'. The Japanese had indicated that they were aware of Decoux's request for British mediation, of the despatch of Jouan for Singapore and of the alleged agreement on gunny bags. 'Japanese expressed concern that while Tokyo negotiations are in progress, Indo-China should be negotiating with us behind their backs, and they accuse Admiral [Decoux] of failing to carry [out] his Government's policy of co-operation with the Axis and therefore with Japan. They added the hint that Japanese army leaders on the spot might be difficult to control ...'. Craigie understood that the ambassador doubted 'wisdom of Admiral entertaining proposal of purely British mediation', and he suggested it should be accepted only if made jointly by the US and the UK. 'This idea has been suggested privately to French Mission. Another proposition which latter are considering is that of joint Anglo–American–Japanese mediation. They consider this would have the advantage of forestalling objections which Japan will certainly raise to British or Anglo-American mediation'.[376] That, Gage thought, might be 'a good way of showing that we are open to reason and do not wish to provoke the Japanese unnecessarily'. But Clarke thought the idea of mediating with the Japanese 'crazy'.[377]

In mid January Thai forces under Prom advanced towards the Cambodian town of Sisophon, but failed to capture it.[378] In a naval engagement the French were the more successful, despite the claims of Thai propaganda. The aged cruiser *Lamotte-Piquet* survived, while the Thais lost one of their two destroyers, the *Thonburi*.[379] At the same time, back in Singapore, Jouan suggested that a settlement might be possible, provided that the Thais made two minor border adjustments in favour of the French.[380] Crosby was not optimistic but thought there might be 'a ray of hope'. Pibun, to whom he relayed Jouan's message, was prepared to receive the Frenchman in Bangkok.[381] Through Vanich, however, Pibun at once informed Futami of the move.[382] 'It would appear that the Thais decided to play off ourselves against the Japanese. A pretty piece of double dealing.'[383]

News of the Thai defeat and of the French démarche was discussed in Japan at a meeting on 19 January. The military pressed for complete control of Indo-China and a military pact with Thailand so that Japan could oust Britain from Southeast Asia; they also argued for a show of force to pre-empt British mediation. Matsuoka, however, got his way: a renewed offer to mediate.[384] The policy paper still, however, spoke of applying military pressure to Indo-China and of obtaining a guarantee of future cooperation from the Thai army. Troops had been moved into Tonkin and warships stationed off Cochin-China.[385] Matsuoka's speech to the Diet on 21 January indicated that 'Japan as the leader in East Asia cannot afford to remain indifferent to such a dispute'.[386] Arsène Henry was confronted with information of Decoux's secret dealing with the British,[387] and Matsuoka said that British interference could not be tolerated.[388] The French gave in. Flandin, the Vichy Foreign Minister, told Leahy, the American ambassador, that Vichy had accepted Japanese mediation. He asked the US to exercise such influence as it could to ensure that no territorial changes ensued.[389] Grew was told to draw Matsuoka's attention to adverse press comment in the US and to the principles of 16 July 1937.[390]

Crosby heard of the mediation proposal from Garreau.[391] 'I am absolutely convinced that there never was the slightest hope of inducing Thai Government to reduce their demands as regards the right bank of Mekong River although I have preached to them consistently the gospel of reason and moderation.' If Vichy had agreed in time, 'the larger question of *left* bank claims need not have loomed up and Thai ambitions could have been satisfied by what would have been a minor concession …'. In its struggle with the Japanese over Thailand Britain suffered from the 'enormous disadvantage that we are unable to fight them ourselves and that America is unwilling to do so'. The British could use only persuasion. The Thais were 'children, and it has not been possible to bring these children to reason with Japan dangling before them the promise of the recovery of their lost provinces ...'.[392] Crosby was, however, also suspicious of Pibun; 'I have a feeling that the Prime Minister has capitulated to the Japanese to a large degree and that he is working secretly in concert with them'. A settlement of the right bank might have been only of 'temporary effect'. Crosby repeated the conviction 'that we have been landed in this mess through the unwillingness of the United States Government to take a strong line against Japan over Indo-China. As it is, I can only recommend the continuance for the time being of our present policy of patience, goodwill and watchfulness towards Thailand.'[393] Continuing a policy of 'tact and friendliness' would depend on the extent to which Thailand sold itself during the mediation, Gage observed. Clarke pointed out that 'tact and friendliness are almost the only shots in our locker in the absence of US support for a more vigorous attitude'.[394] Crosby was told to maintain that policy.[395]

'And it would appear that the Thai leaders in order to acquire their mess of pottage from the prostrate French in Indochina have gone along and deliberately put their heads into the Japanese noose.'[396] Pibun indeed needed no pressure; he responded positively to Futami without even consulting Direck.[397] The latter lamented Japanese mediation and the French intransigence that had led to it. The French, however, tended to blame the British, and especially Crosby, whom they saw, in Stowe's words, as 'conspiring with the Thais to wrest control of Indo-China'.[398] Clarke sought to correct this view by writing to Roché, now in Dublin. Any approach on Indo-China might be construed as evidence of a supposed desire to 'fight to the last Frenchman'. But increasing strength in the Far East might work against this, and the recent agreement with Indo-China indicated a desire 'to co-operate to the best of our ability'.[399] Lack of contact, he told Roché, provoked suspicion. But there was no truth in the idea that 'Crosby instigated, if not invented, the Thai claims on Indo-China'.[400]

The first step was a ceasefire. The French rejected a Japanese proposal to send a peacekeeping force to interpose between the two sides. The Thais deeply disliked the venue of the negotiation, a Japanese ship, the *Natori*, moored at Saigon next to the *Lamotte-Piquet*.[401] Difficult negotiations followed, and the ceasefire agreement, to last until 11 February, was signed only on 31 January.[402] The Thais had to reveal how little their forces had in fact advanced.[403] They had also to accept the stationing of a Japanese destroyer, the *Fumitsuki*, at Paknam,[404] which was where the French man-of-war had been stationed in the crisis of 1893.[405]

The German, American and British ambassadors in Tokyo thought that a new Japanese move was imminent.[406] Roosevelt thought it likely, but the US could do nothing unless its possessions were attacked. Churchill doubted that the Japanese would be so precipitate,[407] although Hitler urged them on.[408]

In fact the Japanese were still divided. The army, especially the Operations Section of the General Staff, saw the mediation simply as a means of extracting agreements from the two parties and wanted to apply pressure on the French. Matsuoka thought precipitate action would provoke the British and the US and taunted his opponents, asking if they were ready to attack Singapore. He also opposed favouring the Thais too much lest this undermined relations with the French.[409] A Liaison Conference met on 30 January. A military plan called for the use of force against Indo-China if Japan's objectives were not met by 31 March. This call was rejected. But the policy finally approved called for a military agreement with Thailand and additional facilities in Indo-China.[410] A conference on 5 February approved Matsuoka's mediation plan. Three proposals were presented. The first would bind France to cede both the enclave opposite Luang Prabang and that opposite Pakse, while the French would retain an area touching on Tonle Sap in Cambodia. The second option would involve all the first enclave but only a part of the second, and the third all the first and a smaller part of the second. Matsuoka also wanted the Thais to make small concessions, such as some disputed islands in the Mekong. Japan would be guarantor of the treaty, secure facilities for carrying out her obligation and participate in the border commission. France and Thailand would make no agreements with third countries and would recognise Japan's leading position in the sphere.[411]

After talking to Prince Wan, the chief Thai negotiator, Grant declared that France would be 'led to the slaughter pen'.[412] In Tokyo he sought the lands lost in the nineteenth century, Laos and Cambodia.[413] The military attaché in Bangkok, Torigoe, argued that Japan should favour Pibun and the pro-Japanese clique.[414] But Matsuoka had no wish to take such a pro-Thai course and wanted his mediation to succeed.[415] The French, of course, rejected Thai demands, and the Japanese, pushing through an extension of the ceasefire to 25 February, tried to scale them down.[416] On 17 February the Japanese put a proposal designed to break the deadlock. France would cede the territories acquired in 1904, the Luang Prabang and Pakse enclaves, all of Battambang, two-thirds of Siem Reap, and a third of Kompong Thom. The Thais would pay France 10 million baht – which implied reciprocity in the agreement, as the French wished – and a demilitarisation zone would be established.[417]

The Thais opposed compensation, and on 21 February Prince Wan indicated that they would drop a demand for Angkor if that proposal were abandoned.[418] On 23 February Arsène Henry said the French were willing to cede the Luang Prabang and Pakse areas and make minor adjustments in the northern part of Cambodia but no more. With naval support Matsuoka persuaded a Liaison Conference, then in session, to extend the ceasefire deadline and to offer another mediation proposal.[419] For this Matsuoka secured the Emperor's sanction on the morning of 24 February. He presented it to the French and Thais in the afternoon. In this proposal the payment was dropped. The cessions would be as in the first proposal of 17 February, but additionally the Cambodian transfers could be demilitarised.[420]

Prince Wan accepted the new plan on 26 February.[421] Matsuoka sought German pressure on Vichy.[422] On 28 February it agreed but attached conditions to its agreement. One condition was that all the territory should be demilitarised. Another was that the decisions should be immutable. Matsuoka took exception to Arsène Henry's statement that France had been intimidated.[423] He revived the idea that France might retain Battambang; a major source, it had been pointed out, of Indochina's rice exports.[424] 'Well anyway this mess-up can hardly be credited to the crafty and perfidious British', Clarke noted.[425] A joint communiqué of 7 March indicated that agreement had been reached in principle.[426] It averted further fighting.[427] The debate over Battambang continued, however, until Tojo's intervention forced Matsuoka to back down.[428]

The mediation plan was signed on 11 March. It called for the return of the west bank enclaves and much of northwestern Cambodia, but not Siem Reap town nor Angkor. The thalweg would form the Mekong frontier, although two islands west of it would be jointly administered. All the cessions would be demilitarised.[429] The Japanese would guarantee the settlement, and neither France nor Thailand would make pacts with third countries that could be considered hostile to Japan.[430]

The treaty took some weeks to conclude. The French sought to include in it a number of detailed provisions designed in part to appease the Laos and Cambodians. They also wanted Thailand to pay for the assets it was acquiring. This Prince Wan refused to do and, at Japan's instance, Pibun gave Vanich, allegedly more malleable, the conduct of the negotiations.[431] In the event the Japanese insisted on total demilitarisation and a payment of 6 million baht by Thailand. So the treaty was signed on 9 May. Pibun was dismayed.[432] Letters exchanged by Matsuoka and the chief delegates stipulated that Japan would guarantee the settlement. They also bound Thailand and Indochina not to make agreements with third countries that might be hostile to Japan.[433]

Arsène Henry had told Grew the mediation was a great blow to Indo-China, but not a fatal one, 'whereas Thailand has suffered an absolutely fatal blow and to all intents and purposes has been reduced to the position of Manchukuo'. He gave Crosby much of the responsibility; he had 'pursued "dragoman diplomacy" in seeking to turn the expansionist interests of Thailand toward Indochina and away from Malaya and the net result had been to throw Thailand directly into the future control of the Japanese military extremists'.[434] Grant had claimed that Crosby had again encouraged the Thais.[435] Matsuoka said that British propaganda 'incited' them to 'most unreasonable demands'.[436] 'Really!' Clarke ex-postulated.[437] In fact the French had been impossibly obstinate, and Crosby was not alone among the British in thinking so.

Thailand was one of the topics Menzies discussed at the Foreign Office on 26 February. He wanted 'an effort to get the Thais on our side and stimulate resistance by Thailand to Japanese demands'. What if the mediation should award Thailand a considerable part of Cambodia? Seymour thought that the Thais had 'a good claim ... and that we should recognise its transfer without making too much fuss'. Butler agreed. But Cadogan pointed to the Prime Minister's declaration about the recognition of transfers before the end of the war. The effect on de Gaulle had also to be considered.[438] He had in fact announced his opposition to cessions to Thailand.[439] If recognition was to be avoided the British still did not wish to oppose Thai claims. That was not, however, the same as promoting them as Grant and the French seemed to think. Nor was encouraging the French to be flexible the same as encouraging the Thais to be demanding.

Before the delegation left for Tokyo Crosby had reminded Pibun of his earlier assurances that Thai independence would not be diminished nor British interests harmed. Thailand should not join the New Order nor enter any military pact nor accept the occupation of bases. Britain was Thailand's most important economic partner. 'Apart from the economic aspect of the case, it is not to be forgotten that the British Empire is a mighty one and that it will not always be preoccupied with military operations in Europe and the Middle East ... A flourishing and a truly independent Thailand is a great desideratum for Britain ...'.[440] He still recommended 'that we should persist in our time-honoured policy of disinterested friendship towards Thailand, in the hope that she will never go so far as to make a break with us inevitable, and that she may one day see the error of her ways and return to the neutral field which she is now to a dangerous extent forsaking'.[441]

The following week Crosby relayed information from an agent of the Government of Burma that the Japanese had been offering Pibun parts of Burma and Malaya in return for his assistance. He wanted to tell Pibun that such proposals were 'a madman's dream ... But are we strong enough to say as much as that?'[442] Only action by the US, Clarke believed, would 'stop the rot in Thailand. But we can hope for nothing from

America at present which would finally convince Thailand that Japan will have to reckon with the United States'. The current efforts to 'obtain some sort of gesture … to impress Japan' would also serve the purpose in regard to Thailand. Could Britain assist Thailand? The COS were in November unwilling to reveal 'the nakedness of the land'. The Far Eastern Committee should discuss this issue again and the question of warning Pibun.[443] The COS reaffirmed their policy of November.[444]

Pibun offered Crosby assurances in mid February. 'Thailand will remain neutral and she regards her independence as sacred. Her policy is to be friends both of Britain and Japan.' But in order to maintain its neutrality and independence Thailand needed money and armaments. He sought a loan, arms and oil. Britain and the US would thus 'win the hearts of the Thai soldiers', counteracting Japan. Crosby concluded that Pibun might not yet have compromised himself with the Japanese altogether, and he favoured a positive response.[445] After a meeting of the Far Eastern Committee Crosby was asked for more details. He was also told to say that any agreement with the Japanese that provided military advantages would be seen as a contravention of the non-aggression pact.[446] In a subsequent conversation Pibun told Crosby that the loan was for development and the arms for protection. The declared policy was to resist any attempt to violate Thailand's neutrality, but 'he could not guarantee that he would oppose Japan by force of arms if she were to attack Malaya or Burma' through Thailand. It might be suicidal to resist unaided, and he did not think the US would go to war with Japan. He pointed to economic pressure from Japan. It wanted Thai tin and rubber, but Malaya could boycott the supply of mining equipment and India the supply of gunny bags.[447] In fact Pibun had pledged raw materials to Japan in return for its supply of arms.[448] Oil had been an issue rather longer. Before the war, with Pibun's support, Vanich had set up a Fuel Oil Department, designed to secure the armed forces supplies independent of the international companies, and he had looked to the Japanese.[449] In July 1939 the foreign companies had pulled out before the Fuel Oil Department was in a position to meet Thailand's needs and at a time when other powers were stockpiling.[450] It had to turn to companies other than those that had formerly traded in Bangkok and to the US, where licences were required.[451]

From Crosby's conversation with the Thai Prime Minister Gage concluded that Pibun felt that Thailand's independence could only 'eventually be maintained by an indication that the US and ourselves – particularly the US – will take effective action to protect it'. The key – he once more declared – was the attitude of the US.[452] At the Far Eastern Committee Butler declared that 'what was really wanted was a line of approach to Washington. The Americans had never taken very much interest in Thailand, and their Minister at Bangkok seemed to be doing a great deal of harm.' Assurance that it would not join an alliance with Japan should be sought in return for a loan and oil, and tin, rubber and rice, normally going to Malaya, should not go to Japan.[453]

Crosby favoured a 'patient long-view policy ... until our armed strength in the Far East is sufficient to justify us in the institution of stronger lines'.[454] The conclusion of the mediation agreement led to further discussion at the Far Eastern Committee. Had Thailand forfeited its claim to assistance? Not yet, it was decided; the object should be to seek American support for assisting Thailand 'in the hope of staving off her final inclusion in the Japanese orbit ... the time was not yet ripe to apply economic pressure ...'.[455]

Grant entirely differed from Crosby; the Thais were pawns and would be puppets. Thailand was now virtually 'allied with the Axis'.[456] American scepticism, E.B. Reynolds argues, 'largely reflected the fundamentally different perspectives of their home countries'. Far away and with little stake in Thailand, the US could take the more detached view.[457] But Grew pointed to the significance of the mediation. Japan had 'at least laid the groundwork for the political, economic, and presumably eventual military control of Indochina and Thailand'. It was also a step in the southward advance.[458] In approaching the US the UK would indeed have to stress that.

Telegrams London sent to Washington at the end of March pointed to the strengthening of Japan's position by the mediation and the undertakings made by French Indo-China and Thailand. It was important economically to prevent Thai rubber and tin going to the Axis and important strategically 'to prevent the Japanese from working round our flank in Malaya'. 'In so far as United States demonstrate solidarity with Great Britain and China and opposition to Japanese aggression effect on Thailand cannot fail to be salutary ...'. It was necessary to awaken the US to the danger and secure its cooperation.[459] The 'most effective way of keeping Thailand ... from falling completely under Japanese influence would be to take suitable naval and military action which would impress her'. Failing that, it was a matter either of economic pressure or of economic assistance. Pressure might deprive Malaya of rice and push Thailand further into the arms of Japan. Assistance could probably not include arms, given US commitments elsewhere. A joint loan might be feasible. The supply of oil could be renewed, but the position was complicated by the withdrawal of the British and American companies from Thailand. Any agreement would have to be accompanied by a Thai undertaking over treaties with other powers similar to that made to Japan, and by guarantees against the diversion of rubber, tin and rice out of the usual trade channels to the benefit of Japan.[460]

Reading these telegrams, Brooke-Popham stressed that the Japanese were infiltrating Thailand with personnel and arms. 'Each day increases their hold and brings nearer the possibility of some form of coup the result of which would probably be a Japanese controlled and occupied Thailand.' To stop the drift 'we can and must show the Thais that we have the forces and the determination to protect our strategic interests in Thailand'. The course of the war in Africa and the Yugoslav coup suggested that Japan had missed its chance. Britain's strength in Malaya was increasing, and he planned to move an air squadron to the Shan states when the diplomatic move was made. He favoured a carrot and stick policy; 'further delay may mean that Thais have lost taste for carrot and feel fortified against stick'.[461] The Far Eastern Committee found the service departments reluctant to approve any moves that might appear provocative to the Japanese. They might follow the diplomatic exchanges with the Thais that might result from the expression of the Americans' views.[462] Bennett favoured preparing a policy that could be used in whatever sense the US responded. That might include 'a very frank and comprehensive talk' between Crosby and Pibun indicating that Britain could assist only if it got satisfactory assurances over relations with the Japanese. If his response was unsatisfactory Britain should start a propaganda campaign about Japanese infiltration then move the squadrons. Even if Pibun's answer were satisfactory the campaign could still be useful in order to create support for him to resist further infiltration.[463]

Before Halifax acted on the telegrams other issues were raised. Crosby pointed out that the US had not compensated the Thais for the planes the delivery of which had been disallowed.[464] Pibun also signalled a desperate need for oil. He could not get tankers to bring it from the US, and supplies were being cut off. He might have to turn to Japan, which, although it had really none to spare, would furnish what it thought Thailand needed. That would only increase Thailand's dependence. Crosby recommended a positive response. 'It may be urged that we run a risk if we allow Thailand to accumulate too much oil, but ... a policy of over-caution may defeat itself and we are bound to take risks if we are going to defeat Japan.' He thought the companies should be left out. The British Government 'in the capacity of big brother' might supply it from Malaya.[465] Diverting rubber, tin and possibly rice to Japan, Crosby was told, would make the supply of oil difficult, and unless assurances were given, it would be difficult to justify it. Indeed the supply of gunnies might be limited.[466] The communications in Washington took these issues into account; so also the Foreign Office's complaint about Grant's 'unhelpful attitude'.[467]

In Washington the embassy made over two aide-mémoires based on the Foreign Office telegrams. One outlined a situation 'full of dangerous possibilities'.[468] The other suggested a loan to Thailand and proposed to regulate its oil supply 'as a means of control which can be made to appear as economic assistance; the British and United States Governments could in conjunction with the oil companies devise practical means of assuring to Thailand balanced supplies of the different types which they are likely to require ...'.[469] In a conversation with Hull Halifax expressed the hope that the US would pay compensation for the planes retained in Manila. Hull said the US would, of course, do so. According to his own memorandum of the conversation, he added that he was 'not at all convinced that the present Thai Government is a real friend of this Government or any other government except the Japanese' and 'that, in my opinion, there exist Japanese–Thai alliances of a more or less military, political and economic nature'.[470] Halifax, according to his account, told Hull

> that we shared all his feelings ... but that I thought the Thais, like a good many other people, had been anxious to eat their cake and have it ... Whatever we might think about their morality, it was clearly to our advantage to help them to resist as long as possible Japanese pressure which they might well dislike as much as we did.

Hull admitted that this was 'possible' but 'clearly was not convinced'.[471] Grant was mentioned. Hull interjected that Crosby was 'a much better man'.[472] On oil Hull suggested a talk with Hornbeck. He told Nevile Butler that the Japanese had 'the inside track in Thailand' and 'that if the British believe that they can hold Thailand in line by supplying commodities and funds it might be well for the British to do the supplying without calling upon us – we being sceptical at least – to participate in that procedure'.[473]

> Until it is proved that the Thais (Siamese) are past praying for we cannot afford to take a view at once so pessimistic and detached as Mr Hull of the position in a country where our vital interests are so much at stake, and we are bound to make another effort to retrieve what we can out of the ruins left by Japanese mediation.

Bennett's suggestions – a talk, propaganda, movement of air squadrons – were outlined to Halifax. The possibility of success would be 'much circumscribed' if there were no American cooperation. Britain could not supply arms or dollar assistance, and oil would be 'our only important inducement'.[474] Pressure was also applied in London. Butler decided to see Hershel Johnson. He could, Clarke suggested, use Brooke-Popham's figure of speech and 'explain that we propose that the carrot should be dangled before the Thai donkey first but that the stick should be visible out of the corner of the donkey's eye'. If the Americans thought inducements too late maybe they would cooperate in applying pressure.[475] Butler expressed concern at the lack of American response on Indo-China and Thailand, both 'rapidly crumbling under Japanese pressure'. That was 'a serious strategic threat both to Burma, including Rangoon and the Burma Road to China, and to Singapore'. Japanese penetration of Thailand might be inhibited by encouragement or pressure or both.[476] 'The British feel ...', Winant reported, 'that until it is proved that Thailand is beyond praying for they cannot afford to abandon their efforts to retrieve what has been left by Japanese mediation.'[477] The British also sought to raise the question of Japanese penetration with the US officers in Singapore.[478]

Casey and Halifax saw Hull and left him another aide-mémoire.[479] The US Government, he said, was 'disposed to feel that Japan had her claws so deeply into Thailand as to make it doubtful whether the position there could be restored'. He finally became 'more sympathetic' to the ideas put forward, but it was 'still evident that he thought the position had gone too far'.[480] As the State Department's own record put it, Thailand was 'at present in the clutches of Japan and ... no one can tell when there may be a separation of these special relations'.[481]

Back from a break in Burma, Crosby found that the situation had deteriorated. For instance, Vanich had joined trade talks to Tokyo.[482] 'Our position in Thailand is starting to disintegrate', Gage wrote, 'and we can no longer afford to defer our action until receipt of the United States Government's views ....'[483] Eden sanctioned the talk with Pibun, coupled, in the event of a suitable reaction, with an offer of early delivery of 150 tons of aviation spirit. 'This is like our Spanish policy but without the same political limelight!' Butler wrote.[484] At the same time Halifax was reminded of the matter.[485] He told Hull the situation was 'slipping'.[486] A few days later he found the Secretary of State 'more sympathetic to my idea of something to help Thailand', but he gave no final decision.[487]

Crosby used 'firm but not provocative' language with Pibun. The Prime Minister 'knew that Japan and the Axis powers were trying to cut Thailand off from Britain and the United States but it was far from his wish that this should happen ...'. He had arranged to supply two million ticals worth of tin to Japan but only in order to secure war matériel. 'It was not himself but the United States Government which were to blame and this difficult situation would not have arisen if Washington had not prohibited the sale of aircraft and war equipment to Thailand.' He was thankful for the offer of aviation spirit. In fact what Thailand currently needed was diesel oil and motor spirit.[488] Pibun said Thailand would resist a Japanese attack. 'He himself could not grant to Japan use of bases in Thailand without being discredited for ever with his own people. (I believe that he meant this at the time but it is another question what his attitude would be if the emergency actually arose).' He did not, however, think Japan would attack Britain through Thailand nor indeed at all; it was afraid of the US and might, like Russia, be waiting to 'reap an easy harvest after both sides in the present war had exhausted themselves'.[489] Crosby suggested sending two months' requirements of diesel oil and motor spirit as a mark of goodwill.[490] That could not be done, the Foreign Office replied. But two small shipments would be sent.[491] Crosby reported that Pibun was grateful.[492]

Direck urged 'immediate help and sympathy' as a means of avoiding a pro-Japanese coup. Crosby thought the Thais should be given 'more than they deserve, bearing in mind that many of our grievances against them are due to their fear of Japan, none of them to hostility towards ourselves'.[493] 'While we should be as forthcoming and friendly ... with the Thais as we can, we ought surely to get some concrete evidence of their good intentions before giving away all our bargaining counters,' Clarke wrote.[494] Bennett, however, commented 'that the fundamental weakness of our policy with Thailand was that we were expecting from the Thai Government a firmness towards Japanese pressure at a time when they had no evidence of our willingness to support them against the consequences of their resistance, or alternatively of our ability to bring similar or greater pressure to bear on them'.[495] Crosby was told that 'we are not prepared to make large concessions before we know where we stand and are beginning to think that pressure rather than concessions may be needed to show Thai Prime Minister where his real interests lie'.[496] Once again the issue was to be put to the United States. If Thailand was prepared to demonstrate its goodwill, 'we should be ready to give some assistance which would lessen her dependence on Japan'. At present Britain could not promise military support. 'To refuse also any support of other kinds could only accelerate the process by which Japan is bringing Thailand under her control. We hardly expect to be able now to check this process finally though we may hope to delay it until we are in a better position to meet the menace.' Apart from the strategic threat there was the danger that all Thai tin and rubber would go to Japan and thence in part to Germany.[497] Hull 'listened with interest to the proposals and felt that even if the chance of success might not be great it was desirable to play for time'.[498] His own record was that he said 'that it was never too late ... to explore the situation and closely observe all developments in the hope that an opportunity may arise to encourage the Thai Government to assert its sovereignty in every way and that this might call for certain economic cooperation, et cetera, et cetera'.[499]

Meanwhile Crosby had been talking to Direck. One suggestion they planned to put to Pibun would be an open market for tin and rubber after the commitments to Japan had been defined and met.[500] Oil should be supplied, and Direck hoped that the promised shipments would soon be despatched. Crosby told his superiors that they should not expect too much. 'Great fear of Japan combined with constant Japanese and German pressure and with the general belief that we cannot win the war are factors which will deter Luang Pibun from asserting his neutrality in the firm and open manner we would like. But we can at least hope for negative result by inducing him not to surrender completely to Japan.' That was why Crosby advocated giving him oil and financial help 'even if we do not get commensurate return in the immediate future'.[501]

Two days later Direck gave Crosby a message from Pibun. Japan sought all Thailand's rubber output, 45 000–48 000 tons p.a., and in return would supply oil. Crosby replied that that would be 'the beginning of the end of her independence economically and politically'. Direck and Crosby discussed two alternatives. One was that Britain would get half the rubber and in return supply oil, while there should be an open market for tin. Another was that Japan would get all the rubber and furnish oil while Britain secured the tin.[502] The Japanese chargé suggested that Japan might ask for 80 per cent of the rubber and 40 per cent of the tin in return for oil and arms. Pibun 'did not want all his eggs in Japanese baskets' but feared coercion if he did not accept. Perhaps, Crosby suggested to the Foreign Office, it would be best to acquiesce in the assignment to Japan of say half the rubber and 25 per cent of the tin. Otherwise Thailand would fall completely into the Co-prosperity Sphere. The supply of gunny bags and mining equipment should be renewed as well as that of oil.[503] Assurance over the promised oil was urgent, he added. 'If we cannot stop the barter agreement with Japan for oil I shall consider that the usefulness of my mission here is virtually at an end ....'[504]

Keeping Japan short of rubber reduced the strength of a potential enemy, the Ministry of Economic Warfare pointed out; it would also prevent its supplying one of Germany's main deficiencies. With supplies from Thailand, as well as from Malaya, Borneo and Netherlands India, and from Indo-China under the agreement recently signed, Japan would be able to meet German requirements. Tin was another Axis deficiency. Japan had already taken its quota from Malaya; it had asked for more from the Dutch and was promised some in the Indo-China agreement. It was important to frustrate its efforts in Thailand. A free market might not help as the Japanese could bid up the prices. Jute was 'a useful bargaining weapon'.[505] Neither of Crosby's suggestions was adequate. Even half the rubber would enable Japan to give Germany its minimum requirements.[506]

The Far Eastern Committee discussed various options on 22 May. One, to encourage the Thais to resist Japanese pressure by a convincing demonstration of Britain's ability to help them against Japanese aggression, was deemed 'impracticable'. Another was to abandon Thailand to Japan, warning it that Britain would take retaliatory action if it acted against British interests. Some argued for this course on the grounds that Thailand would not keep its promises, and supplying it with oil would tend to drain Japan of that commodity. The committee, however, favoured the third option, continued conciliation, as advocated by Crosby. The trade in rubber was important, and some control could be applied through the supply or non-supply of gunny bags. Above all, 'it represented a policy of playing for time, as it would delay the process of Japan gaining complete control of Thailand, and would enable us to consolidate our defensive position in Malaya'. It was decided once more to approach the US, and the COS were asked to review their position.[507]

Crosby thought the Ministry of Economic Warfare was asking the impossible. At most he might be able to limit the amount of rubber and tin that went to Japan. But surely his priority 'must be to prevent Malaya and Borneo from having on their frontiers a Thai passively or actively hostile towards us and likely to become the willing tool in the hands of Japanese Military Party'. Britain 'must avoid anything like a breach with Thailand'.[508] Gage preferred Crosby's policy. Britain should not bully Thailand but eke out supplies such as oil 'with the object of encouraging her to hold off Japan. This policy may fail in the end but it is to my mind the only choice and it may at least delay the evil day.'[509] Bennett said the committee accepted this view. It 'realised that fundamentally our policy was military, and that this applied even to its economic aspect'. It was 'better to gain time than to break with Thailand', and Britain must be content with a compromise on rubber and tin. 'There were no illusions as to our present policy. It might not succeed even in gaining time. But it was worth while to try to gain time during which our military position in Malaya and generally might be strengthened.'[510]

Crosby was told he might offer a regular supply of oil, in return for 75 per cent of the rubber and tin; half the amount if he could secure only 50 per cent.[511] He thought that, so far as rubber was concerned, this was 'wishful thinking', and he reiterated 'with all my soul' that, important though economic issues might be, 'general political issues outweigh them in significance'.[512] Bennett telegraphed: 'Every ton of rubber we can secure from Thailand for ourselves or our friends is a nail in the German coffin'.[513] In fact Pibun told Crosby he had to offer Japan 30 000 tons out of a total production of 48 000; Malaya might have 18 000, and any surplus be divided equally. An open market for tin would apply if Britain furnished Thailand with about 2000 tons to meet what was due to

Japan. In return he expected the normal supply of oil.[514] The 30 000 would meet the Japanese–German requirements, Gage noted.[515] The alternative, Crosby pointed out, was that Japan and Germany might get all the rubber by assignment or by outbidding Britain, that the free export of tin would be stopped, and that Japan will supply oil and thus absorb Thailand into the sphere. Agreement, by contrast, would restore cordial relations with Britain.[516]

At the Far Eastern Committee the Colonial Office representative felt that further concessions involved a loss of face and would only encourage 'further blackmailing demands'. The US would look for results, and the supply of oil would look 'even more suspect'.[517] After the meeting the Foreign Office sought 'one more attempt to drive a harder bargain'.[518] Crosby should try for 50:50; if he had to accept the 30 000, all the rest should go to Malaya. The oil could include only enough aviation spirit for civil airlines.[519]

Crosby thought the telegrams on the negotiations 'unjust to Thailand … I am far from trusting the Thais the whole way but they are not the bunch of crooks the Foreign Office seems to think they are'. If the negotiations were not to be conducted in a tactful atmosphere they should be dropped.

> I have an uneasy feeling that you people in Downing Street live in an ivory tower as regards Thailand and that you fail to realize our colossal loss of prestige in this country as a result of the collapse of France in nearby Indo-China and of the unfavourable course of the war for Britain. Instead of upbraiding Thailand for giving too much to Japan we should be thankful that, with our star almost below the horizon, she still turns to us as much as she does.[520]

Crosby, said Bennett, disliked the bargaining. 'Also it is uncomfortably hot in Bangkok.'[521] He was told that the telegrams represented a collective view. The Foreign Office would try 'not to add to the many odds against which you have had to contend, provided you will not allow yourself to be discouraged and will promise not to throw any more ivory bricks at us'.[522] Perhaps, Bennett had written, Crosby would be feeling better as a result of seeing a telegram from Washington 'showing that at long last the US are waking up about Thailand. We must hope that their awakening has not come too late.'[523]

The State Department had on 17 June indicated that it would offer a loan and commercial credits to Thailand while seeking to obtain tin and rubber and that it would recommend that oil interests participate in a plan to supply Thailand with limited quantities of petroleum products.[524] Duly advised, Crosby told Direck 'that this was the golden opportunity for Thailand to restore former good relations with the United States and with her aid and with that of Britain to avoid becoming the economic vassal of Japan'.[525] The US sought the entire production lest the Thais left the Japanese allocations untouched.[526] Crosby did not know whether the British Government would change its attitude 'now that the war between Russia and Germany makes it impossible for Japan to send tin or rubber to German destinations'.[527] He thought the agreement should be clinched.[528] The British Government agreed. The US would have to attempt to abate the Japanese allocation.[529]

Thai counter proposals sought monthly supplies of oil, including aviation spirit for military as well as civilian purposes, and unrestricted supplies of gunny bags. In return 18 000 tons of rubber would be exported to Malaya, and the tin market would be open and free.[530] Crosby thought that the Thais would press hard for military aviation fuel. 'Has it occurred to you that, if we oblige Thailand to turn to Japan for aviation spirit as well as for aircraft, we may be increasing the possibility of a secret Thai–Japanese military understanding?' On gunny bags, however, he supported the Thais only on condition that the question were linked with some consideration of the supply of rice to the British Empire. He suggested to Direck that all rubber in excess of a total output of 48 000 should go to Malaya; 'otherwise such excess may go to Japan'.[531] The British Government thought the proposals 'highly unsatisfactory'. Given the limited amount of rubber envisaged, it sought to scale down the supply of oil, it declined to supply aviation fuel for military purposes and it made no promise over transportation. It also considered that the agreement should not, as proposed, be for one year but for renewable periods of two months, pending the conclusion of a US–Thailand agreement. The supply of gunny bags would not be covered in the agreement, but an undertaking to supply them might be given if it was required in order to clinch it.[532] A draft agreement was sent to Washington for US concurrence; it was designed, Halifax was told, to avoid prejudicing American negotiations.[533] An addition was suggested by Crosby in view of uncertainty about the next Japanese move: a stipulation that Britain's obligations would cease if a third power was allowed to use any bases in Thailand.[534] The FO approved this in the form of a communication to the Minister of Foreign Affairs.[535]

The US in general approved the British proposals.[536] Its ambassador sought all the rubber and tin not assigned to the UK, a proposal Crosby thought would fail.[537] Grant thought nothing of the new policy. A loan would make no difference. The Japanese could only be blocked by military power, not by 'sops' to Thailand. Moreover, he believed the Japanese and Pibun had an agreement whereby Thailand would ultimately recover Laos and the rest of Cambodia through collaboration. A loan would merely help an aggressor.[538]

The Japanese had gained little by the Tripartite Pact. Their intervention in the Thailand/Indo-China conflict, however, gave them their one substantial success in this phase. Matsuoka had fought off the army elements who pressed for military action and, despite the pledge to uphold the integrity of Indo-China of August 1940, he had been able to secure something for Thailand. It was not all that the Thais had come to seek, although far more than the French had wanted to give. The weakness of French Indo-China was demonstrated, although the Japanese as yet stopped short of formally intervening in the south. Their influence over Thailand was increased. Pibun had been aware of Japan's growing power, apprehensive of its advance in Indo-China and tempted by the prospect of territorial adjustment.

The British and the Americans had reacted differently. The former thought that a limited adjustment might serve to keep the Thais from turning entirely to Japan, which would at once assist its acquisition of raw materials and bring the threat it presented closer to Malaya and Singapore. The Americans were against compromise. They insisted on the status quo and did not consider that the mediation was the kind of peaceful and negotiated change they should accept. They were not, however, prepared to interpose by actions rather than words. Only in June did they prove ready to follow a British proposal to support Thailand economically as a means of keeping it out of the sphere.

That policy the British Government had decided on after rejecting the alternatives. Security guarantees it could not give, and pressure it could not apply. Conciliation seemed to be the answer, although arguments about prestige and about economic warfare tended to attenuate it, and even the Foreign Office at times felt that Crosby went too far. During the Indo-China conflict the French had not responded to the policy but blamed the British for the unfortunate outcome of their own obstinacy. Now the British tried to continue their policy by economic measures. With the growth of Japanese influence they saw it as a delaying action. With good reason they distrusted Pibun, and Crosby tried to work through Direck. On supplies to Thailand, Gage wrote,

> our policy is based not so much on whether, if attacked by Japan, the Thais will put up resistance, but rather on the probability that they are more likely to do so if by strengthening the hands of our friends in Thailand we can make them resist infiltration before such an attack is made. This seems to me a wise policy provided we do not make sacrifices of material we need ourselves.[539]

The United States had not supported the earlier approach. Not only was its minister, Grant, at odds with Crosby; the State Department both insisted on the status quo and indicated that Thailand was a lost cause.

After constant endeavours by the British in Washington it became more flexible. It proposed a bold economic policy, including the buying-up of tin and rubber, rather ironically, perhaps, just before the German attack on the Soviet Union made the landward conveyance of these commodities to the Reich impossible, at least for the time being.

Japanese contacts with Burma

In an interview with Australian journalists on 17 January Matsuoka insisted that Japanese expansion to the south would be peaceful and economic. He included Burma, and Craigie thought it was 'the first time a responsible Japanese statesman' had 'publicly included Burma in the area of southward expansion'. He accordingly took the matter up with the Foreign Minister. He replied that Japan did not enjoy 'equality of economic opportunity in Burma', and that was what it sought. By leadership he meant 'spiritual and intellectual leadership'. Craigie 'observed that the use of the word "expansion" to describe this vague aspiration was bound to arouse hostility and resentment in countries which felt their interests to be threatened and that mention of British Territory in this connection was strongly to be deprecated'. But Matsuoka was 'unrepentant'.[540]

About the same time information from Bangkok led to the internment, to Gage's satisfaction,[541] of a number of Thakins involved with the subversive activity the Japanese promoted. Nothing was done about Kujiro Homma, the chancellor at the Japanese consulate, who was said to form the link between 'the conspirators in Bangkok and their dupes in Burma', but Suzuki had been deported. Aung San and others had not been apprehended but were reported to be in Hainan with the Japanese, who were 'believed to have been pursuing their tactics of trying to obtain disaffected Burmese who would act as their agents and would return to Burma and try to stir up trouble in the event of our going to war with Japan'.[542] Aung San had indeed left in August, shortly after Ba Maw's arrest.[543]

Japanese influence in Portuguese Timor

Concern about Japanese activities extended to Portuguese Timor, and it was shared, of course, by the Australians and the Dutch. At the secret conversations in Singapore in November 1940 the Dutch officers had asked whether Britain could influence Portugal against further concessions to the Japanese.[544] The Portuguese, as Dr Teixeira de Sampayo, Secretary-General of the Foreign Ministry, put it, were 'obliged to walk warily owing to Japanese retaliation against Macao'.[545] Shell and others had taken over an oil concession held by an Australian firm in the eastern part of Portuguese Timor. This the Japanese sought, but the Portuguese were offering instead a right to prospect in the western part, 'believed to be unpromising'. Qantas received the right to establish an air connection with Dili, while the Portuguese had permitted the Japanese to make trial flights.[546]

The Japanese budget also provided for a consul at Dili. The Consul-General at Batavia thought that Britain should send one, too, and Craigie agreed.[547] Dening wanted the British one to arrive first.

> The safety of Macao and Timor depends ultimately on our ability to hold our own against Japan in the event of war. To allow a Japanese consulate and air service to be established will gravely prejudice our position and will assist the Japanese in proceeding to the immediate occupation of Timor after the outbreak of war. Since the Portuguese are themselves in no position to defend their possessions in such an event, the least they can do is to refrain from lessening our ability to do so.[548]

The British Government had suggested that Australia should appoint a consular officer or send someone to report.[549] The Australian Government thought that a consul was not justified; appointing one would only make it difficult for the Portuguese not to accept a Japanese one. Appointing an official representative was preferable.[550] David Ross, of the Department of Civil Aviation, was appointed its agent.[551]

In addition a British consular officer, Archer, was sent to report on Timor. He found Japanese influence had 'made rather less progress than might have been expected'. Japanese ships had been calling since 1934, although it was hardly justified on economic grounds. They had been initially welcomed as breaking the monopoly of the unpopular Dutch Steamship Co., 'and by the time that the political dangers were realised a foothold had been secured'. The government's revenue was based largely on a single product, coffee, the markets for which had been adversely affected by the war. Archer suggested that Britain should make a 'fairly generous' offer for the next crop,

> not as a commercial transaction or because we want the coffee, but because this seems the most convenient and practicable method of enabling the Colonial Government to continue standing on its own feet. It is a British interest for Portuguese Timor to retain some semblance of economic stability, while it is a Japanese interest for the colony to become more and more embarrassed until it is compelled by economic necessity to accept any terms which Japan may choose to dictate.

The military defences of Timor were 'insignificant, alike in numbers, equipment and training'. Probably the capital could be 'seized by thirty or forty determined and well armed men', while the houses of the Japanese residents were 'distributed, by accident or design, so as to be near the leading strategic points'. No doubt the Portuguese had never hoped to do more than 'maintain a guerrilla resistance in the interior until help arrives from outside'. Archer doubted if they could do even so much, given the air menace. 'The Timor natives, from whom the levies are drawn, are a race with no martial traditions at all. With obsolete arms, no gas-equipment, and bare feet, it is difficult to believe that even the mildest dose of frightfulness would fail to break their fighting spirit.'

A number of the leading Portuguese in Timor were 'decidedly Fascist in their sympathies', and Japan gained by being the ally of the Fascist countries of Europe. But Archer believed that the dominant feeling towards Japan was still 'one of dislike and fear'. The feeling towards the British Empire was the 'converse'. Sympathy for Fascism diminished sympathy for Britain, but there was 'still some lingering sentiment for Britain as an ancient ally', and it could be easily 'acquitted of aggressive designs'. The Governor, Ferreira de Carvalho, was anxious to foster trade with Australia. Indeed Ross might profit from being the representative of Australia rather than Britain, 'a tiresome Power which puts pressure on Lisbon, and by her policy of contraband control seriously increases the colony's general difficulties'.

The *Goncalo Velho* had been sent to Timor because of the Japanese threat, but the Governor expressed a 'reasoned optimism'. He did not think the Japanese would raid Timor 'except as part of a general Japanese attack on the British Empire and the Dutch East Indies, and he clearly implied his doubt of Japan feeling strong enough to take this risk'. Even if such a war eventuated 'he felt that Timor was too well screened by more forward British and Dutch possessions to be lightly attacked'. It would be easy to take but difficult to hold. The aerodrome and the harbour were small, and the military gain would not be worth the effort. The only value of Timor would be as a base for flying boats and that only in the western monsoon. The latter opinion Archer questioned.[552]

The recommendations to purchase Timor products – coffee, also manganese – were not taken up.[553] But, while Japanese penetration was less than expected, Archer had emphasised that it would be intensified as the Japanese could threaten Macao and the Germans Portugal itself.[554] The interest in sending a force to Kupang was to suggest a possible need to occupy Dili also.

Reinforcements in Malaya

Reinforcements reached Malaya in March and April.[555] Craigie thought the publicity in Singapore aggravated the situation. 'Apart from the question of provocation ... the deterrent effect of our measures in Malaya will be greater in proportion as they are silent and efficient: all this talk only leads the Japanese public to think that we are whistling to keep up our courage.'[556] 'No doubt the intention is to bolster up local morale', Dening commented, 'and to put heart into Thailand and perhaps even Indo-China'. He and his colleagues agreed, however, that the publicity should be damped down.[557] Cadogan disagreed. 'Perhaps we are not very strong in Malaya, but I can see no possible harm in our giving the impression that we are stronger than we are. I don't know much about the Japanese, but I don't think they are easily "provoked". They do all that for themselves.'[558]

The comments were in keeping with the policy the Foreign Office advocated and pursued in this phase. It was designed to limit Japanese penetration by supporting the friendly and the not too unfriendly. Not much force was available and an ingenious diplomacy had to be used. If any reinforcements became available it was desirable to use it to strengthen the diplomatic course. What might be called provocation was, of course, to come only with the measures of July 1941.

CHAPTER 5

July–December 1941

US–Japan relations

Hitler's invasion of Russia was perhaps the decisive move in World War II. Abandoning any attempt to invade the United Kingdom, he switched his attention to the East and, in June 1941, threw a vast army into the Soviet Union. He failed to gain the decisive victory that he sought; this time blitzkrieg did not work. But that was only the more obvious effect. The move also transformed the position in East Asia. Rather than joining in against the Russians, Japan used their involvement in war as an opportunity to turn south. That move provoked sanctions from the US as well as from the UK and the Netherlands. Sanctions did not bring Japan to a halt. Instead the Japanese resolved on attacking both Britain and the US. That decision precipitated US entry into the war, particularly as Hitler declared war on the US as well.

Before the invasion of Russia the Japanese had remained cautious. There were alarms and excursions, but although the Japanese gained some advantages by their mediation in the Thailand–Indo-China conflict, they appeared to bide their time, awaiting, it was thought, some decisive German move against the British. Their caution perhaps added to the image the West held of their relative weakness and intensified the belief that they would not attempt to attack if the US and the UK showed sufficient resolve. That belief proved to be mistaken.

The British had little room to manoeuvre. Stretched to endurance and almost beyond it in Europe and the Mediterranean, they sought to maintain the status quo in the East. They were, however, unable to make major commitments either in terms of actual forces or in terms of promises. They looked to the US. Only if it made commitments could the British risk them also. If that after all led to war that, it had been decided, might well be acceptable; it would bring the US into the war as a whole and thus ensure the defeat of the Axis.

The Americans had indeed come to see Southeast Asia as important to them, although not, ultimately, essential. It was important as a means of keeping British resistance to the Germans alive and thus fending off the destruction of Atlantic security. It seems clear that Roosevelt hoped to avoid open intervention in the war in Europe if he could. The policy was designed to sustain the status quo in Southeast Asia. The Americans stopped short of committing forces to it and indeed short of making promises. Roosevelt sought to keep the Japanese guessing rather than to intervene openly. At the same time economic restraints would be applied so far as possible in a non-provocative way. The further concept was that a really bold move should be kept in reserve. If it were adopted, it was believed that it would effectively deter Japanese action.

At the same time the US had begun negotiations with Japan. That idea had recurred more than once. In Britain and in Australia some had looked for a general Asian settlement. The major difficulty was always seen to be the risk that any deal would be at China's expense, which, as the British saw, would alienate the Americans. Now the Americans had the same difficulty in negotiating with the Japanese. How would China fit into any settlement that was satisfactory to the Japanese?

The negotiations were not made easier by the way in which the Americans presented their views. Their reaction to Japanese encroach-ments had been in keeping with the tradition of non-recognition going back to Lansing and Stimson. Hull had many times articulated the principles that ought in the American view to underlie the conduct of international relations. They had been seen as a definition of American policies; they had also been seen as a restraint on the Japanese with the idea, too, that, if the restraint did not work, they provided a baseline to which the world, Japan included, might return in saner times. In the attempt to hold the line in Southeast Asia the principles had again been invoked. They might, for example, influence the Thais; they might help to gain time. But when negotiations began they made it difficult to be flexible. How could you accept or condemn some breaches of the principles and not others?

The freezing orders

Churchill promised the Russians aid. 'Any man or state who fights against Nazism will have our aid. Any man or state who marches with Hitler is our foe ... It follows therefore that we shall give whatever help we can to Russia and the Russian people.'[1] There was little aid available, however. The Russians were 'hammered' but did not, as some had expected,

absolutely go 'up in smoke'.[2] On 20 July 1941 the UK sent them 200
fighters.[3] In September, however, Kiev fell. Cadogan wrote: 'Perhaps we
are in a better state than I should, last spring, have expected. But
everything is pretty murky, and how exactly we are going to *win* this war,
I should like someone to explain.'[4] Early in October came the drive for
Moscow. The Germans were to be held just outside it. Eden agreed to
visit Stalin but had little to offer. While he was there Churchill was in
Washington. The war had spread to the Far East.

> So ends 1941 – what a year again! [Cadogan wrote on 31 December]. But it
> does look as if we may be at the turn. Disasters in the Far East cloud the nearer
> scene, but on a long view all that matters is defeat of Germany, and that, with
> her failure in Russia and in Libya, and with entry of US into the war, now seems
> to be coming into sight.[5]

The German attack on Russia reduced the direct threat to Britain and
thus to the US. At the same time the fighting in the west enhanced
Japan's security in the east, and it felt free to expand in Southeast Asia.
The reduced threat in Europe, however, enabled the US to take a firmer
stance in resisting this threat. The survival of Russia, despite the earlier
apprehensions, removed some pressure in regard to the Atlantic.
Roosevelt declined to increase naval support for Britain or to take more
ships back from Hawaii. Assistance to Russia was the President's preferred policy. It would reduce Britain's pressure on him and perhaps
exert some restraint on Japan; 'an ideal compromise for a President
which preferred to contain Hitler by proxy rather than hurriedly to
commit his country to formal war'.6

In that sense the meeting of Churchill and Roosevelt at Placentia Bay,
Newfoundland, on 9–12 August was a disappointment. Despite its subsequent fame, the Atlantic Charter, one of the outputs of the conference,
was a poor substitute for an American commitment to enter the war. The
President had indicated that he would consider parallel declarations
designed to restrain Japan. He would also consider 'a joint general
Declaration of principles', which Cadogan drafted.[7] The two countries
declared that they sought 'no aggrandisement', and that they respected
'the right of all peoples to choose the form of government under which
they will live; and they wish to see Sovereign rights and self-government
restored to those who have been forcibly deprived of them'.[8] 'We didn't
of course get 100% of what we wanted on F[ar] E[ast], but we must
remember that it must be read in conjunction with the Joint Declaration,
which will give the Japanese a jolt.'[9] The British had looked for more.
The 'fluffy flapdoodle', on the other hand, worried Amery.[10]

Churchill told the Cabinet that the President was 'obviously determined that they should come in'.[11] He indicated that the convoying agreement also reached was expected to produce an incident, which would force Hitler to engage in naval war or concede defeat in the Atlantic. Churchill said he had also told Roosevelt 'that he would not answer for the consequences if Russia was compelled to sue for peace and, say, by the Spring of next year, hope died in Britain'. Roosevelt, according to Churchill, would look for an incident that would justify hostilities. On 28 August, however, Churchill had to report to Roosevelt a 'wave of depression' in the Cabinet. Harry L. Hopkins, Roosevelt's personal emissary, told the President that Churchill and others believed that the US would get into the war some time but, 'if they ever reached the conclusion that this was not to be the case, that there would be a very critical moment in the war and the British appeasers might have some influence on Churchill'.[12] The warnings to Japan had been watered down. But Churchill's cable helped, with the U-boat attack on the US destroyer *Greer* on 4 September, to keep the President up to the mark on convoys. Churchill's interpretation of Roosevelt's view was, however, probably mistaken. He wanted, as Reynolds suggests, to avoid a war.[13] It was only the actions of the Japanese and then of Hitler that brought the US into the war. On 11 December Hitler and Mussolini declared war on the US. Churchill 'slept the sleep of the saved and thankful'.[14]

The Germans' attack on Russia found Matsuoka at the Kabuki theatre with Wang Ching-wei.[15] He favoured going along with them despite the neutrality pact he had so recently signed in Moscow. 'Great men change their minds. Previously, I advocated going south, but now I favour north.'[16] The outline of national policies of 2 July, however, involved 'taking steps to advance south'.[17] The Imperial Conference accepted the priority of southward expansion, and Matsuoka was soon after squeezed out of office. This change was certain to alarm the United States, which the Japanese realised.

Nomura called on Admiral Turner, Director of War Plans in the Office of Naval Operations, on 20 July. He wanted to talk to Stark. Evidently he was concerned about US reaction to the occupation of French Indo-China expected in the next few days and conveyed the impression that, if the US were accommodating, 'any action it might take in the Atlantic would not be a matter of great concern to Japan'. Turner replied that the occupation of Indo-China would affect the strategic position of the US. The greatest danger to the US, he told Nomura, lay in the continued military success of Germany. 'If Great Britain were to collapse, German military power might very well be directed against South America, and such moves would cause great difficulties for the United States.' Anything that affected 'the future security of the UK, in any part of the world', was of interest to the US 'from the defensive standpoint'. The occupation of Indo-China was

> particularly important for the defence of the United States since it might threaten the British position in Singapore and the Dutch position in the Netherlands East Indies. Were they to pass out of their present control, a very severe blow would be struck at the integrity of the defense of the British Isles, and these Isles might well then be overcome by the Germans. It can thus be seen what a very close interest, from a military viewpoint, the United States has in sustaining the status quo in the southern portion of the Far East.[18]

The US indeed reacted in more than one way to the changes brought about in East Asia by the German invasion of Russia, and to the subsequent Japanese decision to focus on the south, of which MAGIC intercepts made them promptly aware. Welles showed Halifax some intercepts – 'the monkeys have decided to seize bases in Indo-China'[19] – and he also saw Casey.[20] One move was to reinforce the Philippines. Defence of the islands became part of America's policy. The central feature of the program was the supply of B-17 bombers with a range of 1500 miles, the Flying Fortresses. Based in the Philippines, they might deter the Japanese from attacking either the islands or indeed other parts of Southeast Asia. The build-up would be complete by February or March 1942.[21]

> A strategic opportunity of the utmost importance has suddenly arisen in the southwestern Pacific [Stimson was to write]. From being impotent to influence events in that area, we suddenly find ourselves vested with the possibility of great effective power ... even this imperfect threat, if not promptly called by the Japanese, bids fair to stop Japan's march to the south and secure the safety of Singapore.[22]

Better known are the economic steps the US took. On 26 July 1941 the President issued an executive order freezing Japanese assets in the US, thus bringing 'all financial and import and export trade transactions in which Japanese interests are involved under the control of the Government ...'.[23] Welles thought such steps would 'provoke Japan to war with them before long'.[24] Roosevelt did not intend it to be a complete embargo on oil and gasoline. But officials interpreted it more rigidly than he expected, particularly Dean Acheson and the new Foreign Funds Control Committee. In September Hull confirmed this stance rather than back down.[25]

The prospective reinforcement of the Philippines made gaining time important and, while envisaging economic pressure rather than embargo, the President planned to continue with the Nomura talks. Hull had terminated these talks on 23 July when he learned of the Japanese moves in Indo-China. At Placentia Bay Roosevelt told Churchill he planned to resume the talks, in particular about the conditions the Japanese had attached to an idea he had suggested to Nomura of an international agreement to neutralise Indo-China.

The UK went along with the embargo in July despite the fear that it might provoke the Japanese to move south. Britain must prove its fidelity and then seek a promise of US support in the event of a war. Halifax saw Welles on 2 August with the Australian and South African ministers. The Acting Secretary of State, Welles, said he had on 31 July conveyed to Nomura Roosevelt's proposal that Thailand should be neutralised by general agreement, as proposed for Indo-China, and the same proposal had been conveyed to Grew. The South African minister, R.W. Close, conveyed Smuts' emphasis on 'the importance of United States Government standing with the British Commonwealth against further Japanese advancement'. Casey 'referred to the probability of any Japanese attack falling on us and the Netherlands East Indies and emphasised the importance that Australia would attach in such an event to US support'. Welles' recent statement on the threat to American interests from Japanese action in Indo-China suggested that if there were an attack on the Indies or the British Commonwealth, the US 'would inevitably find themselves involved', and there could be advantage in a further statement by way of warning. Welles

> said he thought he must in the first instance await Japanese reaction to the proposal to neutralise Thailand. He added however that if Japanese response to this was evasive or unsatisfactory it would be further proof to him of what he already felt certain, namely that if the Japanese went into Thailand it would only be because they were contemplating going further.[26]

Churchill followed up at the Placentia meeting. Cadogan drafted parallel notes on 10 August. The one that the US would send would indicate that any further Japanese encroachment in the southwest Pacific would prompt American countermeasures, even though those might lead to war. 'If any Third Power becomes the object of aggression by Japan in consequence of such counter-measures or of their support of them, the President would have the intention to seek authority from Congress to give aid to such a Power.'[27] But Roosevelt and Welles would not accept the second statement. The draft of 15 August indicated that, if the Japanese Government took further steps in pursuance of military domination in the Pacific region, the US would be 'forced to take immediately any and all steps of whatsoever character it deems necessary in its own security notwithstanding the possibility that such further steps on its part may result in conflict between the two countries'.[28] The draft was further watered down in Hull's office, and two documents were given to Nomura on 17 August.[29] An oral statement declared that if Japan took further steps towards military domination of neighbouring countries, the US would 'take immediately any and all steps which it may deem necessary toward safeguarding the legitimate rights and interests of the United States and American nationals and toward insuring the safety and security of the United States'.[30]

> Mr Hull looking very much the benign and courtly old gentleman, told me that when he saw the words agreed at the meeting between the Prime Minister and the President, he said 'Christ – not that' and went on to explain that with the Japanese military extremists in their present jumpy temper he thought it better not to use such crude language.[31]

The statement, moreover, read very generally and did not seem to the British explicitly to warn the Japanese off Thailand. But they had to leave the matter where it was.[32] Churchill's broadcast of 24 August had, however, contained the assurance that, if US attempts to reach a settlement with Japan failed, 'we shall, of course, range ourselves unhesitatingly at the side of the United States'.[33]

The embargo, as enforced, prompted decisions in Tokyo. The longer Japan waited the weaker it would be, and the monsoon would prevent action after November or December. The Imperial Conference of 6 September considered Japan's demands, resolving to go to war if they were not secured, with the first ten days of October as a tentative deadline.[34] 'A number of vital military supplies, including oil, are dwindling day by day', said Admiral Nagano, the Naval Minister.[35]

> The government has decided that if there is no war, the fate of the nation is sealed [he declared]. Even if there is war, the country may be ruined. Nevertheless, a nation which does not fight in this plight has lost its spirit and is already a doomed country. Only if we fight until the last soldier will it be possible to find a way out of this fatal situation.[36]

The Japanese Premier Prince Konoe had picked up an idea put forward by John Doe Associates, that he and Roosevelt might meet. Like the military, he had not expected such a strong American reaction after the move into southern Indo-China. To repair the damage his strategy was, according to Tomita Kenji, to meet FDR and get round any obstruction by cabling direct to the Emperor.[37] But although Grew favoured it, as initially did the President, Hull and his advisers were opposed to such a meeting until basic agreement had been reached: Reynolds suggests that they had Placentia Bay in mind as an example to avoid.[38] 'I was opposed to the first Munich and still more opposed to a second Munich,' Hull himself declared.[39] Konoe fell.

Tojo's new government re-examined Japan's policy. A Liaison conference of 1 November gave the diplomats until 30 November to complete
a settlement. War with the UK and the US would follow if they failed.[40] A
new proposal was submitted on 7 November and rejected. The pursuit of
a modus vivendi was abandoned. At the Imperial Conference on 1
December Tojo declared: 'At the moment our Empire stands at the
threshhold of glory or oblivion …'.[41] 'Sometimes', he believed, 'a man
has to jump with his eyes closed from the temple of Kiyomizu into the
ravine below.'[42]

The negotiations

The conversations initiated earlier in the year had been interrupted by
the move into Indo-China, then resumed after Placentia Bay. Welles had
told Nomura on 23 July that the move must bring the conversations to a
halt.[43] The following day Nomura saw the President. The latter orally
suggested that, if the Japanese refrained from occupying Indo-China or
withdrew its forces, he would endeavour to secure a commitment from
other countries that Indochina should be regarded as a neutralised
country and that the local authorities would remain in control, not
confronted by Gaullist elements. Nomura thought 'that only a very great
statesman would reverse a policy at this time'.[44] The freezing followed.
Until public opinion had cooled, Foreign Minister Toyoda said, 'nothing
could be accomplished along the lines of the President's proposal'.[45]
Welles rejected Nomura's hint of a 'compromise solution'.[46] On 31 July
he told the envoy that the President had learned that Japan was 'making
the same kind of economic and military demands upon the Government
of Thailand which it had recently made upon the French Government
with regard to Indo-China'. Neither threat nor a need for resources
justified them. Roosevelt therefore wanted his proposal to embrace
Thailand as well. If Japan abandoned its present course in Indo-China,
he would seek from other powers the same guarantee for both Indochina
and Thailand.[47]

   In early August the Japanese sought to renew the conversations by
taking up the President's proposal. On the 6th Nomura handed Hull a
Japanese proposal under which Japan would not station further troops
in the southwest Pacific and would withdraw those in Indo-China 'on the
settlement of the China Incident'. It offered to guarantee the neutrality
of the Philippines. The US would suspend its military measures and
advise the British and the Dutch to do so, too. It would restore normal
trade and commerce and cooperate with Japan in procuring the
resources it needed, especially in Netherlands India. The US was to use
its good offices to initiate negotiations between Japan and 'the Chiang
Kai-shek regime' for 'a speedy settlement of the China Incident' and

recognise a special status for Japan in Indo-China even after its troops had left.[48] Hull put the proposal in his pocket and told Nomura that he was 'frankly pessimistic' about getting anywhere with it.[49] The US reply, handed over on 8 August, alluded to its oft-stated views on a 'broad understanding'. Japan was 'well aware of its attitude, of what it is able and willing to do, and of what it cannot do'. The current Japanese proposals were 'lacking in responsiveness to the suggestion made by the President'.[50]

Nomura then revived the idea of a meeting of the responsible heads of government, perhaps in Honolulu. But Hull pointed to the need to reshape Japan's policies.[51] At a conversation with the President on 17 August Nomura again suggested a Roosevelt–Konoe meeting.[52] Roosevelt handed over the post-Placentia warning. He also indicated that the conversations might be resumed if Japan were prepared to 'suspend its expansionist activities' and to 'readjust its position' along the lines of the principles to which the US was committed.[53] On 28 August Nomura made over a message from Konoe, seeking a meeting,[54] and a statement, saying that the principles and 'the practical application thereof, in the friendliest manner possible' were 'the prime requisites of a true peace'.[55] Hull indicated that 'an agreement in principle on the principal questions', including China, was desirable, lest the meeting fail.[56] The President reiterated this on 3 September. The matter would also have to be discussed with the British, the Chinese and the Dutch.[57]

Under Japan's proposals of 6 September it would undertake not to make any military advancement from Indo-China into adjoining areas nor resort to military action against any regions south of Japan 'without any justifiable reason'. If the US entered the European war Japan would decide its interpretation of the Tripartite Pact. Japan would attempt 'the rehabilitation of general and normal relationship between Japan and China' and withdraw its forces when it had done so. Its activities in the southwestern Pacific would be 'carried on by peaceful means and in accordance with the principle of non-discrimination in international commerce'. The US would reciprocate this commitment, abstain from measures prejudicial to Japan's endeavour concerning the settlement of the China Affair, suspend military measures in the East and discontinue the freezing act and the closure of the Panama Canal.[58] As Maxwell Hamilton and his colleagues pointed out, much of this was vague and at odds with earlier statements.[59]

By the end of September no meeting had been arranged. Grew wondered whether reaching a not wholly satisfactory agreement might not be better than Konoe's displacement by 'a military dictatorship'[60] The US reply, however, considered that the Japanese statement would circumscribe the application of the principles. Would a meeting in such circumstances be 'likely to contribute to the advancement of the high purposes which we have mutually had in mind?'[61] China bulked large in the exchanges. Could the question be left in abeyance? Wakasugi, the Minister-Counsellor, asked Welles on 13 October. 'I said it seemed to me that this question was very much like asking whether the play of "Hamlet" could be given on the stage without the character of "Hamlet". The Minister laughed loudly ...'.[62] Hull was 'not very expectant' but resolved to hear what the new Tojo Government had to say.[63]

On 7 November Nomura gave Hull a document focusing on the stationing of forces in China and Indo-China. The former would be withdrawn 'within two years with [sic] the firm establishment of peace and order'; the latter 'as soon as the China Affair is settled or an equitable peace is established in East Asia'.[64] Togo, the new Foreign Minister, told Grew that Japan 'had repeatedly made proposals calculated to approach the American point of view, but the American Government for its part had taken no step toward meeting the Japanese position and had yielded nothing – it had perhaps taken a more advanced position'. The Japanese people, 'if exposed to continued economic pressure, might eventually feel obliged to resort to measures of self-defense'.[65] The same day Nomura called on the President. Roosevelt stressed the need for 'patience'. He 'spoke of a *modus vivendi* as being not merely an expedient and temporary agreement, but also one which takes into account actual human existence'.[66] When Nomura brought his new assistant, Kurusu, to meet Hull on 18 November, the Secretary of State remarked 'that he frankly did not know whether anything could be done on the matter of reaching a satisfactory agreement with Japan; that we can go so far but rather than go beyond a certain point it would be better for us to stand and take the consequences'. He raised the possibility of 'a relaxation of freezing' so as 'to enable the peaceful leaders in Japan to get control of the situation on Japan and to assert their influence'.[67] On 20 November Nomura and Kurusu offered to remove Japanese troops from southern Indo-China, while the US would cooperate in securing commodities from the Indies, drop the freeze, supply oil and refrain from measures prejudicial to endeavours for restoring peace in China.[68] On 22 November Hull told the Japanese of the 'misgivings' among representatives in other countries. 'He repeated that we were doing our best, but emphasised that unless the Japanese were able to do a little there was no use in talking.'[69]

Roosevelt told Churchill of a counter-modus vivendi on 24 November, adding: 'I am not very hopeful and we must all be prepared for real trouble, possibly soon.'[70] Both the Chinese and Dutch ambassadors were critical,[71] Chiang Kai-shek 'greatly agitated'.[72] The British thought a counter proposal should pitch demands high and price low.[73] The draft was finalised on 25 November.[74] Churchill telegraphed Roosevelt. 'Of course, it is for you to handle this business and we certainly do not want an additional war. There is only one point that disquiets us. What about Chiang Kai Shek? Is he not having a very thin diet? ... If they collapse, our joint dangers would enormously increase ...'.[75]

Hull abandoned the modus vivendi.

In view of the opposition of the Chinese Government and either the half-hearted support or the actual opposition of the British, the Netherlands and the Australian Governments, and in view of the wide publicity of the opposition and of the additional opposition that will naturally follow through utter lack of an understanding of the vast importance and value otherwise of the *modus vivendi* [he recommended handing the ambassadors merely a general document, and withholding the modus vivendi], without in any way departing from my views about the wisdom and the benefit of this step.[76]

Halifax asked for an explanation of the change. Welles said that one of the reasons was the 'half-hearted' support of the British. Halifax said they were concerned about the Chinese. Welles ended the conversation by saying that the increase in Japanese forces in Indo-China suggested they were preparing to move 'on a very large scale'.[77] Hull did not think the communications from Churchill and Eden 'would be very helpful in a bitter fight that would be projected by Chiang Kai-shek and carried forward by all of the malcontents in the United States'.[78] Churchill, he told Halifax, might have done better to tell Chiang to 'brace up' rather than passing on his protest without objection. He warned that Japan might move suddenly in 'a desperate gamble'.[79]

On 26 November Hull indicated that the modus vivendi proposals of 20 November would not 'contribute to the ultimate objectives of ensuring peace under law, order and justice' and presented a plan of a broad but simple settlement covering the entire Pacific area that attempted to bridge the gap between the statements of the US and Japanese.[80] This plan provided that both governments would endorse the four principles. Such steps would be taken as the conclusion of a multinational non-aggression pact, an international pledge to respect the integrity of French Indo-China, withdrawal of all Japanese forces from China and Indo-China, negotiation of a US–Japan trade agreement and termination of the freezing restrictions.[81] Kurusu thought his government would 'throw up its hands'. Hull said he had done his best to explore the modus vivendi.[82] '[Hull's] whole attitude was like saying, "No use of discussion," and he would not even give us the time of day,' said Kurusu in his memoirs.[83] A conversation with the President made no progress.[84] Nor did one with Hull on 1 December.[85] At another conversation, Nomura remarked sotto voce 'this isn't getting us anywhere'.[86]

On 7 December Nomura and Kurusu delivered the Japanese Government's comments. Hull expostulated: 'In all my fifty years of public service I have never seen a document that was more crowded with infamous falsehoods and distortions – infamous falsehoods and distortions on a scale so huge that I never imagined until today that any Government on this planet was capable of uttering them.'[87] The attack on Pearl Harbor had already taken place.[88] Roosevelt called 7 December 'a date which will live on in infamy'.[89]

Hull was always very doubtful of the success of the negotiations. In early August he had suggested that the Japanese had either to go forward towards Thailand and the Burma Road or 'turn around and come back toward the road of friendship and peace'. In fact they went forward, making 'fraudulent avowals of peace and friendship' while they 'get ready'. 'Nothing will stop them except force ... The point is how long we can manoeuvre the situation until the military matter in Europe is brought to a conclusion.'[90]

After the war had begun Hull told Halifax that he believed 'that the main decision in Japanese policy was taken early in July and that there was never more than an off-chance of deflecting Japan from it'.[91] 'Japan was probably never doing more than playing for time,' Cadogan noted.[92] The same might be true of the Americans. 'Whether or not Japs decide to attack depends on solidity of democratic front,' Oliver Harvey of the Foreign Office had noted on 11 September.[93] It was possible that the Japanese would not risk it. 'The firmer your attitude and ours the less chance of their taking the plunge,' Churchill had cabled Roosevelt early in November.[94] Hull might have hoped that, if time could be won, this policy might after all work since the US would have reinforced the Far East. That these two lines could not both be pursued is perhaps the real explanation for the collapse of the modus vivendi. Hull nevertheless remained bitter about the criticism of it. He seemed particularly bitter about China and about Britain's support of China. No doubt he recognised the difficulty that the US endorsement of China's integrity and its statement of principles placed in the way even of a modus vivendi.

Was the rigid stance prudent? Akira Iriye has asked. The US would not alter its policy in China but some argue(d) that it made little sense to bring about a war with Japan over China since US interests lay in the Pacific. 'All such ideas miss the essential point, that China was no longer an isolated object of policy but an integral part of America's Asian–Pacific strategy.' Forsaking China would question the ABCD alliance. A temporary expedient was impossible; only a major transformation would do.[95] Hull's frustration may have reflected this dilemma. Maybe he had hoped the British would have helped him out of it.

In the analysis Sir Ronald I. Campbell had offered from Washington in September Hornbeck was presented as the advocate of 'a firmer policy towards Japan', which would keep it 'from expanding and from entering the war' and enable the anti-Axis powers to focus on the West. Hull,

Campbell suggested, had adopted this thesis 'in its general lines', but he recognised 'a certain risk that Japanese extremists will nevertheless plunge into war in a fit of temper'. The UK and the US

are not yet ready for this and ... it is necessary to try to gain time. He is ready and willing therefore to explore the possibilities of preventing a Japanese plunge into war and of procuring a radical change of Japanese policy by negotiations in which he will seek to convince Japan that if she alters her present course she can have access to and a fair share of the good things in the Far East without the expense and risk of war.

Hull was combining 'the idea of firmness with that of persuasion by peaceful negotiation'. He would not, Campbell believed, 'abandon his basic principles' and agree to a settlement at the expense of the Chinese, the Dutch or the British.[96] Cadogan accepted this view. 'We must let the Americans try out their talks ... It may be something to "gain time". What we do gain beyond that, is that America is engaging herself in a discussion of the Pacific situation.'[97]

Hull himself had told Casey in September that 'his principal objective in resuming discussions with Japan was to gain precious time during which United States can improve their position in the Far East. He said he had only a faint hope of success resulting from such discussions.'[98] In the subsequent weeks Hull said little about the talks.[99] The State Department were 'at great pains to conduct conversations with Japan entirely themselves and in the greatest secrecy'.[100] But then he sought to involve them in the modus vivendi initiative, which he described more as Kurusu's than his own.[101] On 23 November Hull discussed the modus vivendi Kurusu proposed with Casey, Halifax and other envoys. He said 'the main thing that we all had to consider was whether we thought such a stop-gap arrangement was worth entering into ... He agreed that it was very doubtful that Japan would accept substantial amendments that he thought it necessary to insist on ... there was perhaps one chance in three'. But two or three months' delay was desirable, certainly in the eyes of army and navy. Hull also read through draft outlines of a 'broad general multilateral agreement ... If we achieved this limited arrangement we would have some time in which to explore the lines of a general agreement provided Japanese Government was willing to use time gained to alter and improve Japanese public opinion towards peaceful solutions and away from aggression.'[102]

Outlining to the envoys of other governments his revision of the modus vivendi on 24 November, Hull 'was clearly exercised in his mind at the prospect of his possibly having to make a decision on his own to present [the] counterproposals to Japanese representatives'. He wanted the other governments to 'express themselves' as early as possible. 'He said that he did not want to have to rely solely on his own judgment in this important matter and that he was turning over in his mind whether or not he should take risk that was entailed in making such a counter proposal to Japanese representatives until our respective Governments had made known their views to him ...'[103]

On 26 November Casey reported that all but the Chinese Government supporting buying time but as cheaply as possible. The Chinese, however, thought a modus vivendi would be 'interpreted in China as sacrificing them for our purposes ...'. Whether or not as a result of this, Casey added, Hull gave the Japanese envoys a document 'detailing fundamental principles on which a general Pacific settlement must be based ... but containing no reference to the modus vivendi'.[104] When Casey saw Hull on 27 November he was

> depressed and upset [wrote Casey]. He blamed the Chinese principally for torpedoing of the modus vivendi. We [he?] said that he would have liked stronger support from British and Dutch Governments but did not stress. He said that it would have been completely impossible to have implemented the modus vivendi in face of strong Chinese opposition and that he had now dropped it entirely.

Hull showed Casey telegrams that he thought indicated that the Japanese would act soon, probably by invading Thailand.[105] Japanese transports had been sighted off Formosa,[106] and MAGIC intercepts had revealed 29 November as the absolute deadline.[107]

The British, too, had an interest in gaining time. They had begun to consider transferring some ships to the East after Placentia Bay. The First Sea Lord was cautious; he would build up a fleet at Trincomalee first, and he would not at first send any modern battleships. Churchill wanted a small modern fleet, based as soon as possible in Singapore, and in October, after Konoe's fall, he got his way. The *Prince of Wales* and the *Repulse* would go to Singapore, to be joined later by other ships. It would deter the Japanese, reassure the Australians and promote cooperation with the US.[108] The US Chiefs of Staff had not approved the ADB report. It seemed that the US Asiatic Fleet could be employed outside the Far East and in support of solely British interests. Nor was there a clear determination to defend the Indies, the 'Malay barrier'.[109] Some of the difficulties were removed at the Atlantic meeting.[110] The Americans, however, rejected a redraft, ABD-2.[111] Instead it was decided to work on the basis of ABC-1 and to promote service coordination on this basis. Sir Tom Phillips was invited to visit Admiral Hart and General MacArthur in Manila.[112] The conversations were interrupted by news of Japanese moves on 6 December.[113]

The British had been prepared to support a counter proposal on the modus vivendi. Churchill wrote to Eden on 23 November:

Our major interest is: no further encroachments and no war, as we have already enough of this latter. The United States will not throw over the Chinese cause, and we may safely follow them in this part of the subject ... Subject to the above, it would be worthwhile to ease up upon Japan economically sufficiently for then [sic] to live from hand to mouth – even if we only get another three months.[114]

'PM ... wants present situation in Far East to endure and not get worse.'[115]

Hull's counter proposal 'struck us in the Foreign Office as being a notable piece of appeasement, and as likely to produce the wrong effect on the Japanese, to say nothing of the blow which it would constitute to the Chinese', Ashley Clarke wrote later of what he thought might be the stuff of a Simon–Stimson controversy. But, while Halifax talked to Hull in terms of the comments on Kurusu's proposal, no comments were made on Hull's other than the PM's message to the President. The effect of the latter, and of Chiang's, was to decide the US 'to throw up all attempts at obtaining a *modus vivendi*' and to put in a statement of principles for a settlement, 'admirable in its way, but which could not be said to constitute an attempt to carry the negotiations any further'. This statement the British Government did not see until some days later.

Whether this was the right course to take only history can judge. At the same time and even in the light of the subsequent successful action of the Japanese it would seem that no serious agreement could have been possible with Japan and it was better that the negotiations should end on the comprehensive statement of principle made by the United States Government rather than tail off into a wrangle about some inglorious and unworkable compromise.[116]

Craigie, by contrast to Clarke, was to be deeply critical of the negative response to Japan's modus vivendi of 20 November. He believed that a more flexible approach could have postponed war; 'had it been possible to reach a compromise with Japan in December 1941 involving the withdrawal of Japanese troops from South Indo-China, war with Japan would not have been inevitable', he wrote in a report to Eden, the Foreign Secretary. Germany's victory had begun to be doubtful, and the risk of Japanese intervention diminished as the certainty of Allied victory became more apparent.[117] Another school of thought, Craigie wrote, argued that 'American participation in the war with Germany was so vital to the Allied cause that it must be secured even at the price of Japan's entry on the other side'. He could not offer an authoritative opinion, but he thought the theory 'highly questionable'. Japan's capacity was so great that American material aid to Britain in and across the Atlantic would have to be 'seriously curtailed'.

The goal of British diplomacy was 'American participation in the war coupled with continued Japanese neutrality'. That, Craigie thought, might have been attained 'given a less uncompromising attitude towards Japan during the concluding stages of the Washington conversations'. Britain could not hold out against a Japanese attack for more than two or three months. Nor could the US assist in the early stages of a war with Japan. American diplomacy often erred 'on the side of rigidity and formality'. Britain should have informed itself of the Anglo-Japanese negotiations so that it might have exerted a 'moderating influence' on the American approach. The Japanese offer of 20 November should have been pursued. The counter proposal the US finally sent had no chance of succeeding; it ignored the fact that Japanese foreign policy had for some years ceased to be founded on the principles enunciated by the counter proposal.

Craigie did not defend Japan's policy, and the American approach to the negotiations was justified on 'purely ethical and ideological grounds'. 'But the burden of my advice during the years 1937 and 1941 has been that we could not afford to follow a purely idealistic policy or to deal with Japan according to her merits so long as we remained under the threat of war with Germany.' That became still more obvious after the fall of France. 'It was the Pétain Government's betrayal of the Allied cause by refusing to continue the fight from the French colonies which, more than any other single event, created in the Japanese mind the belief in the certainty of a German victory and led to the conclusion of the Tripartite Pact.' That pact some saw as committing the Japanese to ultimate intervention, a view Craigie did not share. Pact or no pact, 'I considered that the day of reckoning with Japan should be postponed by every honourable means open to diplomatic technique until a time of our own choosing – our time, that is, not Hitler's. Had that been done, our final settlement with Japan, following upon the defeat and disruption of Germany, might never have required an actual recourse to arms.'

Churchill denounced Craigie's report as giving a 'one-sided and pro-Japanese' account. It betrayed a 'total lack of all sense of proportion' as between 'any British or American slips' and Japan's 'deliberate scheme of war'. Craigie also wrote of the breach with Japan 'as if it were an unmitigated disaster'. It was not.

> It was ... a blessing that Japan attacked the United States and thus brought America wholeheartedly and unitedly into the war. Greater good fortune has rarely happened to the British Empire than this event which has revealed our friends and foes in their true light, and may lead, through the merciless crushing of Japan, to a new relationship of immense benefit to the English speaking countries and to the whole world ...[118]

Hull had never thought that his diplomacy was very likely to be successful. The US policy towards Japan had shifted under the impact of the European war. Earlier it had insisted verbally on the validity of the status quo and on the invalidity of changes to it other than by agreement. Now it found it had to insist on a return to the status quo; anything else appeared inconsistent. Moreover, it would damage the association with other states, China, Britain and the Netherlands, that developed in terms of the principles the US had enunciated. A modus vivendi was thus difficult to pursue, even apart from doubts about the sincerity of the Japanese. Hull nevertheless tended to blame the Chinese, and, even more, the British, for his abandoning the modus vivendi. That seems to echo the dislike of British criticism he had expressed in May rather than a real belief that other countries had undermined his diplomacy. Perhaps, even more, it reflected his disappointment, although his hopes had never been high.

He had justified them in terms of gaining time. That concept, often put forward in London also, was associated with a number of assumptions about Japan's policy. Japan's caution, it was believed, led it to wait on developments in the European war. If Japan's advance in East and Southeast Asia could be postponed until the situation in Europe had improved it might not take place at all. The growing association of the US and the UK, and indeed of the Australians, the Dutch and the Chinese, would add to Japan's caution. The calculation took insufficient account of the impact of the economic sanctions. While some saw the risk that they would provoke Japan to break out, there was a tendency to conclude that it would not, that if it did it would not act as boldly as it did, and that it could be brought to a halt sooner than it was. 'Name me', Hornbeck had asked John Emmerson, then in the Tokyo embassy, 'one country in history which ever went to war in desperation!'[119] 'We're all astounded over Japan. We never thought she would attack us and America at once. She must have gone mad,' wrote Harvey.[120] Ismay heard of Pearl Harbor with 'stunned surprise. It had never occurred to anyone in London, nor I believe in Washington, that such a thing was possible.'[121]

Craigie believed that the modus vivendi negotiations were abandoned too soon. Continuing them would have thrown Japan's plans into confusion and won more time. War might have been postponed for three months or even averted.[122] Abandoning them exposed the other powers to a devastating attack from which the US was in no position immediately to rescue them. His view was not unlike Hull's. But he thought the British were better diplomats and could have played a useful role.

Such views were not popular in London. The British had kept out of these negotiations partly because Hull wanted to keep them out and partly because they believed that allowing the Americans the initiative made it more likely that they would take part if war ensued.[123] Craigie's criticism was unwelcome in this respect. Churchill's rebuttal went much further. The crisis brought the US into the war itself, which ensured victory in Europe and in Asia. What the Prime Minister did not appear to foresee, even after the fall of Singapore, was the difficulty of restoring the fortunes of the British Empire in the East. US help, as Craigie had seen, could have no immediate effect. When it came it was not designed to assist in the restoration of a colonial pattern in which it had never been deeply interested.

Churchill thus saw the Japanese attack, albeit paradoxically, as a stroke of good fortune. He did not congratulate himself on contriving it, and he did not do so. He was prepared to accept that Asia might provide America's route into the European war. He had, however, been cautious over suggesting it, although criticising those who opposed it. He had avoided taking the lead in Asia, although that was partly because he feared that doing so might be counterproductive. As in Europe in 1940, so in Asia in 1941, Churchill played it by ear, listening with a sense of weakness but also of confidence. Like Bismarck, he heard the step of God sounding through events and stepped forth to seize the hem of His garment.[124]

The British thought that, if war came, Japan could be contained. ABD had to be consolidated, the FO argued, and 'Matador', the pre-emptive occupation of Kra, had to be considered. The COS still hesitated; no action should be taken until the US was committed. Churchill agreed. He would commit the UK only to the US. An attack was expected but not one on Pearl Harbor. The question was therefore what the US would do if non-American territory were attacked. The President and his military advisers had agreed on 28 November that the US would have to fight. He told Halifax this in a conversation of 1 December and confirmed it on 3 December. 'We had had very good telegram from Roosevelt about Far East, which removed many of PM's doubts, and he said we could not [read: now] guarantee Dutch.'[125] The UK proceeded to guarantee support to the Dutch, and prepared to guarantee Thailand, and Brooke-Popham was given authority to mount Matador. Roosevelt meanwhile planned to warn Japan in a three-stage process: a message to the Emperor, a warning address to Congress on 9 December, and then, on the 10th, warnings from the British and the Dutch.[126] But Japan's action foreclosed this program. He got only as far as the message to Hirohito. It alluded to the build-up of troops in Indo-China; yet, it added, a withdrawal would result in peace throughout the whole of the South Pacific area.[127] It was, as Graebner puts it, 'a moving appeal to reason and peace, but ultimately on American terms'.[128]

Australia's reactions

'These stupid Dominions of course get cold feet, and don't want to freeze Japanese assets without an assurance of support from US,' Cadogan had written on 24 July. 'They must know that they can't get this.

DO [Dominion Office] wanted to send a telegram agreeing that we should seek it. I watered it down, and we caught A. [Anthony Eden] at 8 p.m. and he, luckily, killed it.'[129] The Australian Government had agreed that the Empire must not lag behind the US. But it emphasised the need for frank exchanges with the US in order to obtain indications of its armed support in the event of war.[130]

> Having regard to constitutional difficulties in the United States [the reply ran] we feel quite certain that to ask the United States Government in terms now to give us such an assurance would be most unwise. Any attempt to attach such a condition to our taking action similar to that which the United States are prepared to take might well discourage the United States from taking action at all and in any case would not, in our view, produce the desired result.

The British Government had considered whether it might be possible to indicate that parallel action would be taken and 'at the same time to make it clear that we are assuming that if, in consequence, an attack on the Netherlands East Indies or ourselves results, they will be prepared to give us armed support'. But the US would make reservations 'which would seriously embarrass us'. In any case the US would, the British Government thought, be compelled to support it. The right line was 'to follow the United States lead boldly and without attaching reservation'. If this led to Japanese threats, then would be the time to seek a guarantee.[131] Menzies insisted that the matter should be raised. He felt that in discussion 'indication of United States attitude will certainly appear. The nature of this in all probability will constitute satisfactory understanding which we feel to be essential ...'.[132] Casey thought that it would be 'impossible to get such undertaking. I believe that events and not logical arguments will drive the United States into belligerency.' His plan was to urge on the carrying-out of the naval plans agreed on in March.[133]

Cranborne told the Commonwealth Government that the British planned to approach the US after the measures had been carried out, seeking an assurance from the Americans 'that we can count on their support if we are attacked by Japan or become involved in war with her through an attack on the Netherlands East Indies'.[134] Menzies wanted it done promptly. 'If the Americans feel in their hearts that in the event of war-like retaliation by Japan they could not remain aloof from the conflict, surely they can be made to see that a plain indication by them to Japan at this stage would probably avoid war.' Australia was perhaps especially conscious of the dangers in the Pacific. The US was in the best position to dispel them. 'The faintest drift in our handling of the Japanese problem may mean that Japan will engage in policies from which at a later stage she cannot withdraw without a serious loss of face.'[135] Hearing of the Placentia meeting, Menzies urged Churchill 'to clarify the Far Eastern position. I do not think that there is any doubt that firm and unequivocal attitude by the United States is the one thing that will deter Japan from continuing in a course leading to war.' He had found Roosevelt 'extremely sympathetic but reluctant to be too precise; and yet precision and firmness are the real antidote to Japan'.[136]

In October the Australian Government welcomed Brooke-Popham to Melbourne. 'He felt that the United Kingdom Chiefs of Staff were not neglecting the Far East and that probably they have made a fair allocation from the resources available.'[137] Plans to send a squadron to the Far East were 'noted with great satisfaction'.[138] Churchill told Australian Prime Minister John Curtin of the decision to send the *Prince of Wales* into the Indian Ocean on 26 October, in respect of home security 'a serious risk for us to run'. It would be 'the best possible deterrent and every effort will be made to spare her permanently'.[139]

In the UK as Special Representative in mid-November, Australian politician Earle Page urged a build-up in air power at Singapore. That might deter Japan; it would also enable the empire to take 'a resolute and determined line', and in turn that might elicit American support.[140] Churchill responded in characteristic manner.

> The United Kingdom were resolute to help Australia if she were menaced with invasion, but ... it would be a grave strategic error to move forces to the Far East – possibly to remain inactive for a year – which were now actively engaged against the Germans and Italians. Our correct strategy was to move our strength from theatre to theatre as the situation changed. At the present time, the theatre in which the forces could be most profitably employed was the Middle East. A policy of spreading our resources to guard against possible but unlikely dangers may be fatal.

Churchill renewed his assurance that if Australia were 'gravely threatened we should [cut] our losses in the Middle East and move in great strength to Australia's assistance'. He went on to discuss Roosevelt's position and his relationship with him. It would be 'a great error ... to press the President to act in advance of American opinion'.[141]

The Australians took a keen interest in the talks when Hull revealed something of them. Inasmuch as, if the negotiations failed, Japan might act against states other than the US, those states, Casey argued, should be involved in shaping the response. Presumably Japan was playing for time. 'If we accept proposals after substantial amendment it would presumably be because we too are playing for time and feel we are likely to be in a more advantageous position should Japan move later. The balance between these advantages and disadvantages is difficult to determine.'[142] Australian Minister for External Affairs H.V. Evatt emphasised that delay was important. The draft of a possible arrangement 'should give opportunities for considerable discussions, amendments, counter-proposals, and further valuable time may be gained thereby'.[143] Hull's revision of the modus vivendi Casey advocated as giving 'some much-needed time'.[144] Canberra thought the occasion 'a favourable one for elaborate negotiation even in relation to temporary modus vivendi'.[145] When Casey reported the opposition of the Chinese to the modus vivendi the Advisory War Council, at Menzies' suggestion, asked Sir Frederic Eggleston, in collaboration with Clark Kerr, to reassure Chungking.[146] Casey suggested to Hull that there might be further discussion with the Chinese, 'but he said that it would be no use now'.[147]

The Australian Government made a further effort. Evatt phoned Casey and telegraphed Eggleston in Chungking.[148] It was 'fundamental' that Hull and the President should not 'abandon attempts reach agreement even at this late stage'.[149] Casey saw Hull on 29 November and 'suggested that I should endeavour through third party to get Kurusu to ask to see me or me to call on them. I would then say apparently the United States, Japan, British countries and Netherlands East Indies were drifting to war.' The US and its friends, he would continue, would 'fight with cohesion and vigour if we had to'. That need not happen. 'I realise relations between Japan and the United States had become such that neither side could initiate further approach to the other. I was in a rather different position and, although I was not acting at suggestion of either British or American Governments, I would be glad to act as an intermediary if he (Kurusu) had any proposal.' Would Hull object? 'Secretary of State was appreciative of the proposal and indicated that he had no objection, although if he were charged publicly with connivance in proposal he would have to deny knowledge of it.' Hull went on to say 'that he believed that situation had gone beyond diplomatic stage'. He thought the Japanese 'would make aggressive moves probably on a wide front in the near future'. Casey tried to arrange the meeting without approaching the embassy direct.[150] Hull's memo was briefer. 'I really gave this matter ['mediation'] no serious attention except to tell him that the diplomatic stage was over and that nothing would come of a move of that kind.'[151] Curtin himself was doubtful in view of the changing situation. If Casey went ahead he would need to preserve 'greatest caution' lest there were a misunderstanding with Halifax. 'It will be far better if Hull could be induced to resume talks.'[152] The idea was mentioned in a telegram to the UK, otherwise about Kra.[153]

In fact Casey, after consulting Halifax, had already talked to Nomura and Kurusu. He had, he said, been following up the phone call of 28 November, urging some way of preventing the breakdown of the conversations. Neither Hull nor Halifax could act, and so Casey decided to run the risk of himself trying to 'reawaken contact between the principal parties'. He had taken the line he had put to Hull. Kurusu 'showed every desire for a peaceful solution' and 'blamed China for the virtual breakdown in the conversations'. Casey pointed out

> that American public opinion towards China made it impossible for American administration to come to [an arrangement] with Japan under which it appeared that China was sacrificed. Kurusu acknowledged this by saying that from the point of view of Japanese public opinion it was equally impossible for Japanese Government to come to an arrangement which inter alia gave one hundred per cent satisfaction to China.

Casey offered to pass on any proposal he wished to make. 'Kurusu had no proposal to make other than that discussions on the limited Japanese proposal should be resumed ....'[154] Casey saw Halifax and then Hull. He told the Secretary of State 'that our respective governments had complete trust in his handling of the situation and that if he was able to revive the conversations directed towards a temporary agreement with Japan on any terms that he believed reasonable our governments would back him'. Hull believed that the Japanese were 'even now, practically speaking, on the march'. He was 'still very bitter against the Chinese. It appears that, in addition to the President having been very impressed with the representations of the Chinese, the Secretary of War [Stimson] and others used their influence in Cabinet here on the side of the Chinese. This finally sealed the fate of the Secretary of State's modus vivendi.'[155] Hull recorded that Casey's talk with Kurusu 'amounted to very little'.[156]

The commitment to the Dutch

Much of the discussion with the Dutch and others had been about an event that in a sense did not occur: the commitment to go to the assistance of the Netherlands Indies if it were attacked first. The Japanese were to take the bolder step of attacking British and American territories first. The discussion had continued almost until the final crisis. Only shortly before it did the British formally undertake the commitment. It followed a commitment from President Roosevelt.

The Foreign Office memorandum that went to the Cabinet on 21 July had opposed the COS recommendations on the ADA report. The Dutch would regard a communication on the lines suggested 'as a flat refusal to give any assurance of support in the event of Japanese aggression, and even as implying that such support would in fact not be given', and the Defence Committee had 'approved the principle of mutual assurances between ourselves and the Dutch'. The Japanese were planning in the next few days to seize bases in Indo-China, a threat to Malaya and Netherlands India. The COS wanted authority from the Dutch to move

Australian forces into Kupang and Ambon, as suggested by the Australians, but had added that the Dutch should be invited to give such authority only if it did not lead them 'to believe that we are going beyond existing political commitments'. This only showed, in the Foreign Office view, the need for a decision on an assurance. The memorandum proposed, after telegraphing to ascertain that the dominions did not object, to inform the Dutch of Britain's general approval of the ADA report. Furthermore, His Majesty's Government would declare its readiness to join the other governments concerned 'to co-operate to the full extent of their available resources in the event of any one of them being forced to take military action to counter armed action by Japanese forces against its territory or mandated territory ...'. Other cases set out in the February report could not involve automatic action but must be the subject of most immediate consultation, machinery for which was being and should be developed.[157]

At the Cabinet Eden put the Foreign Office case, and Churchill, despite the May decision, argued against it. He 'would still prefer to postpone sending a communication on the lines proposed'. He did not expect a Japanese attack on Singapore.

> It might well be that, even if Japan encroached on the Netherlands East Indies, the right policy would be that we should not make an immediate declaration of war on Japan. Once war had been declared, Japanese cruisers would attack our sea communications, and none of our shipping would be safe unless heavily protected by convoys. At the present moment we were not in a position to send an adequate fleet to the Far East ... For all these reasons, he would much prefer to wait and see how the situation developed, and, if a menacing situation should come about, take steps to strengthen our forces in the Far East. He also thought it would be wise to allow time for the American situation to develop. In any event, taking a shorter view, he thought it would be right to wait for a few days and see the result of the action which it now seemed certain that Japan meant to take in Indo-China, which might well have an effect on United States opinion.

Peter Fraser, the New Zealand Prime Minister, thought the US would come into the war if Japan attacked Netherlands India. However, although in favour of a declaration, he went along with a short delay. The Cabinet stood the matter over and asked the COS to review the arrangements for Far Eastern defence in the light of the present situation.[158] 'P.M. digs his toes in against any assurance to the Dutch. He's frightened of nothing but Japan', wrote Cadogan.[159]

The Foreign Secretary brought the matter back to the Cabinet on 28 July. By this time the Dutch, like the British, had followed US initiatives in freezing Japanese assets.[160] They were 'increasingly puzzled as to the reason why we could not ratify the Staff Conversations'. Churchill 'agreed that the action taken by the United States, as the result of Japanese encroachments in Indo-China, rather altered the position. But he still deprecated giving an automatic undertaking to the Netherlands Government that we would go to war with Japan in certain circumstances, irrespective of the attitude of the United States.' The right step was to concentrate on an approach to the US on the Far East, urging a joint or parallel warning to Japan. The probability that American restriction of oil exports to Japan would increase pressure on Netherlands India was 'a strong argument' to use.[161] The Cabinet considered the approach to the US on 31 July. Eden suggested asking whether the Americans would aid Britain or the Netherlands in a war with the Japanese, and whether representations should be made to Japan, joint or parallel, 'warning her that any further action inimical to our interests would lead to trouble, and including aggression against Thailand within the scope of this declaration'.[162] When consulted, John Winant, the American ambassador, suggested that the Prime Minister make the approach directly to the President.[163] This, indeed, Churchill did at the Atlantic meeting a few days later.

Meanwhile Eden and the Foreign Office mounted an approach to the Prime Minister on the reply to the Dutch. The Dutch were allies in the war with Germany, and an attack on the Indies would imperil Singapore and jeopardise communications with Australia and New Zealand. They had aligned themselves with the US in the economic measures against Japan without making conditions. No reply had yet been given to their request for ratification, nor had it been possible to discuss the movement of troops to Kupang and Ambon. All that was now suggested was that the British would let the Dutch know that they would help them in the event of a Japanese attack to the best of their ability. That, as Cadogan said, would avoid any difficulty residing 'in the immediate and automatic obligation to declare war ... If we cannot go that far, we cannot avoid arousing suspicion and distrust.' 'It is this', Eden added, 'which troubles me most.' The Netherlands Foreign Minister 'showed bewilderment. If suspicion follows, as it will, result in the Far East on collaboration between our two countries must be most serious ...'.[164]

In response, Churchill also took up an earlier suggestion, one he had made in February.

> Could you not tell the Dutch that we have already assumed the duty of safeguarding and restoring their possessions and rights to the best of our ability during the war and at the peace? It follows therefore that an attack upon the Netherlands East Indies would lead us to do the utmost in our power. We must however remain the sole judge of what actions or military measures are practicable and likely to achieve our common purpose.
>
> Should the United States be disposed to take supporting action many things would become possible which we cannot undertake now.[165]

This Eden conveyed to the Dutch minister. Clarke wondered whether it should be conveyed to the US. 'The only thing that I should be afraid of is that the Americans might say: "if even you, who have not our constitutional difficulties, cannot give the Dutch more than that, you can imagine how little we are in a position to give you!" '[166] Halifax was told what had passed and in fact did communicate it to the US authorities.[167] Strang had another criticism, the use of the word *restoring*; in the case of Czechs, Poles, Free French, Norway and Belgium, Britain had stopped short of guaranteeing frontiers. '*Peccavi*', Eden admitted, but he blamed Churchill. 'I had much difficulty to get this from PM. Had he been willing to accept FO advice it wouldn't have been needed.'[168]

Gerbrandy, the Dutch Premier, was in fact disappointed.[169] The Foreign Minister again raised the question of the Singapore talks, which were 'all in cold storage'; he asked for no further political commitment, but he wanted the plans updated. 'What he hoped for ... was that our General Staffs would review plans with the Chief of Netherlands Naval Staff and make sure that all was ready so that, if both our governments agreed to press the button, action would follow ...'.[170] Bennett thought van Kleffens was referring to the need for procedures to ensure a prompt decision to take counter-measures if the Japanese made a threatening move. That was already being worked on by the Cabinet secretariat, and he suggested that both this and the statement of 1 August could be worked into a formal reply to the Netherlands Government's earlier request for 'ratification'. The Dutch could also be asked whether they would also agree to placing Australian troops in Ambon and Kupang in the event of a further Japanese advance.[171]

In fact the reply proposed previously was now redrafted to include the undertaking Churchill had suggested and Eden had communicated verbally, and to welcome discussions on procedures with Netherlands service authorities in London.[172] The need for something reassuring was increased by reports of 'despondency' in Batavia, prompted by Welter, which Brooke-Popham found 'most disturbing'.[173] He thought that Berenschot, the Dutch C in C, was 'quite determined to resist Japanese aggression, but doesn't want to lay himself open to accusations which might be passed on to the Germans as indicating an anti-Axis attitude'. He had children in Holland.[174]

'The Dutch may in any event be somewhat encouraged by the President's proposed statement', Seymour thought.[175] Indeed the next developments have to be seen in the context of the Atlantic discussions. There were, as Bennett said, two issues: a US commitment, and a joint or parallel warning to Japan against further penetration into Thailand, the Defence Committee being much concerned with a possible Japanese move on Kra.[176] Former Naval Person got the President to draft a more extensive warning. This warning did not in itself constitute the 'necessary assurance', and further action might be required, perhaps through taking up the proposal, revived by Halifax, of an assurance that Britain and the dominions would range themselves on the US side if the US were at war with Japan. In the meantime how should the British associate themselves with the warning?[177] In the event the US warning was watered down. Churchill made his broadcast nevertheless. But if Churchill participated in the process of 'shaming' the US once mentioned by Chamberlain, it was not by indicating a British commitment to Netherlands India. It was not mentioned.[178] However, the government edged nearer to such a commitment under constant Foreign Office pressure.

Information of Roosevelt's proposed statement had been given to the Netherlands minister,[179] and his government declared it was ready to make a parallel declaration. Eden took the opportunity to give a reassuring verbal message, suggested by Clarke,[180] and originally intended for use with the proposed formal reply on ratification: 'it would be quite wrong if public opinion in the Netherlands East Indies obtained the impression [as a result of non-ratification] that we would not do our utmost to help them if they were the victims of attack ...'.[181] At the end of the month the COS concurred in the draft of the formal reply to the Netherlands minister. They now wanted to ask the Dutch Government whether it would agree to receive Australian forces on Ambon and at Kupang 'in the event of a further deterioration in the situation'. The latter point, Bennett thought, should not be raised at once lest it make the note look like merely a quid pro quo. It was sent on 5 September.[182] The New Zealand Government thought a stronger statement justified. Clarke suggested the matter could be taken up again in face of the 'stubborn' COS when the ADB report had been revised at the Americans' request. At the same time, as the Dutch suggested, the 'automatic' criteria might be considered for partial or full adoption.[183] The Foreign Secretary had himself suggested, on a telegram from Batavia, that 'we should perhaps return to the charge about this soon'.[184]

In Batavia the statement of the Chancellor of the Duchy of Lancaster, Duff Cooper, that Britain would not sit with folded hands if the Indies were attacked did not altogether satisfy the press.[185] Eden indeed returned to the charge. A memorandum prepared for the Cabinet at the end of September compared the Far Eastern position with that in July 1940 when the Chiefs of Staff last considered it as a whole. Stronger reaction to Japan had become possible. In fact the effect of its move into southern Indo-China had been 'to form for the first time something resembling a united front in the Far East' among the United States, the UK and the Netherlands. Japan was 'faced with the prospect of economic isolation unless she makes a real change in her policy' and had to reckon with the possibility of military resistance.

The Japanese hope that the present discussions between themselves and the United States may gain time until the Russian situation is clearer. Possibly they also hope to disrupt the front which is forming against them. While we are not fully informed of the progress of the Washington conversations, we can, I think, be confident that they will not produce the second of these results. There is no sign that the Japanese are prepared for a settlement in China which the United States can accept, and the American pressure on Japan is being fully maintained.

Sooner or later Japan must 'either come to an understanding with the United States and ourselves, or break out, at the risk of war with us both, in order to escape economic strangulation. She is likely to choose according to the amount of combined opposition which threatens to confront her.' Eden believed 'a display of firmness ... more likely to deter Japan from war than to provoke her to it'. The COS should prepare a new appreciation covering the eventuality of Japanese incursions into Siam, Russia and Yunnan.[186]

Netherlands India was not mentioned in this paper. But early in October Eden talked to Churchill. 'The Prime Minister is now in favour', the Far Eastern Department learned, 'of some more definite assurance to the Dutch and the Secretary of State wishes the Department to consider urgently what more can be said to them.' The Dutch Government, Bennett thought, would like either 'an unqualified guarantee of immediate armed support' or an undertaking that Britain would take 'all possible military measures in any of the eventualities listed in the so-called "chalk-line"'. But the COS were unlikely to 'commit themselves to automatic action in these various eventualities unless the United States were to join in, which seems out of the question. The best we can hope for is that the eventualities concerned will be taken as hypotheses on which detailed plans can be based.' Bennett proposed to revert to the formula suggested but not adopted in July, and recommended an exchange of notes on that basis. Sir William Malkin thought this went little, if at all, beyond the September statement, and others agreed. Bennett pointed out that the new statement, which would involve Australia and New Zealand, promised immediate cooperation in the event of an attack on the Indies. 'Admittedly this is not a great advance on what we have already said, but it is something and I doubt if it is possible to be more explicit.' Seymour's view was that 'if we are to go further than we have gone it seems to me that we must go the whole hog and tell the Dutch that we will definitely give them immediate armed support if Japan attacks the NEI. I don't see that anything else would be much good'. A discussion with Eden followed, and Bennett prepared a paper for the Cabinet.[187]

Bennett's paper in fact clearly focused on the need to strengthen defence in the Far East and to seek to deter Japan – where the newly installed Tojo Government would be affected by events in Europe and by the pressure of the freezing measures – 'by consolidating still further the front which we are gradually establishing with the Netherlands and the United States. In particular, it is suggested that the next step should be to close ranks with the Dutch.' The assurance of September was 'somewhat indefinite' and 'secret. It does not provide the basis of that complete understanding and mutual confidence which is vitally necessary to ensure effective co-operation in defence when the attack comes ...'. The COS had been reluctant to give 'a complete guarantee'; Britain's resources were not large, and there was no assurance of US support. But Britain's resources in the Far East were gradually increasing, and American intervention was 'a strong probability, having regard to the direct interest of the United States in these areas, concerning which the United States Government have lately given Japan a solemn warning'. Eden thus proposed a formal defensive agreement promising immediate cooperation in the event of either party's being forced to take military action to counter an attack. He also proposed that it should be public since it might then have a deterrent, but not a provocative, effect. The agreement would have to be announced in such a way that it did not point up the absence of a similar arrangement involving the US; the US should make some statement indicating that the agreement had been made with its knowledge and blessing.[188] C.J. Norton thought the COS were 'somewhat happier' about the Far East but would probably desire 'that the defensive agreement should not be actually signed until the United States agree to say that they support it'.[189]

At a Cabinet meeting on 16 October, which had discussed the possibility of a Japanese war with Russia, Churchill had declared that, although Britain was committed to war with Japan if the US was at war with it,

> we ought not to commit ourselves to any action which would involve us in war with Japan unless the United States was also at war with that country.
> More generally, the Prime Minister said that the Far Eastern situation had undoubtedly changed, and that the United States Government was nearer to commitment than they had been the past. We ought to regard the United States as having taken charge in the Far East. It was for them to take the lead in this area, and we would support them.[190]

A fortnight later the Cabinet discussed the new Foreign Office proposal for a defensive agreement. Eden argued that it was 'increasingly difficult' to explain to the Dutch why Britain would not make a formal agreement and that it would be 'very difficult' otherwise to get them to agree to receive Australian troops. Amery favoured an agreement.

Netherlands India was an outpost of British India's defence. 'Whether or not we made an agreement with the Dutch we should have to fight the Japanese if they attacked the Dutch East Indies. Public opinion here and in America would take it amiss if we stood aloof while Japan attacked the Dutch East Indies.' Churchill thought that the next Japanese move would be against Yunnan, not Netherlands India.

> Our policy in the Far East should be to persuade the United States to cover our weak position in that area. We should not run the risk of finding ourselves at war with Japan without American support. We should therefore press the United States Government to declare that they would take up arms against Japan if she committed any further act of aggression.

Roosevelt had developed such a line orally at the Atlantic meeting. 'No doubt the President would find it necessary to use such language as that in such-and-such circumstances he would find it necessary to seek the support of Congress for the measures required by national security for the United States.' Cranborne thought Australia and New Zealand would react strongly if Britain did not intervene in the event of a Japanese attack on Netherlands India, but Beaverbrook, Ernest Bevin and Alexander agreed with Churchill. The decision was to defer considering the paper for a week, while the Prime Minister would urge the President to make a public declaration.[191]

All this, of course, frustrated the Foreign Office staff. 'We shall have to defend the Dutch East Indies anyway', wrote Clarke, and the US could give

> no prior guarantee of support although the probability of such support amounts almost to a certainty. We therefore lose nothing by having an unambiguous agreement with the Dutch and we gain nothing by making further appeals to the United States. The reluctance which is felt by the Chiefs of Staff to make a frank agreement with the Dutch seems to me like saying that when invasion comes we will defend Hampshire and of course Devonshire, but we are short of anti-tank guns and will therefore not commit ourselves to defend Dorsetshire unless we can get some backing from the President of the United States.

'It is not only, or even mainly, the Chief of Staff (CIGS happens to agree with us) but Admiralty and above all Prime Minister who take this view,' Eden explained. 'I did my utmost for an hour or more in Cabinet but the truth is that many of my colleagues are not prepared to accept Mr Ashley Clarke's contention ...'.[192] But the Foreign Secretary continued to try.

The Dutch Premier wrote to Churchill after hearing the broadcast of the Mansion House speech on 10 November, which announced the strengthening of British naval forces in the East and repeated Britain's readiness to join forces with the US if hostilities broke out.[193] This would, Gerbrandy believed, have a 'sobering' effect on the Japanese. 'Our disposition and determination is exactly the same', he added; the theatres of war in East Asia were inseparable. He hoped that the omission of all mention of Netherlands India in the speech did not mean that the British Government thought differently.[194] Eden used the letter to bring the matter up in Cabinet again. According to Amery's diary, 'Winston took the line that the Dutch had done nothing for us before they were attacked last year and could not claim better treatment from us. I replied rather hotly that if the Dutch had been foolish then that was no reason for our being foolish now.'[195] The official record reads rather differently.

> Mr Eden said that we might be criticised for promising to declare war on Japan in the event of her attacking the United States whilst withholding such a promise from the Dutch if the Dutch East Indies was attacked.
> The Prime Minister said that a serious situation would arise if we were committed to declare war on Japan and were not assured that the United States would come in too. Should the Japanese land in the Dutch East Indies the temperature would immediately rise. It would therefore be wiser to see how the situation developed as a result of such an event than that we should be committed to action beforehand.

Pound, however, said the situation had changed. Sir Tom Phillips, en route to take up his post as Commander-in-Chief Far East, had been authorised to work out revised joint plans with the Americans. No doubt the Dutch could be brought into them.[196]

The next Cabinet was the one attended by Earle Page. His summary had emphasised the strength of Australian feeling on the Indies. 'The reaction in Australia and New Zealand to inaction by Britain if the Netherlands East Indies were attacked would be such as almost to break the Empire.'[197] The phrase does not appear in the Cabinet minutes. The reaction would be 'tense', he is recorded as saying. 'Further the raw materials which the Axis would gain by a successful attack ... would lengthen the war and cost many hundreds of thousands of lives.' Pound responded to Page's wish that the UK might in general take a bolder line. The differences with the US over naval dispositions had been resolved now that Britain was able to strengthen its forces in the Far East.[198]

Invited by Cabinet to tell the Dutch of the proposed naval conversations, Eden indicated that the Dutch would in due course be invited to join in. 'We next reverted to the old question of guarantees and I told my visitors that the Prime Minister was against making any further declarations until the fleet had arrived in Far Eastern waters, when it would be easier to say more.'[199] The Dutch Premier had been told, with Churchill's approval, that 'public utterances have to be limited by what we are able to fulfil. Until we are in a position to say all that we should like to say the PM had thought that you would perhaps prefer that he should not turn the limelight on the Netherlands East Indies and that our collaboration lost nothing by being unobtrusive ...'. Churchill, however, acknowledged the 'admirable spirit' shown in face of Japanese pressure on the Indies and Dutch collaboration in defence and over 'freezing'.[200]

Later in the month Hull's talks with the Japanese came to a halt, the 'modus vivendi' plans were abandoned, and Japanese aggression was anticipated. The Cabinet on 1 December discussed whether Britain should act if, or even before, Japan moved on Kra or if it attacked Netherlands India. The COS were opposed. 'The Prime Minister said that he was still of opinion that we ought not to assume that the outbreak of war between England and Japan would necessarily precipitate the entry of the United States into the war. There was a strong party in the United States who would work up prejudice against being drawn into Britain's war ....' The Foreign Secretary 'was far from happy as to our situation in respect of the Dutch who were co-operating loyally with us and would certainly look to us if they were attacked'. But 'we might at any moment receive an answer from the United States Government which would justify a more forward policy'.[201] As Churchill had said, he had telegraphed the President the previous day, urging 'a plain declaration, secret or public ... , that any further act of aggression by Japan will lead immediately to the gravest consequences'. Britain would make a similar or joint declaration.[202] In fact the US was more forthcoming.

On the same day as the Cabinet meeting, indeed, Roosevelt sent for Halifax and discussed Japanese reinforcement of Indo-China. He had been considering a parallel statement but thought he should first ask the Japanese where the troops were going. But what should be done when their no doubt 'mendacious or evasive' reply was received? The President considered the United States and Great Britain should be clear 'as to what they would do in various hypothetical situations' – an unsatisfactory reply, whether Japanese troops had reached Indo-China or not, or a move on Thailand apart from Kra. The tenor of the conversation, Halifax reported, was

> in the sense that we should both recognise any of these hypothetical actions to be clear prelude to some further action and threat to our common interests, against which we ought to react together at once. At one point he threw in an aside that in the case of any direct attack on ourselves or the Dutch, we should obviously all be together, but he wished to clear up the matters which were less plain ...[203]

Bennett pointed to the aside and, after consulting Eden, prepared a paper for the Cabinet.[204] This urged, among other points, that we should now lose no time in removing the awkwardness which at present exists in our relations with the Dutch owing to our reluctance to promise full and unhesitating support to them if the Netherlands East Indies are attacked. I feel strongly that there should be no further equivocation on this point and that we should inform President Roosevelt of our attitude ...[205]

Bruce and Page had seen Churchill. Again, in regard to Japanese attacks on non-British territory, the Prime Minister had stressed that

we should not anticipate American action but immediately support it. His reason for this is that he feels that American opinion will react favourably to a war which America has entered in defence of her own interests but would be inclined to be antagonistic to the idea of entering a war into which we had already entered and America was coming to our assistance ....

Others, as Bruce reported, maintained 'that American co-operation can best be secured in the event of Japanese aggression by the British Empire immediately resisting'.[206]

The Prime Minister stressed that 'our settled policy' was

not to take forward action in advance of the US. Except in the case of a Japanese attempt to seize the Kra isthmus (which is unlikely), there will be time for the United States to be squarely confronted with a new act of Japanese aggression. If they move, we will move immediately in support. If they do not move we must consider our position afresh ....

An attack on Kra was unlikely. In any case Britain should not take forestalling action without being sure of US support.

A Japanese attack upon the Dutch possessions ... would be a direct affront to the United States following upon their negotiations with Japan. We should tell the Dutch that we should do nothing to prevent the full impact of this Japanese aggression presenting itself to the United States as a direct issue between them and Japan. If the United States declares war on Japan, we follow within the hour. If, after a reasonable interval, the United States is found to be incapable of taking any action, even with our immediate support, we will nevertheless, although alone, make common cause with the Dutch. Having regard to the supreme importance of the United States being foremost, we must be the sole judge of timing the actual moment.

Any attack on British possessions carries with it war with Great Britain as a matter of course.[207]

At the Defence Committee on 3 December Churchill read out this minute. Pound was 'not entirely happy' with the penultimate paragraph.

It would be very awkward if we had to declare war on behalf of the Dutch without the support of the United States.

The Prime Minister thought that we were now bound to go a bit further with the Dutch than we have done up to the present. If the Japanese attacked the Dutch, the impact of the event should be allowed to shock the United States and we should give them a short period in which to make up their minds what to do. If they failed to do anything, then we should face a very awkward situation in this country if we did not act. All he wanted to avoid was being landed in an automatic declaration of war and also he did not wish to step in in front of the United States and give the anti-British party cause for saying that the United States were again being dragged into a British war.

Eden thought the Americans would act. But 'there was a slight danger that the Americans might say that if we were not prepared to act, then why should they? It might possibly be better to tell the President definitely that we were prepared in any event to stand by the Dutch.' Cranborne wondered if Britain could await a Japanese attack on Netherlands India: Dutch resistance might collapse 'while we were making up our minds'. Page 'thought the best thing would be to include a sentence in the reply to Lord Halifax's telegram drawing attention to, and endorsing the President's statement that in the case of a direct attack on the Dutch we were all in it together'. The committee agreed, and a telegram was sent accordingly. But the committee also invited the Foreign Secretary to speak to the Dutch on the lines of Churchill's minute.[208] Bennett was against this; it 'would probably create a crisis in our relations with them and might well be disastrous, particularly if it resulted – as it might – in disclosure to the Americans ...'. He raised other issues, too. Would the air forces of Malaya be available, as the plans envisaged?

> Again, if we do not immediately declare hostilities, should we not at all events immediately break off diplomatic relations? This step, accompanied by military preparations, would conceivably help in hastening a decision by the United States; whereas if we engaged in no military activity and if we allowed Sir R. Craigie to remain in Tokyo and the Japanese Embassy to remain here, the effect not only on the Dutch but in America would surely be very bad.[209]

'PM is defeatist and appeasing where Far East is concerned.'[210] Churchill had long resisted a British commitment before an American one. Now the crisis was at hand, and he admitted that the British must go in. But, although he recognised that it might be unavoidable, he still wished to avoid going in before the Americans. On the whole he could now conclude that the US was likely to come in, but refraining from a promise of automatic action might make it certain. A promise could appear provocative, or it might appear to relieve them of their burden. Churchill's opposition to assurances to the Dutch had been based, for the most part, on considerations of grand strategy. In these last critical days, however, he somewhat shifted his ground, disconcerting Pound. He now thought that opposition to a commitment should be merely temporary, the best tactical means of ensuring US action and thus ultimate, although costly, British victory. His earlier view had been rather negative; the British could not promise unless the Americans promised. Now it was more positive. He was committed to go to help Netherlands India after the situation had been allowed to hit the US. His critics thought that a British initiative would be more helpful.

The President was in fact encouraging on all the points the British raised and assented to the statement of which Page suggested the insertion. Roosevelt thought the Japanese would attack Netherlands India. 'He made comment on this that any action of the kind would prove more easy of presentation to United States public opinion on the ground of threat to the Philippines by encirclement.'[211] At the Cabinet on 4 December the Prime Minister 'said that, in the light of this assurance, we could now say to the Dutch that if any attack was made on them by Japan, we should at once come to their aid, and that we had every confidence that the United States would do so also'. Further steps could be taken on Matador, on assurances to Thailand and on staff talks with the Dutch. The First Lord suggested that the President should be told that the British were making a statement to the Dutch. 'The Foreign Secretary, however, pointed out that this would need to be very carefully phrased, since President Roosevelt was probably under the impression that we had already given assurance on these lines to the Dutch.'[212]

A telegram to Halifax declared that the British had

long felt that we should be bound to go immediately to the assistance of the Netherlands East Indies if attacked, but we have not hitherto felt able to commit ourselves further than to inform the Netherlands Government that we would do the utmost in our power in the event of such an attack, while retaining the complete freedom to judge what action or military measures on our part were practicable and likely to achieve the common purpose. In the face of the present Japanese threat, however, we do not feel that there is any longer room for hesitation, and we are about to propose to the Netherlands Government a mutual understanding whereby each party will undertake to cooperate *immediately* to the fullest extent of its available resources in the event of the other party being forced to take military action to repel an attack any of its territories in the Far East. We feel that President Roosevelt should know this at once. We feel sure that he will agree with us that the Dutch should from now on be brought fully into the frank discussions which we have had regarding the action which we shall all take.[213]

The dominions were also told, and on the same day Cadogan informed the Netherlands Minister, who expressed 'great gratification'. The signature of a declaration by the British, Dutch and dominions was suggested.[214] Van Kleffens was gratified, too,[215] and Australia entirely approved.[216] A draft of a British warning to Japan was given to the Netherlands Minister on 6 December,[217] and late that night he called with the Dutch version.[218] But the next day the attacks began. The Governor-General declared that a state of war existed at 2300 7 December/6.30 8 December.[219]

The reinforcement of the Philippines

The Japanese did not immediately attack Netherlands India, although so much of the discussion among their opponents had been about that prospect. They took a more dramatic course than had been anticipated, indeed one that had been generally discounted: an attack on the British in Malaya and on the Americans. The attack on the latter was delivered at Pearl Harbor itself. After the move into southern Indo-China the Americans had begun to reinforce the Philippines, which, they hoped, would prompt the Japanese to be additionally cautious over any further move into Southeast Asia. For the reinforcement to be effective, however, they needed themselves to win time.

Stimson, the Secretary for War, told Casey of the reinforcement in August. 'There seems to be a noticeable change in the attitude regarding the Philippines.'[220] In October Casey saw Roosevelt himself.

He spoke at length on changeable attitude on the part of the United States army and navy regarding the Philippines ... which have been and are still being reinforced with bombing and fighting aircraft and tanks. From believing Philippines could not be held in the event of war with Japan, army and navy now believe that they could be held at least for a considerable time and indeed that United States air strength would represent formidable deterrent to Japanese movement southward towards Singapore or Netherlands East Indies. He threw out the suggestion ... that Australia might consider [practicability of plans] for Australian air squadrons operating from North Borneo in the event of war with Japan in order to co-operate with the United States air forces based on the Philippines.[221]

This change also affected Quezon's approach. Duff Cooper called on him in early September.

In the course of conversation the President stated ... that the safety of the Philippines, both now and after independence, depended on the victory of the democracies over the axis powers and that, when independence came in 1946, he did not propose to ask for any international or other guarantee for the country. The United States had, at long last, come to realise the economic importance to her of the Far East and the necessity of protecting her large interests out here by maintaining a naval base in the Philippines. It was provided in the Independence Act that this base at Cavite would continue after independence and he felt that the presence of the United States Navy would be ample protection for the Philippines.

He agreed with Duff Cooper that such a base would not be incompatible with independence any more than the lease of bases in the Caribbean was incompatible with British sovereignty.[222]

At the Foreign Office Research Department at Balliol College, Oxford, G.F. Hudson, the Far Eastern specialist, dealt with 'the question whether the Japanese would now ever be likely to move south against Singapore without dealing with the Philippines first'. They would have two alternatives,

> either to attack us directly (or the Dutch, which would involve us), making Singapore their immediate objective, or to invade the Philippines as a preliminary to seizing the central East Indies (particularly the oil of eastern Borneo) and attacking Singapore at a later stage. Politically, the difference is that the first course would be a war against Britain and the Dutch, with the hope that perhaps America would remain non-belligerent; if then America did after all intervene, the Japanese Government of the day would not be responsible for having directly attacked America ...

But the Japanese navy 'would be very likely to insist that it should not be required to take the risk of an advance towards Malaya, Borneo or Celebes leaving American naval and air forces in the Philippines to attack its lines of communication at any moment America might choose for entering the war'. There was a 'dilemma'.[223] What Hudson said about the strategic issue was, of course, true. But the political issue was, of course, to be resolved by the attack on Pearl Harbor.

In August the British ambassador in Montevideo had suggested that it might be 'easy in the present state of public opinion here to start indirectly and untraceably to us, campaign for moral support to Spanish-speaking Latin brothers in the Philippines', and indeed it might start of itself. That might help to break Axis–Latin American relations.[224] Foreign Office officials thought nothing of this idea, 'an absolutely crazy suggestion'. Washington's reactions would be 'violent ... for the proposed campaign, if traced to us, could be interpreted as an attempt to make US–Japan relations even worse than they are and perhaps to get the Americans to fight our battles in the East'. Another official, R.G. Gallop, thought there was some sympathy for the Philippines in Mexico, which Quezon had visited, and possibly elsewhere, but 'rather on a par with that displayed for the other "victim of US imperialism", Porto Rico'. Any move ought to be delayed until Japanese aggression was actual or imminent. Moral support at the moment, J.V. Perowne agreed, could only imply criticism of the US. 'Once the Philippines have been attacked by the Japanese, the US will be in the war, and, in that event, it won't be necessary to hunt for the means to inspire countries like Uruguay to break relations with the Axis.'[225] This was an accurate forecast. In fact Uruguayan foreign policy had been 'pro-Anglo-American'.[226]

By this time, indeed, the US was reinforcing the Philippines. Even so, it failed to act as the insurance for the colonial status quo in Southeast Asia, as in a sense it had since 1898. For Southeast Asia had been drawn into world politics; too much depended on it.

The Japanese move into southern Indo-China

When Hitler began his invasion of the Soviet Union the Japanese re-evaluated their policy and resolved to use the opportunity to intensify the southward advance. They had been expected to renew it when Germany renewed its attacks on Britain. Now the occasion was different. But, while Matsuoka preferred to abandon his treaty and join in against Russia, the decision went against him. The opportunity in the south seemed too great. The British in turn reconsidered options discussed when a Japanese move on southern Indo-China had seemed possible during the Thai–Indo-China conflict earlier in the year.

The *Daily Telegraph* of 4 July carried a report from Shanghai that Japan intended to acquire bases in Indo-China and Thailand. Craigie was instructed to ask the Minister of Foreign Affairs whether the reports were true and to impress on him the seriousness of the situation if they were.[227] The Vice-Minister denied the report.[228] 'The more denials we can collect the better', Clarke noted.[229]

The Cabinet's Far Eastern Committee met, with R.A. Butler in the chair, on the day the *Telegraph* report appeared. No announcement had been made, but it seemed clear that the Japanese had abandoned their intention of attacking Siberia and decided on a policy of southward expansion. 'It appeared most probable that this would take the form of a demand on Indo-China for the use of sea and air bases, followed by military action after the expiry of an ultimatum limited to a few hours.' The British Government, the committee proposed, should take measures, 'as vigorous as possible', immediately after the expected Japanese action. 'Armed action was ruled out by our lack of resources and any strategic moves would be in the nature of warning gestures. They might, however, be accompanied or followed up by economic or propaganda measures.'

The committee recommended the moves to restrict Japanese shipping on the Malayan coast already considered on 12 June. 'It was now agreed that these restrictions should be brought into force without previous warnings in the event of Japanese aggression against Indo-China.' The move of Australian troops to Kupang and Ambon, contemplated only in the event of hostilities, might also be undertaken when Japan took action against Indo-China, but the Dutch would have to be warned. The committee agreed that the Commander-in-Chief China should invite Decoux to send a representative to Singapore, preferably Jouan, to arrange for the withdrawal of French shipping to British or Dutch ports in the event of a Japanese attack.

Denouncing the Anglo-Japanese commercial treaty had also been considered before when too much rubber was found to be going to Germany. It would have a moral effect, bring Britain into line with the US, and 'be an effective reply to Japanese hints that, with the closing of the Siberian route, there was now no obstacle to normal commercial relations'. The Board of Trade had previously criticised it as a mere gesture, and some dominions had misgivings, so that an explanation would be required. Closing the Consulate-General in Singapore would be 'an effective political gesture' but was not recommended for immediate adoption. Blacklisting Mitsui, Mitsubishi and Okura would 'provoke a violent reaction', and most British Empire governments would object. The Australians had suggested restricting Japanese exports as an alternative, and the suggestion that the US should fall into line should be put. The US had hitherto not seen its way to freeze Japanese assets in the US, 'and if it were adopted in the sterling area, the reciprocal action which would follow would have serious consequences for some Empire countries. It would be necessary to ascertain American intentions'.

> The attack on a Vichy colony could be held up to ridicule [in the news] as an act of aggression against a defenceless victim, and an indication might be given that a different and more serious reaction would result if there were any attempt on the territorial integrity of Thailand (Siam). It was realised that such a hint could hardly be given with full Government authority, as it would be largely bluff. Some show of force, however, e.g., a move of the air squadrons in Burma, might give colour to the suggestion if it were effectively timed.

The committee decided that a memorandum should be prepared for Cabinet that stressed, in particular, among the further steps, blacklisting and restricting Japanese exports. If the War Cabinet approved such suggestions Halifax would be instructed to propose 'the adoption of parallel American action'.[230]

The memorandum for the Cabinet, dated 6 July, elaborated some points and modified others. Information indicated that the Japanese, while preparing for all eventualities in Eastern Siberia, had 'decided to acquire points d'appui in Indo-China in order to increase pressure upon Great Britain and the United States of America', perhaps by 'a pretence of negotiation', but by force if necessary. A 'prompt display of interest' might 'disconcert' the Japanese and interfere with their plans. The information could not be used publicly 'without compromising its source'. But Craigie had been instructed to ask the Japanese Government if the Shanghai report were true, and Halifax to suggest a similar inquiry on the part of the US.

In the Far Eastern appreciation of 31 July 1940, the memorandum recalled, the Chiefs of Staff had stated that it was important to try to prevent Japan's gaining one position after another, increasingly threatening the security of Malaya and communications with Australia and New Zealand. A 'marked and swift' reaction was now needed. To prevent 'Trojan Horse' activities in Malaya the Commanders-in-Chief Far East and China had recommended that ships should be prevented from loading at night. This, however, the Japanese might interpret as an economic restriction on their iron exports. The measure should come into force, therefore, only if and when the Japanese made a further demand or move on Indo-China. The Singapore conferences of February and April contemplated reinforcement of Timor and Ambon in the event of hostilities with Japan. The Australian Government suggested subsequently that it would be advisable to undertake it in advance of hostilities, but it was thought 'scarcely feasible' in the absence of a further Japanese move to justify it. A move on southern Indo-China would do so, and an approach to Netherlands India might be made.

In the Tientsin crisis Roosevelt had denounced the US commercial treaty, and the 'political and psychological effect upon the Japanese was considerable'. Denunciation of the British treaty would serve 'as a serious political warning'. It would also bring the British Government into line with the US Government and, unlike the strategic measures, get wide publicity 'and thus appeal to the imagination of the American public'. When it had been earlier considered by the Far Eastern Committee Craigie had wanted to be consulted again, and Australia was doubtful. Consultation was recommended. The closure of the Japanese Consulate-General in Singapore would be 'a serious blow at Japanese intelligence network', but it would 'lead to retaliation', and the action should be held in reserve, the Governor preparing the necessary grounds meanwhile. The purpose of the measures taken would not be lost on the Japanese Government. But publicity should avoid any emphasis on their retaliatory character; each should be justified in its merits, 'security, changed conditions, and the like'.

'Extensive restrictions on the supply of raw materials, particularly those of strategic value, are already in force.' They could be made more stringent. Australia had suggested a restriction on imports from Japan, which would require US cooperation, and Halifax was to sound the American Government. But 'it would require time to organise, and its effect would only become evident at a later stage'. Suggestions approved by the Cabinet would be communicated to Washington, and the US Government would be asked what steps it was contemplating. Indications given by the Under-Secretary of State suggested 'that they may be prepared to react and to apply some form of economic pressure'.[231]

Cabinet considered the memorandum on 7 July, alongside the one from Dalton, the Minister of Economic Warfare, that outlined the economic restrictions against Japan in operation in the empire, in collaboration with the Netherlands and US governments. 'Our policy is based on the inescapable fact that Japan has allied herself with our enemies, and in present circumstances there is no alternative to this policy.' It was not, as the Japanese ambassador claimed, a policy of 'vindictiveness' but one of 'precaution'. It was hoped to 'bring home to an increasing number of Japanese the solid advantages to be gained by renewing Japan's former relations with us and renouncing her connection with the Axis'. But care was taken not to provoke Japan by reducing supplies, e.g. of oil, 'too drastically and suddenly' or striking 'too brusquely' at Japanese enterprises. The closure of the Siberian route did not justify altering the policy.[232]

Eden did not ask for approval for the movement of troops to Ambon and Timor, as the Dutch saw it as premature before the Japanese had taken open action against British or Dutch possessions. He asked for authority in respect of the Malayan proposals and suggested consultation with Craigie and the dominions over denouncing the commercial treaty. 'In discussion it was agreed that the general situation did not justify us in taking strong deterrent measures to prevent further Japanese encroachments. Our policy must therefore be, for the present, to take appropriate counter-action after each encroachment, calculated to play on Japanese reluctance to come into the war against an unbeaten and still formidable country.' The Cabinet approved the Foreign Secretary's proposals and, at Dalton's suggestion, instructed the Far Eastern Committee 'to "tighten the screw" still further against Japan by means of increased economic restrictions, even in the absence of further provocation by that country'.[233]

The dominions were consulted. The Malayan measures, they were told, would reduce Japanese imports from a million to half a million tons of ore, representing only about 5 per cent of Japan's total finished iron and steel output in 1939. But it came on top of other restrictions.[234] Craigie was consulted, in particular about denouncing the commercial treaty. It might, critics suggested, 'have little practical effect and ... only act as an irritant'. But, as the Japanese ambassador had been pressing for an agreement to revive mutual trade, it might have a salutary effect. 'I presume that you do not take the view that this act would be tantamount to prejudicing finally all relations of a political character...'. Craigie was also asked whether he had further suggestions for making restrictions on exports to Japan, except foodstuffs, 'more stringent ... in order to demonstrate that the more the Japanese menace us the less they will get from us in the way of raw materials'.[235]

Germany had shown no regard for Japan, and the Japanese had decided to consider only their own interests, Halifax was told. An attack on Siberia had been abandoned or postponed. Freed from the fear of a Soviet attack, they had decided to proceed to acquire bases in Indo-China. 'They would no doubt argue that this move, however unpopular with us, with the United States and with the Netherlands, would not provoke a state of war. The acquisition of these bases, on the other hand, should place Japan in a much stronger position to attack British or Dutch territory should a favourable opportunity present itself at a later date.' Britain's 'reactions to this contemplated move will be closely watched by the Japanese Government, who may hesitate to proceed further if they are sufficiently vigorous'. But if the reactions were confined to words the Japanese would be encouraged to proceed to the next step, acquiring bases in Thailand, 'or, if the situation in Europe seemed to warrant it, some bolder move'. In any case bases in Indo-China would improve Japan's position in the south while not preventing its intervening in the north if the moment appeared 'propitious'.[236]

Meanwhile Halifax had seen the President, saying he would be speaking to Welles. Roosevelt asked the ambassador to discuss with Welles whether, in the event that the Japanese Government acted as foreshadowed, 'it would or would not be a good thing for the United States Government at once to announce the placing of Japan under all possible economic pressure. The intention to do this might be announced in advance.' Would this 'work as a deterrent' or 'precipitate the Japanese into the Netherlands East Indies, which neither the United States nor Great Britain wanted'? Roosevelt's

> own view was that neither they nor we could fight a war simultaneously in the Atlantic and the Pacific oceans and that if that situation developed we should have to say to Japan that we were busy at the moment with Germany and Europe, but they should make no mistake that when we had finished with the most pressing task we should clear up our differences with them later.[237]

Halifax then spoke to Welles. He said that he had consistently advised the President to place a complete economic embargo on Japan as soon as the Japanese committed any overt act. 'He was not in favour of telling the Japanese in advance that this would be the United States attitude, because he thought that this would have the opposite effect to that which he desired by playing into the hands of the Japanese extremists and weakening the hands of the more moderate elements.' He thought the Japanese were still bargaining with the Germans but would probably move on Indo-China.[238]

'It is not clear ... which way President's mind is working,' the FO commented on the first of the Halifax telegrams. The strong action advocated earlier on seemed inconsistent with 'the very weak line' suggested at the end. 'We naturally agree that object must be to avoid war with Japan. Our own view is that strongest card we hold in this game is fear of war with the United States which ... is both deep and universal in Japan.' The object should thus be 'to keep Japan guessing'. Strengthened economic pressure would be 'warmly welcomed' as a deterrent and a reply to further Japanese moves. This was indeed British policy. 'But we feel that it is safer to maintain Japanese uncertainty as to what the United States or we will or will not do in any given eventuality.' That

> would not preclude of course a statement public or otherwise on the part of the United States Government of their concern in the security of the NEI. Even a general statement from authoritative United States source that United States interests in the Pacific were not less important than in the Atlantic would probably serve to ensure that further economic pressure on Japan did not precipitate Japanese attack on the NEI.

The second telegram arrived as the reply to the first was being drafted. Welles clearly agreed with the FO on the question of prior announcement. Comments on a complete embargo would follow.[239]

It caused considerable debate in the Far Eastern Department. Ashley Clarke thought that the chances that a complete economic embargo would force Japan 'to fall upon the NEI and ourselves without further delay' were considerable. 'We should prefer, I think, that the screws should be turned but not right home.' Dening agreed that it would 'drive Japan to make her final choice, for once she ceases to gain any benefit from association with the democracies, she will either have to sue for terms or go the whole hog in the other direction'. He doubted if the occupation of bases in Indo-China were 'sufficient excuse to drive her to that extreme. There is a risk attached; it may not in fact prove to be a very large one, but I doubt if we want to run it, just yet'. Seymour thought this should be put to the Americans. 'My own belief is that "any overt act" would not cover the acquisition, probably by agreement of bases in Indo-China.'[240]

Clarke's draft of a dispatch to Washington was modified by Bennett. A complete economic embargo would force Japan to come to terms or attack the Indies and/or the British without delay. 'Are the United States Government prepared to force this issue? and are they prepared to give the NEI and ourselves fullest support in the event of Japan's taking the wrong choice?' The President's remarks suggested not. If Japan went for the bases Britain contemplated tightening economic restrictions. 'But until the United States and we are ready to deal with Japan, or unless the latter were to involve herself in hostile action against the Soviet Union, we feel that it would be better to leave the powerful weapon of a total embargo hanging over Japan's head.' There was 'no wish to discourage the Americans from adopting the stiffest measures possible'. But had they fully considered the possible consequences of a complete embargo? Informally Halifax was to put to Welles the 'very serious issues' involved for Britain as well as the US.[241] This modified draft was, however, not sent.

That was a consequence of a further conversation Welles and Halifax held at the former's request. Welles showed the British ambassador a long message from Grew reporting an interview with Matsuoka. There was other information suggesting that an understanding had been reached among Germany, Italy and Japan, and that there would be an immediate Japanese move south and a later attack on Vladivostok.

> Welles repeated definition of United States policy as given me a few days ago. Until the Japanese committed an overt act the United States would make no further communication of minatory kind. As soon as they did so United States would impose embargo on all principal materials that the Japanese wanted, such as lubricants, metals, cotton, but not necessarily on foodstuffs.

Any acquisition of bases in Indo-China would be regarded as an overt act, 'even if done in agreement with Indo-Chinese authorities since this would clearly in effect be under German duress. They would not necessarily so regard acquisition of bases in Thailand where United States judgment would depend on the circumstances.' But similar action would follow an overt act against Russia.[242]

The reply to this telegram modified the draft the Far Eastern Department had prepared, which now explained that the British Government had been 'somewhat disturbed' by the earlier reference to a complete economic embargo. For, imposed at one blow, it would force the Japanese 'either to reverse their policy completely or to exert maximum pressure southwards even to the point of war ... We wondered whether the United States Government were in fact prepared to force this issue and whether they were prepared to give the Netherlands East Indies and ourselves fullest support in the event of Japan's taking wrong choice.' The President's remarks suggested they were not. The further telegrams showed that the embargo was not complete. 'Nevertheless you should bear in mind above considerations in any further discussions.' The Thailand question was, it was hoped, less urgent, but Halifax should ascertain why Welles considered the acquisition of bases there would be less serious. The British planned economic restrictions if Japan went for bases in Indo-China and would welcome parallel American action. Would the embargo be staged? What commodities would it cover?[243]

The Far Eastern Committee had met after the Cabinet meeting, in particular to consider 'suggestions for increasing economic pressure within the framework of the approved policy'. The proposed restrictions on Japanese iron ore ships on the Malayan coast, it was suggested, should be adopted, as originally proposed, for security reasons rather than as a reaction to a Japanese move. Perhaps the C in C FE could 'suggest other measures, e.g. an extension of defence areas in Malaya and restrictions on aliens in the territory to be applied as occasion required, should the Japanese undertake the penetration of Indo-China by stages instead of, as at first thought likely, in a single *coup de main*'. Some response should also be made to the United States approach on tightening restrictions on iron ore exports to Japan: the proposed measures would reduce the output.[244] The telegram to Halifax indicated that the Malayan measures might be enforced in any case, but the British would prefer 'to reserve them for a short time to use as a reprisal'. In referring to the denunciation of the commercial treaty Halifax should not communicate arguments for or against but confine himself to saying 'that we have the American precedent in mind'. Had he any indication that the US had considered the possibility of freezing Japanese assets if the Japanese acquired bases in southern Indo-China?[245]

Halifax saw Welles on 14 July. He set out in a note the actions proposed by the British, and it was agreed that State Department officials would consult the embassy 'on details of points that we might respectively wish to apply'. This, Halifax told the FO, would be the best means of securing inside information about the commodities the US might embargo. The ambassador went on to ask Welles whether the US embargo would be 'imposed all at once and so published. He said that this was so.' No doubt, Halifax went on, Welles had 'considered whether or not pursuance of action involved any serious risk of precipitating Japan into the Netherlands East Indies', and he would 'like to know if he felt able to tell me what would be the United States action if it did'. Welles said that 'technical reasons ... would make it necessary to deal with the matter by fresh executive order rather than by merely tightening up existing orders', but he did not think the effect would be 'any worse'.

> As to the question of precipitating the Japanese into the Netherlands East Indies, he said that of course they recognised the risk, but did not rate it very high. Their information was the Japan had twelve months stock of oil and that so long as she was occupied in China and compelled to make provision against Russia in the north, he did not think, according to United States Staff advice, that Japan was very likely to embark on major adventures in the East Indies.

Halifax also asked Welles the basis of the distinction between the case of Indo-China and that of Thailand.

> To this he said, as I expected, that the case of Indo-China would arise from evident German pressure, whereas Germany had no means of putting such pressure on Thailand. The case, moreover, was difficult [different?] in that

Thailand had more claim than Vichy to rank as an independent power. He added, however, that he did not mean to say that they would not take economic action over the case of Thailand or that the possibility of doing so was excluded. ...

[Halifax] hoped that we were seeing the general problem alike. We were fully alive to the importance of reacting, and being vigorous, and not letting the Japanese think they could get away with anything. On the other hand, we did not want to precipitate trouble. Welles said this was also the United States position.[246]

Characteristically, Bennett would have preferred the emphasis were reversed.[247]

The Australian High Commissioner, Bruce, acknowledged that the US planned an embargo if Japan committed an overt act like acquiring bases, but did not intend to make any further communication of a minatory kind. 'This is understandable if a Japanese move [is] uncertain and time unknown.' But that was not the case. Would it not therefore be wiser for the US to inform Japan of the action it would take if bases were occupied in Indo-China? Should not the UK notify Japan of any action it would take? 'Such joint notification given before Japan is committed might prevent her acting.' But 'given after the occupation it would not cause her to reverse her action'. Bruce had no great hope of success from a joint move, but it could do no harm.[248]

Clarke pointed out that the Vice-Minister for Foreign Affairs had denied press reports. In fact an ultimatum had been presented at Vichy. The US did not favour 'minatory language' with the Japanese in advance.

The only hope of deterring them from executing their plan of the expected move would be if the action which we intended were of an overwhelming character. This is not the case. We cannot expect that the Japanese would be willing to lose face with Vichy to the extent of yielding to such threats as we are in a position at present to make.

'Therefore, our best hope of deterring the Japanese lies in keeping them guessing and multiplying their fears by publicity. We may also hope that any misgivings they may have will be increased by the defence measure which is now being enforced in Malaya.'[249] Bennett, Cadogan and Eden agreed.[250]

The difficulty about a warning, Bruce was told, was that Japan had already committed itself by presenting demands in Vichy. A joint notification would have effect only 'if it foreshadowed action of an overwhelming character. We cannot expect that the Japanese would be willing to lose face with Vichy to the extent of yielding to such threats as we are in a position to make at present. If the United States were ready for a showdown on this business things would of course be different'. But 'all our evidence goes to show that at present they are not so prepared'.[251]

The best hope of deterring the Japanese seemed thus to lie 'in keeping them guessing by such steps as the new defence instructions about the loading of ships at night in Malaya'. Closing Panama for repairs – Welles had told Halifax of this – might have been 'as salutary as any formal warning'.[252]

Halifax's latest interview with the President certainly renewed Foreign Office doubts about US commitment. He saw Roosevelt again on 15 July.

> He said that we should talk over with Mr Welles the possibility of getting Vichy to gain time by discussion. He thought that in view of difficulties, the gaining of time was the principal purpose to which our efforts ought to be directed. He did not believe the Japanese would launch into any large scale adventure at this moment, although he also agreed with me that by establishing themselves in Indo-China they would be better placed for undertaking any adventure that might seem possible later on.

Even if the Japanese did get into Indo-China it would not be 'a very difficult job', the President thought, for the US and UK 'acting together when relieved of their European anxieties, to make it impossible for the Japanese to maintain themselves there. This was of course a reversion to his thought of a week or two ago.'[253] The Japanese cabinet crisis, Foulds commented at the Foreign Office, would gain time. The Americans were in any case better placed to advise Vichy. It was unfortunate, he added, that Roosevelt was 'still harping on the idea that we shall be able to turn the Japanese out of Indo-China after the war: the best policy is to do everything in our power now to dissuade them from giving in'. Cadogan agreed that prevention was better than cure. Eden secured Churchill's permission to send a telegram to Halifax. 'When you next have an opportunity of mentioning subject to him it might be well to suggest that even in these days prevention is better than cure and that the best prevention is fear on the part of the Japanese of immediate war with the United States if they go too far.'[254]

Churchill had repeated on 16 July his conviction 'that Japan will not declare war upon us at the present juncture, nor if the United States enters the war on our side'. He agreed with the Chiefs of Staff 'that we are in no position to declare war upon Japan without the United States being in on our side'. As a result he did not think war between Britain and Japan

> likely at the present time. If contrary to the above views Japan should attack us, I am of opinion that the United States would enter the war as the weight upon us would clearly be too great. Nevertheless, since the threatened Japanese moves in Indo-China are of serious menace to us, further precautions in the Far East should be taken so far as they are possible without condemning us to misfortune in other theatres.[255]

The Far Eastern Department did not entirely endorse this assessment. 'We have no reason to suppose that there is any immediate intention on the part of Japan to declare war on us, though we cannot say what action would follow large-scale attempts to send assistance to the Soviet via Vladivostok.' Other precautions were a matter for the military, although the department suggested closing the Consulate in Singapore.[256] Eden asked whether it agreed with Churchill's minute as a directive to the Chiefs of Staff. 'We should rate the chances of Japan becoming involved in the war against us higher than does the PM. But we should naturally be for any further military precautions that are possible ...'.[257]

The Far Eastern Committee was told on 17 July that it was clear that demands had been made for air and naval bases in Indo-China. 'It was probably now too late to take any action which would deter Japan from the course upon which she had embarked. We were, however, arranging for information to leak into the Press regarding the demands that had been made ...'. There was some doubt about American policy. Welles had said that there would be no action before the Japanese committed an overt act. Then, 'at once and simultaneously', the US would impose a general embargo. But Hornbeck had given Noel Hall of the British Embassy the impression that US policy was 'a good deal less firm'. The committee were also informed that the Dominions had generally agreed to terminate the 1911 treaty in the event of an overt act, although the Australians had seen it as a 'pinprick'. The Americans should be told that it would be important to synchronise any action they took.[258]

On the night of 18 July Bennett had a discussion with Eden, who had asked if machinery were ready for imposing economic restrictions on Japan as soon as it obtained bases:

> it was explained that our attitude depended very much on that of the United States and that we were having difficulty in discovering exactly what the United States proposed to do. It was also explained that some of the measures which the United States were reported to be considering seemed dangerous as liable to drive Japan into further southward moves which might bring about war with the Netherlands East Indies and ourselves, in regard to which we had as yet no guarantee of American support.

Eden saw the risk, but was 'impressed with the alternative risks inherent in discouraging the United States in any action which they might be prepared to take'. If it was prepared to 'force the issue now with Japan, was there not something to be said for doing so' in spite of the COS doctrine 'that we should not allow ourselves to become involved in war with Japan over Indo-China?' Eden wanted this put to Cabinet. A paper was prepared, but Eden then concluded it should be held up as a telegram suggested that the US had no intention of imposing a complete embargo.[259]

Telegrams from Halifax of 19 July still left American proposals open to doubt. Welles thought Indo-China was Japan's 'immediate objective'; for the first time he feared that Singapore was also an objective. At Vichy Admiral Darlan, Minister for National Defence, had told the US ambassador that Japan intended to occupy bases in Indo-China; 'there would be no ultimatum but the Japanese would use force: French would make symbolic defence but would be less able to resist than in Syria'. The Vichy Foreign Office denied, however, that the Japanese had given any indication of designs on Indo-China. Welles had information that Tokyo had pressed Berlin to put pressure on Vichy to 'share' or 'relinquish' bases but did not know whether Berlin had responded.[260] Another telegram described what the Americans proposed to do. A complete embargo was not envisaged; a 'ruthless freezing' of assets was.

At the Foreign Office Bennett prepared another memorandum. He thought that the US did not intend to cut off all Japanese trade, but a ruthless freezing of assets implied that, and the Japanese might well draw that conclusion. 'We and the Dutch must therefore be ready to face the reaction even though we do not ourselves take measures parallel to those proposed by the United States.' Should 'we allow matters to take their course' or, 'at the risk of appearing to discourage action which the United States are prepared to take', again draw US attention to the possibility that the Japanese, thinking themselves likely to be cut off from US imports such as oil, might be tempted to acquire such commodities by expansion, e.g. in Netherlands India? 'We may not have time of course to take action for any such warning, even if we wish, unless Japanese action has been delayed by the Cabinet crisis.' In any case US policy on licences in respect of frozen assets had to be ascertained as it would expect a similar policy in the sterling area.

Bennett drew attention to another immediate issue, the question of a warning, earlier dismissed partly because too little could be threatened. Hitherto the US had been against 'any communication of a minatory kind' until Japan committed an overt act in Indo-China. The UK had concluded that the measures it contemplated as a reaction were not drastic enough to induce Japan to withdraw demands made on Vichy.

> The position is, however, somewhat altered if the United States Government are prepared for really drastic economic action, and if we are prepared to accept and follow their policy. It may be that it is too late for any warning to be either practicable or effective. Nevertheless, there is a chance that if Japan received an indication of the type of action proposed, she might withdraw at the last moment, whereas, if she proceeds without warning to make her move in Indo-China and severe economic action is then taken by the United States

and ourselves, she may have no alternative but to face the challenge and proceed to further extremes. Should we not, therefore, suggest to the United States that they should consider whether it may not be better to face Japan with the issue before she acts, rather than after, if there is still time?[261]

The paper now put to the Cabinet explained that Halifax was trying to elucidate US intentions. A complete embargo or freezing was likely to force Japan either to reverse its pro-Axis policy or to proceed with a move south to the point of war with the Netherlands Indies and the British in an endeavour to secure raw materials; even an embargo on oil might have this effect. Faced with these alternatives, particularly if the British, and perhaps the Dutch, acted in conformity with the US, Japan might well choose the first alternative; 'nevertheless, the risk remains that she would choose war with us, hoping that the United States would not intervene in time.' Were the British prepared to go 'the whole way' with the Americans if they desired to take such drastic action and, if not, should they attempt to restrain them? The COS had consistently advised

that we should not allow ourselves to become involved in war with Japan over Indo-China, and that, in general, we should do everything possible to avoid war with Japan in the absence of a firm guarantee by the United States that they will support us if attacked – a guarantee which, in the nature of American arrangements, constitutional or otherwise, it is probably idle to expect.

But there was danger in 'lagging behind' the US Government, 'a fortiori in our actually attempting to dissuade them from strong action. The risk of creating another Simon–Stimson [1932] incident and of seriously weakening the ties between us and America is real.' The Foreign Secretary thought that

the issue with Japan must be faced sooner or later and that the risk of the United States not intervening in a war between ourselves and Japan is small. The only question is whether we should join with the United States in forcing the issue now in connection with the acquisition of bases in Indo-China (manifestly directed against ourselves and the Netherlands East Indies); or whether we should try to dissuade the United States from forcing it until Japan makes a further and even more threatening move, e.g. in Thailand, or, alternatively, until Japan embarks on hostile action against Russia.

It was not clear that the US would go so far in economic action in these two eventualities. 'Indeed, we have been given an indication that in the case of Thailand they would definitely not be so prepared.' An attack on Russia, however, would make the exertion of economic pressure more effective and less risky. Eden concluded 'that we must on no account discourage any action which the United States may wish to take in pressure on Japan and that we must as far as possible match our action with theirs'; that, although for Britain 'the best moment to force the issue might be when (and if) Japan became involved with Russia, we must, in the paramount interests of Anglo-US co-operation, be prepared to follow a United States lead in forcing the issue over the Indo-Chinese bases'; and that, if Britain was

> called upon to go to lengths which involve a plain risk of war between ourselves and Japan, we should make every effort to obtain the clearest possible indication from the United States that, if war between the British Empire and Japan follows, consequent upon an attack by Japan either on ourselves or on the Dutch, we can count, without reservation, on the active armed support of the United States.[262]

The Cabinet endorsed the recommendations.[263]

This decision was taken to confirm that there would be no warning even though the action might be joint/parallel and drastic. Once in Indo-China, the Commanders-in-Chief observed, the Japanese were in a much better position to attack British, American and Dutch interests and to pressure Thailand.[264] But, as Bennett said, the Cabinet had not favoured a warning. The British had hopes that publicity would have some effect, although they were unable to reveal the source of their information. The press, however, 'has not taken the matter up as we hoped', Bennett wrote on 22 July. He thus suggested a rather fuller reply to a Parliamentary Question than Foulds had drafted. Crosby, he added, had suggested a statement on Thailand. 'Furthermore it would, I think, be well to indicate that the move is likely to affect the security of our possessions. The reason why the press is not interested in Indo-China is that very few people seem to realise this.' Bennett's draft also included a reference to the Free French movement.[265] Seymour preferred the longer draft but with no reference to the security of British territories. 'Our reactions to the Japanese descent cannot be very impressive, and it would perhaps be a mistake to emphasise this aspect of the matter.' Cadogan took out, too, the reference to de Gaulle's restraining the Free French movement. The reply thus insisted that, while the British Government was aware of reports of Japanese designs on Indo-China, it had none. With Thailand Britain's relations were governed by the non-aggression pact.[266]

Clarke had fenced with Yamada, the First Secretary, at lunch on 18 July.

> As I was leaving he drew me aside to say that if this move really was coming off, he felt sure that it would be done quite smoothly with the agreement of Vichy and that the Japanese authorities would carry out the operation 'very carefully'. I said that however carefully the operations were carried out, it would be a threat to us and the effect on us would be bad.[267]

A telegram from the American Embassy in Vichy of 21 July indicated that Darlan had stated that due to 'extremely strong insistence' on the part of the Japanese, he had been 'forced, with regret, to grant permission for Japan to occupy Indo-China. He has, however, asked Japan to make a public declaration of its intention to respect French sovereign rights over the country, and to promise to withdraw its troops when "emergency" has passed.' According to Darlan, it had not been possible to discover Germany's position on the matter.[268]

An American report from Vichy said the Japanese demands had been accompanied by a message from Konoe to Pétain, promising to respect Vichy's sovereignty over Indo-China. Any token resistance would result in the internment of French forces, the proclamation of Annam's 'indépendence' and the assumption of sovereign power by the Japanese. 'Vichy must, therefore, bow quietly to the superior force of the Japanese and try to keep what shadow of authority Japan may allow, however humiliating the situation may be.' The Vichy Foreign Office thought the Germans had approved.[269] Ostorog, an official there, held to the same line of reasoning that Vichy had adopted in the mediation: 'the most important question for France is to remain with some authority on the spot regardless of how restricted such authority may be or how humiliating its curtailment'.[270] Welles said 'that the facts were still very obscure and that until they had been ascertained, which might take three or four days, the United States Government would not take economic counter measures'. The economic program 'would not necessarily be put into force all in one fell swoop', but he planned to keep the British fully informed so that they might, if they wished, 'keep in step'.[271] Foulds thought that Britain could start with denouncing the treaty. But Clarke thought 'the more fell swoop the greater the effect and the less the chance of war', and Cadogan agreed.[272]

The following day Welles as Acting Secretary of State issued a statement drawing attention to the Japanese statements of 1940 on Netherlands India and French Indo-China and the American statement of 23 September that changes were being achieved under duress. Now further changes were being effected under duress. There was no ground for them in self-defence. 'This Government can therefore only conclude that the action of Japan is undertaken because of the estimated value to Japan of bases in that region, primarily for purposes of further and more obvious movements of conquest in adjacent areas.'[273]

Eden also made a statement in the House of Commons. The occupation of the bases was imminent. That it would take place with Vichy consent 'does not obscure the fact that Japan has achieved her object by making demands backed by threats of force if they were not complied with. The miserable plight of the Vichy Government in the face of these demands provides one further example of the blessings of collaboration with the Axis.' The French had to accept Japan's protection against a nonexistent threat. These developments the British Government saw 'as a potential threat to their own territories and interests in the Far East', and it had been in close touch with the governments of the US, the Netherlands and the dominions. The Acting Secretary of State's statement was 'timely and salutary'. Certain defence measures in Malaya had been enforced. Other information would follow.[274]

According to Meiklereid, it seemed likely that, although Decoux had 'a strong indication' that the Japanese would demand facilities in the south, 'he was not aware, until he returned to Hanoi on 21 July, that the demands had for all practical purposes already been accepted by the Vichy Government'. General Mordant, Commander of the French army in Indo-China, had been in favour of refusing Japanese demands, 'if necessary by force of arms, even though it was but a forlorn hope', but 'did not receive much support from the other members of the Government'. General Sumita Raishiro, Nishihara's successor, presented the demands on 22 July, details were settled and the agreement signed on 23 July. It provided for the use of eight air bases in south Vietnam and Cambodia and three naval bases, including Cam Ranh and Saigon. Forty thousand troops would be sent and have freedom of movement. The agreement superseded that of 22 September 1940. Japan guaranteed French sovereignty and the integrity of Indo-China.

On 26 July Sumita arrived at Saigon to superintend the occupation. French aircraft and certain French troops, including the Foreign Legion, were sent north. The Governor-General issued no communiqué, although Vichy issued a message stating that France had made an agreement accepting Japan's cooperation for the defence of Indo-China while stressing its respect for French sovereignty. 'This has by no means deceived the French population of Indo China whose first reaction has been to show a tendency towards increased pro-British sentiment; in the long run however the defeatist spirit, which has been so apparent in the Colony since the collapse of France, cannot fail to be increased.' The effect on the native population was to 'arouse their curiosity; they have collected at street corners as if to watch a procession ...'.[275]

On the evening of 25 July the Japanese Foreign Minister gave Craigie advance information of a statement to be issued the following day on the joint defence agreement reached at Vichy on the 21st. The agreement was made in the light of 'reports of machinations of de Gaullist elements' and 'invasion by Chungking forces'. The Japanese could not 'remain unconcerned if Indo-China were to relapse into a situation resembling that of Syria'. They intended to respect the integrity and sovereignty of Indo-China. The step was not directed against any third country and should not lead to measures against Japan. Craigie read Eden's statements in the House in order 'to bring home the seriousness with which His Majesty's Government viewed this new aggressive step ...'.[276] The Japanese statement, which said that agreement had been reached amicably and without hitch, expressed the hope that the step would not be 'misunderstood' and lead to measures that would add to 'the deep feelings of dissatisfaction ... in the minds of the Japanese people in regard to increased assistance to Chiang Kai-shek's regime and information of an encircling front against Japan'.[277] A subsequent announcement, issued on 26 July, alluded to friendly conversations, respect for the territorial integrity and sovereignty of French Indo-China, and the Greater East Asia Co-Prosperity Sphere.[278]

In his conversation Craigie had drawn attention to Ohashi's categorical denial of 5 July. Such tactics produced 'the worst impression' on the British Government. Furthermore, while occupation of northern Indo-China might be explained, although not justified, as part of the campaign against China, any southward move in Indo-China was 'a potential threat' to British territory. Nor was it justified by baseless reports about the intentions of Britain, or Britain and China, in regard to Indo-China and Thailand. Britain's policy had been 'merely to maintain trade relations with Indo-China and our normal friendly relations with Thailand'. Nor were there de Gaulle movements. In reply the Foreign Minister, Toyoda, pointed to reports of 'military understandings for joint action between the Chungking Government, Burma, Malaya and Netherlands Indies, which constituted a form of encirclement of which Japanese Government were bound to take notice'. The use of the word *encirclement*, Craigie answered, suggested that these 'absurd reports' came from Berlin; 'in any case it was clear that this fresh Japanese initiative would impose further defensive measures upon ourselves'. The Foreign Minister said that the initiative had not been Japan's; 'he referred in particular to the much publicised reinforcement of our military strength in Malaya'. He gave Craigie his word 'as an old friend' that sending troops to southern Indo-China was 'in no sense directed against us, or any other Power with which Japan was at peace, but was purely and simply for defensive purposes'. Craigie commented that while governments came and went, naval bases might be more permanent. The minister 'showed some irritation, saying that if I did not trust his word there was nothing more to be said ...'.[279] He denied that the move in Indo-China had 'any hostile intentions' to Britain.[280] Craigie was told he had spoken 'very well'.[281] The talk of encirclement, Bennett observed, was 'only true in the sense that a man penetrating into a wood is encircled by the trees; and that it is no good blaming the trees'.[282] 'The MFA conveniently forgets that the alleged British threat to Indo-China was one of the reasons for moving in.'[283]

Craigie saw the Foreign Minister again the following day. Groundless reports were the reason given for a step that might be 'fraught with such serious consequences'. It was, however, the actual despatch of troops that would threaten British interests. Could that not be deferred until the Japanese Government had had 'further time to examine the truth of these baseless reports'? The Foreign Minister gave supplementary reasons: 'to ensure the supply to Japan of materials vital to her existence' and to promote the success of the campaign against China. Craigie questioned the latter.[284] Craigie's suggestion came from his Australian colleague, Sir John Latham. He knew the FO preferred to keep Japan guessing, but 'this policy cuts both ways and ... it is important if only as a matter of record, to give most emphatic denials to Japanese allegations of aggressive intentions on our part'. While the last-minute suggestion was unlikely to succeed, its being made 'would place them in an embarrassing position ...'.[285] Latham put it himself as well.[286] The FO agreed that Craigie was right to try the idea if only for propaganda purposes. The Japanese Foreign Minister, Bennett commented, was coming nearer the truth when he spoke of raw materials.[287] Craigie added that he had told the minister that the reference to Syria was a 'red herring'. German planes had used Syrian aerodromes, and French munitions had been sent to Iraqi rebels. There was no parallel in Indo-China. The minister 'merely smiled'.[288]

The Foreign Minister's statement to Grew, to parallel that to Craigie, had mentioned reports that the US might retaliate with economic measures like a freezing of assets and an oil embargo and suggested the need to avoid aggravating Japanese feelings, already excited by failure of the Netherlands Indies negotiations and encirclement.[289] But when Grew saw Toyoda on 26 July after he had just learnt of the American decision to freeze assets, he was 'clearly taken aback and my colleague described him to be as appearing quite crushed by the strength of American reaction, which he had clearly not anticipated'. He did not, however, give 'the slightest indication of any modification being possible in Japanese attitude'. Craigie had the same impression of the minister's 'despondency' as a result of the latest development and the denunciation of the commercial treaty, which he had communicated. 'My surmise is that Japanese Government ... were totally unprepared for anything more than the usual protests', and that the minister, 'new to the job and new to diplomacy, had inherited a policy of whose dangers he was only dimly aware'. Craigie thought he had seen the Emperor before seeing Craigie and Grew.[290] Foulds' comment was that 'action is the only thing which impresses the Japanese. Let us hope that they will seriously ponder the consequences of aggression and stop before it is too late.' The Emperor, he added, was on the side of moderation but had limited influence.[291]

Halifax saw Welles on the morning of 28 July and was shown Grew's report of this interview. Welles said he had seen Nomura on 23 July, when he had spoken on the lines of the statement made public the following day, and the President had seen him on 24 July. 'At this interview the Japanese Ambassador had repeated the usual stuff about encirclement, and the necessity for defensive measures, which the President had dismissed as fantastic.' Roosevelt then made his proposal to Nomura that if the Japanese would stop landing troops in southern Indo-China and abandon the attempt to establish a preferential military or civil position, he would approach the British, the Dutch and the Chinese to secure their concurrence in the plan for a general hands-off policy in Indo-china 'while emergency lasted'. This proposal should meet 'the professed Japanese anxiety about encirclement'. Three days later, on the 27th, Grew found that the Foreign Minister had not yet received the proposal, perhaps as a result of 'deliberate suppression' by extremists in the Japanese FO. Told of it, he was 'non-committal'.[292] These proposals, as Foulds said, were not unlike Craigie's. He agreed that extremists probably suppressed the report in order to ensure ratification of the Indo-China agreement on 26 July, done in the Emperor's presence.[293]

The protocol was concluded at Vichy on 29 July and published on 31 July. It provided for 'mutual co-operation for joint defence of French Indo-China'; measures would be subject to separate arrangements.[294] In effect, a statement made by Welles on 1 August declared, 'this agreement virtually turns over to Japan an important part of the French empire'. There was, as Welles had stated on 24 July, no threat to justify this. Bases were being made over 'to a power whose territorial aspirations are apparent', and the situation had 'a direct bearing upon the vital problem of American security'. The statement pointed out that the French Government did not resist German and Italian use of facilities in Syria. It did not seem to abide by its determination to resist encroachments on its sovereignty.[295]

Darlan remarked to Leahy that the United States had failed to send a squadron to Saigon when he spoke of the deal on 16 July. It made no effort to stop the Japanese; it was 'always too late'. Leahy thought that the decision to admit Japan had been taken well before 16 July. A high French official remarked: 'If the Japanese win or keep out of the war we may be able to save something by co-operation with them. If the Allies are victorious we are confident that the United States will see that we get our colony back.'[296] 'The fallacy ... is that the French will gain nothing from collabn. with the Germans even if the latter win.'[297]

Craigie had two long conversations with Ambassador Shigemitsu, back on leave from London. 'He was convinced that the change in Japanese policy, for which we had all been hoping was at last under way, and it was a tragedy that at this juncture the Indo-China affair should have supervened.' The new government had inherited the Indo-China affair from its predecessors, and 'he urged very earnestly that we should not close any doors'. His conversations with leading Japanese showed 'that there was nowhere any desire in Japan for war with Great Britain or America'. Shigemitsu, Craigie reported, was suggesting

> that we should regard the movement into Southern Indo-China as the last stage of the old policy rather than the first stage of a forward movement sponsored by the new Government. He admitted, however, that the change to a more moderate policy could not be either abrupt or spectacular and that the process of reprisal and counter-reprisal having now been instituted, the steps taken which had led to the recent change in Government might be arrested.

It was thus important 'to handle the situation with calmness and with avoidance of any unnecessary mutual provocation'. Craigie stressed the 'hollowness' of the Japanese case about Indo-China. 'I have also assured him that we have no desire either to go to war with or to humiliate Japan but that we are convinced that an end must be put to these constant Japanese aggressions on the German model and have no intention of allowing our position in south-eastern Asia to be further undermined without hitting back ...'. In his telegram, however, Craigie endorsed Shigemitsu's view 'that, despite the black outlook, it may still be possible, by keeping our measures of retaliation strictly within the economic field, to bring about a change for the better in Japanese foreign policy'.[298]

Foreign Office comments were not sanguine. 'We shall still have to be convinced by Japanese actions that Indo-China represents the end of an old policy rather than the beginning of a new stage,' wrote T.E. Bromley on 1 August. 'The beginnings of pressure on Thailand are disquieting....' The Japanese had no desire for war with Britain and the US, wrote Sir John Brenan, 'provided they can get what they want without war, and it is only the fear of war that is preventing them from going ahead still faster than they are. Nevertheless, they are prepared to take certain risks, and are using all the usual tricks of menace and blandishment to keep us quiet.' Shigemitsu no doubt preferred peaceful expansion, but 'the role of Japanese diplomats is to administer the anaesthetic while the military perform the operation. If we take the chloroform we shall wake up to find the Japanese in Thailand.' Gage was sceptical of Craigie's closing comment. Bennett thought Shigemitsu might yet have an important role in effecting a settlement with Japan. 'But we may have to go through worse crises before we get within sight of that. Meanwhile the plea that it will be all right if only we will accept the latest *fait accompli* is an old Japanese trick.'[299]

After the Cabinet meeting of 24 July the Far Eastern Committee had reviewed the actions taken on the proposals discussed on 4 July. The restriction on Japanese ships had been brought into effect. The Governor of the Straits Settlements, Sir Shenton Thomas, had objected to the closing of the Japanese Consulate-General on 'local security grounds'. The denunciation of the commercial treaty had been approved in the event of an 'overt act'. The US proposed to freeze assets, to subject imports to licensing and to restrict oil exports but not impose a complete embargo. Following the Cabinet decision the US had been told that, 'subject to the concurrence of the Empire Governments concerned', corresponding action would follow in the sterling area.

> It was explained that the United States Government could not be expected to give an unconditional guarantee that they would intervene with armed action; all that was possible was to explain to them that we should expect them to face any consequences which might flow from their own retaliatory measures, even if these involved an attack by Japan either on ourselves or on the Dutch.[300]

On 26 July Halifax outlined the US proposals for administering the freezing order. Specific licences, required to export oil, gas and petroleum products, would for the time being be automatically granted and so would licences for other exports. Imports would be held, and foreign exchange eventually paid to blocked accounts.[301] This caused the British concern. 'If the freezing orders were applied leniently there was danger that this would "add Japanese contempt to Japanese resentment".' If, however, the British pressed the United States to go further than it wished, 'there was danger of American public opinion swinging against us' and, if a warlike situation resulted, a section of American opinion would attribute it to 'our forcing the issue'.

> The Dominions and India were anxious that British policy in relation to Japan should not be in advance of United States policy. Their concern was generally that the policy of the British Empire and the United States should be co-ordinated and that the United States should realise the possibly dangerous implications of that policy in the event of war with Japan resulting.

The Dutch had indicated that the Indies would support the British if there were an attack on British interests in Far East but had no reciprocal assurance. 'They were, therefore, anxious as to the results of the policy being adopted by the British Empire in relation to Japan.' The House of Commons had been given the impression on 30 July that no oil could go to Japan from the British Empire.[302]

An amended telegram was sent to Halifax. 'We were willing to follow [the Americans'] lead by taking the more drastic action which we first supposed them to be about to take but it is obviously undesirable for us to go ahead of them ...'. Any apparent relaxation would create 'a deplorable situation'. The orders had been 'hailed with relief and enthusiasm all over the world as a major economic blow to Japan' and had produced 'a considerable effect' in Japan. If it now turned out that they constituted no very serious blow at all, 'they are unlikely to achieve their object as a deterrent to Japan, disappointment elsewhere will be correspondingly great, and the whole experiment will have a nugatory effect on any future warning action which the United States and we may wish to take ...'. Halifax was urged to put the whole question to the United States Government.[303] In fact the US enforced the sanctions quite sternly, although the British and the Dutch remained nervous lest it relax its restrictions.[304]

From Saigon Meiklereid reported a visit from Jouan on 26 July. Ostensibly he came to complain of Singapore broadcasts, to which Decoux violently objected. He had also arranged to keep Meiklereid informed through the Governor of Cochin-China, but Decoux had issued counter-orders.

Jouan feels that the French in Indo-China will look out for some indication of continued British sympathy even if we cannot maintain Singapore agreement ...

[Jouan] reassured me that if one tanker be allowed to come he would be able to obtain formal undertaking from the Japanese that it would not be interfered with. He feels confident that if the agreement is maintained he will be able to keep us informed of Japanese movements with the consent of the Governor-General ....

Meiklereid thought the 'wireless campaign of personal abuse' gained nothing. He also suggested 'that if it were possible to continue allowing limited supplies to enter Indo-China we might thus maintain friendly influence over French population with little risk of goods falling into the hands of Japanese whose presence is likely to produce an increased feeling of defeatism ...'.[305] The propaganda, the Foreign Office told Meiklereid, was directed at Vichy not at Decoux. Continuance of the agreement would be related to the extent to which Decoux was 'able and willing' still to carry out his obligations especially in respect of rubber.[306]

Some information was made available in mid August before Jouan returned to Hanoi for discussions on Franco-Japanese military collabora-tion. The French General Staff would seek to withdraw French forces to the north, and Jouan and Mordant wanted a 'distinct gap' between Japanese and French forces so that, in the event of an Allied or Japanese attack on Thailand, no French troops would be involved. In the event of hostilities Indo-China would do its 'utmost to remain neutral', fighting only if attacked by the Chinese. 'In the event of the first sign of success against the Japanese, considerable amount of the army may be expected to support us.' About 23 000 troops had landed.[307] 'The French appear to be handing Southern Indo-China over to the Japanese entirely,' Gage commented.[308]

The aim of the French was to preserve the continuity of their rule. They developed some concern about the US–Japan negotiations, which, rather surprisingly, they felt able to express. Vichy told the State Department in September 'that arrangement whereby Japanese forces occupied Indo-China was only intended to be temporary. Vichy expressed the hope that any agreement which might be reached between the United States and Japan would include a stipulation that Indo-China would be evacuated when the present war emergency was over.' This message leaked into the press, whereupon the ambassador expressed his concern to the department 'lest the Japanese, angered by French appeal for United States assistance should retaliate upon Indo-China'.[309] At the Foreign Office Philip Broad thought the French hopes 'very wishful thinking'.[310] Hull certainly expostulated to Henry-Haye,[311] which did not stop the ambassador's going to Welles.[312] Could French humiliation go further? Yes; the Japanese were not sticking to the agreement.

Meiklereid had reported that the Japanese ambassador to Indo-China, Yoshizawa, due in Hanoi on 5 October, was expected to be more exacting than Sumita on the economic front.[313] In early October he reported that Decoux had referred Japanese demands to Vichy as a violation of the military agreement.[314] Additional troops had been arriving, and additional aerodromes were being occupied.[315] At Churchill's suggestion the report was sent to Halifax, inviting him to draw Hull's attention to these activities 'as evidence that the Japanese are not being deterred by their hopes of agreement with the US from extending and consolidating their hold on Indo-China'.[316] In fact, as Craigie reported from Tokyo, Grew had presented the Japanese Foreign Minister 'with a list of actions by Japanese military forces in Indo-China which seemed to indicate an intention to infringe on French sovereignty there, adding that the United States Government find it especially difficult to reconcile these actions with recent declarations by high Japanese officials that actual Japanese foreign policy is based on the maintenance of peace'.[317] Hull was acting on information from Reed, the consul in Hanoi, and from Leahy in Vichy.[318] The Foreign Office agreed that Craigie should support his American colleague.[319]

Craigie gave Toyoda an aide-mémoire on actions of the Japanese military in Indo-China that appeared to infringe and disregard French sovereignty, including demands for additional facilities and arrests and raids. He reminded the minister of his earlier warnings to Matsuoka and the subsequent course of events. 'It seemed to me in highest degree desirable to avoid any aggravation of an already dangerous situation ...'. The minister tried to argue that the actions were taken in agreement with the French and in virtue of the agreement with them, but Craigie said it was clear that they were undertaken despite protests and opposition. He promised to inquire.[320] Craigie's frankness 'must have done some good', wrote Broad.[321] The reply referred to 'fabrications' and 'distortions'. Moreover, these were 'not questions in which third powers should intervene'.[322]

Meanwhile the Foreign Office doubted that Vichy had told Hanoi to resist Japanese demands by force if necessary.[323] Leahy was less than convinced, too.[324] A subsequent report suggested that Decoux had on Vichy instructions refused a Japanese demand to station 50 000 troops in Tonkin. 'A compromise was eventually reached on the basis of previous accord between Generals Martin and Nishimura by which 25 000 Japanese troops would be permitted to enter Tonkin supposedly to support Japanese troops in China.'[325]

Before the Japanese move into southern Indo-China in July the British had avoided a breach with Decoux, although the British believed his commitment to deliver rubber to Japan was against their agreement, and they were anxious to secure the release of Egal. They cut off the oil supply. Decoux urged the need for some encouragement in his policy of limiting the Japanese, for example through the supply of oil and flour; the French, the Commander-in-Chief reported, felt that 'their position is being steadily weakened by shortage of oil and from being forced gradually into the hands of Japanese'.[326] This was how matters stood when the Japanese presented their demands to Vichy. Gage saw little point in supplying oil, as Jouan urged. 'The most effective weapon we have against Japan in this matter is not French resistance but Anglo-American economic reprisals.'[327]

Immediately after Vichy's acceptance of the demands the Far Eastern Committee decided to suspend judgment on continuing the Decoux agreement 'till we see what attitude Adl. Decoux will adopt to the Japanese occupation'.[328] Meiklereid spoke to Jouan. He wanted the agreement maintained. He took the attitude 'that Indo-China could not do other than accept Japanese terms in order to maintain some hope of eventual retention of Indo-China for France as he fears that in the event of Allied victory America and we would share spoils and Empire would disappear'. Gage thought that showed 'a very sorry sense of realism for a Frenchman'. But Clarke thought that the British would 'gain little by breaking the agreement and the absence of it may have substantial disadvantages'.[329]

The Far Eastern Committee favoured continuing the agreement, too. It did not 'unduly restrict our freedom of action' and might enable the US to secure rubber.[330] The Commander-in-Chief also favoured continuing the agreement and supplying oil when a contract was made for supplying 10 000 tons of rubber to the US.[331] Britain was in favour of continuing the agreement, Halifax was told, provided no oil and nothing of military value went to Japan. 'We are anxious to prevent the French authorities from becoming any more dependent on Japan than can possibly be helped, and from actively collaborating with the Japanese to our detriment.'[332] Late in August a contract for the sale of 10 000 tons of rubber to the US was concluded, perhaps, Clarke commented, 'expedited by our attitude to the agreement'.[333]

The agreement was queried again in September. Clarke enunciated its advantages. No ships were seized, and France was the stronger navally. There was no subversive Vichy activity in the Pacific. Supplies were sent to Hong Kong. And the agreement had helped to secure the release of Egal and a contract for rubber for the US. It was a means of securing information and exerting some influence.[334]

> The main point [Bennett added] is that the Agreement serves to maintain some sort of link between ourselves and the French in Indo-China, which may eventually be useful. If the Agreement is scrapped it may well be that Admiral Decoux might refuse any longer to countenance the continued presence in Indo-China of our consular representative and we should be without any official knowledge of what was going on there.[335]

The agreement would become 'progressively more useless' as Japan gained more control in Indo-China, Sir Horace Seymour concluded. 'But it has some advantages still, ... and the time for cancellation doesn't seem to have arrived just yet.'[336]

The Japanese prevented the rubber shipment to the US.[337] The Ministry of Economic Warfare was also concerned over leaks in the blockade caused by shipments from Indo-China through Madagascar and Dakar. A paper presented to the Far Eastern Committee late in October again discussed the Decoux agreement. He had been told that its continuance would depend on his cooperation. The Govenor-General had seemed 100 per cent pro-Vichy, but anti-Japanese sentiment had increased. The Japanese, however, had prevented rubber shipments to the US. The Ministry of Economic Warfare proposed that French ships should be intercepted if suspected of carrying supplies to France, French Africa or Madagascar.[338] The committee noted leaks in the blockade and decided to intercept Indo-China trade in the Sunda Straits, leaving it to the French to denounce the Decoux agreement.[339] The Governor-General did not do so, although, as Meiklereid put it, he gave up 'any pretence of co-operation with us except in so far as economic relations are favourable to Indo-China'. Meiklereid, the Acting Consul-General, still favoured supplying essentials: it would have a 'heartening effect on the people, the majority of whom are still strongly pro-British'.[340]

The C in C China favoured maintaining the agreement by supplying European foodstuffs and continuing the Singapore and Hong Kong trade; in return the French would be required to eliminate anti-British propaganda, stop shipments of contraband to France and be pressed to deliver rubber to the US. A blockade, it was argued, would not help the British cause. A more liberal approach would, however, respond to the public sentiment of the French in Indo-China, 'overwhelmingly pro-British and out of sympathy with the Decoux administration which they consider has let them down unnecessarily on Vichy instructions'. The French were looking to the US and the UK 'to save Indo China for them without any effort on their part and what we need is a weapon to encourage or even draw them to take an active part in standing up to Japanese pressure'.[341]

The Far Eastern Committee, meeting on 5 December, opposed the idea. If war broke out Indo-China would become occupied enemy territory. Even if the crisis relaxed 'another gesture' would have little point. 'Our previous forthcoming attitude had met with no response and no rubber at all had been sent from Indo-China to the United States. It was clear that we would only get out of Indo-China what the Japanese did not want for themselves.' A new gesture would also be 'in direct opposition to United States policy. This would be most undesirable at a time when we were trying to keep as closely as possible in step with the United States ...'. The Committee concluded that, 'even if there were something to be said for putting heart into the population of Indo-China by allowing them supplies, the conclusion of a further arrangement would only strengthen the hand of Admiral Decoux who was well known to carry out all the orders he received from Vichy'. The Committee decided to await the outcome of the crisis and meanwhile tighten economic measures to match those of the Americans.[342]

The crisis, however, ended in war. The British had sought to maintain the status quo even in Decoux's Indo-China. That was now finally ruled out. They had, however, persisted with their gestures, despite some questioning, for almost the whole of the period between the fall of France and the opening of the Pacific war. Their approach towards Thailand offered a number of similarities.

The question of support for Thailand

The main ceremony marking Thailand's take-over of the cessions from Indo-China was at Battambang on 25 July.[343] At the same time Japan assumed military control over the rest of Indo-China, prompting Grant's suspicions that the operations were coordinated.[344] Pibun insisted that they were not.[345] In fact he had been 'very nervous' about his relations with Japan before the transfer took place,[346] and Japan had merely given Pibun a few hours' advance notice of its move on southern Indo-China.[347] Indeed the move was intended to bring pressure on Thailand as well. At the Liaison conference of 12 June General Sugiyama argued that the presence of Japanese troops in southern Indo-China would eliminate the 'scheming intrigues' of the British and Americans in Thailand.[348] Thailand would, in Consul-General Asada's words, 'cease vacillating in her determination to oppose Britain and thus seek emancipation from British power'.[349]

What Pibun had learned of British power was indeed far from reassuring. He had sent a special mission, Thawi Chunlasap and Luang Suranarong, to Singapore on 9 July. Brooke-Popham had said that, if Thailand could hold out until early 1942, the British might be able to provide some equipment.[350] 'The ultimate fate of Thailand is dependent upon the action of a fleet based on Singapore. So long as Britain holds the Singapore naval base Thailand can rely on regaining her independence ultimately. At a later stage British forces might be available for co-operation in the defence of Thailand.' This was the unattractive statement the C in C offered Pibun's emissaries.[351]

The Japanese move on southern Indo-China was expected in Bangkok, and it was also expected, according to Direck, that neither Britain nor the United States would 'proceed beyond verbal protests'. Did that mean that the Thais would get Cambodia and Laos? Crosby asked. Direck replied 'that the matter had not been mentioned recently'. He said the Prime Minister endorsed his view that 'we should assert ourselves and undertake to support Thailand if she resisted Japanese aggression'.[352] 'It is obvious', Gage thought, '… that if we and the US could give Thailand an assurance of military assistance if she were attacked by Japan it would have great effect. Otherwise we must envisage an eventual occupation on the lines of Indo-China.'[353] Information from Singapore suggested that the Japanese had demanded that the Thais should sign no treaty that might endanger the Prosperity Sphere, should recognise Manchukuo, should cease to trade with Russia and, should engage in military co-operation, and, in return, offered that Laos should come under Thai protection.[354] The Deputy Foreign Minister, Crosby found, knew nothing of the offer of territory, but Crosby asked him to warn Pibun of the dangers of accepting it even so.[355] Crosby suggested that Britain and the US should tell Japan that interference with the sovereignty of Indo-China would be a casus belli. That would mean that no offer could be made to Thailand.[356] No such step was, of course, taken. But the Japanese did not dislodge the French in any case.

As Gage observed, however, their moves on Indo-China would make the Thais 'even more fearful of doing anything which might affect

Japan'.[357] The Prime Minister indeed told Crosby on 25 July that he feared increasing pressure from Japan. 'He represented that there would be no end to the aggression of Japan unless, and until, Britain and the United States indicated to her a limit beyond which she could not go without finding herself at war with both those countries …'.[358] The measures now taken against Japan, Gage noted, might 'impress Thailand. But if Japan reacts with demands on Thailand it is perfectly true that the only thing which might make the Thais resist is Anglo-American firmness on the lines suggested by the Thai PM.'[359]

The Thais continued to seek that. 'Nothing less would suffice', both Direck and the Under-Secretary told Sir Josiah Crosby, 'than a public warning to Japan that any attempt by her to violate the territorial integrity or sovereignty of Thailand would involve her in war with Britain and the United States …'. Further, some official statement was required of confidence in Thailand's neutral attitude and readiness to supply it with materials. An American fleet, they urged, should be sent to Singapore as a warning gesture. Crosby agreed with their views. 'I submit that our policy of driving hard bargain with Thailand has been torpedoed by the Japanese occupation of bases in Indo-China and that we must now give to Thailand what she needs generously, quickly and without thought of immediate return if we are to save ourselves by saving her …'.[360] Pibun sent Crosby a message for Eden. 'It is to be expected that Japan will press him to make military and economic concessions and generally to adopt policy which will be incompatible with the position of Thailand as a neutral power and as a friend of Britain.' If he refused Japan might threaten force. 'In that event what would be the attitude of Britain and what courses would His Majesty's Government advise him to follow?'[361]

Craigie supported Crosby. The military had the bit between their teeth, and a 'very determined' attitude was required. The reluctance of the US Government to commit itself in advance might, he thought, have been tempered by the President's offer on Indo-China.[362] In fact Roosevelt was going that way. Grant, of course, wholly disagreed with Crosby. This was in his view a roundabout ploy by the Thais to get American sanction for their aggression in Indo-China.[363] If the US were to make a public statement of support, Grant urged 'that a clear line of demarcation be made between what has already occurred in the matter of the territorial controversy between Thailand and Indo-China and the present situation'. The Thais had not upheld the status quo and might be manoeuvring the Americans into accepting the changes.[364] Willys R. Peck, then in the State Department, agreed. A declaration of support would protect the Thai Government from the accusation that it had pursued a pro-Japanese policy. It would also help the Japanese to allege that the British and the Americans were scheming against them in Thailand.[365] Hull, however, was inclined to think that the importance of the Burma Road, and of Singapore, might 'justify our salvaging what we can' out of 'that original betrayal of everybody by the Siamese to Japan'.[366]

The President told Halifax that he did not think that, if the Japanese took action in Thailand with Thai acquiescence and landed 40 000–50 000 men, it could be a matter for an ultimatum. But Halifax had given Welles a copy of the despatch that had conveyed Pibun's message, and Roosevelt said he intended to discuss with him making the same proposal over Thailand as he had over Indo-China. 'I told him I thought the essential point was for the United States Government by whatever means seemed best to make it plain to the Japanese that any future action of Japan *vis-à-vis* Thailand would be a matter of immediate concern to the United States ...'. Casey and Halifax thought the United States might be asked to say in its communication to the Japanese 'that any further move of the Japanese forces southwards or westwards from Indo-China would leave the United States Government with no option but to give expression to clear trend of public opinion ... in ways that would be even more destructive of good relations ... than those that the United States Government have been obliged already to take'.[367] 'The difficulty is not the reluctance of the USG to make a statement but their reluctance to so prejudice themselves in US public opinion by going ahead of it,' Gage commented.[368]

Halifax saw Welles on 2 August and again on 4 August. What else could be done, the ambassador asked, if the neutralisation proposal did not succeed? 'Was it of any use considering our both making some kindred declaration to the Japanese in terms as strong as we might be prepared to use, expressing our concern about their projected action in Thailand'? Welles thought it might have been useful two months earlier, but now a mere declaration would have no effect. He proposed, however, to tell the Counsellor 'that if Japan pursued their projected plan in Thailand and continued on towards the Netherlands East Indies or Singapore, or northwards (by which I suppose he meant Burma) it was quite inevitable that ... sooner or later the Japanese Government would find themselves involved in war with the United States'. Did this mean, Halifax asked, that 'such a declaration of ultimate result would not apply in the isolated case of Thailand'? That was so, Welles replied, 'since (a) he did not believe the Japanese would go into Thailand unless they had further objectives and (b) it was the further objectives rather than Thailand that mattered to us and to the United States'. Welles associated this with the instructions given to Grew in June 'about the attitude of the United States in the event of Japanese attempt to cut air life line by attack on the

Netherlands East Indies, adding that if the Japanese went for the Netherlands East Indies he had no doubt that would mean war with the British Empire, and that such event it would inevitably mean that the United States would be involved'. He said 'that an attempt by the Japanese on the Dutch or on Singapore would plainly show the Japanese determination to establish hegemony in that vital area which the United States could not tolerate'. Hull, Welles added, proposed to tell the Thai minister that, if the Thais stood up to the Japanese, 'the United States would give them all the help in their power as they had been giving help to China'.[369]

Eden told the House of Commons that a threat to Thailand was of immediate interest to Britain. Hull was less definite. At a press interview on 6 August he alluded to his 'increasing concern'.[370] He told Casey that Japan had linked neutralisation with the end of the China war. What would the US do, Casey asked, if Japan acquired Thai bases? It was considering ejecting consuls, breaking off diplomatic relations, making 'every other difficulty'.[371] At a meeting of 9 August Halifax urged Hull to speak to the Thai minister as he had proposed earlier. 'He repeatedly said that we must not allow any section of the problem, affecting Thailand or Netherlands East Indies to distract our thought from the larger problem arising from Japanese intentions, if these in fact existed, to pursue large policy of southward expansion which might well include Indian Ocean.' Halifax stressed that a move on Thailand would make such designs easier to accomplish.[372] Again, on 13 August, Halifax suggested that the Japanese might have the 'dangerous impression ... that, provided they confined themselves to Thailand, it will not have dangerous reactionary influence'.[373]

While the question of a warning to Japan was meanwhile pursued at Placentia Bay, diplomacy continued at Bangkok. Pibun said he appreciated Hull's statement and added that he would 'welcome more positive action'. He said that he would oppose Japanese aggression by force. He would ratify the non-aggression pact with France and would not press claims for Laos and the rest of Cambodia. He had, he said, decided 'he could not trust the Japanese'.[374] Grant did not believe Pibun. He played with the Japanese 'behind the scenes'.[375] The Thai minister told Peck in Washington, however, that the Thais would resist armed aggression and asked whether the US would render assistance.[376] Hull told the minister that the US would place Thailand in 'the same category' as China.[377]

The British had continued their economic discussions in Bangkok and Washington. The Japanese opposed the negotiations on oil. They sought 35 000 tons of rubber, not 30 000; Pibun contemplated an open market.[378] No reply had been sent to the British proposals for an agreement, and the Ministry of Economic Warfare suggested that a policy of pressure might be more appropriate. The Far Eastern Committee argued the issue again. Threatening Thailand might play into Japan's hands. A guarantee of support could not now be given, but it might be possible later 'if the Thais could be induced to hold out for some months'. 'It was suggested that the economic weapons open to us should be used in a friendly spirit so as to achieve at least a moderate delay before the Thais were finally included in the Japanese orbit.'[379] Oil supplies were to start 'without necessarily awaiting signature of economic agreement, but their continuance will obviously depend on general attitude of Thai Government'.[380] The Ministry of Economic Warfare continued to question the policy: it was, said Troutbeck, 'extremely doubtful whether anything – even a saving of time – will in fact be gained by a policy of giving the Thais everything for nothing'. Supplying oil –'our new bribe to the Thais' – would not 'prevent or even delay their succumbing to Japanese pressure unless we can produce the physical force to stop it ... If an armed bandit puts a revolver to your head, you are not influenced by hopes of an inheritance from an invalid uncle.'[381]

Through Direck Pibun pointed to Japanese pressure and indicated to Crosby, as to Grant, Thailand's determination to resist; he asked for material help, including twelve pursuit aeroplanes.[382] This, the FO thought, would merely provoke Japan.[383] It might be taken as a forerunner of further supplies, Bennett felt, and an indication that the Thais could count on our help. 'We may therefore very quickly find ourselves in the position of having let Thailand down.'[384] 'The supply of driblets of war material to weak countries is a very questionable proposition,' Seymour observed.[385]

The Foreign Office urged the US, to consider not only a warning to Japan but also aid to Thailand.[386] The British Embassy in Washington suggested that pre-emptive buying had to be considered in order to try to keep the Japanese share of rubber down and to keep the US involved.[387] In London it was thought that Japan would be able to get all it wanted so there was no point in paying exaggerated prices for what it did not need.[388] At the State Department, it seemed, there was a 'cleavage of opinion between those who hold that any economic aid to Thailand would merely constitute an undesirable and quite useless measure of appeasement and those who, while distrusting Thailand's promises, would be prepared to maintain United States economic activities there provided nothing is given away except in return for some definite quid pro quo'. A loan would now be 'mistaken for weakness by both Thailand and the Japanese'. Quid pro quo arrangements, such as Britain had been trying to negotiate, were made problematic by the excessive counter-allocation of rubber to Japan. That would leave no room for the US. Hence the suggestion of a pre-emptive purchasing scheme, despite 'its

obvious disadvantages'. The Thais would be permitted to apply the proceeds of it only to purchasing certain approved commodities.[389]

Crosby urged a more generous policy in view of Thailand's indication
that it would resist aggression. Treating it like China might mean waiting
for a Japanese attack, 'tantamount to locking the stable door after the
horse has escaped'.[390] Gage agreed. In the absence of an assurance of
effective support from the US and the UK, the Thais 'cannot be expected
to court the wrath of Japan by coming to a definite arrangement with us
(on our terms) about rubber. We and the Americans should ... supply
Thailand regularly with her vital needs if only to obtain the goodwill of
the Thai people and give the Thai Govt. a handle for their goodwill
towards us ...'.[391] The doubts about the Crosby policy had been revived
in London and Washington not only by distrust of the Thais but also by
the anxiety not to show weakness in respect of the Japanese. But the FO
generally supported the Crosby line.

The decision at Placentia Bay prompted a further effort to win the US
over to it. 'Now that we have got the Americans to give a warning to Japan
covering further action against Thailand', Bennett wrote on 19 August,
'it remains to press on with economic assistance to Thailand, and to try
to get the Americans into line here also.'[392] In spite of 'lingering doubts',
Halifax was told, 'we have reached conclusion that, in the absence of
promise of military assistance, generous policy of economic assistance is
only one now likely to succeed.' It could hardly be described as a 'useless
measure of appeasement'. Denying supplies to Thailand would force it
into closer relations with Japan. Appeasement was hardly the appropriate
term 'since we are dealing not with a powerful aggressor but with a small
country whose independence it is in our strategic interest to maintain if
we can'. The assistance proposed was 'conceived as complementary to
the warnings which we are giving Japan'.[393] 'In the absence of military
support, this was the only policy likely to retard Thailand's progressive
subservience to Japan ....'[394]

The approach to the US crossed a response to earlier approaches. The
authorities in Washington had come down in favour of pre-emptive
purchases of rubber in an open market. This would be done by the
British, but the Thais would be made aware that the US was involved.
Dollar proceeds would go into a special account for purchases in the US,
and oil and other items would be supplied in proportion to rubber
exported.[395] The Ministry of Economic Warfare could see no logic in this.
'If rubber is to be free for everyone to bid for, it is surely unreasonable to
link our purchases of rubber with our supplies to Thailand ...'.[396] 'We
should greatly prefer ... an intimation that the two Governments have
every intention of providing Thailand with economic assistance as long
as she continues to resist Japanese pretensions.'[397] The US accepted this:

'oil and other essential requirements should be furnished to Thailand (Siam) as long as that country continues to resist Japanese aggression and … it is not desirable to make the maintenance of supplies actually contingent upon the amount of rubber delivered to approved destinations'.[398] The Foreign Office suggested that the Thais be told that the US and UK planned to buy and that, as agreed, the East Asiatic Company should start doing so.[399] 'Such a programme', Sir Ronald I. Campbell observed, 'does not appear … to be calculated to provoke the Japanese to do anything more violent than insisting on allocation of their quota.' If they bid up prices, that would drain their exchange and benefit Thailand 'for which we could take credit'.[400] Purchasing began on 18 October.[401]

In the meantime the Thais had again asked for planes. At a dinner for the Air Attaché service leaders sought Buffaloes.[402] On his visit to the Far East Duff Cooper echoed earlier doubts about supplying weak countries.[403] Gage pointed to the advantages : '(1) the stiffening of Thai resistance to Japan especially from the economic point of view and (2) the encouragement to the Thai military to put up a military resistance if attacked. Even if the aircraft did fall into the hands of the Japanese I wonder if they would gain much by it.'[404] Duff Cooper decided to support the idea. The feeling in Bangkok was 'running strongly against Japan', and it was a 'propitious' moment for 'such a gesture'.[405] There was no endorsement for the idea either in London or in Washington where the Thai minister was told that 'demand greatly exceeded production and that aeroplanes would be sent where it was deemed they would be most useful'.[406] Grant's replacement in Bangkok, Peck, suggested that the Thai Government could use the compensation for the planes requisitioned the previous year, but he received little support.[407]

Thai officers visiting Malaya in July had also sought other weapons, and indicated that, if the weapons were supplied, they would welcome British instructors. Twenty-four 4.5-inch howitzers and twelve 75 mm field guns could, it was decided, be made available, provided the Thai Government accepted instructors, including nine officers and twenty-three other ranks, the aim being 'infiltration'. Craigie 'did not feel it would push the Japanese into violent action, but … it would be the kind of resolute step which puzzles the Japanese'.[408] The Thais, it was pointed out, would not accept a British military mission, having resisted a Japanese one. But perhaps they would accept a few instructors for a short period.[409]

Increasingly anxious, perhaps as a result of an initiative by the attaché Tamura,[410] Pibun in mid October pleaded for British and American equipment and aircraft.[411] Through Direck he asked what the British would do if Japan invaded Thailand, and what they would advise the Thais to do for their protection in concert with the British.[412] Concerned

over the defence of Malaya and Singapore, the British had been uncertain as to where the Japanese might strike first.[413] Before the war they
had secretly surveyed Kra,[414] and Pibun had thought the Japanese might
use southern Thailand.[415] With the Japanese in southern Indo-China the
possibility of a Japanese landing there increased. The British thus
prepared Operation Matador, the plan providing for British forces to
cross the border and take up positions around Songkla twenty-four hours
before the Japanese arrived.[416]

'This was the first time', Eden told the Cabinet, 'that the Siamese had
shown any real desire to co-operate with us, and it might be worth while
for the Chiefs of Staff to consider whether this opening was worth
following up.' COS opinion was sought.[417] Until assured of military
support from the US, the COS commented, the UK should undertake no
action, save in defence of its vital interests, that was likely to precipitate
war with Japan. Kra would give Japan a jumping-off ground but would
'not by itself be an attack on our vital interests'. No support could be
given, and no disclosure of Matador should take place.[418]

Clarke doubted that so negative an answer could or should be returned. Could something be concerted along the lines of the operations
envisaged in southern Thailand? If Pibun's request for cooperation and
advice were refused, Bennett added, 'we cannot be surprised if he goes
completely into the Japanese camp'. Even in respect of the Kra operation
Thai opposition ought to be avoided. 'We cannot save Thailand if the
Japanese attack and the most we can hope is to keep the Thais from
giving up in despair, and to get them not to oppose our own operations,
if we are forced to enter the Kra Isthmus.' Seymour thought the British
should take the risk of speaking about the Kra operation. 'There is a
greater risk in letting the Thais slip into the Japanese orbit', Cadogan
believed. '... what we should propose to tell the Thais wd. be rather cold
comfort for them, but it is something.'[419] The COS would offer assistance
only in respect of the defence of Kra.[420]

The UK had continued to consider supplying howitzers and guns and
had consulted the US about that and also about aircraft.[421] Could a few
Vultee aircraft be released?[422] Hornbeck thought a better approach
would be to tell Japan that an armed assault in Thailand would result in
armed support of it from the US and the UK. 'I would rather that we and
the British, with weapons in our hands tell the Japanese that they are not
to invade Thailand than to have the Thais, with our weapons in their
hands, tell the Japanese that', Hornbeck commented.[423] Peck, however,
supported the supply of planes, preferably from Singapore.[424] The State
Department indicated on 6 November that it would agree to Britain's
sending to Thailand planes from Singapore or 'a certain number' of the
planes being supplied to it by the US.[425] But the British felt that they
could not release any.[426]

Peck thought that the Thais were receiving little while a great deal was expected of them.[427] On 10 November Crosby sounded Direck about a secret report that suggested the Japanese would shortly present a quasi-ultimatum seeking economic and military collaboration. There was 'a real danger of the Prime Minister being discouraged and yielding to it if he does not speedily receive some reassuring message from ourselves'.[428] There was little the UK could offer. The reply to Pibun might be held up until the two capital ships sent to Singapore had actually arrived. But 'further delay' was probably undesirable.[429] Pibun was deeply disappointed, and Crosby despaired.[430]

In early November neither the British nor the Americans thought that in fact an attack on Thailand was imminent. The rainy season would deter it. The Americans thought the Burma Road a more likely target.[431] In fact the Japanese had taken their time-limited decision on 5 November. The plan the Liaison Conference received that day had stated that 'close military relations with Thailand will be established just prior to the use of force'.[432] In a question that gave point to a British dilemma over Matador, the Emperor had earlier raised questions about violating Thailand's neutrality.[433] Hara Yoshimichi, President of the Privy Council, now asked how secrecy would be preserved if Thailand were approached ahead of time. Tojo replied that the Japanese had been 'working on' Pibun since the advance into southern Indo-China. 'It is necessary from an operational point of view for us to make landings in Thailand. It will not do to let this be known too early. Therefore, we cannot do other than push this matter by force if they do not agree with us at the talks just before we act.'[434] The Liaison Conference of 12 November received a plan that called for movement of Japanese forces into Thailand, however the Thais responded. The Thais would be expected to do more than merely allow passage and, if they wished, could join a defence pact. Lost territories in Burma and Malaya could be promised. The conference on 22 November adopted a fuller plan.[435]

On 27 November Crosby reported movements of troops in Indo-China. An attack on Kra was expected on 1 December.[436] A similar report came from Meiklereid.[437] A Japanese move seemed imminent as supplies and troops were moved to Hainan and the talks in Washington stalled.[438] Anxious over Matador, Brooke-Popham asked to be kept informed about them. Churchill wanted an American assurance.[439] On 30 November American intelligence revealed a plan to entice Britain into invading Thailand, and that made authorising Matador more difficult. Indeed the Japanese plans of 22 November foresaw the possibility of a prior British invasion.[440]

The President's statement on 1 December prompted the British to give further thought to Kra. Suggesting they be invited in did not commend itself since they could give Thailand little help in protecting the rest of its territory, and the same applied to a promise to guarantee their ultimate sovereignty. A joint public warning to Japan might alone affect Pibun's attitude.[441] Roosevelt's subsequent assurances led the British Government to authorise Brooke-Popham to implement Matador if the Japanese invaded Thailand or appeared to be advancing on Kra.[442] Crosby and Direck appealed against it: Thailand's neutrality must be preserved.[443] That factor contributed to hesitation when news of the departure of the Japanese fleet was received, although in addition its destination was unclear.[444]

Churchill had sought American approval for a message to Pibun: 'There is possibility of imminent Japanese invasion of your country. If you are attacked defend yourself. We shall come to your aid to the utmost of our power and will safeguard independence of your country.'[445] Roosevelt agreed. His own message would indicate that the United States would regard as a hostile act Japanese invasion of Thailand, Malaya, Burma or the Indies. If the Thais did not aid the Japanese, the US and the UK would work for the restoration of Thailand's sovereignty when peace came.[446] The British message was accordingly modified. The third sentence now read: 'The preservation of the full independence and sovereignty of Thailand is a British interest and we shall regard an attack on you as an attack upon ourselves.'[447] On the night of 7 December the Japanese delivered their ultimatum. They also began to bomb Pearl Harbor.[448] Pibun had been absent at the crucial moment. But the Thai Cabinet had ordered a cease-fire before Crosby could deliver Churchill's message.[449]

Grant's remarks had been prophetic:

> I do not take seriously the recent bold announcement of Thai officials to the effect that the Thai would fight aggressors to the last drop of blood. If there should be any show of force against Thailand by the latter, it would only be a gesture for world consumption and we would likely find Luang Phibun still in the saddle under direct Japanese control.[450]

But for the moment Thailand, while permitting the passage of troops, did not pursue the offer of its lost territories.[451]

Burma's search for independence

'By and large it can be said', the new Governor of Burma, Sir Reginald Dorman-Smith, reported on 4 August 1941, 'that no Ministry can consider itself at all secure while it continues to cooperate with us under existing conditions, i.e. without some much more definite promise of "freedom" after the war.'[452] U Saw sought that.

In September 1940 he had overthrown Pu, drawing on his own strength, on a corruption controversy and on his opponent's identification with the war effort. The Atlantic Charter buoyed him up, but it meant, as Amery put it, 'nothing more than we have told them already',[453] and Dorman-Smith could not assure him that it applied to Burma.[454] Saw got nowhere. To obtain a promise of dominion status at the end of the war he visited London in October–November 1941. Amery

> pointed out that all progress in the Empire has been step by step and not by statements in advance and that the most we can do was to make it clear that there would be the fullest discussion immediately after the war, that everything was open and that the object of the discussions was to move in the direction of the ultimate goal, but no statement now could be made which would prejudice the outcome of those discussions.[455]

Saw, Amery told the War Cabinet, had suggested to Dorman-Smith a formula such as that the object of the post-war discussions would be 'the immediate establishment of full self-government in Burma subject to such temporary arrangements as may be necessary in respect of Defence and Foreign Affairs'. This formula could not be accepted because it would 'anticipate and prejudge' a range of topics, including the future of the non-Burman peoples, which could not now be examined. To help him in his political difficulties, and enable him to secure cooperation in the war effort, he should, however, be impressed by the British Government's sincerity. Something in writing would avoid the risk of 'misapprehension ... which might lead him to give a more optimistic picture of these talks than the facts justify and might consequently lead to misunderstanding in Burma'.

Amery submitted a draft that he planned to show Saw to see whether he would consider it helpful. He would then come back to Cabinet.[456] In the draft, which was to be sent on 3 November, Amery acknowledged the statements made by Cochrane up to that of 26 August 1940, envisaging the discussions at the end of the war to promote the attainment of dominion status.

> In the midst of the life-and-death struggle in which this country and Burma and indeed the whole cause of free government in the world are involved, it is not possible ... either to enter upon the detailed examination and discussion required for the solution of these important problems or to anticipate or prejudge conclusions which must themselves be affected by that examination and by the situation at the end of the war...[457]

In his speech at the luncheon next day Amery gave Saw 'the assurance that we sincerely mean what we say when we tell him that in the discussions which we hope will be undertaken as soon as the war is concluded we mean to go as far as we can, and as fast as we can, on the road to that high status …'.[458] 'We were engaged in a struggle for our very lives, and this was not the time to raise such constitutional matters,' Churchill told Saw.[459] Saw was quite unsatisfied and gave 'public expression to his disappointment'. He also distributed a pamphlet, 'Burma's case for full self-Government'.[460]

When he had set out, the Burma Office had been anxious over what Saw might say in public. He had 'little or no experience of European affairs', the British ambassadors in Cairo and Lisbon were told, 'and we are a little anxious, having regard to his views on certain aspects of British policy in relation to Burma, to avoid as far as may be possible his giving interviews or statements *en route* to British or foreign correspondents except in the most general terms …'. He had also said that he proposed to see President Roosevelt, 'but as no approach in regard to such an interview has yet been made through the Foreign Office to the State Department and will not in any case be made until after discussion on his arrival, we should like to avoid any repetition of a definite statement of this character …'.[461]

The plan to visit the US went ahead, however. 'Winston in the small hours of the morning had a sudden brain wave about stopping U Saw from going home via America but I let him know it was too late and that the only result would be to send him really off the deep end whereas I still think he doesn't mean serious mischief,' wrote Amery in his diary.[462] Halifax, indeed, was told that the government would be glad if the President received Saw. It might give the President the opportunity of stressing 'the need for giving the maximum assistance to China' and for Lend-Lease goods to be 'transported without delay and at the least possible cost'. If Saw should ask for an interpretation of Article 3 of the Atlantic Charter, which spoke of the right of peoples to choose their own government, Halifax might suggest that the President should reply

> that while he is not concerned with domestic questions in the British Commonwealth, and while the question primarily in mind at the Atlantic meeting was the restoration of freedom to victims of Nazi aggression, the principles of the joint declaration are in harmony with, and confirm, those which underlie the development of self-government in the various parts of the British Commonwealth and the declarations made on that subject.

Halifax should also explain the constitutional position. Saw's aim had been to obtain a promise that the object of the post-war discussions was 'the immediate establishment of full self-government subject perhaps to temporary reservations in respect of defence and foreign affairs'. The British had been 'unable to give a sweeping promise of this kind'.[463]

Steps were also to be taken to brief the American press on Saw's purpose in visiting Britain and on the constitutional position.[464] It was suggested that Saw might be 'shepherded'.[465] A follow-up telegram conveyed Dorman-Smith's view that Saw should not be encouraged to think that American public opinion was even interested in Burma's struggle for freedom at present.[466] Saw's press conference indeed secured rather meagre coverage. It had been 'ingeniously' arranged for a Saturday, 'when it is hard to find space in the Sunday papers, as they go to bed very early ...'. It was 'sparsely attended, and the propensity of the journalists ... to regard U Saw as a man with a curious name rather than as a Burmese Gandhi was useful. Moreover, he went too far in his obvious desire to annoy and embarrass HMG. His expressed desire to see Kurusu also did not help him ...'.[467]

The government had been keen that Saw should see Roosevelt and that the President should say the right thing. The interview took place. Saw raised with him and with Hull and Hornbeck the issue of Burma's independence and the Atlantic Charter, 'but got no change on any occasion. United States officials as a whole adopted a very polite but non-committal attitude towards U Saw and made it plain to him that their principal interest in Burma was as the channel through which American supplies to China had to flow'.[468] Saw wrote to the President and asked for a further joint declaration that the Atlantic Charter applied to all peoples.[469] But Hull told the President that, as Saw lacked the authority to treat with foreign governments, his request did not require an answer.[470]

The China issue had been discussed in a Balliol paper of 4 November. In the light of Saw's publicly expressed dissatisfaction it questioned whether Burmese nationalist cooperation could be taken for granted if the Japanese attacked through Thailand or if Chinese troops entered to help defend the Burma Road. The easier approach for the Japanese was, it was thought, to cross from Thailand rather than concentrate on Yunnan. The entry of Chinese troops into Burma to meet such a threat might be counter-productive since Burma was

> susceptible to Japanese propaganda cultivating a fear that Anglo-Chinese co-operation for war purposes might grow into some kind of permanent condominium over Burma, involving extensive rights of trade and immigration for China. Such suspicion intensified by U Saw's failure to obtain Dominion Status for Burma might lead to serious clashes between Burmese and Chinese troops and local unrest which could be exploited by a Japanese invasion.[471]

'The extent to which Burmese susceptibilities and their suspicions of China affect the position is perhaps insufficiently appreciated in the USA', wrote Arthur Scott of the Foreign Office. He did not think 'we should get much sympathy there. To the average American it is merely a case of Imperialist Britain denying the reasonable aspirations of the Burmese people, or, at best, refusing to make a concession which is essential to the successful prosecution of resistance to Japan'. Burmese hostility to the entry of Chinese troops would probably not affect the situation much. 'If things go well, there will probably be no difficulty; if things go badly for us at first, we may be in a bit of a "jam".'[472]

The War Office did not think Japan would attack Burma merely to close the Burma Road. 'If Japan decides to go to war with us, her object is far more likely to be Singapore, the fall of which would be decisive, both against us and China, than Burma.' Moreover, to attack Burma, the Japanese would have to occupy Thailand; operations against Rangoon and Kunming were thus not equally open to the Japanese. Finally, there was 'no intention of introducing any Chinese troops into Burma to assist in its defence'.[473] Scott thought that the Japanese might overrun Thailand very quickly: 'an attack on Burma may well be an alternative to an attack on Yunnan'. Maybe the Chinese troops would not be needed. Another possibility was the retreat of Chinese troops into Burma. The debate on this point was abandoned when the war began.[474]

Saw reached Hawaii the day after the Japanese attack. To return to Rangoon he had to turn back via New York, Lisbon, Malta, Cairo and Karachi. Before he got beyond Palestine he was arrested by the British for allegedly making contacts with the Japanese Consul in Lisbon in order to offer his services to lead a rebellion against the British.[475] American intelligence had in fact suggested that he planned to set up a Quisling or Free Burma government.[476] Examination of his baggage and that of Tin Tut, who was with him, found nothing incriminating. Interrogated, Saw denied seeing any Japanese officials in the US. He had, however, learned that Japanese students in the US were being rounded up, and he also heard that American and British citizens were being rounded up and tortured in Japan. He was concerned about Burmese students in Japan especially the son of his election agent at Henzada North. He therefore visited the Japanese Consul-General in Lisbon and asked him 'to send a message to Tokyo to look after the Burmese students there'. Saw thought that he had mentioned the visit while at the British Ambassador's house the same day. 'A little personal explanation is I think necessary – what higher position than my present one would I get by supporting Japan. I say nil. On the contrary it would be a personal loss.'[477] Subsequently it was determined that there was 'no foundation whatever for a successful trial'. Saw's desire to visit Bangkok was not in itself 'criminal or treasonable and if the secret evidence known to Foreign Office cannot be used no treasonable design can be proved'.[478] Saw was detained in Uganda for the duration of the war.

Taylor points out that Saw changed his itinerary for returning home before the war began, inserting Bangkok, and this, he thinks, supports a suggestion that he had arranged to lead an anti-British army.[479] But it is not certain.

His message home at this time the British thought reassuring, but it was not unambiguous. He had, the Foreign Office told Halifax, telegraphed his colleagues 'that while disappointed he wants to make best of it when he gets back and urging them meanwhile to discourage anti-British activities'.[480] The message in fact said that, despite his disappointment with the London talks, he would 'use results to the best advantage' on his return to Burma. He asked Sir Paw Tun as Acting Prime Minister and his colleagues 'to do what they can to create a favourable impression amongst our supporters ... and in view of present international situation to do what is possible to mitigate the risk of strong anti-British feeling being created and the situation getting out of control'.[481] Paw Tun thought that the message would create 'unnecessary and undesirable repercussions'.[482] Saw said in reply on 15 November that the message was not meant for the public but for the Governor.

He now asked for a personal message to the people of Burma, dated Washington 15 November, to be published. It stated that he was confident

> that it cannot be long before Burma finds herself on same status as free nations of the world. But to-day the whole world is passing through a dangerous period and [it] may be that the people of Burma will be called upon to face grave dangers and difficulties and make great sacrifices in the cause of freedom. I call upon my countrymen to stand united and ready for any action and sacrifice.[483]

Although Saw had not yet seen the President, and the war was still three weeks away, the tone of this message might be regarded as at least ambiguous. Saw himself insisted it was drafted 'to reassure public opinion'. Paw Tun had suggested replacing 'dangerous period' with 'period of danger which is brought nearer to Burma by the menacing situation in the Far East'.[484] Saw objected. The dangerous period was for the whole world, and the change would weaken the effect of the sentence.[485]

Whatever Saw had done or said to others, quite clearly he was deeply disappointed over his failure to win further concessions from the British Government over the future of Burma. The British Prime Minister stood in the way. The British did not consider that Burmese opposition would have much effect on the use of the Burma Road. What would have most effect on Burma was the course of the war once it began. Already, indeed, the Thakins, more extreme than Saw, had been recruited by the Japanese in the Minami-Kikan. The initial purpose was indeed to close the Burma Road.[486] But the role of the Thirty Comrades expanded as Japanese ambitions expanded.

The agreement with Sarawak and the defence of Borneo

In another part of their empire quite a different constitutional development had taken place, although again it was unwelcome, as well as being
unexpected. The Colonial Office had taken up the question of appointing a Resident in Sarawak with Lord Lloyd's successor as Colonial Secretary, Lord Moyne. A despatch to Sir Shenton Thomas was authorised,
based on the draft of August 1940.[487] But on 31 March Raja Vyner Brooke
proclaimed that later in the year, when the state celebrated its centenary,
Sarawak would be given a written constitution, prepared by the
Committee of Administration. A legislature was to be set up, and the Raja
would rule with its advice. The aim was said to be, like the first Raja's, 'a
self-governing community and country'.[488] Brooke had been anxious to
provide for his relatives, and the constitution was in this other sense part
of a deal. It had yet another aspect. In a way it forestalled British pressure
already felt in the appointment of a General Adviser. Gent thought that
the Colonial Office had 'missed the boat'.[489] In August, however, Thomas
reported that a British representative would be accepted.[490]

The new agreement was supplementary to that of 1888. A British
representative was to be accredited to the Raja whose advice was to be
asked and acted on in all matters affecting the relations of Sarawak and
foreign states and on all matters of defence. 'The services of the British
Representative shall be available for consultation in matters touching the
general administration of the State', and he would have access to papers
on such matters and attend the Supreme Council. The British Government undertook to take whatever steps it could to protect Sarawak from
hostile attack. Sarawak, Thomas added, was not prepared to follow the
Malay States pattern; but the appointment of a 'Representative' was an
advance, and he would be brought into consultation 'more and more'.[491]
The Colonial Office felt that 'half a loaf is better than no bread' but
wanted the Representative to be able to offer advice on general matters,
and to have papers on such topics.[492] The Sarawak Government agreed
that he could offer advice, but he could have no right to the papers.[493]
The Colonial Office accepted this.[494] 'I personally feel that we have got
all we need,' Gent noted.[495] The agreement was signed on 22
November.[496]

In fact the agreement fell short of what the Colonial Office sought.
The constitution had clearly served to blunt its attack. In 1941 it was
relatively easy to secure powers in defence and foreign relations for the
Representative. The Colonial Office, however, persistently saw its priority
in the longer term. The fact was that within four days of the conclusion
of the supplementary agreement the Japanese began the war.

The defenceless state of North Borneo had been underlined by discussions about the Japanese settled at Tawao.[497] 'No British naval or military aid is available locally, nor is expected to be if war with Japan were to break out.' To remove the Japanese in advance would be 'a very provocative step in an exposed territory where our virtual defenceless-ness makes it especially inadvisable that the Japanese should have excuse to stage an "incident"'. Gent thought that the economic measures against the Japanese in general would reduce their position in North Borneo, stopping exports from their estates and freezing assets.[498] The danger, Bromley thought, was not of an uprising but of 'an uprising timed to coincide with outside help'. Had the War Office decided to abandon North Borneo? Clarke asked. Had the effect on Netherlands India been considered?[499]

The War Office thought it unlikely that the Japanese would deliver major attacks on North Borneo and Malaya concurrently. Britain had to concentrate its deficient forces at the most vital points rather than spread them over large areas. The effect on the Indies had been considered; 'it may be advisable to remember the large numbers of totally unprotected and isolated Dutch islands in this area'.[500] Members of the Far Eastern Department pointed to the risk of a raid, rather than a major attack, and to the proximity of the Dutch oilfields. But it was the War Office's business.[501]

The talks with the Portuguese

In September the Australian Government suggested that 'undue Japanese penetration' of Portuguese Timor had been prevented. But it revived consideration of the possibility that it might be occupied by the Japanese, with or without the agreement of Portugal, whether a war had begun or not. The UK, Australia and the Netherlands should 'agree beforehand on what preventive action is feasible', and conversations should be initiated with the Dutch.[502] A Japanese landing, S.H. Hebble-thwaite at the Foreign Office thought, would 'constitute a most serious threat to our communications'. The COS favoured concerting measures with the Dutch, suggesting that they would involve an Australian commit-ment additional to that in respect of Kupang. It was agreed that the matter should be raised with Portugal, with which military conversations were in prospect.[503] The Australians were asked if they would accept a further commitment should the Portuguese agree to accept reinforce-ments. It was suggested that the Portuguese should be asked whether they would accept 'outside help' if 'the military authorities on the spot' found it necessary, and that they and the Dutch should be asked to agree to discussions with the Australians about preventive action, and about action to be taken 'if a threat should actually eventuate'.[504] The Australian Government agreed.[505]

A Japanese Consul meanwhile arrived in Dili,[506] which prompted the Australians at the suggestion of the British to give Ross consular rank.[507] In addition a commercial aviation agreement was about to be signed.[508] Eden questioned Dr Monteiro, the Portuguese ambassador in London, who said that the Australians had made a similar agreement, which they had failed to implement. It would, Monteiro said, be some time before the agreement came into operation since a technical agreement was also needed. He 'concluded that the position of his Government was a difficult one, since Timor was subject to strong Japanese pressure and was itself so far from Portugal'. But the Portuguese were fully alive to the possibility of infiltration.[509] In fact Qantas had been flying to Dili.[510]

The Foreign Office were nervous about raising the question of military collaboration in Timor lest it scare the Portuguese off conversations that were important for the Atlantic.[511] Their line was that they only granted commercial facilities to the Japanese and were aware of the danger of infiltration. 'They will not therefore readily agree even to discuss the hypothesis of Japanese attack, and still less to go beyond this and entrust the defence of Timor to outside parties.' They were 'so susceptible and touchy' about their empire that the British should not say they were discussing it with the Dutch.[512] 'This will form a very difficult business to handle', Eden felt, although he was 'prepared to try to break the ground with Dr Monteiro. He will surely take the line that Timor is in no danger and will have Macao in mind.'[513] The idea was now to raise the issue as a sequel to the conversation about infiltration.[514]

At a conversation on 4 November Monteiro indicated that the Portuguese would resist an attack. Would Portugal seek Britain's help under the alliance? Eden asked. If so, secret staff conversations might take place.[515] On 10 November Monteiro saw Cadogan. He felt sure Portugal would resist an attack on Timor and be glad of British assistance. Although he had not yet secured a reply from Lisbon, he also thought that his government would want military discussions in London in the first instance.[516] A meeting of staff officers was thus arranged on 12 November.[517] The answer from Lisbon indeed expressed the opinion that 'it would be useful to open conversations in London on the possibility of establishing a joint plan of action in case of need', although it was open to the British to suggest a local venue for talks.[518] Frank Roberts, of the Central Department of the Foreign Office, thought that the Portuguese reaction was favourable enough to justify involving the Dutch and the Australians, 'but if the Portuguese show any signs of taking fright, we should at once offer to restrict the conversations to the Portuguese and ourselves'.[519]

Eden had mentioned his conversations with Monteiro of 21 October and 4 November to van Kleffens who indicated that the Dutch would wish to be involved in any staff talks. The Portuguese, Eden replied, might see difficulties in this; 'nevertheless, I would throw a fly over the Portuguese Ambassador ... and see whether he looked like rising to it'.[520] When the Portuguese had selected their representative Eden thought the British might suggest inviting the Dutch too. 'But this proposal would have to be made with caution.'[521] The C in C FE wanted to assure the Dutch that the British recognised their interest in Timor. Some regret had been expressed in the Indies about 'omission of any reference to them in recent speeches and [it was] most important for the defence of this area to maintain their full co-operation'.[522] Clarke repeated: 'it is a question of handling the Portuguese delicately'.[523] The Foreign Office now prepared an aide-mémoire for Monteiro, formally proposing talks in Singapore and involving the Dutch as well as the Australians.[524] Cadogan gave it to him on 2 December. He had some doubt about discussions with the Dutch. Cadogan said 'that in any event we should be in consultation with the latter, who were our Allies and if we could get into contact with the Portuguese there would then effectively be consultation between the three Powers'.[525]

The Dutch also approached the government in Lisbon and asked the British to support their representations. Cadogan told Michiels that the Portuguese had 'shown some hesitation about discussing the defence of Portuguese Timor with a belligerent with whom they were not allied'. Sir Ronald Campbell should support the Dutch representations, Cadogan decided.[526] In the event Monteiro delivered a reply on 5 December, which indicated that the Portuguese Government had no objection to sending an officer to Singapore to discuss with a representative of the British High Command the question of defending Timor in the event of a Japanese attack arising out of war between Japan and Britain or the US. That officer could be informed, through the British, of the views of the Dutch and could exchange views with a NEI representative 'on the eventualities which might affect that part of Timor belonging to the Netherlands and which, in consequence, would be matters of interest to the defence of Portuguese Timor'.[527] Portuguese Premier Salazar told Baron Pallandt, the Dutch ambassador in Lisbon, of what Campbell called 'this typically Portuguese arrangement'.[528] Clarke thought it should not prevent satisfactory meetings.[529]

If war broke out, Roger Makins had commented on 4 December, it was 'fairly evident that the Dutch will act without waiting on Dr Salazar'.[530] On 10 December Duff Cooper asked if they should.[531] 'We have to go carefully with the Portuguese in view of important discussions now proceeding with them regarding other parts of the Portuguese empire.'[532] At the

Foreign Office Sir Orme Sargent put it to Monteiro that Australian and Dutch troops should help Timor if it was attacked and that, as Japan might act at any moment, the local authorities should be given 'wide latitude so as to ensure that the assistance contemplated was in good time'.[533] The Portuguese Government agreed.[534]

Fear of Japanese submarines prompted action, however. The Portuguese had argued that action would be premature, make them a belligerent, lose them Macao.[535]

> Dr Sampayo was unable to believe that a landing would be forced in opposition to the wishes of the Portuguese Governor who had no authority to permit it in advance of a definite Japanese movement against his territory. When he at length grasped that it might already have occurred ... he said "then you will have reversed the roles and have done the very thing your avoidance of which hitherto has given you the high moral authority which you enjoy among all decent people".[536]

The Portuguese, the Foreign Office concluded, wanted to claim that they had given way to force majeure.[537] The Governor also protested to the Australians.[538]

The Foreign Office saw this as a volte face. In fact the Portuguese had agreed only to accept aid if attacked and were clearly anticipating talks due to be held in Singapore. The Foreign Office itself had wanted to accept that approach because of the importance of other Portuguese possessions, such as the Azores and Cape Verde. What the Consul-General in Batavia called a timely occupation[539] cut short their diplomacy. Salazar was to protest again, and again in vain, when the Japanese invaded Timor late in February 1942.[540] By then Singapore had itself fallen.

Conclusion

It is easy in retrospect to speak of World War II as if it began in 1939. The war of 1939 was, however, a European war. In some sense it indeed contained the possibility of a world war since it held out the prospect of a change in the status quo in Europe that would affect the interests of powers outside Europe. That did not mean that a worldwide war was unavoidable. A change in the status quo in Europe would in particular affect the security of the United States and its relationship with Latin America. If the Germans triumphed the US would lose the security that the British navy had helped to give it. The Americans were to realise this in the great crisis of 1940. Then, indeed, their security seemed to be so threatened by the prospect that the defeat of France would be followed by the defeat of Britain that the US began to put a new emphasis on hemispheric defence. It did, however, retain its concern to keep Britain in the war if there seemed a chance, both moral and material, of its survival. It certainly retained the hope that it could avoid engaging in the war itself. President Roosevelt in particular treasured the possibility that there would be no need to send American forces to Europe as in the war of 1914–18. Measures short of direct involvement might suffice. In a sense it was this anxiety to avoid such a war that in the end led to it by a different route.

The European war had implications for the Japanese too. Faced with Chinese nationalism, Russian communism and the depression, they had increasingly accepted the initiatives of the military despite their long-standing policy of working with the West and their more recent accept-ance of the Washington treaties and Shidehara diplomacy. Nevertheless, they retained something of their old caution and were certainly disposed to stage their initiatives to take advantage of opportunities that the international situation might afford. The move into Manchuria took

363

place at a time when opposition from other powers was unlikely to be forceful, and it resulted not in sanctions but in the Stimson doctrine of non-recognition. The Japanese could conclude that other powers would not forcefully intervene. Turning to China itself, they sought to use alliance with Germany to pressure both the Soviet Union and the maritime powers. Only the following year – and, it seems, with less than full support from the military – did they resort to undeclared war with China. They again faced disapproval from the West, which also afforded limited aid to China. Closer relations with Germany, they thought, might turn the balance. The Nazi–Soviet non-aggression pact that started the war in Europe stunned the Japanese.

They had, however, begun to look to the south. For them it was in particular a source of oil that might render them more independent of American and Caribbean supplies and, in a wider sense, more able to pursue an autonomous policy in face of American disapproval. Even at the time of the Manchuria crisis the Dutch in the Indies had been apprehensive. The Japanese, moreover, began to conceive of Southeast Asia as part of a region in which they might be a leading partner, a sphere that was theirs in a world that seemed increasingly likely to be divided into spheres as the economic depression continued and economic barriers were set up. The south was important for itself. It was also important for the China war. The Japanese conceived that cutting off the KMT regime from outside sources of supply was a way of bringing its resistance to an end.

The 1936 policy had envisaged footsteps in the south. The opening of the war in Europe, despite its initial shock, offered the chance of exerting further pressure on the European powers that dominated much of Southeast Asia. Led by Konoe, the Japanese saw great opportunities in 1940, the year of French defeat. Anxious not to break the continuity of their colonial rule, the French made a deal with the Japanese, and admitted them into northern Indo-China. That action did not prevent a Japanese 'mediation' between Indo-China and Thailand that, while not satisfying the latter, certainly humiliated the former. At the same time the Japanese had pressed additional economic demands on the Netherlands Indies.

The British had been the leading colonial power in Southeast Asia. Their own possessions, Malaya, source of tin and rubber, and Singapore, a commercial entrepôt and naval base, had, however, only become of major importance in the twentieth century. Yet their capacity to uphold the colonial framework, or indeed to use their naval base effectively, had now greatly diminished. The opening of the war reduced their capacity still further, and the defeat of France and the entry of the Italians into the war forced them to focus more attention on the Mediterranean. Singapore became 'an empty garage'.[1] The British resorted to diplomacy. At odds with Vichy elsewhere, they nevertheless endeavoured to sustain the regime in Indo-China that acknowledged Vichy. In Thailand they were tempted to advocate a moderate revision of the status quo in the hope of avoiding a larger disruption. They hoped the Dutch would resist the more extreme demands of the Japanese without provoking them too much. They were not prepared, however, to offer any of these states, even the Dutch, their allies in Europe, a guarantee of support in the event of a Japanese attack. They insisted that such a guarantee could only be given if the US also gave such an undertaking.

The arguments the British rehearsed on this topic almost always revolved on the range of their commitments. Those commitments were said to be so extensive that it was impossible to determine in advance where the limited British force available might best be applied. The argument seems to have been genuine. It combined an appreciation of the actual position of the Dutch with a sense that obligations, if accepted, had to be fulfilled. It did not prevent, and indeed rather encouraged, their suggesting that the Dutch should take the initiative in approaching the Americans, although they did not make the same suggestion to the Australians, to whom they felt themselves bound.

Approaching the Americans was indeed seen as a delicate task. Throughout the 1930s their attitude had helped to determine the approach of the British in East Asia. In particular their interest in the integrity of China – based less on economic interest than on an idealistic world view – had prevented the British coming to terms with Japan. Any such deal would be likely to compromise the future of China and thus alienate the Americans. Yet increasingly the British recognised that it was essential to retain American friendship and the potential of American support not only in respect of Asia but also in respect of Europe. America's views conditioned British policy in another way. Too definite an endeavour to commit the Americans might produce the reverse effect by prompting isolationist or anti-imperialist attitudes.

While the US, however, had endorsed the integrity of China and stated the Stimson doctrine, it had done little to sustain the former or implement the latter. While it retained the Philippines it had set up the Philippines Commonwealth in 1936 and committed itself to granting it independence ten years later. There was no certainty, therefore, that the US would interpose to prevent the further advance of Japanese power. This book argues that the impact of the European war produced a series of actions from the US that the Japanese regarded as drastic, stepped up as they were when, on Hitler's invading Russia, the Japanese turned south. But for the European war the Southeast Asian colonial regimes might have given way to some form of Japanese hegemony. The European war gave the US an interest in colonial Southeast Asia that it had not before had. 'The linkage of American security interests in Asia and Europe was a somewhat paradoxical development.' It 'served to strengthen the American position against Japan', but 'served also to define it as peripheral: a function of America's much greater and more vital interest in the survival of the anti-fascist allies in Europe'.[2]

The survival of the British in Europe – itself seen as desirable for the US and perhaps a means of avoiding direct entry into the war – was connected with its continued access to the resources of Southeast Asia, India and Australasia and the denial of those resources to their opponents. The Americans justified their actions primarily in this interest, so explaining them on occasion even to the Japanese. China was always less important to them than Southeast Asia had now become. The way that they put forward their policy made it impossible, however, to make a deal over the one and not the other. The US had expressed their policy towards China in terms of non-recognition and in terms of principles for the conduct of international relations that validated change only by peaceful negotiation. They also sought to use those doctrines in opposing Japanese moves in regard to Southeast Asia during 1940–41. That approach, and the concerns of China, helped to make it impossible to pursue the modus vivendi to which Hull was attracted in November 1941 and which might have dislodged Japan's decision for war.[3] In some sense this policy was more consistent with the earlier approaches of the British than those of the Americans; it envisaged deferment. Yet now the British were doubtful. The approach would undermine the bolder line of July in which the powers had joined the US in an attempt to block a change in the status quo.

For Hull it was a matter of gaining time. Yet even that should not necessarily be interpreted as gaining time to fight a war more effectively. The US, and indeed the UK, did not believe that the Japanese would go to war with both of them. A remembrance of Japanese caution, a mistaken impression of the fragility of their economy and an absurd underestimation of their determination led to a quite unfounded optimism. The economic measures of July 1941 were widely expected to stop them in their tracks. A firm stand was what Churchill advocated in early November. The view was that, if time were won, reinforcements in Manila and in Singapore would redouble Japanese caution and perhaps defer the crisis. A war in the East might be avoided. The Japanese, however, had adopted a different conclusion and went to war on a bolder scale than the Western leaders had considered possible. The European war was transformed into a world war. Lord Hankey had thought that some incident analogous to the blowing up of the *Maine* in Havana that precipitated the war with Spain in 1898, but bigger, would be needed 'to set American public opinion aflame'.[4] The attack on Pearl Harbor was just that.

Southeast Asia was subjected to war although its inhabitants played the most limited part in the decision. Its resources, not its peoples, were in mind. Only in Burma and the Philippines did the political structures afford them even a limited role. The war was to destroy the colonial regimes and, as the French had perhaps foreseen, they were never to re-establish themselves effectively. The prospect for Southeast Asia was a political independence more real, perhaps, than it might have enjoyed if the process of change had not been so precipitate. 'The Europeanised "Far East" has gone, and the organisation of European activities there in the future will have to be rebuilt on entirely different foundations from those prevailing before 1939.'[5] Quite how different it took time for the Europeans to realise, and it took further struggle, too.

This book has been a study of Britain's diplomacy . That had sought to defer or to avoid war in Asia, while ensuring that, whether or not it came about, the US would be in the war. The policy was unsuccessful in one sense, successful in another. The war in Asia was not put off long enough to avoid a catastrophic defeat, but the US entered the world conflict and so ensured the defeat of Britain's opponents.

There was British diplomacy in Southeast Asia as well as about it. This book has sought to place the former in the context of the latter. It was strikingly active. It sought to limit Japanese penetration in Southeast Asia and to sustain those opposed to it. There were many obstacles. In French Indo-China it was necessary to try to sustain the Vichy authorities despite the relations of their masters with the Germans and of themselves with the Japanese. The policy towards the Thais was largely one of concilia-tion, despite their irredentism and the poor relations with the French and the Americans that it promoted. The British felt unable to offer adequate promises of cooperation to the Dutch in the Indies.

Indeed the diplomacy of the British was always weakened by their demonstrable lack of military and naval strength in the East. The effectiveness of diplomacy ultimately depends on the possession of power. Bluff, as Cadogan recognised, was not enough. The British, how-ever, were ingenious as well as pertinacious in their use of economic and financial resources in the absence of military ones. Their attempts to limit Japanese penetration were in a sense successful. Indo-China more or less excepted, the Japanese had after all to invade Southeast Asia to achieve their objectives.

The book has given less attention to Britain's own territories, although in some sense handling them was a matter of diplomacy, too. One resource was rarely or belatedly called on, the peoples of Southeast Asia themselves. In general the colonial structure was to be defended from outside or not at all.

Confidence, resolution, enterprise and devotion to the cause will inspire every one of us in the fighting services, while from the civilian population, Malay, Chinese, or Indian, we expect that patience, endurance and serenity which is the great virtue of the East and which will go far to assist the fighting men to gain a final and complete victory.[6]

The debacle at Singapore led the British not to abandon their empire in Southeast Asia but to seek to put it on a new footing once regained. 'The Malayan disaster has shocked us into sudden attention to the structure of our colonial empire.'[7] The influential analyst, Margery Perham, drew conclusions from the fall of Singapore that were shared by other policy-makers. They contributed to the plans to reshape Britain's relationships with dependent territories in Southeast Asia and elsewhere in terms of what Lord Hailey called 'partnership'.[8] Paradoxical though the venture was, and indeed had to be, the colonial power planned to engage in 'nation-building'. The empire would come to exist of self-governing dominions on the model of the settler states, cooperating with each other and with Britain at their head. In Asia that was also seen to involve a new relationship between East and West; they had to meet. It was an ambitious as well as a paradoxical policy. The plans the British drew up were rapidly adjusted, if not abandoned, soon after their return. Yet they did not abandon all their aims. They pressed the French and the Dutch to come to terms with nationalism, and they sought to do so themselves. In the final analysis a stable Southeast Asia was their prime objective. It even took preference, in the case of Burma, over keeping a country in the Commonwealth.

The advance of communism made these policies more urgent. Communism had always been seen as a major threat to the empire. It not only threatened subversion within territories; it also challenged the concept that had been the basis of British thinking about the world since the first half of the nineteenth century: that of a world of states the relationships of which were above all economic. After World War II, the threat of communism was demonstrated by Soviet policies in east and central Europe. The triumph of the Chinese communists followed and redoubled Britain's concern about Southeast Asia. What it sought to do in some ways paralleled what it had attempted in regard to the Japanese before the Pacific war. It tried within its limited means to strengthen resistance within Southeast Asia. It also sought to involve the US. But again American power was used in ways that were not entirely consonant with Britain's attitudes nor with its wish to turn to account, as ever in Southeast Asia, the interests of India.

Personalia

Amery Leopold S. Amery (1873–1955). First Lord of the Admiralty, 1922–24; Secretary of State for the Colonies 1924–29, for Dominion Affairs, 1925–29, for India and Byrma, 1940–45.

Bruce Stanley Melbourne Bruce (1883–1967). Prime Minister of Australia, 1923–29; High Commissioner to London 1933–45. Served in Churchill's War Cabinet and on the Pacific War Council, 1942–45.

Butler Richard A. (later Lord) Butler (1902–1982). Parliamentary Under-Secretary at the India Office, 1932–38; at the Foreign Office, 1938–41; Minister of Education, 1941–45; Home Secretary, 1957–62.

Cadogan Alexander Cadogan (1884–1968). British Ambassador at Peking 1935–36; Deputy Under-Secretary at Foreign Office, 1936–37; Permanent Under-Secretary, 1938–46; permanent representative to the UN, 1946–50.

Cooper A. Duff Cooper, later Viscount Norwich (1890–1954). Secretary of State for War, 1935–37; First Lord of the Admiralty, 1937–38; Minister of Information, 1940–41; Minister of State in the Far East, 1941–42; Ambassador to France, 1944–47.

Cranborne Robert Gascoigne-Cecil (1893–1972), Viscount Cranborne, later Marquess of Salisbury. Parliamentary Under-Secretary at the Foreign Office, 1935–38; Secretary of State for the Dominions, 1940–42, 1943–51; Lord President of the Council, 1951–57.

Direck Direck Chaiyanam (1905–67). Secretary to the Thai Cabinet, 1935–40; Deputy Foreign Minister, 1940–41; Foreign Minister, August–December 1941; Ambassador to Tokyo, 1942–43; Ambassador to London, 1947–48.

Eden Anthony Eden (1897–1977). Foreign Secretary, 1935–38, 1940–45, 1951–55; Prime Minister 1955–56.

Grew Joseph C. Grew (1880–1965). US Ambassador to Turkey, 1927–31; to Japan, 1931–34.

Halifax Edward F.L. Wood (1881–1959), Viscount Halifax, later first Earl. Viceroy of India, as Lord Irwin 1926–31; Foreign Secretary, 1938–40; Ambassador to the US, 1941–46.

Hankey Sir Maurice (later Lord) Hankey (1877–1963). Secretary to the Cabinet and CID, 1916–38; Minister without Portfolio, 1939–40; Chancellor of the Duchy of Lancaster, 1940-41; Paymaster-General, 1941–42.

Hornbeck Stanley K. Hornbeck (1883–1966). Chief of Division of Far Eastern Affairs, Department of State, 1928–37; Adviser on Political Relations, 1937–44; Ambassador to the Netherlands, 1944–47.

Latham Sir John Latham (1877–1964). Attorney-General, Australia, 1925–29; Deputy Prime Minister and Minister for External Affairs, 1932–34; leader of the Australian mission to East Indies, China and Japan, 1934; Minister for Australia to Japan, 1940–41; Chief Justice of Australia, 1935–52.

Lothian Philip Kerr (1882–1940), later 11th Marquess of Lothian. Editor, *The Round Table*, 1910–16; secretary to the Prime Minister, 1916–21; Parliamentary Under-Secretary, India Office, 1931–32; Ambassador to the US, 1939–40.

Matsuoka Matsuoka Yosuke (1880–1946). Director, South Manchuria Railway Company, 1921–26; Japanese delegate to League of Nations, 1932–33; president, SMR, 1936–39; Japanese Foreign Minister, 1940–41. Indicted as a war criminal, 1946.

Nagano Nagano Osami (1880–1947). Japanese Navy Minister, 1936–41; Naval Chief of Staff, 1941–44. Indicted as a war criminal, 1946.

Pibun Luang Pibun Songkram (1897–1964). Thai Minister of Defence, 1934–41; Prime Minister, 1938–44; Army Commander, 1939–44; Minister of Foreign Affairs, 1939–August 1941; Prime Minister, 1948–57.

Pound Dudley Pound (1877–1943). C in C, Mediterranean Fleet, 1936–39; First Sea Lord, 1939–43.

Quezon Manuel L. Quezon (1878–1944). Philippines resident commissioner to the US, 1909–16; president of Philippines Senate, 1916–35; first President of the Commonwealth of the Philippines, 1935–44.

Strang William (later Lord) Strang (1893–1978). Assistant Under-Secretary of State, Foreign Office, 1939–43; Permanent Under-Secretary, 1940–53.

Wan Wan Waityakorn Vorovarn (1891–1976), later Prince Narathip, grandson of King Mongkut (19th family). Adviser to Thai Ministry of Foreign Affairs and to Prime Minister, 1933–45; Ambassador to Washington, 1947–52; deputy Prime Minister, 1958–68.

Notes

1 Before September 1939

1 q. N. Meaney, *The Search for Security in the Pacific 1901–14*, Sydney University Press, Sydney, 1976, p. 10. See also p. 205.
2 q. Meaney, p. 252.
3 Meaney, p. 184. Cf M. Bassett, *Sir Joseph Ward*, Auckland University Press, Auckland, 1993, pp. 174ff.
4 Sho Kuwajima, *First World War and Asia: Indian Mutiny in Singapore (1915)*, Author, Osaka, 1988, p. 80.
5 q. S. Murakami, 'Japan's thrust into French Indochina 1940–1945', PhD thesis, New York University, 1981, p. 36.
6 R.J. Moore, *Liberalism and Indian Politics*, Arnold, London, 1966, p. 112.
7 q. N. Tarling, 'The Singapore Mutiny', *Journal of the Royal Asiatic Society Malaysian Branch*, LV, 2 (1982), p. 26.
8 q. Hosoya Chihiro, in Ian Nish (ed.), *Anglo-Japanese Alienation, 1919–1952*, Cambridge University Press, Cambridge, 1982, p. 8.
9 q. Justus D. Doenecke, *The Diplomacy of Frustration*, Hoover Institution Press, Stanford CA, 1981, p. 13.
10 Fiona Venn, *Oil Diplomacy in the Twentieth Century*, Macmillan, London, 1986, p. 88.
11 Yoshitake Oki, *Konoe Fumimaro*, Tokyo, 1983, pp. 10–13, 27–8.
12 David J. Lu, *From the Marco Polo Bridge to Pearl Harbor*, Public Affairs Press, Washington, 1961, p. 35. Cf Michael A. Barnhart, *Japan Prepares for Total War*, Cornell University Press, Ithaca, NY, 1987, pp. 105–6.
13 Minutes by Cadogan, 6 May 1937, Vansittart, s.d. q. M. Murfett, *Fool-proof Relations: The Search for Anglo-American Naval Cooperation during the Chamberlain Years 1937–1940*, Singapore University Press, 1984, p. 17.
14 S. Hornbeck, 13 Apr. 1935, q. K. Martin Friedrich, 'In search of a Far Eastern policy: Joseph Grew, Stanley Hornbeck, and American–Japanese relations, 1937–1941', PhD thesis, Washington State, 1974, p. 43.
15 FRUS J I, p. 326.
16 Paul Gore–Booth, *With Great Truth and Respect*, Constable, London, 1974, p. 146.

17 P. Lowe, 'Great Britain and the coming of the Pacific war, 1939–41', *Transactions of the Royal Historical Society*, 5th Series, 24 (1974), p. 43.
18 Cf Murfett, p. 240.
19 Ashton–Gwatkin, 4 Jan. 1938. FO 371/21041[F11205/615/23], Public Record Office, London.
20 E.M. Andrews, *The Writing on the Wall*, Allen & Unwin, Sydney, 1987, pp. 165–7.
21 q. Andrews, p. 172.
22 Clive–FO, 7 Jan. 1935, 8, confidential, and minutes. FO 371/19359[F1090/483/23].
23 Memorandum, 6 May 1937. FO 371/21024 [F 2638/597/61].
24 Appreciation, 14 June 1937. See Murfett, p. 31.
25 Murfett, p. 20.
26 AFPD, I, pp. 80, 81; Memorandum, 28 May. ibid., I, pp. 90–6.
27 Cf Minute by Cadogan, 1 June. FO 371/21025 [F3281/577/61].
28 Conversation between Davis and Cadogan, 24 Mar 1937. FO 371/21024 [F2348/597/61].
29 Minutes, 5 May 1937. FO 371/21024 [F2586/597/61].
30 Lindsay–Eden, 28 May 1937, 476. FO 371/21025 [F3372/597/61].
31 Dodds–Eden, 17 June 1937, 328. FO 371/21025 [F4002/597/61].
32 q. Murfett, p. 81.
33 D. Reynolds, *The Creation of the Anglo-American Alliance 1937–41*, Europa, London, 1981, p. 61.
34 Murfett, p. 154.
35 B.A. Lee, *Britain and the Sino-Japanese War, 1937–9. A Study in the Dilemmas of British Decline*, Stanford University Press, Stanford, CA,1973, pp. 140–5.
36 Minutes, 2 June 1938. FO 371/22176 [F 5943/5942/61].
37 Statement, 2 Nov. 1938. FRUS J I, p. 478.
38 Lee, p. 172.
39 Murfett, p. 241.
40 R. John Pritchard, 'Far Eastern influences upon British strategy towards the great powers, 1937–1939', PhD thesis, University of London, 1979, p. 180.
41 J.W. Morley, *The China Quagmire*, Columbia University Press, New York, 1983, pp. 356 ff.
42 q. Murfett, p. 254.
43 Jonathan G. Utley, 'The Department of State and the Far East, 1957–41: A study of the ideas behind its Diplomacy', PhD thesis, University of Illinois at Urbana–Champaign, 1970, p. 140.
44 Pritchard, p. 167. See Alvin D. Coox, *Nomonhan Japan against Russia, 1939*, Stanford University Press, Stanford, CA, 1985, ch. 14ff.
45 Minute, 23 Dec. 1938, q. p. Lowe, *Great Britain and the Origins of the Pacific War*, Clarendon Press, Oxford, 1977, p. 53.
46 Cf David E. Omissi, *Air Power and Colonial Control*, Manchester, 1990, p. 51, on south-west Arabia.
47 Cf Chancellor–USFO, 25 July 1922. FO 371/8051[F 2483/2197/23].
48 Memorandum by Ashton-Gwatkin, 4 July 1921. FO 371/6704 [F2840/2840/23].
49 Memorandum by Ridout, 12 Dec. 1919. ibid.
50 Cf P. J.A. Idenburg, 'Het Nederlandse Antwoord op het Indonesisch Nationalisme', in H. Baudet and J.J. Brugmans (eds), *Balans van Beleid*, Van Gorcum, Assen, 1961, p. 124.
51 q. J.A. de Moor, 'A very unpleasant relationship', in G.J.A. Raven and N.A.M. Rodger (eds), *Navies and Armies*, Donald, Edinburgh, 1990, p. 59.

52 C. Smit, *Nederland in de Eerste Wereldoorlog*, Walters-Noordhoff, Groningen, 1971, pp. 202–3.
53 Cf Don Dignan, *The Indian Revolutionary Problem in British Diplomacy 1914–1919*, Allied Publications, New Delhi, 1985, ch.3.
54 Minute by Langley, n.d. FO 371/2691 [235431/31446].
55 Minute by Ashton-Gwatkin, 7 Mar. 1921. FO 371/6696 [F902/902/23].
56 Memorandum, 8 Sept. 1921. FO 371/6696 [F 3600/901/23].
57 Crosby–Henderson, 18 Sept. 1929, 116. FO 371/14146 [W10248/840/29].
58 Russell–Henderson, 6 May 1931, 160. FO 371/15753 [W5373/5373/29].
59 Cf Address to the Society for the Study of Military Science, 13 Nov. 1931, in Russell–Simon, 18 April 1931, 368. FO 371/15752 [W13447/2489/29].
60 Fitzmaurice–FO, 28 Nov 1932, 100. FO 371/16488 [W14012/2193/29]
61 Fitzmaurice–FO, 9 February 1933, 15, Confidential. FO 371/17407 [W1919/1224/29].
62 Russell–Simon, 9 Mar. 1933, 98. FO 371/17165 [F1824/1539/23].
63 Telegram from Russell, 10 Mar., 4 S. FO 371/17165 [F1709/1539/23]; Lindley–Simon, 31Mar. 1933, 192. FO 371/17165 [F2948/1539/23].
64 Fitzmaurice–FO, 1 May 1933, 52. FO 371/17407 [W6671/663/29].
65 Fitzmaurice–FO, 29 June 1933, 77. FO 371/17407 [W9005/663/29].
66 Memorandum, 13 Dec. 1933. FO 371/17407 [A14395/663/29].
67 Carey–DOT, 25 Oct. 1932. FO 371/16489 [W13298/2386/29].
68 Howard Dick, 'Japan's economic expansion in the Netherlands Indies between the First and Second World Wars', *Journal of Southeast Asian Studies*, 22(2) (September 1989), p. 254.
69 Minute by Ashton–Gwatkin, 30 June 1934. FO 371/18571 [W6211/90/29].
70 Minute, 24 July 1934, on Fitzmaurice–FO, 20/6/34, 89, confidential. FO 371/18579 [W6893/6893/29].
71 Memoranda in Dickens–Orde, 22 May 1934. FO 371/18186 [F2996/652/23].
72 Minute, 22 June 1934. ibid.
73 Minute, 26 June. ibid.
74 Minute, 2 July. ibid.
75 Minute, 4 July. ibid.
76 Minute, 6 July. ibid.
77 Minute, 11 July. ibid.
78 Orde–Dickens, 14 August 1934. ibid.
79 Montgomery–Orde, 12 Nov. 1934. ibid.
80 Osborne–Orde, 31 Dec. 1934. FO371/19553[F231/231/23].
81 Memorandum, 16 Feb. 1935. FO 371/19354 [F1234/231/23].
82 Montgomery–Simon, 6 Feb. 1935. FO 371/19353 [F881/231/23].
83 Minute, 3 July 1936. FO 371/20290 [F3828/2328/23].
84 Minute, 22 April 1936. FO 371/20507 [W3351/498/29].
85 Montgomery–Sargent, 11 Apr. 1936, private and secret. ibid.
86 Montgomery–Sargent, 22 Apr. 1936. FO 371/20507 [W3583/498/29].
87 Minute and papers. ibid.
88 Cooper–Eden, 10 June 1936, and minute; Vansittart–Hankey, 2 July. [W5230/498/29]
89 1245–B, 8 July 1936. CAB 4/24, Public Record Office.
90 Minute, 9 July 1936. FO 371/20507 [W6184/498/29].
91 CID, 280th, 10 July 1936. CAB 2/6.
92 Cabinet, 52(36) 7, 15 July. CAB 23/85.
93 Eden–Le Rougetel, 21 July 1936, 298. FO 371/20504 [W6771/252/29].
94 CID 1256–B, 27 July 1936. CAB 4/24.

95 Memorandum, 6 May 1937. FO 371/21024 [F2638/597/61].
96 Minutes on Fitzmaurice/FO, 22 July 1937, 106. FO371/21026 [F5865/1326/61].
97 FO–Montgomery, 13 Dec. 1937. FO 371/21026 [F10516/1326/61].
98 Memorandum, 23 Nov. 1937. FO 371/21026 [F10283/1450/61].
99 Memorandum by Inskip, 7 Jan. 1938. CID 1385/B. CAB 4/27.
100 Minute by Orde, 17 Jan. FO 371/22172 [F545/487/61].
101 Minute, n.d. ibid.
102 CID 307th, 20 Jan. 1938. CAB 2/7.
103 Minute by Ronald, 16 Feb. 1938. FO 371/22172 [F1989/487/61].
104 COS 838, 6 Feb. 1938, circulated as CP 40 (39). CAB 24/283.
105 Fitzmaurice–FO, 10 Apr. 1939, 76. FO 371/23549 [F4495/2644/61].
106 Admiralty–FO, 10 Apr., and minute. FO 371/23550 [F3512/3512/61].
107 Fitzmaurice–FO, 6 Apr., 75. FO 371/23549 [F3961/2742/61].
108 Lambert–FO, 27 July 1939, 154. FO371/23549 [F8465/2742/61].
109 F.B. Harrison, *The Cornerstone of Philippine Independence*, Century, New York, 1922, p. 197.
110 Veto message, 13 Jan. 1933, in Grayson L. Kirk, *Philippine Independence*, Farrer & Rinehart, New York, 1936, pp. 227–34.
111 Memorandum by Ashton–Gwatkin, 25 July 1921. FO 371/6678 [F2839/115/23].
112 Stimson–Bingham, 15 February 1932, in Lindsay–Simon, 6 Apr. 1932, 581. FO371/15876 [A2355/312/45].
113 Lindley–Simon, 20 Apr. 1932, 210. FO 371/15876 [A2837/312/45]
114 q. Carlos Quirino, *Quezon: Paladin of Philippine Freedom*, Filipiniana Book Guild, Manila, 1971, p. 212.
115 Minute, 1 Nov. 1933. FO371/16611 [A7649/89/45].
116 Report, 31 Aug. 1932. FO371/15877 [A6810/312/45].
117 Harrington–FO, 20 Sept. 1933, 49. FO371/16611 [A7649/89/45].
118 Minute by Hogg, 13 June. FO371/17576 [A4667/17/45].
119 Sansom–Orde, 11 May 1934. FO371/17576 [A4667/17/45].
120 Memorandum by Gore-Booth, 17 Oct. 1934. FO371/17576 [A8212/17/45].
121 Minutes by Gore-Booth, 28 Jan; Craigie, 29 Jan. FO371/18762 [A722/722/45].
122 Memorandum by Foulds, 19 Oct. 1934. FO371/17576 [A9645/17/45].
123 Phillips–Craigie, 11 Feb. 1935. FO371/18762 [A1332/722/45].
124 Memorandum, 27 Feb. 1935. FO371/18763 [A2147/1722/45].
125 Osborne–Craigie, 4 Apr. 1935. FO371/18763 [A3505/722/45].
126 Osborne–Craigie, 12 Apr. 1935. FO371/18763 [A3728/722/45].
127 Minutes. ibid.
128 T. Friend, *Between Two Empires*, Yale University Press, New Haven, CT, 1965, p. 187.
129 Blunt–Hoare, 12 Dec. 1935, 101, and minutes, Hohler, 21 Jan., Troutbeck, 28 Jan. FO371/19822 [A533/34/45].
130 Minutes. FO371/19824 [A10298/34/45].
131 Conversation, 19 Feb. 1937. FO371/20650 [A1479/20/4].
132 Mallet–Troutbeck, 5 Mar. 1937. FO371/20650 [A209/20/45].
133 Minute, 18 Dec. 1936. FO371/19824 [A10298/34/45].
134 Hodsoll–Mallet, 15 Feb. 1937, and minute, 6 Mar. FO371/20650 [A1699/20/45].
135 Minute, 26 Mar. 1937. FO371/20650 [A2565/20/45]. CID 1321–B, CAB 4/26.

136 CID, 1331–B 7 June 1937. CAB 4/26.
137 294th, 17 June. CAB 2/6.
138 Minute, 27 April. FO371/21024 [F2214/597/61].
139 Minute, 14 June. FO371/21025 [F3372/597/61].
140 Minute, 15 June. FO371/20651 [A4237/20/45].
141 Minutes, 15, 15, 16 July. FO371/20651 [A4989/20/45].
142 Troutbeck's minute, 15 June; Cadogan–MacDermot, 24 June 1937. [A4237].
143 Turner–Troutbeck, 17 Aug. 1937. FO371/20651 [A7088/20/45].
144 Hodsoll–Thompson, 27 Feb. 1939. FO371/22801 [A2230/63/45].
145 Haigh–Craigie, 2 April 1937. FO371/20650 [A3745/20/45].
146 G.A. Grunder and W.E. Livezey, *The Philippines and the United States*, University of Oklahoma Press, Norman, 1951, pp. 231–2; Friend, pp. 157–9, 190–1.
147 q. John F. Laffey, 'French Far Eastern policy in the 1930s', *Modern Asian Studies*, 23 (1) (1989), p. 121.
148 q. Laffey, p. 130.
149 q. Laffey, p. 131.
150 q. Laffey, p. 133.
151 q. Laffey, p. 134.
152 q. Laffey, p. 136.
153 Cf John E. Dreifort, *Myopic Grandeur*, Kent State University Press, Kent and London, 1991, p. 122.
154 q. Laffey, p. 137.
155 q. Laffey, p. 140.
156 q. Laffey, p. 141.
157 Bullitt–SD, 11 Feb. 1939, FRUS 1939 III, pp. 104–5.
158 Laffey, pp. 142, 142–3n. Bullitt/SofS, 4 April 1939, 4092. FRUS 1939 III, p. 748.
159 Laffey, pp. 143–4.
160 Laffey, pp. 146–7.
161 Dreifort, p. 163.
162 COS (39) 941, 11 Jul. 1939. CAB 53/52; see also Pritchard, pp. 190–3.
163 Likhit Dhiravegin, *Siam and Colonialism*, Thai Watana Panich, Bangkok, BE2518[1974], p. 59.
164 Minute, 22 Mar. 1932. FO371/16261 [F2717/2717/61].
165 Dormer–Simon, 10 Nov. 1933, 196. FO371/17176 [F7922/42/40].
166 Dormer–Simon, 11 Jan. 1934, 13, and minutes. FO371/18206 [F1185/21/40].
167 Minute by Randall, 9 May 1934. FO371/18201 [F2731/2202/40].
168 J. Crosby, *Siam: The Crossroads*, Hollis & Carter, London, 1943, p. 1.
169 Crosby–Orde, 18 Aug. 1934. FO371/18207 [F5730/21/40].
170 Crosby–FO, 25 Sept 1934, 200. FO371/18210 [F6575/3035/40].
171 Minutes, 14 Nov. 1934. ibid.
172 Yatabe/Hirota, 15 Dec. 1935. q. E. Flood, 'Japan's relations with Thailand, 1928–1941', PhD thesis, University of Washington, 1967, pp. 131–2.
173 q. E.B. Reynolds, 'Ambivalent allies: Japan and Thailand, 1941–1945', PhD thesis, University of Hawaii, 1988, p. 68.
174 Judith A. Stowe, *Siam Becomes Thailand*, Hurst, London, 1991, p. 91.
175 Stowe, p. 90.
176 Stowe, p. 102.
177 Stowe, pp. 94–5.
178 Charivat Santaputra, 'Thai foreign policy 1932–1946', PhD thesis, University of Southampton, p. 140.

179 q. Charivat, p. 141, fn 47. He puts *accompanying* for *accommodating*.
180 q. Charivat, pp. 141–2.
181 Flood, p. 183.
182 Stowe, pp. 100–1.
183 Flood, pp. 168–9.
184 P. B. Oblas, 'Siam's efforts to revise the unequal treaty system in the sixth reign (1910–1925)', PhD thesis, Michigan University, 1974, pp. 176–7, 181–2, 215–6.
185 Flood, p. 170.
186 Stowe, pp. 100, 102.
187 Minute, 4 July 1938. FO371/22207 [F7178/113/40].
188 Crosby–Halifax, 5 April 1939, 170. FO371/23593 [F4792/403/40].
189 Stowe, p. 121.
190 Crosby–Halifax, 10 May 1939, 236. FO371/23595 [F4802/186/40].
191 Crosby–Halifax, 16 May 1939, 247. FO371/23595 [F5250/1860/40] 23595/2.
192 FO–Crosby, 28 Jul. 1939. FO371/23595 [F6310/1860/40].
193 Stowe, p. 126.
194 COS(39) 941, CAB 53/52.
195 Note, 24 Jul. FO371/23549 [F7285/2742/61].
196 Extract, Commentary, enclosed in Cornwall–Jones/Howe, 8 Aug. 1939. FO371/23549 [F8630/2742/61].
197 Minute by Welles, 3 Aug. 1939, FRUS 1939, III, pp. 701–2.
198 q. R. Emerson, *Malaysia*, Macmillan, New York, 1937, pp. 174–5.
199 Report of Brig. Gen. Sir Samuel Wilson, March 1933, Cmd 4276, p. 12.
200 Minute on Clementi's letter of 24 Dec. 1931. CO531/24 [92503], Public Record Office, London.
201 Cabinet 42(33), 27 June 1933, Item 7. CAB 23/76.
202 Minutes, 20 Jul. 1938. CO531/28 [53029/3].
203 Thomas–MacDonald, 19 April 1939. CO531/29 [53011/1].
204 Minutes 23, 26 May. ibid.
205 q. by Foulds–Eden, 12 June 1936, 62. FO371/19823 [A6249/34/45].
206 Yuen Choy Leng, 'Japanese rubber and iron investments in Malaya, 1900–1941', JSEAS, V, 1 (March 1974) pp. 18, 24, 27–32.
207 Peter Baugher, 'The contradictions of colonialism: The French experience in Indochina, 1860–1940', PhD, University of Wisconsin–Madison, 1980, p. 93.
208 J.M. Gullick, *Malaya*, Praeger, New York, 1963, p. 144.
209 Nadzan Haron, 'British defence policy in Malaya, 1874–1918', in K.M. de Silva et al (eds), *Asian Panorama*, Vikas, New Delhi, 1990, p. 443.
210 Cf Richard J. Aldrich, *The Key to the South*, Oxford University Press, Kuala Lumpur, 1993, pp. 188–9.
211 Ong Chit Chung, 'Major General William Dobbie and the defence of Malaya, 1935–38', JSEAS, XVII, 2 (September 1986), pp. 293 ff; J. Neidpath, *The Singapore Naval Base and the Defence of Britain's Eastern Empire, 1919–1941*, Clarendon Press, Oxford, 1981, pp. 158 ff.
212 Neidpath, p. 271.
213 FO Minute, 14 Oct. 1938. FO371/22176 [F10819/10819/61].
214 Minute by Fitzmaurice, 26 Jan. 1939, q. Pritchard, p. 132.
215 Memorandum, 27 Jul. 1940. FO371/24708 [F3633/193/61].
216 AFPD, II, pp. 69–73.
217 Chamberlain–Lyons, 20 Mar. 1939. AFPD, II, p. 75.

218 Stirling, Cablegram, 31 Mar. 1939, AFPD, II, p. 92.
219 Pritchard, p. 14.
220 Note, 3 May 1939, AFPD, II, p. 109.
221 Note, 4 May 1939. ibid., p. 112.
222 Menzies–Chamberlain, 24 June 1939, cable. ibid., pp. 139–40.
223 Chamberlain–Menzies, 29 June 1939, cable. ibid., p. 144.
224 Record of Meeting at DO, 11 Jul. 1939. ibid., p. 152.
225 AFPD, II, p. 98.
225 Stirling–Dept. of Ext. Affairs, 20 Mar. 1939, 62. AFPD, II, p. 74.
227 Commonwealth Govt–Inskip, 6 April 1939, 39. ibid., p. 96.

2 September 1939 – June 1940

1 J.G. Utley, 'The Department of State and the Far East, 1937–1941: A study of the ideas behind its diplomacy', PhD thesis, University of Illinois at Urbana–Champaign, 1970, pp. 176–8.
2 Memorandum, 26 Aug. 1939. FRUS 1939 III, p. 212.
3 Cf FRUS 1939 III, pp. 122–3.
4 Utley, p. 188.
5 *The Memoirs of General the Lord Ismay*, Heinemann, London, 1960, p. 104.
6 Eleanor M. Gates, *End of the Affair: The Collapse of the Anglo–French Alliance, 1939–40*, University of California Press, Berkeley and Los Angeles, 1981, p. 26.
7 D. Reynolds, *The Creation of the Anglo–American Alliance 1937–41*, Europa, London, 1981 [hereinafter Reynolds], p. 65.
8 Reynolds, p. 74.
9 E.L. Woodward, *British Foreign Policy in the Second World War*, HMSO, London, 1970, I, p. 181.
10 Cadogan, 11 June 1940. David Dilks (ed.) *The Diaries of Sir Alexander Cadogan*, Cassell, London, 1971 [hereinafter Cadogan], p. 297.
11 D. Reynolds, 'Churchill and the British "decision" to fight on in 1940: Right policy, wrong reasons', in R. Langhorne (ed), *Diplomacy and Intelligence during the Second World War*, Cambridge University Press, Cambridge, 1985, pp. 148–54.
12 *The Ironside Diaries*, ed. R Macleod and D. Kelly, Constable, London, 1962, p. 370.
13 Cf Gates, pp. 259–61.
14 Gates, pp. 301–02, 341–2, 349–51, 355–9; Arthur J. Marder, *From the Dardanelles to Oran*, Oxford University Press, London, 1974, ch. 5.
15 Woodward, II, p. 244.
16 Cadogan, 10 June, p. 296.
17 J. Colville, *The Fringes of Power*, Sceptre, London, 1986, p. 177.
18 Casey/Menzies, 30 May 1940. AFPD, II, pp. 369–70.
19 q. Gates, p. 436.
20 15 June, q. Woodward, I, p. 347. See also PM/FDR via Kennedy, 20 May 1940. Warren S. Kimball, *Churchill and Roosevelt*, Princeton University Press, Princeton, NJ, 1984, p. 40.
21 Robert Dallek, *Franklin D. Roosevelt and American Foreign Policy, 1932–1945*, Oxford University Press, Oxford, 1979, pp. 200–5.
22 Reynolds, pp. 66–71.
23 q. ibid, p. 72.
24 q. ibid, p. 78.

25 q. ibid., p. 79.
26 q. ibid., p. 79.
27 Ibid, pp. 99–100.
28 q. ibid, pp. 119–20.
29 E.L. Woodward and Rohan Butler (eds), *Documents on British Foreign Policy 1919–39*, 3rd Series, IX, London, 1955, p. 526.
30 Utley, pp. 144–6.
31 Lu, p. 65.
32 2 Sept. 1939. q. Lowe, TRHS, p. 44.
33 Lothian to Halifax, 3 Nov. q. Lee, p. 204.
34 FO/Lothian, 27 Nov. 1939, recording Halifax–Kennedy conv, s.d. Kyozo Sato, *Japan and Britain at the Crossroads 1939–41*, Senshu University Press, Tokyo, 1986, p. 38.
35 Memorandum by Hornbeck, 20 June 1940. FRUS IV, p. 29.
36 FRUS J II, pp. 86–8.
37 Memorandum by Grew, 24 June 1940. ibid., p. 88.
38 Memorandum by Grew, 28 June 1940. ibid., p. 90.
39 Oral statement by Arita, 28 June 1940. ibid., p. 92.
40 q. Murakami, p. 48 and in a different translation, Grew–SofS, 29 June, FRUS J II, pp. 93–4.
41 Murakami, p. 49.
42 Eden–Whiskard, 8 Sept. 1939. AFPD II, pp. 250, 251.
43 Whiskard–Eden, 11 Sept. 1939. ibid., pp. 258–60.
44 Eden–Whiskard, 12 Sept. 1939. ibid., p. 263.
45 Note, 21 Sept. 1939. ibid., pp. 279–81.
46 Butler–Bruce, 14 Oct. 1939, ibid., p. 339.
47 Eden–Chamberlain, 3 Nov. 1939. ibid., p. 368.
48 WP(G)(39) 92, 15 Nov. 1939. CAB67/2.
49 Ibid.
50 Casey–Menzies, 17 Nov. 1939. AFPD II, pp. 418–9.
51 Menzies–Savage, 21 Nov. 1939. ibid., pp. 472–3.
52 Casey–Menzies, 23 Nov. 1939, ibid., p. 429.
53 Bruce–Officer, 12 Dec. 1939. ibid., p. 459.
54 Savage–Menzies, 23 Nov. ibid., pp. 424–5.
55 Casey–Menzies, 23 Nov. 1939. ibid., p. 430.
56 Whiskard–DO, 24 Nov. 1939, ibid., p. 433.
57 Cabinet Minute, 28 Nov. 1939, ibid., p. 436.
58 Menzies–Casey, 14 June 1940. AFPD, III, p. 431.
59 COS Memorandum, 13 June, adopted 14 June, sent to Lothian, 18 June. Woodward, I, pp. 351–2. Caldecote–Whiskard, 19 June, quoting memorandum for Lothian. AFPD, III, pp. 458–61.
60 Bruce–Casey, 25 June 1940, ibid., p. 493.
61 Caldecote–Menzies, 26 June 1940, M40. ibid., pp. 501–04.
62 Casey–Menzies, 25 June 1940, ibid., pp. 505–7.
63 Menzies–Caldecote, 27 June 1940, 330. ibid., pp. 511–12.
64 Casey–Menzies, 28 June 1940, pp. 523–4.
65 Aide–mémoire, 27 June 1940. FRUS IV, pp. 365–7.
66 Memorandum of conversation, 28 June 1940. ibid., pp. 369–70.
67 Cf oral statement, 28 June 1940, FRUS 40 IV, p. 372.
68 Ibid., p. 372.
69 Memorandum by Minister of Economic Warfare in FE(41) 136/WP(41) 15, 7 July 1941. CAB 96/4.

70 Commonwealth–Eden, 16 April 1940. AFPD III, p. 201.

71 Fraser–Menzies, 20 April 1940. ibid., pp. 215–16.

72 Eden–Commonwealth, 27 April 1940. ibid., pp. 227 ff; also note on p. 230.

73 Ibid., p. 229n.

74 Hodgson–McEwen, 24 June 1940. ibid., p. 485.

75 A. Vandenbosch, *Dutch Foreign Policy since 1815*, Nijhoff, The Hague, 1959, p. 279.

76 Telegram, 25 Sept. 1939, 1288, and minutes. FO 371/23548 [F10436/1821/61].

77 Cadogan, p. 229.

78 Telegram from Craigie, 12 Nov. 1939, 1487. FO371/23548 [F11831/1821/61].

79 Minutes in F 11831.

80 Telegram from Lothian, 22 Nov. 1939, 810, minutes, and reply, 30 Nov., 835. FO371/23551[F12090/4027/61]. Cf Memorandum by Ag S of S, 21 Nov. 1939. FRUS III, pp. 321–3.

81 Telegram, 9 Dec. 1939, 883. FO371/23551[F12625/4027/61].

82 US Policy in the Far East, Memorandum by V.A.L. Mallet, 8 Dec.1939. FO371/23551[F12709/4027/61].

83 Lambert–FE Dept, 18 Nov. 1939. FO371/23548 [F12717/1821/61].

84 Minutes on Telegram from Craigie, 20 Dec. 1939, 1854. FO371/23562 [F12900/456/23].

85 Memorandum, 6 Mar. 1940. FO371/24708 [F1639/193/61].

86 Telegram from Kerr, 4 Feb. 1940, 44, and minute, 12 Feb. FO371/24708 [F870/193/61].

87 Minute in F983/193/61.

88 Telegram from Lothian, 24 Feb. 1940, 262. FO371/24708 [F1298/193/61].

89 Telegram from Craigie, 15 April 1940, 594. FO371/24716 [F2739/2739/61].

90 Telegram from Craigie, 14 April 1940, 591. FO371/24716 [F2753/2739/61].

91 Telegram from Craigie, 15 April 1940, 596. FO371/24716 [F2740/2739/61].

92 Telegram from Craigie, 15 April 1940, 593. FO371/24716 [F2745/2739/61].

93 Minute [F2740].

94 Bruce–Menzies, 15 April 1940. AFPD III, p. 199.

95 Menzies–Eden, 17 April 1940. ibid., p. 205.

96 Minute by Clarke, 18 April, in F2745.

97 Eden–Commonwealth, 19 April 1940. AFPD III, p. 213; also FO371/24716[F2784/2739/61].

98 Dickover–SofS, 16 April. FRUS 1940 IV, pp. 8–9.

99 Conversation, 22 April 1940. FO371/24716[F2917/2739/61]. H.J. van Mook, *The Netherlands Indies and Japan*, Allen & Unwin, London, 1944, p. 37n.

100 Telegram from Lothian, 18 April 1940, 560. FO371/24716[F2828/2739/61]. Statement in Lothian/FO, 22 April, 353. FO371/24716 [F3208/2739/61]. Vandenbosch, pp. 230–1.

101 Minute by Dening, 15 April, and papers attached. FO371/24716 [F2838/2739/61]. Telegram from Craigie 23 April, 657, and minute by Clarke thereon. FO371/24716[F2911/2739/61]. Conversation between Neths Minister and Butler, 17 April. FO371/24716 [F2876/2739/61].

102 Minute, 20 April 1940, on Craigie telegram, 19 April, 624. FO371/24716 [F2847/2739/61].
103 Telegram from Lothian, 23 April 1940, 591, and minutes. FO371/24716[F2913/2739/61]. PQ 18 April [F2840/2739/61]. Thirty-eight per cent of oil imported into UK in 1937 came from Aruba and Curacao (ultimately from Venezuela). Memorandum by J.R. Garside, 3 Jan. 1938. ADM1/10072, Public Record Office, London.
104 Cf aide–mémoire, French Embassy to State Department, 19 April 1940. FRUS 1940 IV, pp. 9–10.
105 Conversation, 19 April 1940, and minutes. FO371/24716 [F2846/2739/61.
106 Conversation, 22 April. FO371/24716 [F2917/2739/61].
107 Conversation, 26 April. FO371/24716 [F3175/2739/61].
108 Conversation, 26 April. FO371/24716 [F3013/2739/61].
109 Conversation, 1 May 1940, FO371/24716 [F3176/2739/61].
110 Minute, 11 May 1940. FO371/24716 [F3271/2739/61].
111 Minutes [F3271].
112 Telegram, 17 April 1940, 25. FO371/24705 [F2780/6/61].
113 Grew–SofS, 19 April, 262. FRUS 1940 IV, p. 11.
114 Telegram, 11 May 1940, 35. FO371/24705 [F3252/6/61].
115 Walsh–FO, 13 May, No.72. ibid.
116 Telegram from Craigie, 11 May 1940, 744. FO371/24716 [F3253/2739/61].
117 Telegram from Craigie, 11 May 1940, 745. FO 371/24716 [F2740/2739/61].
118 Cf memorandum, 10 May 1940. FRUS IV, p. 13.
119 Telegram from Lothian, 11 May 1940, 693. FO371/24716 [F2913/2739/61].
120 Telegram from Lothian, 13 May, 709. [F2913].
121 Menzies–Bruce, 26 May 1940, 54, relating conversation with Akiyama, 16 May. AFPD II, p. 33.
122 WM 121(40) 5, 14 May. CAB 65/7.
123 Telegram from Lothian, 12 May, 700; telegram to Lothian, 13 May, 756. [F2913].
124 *Times*, 13 May.
125 Telegrams to Craigie, 12 May, 406, 407. [F2740].
126 John A.L. Sullivan, 'The United States, the East Indies and World War II', PhD thesis, University of Massachusetts, 1968, p. 60.
127 E.L. Presseisen, *Germany and Japan: A study in Totalitarian Diplomacy*, Nijhoff, The Hague, 1938, p. 239; F.W. Iklé, *German–Japanese Relations 1936–40*, Bookman Associates, New York, 1956, p. 152.
128 Telegram from Craigie, 13 May, 761. [F2740]. Cf Grew–SofS, 1415, 335. FRUS IV, pp. 17–18.
129 Minute, 13 May 1940; telegrams to Craigie, 13 May, 415, 416. [F2740].
130 Telegram from Craigie, 14 May, 767. FO371/24716[F3271/2739/61].
131 Telegram to Craigie, 15 May, 429. [F3271]. Cf Loudon–SofS, 15 April. FRUS IV, pp. 19–20.
132 Murakami, p. 52.
133 Telegram, 16 May 1940, 784. FO371/24716 [F3279/2739/61].
134 Telegram, 16 May, 785. [F3279].
135 *Times*, 16 May.
136 Telegram 785 [F3279].
137 Telegram, 22 May 1940, 829. FO371/24716 [F3298/2739/61].
138 Telegram, 23 May, 839. FO371/24716 [F3320/2739/61].

139 Telegram from Lothian, 20 May, 769. FO371/24716 [F3298/2739/61].
140 A.C.D. de Graeff (ed.), *Van Vriend tot Vijand*, Elsevier, Amsterdam, 1945, pp. 290-1.
141 Cf Grew–SofS, 12 Mar. 1940, FRUS IV, pp. 7–8. Cf Morley, *The Fateful Choice*, p. 128.
142 Telegram to Craigie, 20 May 1940, 452. FO371/24716 [F3279/2739/61].
143 Howe–Leith-Ross, 18 May. [F3279].
144 Telegram from Craigie, 17 May 1940, 791; minute by Cadogan, 18 May; telegram to Lothian, 25 May, 867; telegram from Lothian, 26 May, 836. FO371/24716 [F3319/2739/61].
145 Minutes, 27, 28 May. [F3319].
146 Telegram to Lothian, 9 June, 1033. [F3319].
147 Telegram from Lothian, 13 June, 983. [F3319].
148 Minute, 17 June. [F3319].
149 Conversation, 3 June 1940. FO371/24716 [F3366/2739/61].
150 Minute, 31 May. FO371/24716[F3342/2739/61].
151 Minutes 6, 7, 8 June on F3366.
152 Utley, p. 183.
153 Hull–Grew, 4 June 1940, FRUS IV, p. 346.
154 q. Utley, p. 186.
155 Telegram from Walsh, 4 June 1940, 50A. FO371/24705 [F3252/6/61].
156 Minute, 6 June 1940. [F3252].
157 Minutes by Cavendish–Bentinck, 6 June, Cadogan, 7 June. [F3252].
158 Note by WSC, 9 June. FO–Ady, WO, 11 June. [F3252].
159 Minute, 7 June. [F3252].
160 WO–FO, 16 June; Admiralty–FO, 25 June; minute, 7 July. FO371/24705 [F3424/6/61].
161 Talks are covered in FRUS J II, pp. 67ff.
162 Murakami, pp. 53–4.
163 Wyatt Smith–Halifax, 12 Sept. 1939, 93. FO371/22802 [A7202/63/45].
164 Smith–Halifax, 7 Oct. 1939, 103. FO371/22802 [A8204/63/45].
165 Minute, 29 Nov. [A8204].
166 Smith–Halifax, 3 Oct. 1939, 96. FO371/22802 [A7919/63/45]. Cf. A. Gopinath, *Manuel L. Quezon*, New Day, Quezon City, 1987, pp. 136–7.
167 Lothian–Halifax, 3 Nov. 1939, 1226. FO371/22802 [A7994/63/45].
168 Smith–Halifax, 7 Oct, 103. [A8204].
169 Smith–Halifax, 28 Oct. 1939, 112. FO371/22802 [A8674/53/45].
170 Ibid.
171 Minutes, 14 Dec., 16 Dec. [A8674].
172 Montgomery, 7 Oct, on Admiralty/FO, 6 Oct. FO371/22802 [A6911/63/45].
173 Smith–Halifax, 3 Nov. 1939, 114. FO371/22802 [A9003/63/45].
174 Minutes, 6 Jan., 7 Jan 1940. [A9003].
175 Smith–Halifax, 26 Jan. 1940, 13; 4 April 1940, 33E. FO371/24252 [A1843/1186/45].
176 Cf memorandum by Dickover, 2 Feb. 1940. FRUS IV, p. 2.
177 Smith–Halifax, 27 Feb. 1940, 22. FO371/24252 [A2310/1186/45].
178 Minute, 20 Mar. [A1843].
179 q. Laffey, p. 147.
180 q. Laffey, p. 148.
181 Reed–SofS, 3 Oct. 1939. FRUS 39 III, pp. 273–4.

182 Grew–SofS, 1 Dec. 1939, 647. FRUS 39 III, p. 766. 11 Dec. 1939, 676. FRUS p. 769. John E. Dreifort, 'Japan's advance into Indochina, 1940: The French response', JSEAS, XIII, 2 (September 1982), pp. 178–80.
183 Cf conversation with Roché, 6 Feb. 1940. FO371/24166 [F873/43/10].
184 Bruce–Menzies, 22 June, 458. AFPD III, p. 476.
185 Caldecote–Whiskard, 20 June, Z 134. ibid., p. 470.
186 Cadogan, p. 311.
187 Cf Hoang Trong Phu, q. Dreifort, JSEAS, p. 281.
188 P. Baudouin, *The Private Diaries (March 1940 to January 1941)*, trans. C. Petrie, Eyre & Spottiswoode, London, 1948, p. 169.
189 G. Catroux, *Deux Actes du Drame Indochinois*, Plon, Paris, 1959, p. 68.
190 Ibid., p. 88.
191 Jean Decoux, *À la barre de l'Indochine*, Plon, Paris, 1949, p. 93. Cf J.W. Morley (ed.), *The Fateful Choice*, Columbia University Press, New York, 1980, pp. 159–60, 164.
192 Baudouin, p. 173.
193 Cypher telegram, 17 June 1940, 18, circular. FO371/24719 [F3474/3429/61].
194 Telegram, 20 June, 9. ibid. Cf Catroux, p. 46.
195 FCP(40) 2nd, 21 June 1940. [F3474].
196 Catroux, p. 57; Decoux, pp. 48–9.
197 Telegrams, 30 June 1940, 103, 164. FO371/24719 [F3526/3429/61].
198 Memorandum by Gage, 19 July. ibid.
199 Telegram, 17 July 1940. ibid.
200 Telegram, 27 June 1940, 1100. FO371/24719 [F3429/3429/61].
201 Telegram, 19 June, 1033. [F3429].
202 Telegram, 19 June, 1039. FO371/24719 [F3526/3429].
203 Telegram, 17 June, 1015. FO371/24719 [F3429/3429/61].
204 Telegram, 19 June, 1039. ibid.
205 Telegram, 21 June, 1058. ibid.
206 Telegram, 28 June, 1109. FO371/24719 [F3526/3429/61].
207 Stowe, p. 130; her words.
208 E.B. Reynolds, 'Ambivalent allies: Japan and Thailand, 1941–1945', PhD thesis, University of Hawaii, 1988, p. 109.
209 Stowe, p. 130.
210 Crosby–Halifax, 7 Sept., 448. FO371/23595 [F10316/1860/40].
211 Minute, 21 Sept. [F10316].
212 Telegram from Crosby, 20 Oct. 1939, 132A. FO371/23595[F11136/1860/40].
213 Crosby–Halifax, 20 Oct. 1939, 519. FO371/23596 [F11460/1860/40].
214 Telegram from Crosby, 27 Oct. 1939, 145. FO371/23595 [F11329/1860/40].
215 Crosby–Halifax, 27 Oct. 1939, 529. FO371/23596 [F11648/1860/40].
216 Minute, 2 Nov. FO371/23596 [F11483/1860/40].
217 Minute, 5 Nov. FO371/23596 [F11460/1860/40].
218 Minute, 4 Nov. FO371/23596 [F11516/1860/40].
219 Telegram from Campbell, 12 Nov. 1939, 845. FO371/23596 [F11808/1860/40].
220 Minute, 14 Nov. [F11808].
221 FO–Campbell, 20 Nov. 1939, 2805. FO371/23596 [F11976/1860/40].
222 Telegram, 30 Dec. 1939, 186. FO371/24750 [F19/19/40].
223 Minute, 2 Jan. [F19].

224 Telegram, 9 Jan, 10. FO371/24750 [F236/19/40].
225 Crosby–Howe, 30 Dec. 1939, P&C. FO371/22754 [F324/324/40].
226 Crosby–Halifax, 30 Dec. 1939, 636. FO371/24750 [F292/9/40].
227 Telegram to Campbell, 7 Jan. 1940, 20. FO371/24750 [F158/19/40].
228 Telegram, 9 Jan., 10. FO371/24750 [F236/19/40].
229 Telegram, 14 Nov. 1939, 158. FO371/23596 [F11850/1860/40].
230 Crosby–Halifax, 6 Jan. 1940, 18. FO371/24750 [F476/19/40].
231 Telegram, 24 Jan. 1940, 19. FO371/24750 [F583/19/40].
232 Telegram from Harvey, 24 Jan. 1940, 63. FO371/24750 [F593/19/40].
233 Telegram, 7 Feb. 1940, 91 Saving. [F593].
234 Telegram from Campbell, 9 Feb. 1940, 109. FO371/24750 [F1048/19/40].
235 Minute, 20 Feb. FO371/24750 [F1212/19/40].
236 Telegram, 16 Mar. 1940, 59. FO371/24750 [F1896/19/40].
237 Crosby–Halifax, 14 April 1940, 147. FO371/24751 [F2877/19/40].
238 Minute by Dean, 25 April. [F2877].
239 FO–Campbell, 1 May 1940, 942. [F2877].
240 Telegram from Campbell, 4 May 1940, 350. FO371/24751 [F3205/19/40].
241 Telegram from Crosby, 17 May, 136. [F3205].
242 Stowe, p. 137.
243 Telegram from Campbell, 20 May, 233. [F3205].
244 Crosby–Halifax, 17 June 1940, 215. FO371/24751 [F2888/19/40].
245 Telegrams from Crosby, 19 June, 171; to Crosby, 24 June. FO371/24751
     [F3395/19/40].
246 Stowe, p. 136.
247 E. Flood, 'Japan's relations with Thailand, 1928–41', PhD thesis, University
     of Washington, 1967, p. 253; also Charivat, p. 186.
248 Flood, pp. 254–6.
249 Note, 14 May on telegram from Coultas, 11 May 1940, 129. FO371/24751
     [F3205/19/40].
250 Flood, pp. 258–9.
251 E. Reynolds, pp. 112–3.
252 q. ibid., pp. 111–12.
253 Crosby–Halifax, 30 June 1940, 233. FO371/24756 [F3690/3268/40].
254 Crosby–Halifax, 7 July 1940, 245. FO371/24756 [F3690/3268/40].
255 Minutes, 5, 7 July. FO371/24756 [F3268/3268/40].
256 Robert H. Taylor, 'Politics in late colonial Burma', *Modern Asian Studies*
     10(2) (1976), p. 173.
257 Taylor, pp. 173–4.
258 Taylor, pp. 175–6.
259 Bruce–Menzies, 19 June 1940. AFPD III, pp. 462–3. Cf Grew–SofS, 19 June,
     470. FRUS IV, p. 267.
260 Bruce–Menzies, 20 June, 450. AFPD III, p. 467. Cf Grew–SofS, 19 June, 473
     FRUS IV, pp. 28–29.
261 Telegram from Craigie, 21 June, 1058. FO371/24719 [F3429/3429/61].
262 Telegrams, 24 June, 1073, 1074. FO371/24666 [F3479/43/10].
263 Telegram, 25 June, 1087. [F3479].
264 Amery–Halifax, 28 June 1940. FO371/24666 [F3544/43/10].
265 Telegram, 27 June, 514. [F3479].
266 Telegram, 2 July, 1215. [F3544].
267 Minute, 2 July. [F3479].
268 Minute, 3 July. [F3479].
269 Telegram to Lothian 2 July, 1348. [F3544].

270 Telegram, 2 July, 635. [F3544].
271 Telegram, 2 July, 634. [F3544].
272 Telegram, 3 July, 1149. [F3544].
273 Telegram, 4 July, 1154. [F3544].
274 Minute by Dening, 7 July. [F3544].
275 Caldecote–Menzies, 26 June, M40. AFPD III, pp. 503–4.
276 Menzies–Caldecote, 27 June, 330. ibid., pp. 511–12.
277 Dilks' editorial in Cadogan, pp. 310–11.
278 *The Empire at Bay: The Leo Amery Diaries 1929–45* (ed. John Barnes and David Nicholson), Hutchinson, London, 1988, pp. 628–9.
279 5 July. Cadogan, p. 311.
280 Caldecote–Commonwealth, 2 July, 234. AFPD IV pp. 5–7.
281 5 July. Cadogan, p. 311.
282 6 July. ibid., p. 311.
283 *The Empire at Bay*, p. 630.
284 Telegram, 6 July, 657. [F3544].
285 Caldecote–Halifax, 6 July. [F3544].
286 WP(40) 263, 9 July. CAB 66/9.
287 Telegram, 9 July, 1196. FO371/24667 [F3568/43/10.
288 Telegram, 10 July, 1203. [F3568].
289 Minute, 10 July [F3568].
290 WM 199(40) 4, 10 July. CAB65/8. For Bruce's view see Bruce–Menzies, 6 July, 520. AFPD, IV pp. 19–20.
291 WM 200(40) 13, 11 July. CAB 65/8.
292 Telegram, 11 July, 671. [F3568].
293 Telegram, 19 July, 350. FO371/24668 [F3943/43/10].
294 14 July, q. Lowe, *Great Britain and the Origins of the Pacific War*, Clarendon Press, Oxford, 1977, p. 149.
295 Memorandum by Hull, 5 July 1940. FRUS IV, p. 40.
296 Telegram, 5 July 1940, 1247. [F3544].
297 Telegram, 9 July, 1286. [F3568].
298 Memorandum of conversation, 12 July. FRUS IV, pp. 46–47.
299 Telegram, 12 July, 1322. FO371/24667 [F3597/43/10].
300 Grew–SofS, 7 July, 544. FRUS IV pp. 40–1.
301 Memorandum by Hornbeck, 13 July 1940. FRUS IV, pp. 583–5.
302 13 July. Cadogan, p. 313.
303 16, 17 July. Cadogan, p. 314.
304 Telegram to Lothian, 18 July, 285 en clair. [F3617]. Churchill, *Speeches*, VI, pp. 6251–2.
305 John Colville, *The Fringes of Power*, Sceptre, London, 1986, I, p. 237.
306 Ibid., p. 235.
307 D. Guyot, 'The political impact of the Japanese occupation of Burma', PhD thesis, Yale University, 1966, pp. 54–5; Won Z. Yoon, *Japan's Scheme for the Liberation of Burma*, Athens, OH, 1973, pp. 19–20.
308 Maung Maung (comp.), *Aung San of Burma*, Nijhoff, The Hague, 1962, p. 55.
309 Director/Secretary, Defence Department, 1 Nov. 1940, in Monteath–Seymour, 3 Feb. 1941. FO371/27773 [F547/54/61].
310 Cf W.R. Louis, *Imperialism at Bay*, Oxford, 1977, pp. 100–01.
311 R.W. Reece, *The Name of Brooke*, Oxford University Press, Kuala Lumpur, 1982, pp. 30–1.
312 A. Brooke to C.V. Brooke, 23 Feb., in Palairet–Stevenson, 27 Feb. 1940. CO531/29 [53011/1].

313 Minute, 8 Mar., 12 Mar. ibid.
314 Telegram, 15 Mar., secret. ibid.
315 Thomas–MacDonald, 19 Mar. 1940, secret. ibid.
316 Item 9 of discussions. CO531/29 [53011/4].
317 Thomas–Jones, 3 July 1940. CO531/29 [53011/1].
318 WP(40), 222, 26 June 1940. CAB66/9; also COS(40) 493. CAB 80/13.
319 WM 183 (4)13, 26 June. CAB 67/5.
320 Caldecote–Commonwealth, 28 June 1940, 228. AFPD III, pp. 517–18.
321 Bruce–Menzies, 3 July, 507. AFPD IV, pp. 10–11.
322 Ismay–Bruce, 4 July, Secret. AFPD IV, pp. 13–14.
323 Bruce–Menzies, 8 July. ibid., pp. 25–8.
324 Menzies–Caldecote, 24 July. ibid., p. 45.
325 Jane Fulcher, *The Nation's Image*, Cambridge University Press, Cambridge, 1988, p. 36.
326 G. Maxwell (comp), *The Civil Defence of Malaya*, London, [?1943], p. 36.
327 Cadogan, p. 308.

3 July–September 1940

1 Grew–Hull, 12 Sept. 1940. FRUS IV, pp. 602–3.
2 Grew–Hull, 13 Sept., 834. FRUS IV, p. 604.
3 q. Murakami, pp. 61–62.
4 Cadogan, p. 317.
5 Ibid., p. 321.
6 Ibid., p. 325.
7 13 Sept. ibid., p. 326.
8 Ibid., p. 328.
9 Ibid., p. 328.
10 Ibid., p. 331.
11 q. D. Reynolds, p. 112.
12 Ibid., p. 114.
13 Ibid., p. 118.
14 Cf Woodward, I, p. 354.
15 James R. Leutze, *Bargaining for Supremacy*, University of North Carolina Press, Chapel Hill, 1977, p. 124.
16 D. Reynolds, pp. 122–5.
17 29 Aug. Cadogan, p. 324.
18 D. Reynolds, p. 132.
19 q. J.R.M. Butler, *Lord Lothian*, Macmillan, London, 1960, p. 298.
20 Speeches, VI, p. 6268.
21 Utley, p. 175.
22 D. Reynolds, p. 135.
23 W.N. Medlicott, *The Economic Blockade*, London, 1959, 1978, II, p. 64.
24 Proclamation 2413, 2 July, following Act, s.d. FRUS J II, pp. 211–13.
25 Proclamation 2417, 26 July. ibid, pp. 216–17.
26 Regulations, 26 July. ibid, pp. 217–18.
27 Utley, p. 197.
28 D. Reynolds, p. 138.
29 J.B. Crowley, *Japan's Quest for Autonomy*, Princeton University Press, Princeton, NJ, 1966, pp. 85–6.
30 Crowley, p. 87.

31 J.M. Meskill, *Hitler and Japan: The Hollow Alliance*, Atherton, New York, 1966, pp. 89–94, 99–100.
32 Conversation, 20 Sept. 1940, FRUS IV, p. 137.
33 Lu, p. 107.
34 Meskill, p. 17.
35 D. Reynolds, p. 138.
36 Meskill, p. 18.
37 D. Reynolds, p. 139; cf Ikle, pp. 175–6.
38 q. by Ikeda Kiyoshi in T.G. Fraser and Peter Lowe (eds), *Conflict and Amity in East Asia*, Macmillan, Basingstoke, 1992, p. 42.
39 Minute by Whitehead, 10 Sept. 1940, FO371/24708 [F3765/193/61].
40 Press release, 25 Sept. FRUS J II, p. 222.
41 Proclamation 2423, 12 Sept. 1940, FRUS J II, pp. 220–1.
42 Press release, FRUS J, II, 222–3.
43 Reynolds, p. 140.
44 Memorandum, 2 Oct. 1940, q. Norman A. Graebner, 'Hoover, Roosevelt and the Japanese', in D. Borg and Shumpei Okamoto, *Pearl Harbor as History*, Columbia University Press, New York and London, 1973, p. 46.
45 Ibid., p. 46.
46 Telegram from Lothian, 4 Oct. 1940, 2197. FO371/24709 [F4556/193/61].
47 Telegram, 29 Sept. 1940, 1905. FO 371/24709 [F4534/193/61].
48 Telegram, 1 Oct. 1940, 2146. FO371/24709 [F4534/193/61].
49 Memorandum, 5 Oct. 1940, FRUS IV pp. 167–8.
50 Conversation, 7 Oct. 1940, FRUS IV, pp. 168–9.
51 William T. Johnsen, 'Forging the foundations of the grand alliance: Anglo-American military collaboration, 1938–1941', PhD thesis, Duke University, 1986, p. 96.
52 Ibid., p. 115.
53 Ibid., pp. 129–39.
54 Cranborne–Whiskard, 12 Oct. 1940, 2303. AFPD IV, p. 221.
55 Casey–Dept, 14 Oct. 1940, 321. ibid., p. 222.
56 Memorandum by Hull, 8 Oct. 1940. FRUS J II, p. 227.
57 Minute, 23 July 1940. FO371/24708 [F3633/193/61].
58 Minute, 25 July. ibid.
59 Memorandum, 27 July 1940, and papers in ibid.
60 P. Lowe, *Great Britain and the Origins of the Pacific War*, Oxford, 1977, pp. 157–60.
61 WM (40) 260th, 27 Sept. CAB 65/9.
62 Minutes, 20 Sept. 1940. FO371/24709 [F4290/193/61].
63 D. Reynolds, p. 142.
64 q. ibid.
65 Ibid.
66 Bruce–Menzies, 18 July 1940, 576. AFPD, IV, pp. 40–1.
67 Menzies–Bruce, 25 July, unnumbered. ibid., pp. 46–7.
68 Fraser–Comm Gt, 30 July 1940. ibid., pp. 56–7.
69 Note of meeting, 31 July. ibid., p. 59.
70 Note, 6 Aug. 1940. ibid., p. 67.
71 Bruce–Menzies, 6 Aug. 1940, 641. ibid., pp. 69–72.
72 Menzies–Bruce, 8 Aug. 1940. ibid., pp. 74–5.
73 Casey–McEwen and Menzies, 10 Aug. 1940. ibid., pp. 79–80.
74 COS(40) 592, 31 July. CAB 66/10; closely followed in Caldecote–Whiskard, 11 Aug. 1940, 2214, extracts. AFPD IV, pp. 89–100.

75 Caldecote–Whiskard, 11 Aug. 1940. AFPD IV, pp. 84–86.
76 Menzies–Caldecote, 29 Aug. 1940. ibid., p. 119.
77 Caldecote–Commonwealth, 18 Sept. 1940, 346. ibid, p. 168.
78 Cranborne–Whiskard, 7 Oct. 1940, Z291. ibid., pp. 209–10.
79 Casey–Menzies, 1 Oct. 1940, 292. ibid., p. 195.
80 Cranborne–Whiskard, 7 Oct. 1940, Z292. ibid., p. 211.
81 Menzies–Cranborne, 10 Oct. 1940, 526. ibid., p. 216.
82 Draft, JP(40) 300, 10 July. FO 371/24722 [F3530/3530/61].
83 COS(40) 592, also WP(40) 302, 31 July. CAB 66/10.
84 JP(40) 300, also COS(40) 555, 19 July. CAB 84/16, CAB 80/15.
85 COS(40) 563, 21 July. CAB 80/15.
86 COS(40) 568 (Revise), also WP(40) 289, 27 July. CAB 80/15, CAB 66/10.
87 COS (40) 230th, 23 July, Item 2. CAB 79/5.
88 COS(40) 572, 25 July. CAB 80/15.
89 COS(40) 234th, 26 July, Item 3. CAB 79/5.
90 COS(40) 236th, 27 July, Item 3. CAB 79/5.
91 In quoting these remarks Dr P. Lowe omits this last sentence, with its important reference to the US. TRHS p. 55n.
92 WM 214(40) 17, 29 July, confidential annexe. CAB 65/14.
93 COS(40) 239th, 240th, 31 July. CAB 79/5.
94 Minute, 7 Aug. 1940. FO371/24708 [F3765/193/61].
95 COS (40) 259th, 10 Aug. CAB 79/6. COS (40) 592 Revise, 15 Aug. CAB 80/15.
96 WP (40) 308; also COS 40 (605), 7 Aug. CAB 66/10, CAB 80/16.
97 WM 222 (40) 4, 8 Aug., confidential annexe. CAB 65/14.
98 Telegram, 11 Aug. 1940, 263. FO 371/24709 [F3819/193/61]. Also Caldecote–Whiskard, 11 Aug., 263. AFPD IV pp. 87–9. New Zealand, Department of Internal Affairs, War History Branch, *Documents Relating to New Zealand's Participation in the Second World War 1939–45*, Wellington, 1963, III, pp. 20–2, 540–52.
99 Conversation, 29 July 1940. FO 371/24717 [F3687/2739/61].
100 Memorandum, 31 July 1940. FRUS IV, p. 59.
101 Halifax–Bland, 3 Aug. 1940, 260 and enc; Bland–Foreign Secretary, 7 Aug., 297. FO 371/24711 [F3704/253/61].
102 Menzies–Bruce, 8 Aug. 1940. AFPD IV, pp. 75–6; FO371/24711 [F3704/253/61].
103 Telegram, 29 Aug. 1940, 457. AFPD IV, p. 121; FO371/24709 [F3941/193/61].
104 Telegram, 15 Aug. 1940, 33. FO371/24709 [F3941/193/61].
105 Telegram, 1 Sept. 1940, 366. FO371/24709 [F4144/193/6]. NZ Documents III, pp. 24–6. M.P. Lissington, *New Zealand and Japan 1900–1941*, Government Printer, Wellington, 1972, p. 153.
106 Bland–Makins, 15 July 1940; note by Gage, 24 July. FO371/24716 [F3391/2739/61].
107 Telegram from Craigie, 29 July 1940, 761. [F3391]; also enclosure in Gore-Booth–Halifax, 9 Aug., 371. FO371/24717 [F4274/2739/61]. Cf van Mook, pp. 29–38; *Documenten betreffende de Buitenlandse Politiek van Nederland 1919–1945*, C, I, The Hague, 1976, pp. 67–72, 145–7, 247–8.
108 Telegram, 13 Aug. 1940, 112. FO371/24717 [F3820/2739/61].
109 Conversation, 13 Aug. 1940. FO371/24717 [F3839/2739/61].
110 Minutes, 14 Aug., 17 Aug. 1940. FO371/24717 [F3678/2339/61].

111 Minutes, 19 Aug., 21 Aug. 1940. FO371/24717 [F3839/2739/61].
112 Bland–Halifax, 28 Aug. 1940, and minute, 5 Sept. FO371/24717 [F3839/2739/61].
113 Reuter, 26 Aug. 1940; Van Mook, p. 39–40.
114 Telegram from Craigie, 11 Sept., 1786. FO371/24717 [F4274/2739/61]; from C-G, 14 Sept, 134. ibid.
115 Minute by Hebblethwaite, 17 Sept. FO371/24717 [F4274/2729/61].
116 Telegram from C–G, 20 Sept. 1940, 141. FO371/24717 [F4368/2739/61].
117 Minute, 13 Aug. 1940. FO371/24709 [F3819/193/61].
118 Minute, 30 Aug. 1940. FO371/24722 [F3982/3982/61].
119 Minutes, 3 Sept., 6 Sept., 7 Sept. FO371/24709 [F391/193/61].
120 Minute, 11 Sept. 1940. FO371/24709 [F4144/193/61].
121 Walsh to Eden, 23 Dec. 1940, No. 187A. FO 371/27846 [F4291/4291/61].
122 Walsh to Foreign Secretary, 19 Sept. 1940, No. 136. FO 371/27785 [F204/141/61].
123 Telegram from Lothian, 21 Aug. 1940, 1783. WP (40) 348, 2 Sept. CAB 66/11.
124 Cf his conversation with Hull, 26 Aug. FRUS IV, pp. 84–5.
125 Telegram, 5 Sept. 1940. FO 371/24709 [F4210/193/61].
126 Memorandum, 5 Sept. 1940. FRUS IV, p. 97.
127 Hull–Foote, 11 Sept. 1940. FRUS IV, p. 109.
128 Telegram to Lothian, 22 Sept. 1940, 2334. FO371/24709 [F4336/193/61].
129 COS (40) 772 (JP), 25 Sept. CAB 80/19.
130 Grew–SofS, substance, 29 Sept. 1940, 916. FRUS J II, p. 171.
131 COS(40) 796, 2 Oct. 1940. CAB 80/19. See also COS (40) 332nd, 3, s.d. CAB 79/7.
132 COS(40) 802, 4 Oct. CAB 80/20.
133 COS(40) 808, 7 Oct. CAB 80/20.
134 Minute, 4 Oct. 1940. FO 371/24709 [F4336/193/61].
135 Kennedy–Hull, 4 Oct. 1940, 3325 enclosing Personal from FNP. FRUS IV, p. 163. Kimball, I, p. 74.
136 Telegram, 4 Oct. 1940. FO371/24709 [F4556/193/61].
137 Telegram, 6 Oct. 1940, 2212. FO371/24716 [F3319/2739/61].
138 WM 267(40) 2, 7 Oct. CAB 65/9.
139 Wyatt Smith–Halifax, 27 Sept. 1940, 73E. FO371/24253 [A4793/1186/45].
140 E. Haas, *Frans Indo-China en de Japanese Expansiepolitiek 1939–1945*, Universitaire Pers Leiden, Leiden, 1956, pp. 56–7. Morley, *The Fateful Choice*, pp. 172–3.
141 Baudouin, pp. 187–9.
142 Ibid., p. 193.
143 Telegram, 5 Aug. 1940. 1620, FO371/24719 [F3710/3429/61].
144 Murphy–Hull, 4 Aug. 1940, 255. FRUS IV, pp. 62–3.
145 Aide-Mémoire, 6 Aug. 1940. FRUS IV, p. 64.
146 Memorandum, 6 Aug. 1940. FRUS IV, p. 65.
147 Welles–Grew, 6 Aug. 1940, 293. FRUS J II, p. 290.
148 Grew–Hull, 7 Aug. 1940, 672. FRUS IV p. 68.
149 Robert Murphy, *Diplomat among Warriors*, Collins, London, 1964, p. 79.
150 q. Dreifort, JSEAS, p. 287.
151 Murphy–Hull, 6 Aug. 1940, 268. FRUS IV, p. 66.
152 Matthews–Hull, 19 Sept. 1940, 591. FRUS IV, p. 133.
153 Baudouin, pp. 193–4.
154 Telegram, 6 Aug. 1940, 54. FO 371/24719 [F3710/3429/61].

155 Minutes, 6, 8 Aug. 1940. ibid.
156 Memorandum, 8 Aug. 1940. FO371/24719[F3526/3429/61].
157 WM (40) 222nd, 8 Aug. 1940. CAB 65/8.
158 Minute, 12 Aug. 1940. FO371/24719[F3474/3429/61].
159 Telegram, 9 Aug. 1940, 819. FO371/24719[F3710/3429/61].
160 Telegram, 9 Aug. 1940, 46. ibid.
161 Baudouin, p. 196.
162 Conversation, 13 Aug. 1940. FO371/24719[F3822/3429/61].
163 Telegram, 10 Aug. 1940, 1674 and minutes thereon. FO371/24719[F3795/3429/61].
164 Telegram, 14 Aug. 1940, 706. FO371/24719[F3831/3429/61].
165 Telegram, 16 Aug. 1940, 1592, and minutes thereon. FO371/24719[F3865/3429/61].
166 Haas, pp. 51–2, 65; Iklé, pp. 166–7.
167 Lu, p. 107.
168 Minutes, 13, 17 Aug. 1940, FO371/24719[F3474/3429/61].
169 Decoux, pp. 49–51.
170 Telegram, 10 Aug. 1940, 58. FO371/24719 [F3767/3429/61].
171 Telegram, 13 Aug. 1940, 49, ibid.
172 Telegram, 18 Aug. 1940, 62. ibid.
173 Telegram, 18 Aug. 1940, 728, and minutes thereon. ibid.
174 Telegram, 21 Aug. 1940, 865. ibid.
175 Telegram, 20 Aug. 1940, 1624, and minutes. ibid.
176 Telegram, 21 Aug. 1940, 874. ibid.
177 Minute, 12 Aug. 1940. FO371/24719[F3789/3429/61].
178 Minutes, 23 July, 26 July, 17 Aug. 1940, FO371/24719[F3651/3429/61].
179 Minute by Clarke, 14 Aug. 1940. ibid.
180 GOC Malaya to War Office, 20 Aug. 1940, 11725. FO371/24719 [F3831/3429/61].
181 Admiralty communication, received 11 July 1940. FO371/24719 [F3583/3429/61].
182 Minute by Gage, 2 Aug. 1940. FO371/24719 [F3655/3429/61].
183 Note, 24 Aug. 1940. FO371/24719 [F4037/3429/61].
184 C in C to Admiralty, 23 Aug. 1940, 379. FO371/24719 [F3795/3429/61].
185 Note, 24 Aug. [F4037].
186 Minute, 14 Aug. [F3651].
187 Telegram, 27 Aug. 1940, 70. FO371/24719 [F3865/3429/61].
188 Conversation, 27 Aug. 1940, FO371/24719[F4040/3429/61].
189 Telegram, 2 Sept. 1940, 1728, and minute, 4 Sept. FO371/24719[F4126/3429/61].
190 Ext Affs–Ballard, 29 Aug. 1940. AFPD IV, p. 118.
191 Murphy–Hull, 17 Aug. 1940, 362. FRUS IV, p. 81.
192 Baudouin, pp. 198–9.
193 Ibid., pp. 203–5.
194 Ibid., p. 218.
195 The letters are printed in Morley, pp. 301–2.
196 Ibid., pp. 174–5.
197 Ibid., pp. 176–7.
198 Decoux, pp. 103–4.
199 Morley, pp. 177–8.
200 Decoux, pp. 108–9.
201 Telegram, 3 Sept. 1940, 3. FO371/24719[F4109/3429/61].

202 Telegram, 3 Sept. 1940, 4. ibid.
203 Telegram, 4 Sept. 1940, 923. ibid.
204 Telegram, 4 Sept. 1940, 2146. ibid.
205 Telegram, 4 Sept. 1940, 164. ibid.
206 Telegram GOC Malaya to War Office, 3 Sept. 1940, 11937. FO371/24719 [F4109/3429/61].
207 Telegram, 4 Sept. 1940, 4. ibid.
208 Hull–Matthews, 26 Aug. 1940, 379. FRUS IV, p. 86.
209 Matthews–Hull, 27 Aug. 1940, 438. FRUS IV, p. 87.
210 Telegram, 3 Sept. 1940, 1902. FO371/24719 [F4109/3429/61]; Hull–Grew, 3 Sept. 1940, 334. FRUS J II, p. 292.
211 Hull–Matthews, 4 Sept., 418. FRUS IV, pp. 95–6.
212 Grew–Hull, 4 Sept., 789, paraphrase. FRUS J II, pp. 292–3.
213 Telegram, 4 Sept. 1940, 1738. FO371/24719[F4206/3429/61].
214 Telegram, 4 Sept. 1940, 1739. FO371/24719[F4171/3429/61].
215 Telegram, 5 Sept. 1940, 1747, FO371/24719[F4207/3429/61].
216 WM(40) 241st, 4 Sept. 1940. CAB 65/9. Telegram, 5/9, 2167. FO371/24719[F4109/3429/61].
217 Foreign Office to Kerr, 4 Sept. 1940, 386. FO371/24719[F4163/3429/61]. Telegram, 7 Sept., 91. ibid.
218 Minute, 4 Sept. 1940, FO371/24719[F4126/3429/61].
219 Morley, *The Fateful Choice*, pp. 182–3.
220 Telegram, 5 Sept. 1940, 5. FO371/24719[F4204/3429/61].
221 Telegram, 7 Sept. 1940, 7. ibid.
222 Telegram, 8 Sept. 1940, 8. ibid.
223 Telegram, 5 Sept. 1940, 78. FO371/24719 [F4165/3429/61].
224 Telegram, 5 Sept. 1940, 79. FO371/24719 [F4215/3429/61].
225 Telegram, 6 Sept. 1940, 1938. FO371/24719[F4165/3429/61].
226 Minutes, 8, 9 Sept. 1940. FO371/24719[F4126/3429/61].
227 Telegrams, 11 Sept., 948, 2214, ibid. Cf aide–mémoire, 12 Sept. 1940. FRUS IV, p. 112.
228 Telegram, 13 Sept. 1940, 1797 [F4126].
229 Minute, 15 Sept. 1940, ibid.
230 Telegram, 15 Sept. 1940, 96. ibid.
231 Telegram, 16 Sept., 1820, and minute, 23 Sept. ibid. Cf Grew–Hull, 16 Sept. FRUS IV, pp. 118–20.
232 Hull–Matthews, 9 Sept. 1940, 440. FRUS IV, p. 105.
233 Memorandum, 11 Sept. 1940, 140. FRUS IV, p. 106.
234 Matthews–Hull, 19 Sept. 1940, 591. FRUS IV, p. 133.
235 Telegram, 4 Sept. 1940, 1911. FO 371/24719[F4165/3429/61].
236 Telegram, 5 Sept. 1940, 1924, and minute, 8 Sept. ibid.
237 Telegram, 16 Sept. 1940, 1810. FO 371/24719 [F3710/3429/61]. Cf. memorandum by Grew, 14 Sept. FRUS II, pp. 293–4.
238 Minute, 22 Sept. 1940. [F3710].
239 Memorandum by Hamilton, 18 Sept. 1940. FRUS IV, p. 124.
240 Hull–Grew, 18 Sept., 385. FRUS IV, pp. 124–5. Telegram, 20 Sept., 1943. FO371/ 24720 [F4330/3429/61].
241 Hull–Grew, 19 Sept. 1940, 357. FRUS J II, p. 294.
242 Memorandum, 20 Sept. 1940. FRUS J II, p. 296.
243 Minute by Butler, 5 Sept. 1940, with note by Halifax, s.d. FO371/24719 [F4219/ 3429/61].

244 Minutes, ibid.; Admiralty communication, 9 Sept. 1940. FO371/24719 [F4226/ 3429/61].
245 CFR (40) 51st, 9 Sept. 1940. CAB 85/22. The planes in Martinique seem to have stayed there. Cf W.L. Langer and Gleason, *The Undeclared War*, Harper, New York, 1953, p. 15n; Haas, p. 90; E.R. Drachman, *United States Policy towards Vietnam, 1940–1945*, Fairleigh Dickinson University Press, Rutherford, NJ, 1970, pp. 17–19.
246 Telegram, 14 Sept. 1940, 13. FO371/24719[F4163/3429/61].
247 Telegram, 6 Sept. 1940, 6. FO371/24719[F4229/3429/61].
248 Telegram, 15 Sept. 1940, 2260. FO371/24719[F4163/3429/61].
249 Minute, 10 Sept. 1940. FO371/24719[F4229/3429/61].
250 Telegram, 7 Sept. 1940, 8. FO371/24719[F4204/3429/61].
251 Telegram GOC Malaya to War Office, 13 Sept. 1940, 12160. FO371/24719[F4248/3429/61].
252 Telegram, 14 Sept. 1940, 2261. FO371/24719[F4229/3429/61].
253 Telegram, 7 Sept, 8. [F4204].
254 Decoux, pp. 108–9.
255 Telegram, 16 Sept. 1940, 2022. FO371/24719[F4204/3429/61]. Cf Haas, p. 77.
256 Telegram, 19 Sept. 1940, 2045. FO371/24719[F4204/3429/61].
257 Casey–Ext Affairs, 19 Sept. 1940, 269. AFPD IV, p. 171.
258 Telegram, GOC Malaya to War Office, 19 Sept. 1940, 12266. FO371/24719. [F4253/3429/61].
259 Telegram, 19 Sept. 1940, 2313. FO371/24719[F4204/3429/61].
260 Conversation, 13 Sept. 1940. FO371/24720[F4309/3429/61].
261 Telegram, 15 Sept. 1940, 13. FO371/24720[F4293/3429/61].
262 Morley, pp. 182–3; Baudouin, pp. 235, 237.
263 Telegram, 18 Sept. 1940, 1829. FO371/24720[F4277/3429/61].
264 Telegram, 20 Sept. 1940, 1840. FO371/24720[F4308/3429/61].
265 Morley, pp. 183–4, 188–9, 192, 194 ff.
266 Telegram, 19 Sept. 1940, 15. FO371/24720[F4308/3429/61].
267 Telegram, 21 Sept. 1940, 19. FO371/24720[F4344/3429/61].
268 Telegram, 22 Sept. 1940, 20, and minute, 23 Sept. FO371/24720 [F4349/3429/61].
269 Telegram, 23 Sept. 1940, 21. FO371/24720 [F4365/3429/61].
270 Telegram, 24 Sept. 1940, 21. FO371/24720[F4399/3429/61].
271 Telegram, 25 Sept. 1940, 24. FO371/24720 [F4401/3429/61].
272 Telegram, 25 Sept. 1940, 24A. FO371/24720[F4430/3429/61].
273 Telegrams, 26 Sept. 1940. FO 371/24720[F4401/3429/61].
274 Decoux, pp. 110ff.
275 Ibid., p. 110.
276 Note, 21 Sept. 1940. FO371/24720[F4308/3429/61].
277 Telegram, 24 Sept. 1940, 21. ibid.
278 Telegram, 27 Sept. 1940, 25. FO371/24720[F4470/3429/61].
279 Telegram, 29 Sept. 1940, 341. FO371/24720[F4467/3429/61].
280 Murphy, p. 103.
281 Minutes, 1, 2 Oct. 1940. FO371/24720[F4470/3429/61].
282 Telegram, 24 Sept. 1940, 400, and minutes thereon. FO371/24720 [F4400/3429/61].
283 Telegram, 25 Sept. 1940, 1869. FO371/24720[F4433/3429/61].
284 Baudouin, p. 239.
285 Telegram, 23 Sept. 1940, 1852. FO371/24720[F4374/3429/61].

286 Telegram, 26 Sept. 1940, 1876, and minutes thereon, 1, 2 Oct. FO371/24720[F4483/3429/61].

287 CFR (40) 53rd, 16 Sept. 1940. CAB 85/22.

288 Morton to Stevenson, 19 Sept. 1940. FO371/24719[F4248/3429/61].

289 CFR (40) 54th, 19 Sept. 1940. CAB 85/22.

290 Minutes, 20, 23 Sept. 1940. FO371/24720[F4585/3249/61].

291 Foreign Office to Colonial Office, 29 Sept. 1940. FO371/24719 [F3651/3249/61].

292 Minute, 3 Oct. 1940. FO371/24719[F4204/3249/61].

293 Telegram, 23 Sept. 1940, 1852. [F4374].

294 Telegram from Kerr, 11 Sept. 1940, 93. FO371/24719[F4204/3429/61].

295 Telegram, 25 Sept. 1940, 106, and minutes thereon. FO371/24720 [F4425/3429/61].

296 Telegram, 28 Sept. 1940, 1890. FO371/24720[F4460/3429/61].

297 Memorandum, 20 Sept. 1940. FRUS J I, pp. 880–1.

298 Telegrams, 23, 24 September 1940, 2081, 2090. FO371/24719 [F4126/3429/61].

299 Ex, 28 Sept. 1940. FRUS J II, pp. 113–14.

300 Murakami, pp. 171–2.

301 Telegram, 9 Oct. 1940, 132. FO371/24720 [F4425/3429/61].

302 Decoux, p. 121.

303 WP (40) 364, 9 Sept. 1940. CAB 66/11; also COS (40), 730. CAB 80/18.

304 Minutes, 20, 22 Sept. 1940. FO371/24720 [F4262/3429/61].

305 Memorandum, 24 Sept. 1940, and note, 8 Oct. FO371/24720[F4406/3429/61].

306 Telegram from Crosby, 4 Aug. 1940, 239. FO371/24756 [F3706/3268/40].

307 Minute, 6 Aug. [F3706].

308 E. Reynolds, p. 116.

309 Stowe, p. 145.

310 Flood, pp. 276–7.

311 Crosby–Halifax, 25 July, 258. FO371/24751 [F3742/19/40].

312 Telegram from Crosby, 7 Aug. 1940, 243. FO371/24756 [F3706/3268/40].

313 Telegram, 8 Aug. 1940, 244. FO371/24756 [F3706/3268/40].

314 Telegram, 14 Aug. 1940, 142. ibid.

315 Telegram from Crosby, 16 Aug. 1940, 258. FO371/24756 [F3894/3268/40].

316 Minutes, 20, 21 Aug. ibid. [F3894].

317 Telegram from Crosby, 30 Aug. 1940, 284. ibid.

318 Telegram, 26 Aug., 271. FO371/24751 [F3395/19/40]. Also message from Churchill, 31 Aug. ibid. Crosby–Halifax, 31 Aug., encg ratification. FO371/24751 [F4629/19/40].

319 Stowe, p. 145.

320 Flood, p. 291.

321 E. Reynolds, p. 121.

322 Stowe, p. 149.

323 Stowe, pp. 149–50. Cf Decoux, pp. 132–3.

324 Minutes. FO371/24756 [F3880/3268/40]. Telegram, 14 Aug, 1494. FO371/24756 [F3706/3268/40].

325 Telegram from Lothian, 22 Aug. 1940, 1796. [F3706].

326 Welles–Grant, 21 Aug. 1940, 37. FRUS IV, p. 84.

327 Telegram, 29 Aug. 1940, 280. FO371/24756 [F3894/3268/40].

328 Grant–Hull, 5 Sept. 1940, 67. FRUS IV, pp. 98–9.

329 Hull–Grant, 5 Sept. 1940, 44. FRUS IV, p. 102.

330 Hull–Grant, 11 Sept. 1940, 46. FRUS IV, pp. 107–8.
331 Stowe, p. 150.
332 Flood, pp. 316, 348.
333 Crosby–Halifax, 16 Sept., 299. FO371/24757 [F4956/3268/40].
334 Telegram from Crosby, 9 Sept. 1940, 308. FO371/24751 [F4158/19/40].
335 Telegram, 12 Sept., 311. FO371/24756 [F4281/3268/40].
336 Minute, 19 Sept. ibid.
337 Telegram, 16 Sept., 316. [F4158]. A–m, 13 Sept., in desp. 299. [F4956].
338 Telegram from Crosby, 19 Sept. 1940, 324. [F4281].
339 Minute, 22 Sept. 1940. FO 371/24756 [F4342/3268/40].
340 Minute, 23 Sept. 1940. ibid.
341 Telegram, 25 Sept. 1940, 188. [F4342].
342 Telegram from Crosby, 27 Sept. 1940, 337. FO371/24751 [F4455/19/40].
343 Minute, 1 Oct. ibid.
344 Note, 3 Oct., on Crosby's telegram of 1 Oct. 1940, 347. FO371/24756[F4471/ 3268/40].
345 Telegram from Crosby, 28 Sept. 1940, 338. ibid.
346 Telegram from Crosby, 28 Sept. 1940, 339. ibid.
347 Minutes, 30 Sept., 3 Oct. 1940. ibid.
348 Grant–Hull, 15 Sept. 1940, 79. FRUS IV, p. 118.
349 Grant–Hull, 20 Sept. 1940, 85. ibid, pp. 135–6.
350 Grant–Hull, 13 Sept. 1940, 75. ibid., pp. 114–15.
351 Grant–Hull, 17 Sept. 1940, 81. ibid., pp. 122–3.
352 Hull–Grant, 18 Sept. 1940, 48. ibid., p. 126.
353 Matthews–Hull, 19 Sept. 1940, 588. ibid., pp. 127–9.
354 Grant–Hull, 25 Sept. 1940, 91. ibid., pp. 152–3.
355 Telegram from Crosby, 1 Oct. 1940, 347. [F4471].
356 E. Reynolds, p. 124.
357 Flood, pp. 323–5; E. Reynolds, p. 125; Charivat, pp. 229–30.
358 Stowe, p. 152.
359 Telegram, 21 Aug. 1940, 1783, attached to WP (40) 348, 2 Sept. CAB 66/11.
360 Telegram, 27 Aug. 1940, 1837. FO371/24669 [F4083/43/10].
361 Minute, 26 Aug. FO371/24669 [F4009/43/10].
362 Telegram to Craigie, 31 Aug. 1940, 913. [F4009].
363 Telegram, 30 Aug. 1940, 1716. FO371/24669 [F4074/43/10].
364 Telegram, 4 Sept., 927. ibid.
365 WP (40) 348 as above.
366 Telegram, 5 Sept. 1940, 1930. FO371/24709 [F4210/193/61].
367 Memorandum, 16 Sept. 1940. FRUS IV, p. 121.
368 Telegram, 16 Sept. 1940, 2027, and minute. FO371/24709 [F4290/193/61]. Cf also Casey–Ext Affs, 16 Sept., 260. AFPD IV, pp. 166–7.
369 Telegram, 8 Sept. 1940, 1763. FO371/24669 [F4238/43/10].
370 Telegram, 9 Sept. 1940, 1765. FO371/24719 [F4243/3429/61].
371 Telegram, 17 Sept. 1940, 1825. FO371/24670 [F4307/43/10].
372 Minute by A. Scott, 12 Sept. 1940. [F4238].
373 Telegram, 17 Sept. 1940, 1821. FO371/24670 [F4334/43/10].
374 Communication, 18 July 1940. FO371/24668. [F3657/43/10].
375 Bruce–Menzies, 3 Sept. 1940. AFPD IV, pp. 136–7.
376 Caldecote–Menzies, 5 Sept. 1940. ibid., pp. 139–41.
377 Policy in the Far East, Memorandum, nd. AFPD IV, pp. 156–60.
378 Menzies–Caldecote, 17 Sept. 1940, 483. ibid., pp. 164–5.
379 Telegram to Lothian, 29 Sept., 2406. FO371/24709 [F4290/193/61].

380 Conversation, 27 Sept. 1940. FRUS, IV, p. 157.
381 WM 264 (40) 4 & 5, 2 Oct. CAB 65/9.
382 Halifax–Churchill, 25 Sept. 1940. FO371/24670 [F4646/43/10].
383 Minute, 27 Sept. ibid.
384 Telegram, 28 Sept. 1940, 2383. ibid.
385 Conversation, 30 Sept. 1940. FRUS IV, p. 160.
386 Minute, 1 Oct. 1940. FO371/24670 [F4489/43/10].
387 WP (40) 400, 2 Oct. 1940. CAB 66/12.
388 WM 265 (40) 3 Oct, Item 5. CAB 65/9.
389 Cf Broadcast, 2 July 1940. I (44) 8, CAB 91/2.
390 Taylor, MAS, p. 177.
391 Telegram from Governor–SofS Burma, 27 Sept. 1940, 828C. FO371/24670 [F4549/43/10].
392 Telegram from Governor, 3 Oct., 849C. ibid.
393 Minute, 11 Oct. FO371/24670 [F4620/43/10].
394 Telegram, 17 Oct. 1940, 2052. FO371/24671 [F4803/43/10].
395 Minute, 21 Oct. ibid.
396 Minute by Gent, 13 Aug. 1940. CO531/29 [53011/4].
397 Draft, August 1940. ibid.
398 Minute by Gent, 1 Nov. ibid.
399 Minute by Parkinson, 6 Mar. 1941. ibid.
400 COS (40) 592, 31 July. CAB 66/10.

4 October 1940 – June 1941

1 31 Dec. 1940. Cadogan, p. 346.
2 Grew–FDR, 14 Dec. 1940. FRUS IV, pp. 469–71.
3 FDR–Grew, 21 Jan. 1941. FRUS 1941 IV, pp. 6–8.
4 Grew–Hull, 14 Feb. 1941, 230. FRUS IV, p. 38. Cf telegram from Craigie, 17 Feb., 255. FO371/27774 [F1043/54/61].
5 Appraisal, 14 Apr. 1941. FRUS IV, pp. 150–2.
6 Cadogan, p. 333.
7 G. St. J. Barclay, *Their Finest Hour*, Weidenfeld & Nicolson, London, 1977, p. 48.
8 31 Nov. Cadogan, p. 336.
9 Ibid., p. 339.
10 24 Feb. 1941. Cadogan, p. 358.
11 Barclay, pp. 106–9.
12 27 May. Cadogan, p. 381.
13 D. Reynolds, p. 189.
14 18 June. Cadogan, p. 389.
15 Ibid., p. 367.
16 31 May. Cadogan, p. 382.
17 2 June. Cadogan, p. 385.
18 D. Reynolds, p. 205.
19 30 June. Cadogan, p. 390.
20 1 July. Cadogan, pp. 390–1.
21 q. D. Reynolds, p. 145.
22 D. Reynolds, pp. 146–7.
23 Ibid., p. 149.
24 q. ibid., p. 150.
25 q. Woodward, I, p. 396.

26 Warren F. Kimball, *The Most Unsordid Act*, Johns Hopkins University Press, Baltimore, MD, 1969, pp. 177 ff.
27 q. D. Reynolds, p. 168.
28 Ibid., p. 183.
29 Ibid., p. 224.
30 Cf Johnsen, pp. 171–7.
31 Ibid., p. 192–3.
32 q. D. Reynolds, p. 185. Cf also Johnsen, p. 179n.
33 D. Reynolds, p. 185.
34 Barclay, p. 39.
35 D. Reynolds, p. 187.
36 q. ibid., p. 201.
37 Ibid., pp. 201–2.
38 President–Former Naval Person, 27 May 1941. Kimball, *Churchill and Roosevelt*, pp. 196–7.
39 28 May 1941. ibid., p. 198.
40 D. Reynolds, pp. 203–4.
41 Casey–Dept, 31 Mar., 241, referring to conversation with Welles. AFPD IV, p. 532.
42 D. Reynolds, p. 224.
43 q. ibid., p. 225.
44 q. ibid.
45 Ibid.
46 Casey–Ext Affairs, 21 Feb. 1941, 151. AFPD IV, pp. 436–7.
47 Reynolds, pp. 227–8. Cf Cranborne–Fadden, 2 May 1941, 308. AFPD IV, pp. 629–31.
48 1 May. Cadogan, p. 375.
49 Minute by Seymour, 5 May. FO371/27756 [F3576/54/61].
50 Cf Casey–Ext Affairs, 8 May 1941, 340. AFPD, pp. 638–9. Cf aide-mémoire, 8 May. FRUS IV, p. 184.
51 James H. Herzog, *Closing the Open Door*, Naval Institute Press, Annapolis, MD, 1973, pp. 130–2.
52 Cf R.J.C. Butow, *The John Doe Associates*, Stanford University Press, Stanford, CA, 1974, ch. 2.
53 Ibid., pp. 164–5.
54 Ibid., pp. 214–5.
55 Conversation, 15 Feb. 1941. FRUS IV, pp. 39–41.
56 Memorandum, 14 April 1941. ibid., p. 149.
57 D. Reynolds, p. 230.
58 Lowe, pp. 252–5.
59 Reynolds' phrase, p. 231.
60 Crowley, pp. 89–90.
61 Ibid., pp. 90–1.
62 Ibid., pp. 91–2.
63 Ibid., pp. 93–4.
64 Report, 31 Oct. 1940. ADM 1/11183.
65 Minute, 25 Nov. 1940. AFPD IV, p. 282.
66 Commonwealth–Cranborne, 1 Dec. 1940, 627. ibid., pp. 285–7.
67 Menzies–Bruce, 3 Dec. 1940, 1464. ibid., p. 289.
68 Cranborne–Commonwealth, 23 Dec. 1940, 510. ibid., pp. 314–16.
69 Fadden–Menzies, 12 Feb. 1941, 57. ibid., p. 386.
70 Memorandum, 12 Feb. 1941. ibid., pp. 387–90.

71 Casey–Ext Affairs, 15 Feb. 1941, 126. ibid., pp. 413–14.
72 *Times*, 4 Mar. 1941.
73 Minute, 5 Mar. 1941. FO371/27774 [F1601/54/61].
74 Minutes, 6 Mar., 6 April. [F1601]. Cf David Day, *Menzies and Churchill*, Angus & Robertson, Sydney, 1986, p. 79.
75 Note of Conversations, 8 Mar. 1941. AFPD IV, pp. 483–4.
76 Memorandum by UK COS (41) 230, 11 April. CAB 80/27. AFPD IV, pp. 568–76.
77 Fadden–Menzies, 23 April 1941, 252. AFPD IV, pp. 608–10.
78 Cranborne–Whiskard, 23 April, Z143. ibid., pp. 612–13.
79 Menzies–Commonwealth, 2 May 1941, M100. ibid., pp. 633–5.
80 Menzies–Churchill, 28 June 1941, 402. ibid., p. 741.
81 Grew–Hull, 7 Feb. 1941, 180–3. FRUS V, p. 63.
82 Cf Casey–Ext Affairs, 24 Feb. 1941, 159. AFPD, p. 440.
83 Ibid., p. 440–1.
84 Memorandum by Minister of Economic Warfare, encd in FE(41) 136/WP (41) 155, 7 July 1941. CAB 96/4. Cf W.N. Medlicott, *The Economic Blockade*, London, 1952/1978, I, pp. 426–8; 1959/1978, II, pp. 68ff.
85 FO Memorandum, 7 July 1941. FE(41) 136/WP (41) 155. CAB 96/4.
86 Stewart–Casey, 9 Dec. 1940, 238. AFPD IV, pp. 293–4.
87 Casey–Dept, 11 Dec. 1940, 424. ibid., p. 297.
88 Cranborne–Commonwealth, 5 April 1941, D 182. ibid., pp. 547–8.
89 Stewart–Latham, 8 April 1941. ibid., pp. 557–8; Commonwealth–Cranborne, 14 May, 290. ibid., pp. 645–6.
90 Telegrams from Lothian, 9 Oct.; 10 Oct. 1940, 2241, 2265, and minute. FO 371/24722 [F4627/4605/61].
91 Minutes in FO371/24717 [F4368/2739/61].
92 Telegram from Lothian, 9 Oct. 1940, 2239, and minute, 12 Oct. FO371/24710 [F4648/193/61].
93 Minute, 14 Oct. 1940. FO371/24722 [F4824/4605/61].
94 COS(40) 829, 13 Oct. 1940. CAB 80/20.
95 Telegram, 14 Oct. 1940, 2645. FO371/24722 [F4627/4605/61].
96 Memorandum, 18 Oct. 1940. FRUS IV, p. 187.
97 Telegrams, 18 Oct. 1940, 2344. FO371/24710 [F4674/193/61]; 16 Oct., 2327 [F4758/193/61].
98 Memorandum, 18 Oct. 1940. FO371/24722 [F4824/4605/61]. Telegram to Butler, 19 Oct., 2728. FO371/24710 [F4698/193/61]. WM 273 (40) 7, 18 Oct. CAB 65/9. Cf Michiels–van Kleffens, 18 Oct. 1940. *Documenten betreffende de Buitenlandse Politiek van Nederland 1919–1945*, Periode C, Deel 1, The Hague, 1976, pp. 517–18.
99 Memorandum by Halifax, 28 Oct. [F4824]; Ady–CinC, 1 Nov., 661. FO371/24710 [F4988/193/61].
100 Memorandum by Bennett, 26 Oct. 1940. [F4824]. Cf also Memorandum by Hornbeck, 30 Oct. FRUS IV, p. 198.
101 Telegram from Butler, 19 Oct. 1940, 2357, and reply, 26 Oct, 2816. FO371/24710 [F4821/193/61]; telegram from Butler, 3 Nov., 2532, and minute, 4 Oct. FO371/24710 [F4975/193/61].
102 Conversation, 6 Nov. 1940. FO371/24717 [F5020/2739/61].
103 COS(40) 383nd, 8 Nov. CAB 79/7.
104 Telegram from Butler, 14 Nov., 2662. FO371/24710 [F5134/193/61].
105 Telegram from C–G, 30 Sept. 1940, 150. FO371/24717 [F4035/2739/61].
106 Telegram from Craigie, 3 Oct. 1940, 1947. FO371/24717 [F4368/2739/61].

107 Walsh–FSy, 25 Oct. 1940, 154; 14 Nov, 163E; 13 Nov., Int. No 6. FO371/24717 [F4984/2739/61].
108 Hull–Grew, 3 Oct. 1940, 376. FRUS IV, p. 161.
109 Memorandum by Welter in FO371/24718 [F5252/2739/61].
110 Minute by Clarke, 27 Nov. 1940. FO371/24718 [F5220/2739/61].
111 Conversation, 19 Nov. 1940. FO371/24718 [F5252/2739/61].
112 Minutes, 22, 25 Nov. 1940. FO371/24722 [F5341/3654/61].
113 Halifax–Bland, 25 Nov. 1940, 273. FO371/24722 [F5341/3654/61].
114 Memorandum 23 Nov. 1940. FO371/24711 [F5359/193/61]. Alexander–Halifax, 29 Nov. ibid.
115 Minute, 19 Nov. 1940. FO371/24757 [F5190/3268/40].
116 Minute, 21 Nov. ibid.
117 Telegram to Lothian, 2 Dec. 1940, 3327. ibid.
118 Telegram to Lothian, 3 Dec. 1940, 3328. FO371/24710 [F5134/193/61].
119 Conversation, 9 Dec. 1940. FO371/24718 [F5465/2739/61].
120 Phillimore–Halifax, 28 Nov. 1940, and minutes. FO371/24711 [F5627/193/61].
121 Minute, 18 Dec. 1940. FO371/24712 [F5642/265/61].
122 Bennett–Hollis, 25 Dec. 1940. [F5627].
123 12 Dec. 1940. ADM 1/11118.
124 Johnsen, pp. 210–11.
125 Minute, 3 Feb. 1941. FO371/27785 [F496/141/61].
126 COS(40) 1055 (JP) (JP (40)797), 19 Dec. CAB80/24.
127 Minute, 4 Jan. 1941. FO371/24711 [F5729/193/61].
128 COS (41) 17 (Final), 7 Jan. 1941. CAB80/25.
129 Memorandum, 3 Jan. 1941. FO371/27773 [F59/54/61].
130 Minutes, 12 Jan. 1941. FO371/27785 [F141/141/61].
131 FE(41) 3, 16 Jan. CAB 96/2.
132 Minute, 26 Jan., 5 Feb. 1941. FO371/27785 [F141/141/61]. COS(41) 49, 21 January. CAB 80/25.
133 WP(41) 24, 5 Feb. 1941. CAB 66/14.
134 WM(41) 4, 6 Feb. CAB 65/17.
135 Minutes of meeting, 7 Feb. 1941. CAB 79/9; also PREM/326/1.
136 *The Empire at Bay*, p. 673.
137 Minutes, 6 Feb., 11 Feb. 1941. PREM 3/326.
138 Minute, 12 Feb. 1941. PREM 3/326.
139 COS (41) 46th, 8 Feb. 1941, Item 4. CAB 79/9.
140 Telegram to Halifax, 11 Feb. 1941, 770. PREM 3/326.
141 Halifax–Hull, 11 Feb. 1941, and encs. FRUS V, pp. 74–7.
142 Conversation with Eden, 10 Feb. 1941. FO371/27785 [F740/141/61].
143 Watt–Dept, cable 114, 12 Feb. 1941. AFPD IV, pp. 398–9.
144 Minute, 13 Feb. 1941. PREM 3/326.
145 Minute, 13 Feb. 1941. PREM 3/326.
146 Minute, 17 Feb. 1941. PREM 3/326.
147 Memorandum, 16 Feb. 1941, in Alexander–Churchill, 18 Feb. PREM 3/326.
148 Minute, 22 Feb. 1941. PREM 3/326.
149 WM 19(41)5. CAB 65/17.
150 Telegram from C in C F E and C in C China, 21 Jan. 1941. FO371/27785 [F496/141/61].
151 Telegram from C in C to Air Ministry, 29 Jan. 1941; from Australian Govt to DO, 29 Jan., 57. FO371/27785 [F496/141/61]. COS(41) 63, 31 Jan. CAB 80/25. See also Walsh–Howe, 28 Jan. FO371/27786 [F2949/141/61].

152 Telegram from GOC Malaya to WO, 9 Feb. 1941. FO371/27785 [F707/141/61].
153 Telegram from Batavia, 22 Feb. 1941, 25. FO371/27786 [F1241/141/61].
154 Conversation, 4 Feb. 1941; minute, s.d. FO 371/27785 [F496/141/61].
155 Conversation, 5 Feb. 1941. [F496].
156 Minute by Bland, 18 Feb. 1941. FO371/27786 [F1141/141/61].
157 Conversation, 20 Feb. 1941. FO371/27786 [F1283/141/61].
158 Conversation, 21 Feb. 1941. FO371/27766 [F1229/141/61].
159 Norman A. Graebner, 'Hoover, Roosevelt and the Japanese' in Borg and Okanioto, *Pearl Harbor as History*, New York and London, 1973, p. 47.
160 Conversation between Netherlands minister and Eden, 31 Jan. 1941. FO371/27785 [F497/141/61]. Walsh–Sy, 23 Jan., 11E, secret. FO371/27786 [F3029/141/61]. Grew–Hull, 10 Feb. 1941, 5363. FRUS J II, pp. 303–4. Pabst–van Kleffens, 4 Feb. 1941. *Documenten*, C, II, pp. 254–6.
161 Telegram from Batavia, 22 Jan. 1941, 10. FO 371/27785 [F247/141/61]. Cf van Mook, pp. 67–8. Also cf Foote–Hull, 22 Feb. FRUS V, pp. 27–8.
162 Second memorandum, 27 Jan. 1941. FO371/27785 [F452/161/61]. Cf van Mook, pp. 68–71.
163 Minutes [F452].
164 van Mook, p. 71; also Grew–Hull, 3 Feb. 1941, 158. FRUS V, p. 54.
165 van Mook, pp. 72–4. Telegram from Batavia, 3 Feb. 1941, 13. FO371/27785 [F452/41/61].
166 Telegram from Walsh, 20 Feb. 1941, 24, and minute. FO371/27786 [F1151/141/61].
167 4th Memorandum, 7 Mar. 1941. FO371/27833 [F1805/1732/61].
168 Telegram from C in C FE to WO, 27 Feb., and minute. FO371/27786 [F1423/141/61].
169 Staff conversations with Officers of NEI, 26–29 Nov. 1940. ADM 1/11118.
170 Telegram from C in C China, 23 Jan. 1941. FO371/27785 [F141/141/61]. COS(41) 68, 31 Jan. CAB 80/25.
171 JP(41) 184, 7 Mar. 1941. CAB 84/28. COS(41) 95th, 12 Mar. CAB 79/9.
172 Minutes, 6 Mar. 1941. FO371/27774 [F2437/54/61].
173 Hart–Stark, 4 Mar. 1941, q. Johnsen p. 221.
174 Conversation, 9 Mar. 1941. FO371/27786 [F1793/141/61].
175 Minute, 27 Mar. 1941. FO371/27786 [F2343/141/61].
176 Menzies–Fadden, telegram, Cairo, 14 Feb., unnumbered. AFPD IV, pp. 405–6.
177 Record, 26 Feb. 1941. AFPD IV, pp. 456–61. Conversation and papers attached, 24 Mar. 1941. [F2343]. Cadogan, p. 359.
178 Memorandum, FE defence. [F2343]. COS(41) 98th, 14 Mar., Item 4. CAB 79/9.
179 Moyne–Butler, 4 April 1941. FO371/27774 [F2677/54/61].
180 Cranborne–Butler, 27 Mar. 1941. FO371/27774 [F2399/54/61].
181 Memorandum, 14 Feb. 1941. *Documenten*, C, II, pp. 284–5.
182 Cranborne–Whiskard, 11 Mar. 1941, Z 66. AFPD, pp. 489–90. Cf 14 Feb. Cadogan, p. 354.
183 Conversation, 8 April 1941. FO371/27775 [F2919/54/61]; also AFPD, p. 567.
184 Hollis–Bennett, 7 April 1941. FO371/27774 [F2719/54/61].
185 *The Empire at Bay*, p. 680.
186 Memorandum, 13 April 1941, and minutes. FO371/27775 [F3164/54/61].
187 Telegram, 19 April, 2105 [F3164].

188 Telegram to dominions, 23 April 1941, 142. FO371/27776 [F3505/54/61]. Cf Winant–Hull, 19 April, 1560. FRUS V, p. 132.
189 WM 42(41) 21 April, Item 3. CAB 65/18. Cf minute on DO comm., 21 April. FO371/ 27789 [F3393/158/61].
190 Note by Bruce, 18 Feb. 1941, and enclosure. AFPD IV, p. 422.
191 Telegram to Halifax, 25 April, 2223 [F3164].
192 Minute by Bennett, 20 April 1941. FO371/27776 [F3456/54/61]. Conversation, 21 April. FO371/27775 [F3257/54/61]. Telegram from Halifax, 26 April, 1848. FO371/27776 [F3446/54/61].
193 Casey–Hull, 22 April 1941. AFPD IV, pp. 602–3; also FRUS V, pp. 137–8.
194 Attachment to minute by Butler, 5 May. FO371/27777 [F3826/54/61].
195 Casey–Dept, 28 April, 313. AFPD IV, p. 622. Hull–Casey conversation, 28 April. FRUS V, pp. 139–40.
196 Telegram from C in C FE to WO, 27 April 1941. COS 41 (272), 30 April. CAB 80/27.
197 Minute, 5 May 1941. FO371/27776 [F3576/54/61].
198 Memorandum, 5 May 1941, and minutes. FO371/27777 [F4128/54/61].
199 MOI communication, 16 May. FO371/27777 [F4122/54/61].
200 Communication, recd 7 May. FO371/27777 [F4017/54/61].
201 Stewart–Casey, 23 May 1941. AFPD, pp. 675–7.
202 Minutes in FO371/27777 [F4130/54/61].
203 WP (41) 101, 12 May 1941. CAB 66/16. Cf Avon, *The Reckoning*, Cassell, London, 1956, p. 310.
204 DO(41) 30th, 15 May. CAB 69/2.
205 Telegram, 22 May 1941, 2756. FO371/27777 [F4130/54/61].
206 22 May, 93. FO371/27847 [F4366/4366/61]; also AFPD IV, p. 667.
207 Telegrams, 26, 31 May, 2372, 2953. FO371/27847 [F4529/4366/61].
208 UK HCSAf–DO, 31 May 1941, 612. FO371/27847 [F4724/4366/61].
209 Conversation, 3 June, and a.m. FRUS V, pp. 166, 167.
210 Telegram, 6 June 1941, 2567. FO371/27778 [F4883/84/61].
211 Casey to Dept, 4 June 1941, 406. AFPD, pp. 702–3.
212 M.P. Lissington, *New Zealand and Japan 1900–1941*, Government Printer, Wellington, 1972, p. 159.
213 Cf Holmes–Bennett, 25 May 1941. FO371/27777 [F4422/54/61].
214 Minute, 12 June 1941. FO371/27778 [F5011/54/61]; also memorandum, 13 June. [F5012/54/61].
215 Telegram from Walsh, 5 Mar. 1941, 33. FO371/27833 [F1732/1732/61].
216 Minute by Gage, 1 April 1941. FO371/27833 [F2429/1732/61].
217 Telegram, 31 Mar. 1941, 60. FO371/27833 [F2513/1732/61].
218 Telegram, 18 Mar. 1941, 27. FO371/27833 [F3690/1732/61].
219 Telegram, 19 May 1941, 89. FO371/27833 [F4311/1732/61].
220 Van Mook, pp. 88–96; telegram from Walsh, 7 June 1941, 105. FO371/27834 [F5079/1732/61]; reply, 6 June. FO371/27834 [F5151/1732/61].
221 Memorandum, 12 June 1941. FO371/27834 [F5151/1732/61].
222 Telegrams, 22 May 1941, 841, 842. FO371/27833 [F4342, 4345/1732/6]. Cf N. Ike, *Japan's Decision for War*, Stanford University Press, Stanford, CA, 1967, p. 38.
223 Minute, 31 May 1941. FO371/27833 [F4376/1732/61]; Telegram to Craigie, 2 June, 654. ibid.
224 JIC(41) 246, 6 June. CAB 79/12.
225 Eden–Bland, 3 June 1941, 22. FO371/27833 [F4545/1732/61].
226 Leith-Ross–Hart, 5 July 1941. FO371/27835 [F5875/1732/61].

227 Hart–Leith-Ross, 15 July 1941. FO371/27835 [F6677/1732/61].
228 Van Mook, pp. 97–9.
229 11 June. Ike, p. 50.
230 Latham–Dept, 12 June 1941, 289. AFPD IV, p. 717.
231 Telegram, 11 June 1941, 967. FO371/27834 [F5083/1732/61].
232 Telegram, 11 June 1941, 968. FO371/27834 [F5148/1732/61].
233 Telegram, 11 June 1941, 969, and minutes, 14 June. FO371/27834 [F5157/1732/61].
234 Telegrams, 14, 16 June 1941, 1000, 1006. FO371/27834 [F5245, F5291/1732/61].
235 Telegram, 18 June 1941, 1022. FO371/27834 [F5402/1732/61].
236 Minute by Clarke, 19 June 1941. FO371/27834 [F5245/1732/61].
237 Telegram from Craigie, 19 June 1941, 1027. FO371/27834 [F5433/1732/61. Cf Cranborne–Menzies, 23 June, M120. AFPD, p. 736, and Hull–Grew, 17 June, 335. FRUS V, p. 177.
238 Memorandum, 2 July 1941. FO371/27778 [F5294/54/61].
239 Conversation, 13 June 1941. FO371/27778 [F5153/54/61].
240 COS (41) 209th, 12 June 1941, Item 6. CAB 79/12.
241 Hollis–Bennett, 18 June 1941. FO371/27778 [F5389/54/61].
242 Minutes, 20, 21 June 1941; telegram, 4 July, 3747. [F5389].
243 WP(41) 150, 3 July 1941. CAB 66/17.
244 Minutes, 26, 27, 29 June, 1 July 1941 [F5389].
245 ADA, 25 Feb. 1941. COS(41) 406, CAB 80/29. JP(41) 503, 1 July. CAB 84/33. ADB, April 1941. COS(41) 387. CAB 80/28. JP(41) 504, 1 July. CAB 84/32. COS(41) 233rd, 3 July, Items 15 and 16. CAB 79/12.
246 COS(41) 414, 5 July. CAB 80/29. COS(41) 238th, 9 July, Item 4. CAB 79/12.
247 COS(41) 239th, 10 July, Item 4. CAB 79/12.
248 Minutes in FO371/27779 [F6172/54/61].
249 Wyatt Smith–Eden, 14 Feb. 1941, 19E. FO371/26232 [A3312/888/45].
250 ADB, April 1941, p. 5.
251 Telegram from Halifax, 19 June 1941, 2853, Gleam 172. FO371/27778 [F5400/54/61].
252 Leahy–Hull, 1 Mar. 1941, 256. FRUS V, p. 100.
253 Telegram to Butler, 16 Nov. 1940, 3059. FO371/24721 [F5219/3429/61].
254 FE (40) 9th, 25 Nov., Item 2. CAB 96/1.
255 FE (40) 11th, 5 Dec., Item 3. CAB 96/1.
256 Telegram, 11 Dec. 1940, 42. FO371/24721 [F5375/3429/61].
257 Telegram from CinC, 28 Dec., 926. FO371/24722 [F5765/3429/61].
258 Note of a meeting at Government House, Singapore, 28 Dec. 1940, in Thomas–Moyne, 18 Feb. 1941. FO371/27761 [F1094/9/61].
259 FO minute, 21 Feb. 1941. FO371/27761 [F1160/9/61]. Cf Medlicott, II, pp. 89–90.
260 CO communication, 29 Dec. 1940; minute, 2 Jan. FO371/27758 [F8/8/61].
261 Telegram, 7 Jan. 1941. FO371/27758 [F185/8/61].
262 Minute by A. Clarke, 14 Jan. 1941. FO371/27758 [F278/8/61].
263 Admiralty communication, 30 Jan. 1941. FO371/27760 [F456/9/61].
264 Telegram to Lampson, 28 Jan. 1941, 228. FO371/27758 [F278/8/61].
265 Admiralty communication, 30 Jan. 1941. [F456].
266 Report on Conditions in Indo-China, encd in E.W. Meiklereid to Eden, 11 July 1941, No. 12, secret. FO371/27767 [F11336/9/61].
267 De Gaulle–Cadogan, 20 Jan. 1941. FO371/27760 [F338/9/61].

268 Telegram, 29 Jan. 1941, 170. FO371/27760 [F466/9/61]; Gage to Banks, 7 Jan., ibid.
269 Air–FO, 8 Feb. 1941. FO371/27760 [F730/9/61].
270 Telegram, 24 Jan. 1941, 128. FO371/27760 [F398/9/61].
271 Minute, 29 Jan. 1941. ibid.
272 Telegram, 27 Jan. 1941, 146. FO371/27760 [F458/9/61].
273 Telegram, 28 Jan. 1941, commd. FO371/27760 [F454/9/61].
274 Telegram, 29 Jan. 1941, 156. Minutes, 31 Jan, 4 Feb. [F454].
275 Telegram, 1 Feb., 505. FO371/27760 [F524/9/61].
276 Minute, 4 Feb. 1941. [F524].
277 Latham–Dept, 4 Feb. 1941, cable 68. AFPD IV, pp. 366–7.
278 Telegram, 3 Feb. 1941, 184. FO 371/27760 [F540/9/61].
279 Minute, 5 Feb. 1941. [F540].
280 WM 13(41) 4, 5 Feb. CAB 65/17.
281 JP(41) 103, 7 Feb. 1941, attached to COS(41) 46th, 8 Feb. CAB 79/9.
282 Minute, 17 Feb. 1941. FO371/27761 [F998/9/61].
283 Minute, 25 Feb. 1941. FO371/27761 [F1094/9/61].
284 Memorandum, 4 Mar. 1941. FO371/27762 [F1624/9/61].
285 Minute, 7 Mar. ibid.
286 Telegram from Craigie, 22 Feb. 1941, 293. FO371/27761 [F1193/9/61].
287 Minute, 26 Feb. 1941. [F1193].
288 Minute, 27 Feb. 1941. [F1193].
289 Telegram, 2 Mar. 1941, 154. FO371/27762 [F1536/9/61].
290 Minutes, 10 Mar., 18 Mar., 19 Mar., 1 April, 3 April; telegram, 4 April 1941, 163. [F1536].
291 Draft, JP (41) 247 (5), 3 April. FO371/27775 [2872/54/61].
292 Medlicott, II, pp. 94–6; A. Gaudel, *L'Indochine Francaise en face du Japon*, Susse, Paris, 1947, pp. 201 ff.
293 Telegram from C in C, China, 21 May 1941, 505. FO371/27826 [F3706/1577/61].
294 Telegram from C in C, China, 1 June 1941, 643. FO371/27827 [F4723/1577/61].
295 Minute, 4 June. [F4723].
296 Minute, 26 June 1941. FO371/27827 [F5644/1577/61].
297 FE(41) 23rd, 26 June, Item 3. CAB96/2.
298 Grant–Hull, 4 Oct. 1940. FRUS IV, p. 166.
299 Stowe, p. 153.
300 Stowe, p. 155. Cf FRUS 1941 V, p. 12.
301 Stowe, p. 155. Cf Hull–Grant, 10 Oct. 1940, 57. FRUS IV, pp. 176–7.
302 Stowe, pp. 148, 158.
303 Telegram GOC Malaya–WO, 7 Oct. 1940, 12643. FO371/24756 [F4625/3268/40].
304 Telegram, 9 Oct., 364. [F4625].
305 Telegram GOC Malaya–WO, 11 Oct. 1940, 12753. [F4625].
306 Telegram to Crosby, 8 Oct., 196. F.L.371/24756 [F4471/3768/40]l.
307 Telegram, 8 Oct. 1940, 363. [F4625].
308 FE (40) 2nd, 9 Oct., 4. CAB 96/1.
309 Minutes by Gage, 11 Oct., Clarke, 13 Oct. [F4625].
310 Minute, 13 Oct. [F4625].
311 FE (40) 3rd, 14 Oct., Item 2. CAB 96/1.
312 Telegram to Crosby, 15 Oct. 1940, 206. [F4625].

313 FE (40) 4th, 18 Oct., Item 3. CAB 96/1.
314 Telegram, 19 Oct. 1940, 381. FO24756 [F4827/3268/40].
315 Telegram, 15 Oct. 1940, 2655. [F4625].
316 Grant–Hull, 11 Oct. 1940, 113. FRUS IV, pp. 177–9.
317 Telegram, 10 Nov. 1940, 424. FO371/24757 [F5064/3268/40].
318 Aide-mémoire, 23 Oct. 1940. FRUS IV, p. 191.
319 FE (40) 5th, 23 Oct. 1940, Item 7. CAB 96/1.
320 Telegram, 29 Oct. 1940, 396. FO371/24721 [F4932/3249/61].
321 Minute, 31 Oct. 1940. [F4932].
322 FE (40) 6th, 31 Oct., Item 2. CAB 96/1.
323 Minute by Clarke, 4 Nov. 1940. [F4932].
324 Minute by Gage, 4 Nov. 1940. FO371/24757 [F4967/3268/40].
325 FE (40) 7th, 7 Nov., Item 2. CAB 96/1. Cf telegram to Crosby, 17 Nov., 248. FO371/28131 [F2803/246/40].
326 Telegram to Butler, 17 Nov. 1940, 3078. FO371/24757 [F5064/3268/40].
327 Memorandum, 18 Nov. 1940. FRUS IV, pp. 214–16.
328 Minute, 27 Nov. FO371/24721 [F4991/3429/61].
329 Stowe, p. 156; Flood, p. 333; Morley, The Fateful Choice, p. 218.
330 Telegram, 1 Nov. 1940, 407. FO371/24757 [F4967/3268/40].
331 Stowe, p. 159.
332 Flood, pp. 337–8.
333 Ibid., pp. 339–40.
334 Ibid., pp. 341–2.
335 E. Reynolds, p. 130.
336 Stowe, p. 160; Richard J. Aldrich, The Key to the South, Oxford University Press, Kuala Lumpur, 1993, p. 275. Cf Memorandum, 11 Nov. DGFP XI, London, 1961, p. 519.
337 Flood, p. 344.
338 Four Ministers, 21 Nov. 1940. Flood, p. 345; Morley, pp. 219–21.
339 Flood, p. 346.
340 Ibid., p. 347.
341 Hull–Murphy, 12 Dec. 1940, 837. FRUS IV, pp. 235–6.
342 Murphy–Hull, 16 Dec. 1940, 1142. ibid., pp. 239–40.
343 E. Reynolds, p. 131.
344 Flood, p. 347.
345 Ibid., p. 367.
346 Stowe, p. 164.
347 Flood, pp. 379–80; E. Reynolds, pp. 132–3.
348 Minute, 1 Dec. 1940. FO371/24757 [F5371/3268/40].
349 Minutes, 2, 2, 3 Dec. [F5371].
350 FE (40) 11th, 5 Dec., Item 4. CAB 96/1.
351 Telegram, 12 Dec. 1940, 284. [F5371].
352 FE (40) 13th, 20 Dec. CAB 96/1.
353 Minute, 20 Dec. 1940. FO371/24757 [F5568/3268/40].
354 Minute, 25 Dec. 1940. [F5568].
355 Minute, 26 Dec. 1940. FO371/24757 [F5489/3268/40].
356 Minute, 22 Dec. 1940. FO371/24722 [F5628/3429/61].
357 Telegram, 30 Dec. 1940, 551. FO371/28108 [F79/5/40].
358 Minute by Clarke, 30 Dec. 1940. FO371/24722 [F5765/3429/61]. Flood, p. 371. Decoux, p. 142.
359 Stowe, p. 165.
360 Telegram to Crosby, 4 Jan. 1941, 6. FO371/28108 [F79/5/40].

361 Conversation, 8 Jan. 1941. FO371/28108 [F175/5/40].
362 Telegram to Butler, 4 Jan. 1941, 57. [F79].
363 Telegram, 8 Jan. 1941, 97 [F79]. Cf aide–mémoire, 6 Jan. FRUS V, pp. 2–5.
364 Telegram, 8 Jan. 1941, 17. FO371/28108 [F142/5/40].
365 Aide–mémoire, 10 Jan. 1941. FRUS V, pp. 10–11.
366 Telegram, 10 Jan. 1941, 146. [F142].
367 Conversation, 13 Jan. 1941. FRUS V, pp. 16–17.
368 Minute, 13 Jan. 1941. [F142].
369 Telegram to Butler, 14 Jan. 1941, 260. [F142].
370 Telegram, 14 Jan. 1941, 261.[F142]. Cf aide–mémoire, 22 Jan. FRUS V, pp. 28–31; also in Butler–FO, 22 Jan. 1941, 90. FO371/28110 [F1277/5/40].
371 Telegram, 22 Jan. 1941, 356. [F142].
372 Memorandum, 24 Jan. 1941. [F142].
373 Telegram 7 Jan. 1941, 7. FO371/27758 [F185/6/23]. Cf also Murphy–Hull, 12 Dec. 1940, 1150. FRUS IV, p. 242.
374 Telegram, 13 Jan. 1941, 31. FO371/27758 [F185/8/61].
375 Minutes, 14, 16 Jan. ibid.
376 Telegram, 17 Jan. 1941, 92. FO371/27758 [F271/8/61].
377 Minutes [F271].
378 E. Reynolds, p. 134.
379 Ibid., p. 134; Charivat, p. 231.
380 Telegram from Governor, 18 Jan. 1941, 22. FO371/28108 [F328/5/40].
381 Telegram from C in C China, 22 Jan. 1941, 1157. FO371/28108 [F306/5/40].
382 Flood, pp. 419–20. Cf Leahy–Hull, 23 Jan. 1941, 98. FRUS V, pp. 38–41.
383 Minute, 30 Jan. 1941. FO371/28109 [F457/5/40].
384 Flood, pp. 422–30.
385 Stowe, pp. 170–1. Morley, pp. 227–8.
386 q. Charivat, p. 235.
387 Stowe, p. 171; also Charivat, p. 235.
388 Leahy–Hull, 22 Jan. 1941, 92. FRUS V, pp. 34–6.
389 Leahy–Hull, 22 Jan. 1941, 91. ibid., pp. 32–4.
390 Hull–Grew, 3 Feb. 1941, 76. ibid., pp. 54–5.
391 Telegram, 25 Jan. 1941, 53. FO371/28109 [F396/5/40].
392 Telegram, 27 Jan. 1941, 59. [F396].
393 Telegram 53, as above.
394 Minutes, 29, 30 Jan. 1941. FO371/28109 [F430/5/40].
395 Telegram, 2 Feb. 1941, 54. [F396].
396 Grant–Hull, 27 Jan. 1941, 48. FRUS V, p. 44.
397 Flood, pp. 434–5.
398 Stowe, p. 172.
399 Minute, 26 Feb. FO371/28110[F1134/5/40].
400 Clarke–Roché, 10 Mar. 1941. [F1134].
401 Stowe, p. 172.
402 Flood, pp. 458–9.
403 Stowe, p. 172.
404 Flood, p. 458.
405 Charivat, p. 236; Stowe, p. 173.
406 Stowe, p. 179. Aide-mémoire, 7 Feb.1941. FRUS V, pp. 61–62.
407 Stowe, p. 179. Cf Churchill–Roosevelt, 15 Feb. 1941. FRUS V, pp. 79–80; Kimball, pp. 135–6.
408 Memorandum, 23 Feb. 1941. DGFP, 1962, XII, p. 44.

409 E. Reynolds, p. 140.
410 Ibid., p. 140.
411 Flood, pp. 465–7.
412 Grant–Hull, 29 Jan. 1941. FRUS V, p. 47.
413 Flood, pp. 476–7.
414 E. Reynolds, p. 143.
415 Ibid., p. 144; Stowe, p. 180.
416 Flood, pp. 477, 481.
417 Ibid., pp. 485–6.
418 Ibid., pp. 492–3.
419 Ibid., pp. 496–501.
420 Ibid., pp. 511–12.
421 E. Reynolds, p. 146.
422 Stowe, p. 183. Ott–FMy, 18 Feb. 1941, 233. DGFP, pp. 115–16; 27 Feb., 287, pp. 178–9. Cf also Leahy–Hull, 1 Mar., 256. FRUS V, p. 99.
423 Flood, pp. 517–18.
424 Stowe, p. 183.
425 Minute, 10 Mar. 1941. FO371/28110 [F1685/5/40].
426 E. Reynolds, p. 147.
427 Charivat, p. 239.
428 Stowe, p. 185.
429 Flood, pp. 553 ff.
430 Reynolds, p. 148.
431 Stowe, pp. 188–9.
432 Stowe, p. 191. Flood, pp. 579 ff.
433 Flood, p. 585.
434 Grew–Hull, 17 Mar. 1941, 423. FRUS V, p. 112.
435 Grant–Hull, 24 Feb. 1941, 107. FRUS V, p. 93.
436 Grew–Hull, 27 Feb., 316. ibid., pp. 93–4.
437 Minute, 1 Mar. 1941. FO371/28131 [F1427/246/40].
438 Conversation, 26 Feb. 1941. AFPD, p. 461.
439 Telegram from Crosby, 24 Feb. 1941, 129. FO371/28120 [F1240/210/40].
440 Enclosure in Crosby–Eden, 3 Feb. 1941, 39. FO371/28110 [F1209/5/40].
441 Crosby–Eden, 1 Feb. 1941, 38. FO371/28120 [F1208/210/40].
442 Telegram, 10 Feb. 1941, 89. FO371/28120/20 [F710/210/40].
443 Minute, 13 Feb. 1941. [F710].
444 FE(41) 8th, 20 Jan. CAB 96/2.
445 Telegram, 14 Feb. 1941, 103. FO371/28135 [F918/438/40].
446 Telegram, 23 Feb., 92. [F918].
447 Telegram, 28 Feb. 1941, 148. FO371/28135 [F1451/438/40].
448 Stowe, p. 165.
449 Ibid., pp. 118–19.
450 Ibid., pp. 124–5.
451 Cf telegram from Halifax, 29 April 1941, 1882. FO371/28138 [F3565/885/40].
452 Memorandum, 2 Mar. 1941. [F1451].
453 FE(41) 10th, 13 Mar., Item 3. CAB 96/2.
454 Telegram, 13 Mar. 1941, 184. FO371/28120 [F1944/210/40].
455 FE (41) 11th, 20 Mar., Item 4. CAB 96/2.
456 Grant–Hull, 19 Mar. 1941, 166. FRUS V, p. 114.
457 E.B. Reynolds, p. 184.
458 Grew–Hull, 24 Mar. 1941, 5463. FRUS V, pp. 117–18.

459 Telegram, 28 Mar. 1941, 1692. FO371/28131 [F2390/246/40].

460 Telegram, 28 Mar. 1941, 1693. [F2390].

461 Telegram to WO, 31 Mar. 1941, GHQ FE 187/2. FO371/28135[F2570/438/40].

462 FE (41) 12th, 3 April. CAB 96/2.

463 Minute, 8 April 1941. [F2570].

464 Telegram, 31 Mar. 1941, 221. FO371/28151 [F2499/1325/40].

465 Telegram, 26 Mar. 1941, 213. FO371/28140 [F2426/1281/40].

466 Telegram, 4 April 1941, 161. [F2426].

467 Telegram, 28 Mar. 1941, 1694. FO371/28151 [F2391/1325/40].

468 Aide-mémoire A, 8 April 1941. FRUS V, p. 121; also in Halifax–FO, 9 April, 370. FO371/28121 [F3539/210/40].

469 Aide–mémoire B, 8 April 1941. FRUS V, p. 123; also in Halifax–FO, 9 April, 369. FO371/28132 [F3540/246/40].

470 Memorandum, 8 April 1941. FRUS V, p. 120.

471 Telegram, 9 April 1941, 1569. FO371/28140 [F2846/1281/40].

472 Telegram, 9 April 1941, 1571. FO371/28151 [F2855/1325/40].

473 Memorandum, 9 May 1941. FRUS V, p. 149.

474 Telegram to Halifax, 18 April 1941, 2101. FO371/28140 [F2846/1281/40].

475 Minute, 20 April. [F2390].

476 Minute by Bennett, 22 April. [F2846].

477 Winant–Hull, 21 April 1941, 1578. FRUS V, p. 133.

478 WO communications, recd 24 April 1941. FO371/27776 [F3346, F3347/54/61].

479 FRUS V, pp. 134–6.

480 Telegram, 22 April, 1769. FO371/28140 [F3285/1281/40].

481 Conversation, 22 April 1941. FRUS V, p. 137.

482 Telegram, 29 April 1941, 267. FO371/28132 [F3509/246/40].

483 Minute, 30 April. [F3509].

484 Minute by Butler, 30 April 1941. Telegram to Crosby, 2 May, 191. [F3509].

485 Telegram, 1 May 1941, 2360. [F3509].

486 Telegram, 4 May, 1975. FO371/28140 [F3687/1281/40].

487 Telegram, 7 May 1941, 2044. FO371/28132 [F3863/246/40].

488 Telegram, 7 May 1941, 285. FO371/28132 [F3852/246/40].

489 Telegram, 7 May 1941, 286. FO371/28132 [F3853/246/40].

490 Telegram, 7 May 1941, 287. FO371/28141 [F3854/1281/40].

491 Telegram, 10 May 1941, 200. FO371/28140 [F3854/1281/40].

492 Telegram, 13 May 1941, 303. FO371/28141 [F4001/1281/40].

493 Telegram, 11 May 1941, 297. FO371/28121 [F3965/210/40].

494 Minute, 14 May. [F3965].

495 Minute, 15 May. [F3965].

496 Telegram, 17 May, 210. [F3965].

497 Telegram, 23 May, 2768. [F3965].

498 Telegram, 4 June 1941, 2554. FO371/28133 [F4881/246/40]. Cf aide-mémoire, 2 June. FRUS V, pp. 163–5.

499 Memorandum, 3 June 1941. FRUS V, p. 166.

500 Telegram, 16 May 1941. FO371/28141 [F4133/1281/40].

501 Telegram, 16 May 1941, 311. FO371/28141 [F4132/1281/40].

502 Telegram, 18 May 1941, 316. FO371/28141 [F4164/1281/40].

503 Telegram, 20 May 1941, 320. FO371/28141 [F4273/1281/40].

504 Telegram, 21 May 1941, 328. FO371/28141 [F4323/1281/40].

505 Telegram, 20 May 1941, 78, ARFAR. FO371/28141 [F4389/1281/40].

506 Memorandum by MEW, 21 May 1941. FO371/28141 [F4423/1281/40].
507 Minute by Clarke, 23 May. [F4423]. FE (41) 18th, 22 May, Item 1. CAB 96/2.
508 Telegram, 25 May 1941, 330. FO371/28141 [F4454/1281/40].
509 Minute, n.d. [F4454].
510 Minute, 29 May 1941. [F4454].
511 Telegram, 30 May 1941, 232. FO371/28141 [F4668/1281/40].
512 Telegram, 3 June 1941, 356. FO371/28142 [F4735/1281/40].
513 Telegram, 4 June, 241. [F4735].
514 Telegram, 4 June 1941, 359. FO371/28142 [F4808/1281/40].
515 Minute, 5 June 1941. FO371/28142 [F4774/1281/40].
516 Telegram, 4 June 1941, 360. FO371/28142 [F4844/1281/40].
517 FE (41) 20th, 6 June, Item 1. CAB 96/2.
518 Telegram, 7 June, 248. [F4844].
519 Telegram, 7 June, 249. [F4844].
520 Telegram, 17 June 1941, 394. FO371/28142 [F5342/1281/40].
521 Minute, 19 June. [F5342].
522 Telegram, 19 June, 271. [F5342].
523 Minute, 19 June, as above.
524 Telegram, 17 June 1941, 2800. FO371/28142 [F5321/1281/40]. Cf Acheson–Hull, 17 June. FRUS V, p. 178.
525 Telegram, 27 June 1941, 425. FO371/28143 [F5651/1281/40].
526 Telegram from Halifax, 28 June 1941, 3029. FO371/28143 [F5726/1281/40].
527 Telegram, 30 June 1941, 433. FO371/28143 [F5774/1281/40].
528 Telegram, 1 July 1941, 434. FO371/28143 [F5775/1281/40].
529 Telegram to Halifax, 7 July 1941, 3841. FO371/28143 [F5908/1281/40].
530 Telegram, 12 July 1941, 460. FO371/28143 [F6128/1281/40].
531 Telegram, 12 July 1941, 461. FO371/28143 [F6158/1281/40].
532 Telegrams, 19 July, 315, 316. [F6158].
533 Telegram, 19 July, 4156. [F6158].
534 Telegram, 16 July 1941, 476. FO371/28144 [F6301/1281/40].
535 Telegram, 19 July, 318. [F6301].
536 Telegram, 24 July 1941, 3467. FO371/28144 [F6703/1281/40].
537 Telegram, 20 July 1941, 487. FO371/28144 [F6509/1281/40].
538 Grant–Hull, 20 July, 356. FRUS V, pp. 219–20.
539 Minute, 19 June 1941. FO 371/28133 [F5150/246/40].
540 Cranborne–Fadden, 3 Feb. 1941, M 17. AFPD IV, pp. 357–8.
541 Minute, 20 Feb. 1941. FO371/27774 [F940/54/61].
542 Extract, Burma Defence Bureau Report, 20 May 1941, in Johnston–Bennett, 26 Aug. 1941. FO371/28124 [F8461/210/40].
543 Ba Maw, *Breakthrough in Burma*, Yale University Press, New Haven, CT, 1968, pp. 97, 103.
544 Cranborne–Whiskard, 3 Jan. 1941, 5. AFPD IV, p. 324.
545 Telegram from Campbell, 14 Feb. 1941, 53. FO371/27792 [F1149/222/61].
546 FO minute, 3 Mar. 1941. FO371/27792 [F1598/222/61].
547 Telegram, 20 Jan. 1941, 104. FO371/27792 [F494/222/61].
548 Minute, 23 Jan. [F494].
549 Minute, 3 Mar. as above; Stirling–Dept., 29 Jan. 1941, 88. AFPD IV, pp. 353–4.
550 Commonwealth–DO, 7 Feb. 1941, 86. FO371/27792 [F732/222/61].
551 Cf submission, 25 Mar. 1941. AFPD IV, pp. 509–11.

552 Report, 5 April 1941, in C–G–FO, 8 April 1941, 38. FO371/27793 [F4268/222/61]. Report, enclosed in Archer–Foreign Secretary, 3 May 1941. FO371/27794 [F7403/222/61].

553 Minute, 31 Aug. FO371/27794 [F7403/222/61].

554 Archer–FSy, 3 May, as above.

555 S.W. Kirby, *The War against Japan*, HMSO, London, 1957, I, p. 57.

556 Telegram, 3 May 1941, 735. FO371/27789 [F3688/158/61].

557 Minutes, 5 May, 6 May. [F3688].

558 Minute, 6 May. [F3688].

5 July–December 1941

1 q. Cadogan commentary, p. 389.

2 2 July. Cadogan, p. 391.

3 D. Reynolds, p. 206.

4 20 Sept. Cadogan, p. 406.

5 31 Dec. Cadogan, p. 425.

6 Reynolds, p. 207.

7 10 Aug. Cadogan, p. 398.

8 Cadogan, pp. 400–1.

9 11 Aug. Cadogan, p. 399.

10 *The Empire at Bay*, p. 710.

11 D. Reynolds, p. 214.

12 q. ibid., p. 215.

13 Ibid., p. 218.

14 q. Reynolds, p. 221.

15 Lu, p. 175.

16 q. Kyozo Sato, *Japan and Britain at the Crossroads*, Senshu University Press, Tokyo, 1956, p. 117.

17 Ike, p. 78.

18 Turner–Stark, 21 July 1941. FRUS J II, pp. 518–19.

19 14 July. Cadogan, p. 392.

20 Casey–Menzies, 9 July 1941, 507. AFPD V, p. 5.

21 H. Conroy and H. Wray, *Pearl Harbor Reexamined*, University of Hawaii Press, Honolulu, 1990, pp. 171–2.

22 Stimson–Roosevelt, 21 Oct. 1941. q. Roberta Wohlstetter, *Pearl Harbor Warning and Decision*, Stanford University Press, Stanford, 1962, pp. 158–9. See also Patrick J. Hearden, *Roosevelt Confronts Hitler*, Northern Illinois University Press, De Kalb, 1987, pp. 216–17.

23 PR, 25 July 1941. FRUS J II, pp. 266–7; Exec Order 8832, 26 July. ibid., p. 267.

24 Casey–Menzies, 9 July 1941, 507. AFPD V, p. 6.

25 Jonathan G. Utley, *Going to War with Japan 1937–1941*, University of Tennessee Press, Knoxville, TN, 1985, pp. 151–6. Medlicott, II, pp. 116–17.

26 DO tel, 4 Aug. 1941, M211. FO371/27822 [F7410/12/23]. Cf Halifax–Welles, 2 Aug. FRUS V, pp. 248–50. Memorandum by Welles, 2 Aug. FRUS IV, pp. 359–60.

27 Draft, 10 Aug. 1941. FO371/27847 [F8011/4366/61].

28 Draft, 15 Aug. 1941, brought to Dept by Welles after the conference. FRUS IV, pp. 370–2.

29 Wilson, *The First Summit*, pp. 241ff; Note by Ballantine, 3 July 1942. FRUS IV, p. 373.

30 Oral statement, 17 Aug. 1941. FRUS J II, pp. 556–7.

31 Campbell–Cadogan, 2 Sept. 1941. FO371/27780 [F9470/54/61].

32 Cf Cranborne–Commonwealth, 12 Sept. 1941, M 304. FO371/27847 [F9350/4366/61]; also AFPD V, pp. 109–11; 19 Sept, M 308. ibid., p. 116–17. WP(41) 220, 16 Sept. CAB 66/18; WM(94)41, 18 Sept., Item 6. CAB 65/19.

33 Churchill, *Speeches*, VIII, p. 6475. Wilson, p. 258. FRUS IV, p. 394.

34 Ike, pp. 135–6.

35 Ibid., p. 139.

36 q. Crowley in J.W. Morley, *Japan's Foreign Policy, 1868–1941*, Columbia University Press, New York and London, 1974, p. 981.

37 Yoshitake Oka, *Konoe Fumimaro*, Tokyo University Press, Tokyo, 1983, pp. 136, 139–40.

38 D. Reynolds, p. 241.

39 q. Butow, *John Doe*, p. 276.

40 Ike, p. 204.

41 Ibid., p. 283.

42 q. Graebner, p. 52.

43 Memorandum, 23 July 1941. FRUS J II, pp. 522–6. Cf conversation with Hull, 23 July, as in memorandum, 24 July. FRUS IV, pp. 339–41.

44 Memorandum by Welles, 24 July 1941. FRUS J II, p. 529.

45 Memorandum by Grew, 27 July. ibid., p. 535.

46 Memorandum, 28 July. ibid., p. 538.

47 Memorandum by Welles, 31 July 1941. FRUS J II, pp. 539–40. Welles–Grew, 1 Aug. FRUS V, p. 245.

48 FRUS J II, pp. 549–50.

49 Memorandum, 6 Aug. 1941. ibid., p. 547.

50 Document, 8 Aug. ibid., pp. 552–3.

51 Memorandum, 8 Aug., ibid., pp. 550–1.

52 Memorandum, 17 Aug. ibid., pp. 554–5.

53 Statement [2nd one], 17 Aug. ibid., pp. 557–9.

54 27 Aug., ibid., pp. 572–3.

55 Statement, 28 Aug. ibid., p. 575.

56 Memorandum, 28 Aug. ibid., pp. 576–9.

57 Memorandum, 3 Sept. ibid., pp. 588–9.

58 Draft, 6 Sept. ibid., pp. 608–9.

59 Memorandum, 10 Sept. ibid., pp. 614–19.

60 Grew–Hull, 29 Sept, 1529 substance. ibid., p. 649.

61 Oral statement, 2 Oct. ibid., pp. 660–1.

62 Memorandum by Welles, 13 Oct. ibid., p. 685.

63 Memorandum, 16–17 Oct. ibid., pp. 687–9.

64 Document, 7 Nov. ibid., pp. 709–10.

65 Memorandum by Grew, 10 Nov. ibid., p. 711.

66 Memorandum, 10 Nov. ibid., p. 718.

67 Conversation, 18 Nov., ibid., pp. 744–50.

68 Draft proposal, 20 Nov. ibid., pp. 755–6.

69 Memorandum, 22 Nov. ibid., pp. 757–62.

70 Hull–Winant, 24 Nov. 1941, 5392, conveying Pt/FNp. FRUS IV, pp. 648–9; Kimball, p. 276.

71 Memorandum, 25 Nov. 1941. FRUS IV, p. 650–1.

72 Currie–Hull, 25 Nov. ibid., pp. 651–2.

73 Memorandum, 25 Nov. ibid., pp. 655–6.
74 Ibid., pp. 661–4.
75 FNP/President, 26 Nov. ibid., p. 665; Kimball, pp. 227–8.
76 Hull–FDR, 26 Nov. FRUS IV, pp. 665–6.
77 Memorandum, 27 Nov. ibid., pp. 666–7.
78 Memorandum, 27 Nov. ibid., p. 668.
79 Conversation, 29 Nov. ibid., pp. 655–7.
80 Oral statement, 26 Nov. FRUS J II, pp. 766–7.
81 Document, 26 Nov. ibid., pp. 768–70.
82 Memorandum, 26 Nov. ibid., pp. 764–6.
83 Kurusu memoirs, q. Sato, p. 173.
84 Memorandum, 27 Nov. 1941. FRUS J II, pp. 770–2.
85 Ibid., pp. 772–7.
86 Memorandum, 5 Dec. ibid., p. 780.
87 Memorandum, 7 Dec. ibid., pp. 786–7. The memorandum is at ibid. pp. 787–92.
88 Statement, 7 Dec. ibid., p. 795.
89 FDR–Congress, 8 Dec. ibid., p. 793.
90 Memorandum by Gray of telephone conversation, 2 Aug. 1941. FRUS IV, pp. 358–9.
91 Minute by Clarke, 4 Jan. 1942. FO371/27914 [F14304/36/23].
92 Minute, 9 Jan. ibid.
93 Harvey, War Diaries, p. 140.
94 q. Graebner, p. 51.
95 Akira Iriye, The Origins of the Second World War in Asia and the Pacific, Longman, London and New York, 1987, pp. 178–9.
96 Campbell–Cadogan, 2 Sept. 1941. FO371/27780 [F9470/54/61].
97 Minute, 2 Oct. q. Lowe, p. 258–9.
98 Casey–Dept, 3 Sept. 1941, 717. AFPD V, p. 96.
99 Casey–Dept, 11 Sept., 734. ibid., p. 109.
100 Casey–Dept, 16 Nov., 981. ibid., p. 204.
101 Casey–Curtin, 18 Nov., 994. ibid., p. 206–8.
102 Casey–Curtin, 23 Nov., 1013. ibid., pp. 216–19.
103 Casey–Curtin, 24 Nov., 1021. ibid., p. 226.
104 Casey–Curtin, 26 Nov., 1037. ibid., pp. 230–1.
105 Casey–Curtin, 27 Nov., 1045. ibid., p. 236.
106 Wohlstetter, p. 243.
107 Utley, Going to War with Japan, p. 174.
108 D. Reynolds, pp. 239, 243. p. Haggie, Britannia at Bay, Clarendon Press, Oxford, 1981, pp. 204–5.
109 COS(41) 414, 5 July 1941. CAB 80/29. COS(41) 238th, 9 July, Item 4. CAB 79/12. Johnsen, pp. 261–4.
110 Ibid., p. 283–91.
111 Ibid., pp. 323–4.
112 Ibid., pp. 325–6. See also DO–telegram, 25 Nov. 1941, 781 & 471. FO371/27847 [F13067/4366/61].
113 Johnsen, p. 330.
114 q. Sato, p. 172.
115 Harvey, War Diaries, p. 66.
116 Minute, 4 Jan. 1942. FO371/27914 [F14304/86/23].
117 Craigie–Eden, 4 Feb.1943. PREM 3/158/4.
118 Minute, 19 Sept. 1943. PREM 3/158/4.

119 q. H. Conroy and H. Wray (eds), *Pearl Harbor Reexamined*, p. 175.
120 Harvey, *War Diaries*, p. 71.
121 Ismay, *Memoirs*, p. 241.
122 Memorandum. PREM 3/158/4, p. 28.
123 Memorandum by Far Eastern Dept, 2 April 1943. PREM 3/158/4, p. 53.
124 Cf M. Balfour, *The Kaiser and His Times*, Cresset, London, 1964, p. 106.
125 6 p.m., 4 Dec. Cadogan, pp. 415–16.
126 D. Reynolds, p. 247; Cf telegram from Halifax, 6 Dec., 5651. FO371/27914 [F133114/86/23].
127 President–Emperor, 6 Dec. FRUS J II, 784–6; Cf telegram from Halifax, 6 Dec. 1941, 5652. FO371/27914 [F13333/86/23].
128 Graebner, p. 51.
129 Cadogan, p. 394.
130 Commonwealth–Cranborne, 23 July 1941, 467. AFPD V, pp. 22–3.
131 Cranborne–Commonwealth, 25 July, M179. ibid., pp. 23–4.
132 Menzies–Cranborne, 25 July, 477. ibid., p. 25.
133 Casey–Ext Affs, 26 July, 562. ibid., pp. 26–7.
134 Cranborne–Commonwealth Gt, 26 July, 515. ibid., p. 28.
135 Menzies–Cranborne, 30 July, 486. ibid., p. 42.
136 Menzies–Churchill, 8 Aug., unnumbered. ibid., p. 63.
137 Advisory War Co. Minute, 16 Oct. 1941, Ex. ibid., p. 144.
138 Curtin–Cranborne, 16 Oct., 686. ibid., p. 149.
139 Churchill–Curtin, 26 Oct. 1941, Winch 1. ibid., p. 154.
140 Page–Curtin, 14 Nov., P3. ibid., pp. 191–6.
141 Page–Curtin, 16 Nov., P4. ibid., pp. 202–3. Cf WM 112(41) 1. CAB 65/24.
142 Casey–Curtin, 23 Nov. 1941, 1014. AFPD V, p. 221.
143 Evatt–Casey, 25 Oct., 1009. ibid., pp. 222–3.
144 Casey–Curtin, 24 Nov., 1021. ibid., p. 227.
145 Dept–Casey, 26 Nov., 1013. ibid., p. 228.
146 War Co Minute 573, 28 Nov. ibid., p. 234.
147 Casey–Curtin, 27 Nov., 1045. ibid., p. 236.
148 Evatt–Eggleston, 29 Nov., 25. ibid., pp. 240–1.
149 Evatt–Casey, 29 Nov., 1025. ibid., p. 241.
150 Casey–Curtin, 29 Nov., 1053. ibid., pp. 245–6.
151 Memorandum, 29 Nov. 1941 FRUS IV, p. 687.
152 Curtin–Casey, 30 Nov. 1941, 132. AFPD V, pp. 246–7.
153 Commonwealth–DO, 1 Dec. 1941, Most Immediate, Most Secret. FO371/27791 [F13081/158/61]. AFPD, V, p. 249.
154 Casey–Curtin, 30 Nov., 1055. ibid., pp. 250–1.
155 Casey–Curtin, 30 Nov., 1057. ibid., pp. 252–3.
156 Memorandum, 30 Nov. 1941. FRUS IV, p. 700.
157 WP(41) 168, 17 July. CAB 66/17. JP(41) 550, 15 July. CAB 84/52. Commonwealth–DO, 10 July, 430. FO371/27847 [F6062/4366/61].
158 WM72(41) 10, 21 July. CAB 65/19 with confidential annexe. CAB 65/23.
159 21 July. Cadogan, p. 393.
160 Van Mook, p. 103.
161 WM 75(41) 6 & 8, 28 July. CAB 65/19, with confidential annexe. CAB 65/23.
162 WM 76(41) 7, 31 July. CAB 65/19.
163 Conversation, 31 July 1941. FO371/27779 [F7244/54/61].
164 FO Memorandum, 30 July 1941. FO371/27780 [F7385/54/61].
165 Minute, 1 Aug. 1941. PREM 3/326/18.

166 Conversation, 1 Aug. 1941, and minute, 6 Aug. FO371/27779 [F7214/54/61].

167 Telegram to Halifax, 5 Aug., 4415. FO371/27779 [F6902/54/61]. Minute, 9 Aug. FO371/27780 [F7526/54/61]. Memorandum, 9 Aug. FRUS IV, p. 363.

168 Minutes, 15, 17 Aug. [F7526].

169 Gerbrandy–Biddle, 6 Aug. 1941. FRUS V, pp. 260–2.

170 Conversation, 8 Aug. [F7526]. Cf memorandum by Biddle, 8 Aug. 1941. FRUS V, p. 266.

171 Minute, 9 Aug. [F7526].

172 Draft. [F7526].

173 Telegram, 12 Aug. 1941, 158. FO371/27780 [F7658/54/61]; C in C FE–WO, 13 Aug. FO371/27780 [F7744/54/61].

174 Brooke-Popham–Ismay, 15 July. FO371/27780 [F8086/54/61].

175 Minute, 14 Aug. [F7658].

176 DO(41) 55th, 56th meetings, 7, 8 Aug. CAB 69/2.

177 Memorandum, 15 Aug. 1941. FO371/27847 [F7812/4366/61].

178 Minute, 9 Sept. 1941. FO 371/27780 [F9065/54/61].

179 WM 83(41) 4, 18 Aug., Confidential annexe. CAB 65/23.

180 Minute, 13 Aug. 1941. FO 371/27780 [F7658/54/61].

181 Conversation, 20 Aug. 1941. FO371/27780 [F8169/54/61].

182 Hollis–Bennett, 29 Aug. 1941, & attached papers. FO371/27847 [F8675/ 4366/61].

183 HMGNZ/DO, 16 Sept. 1941, 388, and minute. FO371/27780 [F9472/54/ 61]. Lissington, p. 167.

184 Note, on Telegram from Walsh, 5 Sept. 1941, 187. FO371/27780 [F8938/ 54/61].

185 Report, in Walsh–Foreign Secretary, 7 Nov. 1941, 148. FO371/31751 [F90/ 90/61].

186 WP (41) 230, 30 Sept. CAB 66/19.

187 Minutes. FO371/27781 [F10561/54/61].

188 WP (41) 254, 31 Oct. CAB 66/19.

189 Minute, 30 Oct. [F10561].

190 WM 103 (41) 5, 16 Oct., Confidential annexe. CAB 65/23.

191 WM 108 (41) 5, 3 Nov., Confidential annexe. CAB 65/24.

192 Minutes. FO371/27847 [F11734/4366/61].

193 Churchill, *Speeches*, VI, pp. 6502–5.

194 Gerbrandy–Churchill, 11 Nov. 1941. PREM 3/326.

195 *The Empire at Bay*, p. 744.

196 WM 111 (41) 3, 11 Nov. Confidential annexe. CAB 65/24. Cf telegram from B.A.D., 14 Nov., Gleam 163. FO371/27781 [F12292/54/61].

197 AFPD V, p. 193.

198 WM 112 (41) 1, 12 Nov., Confidential annexe. CAB 65/24.

199 Conversation, 17 Nov. 1941. FO371/27781 [F12472/54/61].

200 Eden–Gerbrandy, 15 Nov. 1941. PREM 3/326.

201 WM 122 (41) 3, 1 Dec., Confidential annexe. CAB 65/24.

202 FNP–President, 30 Nov. 1941. FO371/27913 [F13053/86/23]. Kimball, pp. 278–9.

203 Telegram, 1 Dec. 1941, 5519. FO371/27913 [F13114/86/23]. Cf Casey–Dept, 1 Dec., 1064. AFPD V, pp. 259–61.

204 Minutes, 2 Dec. [F13114].

205 WP (41) 296, 2 Dec. CAB 66/20.

206 Bruce–Curtin, 1 Dec., 112. AFPD V, p. 255. Cf P. Hasluck, *The Government and the People 1939–1941*, Australian War Memorial, Canberra, 1952, p. 554.
207 Memorandum, 2 Dec. [F13114].
208 DO (41) 71st, 3 Dec. CAB 69/2.
209 Minute, 4 Dec. 1941. FO371/27781 [F13232/56/61].
210 Harvey, 2 Dec. 1941. *War Diaries*, p. 68.
211 Telegram, 3 Dec. 1941, 5577. FO371/27914 [F13219/86/23].
212 WM 124 (41) 4, 4 Dec., Confidential annexe. CAB 65/24.
213 Telegram, 5 Dec. 1941, 6711. FO371/27914 [F13219/86/23]
214 Minute by Cadogan, 5 Dec. 1941; note, s.d. FO371/27781 [F13254/54/61].
215 Van Kleffens–Eden, 6 Dec. 1941. FO371/27781 [F13587/54/61].
216 Telegram, 6 Dec. 1941, 773. FO371/27781 [F13313/54/61]. Cf AFPD V, p. 274n.
217 Memorandum, 6 Dec. 1941. FO371/27847 [F13499/86/23].
218 Conversation, 6 Dec. 1941. FO371/27847 [F13423/4366/61].
219 Telegram, 8 Dec. 1941, 252. FO371/28056 [F13421/13421/23].
220 Casey–Dept, 15 Aug. 1941, 642. AFPD V, p. 81.
221 Casey–Dept, 11 Oct., 848. ibid., p. 131.
222 Smith–Eden, 13 Sept. 1941, 34. FO371/26233 [A9389/888/45].
223 Hudson–Bennett, 9 Oct. 1941. FO371/27884 [F10682/12/23].
224 Telegram, 6 Aug. 1941, 237. FO371/26295 [A6223/244/46].
225 Minutes, 8, 8, 9 Aug. [A6223].
226 R.A. Humphreys, *Latin America and the Second World War*, Athlone, London, 1981, I, p. 146.
227 DT, 4 July 1941. Telegram to Craigie, 4 July, 788. FO371/27881 [F5904/12/23].
228 Telegram from Craigie, 5 July 1941. FO371/27881 [F5905/12/23].
229 Minute, 6 July. [F5905].
230 FE(41) 24th, 4 July, Item 1. CAB 98/2.
231 WP(41) 154, 6 July. CAB 66/17. Draft with some amendments by Eden in FO371/27763 [F5933/9/61].
232 WP(41) 155, 7 July. CAB 96/4.
233 WM 66 (41) 7, 7 July 1941. CAB 65/19.
234 Telegram, 9 July, M 140. FO371/27763 [F6056/9/61].
235 Telegram to Craigie, 10 July 1941, 809. FO371/27763 [F5933/9/61].
236 Telegram to Halifax, 10 July 1941, 3900. FO371/27763 [F5953/9/61].
237 Telegram from Halifax, 7 July 1941, 3164. FO371/27763 [F5957/9/61].
238 Telegram from Halifax, 8 July 1941, 3190. FO371/27763 [F6022/9/61].
239 Telegram to Halifax, 11 July 1941, 3957. FO371/27763 [F5957/9/61].
240 Minutes. [F6022].
241 Draft. [F6022].
242 Telegram from Halifax, 10 July 1941, 3255. FO371/27881 [F6101/12/23]. Cf memorandum by Welles, 10 July. FRUS IV, pp. 300–3.
243 Telegram to Halifax, 13 July 1941, 4016. FO371/27881 [F6101/12/23].
244 FE (41) 25th, 10 July 1941. CAB 96/2.
245 Telegram to Halifax, 12 July 1941, 4000. FO371/27881 [F5868/12/23].
246 Telegram from Halifax, 14 July 1941, 3304. FO371/27882 [F6272/12/23]. Memorandum by Welles, 14 July, does not cover all this. FRUS IV, pp. 826–7.
247 Minute, 16 July. [F6272].
248 Bruce–Eden, 15 July 1941. FO371/27764 [F6733/9/61].
249 Minute by Clarke, 16 July. [F6733].

250 Ibid.

251 Eden's version, a bit tougher than Bennett's.

252 Eden–Bruce, 19 July. [F6733].

253 Telegram from Halifax, 15 July 1941, 3319. FO371/27763 [F6273/9/61].

254 Minutes, 17 July; telegram to Halifax, 22 July, 4178. [F6273].

255 PM's minute, 16 July 1941, M745/1. FO371/27764 [F6606/9/61].

256 Minute, 16 July. [F6606].

257 Minutes by Eden, 16 July; Seymour, 17 July. [F6606].

258 FE (41) 26th, 17 July, Item 1. CAB 96/2. PM's Dept–Bruce, 16 July 1941, 3769. AFPD V, pp. 15–16. Cf Hornbeck–Hall conversations, as recorded by Hornbeck, 16 July. FRUS IV, pp. 828–32.

259 Minutes by Bennett, 19 July 1941; Eden, 20 July. FO371/27764 [F6734/9/61].

260 Telegram, 19 July 1941, 3393. FO371/27763 [F6473/9/61]. Cf Leahy–Hull, 16 July, 888. FRUS V, pp. 213–14.

261 Minute, 20 July 1941. FO371/27763 [F6473/9/61].

262 WP (41) 172, 20 July 1941. CAB 66/17.

263 WM 72 (41), 21 July. CAB 65/19.

264 Telegram, 21 July 1941, 53/4. FO371/27764 [F6597/9/61].

265 Minute, 22 July 1941. FO371/27764 [F6731/9/61].

266 Answered 23 July. [F6731].

267 Minute, 18 July 1941. FO371/27764 [F6642/9/61].

268 Telegram from Halifax, 22 July 1941, 3437. FO371/27764 [F6621/9/61]. Cf Leahy–Hull, 21 July, 919. FRUS V, pp. 220–1. Morley, p. 238.

269 Telegram from Halifax, 28 July 1941, 196 Saving. FO371/27766 [F7446/9/61].

270 Leahy–Hull, 22 July 1941, 921. FRUS V, pp. 221–2.

271 Telegram from Halifax, 23 July, 3458. FO371/27764 [F6663/9/61].

272 Minute, 25 July. [F6663].

273 Telegram from Halifax, 24 July 1941, 3477. FO371/27764 [F6745/9/61]. The statement is in FRUS J II, pp. 315–17.

274 House of Commons, 25 July. FO371/27765 [F6834/9/61].

275 Meiklereid–FSy, 17 Sept. 1941, 23, airmail, recd 5 Dec. FO371/27767 [F13264/9/61].

276 Telegram, 25 July 1941, 1264. FO371/27764 [F6756/9/61].

277 Telegram, 26 July 1941, 1265. FO371/27764 [F6797/9/61].

278 Telegram, 26 July 1941, 1275. FO371/27765 [F6820/9/61].

279 Telegram, 26 July 1941, 1268, 2 pts. FO371/27765 [F6799/9/61].

280 Telegram, 26 July 1941, 1273. FO371/27882 [F6864/12/73].

281 Telegram, 28 July 1941, 911. FO371/27765 [F6799/12/23].

282 Minute, 27 July. [F6799].

283 Minute by Bromley, 29 July. [F6864].

284 Telegram, 26 July 1941, 1278. FO371/27765 [F6810/9/61].

285 Telegram, 26 July 1941, 1279. [F6810].

286 Latham–Stewart, 29 July, S–69. AFPD V, pp. 36–41.

287 Minutes. [F6810].

288 Telegram from Craigie, 27 July 1941, 1287. FO371/27705 [F6875/9/61]. For the situation in Syria, where de Gaullist elements had been associated with the British moves to eliminate Vichy authorities helpful to the Germans, see S.H. Longrigg, *Syria and Lebanon under the French Mandate*, Oxford University Press, London, 1958, pp. 305 ff.

289 Telegram from Craigie, 26 July 1941, 1276. FO371/27765 [F6890/9/61].
290 Telegram, 26 July 1941, 1281. FO371/27765 [F6811/9/61]. Cf memorandum by Grew, 26 July. FRUS J II, pp. 532–4.
291 Minute, 27 July. [F6811].
292 Telegram from Halifax, 28 July 1941, 3540. FO371/27765 [F6884/9/61].
293 Minute by Foulds, 29 July. [F6884].
294 Telegram from Craigie, 1 Aug. 1941, 1338. FO371/27765 [F7163/9/61].
295 Press statement 374, 1 Aug. 1941, dated 2 Aug. in FRUS J II, pp. 320–1. Halifax–Eden, 5 Aug., 767. FO371/27766 [F7793/9/61].
296 Telegram from Halifax, 5 Aug. 1941, 218 Saving. FO371/27766 [F7794/9/61]. Cf Leahy–Hull, 1 Aug., 966, 970. FRUS V, pp. 244–5, 246–7.
297 Minute by Clarke, 16 Aug. [F7794].
298 Telegram, 29 July 1941, 1304. FO371/27882 [F7098/12/23].
299 Minutes. [F7098].
300 FE (41) 27th, 24 July. CAB 96/2.
301 Telegram from Halifax, 26 July 1941, 3510. FO371/27765 [F6802/9/61].
302 FE (41) 28th, 31 July. CAB 96/2.
303 Telegram to Halifax, 1 Aug. 1941, 4353. FO371/27765 [F6802/9/61].
304 FE (41) 33rd, 11 Sept., Item 1. CAB 96/2.
305 Telegram, 26 July 1941, 151Pt 1. FO371/27765 [F6800/9/61].
306 Telegram, 29 July, 108. [F6800].
307 Telegram from Ag C–G, 17 Aug. 1941, 174. FO371/27766 [F7888/9/61].
308 Minute, 18 Aug. [F7888].
309 Telegram, 25 Sept. 1941, 4424. FO371/27766 [F9925/9/61]. Cf memorandum by Berle, 12 Sept. FRUS V, pp. 287–9. Leahy–Hull, 15 Sept., 1184. FRUS IV, p. 452.
310 Minute, 27 Sept. [F9925].
311 Memorandum, 16 Sept. 1941. FRUS IV, pp. 452–4.
312 Memorandum, 23 Sept. 1941. FRUS V, pp. 291–2.
313 Telegram, 14 Sept. 1941, 198. FO371/27766 [F9351/9/61].
314 Telegram, 7 Oct. 1941, 210. FO371/27766 [F10468/9/61].
315 Telegram, 5 Oct. 1941, 209. FO371/27766 [F10389/9/61].
316 Telegram, 8 Oct., 5452. [F10389].
317 Telegram, 10 Oct. 1941, 1950. FO371/27766 [F10631/9/61].
318 Hull–Grew, 2 Oct. 1941. FRUS V, pp. 304–5; Grew–Hull, 8 Oct., 1587. ibid., p. 315.
319 Telegram, 13 Oct., 1315. [F10631].
320 Telegrams, 29 Oct. 1941, 2159. FO371/27767 [F11592/9/61]; 30 Oct., 2164. [F11621/9/61].
321 Minute, 1 Nov. [F11592].
322 Telegram, 26 Nov. 1941, 2403. FO371/27767 [F12941/9/61].
323 Telegram, nd, recd 11 Oct. 1941, 215. FO371/27766 [F10653/9/61]. Cf minute by Broad, 14 Oct.
324 Leahy–Hull, 8 Oct. 1941, 1283. FRUS V, pp. 313–14.
325 Telegram from Ag CG, 27 Oct. 1941, 229. FO371/22767 [F11421/9/61]. Cf Reid–Hull, 29 Oct. 1941, 170. FRUS V, p. 331.
326 Telegram from Meiklereid, 15 July 1941, 134. FO371/27828 [F6295/1577/61]. Telegram from C in C China, 14 July, 878. FO371/27828 [F6386/1577/61].
327 Minute, 23 July 1941. FO371/27828 [F6565/1577/61].

328 FE (41) 24 July, Item 2. CAB 96/2; Minute by Clarke, 26 July. FO371/27828 [F6603/1577/61].

329 Telegram, 3 Aug. 1941, 161. Minutes, 5, 6 Aug. FO371/27828 [F7269/1577/61].

330 FE (41) 29th, 7 Aug., Item 5. CAB 96/2.

331 Telegram, 10 Aug. 1941, 47. FO371/27828 [F7653/1577/61].

332 Telegram, 11 Aug. 1941, 4499. FO371/27828 [F7572/1577/61].

333 Telegram from Meiklereid, 30 Aug. 1941, 184. FO371/27829 [F8653/1577/61]. Minute, 5 Nov. FO371/27829 [F8809/1577/61].

334 Minute, 11 Sept. 1941. FO371/27829 [F9381/1577/61].

335 Minute, 11 Sept. [F9381].

336 Minute, 12 Sept. [F9381].

337 Cf Leahy–Hull, 26 Sept. 1941, 1228. FRUS V, pp. 294–6.

338 FE (41) 220, 28 Oct. CAB 96/3.

339 FE (41) 36th, 31 Oct, Item 3. CAB 96/2.

340 Telegram, 17 Nov. 1941, 253. FO371/27830 [F12451/1577/61].

341 Telegram, 1 Dec. 1941, 716. FO371/27830 [F13122/1577/61].

342 FE (41) 38th, 5 Dec., Item 2. CAB 96/2.

343 Stowe, p. 193.

344 Grant–Hull, 28 July 1941. FRUS V, pp. 236–7.

345 Telegram from Crosby, 29 July 1941, 507. FO371/28112 [F6972/5/40].

346 Telegram, 8 July 1941, 456. FO371/28123 [F6252/210/40].

347 Stowe, p. 195.

348 Flood, p. 612.

349 Ibid., p. 189.

350 Ibid., p. 195 fn 47.

351 Ibid., fn 48.

352 Telegram, 23 July 1941, 495. FO371/28123 [F6695/210/40].

353 Minute, 24 July. [F6695].

354 Telegram to Halifax, 1 Aug. 1941, 4363. FO371/28135 [F6812/438/40].

355 Telegram, 29 July 1941, 508. FO371/28135 [F6983/438/40].

356 Telegram, 27 July 1941, 505. FO371/28135 [F6812/438/40].

357 Minute, 25 July 1941. FO371/28144 [F6707/1281/40].

358 Telegram, 26 July 1941, 502. FO371/28134 [F6870/246/40].

359 Minute, 28 July. [F6870].

360 Telegram, 29 July 1941, 509. FO371/28123 [F7085/210/40].

361 Telegram, 30 July 1941, 512. FO371/28123 [F7027/210/40].

362 Telegram, 1 Aug. 1941, 1358. FO371/28125 [F7205/438/40].

363 E. Reynolds, p. 196.

364 Grant–Hull, 28 July 1941, 371. FRUS V, pp. 236–7.

365 Memorandum, 30 July 1941. FRUS V, p. 240.

366 Memorandum, 31 July 1941. FRUS V, p. 242.

367 Telegram, 31 July 1941, 3614. FO371/28123 [F7171/210/40].

368 Minute, 2 Aug. [F7171].

369 Telegram, 4 Aug. 1941, 3683. FO371/28123 [F7301/210/40].

370 Telegram, 7 Aug. 1941, 3715. FO371/28123 [F7562/210/40]. Hull–Grew, 7 Aug., 91. FRUS V, pp. 264–5.

371 Telegram, 7 Aug. 1941, 3726. FO371/28123 [F7491/210/40].

372 Telegram, 10 Aug. 1941, 3740. FO371/28124 [F7581/210/40].

373 Telegram, 13 Aug. 1941, 3795. FO371/28124 [F7796/210/40].

374 Grant–Hull, 9 Aug. 1941, 405. FRUS V, pp. 266–7.

375 Grant–Hull, 12 Aug. 1941, 412. ibid., pp. 269–70.
376 Memorandum, 14 Aug. 1941. FRUS V, pp. 271–3.
377 Memorandum, 18 Aug. 1941. FRUS V, p. 277.
378 Telegram from Crosby, 26 July 1941, 501. FO371/28144 [F6798/1281/40].
Grant to Hull, 26 July, 367. FRUS V, pp. 233–4.
379 FE (41) 28th, 31 July, Item 3. CAB 96/2.
380 Telegram, 1 Aug. 1941, 343. FO371/28182 [F7027/210/40].
381 Troutbeck–Bennett, 2 Aug. 1941. FO371/28145 [F7351/1281/40].
382 Telegram, 2 Aug. 1941, 520. FO371/28123 [F7206/210/40].
383 Telegram, 3 Aug., 358. [F7206].
384 Minute, 6 Aug. 1941. FO371/28123 [F7248/210/40].
385 Minute, 6 Aug. [F7248].
386 Telegram, 2 Aug. 1941, 4380. FO371/28123 [F7027/210/40].
387 Telegram, 4 Aug. 1941, 3672. FO371/28144 [F7275/1281/40].
388 Telegram, 6 Aug., 4429. [F7275].
389 Telegram, 7 Aug. 1941, 3712. FO371/28145 [F7515/1281/40].
390 Telegram, 10 Aug. 1941, 552. FO371/28145 [F7580/1281/40].
391 Minute, 15 Aug. 1941. FO371/28145 [F7767/1281/40].
392 Minute, 19 Aug. 1941. FO371/28145 [F7805/1281/40].
393 Telegram, 20 Aug., 4646. [F7805].
394 FE (41) 31st, 21 Aug., Item 2. CAB 96/2.
395 Telegram, 18 Aug. 1941, 3847. FO371/28145 [F7970/1281/40].
396 MEW paper, 21 Aug. [F7970].
397 Telegram, 26 Aug. 1941, 473. FO371/28146 [F8242/1281/40].
398 Telegram, 12 Sept. 1941, 4206. FO371/28147 [F9303/1281/40]. Cf aide-mémoire, 11 Sept. FRUS V, p. 287.
399 Telegram, 19 Sept. 1941, 5136. FO371/28147 [F9446/1281/40].
400 Telegram, 18 Sept. 1941, 4325. FO371/28147 [F9573/1281/40].
401 Telegram, 18 Oct. 1941, 735. FO371/28148 [F10983/1281/40].
402 Telegram, 9 Sept. 1941, 651. FO371/28147 [F9220/1281/40].
403 Telegram, Cooper–Colonial Secretary, 13 Sept. 1941, Duchy 8. FO371/28147 [F9313/1281/40].
404 Minute, 15 Sept. [F9313].
405 Telegram, 16 Sept. 1941, 663. FO371/28147 [F9486/1281/40]. Cf Asada's report, mentioned in William L. Swan, 'Thai–Japanese relations at the start of the Pacific War: New insight into a controversial period', JSEAS, XVIII, 2 (September 1987), p. 273.
406 Telegram, 6 Oct. 1941, 4576. FO371/28148 [F10458/1281/40].
407 Peck–SofS, 4 Oct. 1941, 465. FRUS V, p. 309, p. 309n.
408 Memorandum & minute by Broad, 25 Sept. 1941. FO371/28147 [F9764/1281/40].
409 FE (41) 35th, 9 Oct., Item 2. CAB 96/2.
410 E. Reynolds, pp. 229–30.
411 Stowe, p. 202.
412 Telegram, 15 Oct. 1941, 724. FO371/28125 [F10827/210/40]. Peck–Hull, 15 Oct., 476. FRUS V, pp. 320–2.
413 Stowe, p. 202.
414 Ibid., p. 101.
415 Ibid., p. 137.
416 Ibid., p. 202. Cf S.W. Kirby, The War Against Japan, HMSO, London, 1957, I, p. 76. Louis Allen, Singapore 1941–1942, Cass, London, 1977, pp. 92–4.
417 WM 103 (41), 16 Oct., Item 5, Annexe. CAB 65/23.

418 Price–Seymour, 18 Oct. 1941. FO371/28126 [F10967/210/40].

419 Minutes. [F10962].

420 Aldrich, p. 341.

421 Minute by Broad, 11 Nov. 1941. FO371/28126 [F12040/210/40].

422 Aide-mémoire, 25 Oct. 1941. FRUS V pp. 326–7.

423 Memorandum, 28 Oct. 1941. FRUS V, pp. 327–9.

424 Peck–SofS, 29 Oct. 1941, 495. ibid., pp. 330–1.

425 Memorandum to British Embassy, 6 Nov. 1941. FRUS V, pp. 333–4.

426 Telegram, 14 Nov. 1941, 6192. [F12040].

427 Peck–SofS, 6 Nov. 1941, 504. FRUS V, pp. 335–7.

428 Telegram, 10 Nov., 798. [F12040].

429 Telegram, 14 Nov., 535. [F12040].

430 Aldrich, p. 343.

431 Stowe, p. 203.

432 E. Reynolds, p. 232.

433 Ibid., p. 233. Cf Stowe, p. 101.

434 q. E. Reynolds, p. 233. Cf Ike, p. 281.

435 E. Reynolds, pp. 233–6.

436 Telegram, 27 Nov., 861. FO371/27767 [F12923/9/61].

437 Telegram, 26 Nov., 266. FO371/27767 [F12823/9/61].

438 Stowe, p. 205.

439 Allen, pp. 95–7.

440 Flood, p. 666.

441 Cranborne–Curtin, 3 Dec., M418. AFPD V, pp. 268–70.

442 Cranborne–Curtin, 5 Dec., M424. ibid., p. 275.

443 Stowe, p. 206.

444 Ibid., p. 208.

445 q. Charivat, p. 260.

446 Ibid., p. 260. Cf telegram from Halifax, 5 Dec. 1941, 5603. FO371/27914 [F13280/86/23].

447 q. Charivat, p. 261. See also Stowe, p. 224.

448 Stowe, pp. 210–11.

449 Charivat, p. 278.

450 Grant–Hull, 12 Aug. 1941, 412. FRUS V, p. 270.

451 Telegram, 8 Dec. 1941, 903. FO371/28127 [F13492/210/40].

452 Robert H. Taylor, 'Politics in late colonial Burma', MAS, 10, 2 (1976) p. 183.

453 *The Empire at Bay*, p. 710.

454 Taylor, 'Politics in late colonial Burma', p. 190.

455 *The Empire at Bay*, p. 739.

456 WP (G) (41) 122, 28 Oct. 1941. FO371/27863 [F12163/9889/61].

457 Letter, 3 Nov. I (44) 8, 22 Dec. 1944. CAB 91/2.

458 4 Nov. I (44) 8.

459 R.H. Taylor, 'The relationship between Burmese social classes and British–Indian policy on the behaviour of the Burmese political élite, 1937–42', PhD thesis, Cornell University, p. 627.

460 Telegram, 10 Nov. 1941, 6094. FO371/27863 [F12136/9889/61].

461 Telegrams, 25 Sept. 1941, 3349, 1504. FO371/27863 [F9889/9889/61].

462 *The Empire at Bay*, p. 742.

463 Telegram, 5 Nov. 1941, 5991. FO371/27863 [F12135/9889/61].

464 Telegram to New York, 6 Nov. 1941, 1120. FO371/27863 [F11780/9889/61].

465 Telegram, 6 Nov. 1941, 6023. [F11780].

466 Telegram to Halifax, 20 Nov. 1941, 6319. FO371/27863 [F12137/9889/61].
467 Hayter–Nevile Butler, 24 Nov. 1941. FO371/27863 [F13443/9889/61].
468 Telegram from Halifax, 22 Nov. 1941, 5331. FO371/27863 [F12650/9889/61].
469 John A.L. Sullivan, 'The United States the East Indies and World War II', PhD, University of Massachusetts, 1968, p. 94.
470 Memorandum, 15 Dec. 1941. q. Sullivan p. 94.
471 Memorandum, 4 Nov. 1941 FO371/27844 [F11822/3019/61].
472 Minute, 7 Nov. [F11822].
473 WO–FO, 24 Nov. 1941, 2452, M.1.2. FO371/27844 [F12794/3019/61].
474 Minutes, 27 Nov., 13 Dec. [F12794].
475 Taylor, 'Politics in late colonial Burma', pp. 190–1.
476 Grey 253, 7 Jan. 1942, Hush–Most Secret. FO371/31776 [F1740/662/61].
477 Telegram C in C ME/WO, 15 Jan., 49631, 2. [F1740].
478 Telegram, C in C ME/WO, 5 Feb. 1942, 58056. FO371/31776 [F1347/662/61].
479 Taylor, 'Politics in late colonial Burma', pp. 190, 191n.
480 Telegram, 10 Nov. 1941, 6094. FO371/27863 [F12136/9889/61].
481 Telegram from Sir R. Campbell, 8 Nov. 1941, 1373. FO371/27863 [F11963/9889/61].
482 Telegram, 13 Nov. 1941, 225. FO371/27863 [F12310/9889/61].
483 Telegram from Halifax, 15 Nov. 1941, 5206. FO371/27863 [F12397/9889/61].
484 Telegram to Halifax, 24 Nov., 6410. [F12397].
485 Telegram from Halifax, 1 Dec. 1941, 5517. FO371/27863 [F13132/9889/61].
486 Yoon Won Zoon, 'Japan's occupation of Burma 1941–1945', PhD thesis, New York University, 1971, p. 92.
487 CO–Thomas, 13 Mar. 1941. CO531/29 [53011/4].
488 R.H.W. Reece, The Name of Brooke, Oxford University Press, Kuala Lumpur, 1982, p. 72.
489 Minute, 5 April 1941. CO 531/30 [53011/4].
490 Telegram, 15 Aug. 1941, 44. CO 531/30 [53011/4].
491 Telegram, 28 Aug., Borneo 47. CO531/30 [53011/4].
492 Minute by Monson, 29 Aug. 1941. CO531/30 [53011/4].
493 Telegram, 31 Oct. 1941, 64. CO531/30 [53011/4].
494 Telegram, 10 Nov. 1941. CO 531/30 [53011/4].
495 Minute, 4 Nov. 1941. CO531/30 [53011/4].
496 Telegram, 25 Nov. 1941, 72. CO531/30 [53011/4].
497 Cf papers in FO371/27814.
498 Gent–Bennett, 16 Aug. 1941. FO371/27791 [F7917/158/61].
499 Minutes, 22, 24, 27 Aug. [F7917].
500 Scott–Bennett, 31 Aug. FO371/27791 [F8830/158/61].
501 Minutes 7, 14 Sept. [F8830].
502 Telegram Commonwealth–DO, 8 Sept., 588. FO371/27794 [F9212/222/61]. AFPD V, pp. 102–3.
503 Minutes 13, 23 Sept., 23 Sept. [F9212].
504 DO telegram, 13 Oct. 1941, 689. FO371/27794 [F10787/222/61]. AFPD V, pp. 136–7.
505 Telegram, 16 Oct. 1941, 68B. FO371/27794 [F10890/222/61]. AFPD V, p. 147.

506 Telegrams from Walsh, 2 Oct. 1941, 209. FO371/27794 [F10302/222/61]; Campbell, 8 Oct, 1188. [F10540].
507 Clarke–Costley-White, 13 Oct. [F10540]. Cranborne–Commonwealth, 17 Oct, 707. AFPD V, pp. 151–2. Telegram from Australia, 23 Oct., 694. FO371/27795 [F11307/222/61]. Evatt–Ferrara, 5 Nov. AFPD V, p. 164.
508 Telegram from Campbell, 7 Oct. 1941, 388. FO371/27794 [F10547/222/61].
509 Eden–Balfour, 21 Oct. 1941, 427. FO371/27795 [F11166/222/61].
510 Telegram to Campbell, 11 Nov. 1941, 704. FO371/27796 [F12165/222/61].
511 Minute by Roberts, 20 Oct. 1941. FO371/27794 [F10890/222/61].
512 Minute by Roberts, 26 Oct. [F10890].
513 Minute, 29 Oct. [F10890].
514 Brief, 28 Oct. [F10890].
515 Eden–Campbell, 4 Nov. 1941, 453. FO371/27795 [F11814/222/61].
516 Conversation, 10 Nov. 1941. FO371/27796 [F12104/222/61].
517 Eden–Campbell, 15 Nov., 465. FO371/27796 [F12289/222/61]
518 Minute by Cadogan, 13 Nov. 1941. FO371/27790 [F12290/222/61]. Eden–Campbell, 15 Nov., 465. [F12289].
519 Minute, 14 Nov. 1941. FO371/27796 [F12289/222/61].
520 Eden–Bland, 6 Nov. 1941, 97. FO371/27796 [F12142/222/61].
521 Conversation with van Kleffens, 17 Nov. 1941. FO371/27796 [F12476/222/61]; also FO371/27781 [F12472/54/61].
522 Telegram, 21 Nov. 1941, 21916. FO371/27796 [F12731/222/61].
523 Minute, 26 Nov. 1941. FO371/27796 [F12732/222/61].
524 Aide-mémoire, 27 Nov. [F12732].
525 Memorandum, 3 Dec. 1941. FO371/27796 [F13304/222/61].
526 Minute by Makins, 4 Nov. 1941. FO371/27796 [F13305/222/61]. Cf telegram from Campbell, 5 Dec., 1566. FO371/27796 [F13283/222/61].
527 Aide-mémoire, 5 Dec. 1941. FO371/27796 [F13306/222/61].
528 Telegram, 6 Dec. 1941, 1570. FO371/27796 [F13315/222/61].
529 Minute, 7 Dec. [F13315].
530 Minute, 4 Dec. [F13305].
531 Telegram, 10 Dec. 1941. FO371/27797 [F13517/222/61].
532 Telegram, 11 Dec., 35. [F13517].
533 Minute, 11 Dec. 1941. FO371/27797 [F13579/222/61].
534 Telegram to Cooper, 14 Dec. 1941, 55. [F13579].
535 Telegram, 16 Dec. 1941, 1644. FO371/27797 [F13808/222/61];
536 Telegram, 17 Dec. 1941, 1659. FO371/27797 [F13860/222/61].
537 Telegram to Halifax, 17 Dec. 1941, 6992. [F13808].
538 Geoffrey C. Gunn, *Wartime Portuguese Timor: The Azores Connection*, Monash University Centre for Southeast Asian Studies [Melbourne], 1988, p. 4.
539 Telegram, 19 Dec. 1941, 259. FO371/28056 [F14033/13421/23].
540 Sullivan, pp. 164–5; Hugh Kay, *Salazar and Modern Portugal*, Eyre & Spottiswoode, London, 1970, p. 165.

Conclusion

1 AFPD, V. p. 34.
2 James C. Thomson, Jr, Peter W. Stanley, John Curtis Perry, *Sentimental Imperialists. The American Experience in East Asia*, Harper, New York, 1981, pp. 192–3.

3 Cf Chihiro Hosoya, 'Twenty-five years after Pearl Harbor', in Grant K. Goodman (ed.), *Imperial Japan and Asia: A Reassessment*, Columbia University East Asia Institute, New York, 1967, p. 63.
4 S. Roskill, *Hankey: Man of Secrets*, Collins, London, 1974, III, p. 531.
5 Walsh–Foreign Secretary, 26 Mar. 1942, secret. FO371/31751 [F4969/90/61].
6 Order of the day, 8 Dec. 1941, q. Maxwell, *The Civil Defence of Malaya*, p. 73.
7 q. William Roger Louis, *Imperialism at Bay*, Oxford, 1977, p. 136.
8 John W. Cell, *Hailey: A Study in British Imperialism*, Cambridge and New York, 1992, p. 267.

Bibliography

Documentary sources

Unpublished records at the Public Record Office, Kew

ADM 1 series
FO 371 series
CAB 2, 4, 23, 53, 65, 66, 67, 69, 79, 80, 84, 85, 91, 96 series
CO 531 series
PREM 3

Published

Documenten betreffende de Buitenlandse Politiek van Nederland 1919–45. Periode C 1940–1945. 1940–1, 3 vols, The Hague, Nijhoff, 1976, 1977, 1980.
Documents of Australian Foreign Policy, 1937–49 [AFPD]. 1939–42, vols 2–5, Canberra, Australian Government Publishing Service, 1976, 1979, 1980, 1982.
Documents on British Foreign Policy 1919–39, ed. E.L. Woodward and R. Butler. 3rd Series, vols. 1–9 (1949–55).
Documents on German Foreign Policy [DGFP]. Series D (1937–45) vols 8–13, Government Printing Office, Washington and London, HMSO, 1954, 1956, 1957, 1961, 1962, 1964.
Documents Relating to New Zealand's Participation in the Second World War 1939–45. 3 vols, Wellington, Dept of Internal Affairs, 1949, 1951, 1963.
Foreign Relations of the United States [FRUS]. Washington, Government Printing Office, Japan I and II (1943), 1939 III (1955), 1940 IV (1955), 1941 IV & V (1956).

Memoirs, monographs, theses and articles

Aldrich, Richard J. *The Key to the South*, Oxford University Press, Kuala Lumpur, 1993.
Allen, Louis *Singapore 1941–1942*, Cass, London, 1977.
Andrews, E.M. *The Writing on the Wall*, Allen and Unwin, Sydney, 1987.

Avon, Lord. *The Reckoning*, Cassell, London, 1965.

Ba Maw *Breakthrough in Burma*, Yale University Press, New Haven, CT, 1968.

Balfour, M. *The Kaiser and His Times*, Cresset, London, 1964.

Barclay, G. St J. *Their Finest Hour*, Weidenfeld and Nicolson, London, 1977.

Barmé, Scot. *Luang Wichit Wathakan and the Creation of a Thai Identity*, Singapore, 1993.

Barnes, John and David Nicholson (eds), *The Empire at Bay: The Leo Amery Diaries 1939–1945*, Hutchinson, London, 1988.

Barnhart, Michael A. *Japan Prepares for Total War*, Cornell University Press, Ithaca, NY, 1987.

Bassett, M. *Sir Joseph Ward*, Auckland University Press, Auckland, 1993.

Baudet, H. and J.J. Brugmans (eds) *Balans van Beleid*, Van Gorcum, Assen, 1961.

Baudouin, P. *The Private Diaries (March 1940 to January 1941)*, trans. C. Petrie, Eyre and Spottiswoode, London, 1948.

Baugher, Peter, 'The contradictions of colonialism: The French experience in Indochina, 1860–1940', PhD thesis, University of Wisconsin–Madison, 1980.

Borg, D. and S. Okamoto (eds) *Pearl Harbor as History: Japanese–American Relations 1931–1941*, Columbia University Press, New York and London, 1973.

Braddell, Roland St J. *The Lights of Singapore*, Methuen, London, 1934.

Brailey, N.J. *Thailand and the Fall of Singapore*, Westview, Boulder, CO and London, 1986.

Burns, Richard D. and E.M. Bennett, *Diplomats in Crisis: US–Chinese–Japanese Relations 1919–41*, ABC–Clio, Santa Barbara, CA, 1974.

Butler, J.R.M. *Lord Lothian*, Macmillan, London, 1960.

Butow, R.C.J. *Tojo and the Coming of the War*, Princeton University Press, Princeton, NJ, 1961.

Butow, R.J.C. *The John Doe Associates*, Stanford University Press, Stanford, CA, 1974.

Cadogan, A.C. *The Diaries, 1938–1945*, ed. D. Dilks, Cassell, London, 1971.

Catroux, G. *Deux Actes du Drame Indochinois*, Plon, Paris, 1959.

Charivat Santaputra, 'Thai foreign policy, 1932–1946', PhD thesis, University of Southampton, 1982.

Colville, J. *The Fringes of Power*, Sceptre, London, 1986.

Conroy, H., and H. Wray (eds), *Pearl Harbor Reexamined*, University of Hawaii Press, Honolulu, 1990.

Coox, Alvin D. *Nomonhan Japan Against Russia: 1939*, Stanford University Press, Stanford, CA, 1985.

Cowling, M. *The Impact of Hitler: British Politics and British Policy, 1933–40*, Cambridge University Press, Cambridge, 1975.

Crowley, James B. *Japan's Quest for Autonomy*. Princeton University Press, Princeton, NJ, 1966.

Crosby, Josiah. *Siam: The Crossroads*, Hollis and Carter, London, 1945.

Dallek, Robert. *Franklin D. Roosevelt and American Foreign Policy, 1932–1945*, Oxford University Press, New York, 1979.

Day, David. *Menzies and Churchill*, Angus & Robertson, Sydney, 1986.

Decoux, Jean. *A la barre de L'Indochine*, Plon, Paris, 1949.

de Silva, K.M., et al (eds), *Asian Panorama*, Vikas, New Delhi, 1990.

Dignan, Don K. *The Indian Revolutionary Problem in British Diplomacy 1914–1919*, Allied Publishers, New Delhi, 1985.

Direck Jayanama. *Thailand im Zweiten Weltkrieg*, Erdman, Tubingen, 1970.

Doenecke, Justus D. *The Diplomacy of Frustration.* Hoover Institution Press, Stanford, CA, 1981.

Drachman, E.R. *United States Policy Toward Vietnam, 1940–1945,* Fairleigh Dickinson University Press, Rutherford, NJ, 1970.

Dreifort, John E. 'Japan's advance into Indochina, 1940: The French response', *Journal of South East Asian Studies,* 13 (2) September 1982, pp. 279–95.

Dreifort, John E. *Myopic Grandeur,* Kent State University Press, Kent and London, 1991.

Emerson, Rupert. *Malaysia,* Macmillan, New York, 1937.

Flood, E.T. 'Japan's relations with Thailand, 1928–41', PhD thesis, University of Washington, 1967.

Fraser, T.G. and Peter Lowe (eds) *Conflict and Amity in East Asia. Essays in Honour of Ian Nish,* Macmillan, Basingstoke, 1992.

Friend, Theodore F. *Between Two Empires,* Yale University Press, New Haven, CT, 1965.

Fulcher, Jane. *The Nation's Image,* Cambridge University Press, Cambridge, 1988.

Gates, Eleanor M. *End of the Affair: The Collapse of the Anglo-French Alliance, 1939–40,* University of California Press, Berkeley and Los Angeles, 1981.

Gaudel, A. *L'Indochine Française en face du Japon,* Susse, Paris, 1947.

Goodman, Grant K. (ed.) *Imperial Japan and Asia: A Reassessment,* Columbia University East Asia Institute, New York, 1967.

Gopinath, A. *Manuel L. Quezon,* New Day, Quezon City, 1987.

Gore-Booth, P. *With Great Truth and Respect,* Constable, London, 1974.

Graebner, Norman A. 'Hoover, Roosevelt and the Japanese', in Borg and Okamoto, q.v.

Graeff, A.C.D. de. *Van Vriend tot Vijand,* Elsevier, Amsterdam, 1945.

Grunder, G.A. and Livezey, W.E. *The Philippines and the United States,* University of Oklahoma Press, Norman, 1951.

Gullick, J.M. *Malaya,* Praeger, New York, 1963.

Gunn, Geoffrey C. *Wartime Portuguese Timor: The Azores Connection,* Monash University Centre of Southeast Asian Studies, Working Paper No. 50, [Melbourne,] 1988.

Guyot, D. 'The political impact of the Japanese occupation of Burma', PhD thesis, Yale University, 1966.

Haas, E. *Frans Indo-China en de Japanese Expansiepolitiek 1939–1945,* Universitaire Pers Leiden, Leiden, 1956.

Haggie, P. *Britannia at Bay,* Clarendon Press, Oxford, 1981.

Hamill, I. *The Strategic Illusion,* Singapore University Press, Singapore, 1981.

Harrison, F.B. *The Cornerstone of Philippine Independence,* Century, New York, 1922.

Harvey, Oliver. *The War Diaries, 1941–1945,* Collins, London, 1978.

Hasluck, P. *The Government and the People, 1939–1941,* Australian War Memorial, Canberra, 1952.

Hearden, Patrick J. *Roosevelt Confronts Hitler: America's Entry into World War II.* Northern Illinois University Press, De Kalb, 1987.

Herzog, James H. *Closing the Open Door,* Naval Institute Press, Annapolis, MD, 1973.

Hess, Gary R. *The United States' Emergence as a Southeast Asian Power, 1940–1950,* Columbia University Press, New York, 1987.

Humphreys, R.A. *Latin America and the Second World War,* Athlone, London, 1981.

Ike, N. (ed.) *Japan's Decision for War,* Stanford University Press, Stanford, CA, 1967.

Iklé, F.W. *German–Japanese Relations 1936–40*, Bookman Associates, New York, 1956.

Iriye, Akira. *Power and Culture: The Japanese–American War 1941–1945*, Harvard University Press, Cambridge, MA, 1981.

Iriye, Akira. *The Origins of the Second World War in Asia and the Pacific*, Longman, London and New York, 1987.

The Ironside Diaries, ed. R. Macleod and D. Kelly, Constable, London, 1962.

Ismay, Lord. *The Memoirs of General the Lord Ismay*, Heinemann, London, 1960.

Johnsen, William T. 'Forging the foundations of the grand alliance: Anglo-American military collaboration, 1938–1941', PhD thesis, Duke University, 1986.

Jones, F.C. *Japan's New Order in East Asia*, Oxford University Press, London, 1954.

Kay, Hugh. *Salazar and Modern Portugal*, Eyre and Spottiswoode, London, 1970.

Kersten, A.E. (ed.) *Het Dagboek van dr. G.H.C. Hart, Londen mei 1940–mei 1941*, Nijhoff, The Hague, 1976.

Kimball, Warren F. *The Most Unsordid Act*, Johns Hopkins University Press, Baltimore, 1969.

Kirby, S.W. *The War against Japan*, 5 vols, HMSO, London, 1957–69.

Kirby, S.W. *Singapore: The Chain of Disaster*, Cassell, London, 1971.

Kirk, G.L. *Philippine Independence*, Farrar and Rinehart, New York, 1936.

Kuwajuma Sho. *First World War and Asia: Indian Mutiny in Singapore (1915)*, Author, Osaka, 1988.

Laffey, John F. 'French Far Eastern policy in the 1930s', *Modern Asian Studies*, 23 (1) 1989, pp. 117–49.

Langer, W.L. *The Undeclared War*, Harper, New York, 1953.

Langhorne, R. (ed.) *Diplomacy and Intelligence during the Second World War*, Cambridge University Press, Cambridge, 1985.

Lee, Bradford A. *Britain and the Sino–Japanese War, 1937–9*, Stanford University Press, Stanford, CA, 1973.

Leutze, James R. *Bargaining for Supremacy*, University of North Carolina Press, Chapel Hill, 1977.

Likhit Dhiravegin, *Siam and Colonialism*, Thai Watana Panich, Bangkok, BE 2518 [1974].

Lissington, M.P. *New Zealand and Japan 1900–1941*, Government Printer, Wellington, 1972.

Longrigg, S.H. *Syria and Lebanon under the French Mandate*, Oxford University Press, London, 1958.

Louis, W. R. *British Strategy in the Far East 1919–1939*, Clarendon Press, Oxford, 1971.

Lowe, P. 'Great Britain and the coming of the Pacific war, 1939–41', *Transactions of the Royal Historical Society*, 5th Series, 24 (1974), pp. 43–62.

Lowe, P. *Great Britain and the Origins of the Pacific War*, Clarendon Press, Oxford, 1977.

Lu, David J. *From the Marco Polo Bridge to Pearl Harbor*, Public Affairs Press, Washington, 1961.

Marder, Arthur J. *From the Dardanelles to Oran*, Oxford University Press, London, 1974.

Maung Maung, comp., *Aung San of Burma*, Nijhoff, The Hague, 1962.

McIntyre, W.D. *The Rise and Fall of the Singapore Naval Base*, Macmillan, London, 1980.

Meaney, N. *The Search for Security in the Pacific, 1901–14*, Sydney University Press, Sydney, 1976.

Meskill, J.M. *Hitler and Japan: the Hollow Alliance*, Atherton, New York, 1966.

Michelson, Mark C. 'A place in the sun : The Foreign Ministry and perceptions and policies in Japan's international relations, 1931–1941', PhD thesis, University of Illinois at Urbana–Champaign, 1979.

Miner, Deborah N. 'United States policy toward Japan 1941: the assumption that South East Asia was vital to the British War Effort', PhD thesis, Columbia University, 1976.

Mook, H.J. van *The Netherlands Indies and Japan*, Allen & Unwin, London, 1944.

Moore, R.J. *Liberalism and Indian Politics*, Arnold, London, 1966.

Moore, R.J. *Churchill, Cripps and India*, Clarendon Press, Oxford, 1979.

Morley, J.W. (ed.) *Japan's Foreign Policy 1868–1941: A Research Guide*, Columbia University Press, New York, 1974.

Morley, J.W. (ed.) *The Fateful Choice*, Columbia University Press, New York, 1980.

Morley, J.W. (ed.) *The China Quagmire*, Columbia University Press, New York, 1983.

Murfett, M. *Fool-Proof Relations: The Search for Anglo-American Naval Cooperation during the Chamberlain Years 1937–1940*, Singapore University Press, Singapore, 1984.

Murphy, Robert D. *Diplomat Among Warriors*, Collins, London, 1964.

Neidpath, J. *The Singapore Naval Base and the Defence of Britain's Eastern Empire, 1919–1941*, Clarendon Press, Oxford, 1981.

Nish, Ian *Japanese Foreign Policy, 1869–1941: Kasamigaseki to Miyakezaka*, Routledge, London, 1977.

Nish, Ian (ed.) *Anglo-Japanese Alienation, 1919–1952*, Cambridge University Press, Cambridge, 1982.

Oblas, P. 'Siam's efforts to revise the unequal treaty system in the sixth reign (1910–1925)', PhD thesis, University of Michigan, 1974.

Oka Yoshitake. *Konoe Fumimaro*, Tokyo University Press, Tokyo, 1983.

Olu Agbi, S. 'The Pacific war controversy in Britain: Sir Robert Craigie versus the Foreign Office', *Modern Asian Studies*, 17 (3) 1983, pp. 489–517.

Omissi, David E. *Air Power and Colonial Control*, Manchester University Press, Manchester, 1990.

Ong Chit Chung, 'Major General William Dobbie and the Defence of Malaya, 1935–38', *Journal of South East Asian Studies*, 17, 2, September 1986.

Pelz, Stephen E. *Race to Pearl Harbor*, Harvard University Press, Cambridge, 1974.

Presseisen, E.L. *Germany and Japan: A Study in Totalitarian Diplomacy*, Nijhoff, The Hague, 1958.

Pritchard, R. John. 'Far Eastern influences upon British strategy towards the great powers, 1937–1939', PhD thesis, University of London, 1979.

Quirino, Carlos. *Quezon: Paladin of Philippine Freedom*, Filipiniana Book Guild, Manila, 1971.

Raven, G.J.A. and N.A.M. Rodger (eds) *Navies and Armies: The Anglo-Dutch Relationship in War and Peace*, Donald, Edinburgh, 1990.

Reece, R.H.W. *The Name of Brooke*, Oxford University Press, Kuala Lumpur, 1982.

Reynolds, D. *The Creation of the Anglo-American Alliance 1937–41*, Europa, London, 1981.

Reynolds, E.B. 'Ambivalent allies. Japan and Thailand, 1941–1945', PhD thesis, University of Hawaii, 1988.

Roskill, S.W. *Hankey: Man of Secrets*, 3 vols, Collins, London, 1970–1974.

Rusbridger, James and Eric Nave. *Betrayal at Pearl Harbor*, Simon & Schuster, New York, 1992.

Sansom, K. *Sir George Sansom and Japan: A Memoir*, Diplomatic Press, Tallahassee, FL, 1972.

Sato Kyozo. *Japan and Britain at the Crossroads 1939–1941*, Senshu University Press, Tokyo, 1986.

Schneider, James C. *Should America Go to War? The Debate over Foreign Policy in Chicago*, University of North Carolina Press, Chapel Hill, 1989.

Schroeder, Paul W. *The Axis Alliance and Japanese–American Relations 1941*, Cornell University Press, Ithaca, NY, 1958.

Shai, Aron. *Origins of the War in the East: Britain, China and Japan, 1937–1939*, London, Croom Helm, 1976.

Smit, C. *Nederland in de Eerste Wereldoorlog*, Wolters-Noordhoff, Groningen, 1971.

Smyth, John. *Percival and the Tragedy of Singapore*, Macdonald, London, 1971.

Stowe, Judith A. *Siam Becomes Thailand*, Hurst, London, 1991.

Sullivan, John A.L. 'The United States, the East Indies and World War II', PhD thesis, Massachusetts University, 1968.

Swan, William L. 'Thai–Japanese relations at the start of the Pacific war: New Insight into a controversial period', *Journal of South East Asian Studies*, 18, (2) September, 1987.

Tarling, N. 'The Singapore Mutiny', *Journal of the Malaysian Branch Royal Asiatic Society*, 55 (2) 1982.

Taylor, Robert H. 'Politics in late colonial Burma', *Modern Asian Studies*, 10 (2) 1976, pp. 161–193.

Thomson, James C., et al., *Sentimental Imperialists: The American Experience in East Asia*, Harper, New York, 1981.

Trotter, Ann *Britain and East Asia 1933–1937*, Cambridge University Press, Cambridge, 1975.

Utley, Jonathan G. 'The Department of State and the Far East, 1937–41: A study of the ideas behind its diplomacy', PhD thesis, University of Illinois at Urbana–Champaign, 1970.

Utley, Jonathan G. *Going to War with Japan 1937–1941*, University of Tennessee Press, Knoxville, 1985.

Vandenbosch, A. *Dutch Foreign Policy Since 1815*, Nijhoff, The Hague, 1959.

Venn, Fiona. *Oil Diplomacy in the Twentieth Century*, Macmillan, Basingstoke, 1986.

Vivat Sethachuay, 'United States–Thailand diplomatic relations during World War II', PhD thesis, Brigham Young University, 1977.

Watt, D.C. *Succeeding John Bull*, Cambridge University Press, Cambridge, 1984.

Wilson, Theodor A. *The First Summit*, Macdonald, London, 1970.

Wohlstetter, Roberta. *Pearl Harbor Warning and Decision*, Stanford University Press, Stanford, CA, 1962.

Wolthuis, Robert K. 'United States foreign policy towards the Netherlands Indies: 1937–1945', PhD thesis, Johns Hopkins University, 1968.

Woodward, E.L. *British Foreign Policy in the Second World War*, 5 vols, HMSO, London, 1970–6.

Yoon, Won Z. *Japan's Scheme for the Liberation of Burma*, Athens, OH, 1973.

Yuen Choy Leng. 'Japanese rubber and iron investments in Malaya, 1900–1941', *Journal of South East Asian Studies*, 5(1) (March 1974), pp. 18–36.

Index

427